English Grammar in Use

A self-study reference and practice book
for intermediate learners of English

Fourth Edition

with answers

Raymond Murphy

CAMBRIDGE
UNIVERSITY PRESS

CAMBRIDGE
UNIVERSITY PRESS

University Printing House, Cambridge CB2 8BS, United Kingdom

One Liberty Plaza, 20th Floor, New York, NY 10006, USA

477 Williamstown Road, Port Melbourne, VIC 3207, Australia

4843/24, 2nd Floor, Ansari Road, Daryaganj, Delhi – 110002, India

79 Anson Road, #06–04/06, Singapore 079906

Cambridge University Press is part of the University of Cambridge.

It furthers the University's mission by disseminating knowledge in the pursuit of education, learning and research at the highest international levels of excellence.

www.cambridge.org
Information on this title: www.cambridge.org/englishgrammarinuse

Fourth Edition © Cambridge University Press 2012

English Grammar in Use first published 1985
Fourth edition 2012
40 39 38 37 36 35 34 33 32 31 30 29 28 27 26 25 24

Printed in Italy by Rotolito S.p.A.

A catalogue record for this publication is available from the British Library

ISBN 978-0-521-18906-4 Edition with answers
ISBN 978-0-521-18908-8 Edition without answers
ISBN 978-0-521-18939-2 Edition with answers and CD-ROM
ISBN 978-0-511-96173-1 Online access code pack
ISBN 978-1-107-64138-9 Online access code pack and book with answers

Contents

IF YOU ARE NOT SURE WHICH UNITS YOU NEED TO STUDY, USE THE **STUDY GUIDE** ON PAGE 326.

iii

IF YOU ARE NOT SURE WHICH UNITS YOU NEED TO STUDY, USE THE **STUDY GUIDE** ON PAGE 326.

IF YOU ARE NOT SURE WHICH UNITS YOU NEED TO STUDY, USE THE **STUDY GUIDE** ON PAGE 326.

IF YOU ARE NOT SURE WHICH UNITS YOU NEED TO STUDY, USE THE **STUDY GUIDE** ON PAGE 326.

Thanks

This is the fourth edition of *English Grammar in Use*. I wrote the original edition when I was a teacher at the Swan School of English, Oxford. I would like to repeat my thanks to my colleagues and students at the school for their help, encouragement and interest at that time.

Regarding the production of this fourth edition, I am grateful to Nóirín Burke, Annabel Marriott, Matthew Duffy, Liz Driscoll, Jane Walsh, Jeanette Alfoldi and Kamae Design. I would like to thank Cambridge University Press for permission to access the Cambridge International Corpus.

Thank you also to the following illustrators: Humberto Blanco, Paul Fellows, Sophie Joyce, Katie Mac, Ian Mitchell, Gillian Martin, Sandy Nicholls, Roger Penwill, Lisa Smith, Dave Whamond and Simon Williams.

To the student

This book is for students who want help with English grammar. It is written for you to use without a teacher.

The book will be useful for you if you are not sure of the answers to questions like these:

- What is the difference between *I did* and *I have done*?
- When do we use *will* for the future?
- What is the structure after *I wish*?
- When do we say *used to do* and when do we say *used to doing*?
- When do we use *the*?
- What is the difference between *like* and *as*?

These and many other points of English grammar are explained in the book and there are exercises on each point.

Level

The book is intended mainly for *intermediate* students (students who have already studied the basic grammar of English). It concentrates on those structures which intermediate students want to use, but which often cause difficulty. Some advanced students who have problems with grammar will also find the book useful.

The book is *not* suitable for elementary learners.

How the book is organised

There are 145 units in the book. Each unit concentrates on a particular point of grammar. Some problems (for example, the present perfect or the use of *the*) are covered in more than one unit. For a list of units, see the *Contents* at the beginning of the book.

Each unit consists of two facing pages. On the left there are explanations and examples; on the right there are exercises. At the back of the book there is a Key for you to check your answers to the exercises (page 336).

There are also seven *Appendices* at the back of the book (pages 292–301). These include irregular verbs, summaries of verb forms, spelling and American English.

Finally, there is a detailed *Index* at the back of the book (page 373).

How to use the book

The units are *not* in order of difficulty, so it is *not* intended that you work through the book from beginning to end. Every learner has different problems and you should use this book to help you with the grammar that *you* find difficult.

It is suggested that you work in this way:

- Use the *Contents* and/or *Index* to find which unit deals with the point you are interested in.
- If you are not sure which units you need to study, use the *Study guide* on page 326.
- Study the explanations and examples on the left-hand page of the unit you have chosen.
- Do the exercises on the right-hand page.
- Check your answers with the *Key*.
- If your answers are not correct, study the left-hand page again to see what went wrong.

You can of course use the book simply as a reference book without doing the exercises.

Additional exercises

At the back of the book there are *Additional exercises* (pages 302–325). These exercises bring together some of the grammar points from a number of different units. For example, Exercise 16 brings together grammar points from Units 26–36. You can use these exercises for extra practice after you have studied and practised the grammar in the units concerned.

To the teacher

English Grammar in Use was written as a self-study grammar book, but teachers may also find it useful as additional course material in cases where further work on grammar is necessary.

The book will probably be most useful at middle- and upper-intermediate levels (where all or nearly all of the material will be relevant), and can serve both as a basis for revision and as a means for practising new structures. It will also be useful for some more advanced students who have problems with grammar and need a book for reference and practice. The book is not intended to be used by elementary learners.

The units are organised in grammatical categories (*Present and past*, *Articles and nouns*, *Prepositions* etc.). They are not ordered according to level of difficulty, so the book should not be worked through from beginning to end. It should be used selectively and flexibly in accordance with the grammar syllabus being used and the difficulties students are having.

The book can be used for immediate consolidation or for later revision or remedial work. It might be used by the whole class or by individual students needing extra help. The left-hand pages (explanations and examples) are written for the student to use individually, but they may of course be used by the teacher as a source of ideas and information on which to base a lesson. The student then has the left-hand page as a record of what has been taught and can refer to it in the future. The exercises can be done individually, in class or as homework. Alternatively (and additionally), individual students can be directed to study certain units of the book by themselves if they have particular difficulties not shared by other students in their class. Don't forget the *Additional exercises* at the back of the book (see **To the student**).

This fourth edition of *English Grammar in Use* has been revised and updated. There are no new units, but some of the exercises have been rewritten or replaced.

An edition of *English Grammar in Use* without the Key is available. Some teachers may prefer this for use with their students.

An online version of *English Grammar in Use* is also available.

English Grammar in Use

Present continuous (**I am doing**)

Study this example situation:

Sarah is in her car. She is on her way to work.
She **is driving** to work.

This means: she is driving *now*, at the time of speaking.
The action is not finished.

Am/is/are + -ing is the *present continuous*:

I	**am**	(= I**'m**)	**driving**
he/she/it	**is**	(= he**'s** etc.)	**working**
we/you/they	**are**	(= we**'re** etc.)	**doing** etc.

I am doing something = I'm in the middle of doing it; I've started doing it and I haven't finished:
- ☐ Please don't make so much noise. **I'm trying** to work. (*not* I try)
- ☐ 'Where's Mark?'   'He**'s having** a shower.' (*not* He has a shower)
- ☐ Let's go out now. It **isn't raining** any more. (*not* It doesn't rain)
- ☐ *(at a party)* Hi, Jane. **Are** you **enjoying** the party? (*not* Do you enjoy)
- ☐ What's all that noise? What**'s going** on? (= What's happening?)

Sometimes the action is not happening at the time of speaking. For example:

Steve is talking to a friend on the phone. He says:

I'm reading a really good book at the moment.
It's about a man who …

Steve is not reading the book at the time of speaking.
He means that he has started it, but has not finished it yet.
He is in the middle of reading it.

Some more examples:
- ☐ Kate wants to work in Italy, so she**'s learning** Italian. (but perhaps she isn't learning Italian at the time of speaking)
- ☐ Some friends of mine **are building** their own house. They hope to finish it next summer.

You can use the present continuous with **today / this week / this year** etc. (periods around now):
- ☐ A: You**'re working hard today**. (*not* You work hard today)
  B: Yes, I have a lot to do.
- ☐ The company I work for **isn't doing** so well **this year**.

We use the present continuous when we talk about changes happening around now, especially with these verbs:

> get   change   become   increase   rise   fall   grow   improve   begin   start

- ☐ **Is** your English **getting** better? (*not* Does your English get better)
- ☐ The population of the world **is increasing** very fast. (*not* increases)
- ☐ At first I didn't like my job, but I**'m beginning** to enjoy it now. (*not* I begin)

Present continuous and present simple ➔ Units 3–4   Present tenses for the future ➔ Unit 19

Exercises

1.1 The sentences on the right follow those on the left. Which sentence goes with which?

1 Please don't make so much noise.	a It's getting late.
2 I need to eat something soon.	b They're lying.
3 I don't have anywhere to live right now.	c It's starting to rain.
4 We need to leave soon.	d They're trying to sell it.
5 They don't need their car any more.	e I'm getting hungry.
6 Things are not so good at work.	f I'm trying to work.
7 It isn't true what they said.	g I'm looking for an apartment.
8 We're going to get wet.	h The company is losing money.

1   *f*
2   ....
3   ....
4   ....
5   ....
6   ....
7   ....
8   ....

1.2 Complete the conversations.

1 A: I saw Brian a few days ago.
   B: Oh, did you?   ___What's he doing___ these days?   (what / he / do)
   A: He's at university.
   B: .... ?   (what / he / study)
   A: Psychology.
   B: .... it?   (he / enjoy)
   A: Yes, he says it's a very good course.

2 A: Hi, Nicola. How .... ?   (your new job / go)
   B: Not bad. It wasn't so good at first, but .... better now.
      (it / get)
   A: What about Daniel? Is he OK?
   B: Yes, but .... his work right now.   (he / not / enjoy)
      He's been in the same job for a long time and .... to get bored
      with it.   (he / begin)

1.3 Put the verb into the correct form, positive (**I'm doing** etc.) or negative (**I'm not doing** etc.).

1 Please don't make so much noise.   ___I'm trying___ (I / try) to work.
2 Let's go out now.   ___It isn't raining___ (it / rain) any more.
3 You can turn off the radio.   .... (I / listen) to it.
4 Kate phoned me last night. She's on holiday in France.   .... (she / have)
   a great time and doesn't want to come back.
5 I want to lose weight, so this week .... (I / eat) lunch.
6 Andrew has just started evening classes.   .... (he / learn) Japanese.
7 Paul and Sally have had an argument.   .... (they / speak)
   to each other.
8 .... (I / get) tired. I need a rest.
9 Tim .... (work) today. He's taken the day off.
10 .... (I / look) for Sophie. Do you know where she is?

1.4 Complete the sentences using the following verbs:

start   get   increase   change   rise

1 The population of the world   ___is increasing___ very fast.
2 The world .... Things never stay the same.
3 The situation is already bad and it .... worse.
4 The cost of living .... Every year things are more expensive.
5 The weather .... to improve. The rain has stopped, and the wind isn't
   as strong.

A

Study this example situation:

Alex is a bus driver, but now he is in bed asleep.
He is not driving a bus.   (He is asleep.)

but   He **drives** a bus.   (He is a bus driver.)

Drive(s)/**work**(s)/**do**(es) etc. is the *present simple*:

I/we/you/they	**drive/work/do** etc.
he/she/it	**drives/works/does** etc.

B

We use the present simple to talk about things in general. We use it to say that something happens all the time or repeatedly, or that something is true in general:
- ○ Nurses **look** after patients in hospitals.
- ○ I usually **go** away at weekends.
- ○ The earth **goes** round the sun.
- ○ The café **opens** at 7.30 in the morning.

Remember:

    I **work** …   *but*   He **works** …   They **teach** …   *but*   My sister **teaches** …

For spelling (**-s** or **-es**), see Appendix 6.

C

We use **do/does** to make questions and negative sentences:

do does	I/we/you/they he/she/it	**work**? **drive**? **do**?		I/we/you/they he/she/it	**don't** **doesn't**	**work** **drive** **do**

- ○ I come from Canada. Where **do** you **come** from?
- ○ I **don't go** away very often.
- ○ What **does** this word **mean**?   (*not* What means this word?)
- ○ Rice **doesn't grow** in cold climates.

In the following examples, **do** is also the main verb (do you **do** / doesn't **do** etc.):
- ○ 'What **do** you **do**?' 'I work in a shop.'
- ○ He's always so lazy. He **doesn't do** anything to help.

D

We use the present simple to say how often we do things:
- ○ I **get** up at 8 o'clock **every morning**.
- ○ **How often** do you **go** to the dentist?
- ○ Julie **doesn't drink** tea **very often**.
- ○ Robert usually **goes** away **two or three times a year**.

E

I promise / I apologise etc.

Sometimes we do things by saying something. For example, when you *promise* to do something, you can say '**I promise** …'; when you *suggest* something, you can say '**I suggest** …':
- ○ **I promise** I won't be late.   (*not* I'm promising)
- ○ 'What do you **suggest** I do?' '**I suggest** that you …'

In the same way we say: **I apologise** … / **I advise** … / **I insist** … / **I agree** … / **I refuse** … etc.

Present simple and present continuous ➜ **Units 3–4**   Present tenses for the future ➜ **Unit 19**

Exercises

2.1 Complete the sentences using the following verbs:

| cause(s) | connect(s) | drink(s) | live(s) | open(s) | ~~speak(s)~~ | take(s) |

1 Tanya ....*speaks*.... German very well.
2 I don't often .... coffee.
3 The swimming pool .... at 7.30 every morning.
4 Bad driving .... many accidents.
5 My parents .... in a very small flat.
6 The Olympic Games .... place every four years.
7 The Panama Canal .... the Atlantic and Pacific oceans.

2.2 Put the verb into the correct form.

1 Julie ...*doesn't drink*... (not / drink) tea very often.
2 What time .... (the banks / close) here?
3 I've got a car, but I .... (not / use) it much.
4 'Where .... (Ricardo / come) from?' 'From Cuba.'
5 'What .... (you / do)?' 'I'm an electrician.'
6 It .... (take) me an hour to get to work. How long .... (it / take) you?
7 Look at this sentence. What .... (this word / mean)?
8 David isn't very fit. He .... (not / do) any sport.

2.3 Use the following verbs to complete the sentences. Sometimes you need the negative:

| believe | eat | flow | ~~go~~ | ~~grow~~ | make | rise | tell | translate |

1 The earth ...*goes*... round the sun.
2 Rice ...*doesn't grow*... in Britain.
3 The sun .... in the east.
4 Bees .... honey.
5 Vegetarians .... meat.
6 An atheist .... in God.
7 An interpreter .... from one language into another.
8 Liars are people who .... the truth.
9 The River Amazon .... into the Atlantic Ocean.

2.4 You ask Lisa questions about herself and her family. Write the questions.

1 You know that Lisa plays tennis. You want to know how often. Ask her.
   How often ...*do you play tennis*... ?
2 Perhaps Lisa's sister plays tennis too. You want to know. Ask Lisa.
   .... your sister .... ?
3 You know that Lisa reads a newspaper every day. You want to know which one. Ask her.
   .... ?
4 You know that Lisa's brother works. You want to know what he does. Ask Lisa.
   .... ?
5 You know that Lisa goes to the cinema a lot. You want to know how often. Ask her.
   .... ?
6 You don't know where Lisa's grandparents live. You want to know. Ask Lisa.
   .... ?

2.5 Complete using the following:

| I apologise | I insist | I promise | I recommend | ~~I suggest~~ |

1 Mr Evans is not in the office today. ...*I suggest*... you try calling him tomorrow.
2 I won't tell anybody what you said. ....
3 *(in a restaurant)* You must let me pay for the meal. ....
4 .... for what I did. It won't happen again.
5 The new restaurant in Hill Street is very good. .... it.

Present continuous and present simple 1 (**I am doing** and **I do**)

A

Compare:

Present continuous (**I am doing**)

We use the continuous for things happening at or around the time of speaking.
The action is not complete.

	I am doing	
past	*now*	*future*

- ☐ The water **is boiling**. Can you turn it off?
- ☐ Listen to those people. What language **are** they **speaking**?
- ☐ Let's go out. It **isn't raining** now.
- ☐ 'I'm busy.' 'What **are** you **doing**?'
- ☐ I**'m getting** hungry. Let's go and eat.
- ☐ Kate wants to work in Italy, so she**'s learning** Italian.
- ☐ The population of the world **is increasing** very fast.

We use the continuous for *temporary* situations:
- ☐ I**'m living** with some friends until I find a place of my own.
- ☐ A: You**'re working** hard today.
  B: Yes, I have a lot to do.

See Unit 1 for more information.

Present simple (**I do**)

We use the simple for things in general or things that happen repeatedly.

	I do	
past	*now*	*future*

- ☐ Water **boils** at 100 degrees Celsius.
- ☐ Excuse me, **do** you **speak** English?
- ☐ It **doesn't rain** very much in summer.
- ☐ What **do** you usually **do** at weekends?
- ☐ I always **get** hungry in the afternoon.
- ☐ Most people **learn** to swim when they are children.
- ☐ Every day the population of the world **increases** by about 200,000 people.

We use the simple for *permanent* situations:
- ☐ My parents **live** in London. They have lived there all their lives.
- ☐ Joe isn't lazy. He **works** hard most of the time.

See Unit 2 for more information.

B

I always do and **I'm always doing**

I **always do** (something) = I do it every time:
- ☐ I **always go** to work by car. (*not* I'm always going)

'I**'m always** doing something' has a different meaning. For example:

I've lost my phone again. I**'m always losing** things.

I**'m always losing** things = I lose things very often, perhaps too often, or more often than normal.

More examples:
- ☐ You**'re always playing** computer games. You should do something more active.
  (= You play computer games too often)
- ☐ Tim is never satisfied. He**'s always complaining**. (= He complains too much)

Present continuous and simple 2 ➜ **Unit 4**   Present tenses for the future ➜ **Unit 19**

Exercises

3.1 Are the <u>underlined</u> verbs right or wrong? Correct them where necessary.

1 Water <u>boils</u> at 100 degrees Celsius.   *OK*
2 The water <u>boils</u>. Can you turn it off?   *is boiling*
3 Look! That man <u>tries</u> to open the door of your car.
4 Can you hear those people? What <u>do they talk</u> about?
5 The moon <u>goes</u> round the earth in about 27 days.
6 I must go now. <u>It gets</u> late.
7 <u>I usually go</u> to work by car.
8 'Hurry up! It's time to leave.' 'OK, <u>I come</u>.'
9 I hear you've got a new job. How <u>do you get</u> on?
10 Paul is never late. <u>He's always getting</u> to work on time.
11 They don't get on well. <u>They're always arguing</u>.

3.2 Put the verb into the correct form, present continuous or present simple.

1 Let's go out. ___It isn't raining___ (it / not / rain) now.
2 Julia is very good at languages. ___She speaks___ (she / speak) four languages very well.
3 Hurry up! _____ (everybody / wait) for you.
4 '_____ (you / listen) to the radio?' 'No, you can turn it off.'
5 '_____ (you / listen) to the radio every day?' 'No, just occasionally.'
6 The River Nile _____ (flow) into the Mediterranean.
7 The river _____ (flow) very fast today – much faster than usual.
8 _____ (we / usually / grow) vegetables in our garden, but this year
   _____ (we / not / grow) any.
9 A: How's your English?
   B: Not bad. I think _____ (it / improve) slowly.
10 Rachel is in New York right now. _____ (she / stay) at the Park Hotel.
   _____ (she / always / stay) there when she's in New York.
11 Can we stop walking soon? _____ (I / start) to feel tired.
12 A: Can you drive?
   B: _____ (I / learn). My father _____ (teach) me.
13 Normally _____ (I / finish) work at five, but this week
   _____ (I / work) until six to earn a little more money.
14 My parents _____ (live) in Manchester. They were born there and have never
   lived anywhere else. Where _____ (your parents / live)?
15 Sonia _____ (look) for a place to live. _____ (she / stay)
   with her sister until she finds somewhere.
16 A: What _____ (your brother / do)?
   B: He's an architect, but _____ (he / not / work) at the moment.
17 (at a party) _____ (I / usually enjoy) parties, but
   _____ (I /not / enjoy) this one very much.

3.3 Finish B's sentences. Use **always -ing**.

1 A: I've lost my phone again.
   B: Not again! ___You're always losing your phone___ .
2 A: The car has broken down again.
   B: That car is useless. It _____ .
3 A: Look! You've made the same mistake again.
   B: Oh no, not again! I _____ .
4 A: Oh, I've forgotten my glasses again.
   B: Typical! _____ .

Present continuous and present simple 2
(I am doing and I do)

A

We use continuous forms for actions and happenings that have started but not finished (they **are eating** / it **is raining** etc.). Some verbs (for example, **know** and **like**) are not normally used in this way. We don't say 'I am knowing' or 'they are liking'; we say 'I **know**', 'they **like**'.

The following verbs are not normally used in the present continuous:

like	want	need	prefer			
know	realise	suppose	mean	understand	believe	remember
belong	fit	contain	consist	seem		

- ○ I'm hungry. I **want** something to eat. (*not* I'm wanting)
- ○ **Do** you **understand** what I **mean**?
- ○ Anna **doesn't seem** very happy at the moment.

B Think

When **think** means 'believe' or 'have an opinion', we do not use the continuous:
- ○ I **think** Mary is Canadian, but I'm not sure. (*not* I'm thinking)
- ○ What **do** you **think** of my plan? (= What is your opinion?)

When **think** means 'consider', the continuous is possible:
- ○ I**'m thinking** about what happened. I often **think** about it.
- ○ Nicky **is thinking** of giving up her job. (= she is considering it)

C See hear smell taste

We normally use the present simple (not continuous) with these verbs:
- ○ **Do** you **see** that man over there? (*not* Are you seeing)
- ○ This room **smells**. Let's open a window.

We often use **can + see/hear/smell/taste**:
- ○ **I can hear** a strange noise. **Can** you **hear** it?

D Look feel

You can use the present simple or continuous to say how somebody looks or feels now:
- ○ You **look** well today. *or* You**'re looking** well today.
- ○ How **do** you **feel** now? *or* How **are** you **feeling** now?

but
- ○ I usually **feel** tired in the morning. (*not* I'm usually feeling)

E He is selfish and He is being selfish

He**'s being** = He's behaving / He's acting. Compare:
- ○ I can't understand why he**'s being** so selfish. He isn't usually like that.
  (**being** selfish = behaving selfishly at the moment)
- ○ He never thinks about other people. He **is** very selfish. (*not* He is being)
  (= He is selfish generally, not only at the moment)

We use **am/is/are being** to say how somebody is *behaving*. It is not usually possible in other sentences:
- ○ It**'s** hot today. (*not* It is being hot)
- ○ Sarah **is** very tired. (*not* is being tired)

Present continuous and simple 1 → Unit 3   Have → Unit 17   Present tenses for the future → Unit 19

Exercises

4.1 Put the verb into the correct form, present continuous or present simple.

1 Are you hungry? _Do you want_ (you / want) something to eat?
2 Don't put the dictionary away. .... (I / use) it.
3 Don't put the dictionary away. .... (I / need) it.
4 Who is that man? What .... (he / want)?
5 Who is that man? Why .... (he / look) at us?
6 Alan says he's 80 years old, but nobody .... (believe) him.
7 She told me her name, but .... (I / not / remember) it now.
8 .... (I / think) of selling my car. Would you be interested in buying it?
9 .... (I / think) you should sell your car.
   .... (you / not / use) it very often.
10 Air .... (consist) mainly of nitrogen and oxygen.

4.2 Use the words in brackets to make sentences. (You should also study Unit 3 before you do this exercise.)

① (you / not / seem / very happy today)
You don't seem
very happy today.

② (what / you / do?)
....
Be quiet! (I / think)

③ (who / this umbrella / belong to?)
....
I have no idea.

④ (the dinner / smell / good)
....

⑤ Excuse me. (anybody / sit / there?)
....
No, it's free.

⑥ (these gloves / not / fit / me)
....
They're too small.

GLOVES

4.3 Are the <u>underlined</u> verbs right or wrong? Correct them where necessary.

1 Nicky <u>is thinking</u> of giving up her job.   _OK_
2 <u>Are</u> you <u>believing</u> in God? ....
3 <u>I'm feeling</u> hungry. Is there anything to eat? ....
4 This sauce is great. <u>It's tasting</u> really good. ....
5 <u>I'm thinking</u> this is your key. Am I right? ....

4.4 Complete the sentences using the most suitable form of **be**. Use **am/is/are being** (continuous) where possible; otherwise use **am/is/are** (simple).

1 I can't understand why _he's being_ so selfish. He isn't usually like that.
2 Sarah .... very nice to me at the moment. I wonder why.
3 You'll like Sophie when you meet her. She .... very nice.
4 You're usually very patient, so why .... so unreasonable about waiting ten more minutes?
5 Why isn't Steve at work today? .... ill?

9

A Study this example:

> Wolfgang Amadeus Mozart **was** an Austrian musician and composer. He **lived** from 1756 to 1791. He **started** composing at the age of five and **wrote** more than 600 pieces of music. He **was** only 35 years old when he **died**.
>
> **Lived/started/wrote/was/died** are all *past simple*.

W.A. MOZART

1756-1791

B Very often the past simple ends in **-ed** (*regular* verbs):
- ○ I work in a travel agency now. Before that I **worked** in a department store.
- ○ We **invited** them to our party, but they **decided** not to come.
- ○ The police **stopped** me on my way home last night.
- ○ Laura **passed** her exam because she **studied** very hard.

For spelling (sto**pp**ed, stud**ied** etc.), see Appendix 6.

But many verbs are *irregular*. The past simple does *not* end in **-ed**. For example:

write	→	**wrote**	○ Mozart **wrote** more than 600 pieces of music.
see	→	**saw**	○ We **saw** Tanya in town a few days ago.
go	→	**went**	○ I **went** to the cinema three times last week.
shut	→	**shut**	○ It was cold, so I **shut** the window.

For a list of irregular verbs, see Appendix 1.

C In questions and negatives we use **did/didn't** + *infinitive* (**enjoy/see/go** etc.):

I	**enjoyed**			you	**enjoy?**			I		**enjoy**
she	**saw**		**did**	she	**see?**			she	**didn't**	**see**
they	**went**			they	**go?**			they		**go**

- ○ A: **Did** you **go** out last night?
  B: Yes, I **went** to the cinema, but I **didn't enjoy** the film much.
- ○ 'When **did** Mr Thomas **die**?' 'About ten years ago.'
- ○ They **didn't invite** us to the party, so we **didn't go**.
- ○ '**Did** you **have** time to do the shopping?' 'No, I **didn't**.'

In the following examples, **do** is the main verb in the sentence (**did … do / didn't do**):
- ○ What **did** you **do** at the weekend? (*not* What did you at the weekend?)
- ○ I **didn't do** anything. (*not* I didn't anything)

D The past of **be** (**am/is/are**) is **was/were**:

I/he/she/it	**was/wasn't**		**was**	I/he/she/it?
we/you/they	**were/weren't**		**were**	we/you/they?

Note that we do not use **did** in negatives and questions with **was/were**:
- ○ I **was** angry because they **were** late.
- ○ **Was** the weather good when you **were** on holiday?
- ○ They **weren't** able to come because they **were** so busy.
- ○ Did you go out last night or **were** you too tired?

Past simple and past continuous ➔ Unit 6   Past simple and present perfect ➔ Units 12–14

Exercises

5.1 Read what Laura says about a typical working day:

I usually get up at 7 o'clock and have a big breakfast. I walk to work, which takes me about half an hour. I start work at 8.45. I never have lunch. I finish work at 5 o'clock. I'm always tired when I get home. I usually cook a meal in the evening. I don't usually go out. I go to bed at about 11 o'clock, and I always sleep well.

Laura

Yesterday was a typical working day for Laura. Write what she did or didn't do yesterday.

1 *She got up* .... at 7 o'clock.
2 She .... a big breakfast.
3 She ....
4 It .... to get to work.
5 .... at 8.45.
6 .... lunch.
7 .... at 5 o'clock.
8 .... tired when .... home.
9 .... a meal yesterday evening.
10 .... out yesterday evening.
11 .... at 11 o'clock.
12 .... well last night.

5.2 Complete the sentences using the following verbs in the correct form:

| buy | catch | cost | fall | hurt | sell | spend | teach | throw | ~~write~~ |

1 Mozart .....*wrote*..... more than 600 pieces of music.
2 'How did you learn to drive?' 'My father .... me.'
3 We couldn't afford to keep our car, so we .... it.
4 Dave .... down the stairs this morning and .... his leg.
5 Joe .... the ball to Sue, who .... it.
6 Ann .... a lot of money yesterday. She .... a dress which .... £100.

5.3 You ask James about his holiday. Write your questions.

　　Hi. How are things?
　　　　　　Fine, thanks. I've just had a great holiday.
1 Where *did you go* ?
　　　　　　To the U.S. We went on a trip from San Francisco to Denver.
2 How .... ? By car?
　　　　　　Yes, we hired a car in San Francisco.
3 It's a long way to drive. How long .... to get to Denver?
　　　　　　Two weeks.
4 Where .... ? In hotels?
　　　　　　Yes, small hotels or motels.
5 .... good?
　　　　　　Yes, but it was very hot – sometimes too hot.
6 .... the Grand Canyon?
　　　　　　Of course. It was wonderful.

5.4 Complete the sentences. Put the verb into the correct form, positive or negative.

1 It was warm, so I ....*took*.... off my coat. (take)
2 The film wasn't very good. I ...*didn't enjoy*... it much. (enjoy)
3 I knew Sarah was busy, so I .... her. (disturb)
4 We were very tired, so we .... the party early. (leave)
5 The bed was very uncomfortable. I .... well. (sleep)
6 The window was open and a bird .... into the room. (fly)
7 The hotel wasn't very expensive. It .... much to stay there. (cost)
8 I was in a hurry, so I .... time to phone you. (have)
9 It was hard carrying the bags. They .... very heavy. (be)

A Study this example situation:

Yesterday Karen and Jim played tennis. They started at 10 o'clock and finished at 11.30.
So, at 10.30 they **were playing** tennis.

They **were playing** = they were in the middle of playing. They had not finished playing.
Was/were -ing is the *past continuous*:

I/he/she/it	**was**	**playing**
we/you/they	**were**	**doing**
		working etc.

B I **was doing** something = I was in the middle of doing something at a certain time. The action or situation had already started before this time, but had not finished:

I started doing   **I was doing**   **I finished doing**

past   *past*   *now*

- ○ This time last year I **was living** in Brazil.
- ○ What **were** you **doing** at 10 o'clock last night?
- ○ I waved to Helen, but she **wasn't looking**.

C Compare the *past continuous* (I **was doing**) and *past simple* (I **did**):

Past continuous (in the middle of an action)	*Past simple* (complete action)
○ I **was walking** home when I met Dan. (in the middle of walking home)	○ I **walked** home after the party last night. (= all the way, completely)
○ Kate **was watching** TV when we arrived.	○ Kate **watched** TV a lot when she was ill last year.

D We often use the past simple and the past continuous together to say that something happened in the middle of something else:

- ○ Matt **phoned** while we **were having** dinner.
- ○ It **was raining** when I **got** up.
- ○ I **saw** you in the park yesterday. You **were sitting** on the grass and **reading** a book.
- ○ I **hurt** my back while I **was working** in the garden.

But we use the past simple to say that one thing happened after another:

- ○ I **was walking** along the road when I **saw** Dan. So I **stopped**, and we **had** a chat.

Compare:

○ When Karen arrived, we **were having** dinner. (= we had already started before she arrived)	○ When Karen arrived, we **had** dinner. (= Karen arrived, and then we had dinner)

E Some verbs (for example, **know** and **want**) are not normally used in the continuous (see Unit 4A):

- ○ We were good friends. We **knew** each other well. (*not* We were knowing)
- ○ I was enjoying the party, but Chris **wanted** to go home. (*not* was wanting)

Exercises

6.1 What were you doing at these times? Write sentences as in the examples. The past continuous is not always necessary (see the second example).

1 (at 8 o'clock yesterday evening) _I was having dinner._
2 (at 5 o'clock last Monday) _I was on a bus on my way home._
3 (at 10.15 yesterday morning) ....
4 (at 4.30 this morning) ....
5 (at 7.45 yesterday evening) ....
6 (half an hour ago) ....

6.2 Use your own ideas to complete the sentences. Use the past continuous.

1 Matt phoned while we _were having dinner_ .
2 The doorbell rang while I ....
3 The car began to make a strange noise when we ....
4 Jessica fell asleep while she ....
5 The television was on, but nobody ....

6.3 Put the verb into the correct form, past continuous or past simple.

1	2 Gates 1–10	3
I _saw_ (see) Sue in town yesterday, but she .... (not / see) me. She .... (look) the other way.	I .... (meet) Tom and Jane at the airport a few weeks ago. They .... (go) to Paris and I .... (go) to Rome. We .... (have) a chat while we .... (wait) for our flights.	I .... (cycle) home yesterday when a man .... (step) out into the road in front of me. I .... (go) quite fast, but luckily I .... (manage) to stop in time and .... (not / hit) him.

6.4 Put the verb into the correct form, past continuous or past simple.

1 Jenny _was waiting_ (wait) for me when I _arrived_ (arrive).
2 'What .... (you / do) at this time yesterday?' 'I was asleep.'
3 '.. (you / go) out last night?' 'No, I was too tired.'
4 How fast .... (you / drive) when the accident .... (happen)?
5 Sam .... (take) a picture of me while I .... (not / look).
6 We were in a very difficult position. We .... (not / know) what to do.
7 I haven't seen Alan for ages. When I last .... (see) him, he .... (try) to find a job.
8 I .... (walk) along the street when suddenly I .... (hear) footsteps behind me. Somebody .... (follow) me. I was scared and I .... (start) to run.
9 When I was young, I .... (want) to be a pilot.
10 Last night I .... (drop) a plate when I .... (do) the washing-up. Fortunately it .... (not / break).

→ Additional exercise 1 (page 302)

Present perfect 1 (I have done)

A Study this example situation:

I've lost my key.

Tom is looking for his key. He can't find it.
He **has lost** his key.

He **has lost** his key = He lost it recently, and he still
doesn't have it.

Have/has lost is the *present perfect simple:*

I/we/they/you **have** (= I've etc.)	**finished**
	lost
he/she/it **has** (= he's etc.)	**done**
	been etc.

The present perfect simple is **have/has** + *past participle*. The past participle often ends in -**ed**
(finish**ed**/decid**ed** etc.), but many important verbs are *irregular* (**lost/done/written** etc.).

For a list of irregular verbs, see Appendix 1.

B When we say that 'something **has happened**', this is usually new information:
- ☐ Ow! I**'ve cut** my finger.
- ☐ The road is closed. There**'s been** (there **has been**) an accident.
- ☐ *(from the news)* Police **have arrested** two men in connection with the robbery.

When we use the present perfect, there is a connection with *now*. The action in the past has a result *now:*
- ☐ 'Where's your key?' 'I don't know. I**'ve lost** it.' (= I don't have it *now*)
- ☐ He told me his name, but I**'ve forgotten** it. (= I can't remember it *now*)
- ☐ 'Is Sally here?' 'No, she**'s gone** out.' (= she is out *now*)
- ☐ I can't find my bag. **Have** you **seen** it? (= Do you know where it is *now*?)

C Note the difference between **gone (to)** and **been (to)**:
- ☐ James is on holiday. He **has gone to** Italy. (= he is there now or on his way there)
- ☐ Jane is back home now. She **has been to** Italy. (= she has now come back)

D You can use the present perfect with **just**, **already** and **yet**.

Just = a short time ago:
- ☐ 'Are you hungry?' 'No, I**'ve just had** lunch.'
- ☐ Hello. **Have** you **just arrived**?

We use **already** to say that something happened sooner than expected:
- ☐ 'Don't forget to pay your electricity bill.' 'I**'ve already paid** it.'
- ☐ 'What time is Mark leaving?' 'He**'s already left**.'

Yet = until now. **Yet** shows that the speaker is expecting something to happen. Use **yet** only in
questions and negative sentences:
- ☐ **Has** it **stopped** raining **yet**?
- ☐ I've written the email, but I **haven't sent** it **yet**.

E You can also use the past simple (**did**, **went**, **had** etc.) in the examples on this page. So you can say:
- ☐ 'Is Sally here?' 'No, she **went** out.' *or* 'No, she**'s gone** out.'
- ☐ 'Are you hungry?' 'No, I **just had** lunch.' *or* 'No, I**'ve just had** lunch.'

Present perfect ➔ Units 8, 11   Been to ➔ Units 8A, 126A   Present perfect continuous ➔ Units 9–10
Present perfect and past ➔ Units 12–14   Yet and already ➔ Unit 111   American English ➔ Appendix 7

Exercises

7.1 Read the situations and write sentences. Use the following verbs in the present perfect:

| arrive | break | fall | go up | grow | improve | ~~lose~~ |

1 Tom is looking for his key. He can't find it.   Tom *has lost his key.*
2 Lisa can't walk and her leg is in plaster.   Lisa ....
3 Last week the bus fare was £1.80. Now it is £2.   The bus fare ....
4 Maria's English wasn't very good. Now it is better.   Her English ....
5 Dan didn't have a beard before. Now he has a beard.   Dan ....
6 This morning I was expecting a letter. Now I have it.   The letter ....
7 The temperature was 20 degrees. Now it is only 12.   The ....

7.2 Put in **been** or **gone**.

1 James is on holiday. He's ....*gone*.... to Italy.
2 Hello! I've just .... to the shops. I've bought lots of things.
3 Alice isn't here at the moment. She's .... to the shop to get a newspaper.
4 Tom has .... out. He'll be back in about an hour.
5 'Are you going to the bank?' 'No, I've already .... to the bank.'

7.3 Complete B's sentences. Make sentences from the words in brackets.

	A	B
1	Would you like something to eat?	No, thanks. *I've just had lunch.* (I / just / have / lunch)
2	Do you know where Julia is?	Yes, ... (I / just / see / her)
3	What time is David leaving?	.... (he / already / leave)
4	What's in the newspaper today?	I don't know. .... (I / not / read / it yet)
5	Is Sue coming to the cinema with us?	No, ... (she / already / see / the film)
6	Are your friends here yet?	Yes, ... (they / just / arrive)
7	What does Tim think about your plan?	.... (we / not / tell / him yet)

7.4 Read the situations and write sentences with **just**, **already** or **yet**.

1 After lunch you go to see a friend at her house. She says, 'Would you like something to eat?'
   You say: No thank you. ....*I've just had lunch*.... . (have lunch)
2 Joe goes out. Five minutes later, the phone rings and the caller says, 'Can I speak to Joe?'
   You say: I'm afraid .... (go out)
3 You are eating in a restaurant. The waiter thinks you have finished and starts to take your
   plate away. You say: Wait a minute! .... (not / finish)
4 You plan to eat at a restaurant tonight. You phoned to reserve a table. Later your friend says,
   'Shall I phone to reserve a table?' You say: No, ... (do it)
5 You know that a friend of yours is looking for a place to live. Perhaps she has been successful.
   Ask her. You say: .... ? (find)
6 You are still thinking about where to go for your holiday. A friend asks, 'Where are you going
   for your holiday?' You say: .... (not / decide)
7 Linda went shopping, but a few minutes ago she returned. Somebody asks, 'Is Linda still out
   shopping?' You say: No, ... (come back)

Present perfect 2 (I have done)

A

Study this example conversation:

DAVE: **Have** you **travelled** a lot, Jane?
JANE: Yes, I**'ve been** to lots of places.
DAVE: Really? **Have** you ever **been** to China?
JANE: Yes, I**'ve been** to China twice.
DAVE: What about India?
JANE: No, I **haven't been** to India.

Jane's life
(a period until now)

past   *now*

When we talk about a period of time that continues from the past until now, we use the *present perfect* (**have been / have travelled** etc.). Here, Dave and Jane are talking about the places Jane has visited in her life, which is a period that continues until now.

Some more examples:
- **Have** you ever **eaten** caviar?
- We**'ve** never **had** a car.
- '**Have** you **read** *Hamlet*?' 'No, I **haven't read** any of Shakespeare's plays.'
- Susan really loves that film. She**'s seen** it eight times!
- What a boring film! It's the most boring film I**'ve ever seen**.

Been (to) = visited:
- I**'ve** never **been to** China. Have you **been** there?

B

In the following examples too, the speakers are talking about a period that continues until now (**recently / in the last few days / so far / since breakfast** etc.):
- **Have** you **heard** anything from Brian **recently**?
- I**'ve met** a lot of people **in the last few days**.
- Everything is going well. We **haven't had** any problems **so far**.
- I'm hungry. I **haven't eaten** anything **since breakfast**. (= from breakfast until now)
- It's good to see you again. We **haven't seen** each other **for a long time**.

——— recently ———→
— in the last few days —→
——— since breakfast ——→

past   *now*

C

In the same way we use the present perfect with **today / this evening / this year** etc. when these periods are not finished at the time of speaking (see also Unit 14B):
- I**'ve drunk** four cups of coffee today.
- **Have** you **had** a holiday **this year**?
- I **haven't seen** Tom **this morning**. **Have** you?
- Rob **hasn't worked** very hard **this term**.

——— today ———→
past   *now*

D

We say: It's the (first) time something **has happened**. For example:
- Don is having a driving lesson. It's his first one.
  It's the first time he **has driven** a car. (*not* drives)
- *or* He **has never driven** a car **before**.

- Sarah has lost her passport again. This is the second time this **has happened**. (*not* happens)
- Bill is phoning his girlfriend again. That's the third time he**'s phoned** her **this evening**.

This is the first time
I**'ve driven** a car.

DRIVING SCHOOL

KT09 GYR

Present perfect 1 → **Unit 7**   Present perfect + **for/since** → **Units 11–12**
Present perfect and past → **Units 12–14**

Exercises

8.1 You ask people about things they have done. Write questions with **ever**.

1 (ride / horse?)   _Have you ever ridden a horse?_
2 (be / California?)   Have ....
3 (run / marathon?)   ....
4 (speak / famous person?)   ....
5 (most beautiful place / visit?)   What's ....

8.2 Complete B's answers. Some sentences are positive and some negative. Use these verbs:

be	be	eat	happen	~~have~~	have	~~meet~~	play	read	see	try

A

1 What's Mark's sister like?
2 Is everything going well?
3 Are you hungry?
4 Can you play chess?
5 Are you enjoying your holiday?

6 What's that book like?
7 Is Brussels an interesting place?
8 I hear your car broke down again yesterday.
9 Do you like caviar?
10 Mike was late for work again today.

11 Who's that woman by the door?

B

1 I've no idea.   _I've never met_ her.
2 Yes, we _haven't had_ any problems so far.
3 Yes.   I .... much today.
4 Yes, but .... for ages.
5 Yes, it's the best holiday .... for a long time.
6 I don't know. .... it.
7 I've no idea. .... there.
8 Yes, it's the second time .... this month.
9 I don't know. .... it.
10 Again?   He .... late every day this week.
11 I don't know. .... her before.

8.3 Write four sentences about yourself. Use **I haven't** and choose from the boxes.

used a computer	travelled by bus	eaten any fruit
been to the cinema	read a book	lost anything

today
this week
recently
for ages
since ...
this year

1   _I haven't used a computer today._ ....
2   ....
3   ....
4   ....
5   ....

8.4 Read the situations and write sentences as shown in the example.

1 Jack is driving a car, but he's very nervous and not sure what to do.
   You ask: _Have you driven a car before?_
   He says: _No, this is the first time I've driven a car._
2 Ben is playing tennis. He's not good at it and he doesn't know the rules.
   You ask: Have ....
   He says: No, this is the first ....
3 Sue is riding a horse. She doesn't look very confident or comfortable.
   You ask: ....
   She says: ....
4 Maria is in Japan. She has just arrived and it's very new for her.
   You ask: ....
   She says: ....

Present perfect continuous (**I have been doing**)

A   It has been raining

Study this example situation:

Is it raining?
No, but the ground is wet.
It has been raining.

Have/has been -ing is the *present perfect continuous:*

I/we/they/you **have** (= I**'ve** etc.)		
he/she/it **has** (= he**'s** etc.)	**been**	**doing** **waiting** **playing** etc.

We use the present perfect continuous for an activity that has recently stopped or just stopped. There is a connection with *now:*

- You're out of breath. **Have** you **been running**? (= you're out of breath *now*)
- Paul is very tired. He**'s been working** very hard. (= he's tired *now*)
- Why are your clothes so dirty? What **have** you **been doing**?
- I**'ve been talking** to Amanda about the problem and she agrees with me.
- Where have you been? I**'ve been looking** for you everywhere.

B   It has been raining for two hours.

Study this example situation:

It began raining two hours ago and it is still raining.
How long **has** it **been raining**?
It **has been raining** for two hours.

We use the present perfect continuous in this way especially with **how long**, **for** … and **since** … . The activity is still happening (as in this example) or has just stopped.

- **How long have** you **been learning** English? (= you're still learning English)
- Tim is still watching TV. He**'s been watching** TV **all day**.
- Where have you been? I**'ve been looking** for you **for the last half hour**.
- Chris **hasn't been feeling** well **recently**.

You can use the present perfect continuous for actions repeated over a period of time:

- Silvia is a very good tennis player. She**'s been playing since she was eight**.
- Every morning they meet in the same café. They**'ve been going** there **for years**.

C   Compare **I am doing** (see Unit 1) and **I have been doing**:

I am doing
present continuous

now

I have been doing
present perfect continuous

now

- Don't disturb me now. I**'m working**.

- We need an umbrella. It**'s raining**.
- Hurry up! We**'re waiting**.

- I**'ve been working** hard. Now I'm going to have a break.
- The ground is wet. It**'s been raining**.
- We**'ve been waiting** for an hour.

Present perfect continuous and simple ➜ **Units 10–11**   Present perfect + for/since ➜ **Units 11–12**

Exercises

9.1 **What have these people been doing or what has been happening?**

1 earlier / now

They **'ve been shopping.**

2 earlier / now

She ....

3 earlier / now

They ....

4 earlier / now

He ....

9.2 **Write a question for each situation.**

1 You meet Paul as he is leaving the swimming pool.
You ask: (you / swim?)   **Have you been swimming?**

2 You have just arrived to meet a friend who is waiting for you.
You ask: (you / wait / long?) ....

3 You meet a friend in the street. His face and hands are very dirty.
You ask: (what / you / do?) ....

4 A friend of yours is now working in a shop. You want to know how long.
You ask: (how long / you / work / there?) ....

5 A friend tells you about his job – he sells mobile phones. You want to know how long.
You ask: (how long / you / sell / mobile phones?) ....

9.3 **Read the situations and complete the sentences.**

1 It's raining. The rain started two hours ago.
It **'s been raining** for two hours.

2 We are waiting for the bus. We started waiting 20 minutes ago.
We .... for 20 minutes.

3 I'm learning Spanish. I started classes in December.
I .... since December.

4 Jessica is working in a supermarket. She started working there on 18 January.
.... since 18 January.

5 Our friends always spend their holidays in Italy. They started going there years ago.
.... for years.

9.4 **Put the verb into the present continuous (I am -ing) or present perfect continuous
(I have been -ing).**

1 **Maria has been learning** (Maria / learn) English for two years.

2 Hello, Tom. .... (I / look) for you. Where have you been?

3 Why .... (you / look) at me like that? Stop it!

4 Linda is a teacher. .... (she / teach) for ten years.

5 .... (I / think) about what you said and I've decided to take
your advice.

6 'Is Paul on holiday this week?' 'No, ... (he / work).'

7 Sarah is very tired. .... (she / work) very hard recently.

Present perfect continuous and simple
(I have been doing and I have done)

A Study this example situation:

I've been painting my bedroom.

I've painted my bedroom.

There is paint on Kate's clothes.
She **has been painting** her bedroom.

Has been painting is the *present perfect continuous.*

We are thinking of the activity. It does not matter whether it has been finished or not. In this example, the activity (painting the bedroom) has not been finished.

Her bedroom was green. Now it is yellow.
She **has painted** her bedroom.

Has painted is the *present perfect simple.*

Here, the important thing is that something has been finished. **Has painted** is a completed action. We are interested in the result of the activity (the painted bedroom), not the activity itself.

B Compare these examples:

- ◻ My hands are very dirty. **I've been repairing** my bike.
- ◻ Joe **has been eating** too much recently. He should eat less.
- ◻ It's nice to see you again. What **have** you **been doing** since we last met?
- ◻ Where have you been? **Have** you **been playing** tennis?

- ◻ My bike is OK again now. **I've repaired** it.
- ◻ Somebody **has eaten** all the chocolates. The box is empty.
- ◻ Where's the book I gave you? What **have** you **done** with it?
- ◻ **Have** you ever **played** tennis?

C We use the continuous to say *how long* (for something that is still happening):

- ◻ How long **have** you **been reading** that book?
- ◻ Lisa is writing emails. She**'s been writing** emails all morning.
- ◻ They**'ve been playing** tennis since 2 o'clock.
- ◻ I'm learning Arabic, but **I haven't been learning** it very long.

We use the simple to say *how much, how many* or *how many times:*

- ◻ How much of that book **have** you **read**?
- ◻ Lisa is writing emails. She**'s sent** lots of emails this morning.
- ◻ They**'ve played** tennis three times this week.
- ◻ I'm learning Arabic, but I **haven't learnt** very much yet.

D Some verbs (for example, **know/like/believe**) are not normally used in the continuous:

- ◻ I**'ve known** about the problem for a long time. (*not* I've been knowing)
- ◻ How long **have** you **had** that camera? (*not* have you been having)

For a list of these verbs, see Unit 4A. For **have**, see Unit 17.
But note that you *can* use **want** and **mean** in the present perfect continuous:

- ◻ I**'ve been meaning** to phone Jane, but I keep forgetting.

Present perfect simple ➜ Units 7–8   Present perfect continuous ➜ Unit 9
Present perfect + **for/since** ➜ Units 11–12

Exercises

10.1 Read the situation and complete the sentences. Use the verbs in brackets.

1 Tom started reading a book two hours ago. He is still reading it and now he is on page 53.
   <u>He has been reading</u> for two hours. (read)
   <u>He has read</u> 53 pages so far. (read)

2 Rachel is from Australia. She is travelling round Europe at the moment. She began her trip three months ago.
   She .... for three months. (travel)
   .... six countries so far. (visit)

3 Patrick is a tennis player. He began playing tennis when he was ten years old. This year he won the national championship again – for the fourth time.
   .... the national championship four times. (win)
   .... since he was ten. (play)

4 When they left college, Lisa and Sue started making films together. They still make films.
   They .... films since they left college. (make)
   .... five films since they left college. (make)

10.2 For each situation, ask a question using the words in brackets.

1 You have a friend who is learning Arabic. You ask:
   (how long / learn / Arabic?) <u>How long have you been learning Arabic?</u>
2 You have just arrived to meet a friend. She is waiting for you. You ask:
   (wait / long?) Have ....
3 You see somebody fishing by the river. You ask:
   (catch / any fish?) ....
4 Some friends of yours are having a party next week. You ask:
   (how many people / invite?) ....
5 A friend of yours is a teacher. You ask:
   (how long / teach?) ....
6 You meet somebody who is a writer. You ask:
   (how many books / write?) ....
   (how long / write / books?) ....
7 A friend of yours is saving money to go on a world trip. You ask:
   (how long / save?) ....
   (how much money / save?) ....

10.3 Put the verb into the more suitable form, present perfect simple (**I have done**) or continuous (**I have been doing**).

1 Where have you been? <u>Have you been playing</u> (you / play) tennis?
2 Look! .... (somebody / break) that window.
3 You look tired. .... (you / work) hard?
4 '.. (you / ever / work) in a factory?' 'No, never.'
5 'Liz is away on holiday.' 'Is she? Where .... (she / go)?'
6 My brother is an actor. .... (he / appear) in several films.
7 'Sorry I'm late.' 'That's all right. .... (I / not / wait) long.'
8 'Is it still raining?' 'No, ... (it / stop).'
9 .... (I / lose) my phone. .... (you / see) it anywhere?
10 .... (I / read) the book you lent me, but .... (I / not / finish) it yet. It's very interesting.
11 .... (I / read) the book you lent me, so you can have it back now.
12 This is a very old book. .... (I / have) it since I was a child.

A

Study this example situation:

Dan and Jenny are married. They got married exactly 20 years ago, so today is their 20th wedding anniversary.

They **have been** married **for 20 years**.

We say: They **are** married.   (*present*)

but   **How long have** they **been** married?   (*present perfect*)
(*not* How long are they married?)
They **have been** married **for 20 years**.
(*not* They are married for 20 years)

We use the *present perfect* to talk about something that began in the past and still continues now. Compare the *present* and the *present perfect*:

○	Paul is in hospital.
but	He**'s been** in hospital **since Monday**. (= He **has** been ...) (*not* He's in hospital since Monday)
○	**Do** you **know** each other well?
but	**Have** you **known** each other **for a long time**? (*not* Do you know)
○	She**'s waiting** for somebody.
but	She**'s been waiting all morning**.
○	**Do** they **have** a car?
but	**How long have** they **had** their car?

present
he is
do you know
she is waiting

present perfect
he has been
have you known
she has been waiting

past   *now*

B

I have known/had/lived etc. is the *present perfect simple*.
I have been learning / been waiting / been doing etc. is the *present perfect continuous*.

When we ask or say 'how long', the continuous is more usual (see Unit 10):

○ I**'ve been learning** English **for six months**.
○ It**'s been raining since lunchtime**.
○ Richard **has been doing** the same job **for 20 years**.
○ '**How long have** you **been driving**?'   'Since I was 17.'

Some verbs (for example, **know/like/believe**) are not normally used in the continuous:

○ How long **have** you **known** Jane?   (*not* have you been knowing)
○ I**'ve had** a pain in my stomach all day.   (*not* I've been having)

See also Units 4A and 10C. For **have**, see Unit 17.

C

You can use either the present perfect continuous or simple with **live** and **work**:

○ Julia **has been living / has lived** here for a long time.
○ How long **have** you **been working / have** you **worked** here?

But use the simple (**I've lived / I've done** etc.) with **always**:

○ I**'ve always lived** in the country.   (*not* always been living)

D

We say '**I haven't done** something **since/for** ...' (*present perfect simple*):

○ I **haven't seen** Tom since Monday.   (= Monday was the last time I saw him)
○ Sarah **hasn't phoned** for ages.   (= the last time she phoned was ages ago)

I haven't ... since/for ➜ Unit 8B   .   Present perfect continuous ➜ Units 9–10   For and since ➜ Unit 12A

Exercises

11.1 Are the <u>underlined</u> verbs right or wrong? Correct them where necessary.

1 Ben is a friend of mine. <u>I know him</u> very well.   *OK*
2 Ben is a friend of mine. <u>I know him</u> for a long time.   *I've known him*
3 Sarah and Adam <u>are married</u> since July.
4 The weather is awful. <u>It's raining</u> again.
5 The weather is awful. <u>It's raining</u> all day.
6 I like your house. How long <u>are you living</u> there?
7 Gary <u>is working</u> in a shop for the last few months.
8 <u>I don't know</u> Tom well. We've only met a few times.
9 I gave up drinking coffee. <u>I don't drink</u> it for a year.
10 That's a very old bike. How long <u>do you have</u> it?

11.2 Read the situations and write questions from the words in brackets.

1 A friend tells you that Paul is in hospital. You ask him:
(how long / be / in hospital?)   *How long has Paul been in hospital?*
2 You meet a woman who tells you that she teaches English. You ask her:
(how long / teach / English?)
3 You know that Jane is a good friend of Katherine's. You ask Jane:
(how long / know / Katherine?)
4 Your friend's brother went to Australia some time ago and he's still there. You ask your friend:
(how long / be / in Australia?)
5 Tom always wears the same jacket. It's a very old jacket. You ask him:
(how long / have / that jacket?)
6 You are talking to a friend about Joe. Joe now works at the airport. You ask your friend:
(how long / work / at the airport?)
7 A friend of yours is having guitar lessons. You ask him:
(how long / have / guitar lessons?)
8 You meet somebody on a plane. She says that she lives in Chicago. You ask her:
(always / live / in Chicago?)

11.3 Complete B's answers to A's questions.

	A	B
1	Paul is in hospital, isn't he?	Yes, he _has been_ in hospital since Monday.
2	Do you see Ann very often?	No, I _haven't seen_ her for three months.
3	Is Amy married?	Yes, she _____ married for ten years.
4	Are you waiting for me?	Yes, I _____ for the last half hour.
5	You know Mel, don't you?	Yes, we _____ each other a long time.
6	Do you still play tennis?	No, I _____ tennis for years.
7	Is Joe watching TV?	Yes, he _____ TV all evening.
8	Do you watch TV a lot?	No, I _____ TV for ages.
9	Do you have a headache?	Yes, I _____ a headache all morning.
10	Adrian is never ill, is he?	No, he _____ ill since I've known him.
11	Are you feeling ill?	Yes, I _____ ill all day.
12	Sue lives in Berlin, doesn't she?	Yes, she _____ in Berlin for the last few years.
13	Do you go to the cinema a lot?	No, I _____ to the cinema for ages.
14	Would you like to go to New York one day?	Yes, I _____ to go to New York. (*use* **always / want**)

A

We use **for** and **since** to say how long something has been happening.

We use **for** + a period of time (**two hours, six weeks** etc.):	We use **since** + the start of a period (**8 o'clock, Monday, 1999** etc.):
☐ I've been waiting **for two hours**.	☐ I've been waiting **since 8 o'clock**.

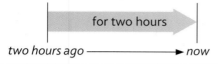

for two hours

two hours ago ──────→ now

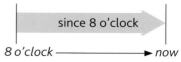

since 8 o'clock

8 o'clock ──────→ now

for		
two hours	20 minutes	five days
a long time	six months	50 years
a week	ages	years

since		
8 o'clock	Monday	12 May
April	2001	Christmas
lunchtime	we arrived	I got up

☐ Sally has been working here **for six months**. (*not* since six months)
☐ I haven't seen Tom **for three days**.

☐ Sally has been working here **since April**. (= from April until now)
☐ I haven't seen Tom **since Monday**.

It is possible to leave out **for** (but not usually in negative sentences):
☐ They've been married (for) **ten years**. (with or without **for**)
☐ They **haven't had** a holiday **for** ten years. (you must use **for**)

We do *not* use **for** + **all** ... (**all day / all my life** etc.):
☐ I've lived here **all my life**. (*not* for all my life)

You can use **in** instead of **for** in negative sentences (**I haven't** ... etc.):
☐ They **haven't had** a holiday **in ten years**. (= for ten years)

B

Compare **when** ... ? (+ *past simple*) and **how long** ... ? (+ *present perfect*):

A: **When** did it start raining?
B: It started raining **an hour ago / at 1 o'clock**.

A: **How long** has it been raining?
B: It's been raining **for an hour / since 1 o'clock**.

A: **When** did Joe and Carol first meet?
B: They first met { **a long time ago**.
            { **when they were at school**.

A: **How long** have they known each other?
B: They've known each other { **for a long time**.
                 { **since they were at school**.

C

We say:

It's (= It **is**) *or* **It's been** (= It **has been**)	**a long time** **six months** (etc.)	since something happened

☐ **It's two years since** I last saw Joe. *or* **It's been two years since** ...
(= I haven't seen Joe for two years)
☐ **It's ages since** we went to the cinema. *or* **It's been ages since** ...
(= We haven't been to the cinema for ages)
☐ **How long is it since** Mrs Hill died? *or* **How long has it been since** ... ?
(= When did Mrs Hill die?)

How long have you (been) ... ? ➜ Unit 11

Exercises

12.1 Write **for** or **since**.

1 It's been raining ..._since_.. lunchtime.
2 Sarah has lived in Paris .... 1995.
3 Paul has lived in Brazil .... ten years.
4 I'm tired of waiting. We've been sitting here .... an hour.
5 Kevin has been looking for a job .... he left school.
6 I haven't been to a party .... ages.
7 I wonder where Joe is. I haven't seen him .... last week.
8 Jane is away. She's been away .... Friday.
9 The weather is dry. It hasn't rained .... a few weeks.

12.2 Write questions with **how long** and **when**.

1 It's raining.
(how long?) ..._How long has it been raining?_...
(when?) ..._When did it start raining?_...
2 Kate is learning Japanese.
(how long / learn?) ....
(when / start?) ....
3 I know Simon.
(how long / you / know?) ....
(when / you / first / meet?) ....
4 Rebecca and David are married.
(how long?) ....
(when?) ....

12.3 Read the situations and complete the sentences.

1 It's raining. It's been raining since lunchtime. It ..._started raining_.. at lunchtime.
2 Ann and Jess are friends. They first met years ago. They've ..._known each other for_.. years.
3 Mark is ill. He became ill on Sunday. He has .... Sunday.
4 Mark is ill. He became ill a few days ago. He has .... a few days.
5 Sarah is married. She's been married for a year. She got ....
6 You have a headache. It started when you woke up.
I've .... I woke up.
7 Sue has been in Italy for the last three weeks.
She went ....
8 You're working in a hotel. You started six months ago.
I've ....

12.4 Write B's answers to the questions.

1 A: Do you often go on holiday?
B: No, ..._I haven't had a holiday for_.. five years.
2 A: Do you often see Laura?
B: No, I .... about a month.
3 A: Do you often go to the cinema?
B: No, ... a long time.
4 A: Do you often eat in restaurants?
B: No, ... ages.

Now write B's answers again. This time use **It's … since … .**

5 (1) ..._No, it's five years since I had a holiday._..
6 (2) No, it's ....
7 (3) No, ...
8 (4) ....

A

Study this example situation:

Tom is looking for his key. He can't find it.

He **has lost** his key. *(present perfect)*

This means that he doesn't have his key *now*.

Ten minutes later:

Now Tom **has found** his key. He has it now.

Has he **lost** his key?   No, he **has found** it.

Did he **lose** his key?   Yes, he **did**.

He **lost** his key *(past simple)*

but now he **has found** it. *(present perfect)*

The present perfect (something **has happened**) is a *present* tense. It always tells us about the situation *now*. 'Tom **has lost** his key' = he doesn't have his key *now* (see Unit 7).

The past simple (something **happened**) tells us only about the *past*. If somebody says 'Tom **lost** his key', this doesn't tell us whether he has the key now or not. It tells us only that he lost his key at some time in the past.

Do *not* use the present perfect if the situation now is different. Compare:
- They**'ve gone** away. They'll be back on Friday.   (they are away *now*)
  They **went** away, but I think they're back at home now.   (*not* They've gone)
- It **has stopped** raining now, so we don't need the umbrella.   (it isn't raining *now*)
  It **stopped** raining for a while, but now it's raining again.   (*not* It has stopped)

B

You can use the present perfect for new or recent happenings:
- 'I**'ve repaired** the washing machine. It's working OK now.'   'Oh, that's good.'
- 'Sally **has had** a baby! It's a boy.'   'That's great news.'

Usually, you can also use the past simple:
- I **repaired** the washing machine. It's working OK now.

Use the past simple (*not* the present perfect) for things that are not recent or new:
- Mozart **was** a composer. He **wrote** more than 600 pieces of music.
  (*not* has been … has written)
- My mother **grew** up in Italy.   (*not* has grown)

Compare:
- Did you know that somebody **has invented** a new type of washing machine?
- Who **invented** the telephone?   (*not* has invented)

C

We use the present perfect to give new information (see Unit 7). But if we continue to talk about it, we normally use the past simple:
- A: Ow! I**'ve burnt** myself.
  B: How **did** you **do** that?   (*not* have you done)
  A: I **picked** up a hot dish.   (*not* have picked)

- A: Look! Somebody **has spilt** something on the sofa.
  B: Well, it **wasn't** me. I **didn't do** it.   (*not* hasn't been … haven't done)

Past simple → Unit 5   Present perfect → Units 7–8   Present perfect and past 2 → Unit 14
American English → Appendix 7

Exercises

13.1 Complete the sentences using the verbs in brackets. Use the present perfect where possible. Otherwise use the past simple.

1. I can't get in. I __'ve lost__ (lose) my key.

2. The office is empty now. Everybody .... (go) home.

3. I meant to call you last night, but I .... (forget).

4. Helen .... (go) to Egypt for a holiday, but she's back home in England now.

   HELEN

5. Are you OK?
   Yes, I .... (have) a headache, but I'm fine now.

6. Can you help us? Our car .... (break) down.

13.2 Are the <u>underlined</u> parts of these sentences right or wrong? Correct them where necessary.

1. Did you hear about Sue? <u>She's given</u> up her job.   *OK*
2. My mother <u>has grown</u> up in Italy.   *grew*
3. How many poems <u>has William Shakespeare written</u>?   ....
4. Ow! <u>I've cut</u> my finger. It's bleeding.   ....
5. Drugs <u>have become</u> a big problem everywhere.   ....
6. Who <u>has invented</u> paper?   ....
7. Where <u>have you been born</u>?   ....
8. Ellie isn't at home. <u>She's gone</u> shopping.   ....
9. Albert Einstein <u>has been</u> the scientist who   ....
   <u>has developed</u> the theory of relativity.   ....

13.3 Put the verb into the correct form, present perfect or past simple.

1. __It stopped__ raining for a while, but now it's raining again. (it / stop)
2. The town where I live is very different now. __It has changed__ a lot. (it / change)
3. I studied German at school, but .... most of it now. (I / forget)
4. The police .... three people, but later they let them go. (arrest)
5. What do you think of my English? Do you think ....? (it / improve)
6. A: Are you still reading the paper?
   B: No, ... with it. You can have it. (I / finish)
7. .... for a job as a tourist guide, but I wasn't successful. (I / apply)
8. Where's my bike? .... outside the house, but it's not there now. (it / be)
9. Quick! We need to call an ambulance. .... an accident. (there / be)
10. A: Have you heard about Ben? .... his arm. (he / break)
    B: Really? How ....? (that / happen)
    A: .... off a ladder. (he / fall)

27

Present perfect and past 2 (**I have done** and **I did**)

Do not use the present perfect (**I have done**) when you talk about a *finished* time (for example, **yesterday / ten minutes ago / in 2005 / when I was a child**). Use a past tense:

- ○ It **was** very cold **yesterday**. (*not* has been)
- ○ Paul and Lucy **arrived ten minutes ago**. (*not* have arrived)
- ○ **Did** you **eat** a lot of sweets **when you were a child**? (*not* have you eaten)
- ○ I **got** home late **last night**. I **was** very tired and **went** straight to bed.

Use the past to ask **When** ... ? or **What time** ... ?:

- ○ **When did** your friends **arrive**? (*not* have ... arrived)
- ○ **What time did** you **finish** work?

Compare:

Present perfect	*Past simple*
○ Tom **has lost** his key. He can't get into the house.	○ Tom **lost** his key **yesterday**. He couldn't get into the house.
○ Is Carla here or **has she left**?	○ **When did** Carla **leave**?

Compare:

Present perfect (**have done**)	*Past simple* (**did**)
○ I**'ve done** a lot of work **today**.	○ I **did** a lot of work **yesterday**.

We use the present perfect for a period of time that continues *until now*. For example: **today / this week / since 2007**.	We use the past simple for a *finished* time in the past. For example: **yesterday / last week / from 2007 to 2010**.

○ It **hasn't rained this week**.	○ It **didn't rain last week**.
○ **Have** you **seen** Anna **this morning**? (it is still morning)	○ **Did** you **see** Anna **this morning**? (it is now afternoon or evening)
○ **Have** you **seen** Tim **recently**?	○ **Did** you **see** Tim **on Sunday**?
○ I don't know where Lisa is. I **haven't seen** her. (= I haven't seen her recently)	○ A: **Was** Lisa at the party **on Sunday**? B: I don't think so. I **didn't** see her.
○ We**'ve been waiting** for an hour. (we are still waiting now)	○ We **waited** (*or* **were waiting**) for an hour. (we are no longer waiting)
○ Jack lives in Los Angeles. He **has lived** there for seven years.	○ Jack **lived** in New York for ten years. Now he lives in Los Angeles.
○ I **have never played** golf. (in my life)	○ I **didn't play** golf **last summer**.
○ *It's the last day of your holiday. You say*: It**'s been** a really good holiday. I**'ve** really **enjoyed** it.	○ *After you come back from holiday you say*: It **was** a really good holiday. I really **enjoyed** it.

Past simple ➜ Unit 5   Present perfect ➜ Units 7–8   Present perfect and past 1 ➜ Unit 13

Exercises

14.1 Are the <u>underlined</u> parts of these sentences right or wrong? Correct them where necessary.

1 <u>I've lost</u> my key. I can't find it anywhere.   *OK*
2 <u>Have you eaten</u> a lot of sweets when you were a child?   *Did you eat*
3 <u>I've bought</u> a new car. You must come and see it.
4 <u>I've bought</u> a new car last week.
5 Where <u>have you been</u> yesterday evening?
6 Lucy <u>has left</u> school in 1999.
7 I'm looking for Mike. <u>Have you seen</u> him?
8 '<u>Have you been</u> to Paris?' 'Yes, many times.'
9 I'm very hungry. <u>I haven't eaten</u> much today.
10 When <u>has this book been</u> published?

14.2 Make sentences from the words in brackets. Use the present perfect or past simple.

1 (it / not / rain / this week)   *It hasn't rained this week.*
2 (the weather / be / cold / recently) The weather
3 (it / cold / last week) It
4 (I / not / read / a newspaper yesterday) I
5 (I / not / read / a newspaper today)
6 (Emily / earn / a lot of money / this year)
7 (she / not / earn / so much / last year)
8 (you / have / a holiday recently?)

14.3 Put the verb into the correct form, present perfect or past simple.

1 'What's Madrid like?' 'I don't know.   *I haven't been*   (I / not / be) there.'
2 When   *I got*   (I / get) home last night,   *I was*   (I / be)
   very tired and   *I went*   (I / go) straight to bed.
3 A: .... (you / see) Lisa recently?
   B: Yes, ... (I / see) her a few days ago.
4 I'm tired. .... (I / not / sleep) well last night.
5 The bus drivers were on strike last week. .... (there / be) no buses.
6 Mr Lee .... (work) in a bank for 15 years. Then .... (he / give)
   it up. Now he works as a gardener.
7 Mary lives in Dublin. .... (she / live) there all her life.
8 A: .... (you / go) to the cinema last night?
   B: Yes, but .... (it / be) a mistake. The film .... (be) awful.
9 My grandfather .... (die) before I was born. ....
   (I / never / meet) him.
10 I don't know Karen's husband. .... (I / never / meet) him.
11 It's nearly lunchtime, and .... (I / not / see) Martin all morning.
   I wonder where he is.
12 'Where do you live?' 'In Boston.'
   'How long .... (you / live) there?' 'Five years.'
   'Where .... (you / live) before that?' 'In Chicago.'
   'And how long .... (you / live) in Chicago?' 'Two years.'

14.4 Write sentences about yourself using the ideas in brackets.

1 (something you haven't done today)   *I haven't eaten any fruit today.*
2 (something you haven't done today)
3 (something you didn't do yesterday)
4 (something you did yesterday evening)
5 (something you haven't done recently)
6 (something you've done a lot recently)

Past perfect (**I had done**)

A   Study this example situation:

at 10.30   *at 11.00*

Bye!

Hi!

PAUL   SARAH

Sarah went to a party last week. Paul went to the party too, but they didn't see each other. Paul left the party at 10.30 and Sarah arrived at 11 o'clock. So:

When Sarah arrived at the party, Paul wasn't there.

He **had gone** home.

Had gone is the *past perfect (simple):*

I/we/they/you he/she/it	**had**	(= I**'d** etc.) (= he**'d** etc.)	**gone** **seen** **finished** etc.

The past perfect simple is **had** + *past participle* (**gone/seen/finished** etc).

Sometimes we talk about something that happened in the past:
- ○   Sarah **arrived** at the party.

This is the starting point of the story. Then, if we want to talk about things that happened *before* this time, we use the past perfect (**had** …):
- ○   When Sarah arrived at the party, Paul **had** already **gone** home.

Some more examples:
- ○   When we got home last night, we found that somebody **had broken** into the flat.
- ○   Karen didn't want to go to the cinema with us because she**'d** already **seen** the movie.
- ○   At first I thought I**'d done** the right thing, but I soon realised that I**'d made** a big mistake.
- ○   The man sitting next to me on the plane was very nervous. He **hadn't flown** before.
  or   … He **had** never **flown** before.

B   Compare the *present perfect* (**have seen** etc.) and the *past perfect* (**had seen** etc.):

Present perfect

have seen

past   now

- ○   Who is that woman? I**'ve seen** her before, but I can't remember where.
- ○   We aren't hungry. We**'ve** just **had** lunch.
- ○   The house is dirty. They **haven't cleaned** it for weeks.

Past perfect

had seen

past   now

- ○   I wasn't sure who she was. I**'d seen** her before, but I couldn't remember where.
- ○   We weren't hungry. We**'d** just **had** lunch.
- ○   The house was dirty. They **hadn't cleaned** it for weeks.

C   Compare the *past simple* (**left**, **was** etc.) and the *past perfect* (**had left**, **had been** etc.):

- ○   A: Was Tom there when you arrived?
  B: Yes, but he **left** soon afterwards.

- ○   Kate **wasn't** at home when I phoned. She **was** at her mother's house.

- ○   A: Was Tom there when you arrived?
  B: No, he **had** already **left**.

- ○   Kate **had** just **got** home when I phoned. She **had been** at her mother's house.

Past perfect continuous → Unit 16   Irregular verbs (**gone/seen** etc.) → Appendix 1

Exercises

15.1 **Read the situations and write sentences from the words in brackets.**

1 You went to Sue's house, but she wasn't there.
   (she / go / out)   _She had gone out._

2 You went back to your home town after many years. It wasn't the same as before.
   (it / change / a lot) _____

3 I invited Rachel to the party, but she couldn't come.
   (she / arrange / to do something else) _____

4 You went to the cinema last night. You got to the cinema late.
   (the film / already / start) _____

5 It was nice to see Daniel again after such a long time.
   (I / not / see / him for five years) _____

6 I offered Sue something to eat, but she wasn't hungry.
   (she / just / have / breakfast) _____

15.2 **For each situation, write a sentence ending with never … before. Use the verb in brackets.**

1 The man sitting next to you on the plane was very nervous. It was his first flight.
   (fly)   _He'd never flown before._

2 Somebody sang a song. I didn't know it.
   (hear) I _____ before.

3 Sam played tennis yesterday. He wasn't very good at it because it was his first game.
   (play) He _____

4 Last year we went to Mexico. It was our first time there.
   (be there)   We _____

15.3 **Use the sentences on the left to complete the paragraphs on the right. These sentences are
in the order in which they happened – so (a) happened before (b), (b) before (c) etc. But your
paragraph begins with the underlined sentence, so sometimes you need the past perfect.**

1 (a) Somebody broke into the office during
        the night.
   (b) <u>We arrived at work in the morning.</u>
   (c) We called the police.

   We arrived at work in the morning and
   found that _somebody had broken_
   into the office during the night. So
   _____ the police.

2 (a) Laura went out this morning.
   (b) <u>I rang her doorbell.</u>
   (c) There was no answer.

   I went to Laura's house this morning and
   rang her doorbell, but _____ no
   answer. _____ out.

3 (a) Jim came back from holiday a few
        days ago.
   (b) <u>I met him the same day.</u>
   (c) He looked very well.

   I met Jim a few days ago. _____
   just _____ holiday.
   _____ very well.

4 (a) Kevin sent Sally lots of emails.
   (b) She never replied to them.
   (c) <u>Yesterday he got a phone call from her.</u>
   (d) He was very surprised.

   Yesterday Kevin _____ from
   Sally. _____ very surprised.
   _____ lots of emails,
   but _____ .

15.4 **Put the verb into the correct form, past perfect (I had done) or past simple (I did).**

1 'Was Paul at the party when you arrived?' 'No, he _had gone_ (go) home.'

2 I felt very tired when I got home, so I _____ (go) straight to bed.

3 The house was very quiet when I got home. Everybody _____ (go) to bed.

4 Sorry I'm late. The car _____ (break) down on my way here.

5 We were driving along the road when we _____ (see) a car which
   _____ (break) down, so we _____ (stop) to help.

→ Additional exercises 5–8 (pages 304–07)   **31**

Past perfect continuous (**I had been doing**)

Study this example situation:

yesterday morning

Yesterday morning I got up and looked out of the window. The sun was shining, but the ground was very wet.

It **had been raining**.

It was *not* raining when I looked out of the window; the sun was shining. But it **had been** raining before.

Had been -ing is the *past perfect continuous*:

I/we/you/they he/she/it	**had**	(= I**'d** etc.) (= he**'d** etc.)	**been**	**doing working playing** etc.

Some more examples:
- ○ When the boys came into the house, their clothes were dirty, their hair was untidy and one of them had a black eye. They**'d been fighting**.
- ○ I was very tired when I got home. I**'d been working** hard all day.
- ○ When I went to Madrid a few years ago, I stayed with a friend of mine. She **hadn't been living** there very long, but she knew the city very well.

You can say that something **had been happening** for a period of time before something else happened:
- ○ We**'d been playing** tennis for about half an hour when it started to rain heavily.
- ○ Paul went to the doctor last Friday. He **hadn't been feeling** well for some time.

Compare **have been -ing** (*present perfect continuous*) and **had been -ing** (*past perfect continuous*):

Present perfect continuous

I have been -ing

past   *now*

- ○ I hope the bus comes soon. I**'ve been waiting** for 20 minutes. *(before now)*
- ○ James is out of breath. He **has been running**.

Past perfect continuous

I had been -ing

past   *now*

- ○ At last the bus came. I**'d been waiting** for 20 minutes. *(before the bus came)*
- ○ James was out of breath. He **had been running**.

Compare **was -ing** (*past continuous*) and **had been -ing**:
- ○ It **wasn't raining** when we went out. The sun **was shining**. But it **had been raining**, so the ground was wet.
- ○ Katherine **was sitting** in an armchair resting. She was tired because she**'d been working** very hard.

Some verbs (for example, **know** and **like**) are not normally used in the continuous:
- ○ We were good friends. We **had known** each other for years. (*not* had been knowing)
- ○ I was surprised when Lisa cut her hair. She**'d had** long hair since I first met her. (*not* she'd been having)

For a list of these verbs, see Unit 4A. For **have**, see Unit 17.

Present perfect continuous ➜ Unit 9–10   Past perfect simple ➜ Unit 15

Exercises

16.1 Read the situations and make sentences from the words in brackets.

1 I was very tired when I arrived home.
(I / work / hard all day) _I'd been working hard all day._

2 The two boys came into the house. They had a football and they were both very tired.
(they / play / football) ....

3 I was disappointed when I had to cancel my holiday.
(I / look / forward to it) ....

4 Ann woke up in the middle of the night. She was frightened and didn't know where she was.
(she / dream) ....

5 When I got home, Mark was sitting in front of the TV. He had just turned it off.
(he / watch / a film) ....

16.2 Read the situations and complete the sentences.

1 We played tennis yesterday. Half an hour after we began playing, it started to rain.
We _had been playing for half an hour_ when _it started to rain_ .

2 I had arranged to meet Tom in a restaurant. I arrived and waited for him. After 20 minutes
I realised that I was in the wrong restaurant.
I .... for 20 minutes when I ....
.... the wrong restaurant.

3 Sarah got a job in a factory. Five years later the factory closed down.
At the time the factory ...., Sarah ....
.... there for five years.

4 I went to a concert last week. The orchestra began playing. After about ten minutes a man in
the audience suddenly started shouting.
The orchestra .... when

This time make your own sentence:

5 I began walking along the road. I ....
when ....

16.3 Put the verb into the most suitable form, past continuous (**I was doing**), past perfect
(**I had done**) or past perfect continuous (**I had been doing**).

1 It was very noisy next door. Our neighbours _were having_ (have) a party.

2 We were good friends. _We'd known_ (we / know) each other for years.

3 John and I went for a walk. I had difficulty keeping up with him because
.... (he / walk) so fast.

4 Sue was sitting on the ground. She was out of breath. .... (she / run).

5 When I arrived, everybody was sitting round the table with their mouths full.
.... (they / eat).

6 When I arrived, everybody was sitting round the table and talking. Their mouths were empty,
but their stomachs were full. .... (they / eat).

7 James was on his hands and knees on the floor. .... (he / look) for his
contact lens.

8 When I arrived, Kate .... (wait) for me. She was annoyed because I was
late and .... (she / wait) for a long time.

9 I was sad when I sold my car. .... (I / have) it for a very long time.

10 We were extremely tired at the end of the journey. .... (we / travel) for
more than 24 hours.

A

Have and **have got** (= for possession, relationships, illnesses etc.)

You can use **have** or **have got**. There is no difference in meaning:
- They **have** a new car. *or* They**'ve got** a new car.
- Lisa **has** two brothers. *or* Lisa**'s got** two brothers.
- I **have** a headache. *or* I**'ve got** a headache.
- Our house **has** a small garden. *or* Our house **has got** a small garden.
- He **has** a few problems. *or* He**'s got** a few problems.

With these meanings (possession etc.), you cannot use continuous forms (**am having** etc.):
- We're enjoying our holiday. We **have** / We**'ve got** a nice room in the hotel. (*not* We're having a nice room)

For the past we use **had** (without **got**):
- Lisa **had** long hair when she was a child. (*not* Lisa had got)

B

In questions and negative sentences there are three possible forms:

Do you have any questions?	I **don't have** any questions.
Have you got any questions?	I **haven't got** any questions.
Have you any questions? *(less usual)*	I **haven't** any questions. *(less usual)*
Does she have a car?	She **doesn't have** a car.
Has she got a car?	She **hasn't got** a car.
Has she a car? *(less usual)*	She **hasn't** a car. *(less usual)*

In past questions and negative sentences we use **did/didn't**:
- **Did** you **have** a car when you were living in Paris?
- I **didn't have** my phone, so I couldn't call you.
- Lisa **had** long hair, **didn't** she?

C

Have breakfast / **have** a shower / **have** a good time etc.

We also use **have** (*but not* have got) for many actions and experiences. For example:

have	**breakfast / dinner / a cup of coffee / something to eat** etc.
	a bath / a shower / a swim / a break / a rest / a party / a holiday
	an accident / an experience / a dream
	a look (at something)
	a chat / a conversation / a discussion (with somebody)
	trouble / difficulty / fun / a good time etc.
	a baby (= give birth to a baby)

Have got is *not* possible in the expressions in the box. Compare:
- Sometimes I **have** (= eat) a sandwich for my lunch. (*not* I've got)

but I**'ve got** / I **have** some sandwiches. Would you like one?

You can use continuous forms (**am having** etc.) with the expressions in the box:
- We're enjoying our holiday. We**'re having** a great time. (*not* We have)
- Mark **is having** a shower at the moment. He has a shower every day.

In questions and negative sentences we use **do/does/did**:
- I **don't** usually **have** a big breakfast. (*not* I usually haven't)
- What time **does** Chris **have** lunch? (*not* has Chris lunch)
- **Did** you **have** trouble finding a place to live?

Have (got) to ... → Unit 31   American English → Appendix 7

Exercises

Unit
17

17.1 Write negative sentences with **have**. Some are present and some are past.

1 I can't get into the house.   (a key)   I haven't got a key.
2 I couldn't read the letter.   (my glasses)   I didn't have my glasses.
3 I can't get onto the roof.   (a ladder)   I
4 We couldn't visit the museum.   (enough time)   We
5 He couldn't find his way to our house.   (a map)
6 She can't pay her bills.   (any money)
7 I can't go swimming today.   (enough energy)
8 They couldn't take any pictures.   (a camera)

17.2 Which alternatives are correct? Sometimes two alternatives are possible, sometimes only one.

1 Excuse me, ... a pen I could borrow?
   (A) have you got   **B** are you having   **(C)** do you have   (*both* A *and* C *are correct*)

2 .... time to go to the bank yesterday?
   A Had you got   **B** Did you have   **C** Had you

3 I need a stamp for this letter. .... one?
   A Do you have   **B** Are you having   **C** Have you got

4 What does Jack do? .... a job?
   A Does he have   **B** Is he having   **C** Has he got

5 .... a lot of friends when you were a child?
   A Did you have   **B** Were you having   **C** Had you

6 When you worked in your last job, ... your own office?
   A had you   **B** have you got   **C** did you have

17.3 Are the <u>underlined</u> verbs OK? Change them where necessary.

1 Is there anything you want to ask? <u>Do you have</u> any questions?   OK
2 Lisa <u>had got</u> long hair when she was a child.   Lisa had long hair.
3 Tom couldn't contact us because <u>he hadn't</u> our number.
4 'Are you feeling OK?' 'No, <u>I'm having</u> a toothache.'
5 Are you enjoying yourself? <u>Are you having</u> a good time?
6 It started to rain. I got wet because <u>I hadn't</u> an umbrella.
7 Will can't drive. <u>He doesn't have</u> a driving licence.
8 Did your trip go OK? <u>Had you</u> any problems?
9 My friend called me when <u>I was having</u> breakfast.

17.4 Complete the sentences. Use an expression from the list with **have** in the correct form.

have a baby	have a break	have a chat	have trouble	have a good flight
have a look	~~have lunch~~	have a party	have a nice time	have a shower

1 I don't eat much during the day. I never   have lunch   .
2 David starts work at 8 o'clock and .... at 10.30.
3 We .... last week. It was great – we invited lots of people.
4 Excuse me, can I .... at your newspaper, please?
5 Jim is away on holiday at the moment. I hope he ....
6 I met Ann in the supermarket yesterday. We stopped and ....
7 A: .... finding the book you wanted?
   B: No, I found it OK.
8 Suzanne .... a few weeks ago. It's her second child.
9 A: Why didn't you answer the phone?
   B: I ....
10 *You meet your friend Sally at the airport. She has just arrived. You say:*
   Hi, Sally. How are you? .... ?

35

Used to (do)

A Study this example situation:

a few years ago

these days

Nicola doesn't travel much these days.
She prefers to stay at home.

But she **used to travel** a lot.
She **used to go** away two or three times a year.

She **used to travel** a lot = she travelled a lot often in the past, but she doesn't do this any more.

← she used to travel →	she doesn't travel
past	*now*

B Something **used to** happen = it happened often in the past, but no longer happens:

- ○ I **used to play** tennis a lot, but I don't play very much now.
- ○ David **used to spend** a lot of money on clothes. These days he can't afford it.
- ○ 'Do you go to the cinema much?' 'Not now, but I **used to**.' (= I used to go)

We also use **used to** … for things that were true, but are not true any more:

- ○ This building is now a furniture shop. It **used to be** a cinema.
- ○ I **used to think** Mark was unfriendly, but now I realise he's a very nice person.
- ○ I've started drinking tea recently. I never **used to like** it before.
- ○ Lisa **used to have** very long hair when she was a child.

C 'I **used to** do something' is past. There is no present. You cannot say 'I use to do'.
To talk about the present, use the present simple (I **do**).

Compare:

past	he **used to play**	we **used to live**	there **used to be**
present	he **plays**	we **live**	there **is**

- ○ We **used to live** in a small village, but now we **live** in London.
- ○ There **used to be** four cinemas in the town. Now there **is** only one.

D The normal question form is **did** (you) **use to** … ?:

- ○ **Did** you **use to eat** a lot of sweets when you were a child?

The negative form is **didn't use to** … (**used not to** … is also possible):

- ○ I **didn't use to like** him. (*or* I **used not to like** him.)

E Compare **I used to do** and **I was doing**:

- ○ I **used to watch** TV a lot. (= I watched TV often in the past, but I no longer do this)
- ○ I **was watching** TV when Rob called. (= I was in the middle of watching TV)

F Do not confuse **I used to do** and **I am used to doing** (see Unit 61). The structures and meanings are different:

- ○ I **used to live** alone. (= I lived alone in the past, but I no longer live alone)
- ○ I **am used** to **living** alone. (= I live alone, and I don't find it strange or difficult because I've been living alone for some time)

Past continuous (**I was doing**) → Unit 6   Would (= **used to**) → Unit 36
Be/get used to (doing) something → Unit 61

Exercises

18.1 Complete the sentences with **use(d) to** + a suitable verb.

1 Nicola doesn't travel much now. She ___used to travel___ a lot, but she prefers to stay at home these days.
2 Sophie _____ a motorbike, but last year she sold it and bought a car.
3 We moved to Spain a few years ago. We _____ in Paris.
4 I rarely eat ice-cream now, but I _____ it when I was a child.
5 Jackie _____ my best friend, but we aren't good friends any more.
6 It only takes me about 40 minutes to get to work now that the new road is open. It _____ more than an hour.
7 There _____ a hotel near the airport, but it closed a long time ago.
8 When you lived in New York, _____ to the theatre very often?

18.2 Compare what Karen said five years ago and what she says today:

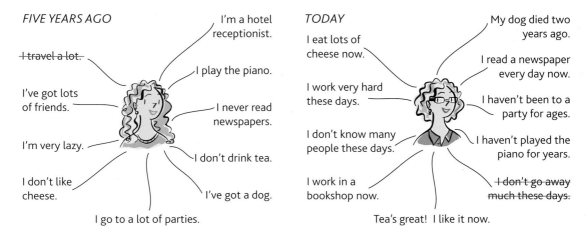

FIVE YEARS AGO

I travel a lot.

I've got lots of friends.

I'm very lazy.

I don't like cheese.

I go to a lot of parties.

I'm a hotel receptionist.

I play the piano.

I never read newspapers.

I don't drink tea.

I've got a dog.

TODAY

I eat lots of cheese now.

I work very hard these days.

I don't know many people these days.

I work in a bookshop now.

My dog died two years ago.

I read a newspaper every day now.

I haven't been to a party for ages.

I haven't played the piano for years.

I don't go away much these days.

Tea's great! I like it now.

Now write sentences about how Karen has changed. Use **used to / didn't use to / never used to** in the first part of your sentence.

1 ___She used to travel a lot,___ but ___she doesn't go away much these days.___
2 She used _____ but _____
3 _____ but _____
4 _____ but _____
5 _____ but _____
6 _____ but _____
7 _____ but _____
8 _____ but _____
9 _____ but _____
10 _____ but _____

18.3 Write sentences about yourself like the examples. Begin **I used to ...** (**I used to be/work/like/play/read** etc.).

1 ___I used to live in a small village, but now I live in London.___
2 ___I used to play tennis a lot, but I don't play any more.___
3 I used _____, but _____
4 I _____
5 _____

Now begin with **I didn't use to ... .**

6 ___I didn't use to read a lot, but I do now.___
7 I didn't _____
8 _____

➔ Additional exercise 9 (page 307)

Present tenses (**I am doing** / **I do**) for the future

A | *Present continuous* (**I am doing**) with a future meaning

This is Ben's diary for next week.

He **is playing** tennis on Monday afternoon.
He **is going** to the dentist on Tuesday morning.
He **is having** dinner with Kate on Friday.

In all these examples, Ben has already decided and arranged to do these things.

I'm doing something (tomorrow) = I have already decided and arranged to do it:

- ○ A: What **are** you **doing** on Saturday evening? (*not* What do you do)
  B: **I'm going** to the theatre. (*not* I go)
- ○ A: What time **is** Katherine **arriving** tomorrow?
  B: Half past ten. **I'm meeting** her at the station.
- ○ **I'm not working** tomorrow, so we can go out somewhere.
- ○ Steve **isn't playing** football next Saturday. He's hurt his leg.

'I'm **going to** (do)' is also possible in these sentences:

- ○ What **are** you **going to do** on Saturday evening?

But the present continuous is more natural when we talk about arrangements. See Unit 20B.

Do not use **will** to talk about what you have arranged to do:

- ○ What **are** you **doing** this evening? (*not* What will you do)
- ○ Alex **is getting** married next month. (*not* will get)

You can also use the present continuous for an action *just before you begin to do it*. This happens especially with verbs of movement (**go/come/leave** etc.):

- ○ I'm tired. **I'm going** to bed now. Goodnight. (*not* I go to bed now)
- ○ 'Jess, are you ready yet?' 'Yes, **I'm coming**.' (*not* I come)

B | *Present simple* (**I do**) with a future meaning

We use the present simple when we talk about timetables, programmes etc. (for public transport, cinemas etc.):

- ○ My train **leaves** at 11.30, so I need to be at the station by 11.15.
- ○ What time **does** the film **start** this evening?
- ○ It**'s** Wednesday tomorrow. / Tomorrow **is** Wednesday.

You can use the present simple to talk about people if their plans are fixed like a timetable:

- ○ I **start** my new job on Monday.
- ○ What time **do** you **finish** work tomorrow?

But the continuous is more usual for personal arrangements:

- ○ What time **are** you **meeting** Ann tomorrow? (*not* do you meet)

Compare:

Present continuous	*Present simple*
○ What time **are you arriving**?	○ What time **does the train arrive**?
○ **I'm going** to the cinema this evening.	○ **The film starts** at 8.15 (this evening).

I'm going to ➜ Units 20, 23   Will ➜ Units 21–22   Present simple after when/if etc. ➜ Unit 25

Exercises

19.1 A friend of yours is planning to go on holiday soon. You ask her about her plans.
Use the words in brackets to make your questions.

1 (where / go?)   _Where are you going?_   Scotland.
2 (how long / go for?) .... Ten days.
3 (when / leave?) .... Next Friday.
4 (go / alone?) .... No, with a friend.
5 (travel / by car?) .... No, by train.
6 (where / stay?) .... In a hotel.

19.2 Tom wants you to visit him, but you are very busy. Look at your diary for the next few days and
explain to him why you can't come.

5-Monday:
Volleyball 7.30 pm
6-Tuesday:
Work late (till 9 pm)
7-Wednesday:
Theatre
8-Thursday:
Meet Julia 8 pm

TOM: Can you come on Monday evening?
YOU: Sorry, but __I'm playing volleyball__ .... (1)
TOM: What about Tuesday evening then?
YOU: No, not Tuesday. I .... (2)
TOM: And Wednesday evening?
YOU: .... (3)
TOM: Well, are you free on Thursday?
YOU: I'm afraid not. .... (4)

19.3 Have you arranged to do anything at these times? Write sentences about yourself.

1 (this evening)   _I'm going out this evening._   **or**   _I'm not doing anything this evening._
2 (tomorrow morning) I ....
3 (tomorrow evening) ....
4 (next Sunday) ....
5 *(choose another day or time)* ....

19.4 Put the verb into the more suitable form, present continuous or present simple.

1 ___I'm going___ (I / go) to the cinema this evening.
2 ___Does the film start___ (the film / start) at 3.30 or 4.30?
3 .... (we / have) a party next Saturday. Would you like to come?
4 The art exhibition .... (finish) on 3 May.
5 .... (I / not / go) out this evening.
 (I / stay) at home.
6 '... (you / do) anything tomorrow morning?'   'No, I'm free. Why?'
7 .... (we / go) to a concert tonight. ....
 (it / start) at 7.30.
8 .... (I / leave) now. I've come to say goodbye.
9 A: Have you seen Liz recently?
 B: No, but .... (we / meet) for lunch next week.
10 *You are on the train to London and you ask another passenger:*
 Excuse me. What time .... (this train / get) to London?
11 *You are talking to Helen:*
 Helen, ... (I / go) to the supermarket. .... (you / come)
 with me?
12 *You and a friend are watching television. You say:*
 I'm bored with this programme. What time .... (it / end)?
13 .... (I / not / use) the car this evening, so you can have it.
14 Sue .... (come) to see us tomorrow. ....
 (she / travel) by train and her train .... (arrive) at 10.15.

→ Additional exercises 10–13 (pages 308–10)

(I'm) going to (do)

A

I **am going to do** something = I have already decided to do it, I intend to do it:

- ○ '**Are** you **going to eat** anything?' 'No, I'm not hungry.'
- ○ A: I hear Sarah has won some money. What **is** she **going to do** with it?
  B: She**'s going to buy** a new car.
- ○ I**'m** just **going to make** a quick phone call. Can you wait for me?
- ○ This cheese smells horrible. I**'m not going to eat** it.

B

I am doing and **I am going to do**

We use **I am doing** (*present continuous*) when we say what we have *arranged* to do – for example, arranged to meet somebody, arranged to go somewhere:

- ○ What time **are** you **meeting** Ann this evening?
- ○ I**'m leaving** tomorrow. I've got my plane ticket.

I **am going to do** something = I've decided to do it (but perhaps not *arranged* to do it):

- ○ 'Your shoes are dirty.' 'Yes, I know. I**'m going to clean** them.' (= I've decided to clean them, but I haven't *arranged* to clean them)
- ○ I've decided not to stay here any longer. Tomorrow I**'m going to look** for somewhere else to stay.

Often the difference is very small and either form is possible.

C

You can also say that 'something **is going to happen**' in the future. For example:

The man isn't looking where he is going.

He **is going to walk** into the wall.

When we say that 'something **is going to happen**', the situation *now* makes this clear. The man is walking towards the wall now, so we can see that he **is going to walk** into it.

 going to

situation now *future happening*

Some more examples:

- ○ Look at those black clouds! It**'s going to rain**. (the clouds are there now)
- ○ I feel terrible. I think I**'m going to be** sick. (I feel terrible now)
- ○ The economic situation is bad now and things **are going to get** worse.

D

I **was going to** do something = I intended to do it, but didn't do it:

- ○ We **were going to travel** by train, but then we decided to go by car instead.
- ○ Peter **was going to do** the exam, but he changed his mind.
- ○ I **was** just **going to cross** the road when somebody shouted 'Stop!'

You can say that 'something **was going to happen**' (but didn't happen):

- ○ I thought it **was going to rain**, but it didn't.

I am doing for the future ➜ Unit 19A   **I will** and **I'm going to** ➜ Unit 23

Exercises

20.1 **Write a question with going to for each situation.**

1 Your friend has won some money. You ask:
(what / do with it?)   _What are you going to do with it?_
2 Your friend is going to a party tonight. You ask:
(what / wear?) ....
3 Your friend has just bought a new table. You ask:
(where / put it?) ....
4 Your friend has decided to have a party. You ask:
(who / invite?) ....

20.2 **Read the situations and complete the dialogues. Use going to.**

1 You have decided to clean your room this morning.
FRIEND: Are you going out this morning?
YOU: No, _I'm going to clean my room._
2 You bought a sweater, but it doesn't fit you very well. You have decided to take it back
to the shop.
FRIEND: That sweater is too big for you.
YOU: I know. ....
3 You have been offered a job, but you have decided not to accept it.
FRIEND: I hear you've been offered a job.
YOU: That's right, but ....
4 You have to phone Sarah. It's morning now, and you have decided to phone her tonight.
FRIEND: Have you phoned Sarah yet?
YOU: No, ...
5 You are in a restaurant. The food is awful and you've decided to complain.
FRIEND: This food is awful, isn't it?
YOU: Yes, it's disgusting. ....

20.3 **What is going to happen in these situations? Use the words in brackets.**

1 There are a lot of black clouds in the sky.
(rain)   _It's going to rain._
2 It is 8.30. Tom is leaving his house. He has to be at work at 8.45, but the journey takes 30
minutes.
(late)   He ....
3 There is a hole in the bottom of the boat. A lot of water is coming in through the hole.
(sink)   The boat ....
4 Lucy and Chris are driving. There is very little petrol left in the tank. The nearest petrol station is
a long way away.
(run out)   They ....

20.4 **Complete the sentences with was/were going to + the following verbs:**

| buy   give up   phone   play   say   ~~travel~~ |

1 We _were going to travel_ by train, but then we decided to go by car instead.
2 I .... some new clothes yesterday, but I was very busy and
didn't have time to go to the shops.
3 Oliver and I .... tennis last week, but he had to cancel
because he'd hurt his knee.
4 I .... Jane, but I decided to email her instead.
5 A: When I last saw Tim, he .... his job.
B: That's right, but in the end he decided to stay where he was.
6 I'm sorry I interrupted you. What .... you .... ?

Will/shall 1

A We use **I'll** (= **I will**) when we've just decided to do something. When we say '**I'll** do something', we announce our decision:

- ○ Oh, I've left the door open. **I'll go** and shut it.
- ○ 'What would you like to drink?' '**I'll have** an orange juice, please.'
- ○ 'Did you phone Lucy?' 'Oh no, I forgot. **I'll phone** her now.'

You cannot use the *present simple* (**I do** / **I go** etc.) in these sentences:

- ○ **I'll go** and shut the door. (*not* I go and shut)

We often use **I think I'll** … and **I don't think I'll** … :

- ○ I feel a bit hungry. **I think I'll have** something to eat.
- ○ **I don't think I'll go** out tonight. I'm too tired.

In spoken English the negative of **will** is usually **won't** (= **will not**):

- ○ I can see you're busy, so **I won't stay** long.

B Do *not* use **will** to talk about what you decided before (see Units 19–20):

- ○ **I'm going** on holiday next Saturday. (*not* I'll go)
- ○ **Are** you **working** tomorrow? (*not* Will you work)

C We often use **will** in these situations:

Offering to do something
- ○ That bag looks heavy. **I'll help** you with it. (*not* I help)

Agreeing to do something
- ○ A: Can you give Tim this book?
- ○ B: Sure, **I'll give** it to him when I see him this afternoon.

Promising to do something
- ○ Thanks for lending me the money. **I'll pay** you back on Friday.
- ○ **I won't tell** anyone what happened. I promise.

Asking somebody to do something (**Will you** … ?)
- ○ **Will you** please turn the music down? I'm trying to concentrate.

You can use **won't** to say that somebody refuses to do something:

- ○ I've tried to give her advice, but she **won't listen**.
- ○ The car **won't start**. (= the car 'refuses' to start)

D **Shall I** … ? **Shall we** … ?

Shall is used mostly in the questions **shall I** … ? / **shall we** … ?
We use **shall I** … ? / **shall we** … ? to ask somebody's opinion (especially in offers or suggestions):

- ○ **Shall I** open the window? (= Do you want me to open the window?)
- ○ I've got no money. What **shall I** do? (= What do you suggest?)
- ○ '**Shall we** go?' 'Just a minute. I'm not ready yet.'
- ○ 'Where **shall we** have lunch?' 'Let's go to Marino's.'

Compare **shall I** … ? and **will you** … ?:

- ○ **Shall I** shut the door? (= Do you want me to shut it?)
- ○ **Will you** shut the door? (= I want you to shut it)

Will/shall 2 → Unit 22   I will and I'm going to → Unit 23   American English → Appendix 7

Exercises

21.1 Complete the sentences with **I'll + a suitable verb.**

1 I'm too tired to walk home. I think ___I'll take___ a taxi.
2 'It's cold in this room.' 'Is it? _____ on the heating then.'
3 'Bye! Have a nice holiday!' 'Thanks. _____ you a postcard.'
4 'Shall I do the washing-up?' 'No, it's all right. _____ it later.'
5 'I don't know how to shut down this computer.' 'OK, _____ you.'
6 'Would you like tea or coffee?' '_____ coffee, please.'
7 'Are you coming with us?' 'No, I think _____ here.'
8 Thanks for lending me the money. _____ it back as soon as possible, OK?
9 A: I know you're busy, but can you finish this report this afternoon?
    B: Well, _____ , but I can't promise.

21.2 Read the situations and write sentences with **I think I'll ...** or **I don't think I'll ...** .

1 It's a bit cold. The window is open and you decide to close it. You say:
   ___I think I'll close the window.___
2 You are feeling tired and it's getting late. You decide to go to bed. You say:
   I think _____
3 A friend of yours offers you a lift in his car, but you decide to walk. You say:
   Thank you, but _____
4 You were going to have lunch. Now you decide that you don't want to eat anything. You say:
   I don't think _____
5 You planned to go swimming. Now you decide that you don't want to go. You say:
   _____

21.3 Which is correct? (If necessary, study Units 19–20 first.)

1 'Did you phone Lucy?' 'Oh no, I forgot. ~~I phone~~ / I'll phone her now.' (I'll phone is correct)
2 I can't meet you tomorrow. I'm playing / ~~I'll play~~ tennis. (I'm playing is correct)
3 I meet / I'll meet you outside the hotel in half an hour, OK?' 'Yes, that's fine.'
4 'I need some money.' 'OK, I'm lending / I'll lend you some. How much do you need?'
5 I'm having / I'll have a party next Saturday. I hope you can come.
6 'Remember to get a newspaper when you go out.' 'OK, I don't forget / I won't forget.'
7 What time does your train leave / will your train leave tomorrow?
8 I asked Sue what happened, but she doesn't tell / won't tell me.
9 Are you doing / Will you do anything tomorrow evening?' 'No, I'm free. Why?'
10 I don't want to go out alone. Do you come / Will you come with me?

21.4 What do you say in these situations? Write sentences with **shall I ... ?** or **shall we ... ?**

1 You and a friend want to do something this evening, but you don't know what.
   You ask your friend: ___What shall we do this evening?___
2 You try on a jacket in a shop. You are not sure whether to buy it or not.
   You ask a friend for advice: _____ it?
3 It's Helen's birthday next week. You want to give her a present, but you don't know what.
   You ask a friend for advice:
   What _____
4 You and a friend are going on holiday together, but you have to decide where.
   You ask him/her: _____
5 You and a friend are going out. You have to decide whether to go by car or to walk.
   You ask him/her: _____ or _____
6 Your friend wants you to come and see her. You don't know what time to come.
   You ask her: _____

➜ Additional exercises 10–13 (pages 308–10)

A

We do not use **will** to say what somebody has already arranged or decided to do:

- Diane **is working** next week. (*not* Diane will work)
- **Are** you **going to watch** anything on TV this evening? (*not* Will you watch)

For '**is working**' and '**Are** you **going to** … ?', see Units 19–20.

But often, when we talk about the future, we are *not* talking about what somebody has decided to do. For example:

Kate is doing an exam next week. Chris and Joe are talking about it.

Do you think Kate **will pass** the exam?

CHRIS

Yes, she**'ll pass** easily.

JOE

She'll pass does *not* mean 'she has decided to pass'. Joe is saying what he knows or believes will happen.

He is *predicting* the future.

When we predict a future happening or situation, we use **will/won't**.

Some more examples:

- They've been away a long time. When they return, they**'ll find** a lot of changes here.
- 'Where **will** you **be** this time next year?' 'I**'ll be** in Japan.'
- That plate is hot. If you touch it, you**'ll burn** yourself.
- Tom **won't pass** the exam. He hasn't studied hard enough.
- Anna looks completely different now. You **won't recognise** her.
- When **will** you **get** your exam results?

B

We often use **will** ('**ll**) with:

probably	◯ I**'ll probably** be home late tonight.
(I'm) **sure**	◯ Don't worry about the exam. I'm **sure** you**'ll** pass.
(I) **think**	◯ Do you **think** Sarah **will** like the present we bought her?
(I) **don't think**	◯ I **don't think** the exam **will** be very difficult.
I **wonder**	◯ **I wonder** what **will** happen.

After **I hope**, we generally use the present (**will** is also possible):

- I hope Kate **passes** the exam. (*or* I hope Kate **will pass** …)
- I hope it **doesn't rain** tomorrow.

C

Generally we use **will** to talk about *the future*, but sometimes we use **will** to talk about *now*. For example:

- Don't phone Ann now. She**'ll be** busy. (= she'll be busy *now*)

D

I shall … / we shall …

Normally we use **shall** only with **I** and **we**. You can say:

I shall *or* **I will** (**I'll**)   **we shall** *or* **we will** (**we'll**)

- **I shall** be late this evening. (*or* **I will** be)
- **We shall** probably go to France in June. (*or* We **will** probably go)

In spoken English we normally use **I'll** and **we'll**:

- **We'll** probably go to France.

The negative of **shall** is **shall not** or **shan't**:

- I **shan't** be here tomorrow. (*or* I **won't** be)

Do not use **shall** with **he/she/it/you/they**:

- She **will** be very angry. (*not* She shall be)

| Will/shall 1 ➜ Unit 21 | I will and I'm going to ➜ Unit 23 | Will be doing and will have done ➜ Unit 24 |
| Will have to ➜ Unit 31A | The future ➜ Appendix 3 | American English ➜ Appendix 7 |

Exercises

22.1 Which form of the verb is better in these sentences? The verbs are <u>underlined</u>.

1 Diane isn't free on Saturday. ~~She'll work~~ / She's working. (She's working *is correct*)
2 <u>I'll go / I'm going</u> to a party tomorrow night. Would you like to come too?
3 I think Amy <u>will get / is getting</u> the job. She has a lot of experience.
4 I can't meet you this evening. A friend of mine <u>will come / is coming</u> to see me.
5 A: Have you decided where to go for your holidays?
   B: Yes, <u>we'll go / we're going</u> to Italy.
6 Don't be afraid of the dog. <u>It won't hurt / It isn't hurting</u> you.

22.2 Put in **will ('ll)** or **won't**.

1 Can you wait for me? I __won't__ be long.
2 Don't ask Amanda for advice. She _____ know what to do.
3 I'm glad you're coming to see us next week. It _____ be good to see you again.
4 I'm sorry about what happened yesterday. It _____ happen again.
5 You don't need to take an umbrella with you. I don't think it _____ rain.
6 I've got some incredible news! You _____ believe it.

22.3 Complete the sentences using **will ('ll)**. Choose from the following:

it / be	she / come	you / get	you / like
people / live	it / look	we / meet	~~you / pass~~

1 Don't worry about your exam. I'm sure __you'll pass__ .
2 Why don't you try on this jacket? _____ nice on you.
3 You must meet Daniel sometime. I think _____ him.
4 It's raining. Don't go out. _____ wet.
5 Do you think _____ longer in the future?
6 Bye! I'm sure _____ again before long.
7 I've invited Anna to the party, but I don't think _____ .
8 It takes me an hour to get to work at the moment, but when the new road is finished,
   _____ much quicker.

22.4 Write questions using **do you think ... will ... ?** + the following:

be back	cost	end	get married	happen	~~like~~	rain

1 I've bought this picture for Karen.   _Do you think she'll like it_ ?
2 The weather doesn't look very good.   Do you _____ ?
3 The meeting is still going on.   When do you _____ ?
4 My car needs to be repaired.   How much _____ ?
5 Sally and David are in love.   Do _____ ?
6 'I'm going out now.'   'OK. What time _____ ?'
7 The future situation is uncertain.   What _____ ?

22.5 Where do you think you will be at these times? Write true sentences about yourself. Use:
I'll be ... *or* **I'll probably be ...** *or* **I don't know where I'll be**

1 (next Monday evening at 7.45)   _I'll be at home._
                                    or _I'll probably be at home._
                                    or _I don't know where I'll be._

2 (at 5 o'clock tomorrow morning)   _____

3 (at 10.30 tomorrow morning)   _____

4 (next Saturday afternoon at 4.15)   _____

5 (this time next year)   _____

I will and I'm going to

Future actions

Study the difference between **will** and **(be) going to**:

Sarah is talking to Helen:

Let's have a party.

That's a great idea.
We'**ll invite** lots of people.

SARAH   HELEN

will ('**ll**): We use **will** to announce a new decision. The party is a new idea.

decision
now

We'll ...

past   now   future

Later that day, Helen meets Dan:

Sarah and I have decided to have a party.
We'**re going to invite** lots of people.

HELEN   DAN

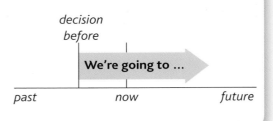

(be) going to: We use **(be) going to** when we have *already decided* to do something. Helen had already decided to invite lots of people *before* she spoke to Dan.

decision
before

We're going to ...

past   now   future

Compare:
- 'Gary phoned while you were out.'   'OK. I'**ll call** him back.'
  'Gary **phoned** while you were out.'   'Yes, I know. I'**m going to call** him back.'
- 'Anna is in hospital.'   'Oh really? I didn't know. I'**ll go** and visit her.'
  'Anna is in hospital.'   'Yes, I know. I'**m going to visit** her this evening.'

Future happenings and situations (predicting the future)

We use both **will** and **going to** to predict future happenings and situations. So you can say:
- I think **the weather will be** nice later. *or*
  I think **the weather is going to be** nice later.
- Those shoes are well-made. **They'll last** a long time. *or*
  Those shoes are well-made. **They're going to last** a long time.

When we say something **is going to** happen, we know this from the situation *now*. What is happening *now* shows that something **is going to** happen in the future. For example:
- Look at those black clouds. It'**s going to rain**. (*not* It will rain)
  (We can see that it **is going to rain** from the clouds that are in the sky *now*.)
- I feel terrible. I think I'**m going to be** sick. (*not* I think I'll be sick)
  (I think I'**m going to be** sick because I feel terrible *now*.)
Do not use **will** in this type of situation.

I'm going to ➜ Unit 20   Will ➜ Units 21–22   The future ➜ Appendix 3

Exercises

23.1 Complete the sentences using **will ('ll)** or **going to**.

1 A: Why are you turning on the TV?
   B: _I'm going to watch_ the news. (I / watch)
2 A: Oh, I've just realised. I haven't got any money.
   B: Haven't you? Well, don't worry. .... you some. (I / lend)
3 A: I've got a headache.
   B: Have you? Wait a second and .... an aspirin for you. (I / get)
4 A: Why are you filling that bucket with water?
   B: .... the car. (I / wash)
5 A: I've decided to repaint this room.
   B: Oh, have you? What colour .... it? (you / paint)
6 A: Where are you going? Are you going shopping?
   B: Yes, ... some things for dinner. (I / buy)
7 A: I don't know how to use the washing machine.
   B: It's easy. .... you. (I / show)
8 A: What would you like to eat?
   B: .... a pizza, please. (I / have)
9 A: Did you call Lisa?
   B: Oh, no. I completely forgot. .... her now. (I / call)
10 A: Has Dan decided what to do when he leaves school?
   B: Yes. Everything is planned. .... a holiday for a few weeks.
      (he / have) Then .... a management training course. (he / do)

23.2 Read the situations and complete the sentences using **will ('ll)** or **going to**.

1 The phone rings and you answer. Somebody wants to speak to John.
   CALLER: Hello. Can I speak to John, please?
   YOU: Just a moment. _I'll get_ him. (I / get)
2 It's a nice day, so you have decided to take a walk. Just before you go, you tell your friend.
   YOU: The weather's too nice to stay in. .... a walk. (I / take)
   FRIEND: Good idea! I think .... you. (I / join)
3 Your friend is worried because she has lost her driving licence.
   YOU: Don't worry. I'm sure .... it. (you / find)
   FRIEND: I hope so.
4 There was a job advertised in the paper recently. At first you were interested, but then you
   decided not to apply.
   FRIEND: Have you decided what to do about that job you were interested in?
   YOU: Yes, ... for it. (I / not / apply)
5 You and a friend are stuck in traffic. You have to be in a meeting in five minutes and you need at
   least another 20 minutes to get there.
   YOU: The meeting begins in five minutes. .... (we / be late)
6 Ann and Sam are staying at a hotel. Their room is in very bad condition, especially the ceiling.
   ANN: The ceiling doesn't look very safe, does it?
   SAM: No, it looks as if .... (it / fall down)
7 Paul has to go to the airport to catch a plane tomorrow morning.
   PAUL: Kate, I need somebody to take me to the airport tomorrow morning.
   KATE: That's no problem. .... you. (I / take)   What time is your flight?
   PAUL: 10.30.
   KATE: OK, ... you up at your house at about 8 o'clock then. (I / pick)
   Later that day, Joe offers to take Paul to the airport.
   JOE: Paul, do you want me to take you to the airport?
   PAUL: No thanks, Joe. .... me. (Kate / take)

➜ Additional exercises 10–13 (pages 308–10)

A Study this example situation:

These people are standing in a queue to get into the cinema.

now

Half an hour from now, the cinema will be full.
Everyone **will be watching** the film.

half an hour from now

Three hours from now, the cinema will be empty.
The film **will have finished**.
Everyone **will have gone** home.

three hours from now

B I **will be doing** something *(future continuous)* = I will be in the middle of doing it:
- ○ This time next week I'll be on holiday. **I'll be lying** on the beach or **swimming** in the sea.
- ○ You have no chance of getting the job. You**'ll be wasting** your time if you apply for it.

Compare **will be** (do)**ing** and **will** (do):
- ○ Don't phone between 7 and 8. We**'ll be having** dinner.
- ○ Let's wait for Liz to arrive and then we**'ll have** dinner.

Compare **will be -ing** with other continuous forms:
- ○ At 10 o'clock yesterday, Sally **was** in her office. She **was working**. *(past)*
  It's 10 o'clock now. She **is** in her office. She **is working**. *(present)*
  At 10 o'clock tomorrow, she **will be** in her office. She **will be working**.

C We also use **will be -ing** to talk about complete actions in the future.
For example:
- ○ The government **will be making** a statement about the crisis later today.
- ○ **Will** you **be going** away this summer?
- ○ Later in the programme, I**'ll be talking** to the Minister of Education …
- ○ Our best player is injured and **won't be playing** in the game on Saturday.

Later in the programme.
I'll be talking to …

In these examples **will be -ing** is similar to (**be**) **going to** … .

D We use **will have** (**done**) *(future perfect)* to say that something will already be complete before a time in the future. For example:
- ○ Sally always leaves for work at 8.30 in the morning. She won't be at home at 9 o'clock – she**'ll have gone** to work.
- ○ We're late. The film **will** already **have started** by the time we get to the cinema.

Compare **will have** (done) with other perfect forms:
- ○ Ted and Amy **have been** married for 24 years. *(present perfect)*
  Next year they **will have been** married for 25 years.
  When their son was born, they **had been** married for three years. *(past perfect)*

Will ➜ Units 21–22   By then / by the time ➜ Unit 120   The future ➜ Appendix 3

Exercises

24.1 Read about Andy. Then tick (✓) the sentences which are true. In each group of sentences at least one is true.

Andy goes to work every day. He leaves home at 8 o'clock and arrives at work at about 8.45. He starts work immediately and continues until 12.30 when he has lunch (which takes about half an hour). He starts work again at 1.15 and goes home at exactly 4.30. Every day he follows the same routine and tomorrow will be no exception.

1  **At 7.45**
   a he'll be leaving the house
   b he'll have left the house
   c he'll be at home ✓
   d he'll be having breakfast ✓

4  **At 12.45**
   a he'll have lunch
   b he'll be having lunch
   c he'll have finished his lunch
   d he'll have started his lunch

2  **At 8.15**
   a he'll be leaving the house
   b he'll have left the house
   c he'll have arrived at work
   d he'll be arriving at work

5  **At 4 o'clock**
   a he'll have finished work
   b he'll finish work
   c he'll be working
   d he won't have finished work

3 **At 9.15**
   a he'll be working
   b he'll start work
   c he'll have started work
   d he'll be arriving at work

6  **At 4.45**
   a he'll leave work
   b he'll be leaving work
   c he'll have left work
   d he'll have arrived home

24.2 Put the verb into the correct form, **will be (do)ing** or **will have (done)**.

1 Don't phone between 7 and 8. _____We'll be having_____ dinner then. (we / have)
2 Phone me after 8 o'clock. _____ dinner by then. (we / finish)
3 Tomorrow afternoon we're going to play tennis from 3 o'clock until 4.30. So at 4 o'clock,
_____ tennis. (we / play)
4 A: Can we meet tomorrow?
  B: Yes, but not in the afternoon. _____ . (I / work)
5 *B has to go to a meeting which begins at 10 o'clock. It will last about an hour.*
  A: Will you be free at 11.30?
  B: Yes, _____ by then. (the meeting / end)
6 Ben is on holiday and he is spending his money very quickly. If he continues like this,
_____ all his money before the end of his holiday. (he / spend)
7 Do you think _____ the same job in ten years' time?
  (you / still / do)
8 Lisa is from New Zealand. She is travelling around Europe at the moment. So far she has
  travelled about 1,000 miles. By the end of the trip, _____ more
  than 3,000 miles. (she / travel)
9 If you need to contact me, _____ at the Lion Hotel until Friday.
  (I / stay)
10 A: _____ Laura tomorrow? (you / see)
  B: Yes, probably. Why?
  A: I borrowed this DVD from her. Can you give it back to her?

→ Additional exercises 12–13 (pages 309–10)

When I do / When I've done   When and if

A

Study this example:

Will you phone me tomorrow?

Yes, I'll phone you **when I get** home from work.

'I'll phone you when I get home' is a sentence with two parts:

the *main part*:   I'**ll** phone you
and   *the* **when**-*part*:   **when** I **get** home

The time in the sentence is future (tomorrow), but we use a *present* tense (I **get**) in the **when**-part of the sentence.

We do *not* use **will** in the **when**-part of the sentence.

Some more examples:
- We'**ll go** out **when** it **stops** raining. (*not* when it will stop)
- **When** you **are** in London again, come and see us. (*not* When you will be)
- (*said to a child*) What do you want to be **when** you **grow** up? (*not* will grow)

The same thing happens after **while / before / after / as soon as / until** or **till**:
- What are you going to do **while** I'**m** away? (*not* while I will be)
- I'll probably go back home on Sunday. **Before** I **go**, I'd like to visit the museum.
- Wait here **until** (*or* **till**) I **come** back.

B

You can also use the present perfect (**have done**) after **when / after / until / as soon as**:
- Can I borrow that book **when** you'**ve finished** with it?
- Don't say anything while Ian is here. Wait **until** he **has gone**.

If you use the present perfect, one thing must be complete *before* the other (so the two things do *not* happen together):
- **When** I'**ve phoned** Kate, we can have dinner.
  (= First I'll phone Kate and *after that* we can have dinner.)

Do not use the present perfect if the two things happen together:
- **When** I **phone** Kate, I'll ask her about the party. (*not* When I've phoned)

It is often possible to use either the present simple or the present perfect:
- I'll come **as soon as I finish**.   *or*   I'll come **as soon as I've finished**.
- You'll feel better **after you have**   *or*   You'll feel better **after you've had**
  something to eat.   something to eat.

C

After **if**, we normally use the present simple (**if I do / if I see** etc.) for the future:
- It's raining hard. We'll get wet **if** we **go** out. (*not* if we will go)
- I'll be angry **if** it **happens** again. (*not* if it will happen)
- Hurry up! **If** we **don't hurry**, we'll be late.

D

When and **if**

We use **when** for things which are *sure* to happen:
- I'm going out later. (for sure)   **When** I go out, I'll get some bread.

We use **if** (*not* when) for things that will *possibly* happen:
- I might go out later. (it's possible)   **If** I go out, I'll get some bread.
- **If** it is raining this evening, I won't go out. (*not* When it is raining)
- Don't worry **if** I'm late tonight. (*not* when I'm late)
- **If** they don't come soon, I'm not going to wait. (*not* When they don't come)

If ➔ Units 38–40   Even if / even when ➔ Unit 112D   Unless ➔ Unit 115

Exercises

25.1 Complete the sentences using the verbs in brackets. All the sentences are about the future. Use **will/won't** or the present simple (**I see / he plays / it is** etc.).

1 When ___you are___ (you / be) in London again, come and see us.
2 I want to see Sophie before .... (she / go) out.
3 Call me when .... (you / know) what time you're going to get here.
4 I'm going out now. .... (you / be) here when
.... (I / get) back?
5 I think everything will be fine, but if .... (there / be) any problems,
.... (I / call) you, OK?
6 We must do something soon before .... (it / be) too late.
7 Anna looks very different now. When .... (you / see) her again,
.... (you / not / recognise) her.
8 Steve has applied for the job, but he isn't really qualified for it. .... (I / be)
surprised if .... (he / get) it.
9 I'm going to be away for a few days. If .... (you / need) to
contact me while .... (I / be) away, here's my mobile number.
10 I don't want to go without you. .... (I / wait) for you until
.... (you / be) ready.

25.2 Make one sentence from two.

1 It will stop raining soon. Then we'll go out.
    ___We'll go out___ when ___it stops raining.___
2 I'll find somewhere to live. Then I'll give you my address.
    I .... when ....
3 I'll do the shopping. Then I'll come straight back home.
    .... after ....
4 It's going to get dark. Let's go home before that.
    .... before ....
5 She must apologise to me first. I won't speak to her until then.
    .... until ....

25.3 Read the situations and complete the sentences.

1 A friend of yours is going on holiday. You want to know what she is going to do.
    You ask: What are you going to do when ___you are on holiday___ ?
2 A friend is visiting you. She has to go soon, but you'd like to show her some pictures.
    You ask: Do you have time to look at some pictures before .... ?
3 You want to sell your car. Mark is interested in buying it, but he hasn't decided yet.
    You ask: Can you let me know as soon as .... ?
4 Your friends are going to Hong Kong soon. You want to know where they're going to stay.
    You ask: Where are you going to stay when .... ?
5 The traffic is very bad in your town, but they are going to build a new road.
    You say: I think things will be better when they ....

25.4 Put in **when** or **if**.

1 Don't worry ___if___ I'm late tonight.
2 Be careful. You'll hurt yourself .... you fall.
3 I'm going to Rome next week. .... I'm there, I hope to visit a friend of mine.
4 I'm going shopping. .... you want anything, I can get it for you.
5 .... I don't see you tomorrow, when will I see you again?
6 I'm going away for a few days. I'll call you .... I get back.
7 I hope Sarah can come to the party. It will be a shame .... she can't come.
8 We can eat at home or, ... you prefer, we can go to a restaurant.

→ Additional exercises 12–15 (pages 309–11), 32 (page 321)

Can, could and (be) able to

A

We use **can** to say that something is possible or allowed, or that somebody has the ability to do something. We use **can** + *infinitive* (**can do / can see** etc.):

- ○ We **can see** the lake from our hotel.
- ○ 'I don't have a pen.' 'You **can use** mine.'
- ○ **Can** you **speak** any foreign languages?
- ○ I **can come** and see you tomorrow if you like.
- ○ The word 'dream' **can be** a noun or a verb.

The negative is **can't** (= **cannot**):

- ○ I'm afraid I **can't come** to the party on Friday.

B

You can say that somebody **is able to** do something, but **can** is more usual:

- ○ We **are able to see** the lake from our hotel.

But **can** has only two forms: **can** *(present)* and **could** *(past)*. So sometimes it is necessary to use (**be**) **able to**. Compare:

○ I **can't** sleep.	○ I **haven't been able to** sleep recently.
○ Tom **can** come tomorrow.	○ Tom **might be able to** come tomorrow.
○ Maria **can** speak French, Spanish and English.	○ Applicants for the job **must be able to** speak two foreign languages.

C Could

Sometimes **could** is the past of **can**. We use **could** especially with:

    see   **hear**   **smell**   **taste**   **feel**   **remember**   **understand**

- ○ We had a lovely room in the hotel. We **could see** the lake.
- ○ As soon as I walked into the room, I **could smell** gas.
- ○ I was sitting at the back of the theatre and **couldn't hear** very well.

We also use **could** to say that somebody had the general ability or permission to do something:

- ○ My grandfather **could speak** five languages.
- ○ We were totally free. We **could do** what we wanted. (= we were allowed to do)

D Could and was able to

We use **could** for *general* ability. But if you want to say that somebody did something in a specific situation, use **was/were able to** or **managed to** (*not* **could**):

- ○ The fire spread through the building very quickly, but fortunately everybody **was able to escape / managed to escape**. (*not* could escape)
- ○ We didn't know where David was, but we **managed to find / were able to find** him in the end. (*not* could find)

Compare:

- ○ Jack was an excellent tennis player when he was younger. He **could beat** anybody.
  (= he had the *general* ability to beat anybody)
but   Jack and Andy played a match yesterday. Andy played well, but Jack **managed to beat** him.
        (= he managed to beat him this time)

The negative **couldn't** (**could not**) is possible in all situations:

- ○ My grandfather **couldn't swim**.
- ○ We looked for David everywhere, but we **couldn't find** him.
- ○ Andy played well, but he **couldn't beat** Jack.

Could (do) and could have (done) ➜ Unit 27   Must and can't ➜ Unit 28
Can/could you … ? ➜ Unit 37

Exercises

26.1 Complete the sentences using **can** or **(be) able to**. Use **can** if possible; otherwise use **(be) able to**.

1 Gary has travelled a lot. He ___can___ speak five languages.
2 I haven't ___been able to___ sleep very well recently.
3 Nicole _____ drive, but she doesn't have a car.
4 I used to _____ stand on my head, but I can't do it any more.
5 I can't understand Mark. I've never _____ understand him.
6 I can't see you on Friday, but I _____ meet you on Saturday morning.
7 Ask Katherine about your problem. She might _____ help you.

26.2 Write sentences about yourself using the ideas in brackets.

1 (something you used to be able to do)
   ___I used to be able to sing well.___
2 (something you used to be able to do)
   I used _____
3 (something you would like to be able to do)
   I'd _____
4 (something you have never been able to do)
   I've _____

26.3 Complete the sentences with **can/can't/could/couldn't** + the following:

~~come~~ eat hear run sleep wait

1 I'm afraid I ___can't come___ to your party next week.
2 When Dan was 16, he _____ 100 metres in 11 seconds.
3 'Are you in a hurry?' 'No, I've got plenty of time. I _____ .'
4 I was feeling sick yesterday. I _____ anything.
5 Can you speak a little louder? I _____ you very well.
6 'You look tired.' 'Yes, I _____ last night.'

26.4 Complete the answers to the questions with **was/were able to** … .

1 A: Did everybody escape from the fire?
   B: Yes, although the fire spread quickly, everybody ___was able to escape___ .
2 A: Did you finish your work this afternoon?
   B: Yes, there was nobody to disturb me, so I _____ .
3 A: Did you have problems finding our house?
   B: Not really. Your directions were good and we _____ .
4 A: Did the thief get away?
   B: Yes. No-one realised what was happening and the thief _____ .

26.5 Complete the sentences using **could, couldn't** or **managed to**.

1 My grandfather travelled a lot. He ___could___ speak five languages.
2 I looked everywhere for the book, but I ___couldn't___ find it.
3 They didn't want to come with us at first, but we ___managed to___ persuade them.
4 Laura had hurt her leg and _____ walk very well.
5 I ran my first marathon recently. It was very hard, but I _____ finish.
6 I looked very carefully and I _____ see somebody in the distance.
7 I wanted to buy some tomatoes. The first shop I went to didn't have any, but I
   _____ get some in the next shop.
8 My grandmother loved music. She _____ play the piano very well.
9 A girl fell into the river, but fortunately we _____ pull her out.
10 I had forgotten to bring my camera, so I _____ take any pictures.

Could (do) and could have (done)

A

We use **could** in a number of ways. Sometimes **could** is the past of **can** (see Unit 26):
- ○ Listen. I **can hear** something. *(now)*
- ○ I listened. I **could hear** something. *(past)*

But **could** is not only used in this way. We also use **could** to talk about possible actions now or in the future (especially to make suggestions). For example:

- ○ A: What shall we do tonight?
  B: We **could go** to the cinema.

- ○ A: When you go to Paris next month, you **could stay** with Sarah.
  B: Yes, I suppose I **could**.

What shall we do tonight?

We **could go** to the cinema.

WHAT'S ON

Can is also possible in these sentences ('We **can** go to the cinema.' etc.). **Could** is less sure than **can**.

B

We also use **could** (*not* can) for actions that are not realistic. For example:
- ○ I'm so tired, I **could sleep** for a week. *(not* I can sleep for a week)

Compare **can** and **could**:
- ○ I **can stay** with Sarah when I go to Paris. (realistic)
- ○ Maybe I **could stay** with Sarah when I go to Paris. (possible, but less sure)
- ○ This is a wonderful place. I **could stay** here forever. (unrealistic)

C

We also use **could** (*not* can) to say that something (a situation or a happening) is possible now or in the future. The meaning is similar to **might** or **may** (see Unit 29):
- ○ The story **could be** true, but I don't think it is. (*not* can be true)
- ○ I don't know what time Lisa is coming. She **could get** here at any time.

Compare **can** and **could**:
- ○ The weather **can** change very quickly in the mountains. (in general)
- ○ The weather is nice now, but it **could** change. (the weather now, not in general)

D

We use **could have** (done) to talk about the past. Compare:
- ○ I'm so tired, I **could sleep** for a week. *(now)*
  I was so tired, I **could have slept** for a week. *(past)*
- ○ The situation is bad, but it **could be** worse. *(now)*
  The situation was bad, but it **could have been** worse. *(past)*

Something **could have** happened = it was possible but did *not* happen:
- ○ Why did you stay at a hotel when you were in Paris? You **could have stayed** with Sarah. (you didn't stay with her)
- ○ David was lucky. He **could have hurt** himself when he fell, but he's OK.

E

We use **couldn't** to say that something would not be possible:
- ○ I **couldn't live** in a big city. I'd hate it. (= it wouldn't be possible for me)
- ○ Everything is fine right now. Things **couldn't be** better.

For the past we use **couldn't have** (done):
- ○ We had a really good holiday. It **couldn't have been** better.
- ○ The trip was cancelled last week. Paul **couldn't have gone** anyway because he was ill.
  (= it would not have been possible for him to go)

Couldn't have (done) → Unit 28B   Could and might → Unit 29C   Could I/you ... ? → Unit 37
Could with if → Units 38C, 39E, 40D   Modal verbs (can/could/will/would etc.) → Appendix 4

Exercises

27.1 Answer the questions with a suggestion. Use **could**.

1	Where shall we go for our holidays?	(to Scotland) _We could go to Scotland._
2	What shall we have for dinner tonight?	(fish) We ....
3	When shall I phone Vicky?	(now) You ....
4	What shall I give Ann for her birthday?	(a book) ....
5	Where shall we hang this picture?	(in the kitchen) ....

27.2 In some of these sentences, you need **could** (not **can**). Change the sentences where necessary.

1 The story can be true, but I don't think it is.   _could be true_
2 It's a nice day. We can go for a walk.   _OK (could go is also possible)_
3 I'm so angry with him. I can kill him!
4 If you're hungry, we can have dinner now.
5 It's so nice here. I can stay here all day, but
 unfortunately I have to go.
6 A: Where's my bag? Have you seen it?
 B: No, but it can be in the car.
7 Peter is a keen musician. He plays the flute
 and he can also play the piano.
8 A: I need to borrow a camera.
 B: You can borrow mine.
9 Be careful climbing that tree. You can fall.

27.3 Complete the sentences. Use **could** or **could have** + a suitable verb.

1 A: What shall we do this evening?
 B: I don't mind. We __could go__ to the cinema.
2 A: I spent a very boring evening at home yesterday.
 B: Why did you stay at home? You .... out with us.
3 A: Have you seen this job advertised in the paper? You .... for it.
 B: What sort of job? Show me the advertisement.
4 A: How was your exam? Was it difficult?
 B: It wasn't so bad. It .... worse.
5 A: I got very wet walking home in the rain last night.
 B: Why did you walk? You .... a taxi.
6 A: Where shall we meet tomorrow?
 B: Well, I .... to your house if you like.

27.4 Complete the sentences. Use **couldn't** or **couldn't have** + these verbs (in the correct form):

be   be   come   find   get   live   wear

1 I __couldn't live__ in a big city. I'd hate it.
2 We had a really good holiday. It __couldn't have been__ better.
3 I .... that hat. I'd look silly and people would laugh at me.
4 We managed to find the restaurant you recommended, but we .... it
 without the map that you drew for us.
5 Paul has to get up at 4 o'clock every morning. I don't know how he does it. I ....
 .... up at that time every day.
6 The staff at the hotel were really nice when we stayed there last summer. They ....
 .... more helpful.
7 A: I tried to phone you last week. We had a party and I wanted to invite you.
 B: That was nice of you, but I .... anyway. I was away all last week.

A

Study this example:

My house is very near the motorway.

It **must be** very noisy.

You can use **must** to say that you believe something is certain:

- ○ You've been travelling all day. You **must be** tired. (Travelling is tiring and you've been travelling all day, so you **must** be tired.)
- ○ 'Joe is a hard worker.' 'Joe? You **must be joking**. He doesn't do anything.'
- ○ Louise **must get** very bored in her job. She does the same thing every day.
- ○ I'm sure Sally gave me her address. I **must have** it somewhere.

You can use **can't** to say that you believe something is not possible:

- ○ You've just had lunch. You **can't be** hungry already. (People are not normally hungry just after eating a meal. You've just eaten, so you **can't** be hungry.)
- ○ They haven't lived here for very long. They **can't know** many people.

Study the structure:

I/you/he (etc.)	must can't	**be** (tired / hungry / at work etc.) **be** (**doing** / **going** / **joking** etc.) **do** / **get** / **know** / **have** etc.

B

For the past we use **must have** (**done**) and **can't have** (**done**).
Study this example:

There's nobody at home. They **must have gone** out.

Martin and Lucy are standing at the door of their friends' house.
They have rung the doorbell twice, but nobody has answered. Lucy says:

They **must have gone** out.

- ○ 'We used to live very near the motorway.' 'Did you? It **must have been** noisy.'
- ○ 'I've lost one of my gloves.' 'You **must have dropped** it somewhere.'
- ○ Sarah hasn't contacted me. She **can't have got** my message.
- ○ Tom walked into a wall. He **can't have been looking** where he was going.

Study the structure:

I/you/he (etc.)	must can't	have	**been** (asleep / at work etc.) **been** (**doing** / **looking** etc.) **gone** / **got** / **known** etc.

You can use **couldn't have** instead of **can't have**:

- ○ Sarah **couldn't have got** my message.
- ○ Tom **couldn't have been looking** where he was going.

Can't ('I can't swim' etc.) ➔ Unit 26   **Must** ('I must go' etc.) ➔ Units 31–32
Modal verbs (**can/could/will/would** etc.) ➔ Appendix 4   American English ➔ Appendix 7

Exercises

28.1 Put in **must** or **can't**.

1 You've been travelling all day. You _____must_____ be tired.
2 That restaurant _____ be very good. It's always full of people.
3 That restaurant _____ be very good. It's always empty.
4 I'm sure I gave you the key. You _____ have it. Have you looked in your bag?
5 I often see that woman walking along this street. She _____ live near here.
6 It rained every day during their holiday, so they _____ have had a very nice time.
7 Congratulations on passing your exam. You _____ be very pleased.
8 You got here very quickly. You _____ have walked very fast.
9 Bill and Sue always stay at luxury hotels, so they _____ be short of money.

28.2 Complete each sentence with a verb (one or two words).

1 I've lost one of my gloves. I must _have dropped_ it somewhere.
2 Their house is very near the motorway. It must _be_ very noisy.
3 Sarah knows a lot about films. She must _____ to the cinema a lot.
4 I left my bike outside the house last night and now it's gone. Somebody must _____ it.
5 'How old is Ted?' 'He's older than me. He must _____ at least 40.'
6 I didn't hear the phone ring. I must _____ asleep.
7 A: You're going on holiday soon. You must _____ forward to it.
   B: Yes, it will be really good to get away.
8 The police have closed the road, so we have to go a different way. There must _____ an accident.
9 I'm sure you know this song. You must _____ it before.
10 There is a man walking behind us. He has been walking behind us for the last 20 minutes. He must _____ us.

28.3 Read the situations and use the words in brackets to write sentences with **must have** and **can't have**.

1 We went to their house and rang the doorbell, but nobody answered. (they / go out)
   They must have gone out.
2 Sarah hasn't contacted me. (she / get / my message)
   She can't have got my message.
3 The jacket you bought is very good quality. (it / very expensive)
   _____
4 I haven't seen our neighbours for ages. (they / go away)
   _____
5 I can't find my umbrella. (I / leave / it in the restaurant last night)
   _____
6 Amy was in a very difficult situation when she lost her job. (it / easy for her)
   _____
7 There was a man standing outside the café. (he / wait / for somebody)
   _____
8 Rachel did the opposite of what I asked her to do. (she / understand / what I said)
   _____
9 When I got back to my car, the door was unlocked. (I / forget / to lock it)
   _____
10 I was woken up in the night by the noise next door. (my neighbours / have / a party)
   _____
11 The light was red, but the car didn't stop. (the driver / see / the red light)
   _____

→ Additional exercises 16–18 (pages 311–13)

May and **might** 1

Study this example situation:

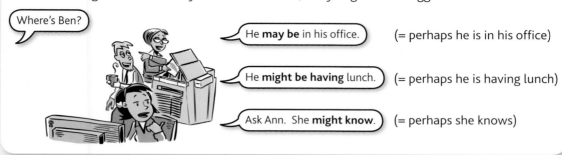

You are looking for Ben. Nobody is sure where he is, but you get some suggestions.

Where's Ben?

He **may be** in his office.　(= perhaps he is in his office)

He **might be having** lunch.　(= perhaps he is having lunch)

Ask Ann. She **might know**.　(= perhaps she knows)

We use **may** or **might** to say that something is possible. Usually you can use **may** or **might**, so you can say:
- ○　It **may** be true.　*or*　It **might** be true.　(= perhaps it is true)
- ○　She **might** know.　*or*　She **may** know.

The negative forms are **may not** and **might not** (*or* **mightn't**):
- ○　It **may not** be true.　(= perhaps it isn't true)
- ○　She **might not** work here any more.　(= perhaps she doesn't work here)

Study the structure:

I/you/he (etc.)	**may** **might**	(**not**)	**be** (true / in his office etc.) **be** (**doing** / **working** / **having** etc.) **know** / **work** / **want** etc.

For the past we use **may have** (**done**) or **might have** (**done**):
- ○　A: I wonder why Kate didn't answer her phone.
  　B: She **may have been** asleep.　(= perhaps she was asleep)
- ○　A: I can't find my phone anywhere.
  　B: You **might have left** it at work.　(= perhaps you left it at work)
- ○　A: Why wasn't Amy at the meeting yesterday?
  　B: She **might not have known** about it.　(= perhaps she didn't know)
- ○　A: I wonder why David was in such a bad mood yesterday.
  　B: He **may not have been feeling** well.　(= perhaps he wasn't feeling well)

Study the structure:

I/you/he (etc.)	**may** **might**	(**not**) **have**	**been** (asleep / at home etc.) **been** (**doing** / **working** / **feeling** etc.) **known** / **had** / **wanted** / **left** etc.

Could is similar to **may** and **might**:
- ○　It's a strange story, but it **could be** true.　(= it is possible that it's true)
- ○　You **could have left** your phone at work.　(= it's possible that you left it there)

But **couldn't** (*negative*) is different from **may not** and **might not**. Compare:
- ○　Sarah **couldn't have** got my message. Otherwise she would have replied.
  　(= it is not possible that she got my message)
- ○　I wonder why Sarah hasn't replied to my message. I suppose she **might not have** got it.
  　(= it's possible that she didn't get it – so perhaps she did, perhaps she didn't)

Could → Unit 27　　May/might 2 → Unit 30　　May I … ? → Unit 37C
Might with if → Units 30B, 38C, 40D　　Modal verbs (**can/could/will/would** etc.) → Appendix 4

Exercises

29.1 Write these sentences in a different way using **might**.

1 Perhaps Helen is in her office.   _She might be in her office._
2 Perhaps Helen is busy.   ....
3 Perhaps she is working.   ....
4 Perhaps she wants to be alone.   ....
5 Perhaps she was ill yesterday.   ....
6 Perhaps she went home early.   ....
7 Perhaps she had to go home early.   ....
8 Perhaps she was working yesterday.   ....

In sentences 9–11 use **might not**.

9 Perhaps she doesn't want to see me.   ....
10 Perhaps she isn't working today.   ....
11 Perhaps she wasn't feeling well yesterday.   ....

29.2 Complete each sentence with a verb in the correct form.

1 'Where's Ben?'   'I'm not sure. He might ___be having___ lunch.'
2 'Who is that man with Anna?'   'I'm not sure. It might .... her brother.'
3 A: Who was the man we saw with Anna yesterday?
   B: I'm not sure. It may .... her brother.
4 A: What are those people doing by the side of the road?
   B: I don't know. I suppose they might .... for a bus.
5 'Is Sarah here?'   'I can't see her. She may not .... yet.'

29.3 Read the situation and make sentences from the words in brackets. Use **might**.

1 I can't find Jeff anywhere. I wonder where he is.
   a (he / go / shopping)   _He might have gone shopping._
   b (he / play / tennis)   _He might be playing tennis._
2 I'm looking for Sophie. Do you know where she is?
   a (she / watch / TV)   ....
   b (she / go / out)   ....
3 I can't find my umbrella. Have you seen it?
   a (it / be / in the car)   ....
   b (you / leave / in the restaurant)   ....
4 Why didn't Dan answer the doorbell? I'm sure he was at home at the time.
   a (he / go / to bed early)   ....
   b (he / not / hear / the doorbell)   ....
   c (he / be / in the shower)   ....

29.4 Complete the sentences using **might not have** … or **couldn't have** … .

1 A: Do you think Sarah got the message I sent her?
   B: No, she would have replied.   _She couldn't have got it_ .
2 A: I was surprised Amy wasn't at the meeting. Perhaps she didn't know about it.
   B: That's possible.   _She might not have known about it_ .
3 A: I wonder why they haven't replied to the email I sent. Do you think they received it?
   B: Maybe not. They ....
4 A: I wonder how the fire started. Was it an accident?
   B: No, the police say it ....
5 A: Mike says he needs to see you. He tried to find you yesterday.
   B: Well, he .... very hard. I was in my office all day.
6 A: The man you spoke to – are you sure he was American?
   B: No, I'm not sure. He ....

→ Additional exercises 16–18 (pages 311–13)

May and might 2

A

We use **may** and **might** to talk about possible actions or happenings in the future:

- ○ I haven't decided yet where to go on holiday. I **may go** to Ireland. (= perhaps I will go there)
- ○ Take an umbrella with you. It **might rain** later. (= perhaps it will rain)
- ○ The bus isn't always on time. We **might have** to wait a few minutes. (= perhaps we will have to wait)

The negative forms are **may not** and **might not** (**mightn't**):

- ○ Amy **may not go** out tonight. She isn't feeling well. (= perhaps she will not go out)
- ○ There **might not be** enough time to discuss everything at the meeting. (= perhaps there will not be enough time)

Compare **will** and **may/might**:

- ○ I**'ll** be late this evening. (for sure)
- ○ I **may/might** be late this evening. (possible)

B

Usually you can use **may** or **might**. So you can say:

- ○ I **may go** to Ireland. *or* I **might go** to Ireland.
- ○ Jane **might be** able to help you. *or* Jane **may be** able to help you.

But we use only **might** (*not* may) when the situation is *not real*:

- ○ If they paid me better, I **might** work harder. (*not* I may work)

The situation here is not real because they do *not* pay me well, so I'm not going to work harder.

C

There is a continuous form: **may/might be -ing**. Compare this with **will be -ing**:

- ○ Don't phone at 8.30. I**'ll be watching** the football on television.
- ○ Don't phone at 8.30. I **might be watching** (*or* I **may be watching**) the football on TV. (= perhaps I'll be watching it)

We also use **may/might be -ing** for possible plans. Compare:

- ○ I**'m going** to Ireland in July. (for sure)
- ○ I **might be going** (*or* I **may be going**) to Ireland soon. (possible)

But you can also say 'I **might go** / I **may go** …' with little difference in meaning.

D

Might as well

Helen and Clare have just missed the bus. The buses run every hour.

> What shall we do? Shall we walk?

> We **might as well**. It's a nice day and I don't want to wait here for an hour.

We **might as well** do something = We should do it because there is no better alternative. There is no reason not to do it.

May as well is also possible.

- ○ A: What time are you going out?
  B: Well, I'm ready, so I **might as well go** now.
- ○ Buses are so expensive these days, you **might as well get** a taxi. (= taxis are as good, no more expensive)

Will be -ing → Unit 24   May/might 1 → Unit 29   May I … ? → Unit 37C
Might with if → Units 38C, 40D

Exercises

30.1 Write sentences with **might**.

1 Where are you going for your holidays? (to Ireland???)
I haven't decided yet.   *I might go to Ireland.*

2 What sort of car are you going to buy? (a Honda???)
I'm not sure yet.   I _____

3 When is Tom coming to see us? (on Saturday???)
He hasn't said yet. _____

4 Where are you going to hang that picture? (in the dining room???)
I haven't made up my mind yet. _____

5 What is Tanya going to do when she leaves school? (go to university???)
She's still thinking about it. _____

30.2 Complete the sentences using **might** + the following:

> bite   break   need   ~~rain~~   slip   wake

1 Take an umbrella with you when you go out.   It _*might rain*_ later.
2 Don't make too much noise.   You _____ the baby.
3 Be careful of that dog.   It _____ you.
4 Don't throw that letter away.   We _____ it later.
5 Be careful. The footpath is very icy.   You _____ .
6 Don't let the children play in this room.   They _____ something.

30.3 Complete the sentences. Use **might be able to** or **might have to** + one of the following:

> fix   ~~help~~   leave   meet   sell   work

1 Tell me about your problem.   I _*might be able to help*_ you.
2 I'm not free this evening, but I _____ you tomorrow.
3 I don't know if I'll be free on Sunday.   I _____ .
4 I can come to the meeting, but I _____ before the end.
5 I'm short of money. I want to keep my car, but I _____ it.
6 A: There's something wrong with my bike.
  B: Let me have a look.   I _____ it.

30.4 Write sentences with **might not**.

1 I'm not sure that Liz will come to the party.
   Liz might not come to the party.

2 I'm not sure that I'll go out this evening.
   I _____

3 I'm not sure that we'll be able to get tickets for the game.
   We _____

4 I'm not sure that Sam will be able to go out with us tonight.
   _____

30.5 Read the situations and make sentences with **might as well**.

1 You and a friend have just missed the bus. The buses run every hour.
   You say: We'll have to wait an hour for the next bus.   *We might as well walk.*

2 You've been invited to a party. You're not very excited about it, but you decide to go.
   You say: I'm not doing anything else, so I _____ to the party.

3 You've just painted your kitchen. You still have a lot of paint, so why not paint the bathroom too?
   You say: We _____ . There's plenty of paint left.

4 You and a friend are at home. You're bored. There's a film on TV starting in a few minutes.
   You say: _____ . There's nothing else to do.

→ Additional exercises 16–18 (pages 311–13)

A

I **have to** do something = it is necessary to do it, I am obliged to do it:

- ◯ You can't turn right here. You **have to turn** left.
- ◯ I **have to wear** glasses for reading.
- ◯ Robert can't come out with us this evening.
  He **has to work** late.
- ◯ Last week Tina broke her arm and **had to go** to hospital.
- ◯ I haven't **had to go** to the doctor for ages.

You **have to turn** left here.

We use **do/does/did** in questions and negative sentences (for the present and past simple):

- ◯ What **do** I **have to do** to get a new driving licence?   (*not* What have I to do?)
- ◯ Karen **doesn't have to work** Saturdays. (*not* Karen hasn't to)
- ◯ Why **did** you **have to leave** early?

You can say I**'ll have to** … , I**'m going to have to** … and I **might** / I **may have to** … :

- ◯ They can't fix my computer, so I**'ll have to buy** a new one. *or*
  I**'m going to have to buy** a new one.
- ◯ Tom **might have to work** late tomorrow. *or* Tom **may have to work** …
  (= it's possible that he will have to)

B

Must is similar to **have to**:

- ◯ It's later than I thought. I **must go**. *or* I **have to go**.

You can use **must** or **have to** to give your own opinion (for example, to say what *you* think is necessary, or to recommend someone to do something):

- ◯ I haven't spoken to Sue for ages. I **must phone** her. / I **have to phone** her.
  (= I say this is necessary)
- ◯ Mark is a really nice person. You **must meet** him. / You **have to meet** him.
  (I recommend this)

We use **have to** (*not usually* **must**) to say what someone is *obliged* to do. The speaker is not giving his/her own opinion:

- ◯ I **have to work** from 8.30 to 5.30 every day.   (a fact, not an opinion)
- ◯ Jane **has to travel** a lot for her work.

But **must** is used in written rules and instructions:

- ◯ Applications for the job **must be received** by 18 May.
- ◯ (*exam instruction*) Answer all the questions. You **must write** your answers in ink.

You cannot use **must** to talk about the past:

- ◯ We didn't have much time. We **had** to hurry. (*not* we must hurry)

C

Mustn't and **don't have to** are completely different:

You **mustn't** do something = it is necessary that you do *not* do it (so don't do it):
- ◯ You **must keep** this a secret. You **mustn't tell** anyone. (= don't tell anyone)
- ◯ I promised I would be on time. I **mustn't be** late. (= I must be on time)

You **don't have to** do something = you don't need to do it (but you can if you want):
- ◯ You **don't have to tell** Tom what happened. I can tell him myself.
- ◯ I **don't have to be** at the meeting, but I think I'll go anyway.

D

You can use **have got to** instead of **have to**. So you can say:

- ◯ I**'ve got to** work tomorrow. *or* I **have to** work tomorrow.
- ◯ When **has** Helen **got to** go? *or* When **does** Helen **have to** go?

Must ('You must be tired') ➜ Unit 28   Must/mustn't/needn't ➜ Unit 32

Exercises

31.1 Complete the sentences using **have to / has to / had to**.

1 Bill starts work at 5 a.m.   <u>He has to get up</u> at four.   (he / get up)
2 'I broke my arm last week.'   ' <u>Did you have to go</u> to hospital?'   (you / go)
3 There was a lot of noise from the street.   .... the window.   (we / close)
4 Karen can't stay for the whole meeting.   .... early.   (she / leave)
5 How old .... to drive in your country?   (you / be)
6 I don't have much time.   .... soon.   (I / go)
7 How is Paul enjoying his new job?   .... a lot?   (he / travel)
8 'I'm afraid I can't stay long.'   'What time .... ?'   (you / go)
9 'The bus was late again.'   'How long .... ?'   (you / wait)
10 There was nobody to help me.   .... everything by myself.   (I / do)

31.2 Complete the sentences using **have to** + the verbs in the list. Some sentences are positive
(**I have to** … etc.) and some are negative (**I don't have to** … etc.):

| ask | do | drive | ~~get up~~ | go | make | make | pay | ~~show~~ |

1 I'm not working tomorrow, so I <u>don't have to get up</u> early.
2 Steve didn't know how to turn off the computer, so I <u>had to show</u> him.
3 Excuse me a moment – I .... a phone call. I won't be long.
4 I'm not too busy. I have a few things to do, but I .... them now.
5 I couldn't find the street I wanted.   I .... somebody for directions.
6 The car park is free. You .... to park your car there.
7 A man was injured in the accident, but he .... to hospital because it
wasn't serious.
8 Jane has a senior position in the company. She .... important decisions.
9 When Patrick starts his new job next month, he .... 50 miles to
work every day.

31.3 In some of these sentences, **must** is wrong or unnatural. Correct the sentences where necessary.

1 It's later than I thought. I must go.   <u>OK</u> (have to *is also correct*)
2 I must work every day from 8.30 to 5.30.   <u>I have to work</u>
3 You must come and see us again soon.   ....
4 Tom can't meet us tomorrow. He must work.   ....
5 I must work late yesterday evening.   ....
6 I must get up early tomorrow. I have a lot to do. ....
7 Julia wears glasses. She must wear glasses   ....
   since she was very young.

31.4 Complete the sentences with **mustn't** or **don't/doesn't have to**.

1 I don't want anyone to know about our plan. You <u>mustn't</u> tell anyone.
2 Richard <u>doesn't have to</u> wear a suit to work, but he usually does.
3 I can sleep late tomorrow morning because I .... go to work.
4 Whatever you do, you .... touch that switch. It's very dangerous.
5 There's a lift in the building, so we .... climb the stairs.
6 You .... forget what I told you. It's very important.
7 Silvia .... get up early, but she usually does.
8 Don't make so much noise. We .... wake the children.
9 I .... eat too much. I'm supposed to be on a diet.
10 You .... be a good player to enjoy a game of tennis.

→ Additional exercise 16 (page 311)

Must   mustn't   needn't

A   Must and mustn't

You **must** do something = it is necessary that you do it:
- ○ Don't tell anybody what I said. You **must** keep it a secret.
- ○ We haven't got much time. We **must** hurry.

You **mustn't** do something = it is necessary that you do *not* do it (so don't do it):
- ○ You **must** keep it a secret. You **mustn't** tell anyone.   (= don't tell anyone)
- ○ We **must** be very quiet. We **mustn't** make any noise.

B   Needn't and don't need to

You **needn't** do something = it's not necessary to do it (but you can if you like):
- ○ We've got plenty of time. We **needn't hurry**.   (= it is not necessary to hurry)
- ○ Joe can stay here. He **needn't come** with us.   (= it is not necessary for him to come)

You can also use **don't/doesn't need to**:
- ○ We **don't need to** hurry.

Remember that we say **don't need to do / doesn't need to do**, but **needn't do** (*without* **to**).

C   Needn't have (done)

Study this example situation:

Hello, can I reserve a table for two, please?

RESTAURA

later

We **needn't have reserved** a table.

Paul and Sue decided to go to a restaurant.
They reserved a table.

But the restaurant was almost empty.
So they **needn't have reserved** a table.

They **needn't have reserved** a table. = They reserved a table, but this was not necessary.

Compare **needn't** (do) and **needn't have** (done):
- ○ Everything will be OK. You **needn't worry**.   (it is not necessary)
- ○ Everything was OK. You **needn't have worried**.   (you worried, but it was not necessary)

D   Needn't have (done) and didn't need to (do)

He **needn't have done** something = he did it, but now we know that it was not necessary:
- ○ Why did he get up at 5 o'clock? He **needn't have got** up so early. He could have stayed in bed longer.

He **didn't need to** do something = it was not necessary to do it. It doesn't matter whether he did it or not:
- ○ He **didn't need to** get up early, so he didn't.
- ○ He **didn't need to** get up early, but it was a beautiful morning, so he did.

He didn't have to … is also possible in these examples.

Must ('You must be tired') ➜ Unit 28   Have to and must ➜ Unit 31
Modal verbs (**can/could/will/would** etc.) ➜ Appendix 4   American English ➜ Appendix 7

Exercises

32.1 **Which is correct?**

1 We haven't got much time. We <u>must / mustn't</u> hurry. (<u>must</u> *is correct*)
2 We've got plenty of time. We <u>mustn't / don't need to</u> hurry.
3 I have to talk to Gary. I <u>must / mustn't</u> remember to call him.
4 I have to talk to Gary. I <u>mustn't / needn't</u> forget to call him.
5 There's plenty of time for you to make up your mind. You <u>mustn't / don't need to</u> decide now.
6 We <u>needn't / mustn't</u> wash these tomatoes. They've already been washed.
7 This is a valuable book. You <u>must / needn't</u> take good care of it and you <u>mustn't / don't need to</u> lose it.
8 A: What sort of house do you want to buy? Something big?
   B: Well, it <u>mustn't / needn't</u> be big – that's not so important. But it <u>must / mustn't</u> have a nice garden – that's essential.

32.2 **Complete the sentences. Use needn't + one of these verbs:**

> ask   come   explain   ~~leave~~   walk

1 We've got plenty of time. We ....*needn't leave*.... yet.
2 I can manage the shopping alone. You .... with me.
3 We .... all the way home. We can get a taxi.
4 Just help yourself if you'd like more to eat. You .... first.
5 I understand the situation perfectly. You .... further.

32.3 **Write two sentences for each situation. Use needn't have in the first sentence and could have in the second (as in the example). For could have, see Unit 27.**

1 Why did you rush? Why didn't you take your time?
   You needn't have rushed. You could have taken your time.
2 Why did you walk home? Why didn't you take a taxi?
   ....

3 Why did you stay at a hotel? Why didn't you stay with us?
   ....

4 Why did she phone me in the middle of the night? Why didn't she wait until the morning?
   ....

5 Why did you shout at me? Why weren't you more patient?
   ....

6 Why did you leave without saying anything? Why didn't you say goodbye to me?
   ....

32.4 **Correct the sentences where necessary.**

1 We have plenty of time. <u>We don't need hurry</u>.   *We don't need to hurry.*
2 You must keep it a secret. <u>You mustn't tell</u> anybody else.   *OK*
3 I'll be all right. <u>You needn't to worry</u> about me. ....
4 <u>You mustn't wait</u> for me. You go on and I'll join you later. ....
5 <u>You don't need to keep</u> these emails. You can delete them. ....
6 <u>I needn't have gone</u> out, so I stayed at home. ....
7 <u>I needn't have bought</u> eggs. We had some already. ....

→ **Additional exercises 16–17** (pages 311–12)

Should 1

A

You **should do** something = it is a good thing to do or the right thing to do. You can use **should** to give advice or to give an opinion:

- ◯ You look tired. You **should go** to bed.
- ◯ The government **should do** more to improve education.
- ◯ '**Should** we **invite** Stephanie to the party?' 'Yes, I think we **should**.'

We often use **should** with **I think / I don't think / Do you think** … ?:

- ◯ **I think** the government **should do** more to improve education.
- ◯ **I don't think** you **should work** so hard.
- ◯ '**Do you think** I **should apply** for this job?' 'Yes, **I think you should**.'

You **shouldn't** do something = it isn't a good thing to do:

- ◯ You **shouldn't believe** everything you read in the newspapers.

Should is not as strong as **must** or **have to**:

- ◯ You **should** apologise. (= it would be a good thing to do)
- ◯ You **must** apologise. / You **have to** apologise. (= you have no alternative)

B

You can use **should** when something is not right or what you expect:

- ◯ Where's Tina? She **should be** here by now.
  (= she isn't here yet, and this is not normal)
- ◯ The price on this packet is wrong. It **should be** £2.50, not £3.50.
- ◯ That man on the motorbike **should be wearing** a helmet.

We also use **should** to say that we expect something to happen:

- ◯ Helen has been studying hard for the exam, so she **should pass**.
  (= I expect her to pass)
- ◯ There are plenty of hotels in the town. It **shouldn't be** hard to find a place to stay.
  (= I don't expect it to be hard)

He **should be wearing** a helmet.

C

You **should have done** something = you didn't do it, but it would have been the right thing to do:

- ◯ You missed a great party last night. You **should have come**. Why didn't you?
  (= you didn't come, but it would have been good to come)
- ◯ I wonder why they're so late. They **should have got** here long ago.

You **shouldn't have done** something = you did it, but it was the wrong thing to do:

- ◯ I'm feeling sick. I **shouldn't have eaten** so much. (= I ate too much)
- ◯ She **shouldn't have been listening** to our conversation. It was private.
  (= she was listening)

Compare **should** (do) and **should have** (done):

- ◯ You look tired. You **should go** to bed now.
- ◯ You went to bed very late last night. You **should have gone** to bed earlier.

D

Ought to …

You can use **ought to** instead of **should** in the sentences on this page. We say 'ought **to** do' (with **to**):

- ◯ Do you think I **ought to apply** for this job? (= Do you think I **should apply** … ?)
- ◯ Jack **ought not to go** to bed so late. (= Jack **shouldn't go** …)
- ◯ It was a great party last night. You **ought to have come**.
- ◯ Helen has been studying hard for the exam, so she **ought to pass**.

Should 2 ➔ Unit 34   Should and had better ➔ Unit 35B
Modal verbs (can/could/will/would etc.) ➔ Appendix 4

Exercises

33.1 For each situation, write a sentence with **should** or **shouldn't** + one of the following:

| ~~go away for a few days~~ | go to bed so late | look for another job |
| put some pictures on the walls | take a photo | use her car so much |

1 Anna needs a change.   *She should go away for a few days.*
2 Your salary is very low.   You _____
3 Jack always finds it hard to get up.   He _____
4 What a beautiful view!   You _____
5 Sue drives everywhere. She never walks.   She _____
6 Dan's room isn't very interesting.

33.2 Read the situations and write sentences with **I think / I don't think** ... **should** ... .

1 Joe and Catherine are planning to get married. You think it's a bad idea.
   I don't think they should get married.
2 Jane has a bad cold, but plans to go out tonight. You don't think this is a good idea. You say to her: _____
3 Peter needs a job. He's just seen an advert for a job which you think would be ideal for him, but he's not sure whether to apply or not. You say to him: _____

4 The government wants to increase taxes, but you don't think this is a good idea. _____

33.3 Complete the sentences with **should (have)** + the verb in brackets.

1 Helen ___*should pass*___ the exam. She's been studying very hard. (pass)
2 You missed a great party last night. ___*You should have come*___. (come)
3 We don't see you enough. You _____ and see us more often. (come)
4 I'm in a difficult position. What do you think I _____ now? (do)
5 I'm sorry that I didn't take your advice. I _____ what you said. (do)
6 We lost the game yesterday, but we _____. We were the better team. (win)
7 Tanya has a tennis match against Jane tomorrow. Jane _____ – she's much better than Tanya. (win)
8 'Is Joe here yet?' 'Not yet, but he _____ here soon.' (be)
9 We went the wrong way and got lost. We _____ right, not left. (turn)

33.4 Read the situations and write sentences with **should/shouldn't**. Some of the sentences are past and some are present.

1 I'm feeling sick. I ate too much. ___*I shouldn't have eaten so much.*___
2 That man on the motorbike isn't wearing a helmet. That's dangerous.
   He ___*should be wearing a helmet.*___
3 When we got to the restaurant, there were no free tables. We hadn't reserved one.
   We _____
4 The notice says that the shop is open every day from 8.30. It is 9 o'clock now, but the shop isn't open yet. _____
5 The speed limit is 30 miles an hour, but Kate is doing 50.
   She _____
6 Laura told me her address, but I didn't write it down. Now I can't remember the house number.
   I _____
7 I was driving behind another car. Suddenly, the driver in front stopped without warning and I drove into the back of his car. It wasn't my fault.
   The driver in front _____
8 I walked into a wall. I was looking behind me. I wasn't looking where I was going.

→ Additional exercises **16–18** (pages 311–13)   **67**

A

You can use **should** after:

insist   recommend   suggest   demand   propose

- ○ I **insisted** that he **should apologise**.
- ○ Doctors **recommend** that everyone **should eat** plenty of fruit.
- ○ What do you **suggest** we **should do**?
- ○ Many people are **demanding** that something **should be done** about the problem.

also

It's important/vital/necessary/essential that … **should** … :
- ○ It's **essential** that everyone **should be** here on time.

B

You can also leave out **should** in the sentences in section A. So you can say:

- ○ It's **essential** that everyone **be** here on time.   (= … that everyone **should be** here)
- ○ I **insisted** that he **apologise**.   (= … that he **should apologise**)
- ○ What do you **suggest** we **do**?
- ○ Many people are **demanding** that something **be done** about the problem.

This form (**be/do/apologise** etc.) is called the *subjunctive*. It is the same as the *infinitive* (without **to**).
You can also use normal present and past tenses:
- ○ It's **essential** that everyone **is** here on time.
- ○ I **insisted** that he **apologised**.

C

After **suggest**, you cannot use **to** … ('to do / to buy' etc.). You can say:
- ○ What do you **suggest we should do**?
- *or*   What do you **suggest we do**? (*but not* What do you suggest us to do?)
- ○ Jane won the lottery.
  I **suggested** that she **should buy** a car with the money she'd won.
- *or*   I **suggested** that she **buy** a car.
- *or*   I **suggested** that she **bought** a car.   (*but not* I suggested her to buy)

You can also use **-ing** after **suggest** (What do you **suggest doing**?). See Unit 53.

D

You can use **should** after a number of adjectives, especially:

strange   odd   funny   typical   natural   interesting   surprised   surprising

- ○ It's **strange** that he **should be** late. He's usually on time.
- ○ I was **surprised** that he **should say** such a thing.

E

You can say '**If** something **should** happen …'. For example:
- ○ We have no jobs at present, but **if** the situation **should change**, we will contact you.

You can also begin with **should** (**Should** something happen …):
- ○ **Should** the situation **change**, we will contact you.

This means the same as '**If** the situation **changes**, …'. With **should**, the speaker feels that the possibility is smaller.

F

You can use **I should** … / **I shouldn't** … to give somebody advice. For example:
- ○ 'Shall I leave now?' 'No, **I should wait** a bit.'

Here, **I should wait** = I would wait if I were you, I advise you to wait.
More examples:
- ○ 'I'm going out now. Is it cold out?'   'Yes, **I should wear** a coat.'
- ○ **I shouldn't stay** up too late. You have to be up early tomorrow.

Should 1 ➜ Unit 33   American English ➜ Appendix 7

Exercises

34.1 Write a sentence (beginning in the way shown) that means the same as the first sentence.

1 'I think it would be a good idea to see a specialist,' the doctor said to me.
   The doctor recommended that ___I should see a specialist___ .

2 'You really must stay a little longer,' she said to me.
   She insisted that I _____ .

3 'Why don't you visit the museum after lunch?' I said to them.
   I suggested that _____ .

4 'You must pay the rent by Friday,' the landlord said to us.
   The landlord demanded that _____ .

5 'Why don't we go away for a few days?' Jack said to me.
   Jack suggested that _____ .

34.2 Are these sentences right or wrong?

1 a Tom suggested that I should look for another job. ___OK___
   b Tom suggested that I look for another job. _____
   c Tom suggested that I looked for another job. _____
   d Tom suggested me to look for another job. _____
2 a Where do you suggest I go for my holiday? _____
   b Where do you suggest me to go for my holiday? _____
   c Where do you suggest I should go for my holiday? _____

34.3 Complete the sentences using **should** + the following:

> ask   ~~be~~   leave   listen   say   worry

1 It's strange that he ___should be___ late. He's usually on time.
2 It's funny that you _____ that. I was going to say the same thing.
3 It's only natural that parents _____ about their children.
4 Isn't it typical of Joe that he _____ without saying goodbye to anybody?
5 I was surprised that they _____ me for advice. What advice could I give them?
6 I'm going to give you all some essential information, so it's important that everybody
   _____ very carefully.

34.4 Use the words in brackets to complete these sentences. Use **If … should … .**

1 We have no jobs at present.   (the situation / change)
   ___If the situation should change___ , we will contact you.
2 I've hung the washing out to dry on the balcony.   (it / rain)
   _____ , can you bring the washing in, please?
3 I think everything will be OK.   (there / be / any problems)
   _____ , I'm sure we'll be able to solve them.
4 I don't want anyone to know where I'm going.   (anyone / ask)
   _____ , just say that you don't know.

Write sentences 3 and 4 again, this time beginning with **Should**.

5 (3) Should _____ , I'm sure we'll be able to solve them.
6 (4) _____ , just say that you don't know.

34.5 (Section F) Complete the sentences using **I should** + the following:

> get   keep   phone   ~~wait~~

1 'Shall I leave now?' 'No, ___I should wait___ a bit.'
2 'Shall I throw these things away?'   'No, _____ them. You may
   need them.'
3 'Shall I go and see Paul?' 'Yes, but _____ him first.'
4 'Is it worth getting this TV repaired?' 'No, _____ a new one.'

A   Had better (I'd better / you'd better etc.)

I'd better do something = it is advisable to do it. If I don't do it, there will be a problem or a danger:
- ○ I have to meet Amy in ten minutes. **I'd better go** now or I'll be late.
- ○ 'Shall I take an umbrella?'   'Yes, **you'd better**. It might rain.'
- ○ **We'd better stop** for petrol soon. The tank is almost empty.

The negative is **I'd better not** (= I **had** better not):
- ○ 'The jacket looks good on you. Are you going to buy it?'   '**I'd better not**. It's too expensive.'
- ○ You don't look very well. **You'd better not go** out tonight.

Remember that:

> The form is '**had** better' (usually '**I'd** better / **you'd** better' etc. in spoken English).
> - ○ **I'd better** phone Chris, **hadn't** I?
>
> **Had** is normally past, but the meaning of **had better** is present or future, *not* past.
> - ○ **I'd better go** to the bank **now** / **tomorrow**.
>
> We say 'I'd better **do**' (*not* to do):
> - ○ It might rain. We'd better **take** an umbrella.   (*not* We'd better to take)

B   Had better and should

Had better is similar to **should**, but not exactly the same. We use **had better** only for a specific situation, not for things in general. You can use **should** in all types of situations to give an opinion or give advice:
- ○ It's late. You**'d better go**. / You **should go**.   (a specific situation)
- ○ You're always at home. You **should go** out more often.   (in general – *not* 'had better go')

Also, with **had better**, there is always a danger or a problem if you don't follow the advice.
Should means only 'it is a good thing to do'. Compare:
- ○ It's a great film. You **should** go and see it.   (but no problem if you don't)
- ○ The film starts at 8.30. You**'d better** go now or you'll be late.

C   It's time ...

You can say **It's time** (for somebody) **to** ... :
- ○ It's time **to go** home. / It's time for us **to go** home.

But you can also say:
- ○ It's late. It's time **we went** home.

When we use **it's time** + past (we **went** / I **did** / they **were** etc.), the meaning is present, *not* past:
- ○ **It's time** they **were** here. Why are they so late?   (*not* It's time they are here)

It's time somebody **did** something = they should have already done it or started it. We often use this structure to criticise or to complain:
- ○ This situation can't continue. **It's time** you **did** something about it.
- ○ He's very selfish. **It's time** he **realised** that he isn't the most important person in the world.

You can also say **It's about time** ... . This makes the criticism stronger:
- ○ Jack is a great talker. But **it's about time** he **did** something instead of just talking.

Should 1 ➜ Unit 33

Exercises

35.1 Read the situations and write sentences with **had better** or **had better not**. Use the words in brackets.

1 You're going out for a walk with Tom. It looks as if it might rain. You say to Tom:
   (an umbrella)   *We'd better take an umbrella.*
2 Oliver has just cut himself. It's a bad cut. You say to him:
   (a plaster) ....
3 You and Kate plan to go to a restaurant this evening. It's a popular restaurant. You say to Kate:
   (reserve)   We ....
4 Rebecca doesn't look very well this morning – not well enough to go to work. You say to her:
   (work) ....
5 You received your phone bill four weeks ago, but you haven't paid it yet. If you don't pay soon, you could be in trouble. You say to yourself:
   (pay) ....
6 You want to ask your boss something, but he's very busy and you know he doesn't like to be disturbed. You say to a colleague:
   (disturb)   I ....

35.2 Put in **had better** where suitable. If **had better** is not suitable, use **should**.

1 I have an appointment in ten minutes. I ...*'d better*... go now or I'll be late.
2 It's a great film. You ...*should*... go and see it. You'll really like it.
3 You .... set your alarm. You'll never wake up on time if you don't.
4 When people are driving, they .... keep their eyes on the road.
5 I'm glad you came to see us. You .... come more often.
6 She'll be upset if we don't invite her to the party, so we .... invite her.
7 These biscuits are delicious. You .... try one.
8 I think everybody .... learn a foreign language.

35.3 Complete the sentences. Sometimes you need only one word, sometimes two.

1 a I have a toothache. I'd better ...*go*... to the dentist.
   b John is expecting you to phone him. You .... better phone him now.
   c 'Shall I leave the window open?' 'No, you'd better .... it.'
   d We'd better leave as soon as possible, ... we?

2 a It's time the government .... something about the problem.
   b It's time something .... about the problem.
   c I think it's about time you .... about other people instead of only thinking about yourself.

35.4 Read the situations and write sentences with **It's time** (somebody **did** something).

1 You think the oil in the car needs to be changed. It hasn't been changed for a long time.
   It's time we changed the oil in the car.
2 You haven't had a holiday for a very long time. You need one now.
   It's time I ....
3 You're sitting on a train waiting for it to leave the station. It's already five minutes late.
   ....
4 You enjoy having parties. You haven't had one for a long time.
   ....
5 The company you work for has been badly managed for a long time. You think some changes should be made.
   ....
6 Andrew has been doing the same job for the last ten years. He should try something else.
   ....

→ Additional exercise 16 (page 311)

A

We use **would** ('d) / **wouldn't** when we *imagine* a situation or action (= we think of something that is not real):

- It **would be** nice to buy a new car, but we can't afford it.
- I**'d love** to live by the sea.
- A: Shall I tell Chris what happened?
  B: No, I **wouldn't say** anything.
  (= I wouldn't say anything in your situation)

We use **would have** (**done**) when we imagine situations or actions in the past (= things that didn't happen):

- They helped us a lot. I don't know what we**'d have done** (= we **would have done**) without their help.
- I didn't tell Sam what happened. He **wouldn't have been** pleased.

Compare **would** (**do**) and **would have** (**done**):

- I **would call** Lisa, but I don't have her number. *(now)*
  I **would have called** Lisa, but I didn't have her number. *(past)*
- I'm not going to invite them to the party. They **wouldn't come** anyway.
  I didn't invite them to the party. They **wouldn't have come** anyway.

We often use **would** in sentences with **if** (see Units 38–40):

- I **would call** Lisa **if** I had her number.
- I **would have called** Lisa **if** I'd had her number.

B

Compare **will** ('ll) and **would** ('d):

- I**'ll stay** a little longer. I've got plenty of time.
  I**'d stay** a little longer, but I really have to go now. (so I can't stay longer)
- I**'ll call** Lisa. I have her number.
  I**'d call** Lisa, but I don't have her number. (so I can't call her)

Sometimes **would/wouldn't** is the past of **will/won't**. Compare:

present	past
TOM: I**'ll call** you on Sunday. →	Tom said he**'d call** me on Sunday.
AMY: I promise I **won't be** late. →	Amy promised that she **wouldn't be** late.
LISA: Damn! The car **won't start**. →	Lisa was annoyed because her car **wouldn't start**.

Somebody **wouldn't do** something = he/she refused to do it:

- I tried to warn him, but he **wouldn't listen** to me. (= he refused to listen)
- The car **wouldn't start**. (= it 'refused' to start)

C

You can also use **would** to talk about things that happened regularly in the past:

- When we were children, we lived by the sea. In summer, if the weather was fine, we **would** all get up early and go for a swim. (= we did this regularly)
- Whenever Richard was angry, he **would** walk out of the room.

With this meaning, **would** is similar to **used to** (see Unit 18):

- Whenever Richard was angry, he **used to walk** out of the room.

Will ➔ Units 21–22   Would you … ? ➔ Unit 37A   Would … if ➔ Units 38–40
Wish … would ➔ Unit 41   Would like ➔ Units 37E, 58   Would prefer / would rather ➔ Unit 59
Modal verbs ➔ Appendix 4

Exercises

36.1 Write sentences about yourself. Imagine things you would like or wouldn't like.

1 (a place you'd love to live)   *I'd love to live by the sea.*
2 (a job you wouldn't like to do) ....
3 (something you would love to do) ....
4 (something that would be nice to have) ....
5 (a place you'd like to go to) ....

36.2 Complete the sentences using **would** + the following verbs (in the correct form):

> be   be   ~~do~~   do   enjoy   enjoy   have   pass   stop

1 They helped us a lot. I don't know what we .....*would have done*..... without their help.
2 You should go and see the film. You .... it.
3 It's a pity you couldn't come to the party last night. You .... it.
4 Shall I apply for the job or not? What .... you .... in my position?
5 I was in a hurry when I saw you. Otherwise I .... to talk.
6 We took a taxi home last night, but got stuck in the traffic. It ....
   quicker to walk.
7 Why don't you go and see Clare? She .... very pleased to see you.
8 Why didn't you do the exam? I'm sure you .... it.
9 In an ideal world, everybody .... enough to eat.

36.3 Each sentence on the right follows a sentence on the left. Which follows which?

1 ~~I'd like to go to Australia one day.~~	a It wouldn't have been very nice.	1 .....c.....
2 I wouldn't like to live on a busy road.	b It would have been fun.	2 ....
3 I'm sorry the trip was cancelled.	c ~~It would be nice.~~	3 ....
4 I'm looking forward to going out tonight.	d It won't be much fun.	4 ....
5 I'm glad we didn't go out in the rain.	e It wouldn't be very nice.	5 ....
6 I'm not looking forward to the trip.	f It will be fun.	6 ....

36.4 Write sentences using **promised** + would/wouldn't.

1 I wonder why Laura is late.   *She promised she wouldn't be late.*
2 I wonder why Steve hasn't called me. He promised ....
3 Why did you tell Jane what I said? You ....
4 I'm surprised they didn't wait for us. They ....

36.5 Complete the sentences. Use **wouldn't** + a suitable verb.

1 I tried to warn him, but he .....*wouldn't listen*..... to me.
2 I asked Amanda what had happened, but she .... me.
3 Paul was very angry about what I'd said and .... to me for two weeks.
4 Martina insisted on carrying all her luggage. She .... me help her.

36.6 These sentences are about things that often happened in the past. Complete the sentences
using **would** + these verbs:

forget   help   shake   share   ~~walk~~

1 Whenever Richard was angry, he .....*would walk*..... out of the room.
2 We used to live next to a railway line. Every time a train went past, the house ....
3 Alan was a very kind man. He .... always .... you if you had a problem.
4 Katherine was always very generous. She didn't have much, but she ....
   what she had with everyone else.
5 You could never rely on Joe. It didn't matter how many times you reminded him to do
   something, he .... always ....

→ Additional exercises 16–18 (page 311–13)   **73**

Can/Could/Would you ... ? etc.
(Requests, offers, permission and invitations)

A Asking people to do things (requests)

We use **can** or **could** to ask people to do things:
- ○ **Can you** wait a moment, please?
- *or* **Could you** wait a moment, please?
- ○ Helen, **can you** do me a favour?
- ○ Excuse me, **could you** tell me how to get to the airport?

> **Could you** open the door, please?

Note that we say **Do you think** you **could** ... ? (*not* can):
- ○ **Do you think you could** take me to the station?

We also use **will** and **would** to ask people to do things (but **can/could** are more usual):
- ○ Helen, **will you** do me a favour?
- ○ **Would you** please be quiet? I'm trying to concentrate.

B Asking for things

To ask for something, we use **Can I have** ... ? / **Could I have** ... ? or **Can I get** ... ?:
- ○ *(in a shop)* **Can I have** these postcards, please? *or*
  Can I get these postcards, please?
- ○ *(during a meal)* **Could I have** the salt, please?

May I have ... ? is also possible:
- ○ **May I have** these postcards, please?

C Asking to do things

To ask to do something, we use **can**, **could** or **may**:
- ○ *(on the phone)* Hello, **can I** speak to Steve, please?
- ○ '**Could I** use your phone?' 'Sure.'
- ○ **Do you think I could** borrow your bike?
- ○ '**May I** come in?' 'Yes, please do.'

May is more formal than **can** or **could**.

> **Could I** use your phone? Sure.

To ask to do something, you can also say **Do you mind if I** ... ?
or **Is it all right / Is it OK if I** ... ?:
- ○ '**Do you mind if I** use your phone?' 'Sure. Go ahead.'
- ○ '**Is it all right if I** come in?' 'Yes, of course.'

D Offering to do things

To offer to do something, we use **Can I** ... ?:
- ○ '**Can I** get you a cup of coffee?' 'That would be nice.'
- ○ '**Can I** help you?' 'No, it's all right. I can manage.'

E Offering and inviting

To offer or to invite, we use **Would you like** ... ? (*not* Do you like):
- ○ '**Would you like** a cup of coffee?' 'Yes, please.'
- ○ '**Would you like** to eat with us tonight?' 'I'd love to.'

I'd like ... is a polite way of saying what you want:
- ○ *(at a tourist information office)* **I'd like** some information about hotels, please.
- ○ *(in a shop)* **I'd like** to try on this jacket, please.

Can and could → Units 26–27   Mind -ing → Unit 53   Would like → Units 55A, 58B
Modal verbs (can/could/will/would etc.) → Appendix 4

Exercises

37.1 Read the situations and write questions beginning **Can** ... or **Could** ... .

1 You're carrying a lot of things. You can't open the door yourself. There's a man standing near the door. You say to him: *Could you open the door, please?*

2 You phone Kate's office, but somebody else answers. Kate isn't there. You want to leave a message for her. You say: ....

3 You're a tourist. You want to go to the station, but you don't know how to get there. You ask at your hotel: ....

4 You are in a clothes shop. You see some trousers you like and you want to try them on. You say to the shop assistant: ....

5 You have a car. You have to go the same way as Steve, who is on foot. You offer him a lift. You say to him: ....

37.2 Read the situation and write a question using the word in brackets.

1 You want to borrow your friend's bike. What do you say to him?
(think)   *Do you think I could borrow your bike?*

2 You are staying at a friend's house and you would like to make some coffee. What do you say?
(all right)   *Is it all right if I make some coffee?*

3 You've filled in some forms in English. You want your friend to check them for you. What do you ask?
(think) ....

4 You want to leave work early. What do you ask your boss?
(mind) ....

5 The woman in the next room is playing music. It's very loud. You want her to turn it down. What do you say to her?
(think) ....

6 You're on a train. The window is open and you're feeling cold. You'd like to close it, but first you ask the woman next to you.
(OK) ....

7 You're still on the train. The woman next to you has finished reading her paper, and you'd like to have a look at it. You ask her.
(think) ....

37.3 What would you say in these situations?

1 Paul has come to see you in your flat. You offer him something to eat.
YOU: *Would you like something to eat* ?
PAUL: No, thank you. I've just eaten.

2 You need help to charge the battery in your camera. You ask Kate.
YOU: I don't know how to charge the battery. .... ?
KATE: Sure. It's easy. All you have to do is this.

3 You're on a bus. You have a seat, but an elderly man is standing. You offer him your seat.
YOU: .... ?
MAN: Oh, that's very kind of you. Thank you very much.

4 You're the passenger in a car. Your friend is driving very fast. You ask her to slow down.
YOU: You're making me very nervous. .... ?
DRIVER: Oh, I'm sorry. I didn't realise I was going so fast.

5 You've finished your meal in a restaurant and now you want the bill. You ask the waiter:
YOU: .... ?
WAITER: Sure. I'll get it for you now.

6 A friend of yours is interested in one of your books. You invite him to borrow it.
FRIEND: This looks very interesting.
YOU: Yes, it's a good book. .... ?

A

Compare these examples:

(1) LISA: Shall we go by bus or by train?
JESS: **If we go** by bus, it **will** be cheaper.

For Jess, it is possible that they will go by bus,
so she says:
If we **go** by bus, it **will** be ...

If we go by bus, it will be cheaper.

LISA   JESS

(2) Lisa and Jess decide to go by train.
Later, Jess talks to Joe.

JOE: How are you going to travel?
JESS: We're going by train. **If we went** by bus,
it **would** be cheaper, but the train is quicker.

Now Jess knows they are not going to travel by bus,
so she says:
If we **went** by bus, it **would** be ... (*not* If we go ...)

If we went by bus, it would be cheaper.

JOE   JESS

When we imagine something that will not happen, or we
don't expect that it will happen, we use **if** + *past*
(**if** we **went** / **if** there **was** / **if** you **found** etc.).
But the meaning is *not* past:
- ○ What would you do **if** you **won** a lot of money?
  (we don't really expect this to happen)
- ○ **If** there **was** (*or* were) an election tomorrow,
  who would you vote for?

For **if** ... **was/were**, see Unit 39C.

If I won a lot of money ...

Compare **if I find** and **if I found**:
- ○ I think I left my watch at your house. **If you find** it,
  can you call me?
but   **If you found** a wallet in the street, what would you do with it?

B

We do not normally use **would** in the **if**-part of the sentence:
- ○ I'd be very scared **if** somebody **pointed** a gun at me. (*not* if somebody would point)
- ○ **If we went** by bus, it would be cheaper. (*not* If we would go)

But you can use **if** ... **would** when you ask somebody to do something:
- ○ (*from a formal letter*) I would be grateful **if** you **would let** me know your decision as soon
  as possible.

C

In the other part of the sentence (not the **if**-part) we use **would** ('d) / **wouldn't**:
- ○ What **would** you **do** if you were bitten by a snake?
- ○ I'm not going to bed yet. I'm not tired. If I went to bed now, I **wouldn't sleep**.
- ○ **Would** you **mind** if I used your phone?

Could and **might** are also possible:
- ○ If I won a lot of money, I **might buy** a house. (= it is possible that I would buy a house)
- ○ If it stopped raining, we **could go** out. (= we would be able to go out)

Will → Units 21–22   If and when → Unit 25D   Would → Unit 36   If I knew → Unit 39
If I had known → Unit 40

Exercises

38.1 What do you say in these situations?

1 Of course you don't expect to win the lottery. Which do you say?
  a If I win the lottery, I'll buy a big house. ☐
  b If I won the lottery, I'd buy a big house. ☑ (b *is correct*)
2 You're not going to sell your car because it's old and not worth much. Which do you say?
  a If I sell my car, I won't get much money for it. ☐
  b If I sold my car, I wouldn't get much money for it. ☐
3 You often see Sarah. A friend of yours wants to contact her. Which do you say?
  a If I see Sarah, I'll tell her to call you. ☐
  b If I saw Sarah, I'd tell her to call you. ☐
4 You don't expect that there will be a fire in the building. Which do you say?
  a What will you do if there is a fire in the building? ☐
  b What would you do if there was a fire in the building? ☐
5 You've never lost your passport. You can only imagine it.
  a I don't know what I'll do if I lose my passport. ☐
  b I don't know what I'd do if I lost my passport. ☐
6 Somebody stops you and asks the way to a bank. Which do you say?
  a If you go right at the end of this street, you'll see a bank on your left. ☐
  b If you went right at the end of this street, you'd see a bank on your left. ☐
7 You're in a lift. There is an emergency button. Nobody is going to press it. Which do you say?
  a What will happen if somebody presses that button? ☐
  b What would happen if somebody pressed that button? ☐

38.2 Put the verb into correct form.

1 I'd be very scared if somebody ....*pointed*.... (point) a gun at me.
2 I can't afford to buy a car. If I .... (buy) a car, I'd have to borrow the money.
3 Don't lend Amy your car. If she .... (ask) me, I wouldn't lend her mine.
4 If the computer factory closed down, many people .... (lose) their jobs.
5 I don't think Gary and Emma will get married. I .... (be) amazed if they did.
6 What would you do if you .... (be) in a lift and it .... (stop) between floors?
7 If somebody .... (give) me £10,000, I .... (have) a very long holiday.

38.3 Write sentences beginning If … .

1 We've decided not to catch the 10.30 train. (arrive too early)
   If we caught the 10.30 train, we'd arrive too early.
2 Kevin is not going to do his driving test now. (fail)
   If he ....
3 We've decided not to stay at a hotel. (cost too much)
   If ....
4 Sally isn't going to leave her job. (not / get another one)
   ....
5 We've decided not to invite Ben to the party. (have to invite his friends too)
   ....
6 I'm not going to tell him what happened. (not / believe me)
   ....

38.4 Use your own ideas to complete these sentences.

1 If I won a lot of money, ...*I'd buy a house.*....
2 I'd be very angry if ....
3 If you bought a car, ...
4 I'd be surprised if ....
5 Would you mind if ....

If I knew ...   I wish I knew ...

A

Study this example situation:

Sarah wants to phone Paul, but she can't do this because she doesn't know his number. She says:

If I knew his number, I **would phone** him.

Sarah says: **If I knew** his number … . This tells us that she *doesn't* know his number. She is imagining the situation. The *real* situation is that she doesn't know his number.

> **If I knew** his number …

When we imagine a situation like this, we use **if** + *past* (**if** I **knew** / **if** you **were** / **if** we **didn't** etc.). But the meaning is present, *not* past:
- ○ There are many things I'd like to do **if** I **had** more time. (but I don't have time)
- ○ **If** I **didn't** want to go to the party, I wouldn't go. (but I want to go)
- ○ We wouldn't have any money **if** we **didn't** work. (but we work)
- ○ **If** you **were** in my position, what would you do?
- ○ It's a pity he can't drive. It would be useful **if** he **could**.

B

We use the past in the same way after **wish** (I **wish** I **knew** / I **wish** you **were** etc.). We use **wish** to say that we regret something, that something is not as we would like it to be:
- ○ I **wish** I **knew** Paul's phone number.
  (= I don't know it and I regret this)
- ○ Do you ever **wish** you **could** fly?
  (you can't fly)
- ○ It rains a lot here. I **wish** it **didn't** rain so much.
- ○ It's very crowded here. I **wish** there **weren't** so many people. (there are a lot of people)
- ○ I **wish** I **didn't** have to work tomorrow, but unfortunately I do.

> I **wish** I **had** an umbrella.

C

If I **were** / if I **was**

After **if** and **wish**, you can use **were** instead of **was** (**if** I **were** / I **wish** it **were** etc.).
If I **was** / I **wish** it **was** are also possible. So you can say:
- ○ **If I were** you, I wouldn't buy that coat.   *or*   **If I was** you, …
- ○ I'd go for a walk **if it weren't** so cold.   *or*   … **if it wasn't** so cold.
- ○ I **wish she were** here.   *or*   I **wish she was** here.

D

We do not normally use **would** in the **if**-part of the sentence or after **wish**:
- ○ **If** I **were** rich, I **would** travel a lot. (*not* If I would be rich)
- ○ Who **would** you ask **if** you **needed** help? (*not* if you would need)
- ○ I **wish** I **had** something to read. (*not* I wish I would have)

Sometimes **wish** … **would** is possible: **I wish you would listen**. See Unit 41.

E

Could sometimes means 'would be able to' and sometimes 'was/were able to':
- ○ She **could** get a better job   (she **could** get = she would be able to get)
  if she **could** speak English.   (if she **could** speak = if she was/were able to speak)
- ○ I wish I **could** help you.   (I wish I **could** = I wish I was able)

> Could → Units 26–27   If I do / if I did → Unit 38
> If I had known / I wish I had known → Unit 40   Wish → Unit 41

Exercises

39.1 **Put the verb into the correct form.**

1 If ___I knew___ (I / know) his number, I would phone him.
2 ___I wouldn't buy___ (I / not / buy) that coat if I were you.
3 .... (I / help) you if I could, but I'm afraid I can't.
4 We don't need a car at present, but we would need a car if .... (we / live)
   in the country.
5 If we had the choice, ... (we / live) in the country.
6 This soup isn't very good. .... (it / taste) better if it wasn't so salty.
7 I wouldn't mind living in England if the weather .... (be) better.
8 If I were you, ... (I / not / wait). .... (I / go) now.
9 You're always tired. If .... (you / not / go) to bed so late every night,
   you wouldn't be tired all the time.
10 I think there are too many cars. If .... (there / not / be) so many cars,
   .... (there / not / be) so much pollution.

39.2 **Write a sentence with if … for each situation.**

1 We don't see you very often because you live so far away.
   ___If you didn't live so far away, we'd see you more often.___
2 It's a nice book but it's too expensive, so I'm not going to buy it.
   I .... it if .... so ....
3 We don't go out very often – we can't afford it.
   We .... more often
4 I can't meet you tomorrow – I have to work late.
   If ....
5 It would be nice to have lunch outside but it's raining, so we can't.
   We ....
6 I don't want his advice, and that's why I'm not going to ask for it.
   If ....

39.3 **Write sentences beginning I wish … .**

1 I don't know many people (and I'm lonely). ___I wish I knew more people.___
2 I don't have a computer (and I need one). I wish ....
3 Helen isn't here (and I need to see her). ....
4 It's cold (and I hate cold weather). ....
5 I live in a big city (and I don't like it). ....
6 I can't go to the party (and I'd like to). ....
7 I have to get up early tomorrow (but I'd like to sleep late).
   ....
8 I don't know anything about cars (and my car has just broken down).
   ....
9 I'm not feeling well (and it's not nice).
   ....

39.4 **Write your own sentences beginning I wish … .**

1 (somewhere you'd like to be now – on the beach, in New York, in bed etc.)
   I wish I ....
2 (something you'd like to have – a motorbike, more friends, lots of money etc.)
   ....
3 (something you'd like to be able to do – sing, travel more, cook etc.)
   ....
4 (something you'd like to be – beautiful, strong, younger etc.)
   ....

→ **Additional exercises 19–21** (pages 313–14)

If I had known ...   I wish I had known ...

Study this example situation:

> Last month Gary was in hospital for a few days. Rachel didn't know this, so she didn't go to visit him. They met a few days ago.
>
> Rachel said:
>
> **If I'd known** you were in hospital, I **would have gone** to see you.
>
> Rachel said: **If I'd known** (= If I **had** known) you were in hospital. This tells us that she *didn't* know.

We use **if + had** (**'d**) ... to talk about the past (**if I had known/been/done** etc.):

- ○ I didn't see you when you passed me in the street. **If I'd seen** you, of course I would have said hello.   (but I didn't see you)
- ○ I didn't go out last night. I would have gone out **if I hadn't been** so tired.   (but I was tired)
- ○ **If** he **had been looking** where he was going, he wouldn't have walked into the wall.   (but he wasn't looking)
- ○ The view was wonderful. **If I'd had** a camera with me, I would have taken some pictures.   (but I didn't have a camera)

Compare:

- ○ I'm not hungry. **If** I **was** hungry, I would eat something.   *(now)*
- ○ I wasn't hungry. **If** I **had been** hungry, I would have eaten something.   *(past)*

Do not use **would** in the **if**-part of the sentence. We use **would** in the other part of the sentence:

- ○ **If** I **had seen** you, I **would have said** hello.   (*not* If I would have seen you)

Note that **'d** can be **would** or **had**:

- ○ If I**'d seen** you,   (I**'d** seen = I **had** seen)
- ○ I**'d have said** hello.   (I**'d** have said = I **would** have said)

We use **had** (**done**) in the same way after **wish**. I **wish** something **had happened** = I am sorry that it didn't happen:

- ○ I **wish** I**'d known** that Gary was ill. I would have gone to see him.   (but I didn't know)
- ○ I feel sick. I **wish** I **hadn't eaten** so much cake.   (I ate too much cake)
- ○ Do you **wish** you**'d studied** science instead of languages?   (you didn't study science)

Do not use **would have** ... after **wish**:

- ○ The weather was cold when we were on holiday. I wish it **had been** warmer.   (*not* I wish it would have been)

Compare **would** (**do**) and **would have** (**done**):

- ○ If I'd gone to the party last night, I **would be** tired now.   (I am not tired now – *present*)
- ○ If I'd gone to the party last night, I **would have met** lots of people.   (I didn't meet lots of people – *past*)

Compare **would have**, **could have** and **might have**:

- ○ If the weather hadn't been so bad, { we **would have gone** out.
  we **could have gone** out.
  (= we would have been able to go out)
  we **might have gone** out.
  (= perhaps we would have gone out) }

Had done → Unit 15   **If I do / if I did → Unit 38**   **If I knew / wish I knew → Unit 39**
Wish → Unit 41

Exercises

40.1 **Put the verb into the correct form.**

1 I didn't see you when you passed me in the street. If ___I'd seen___ (I / see) you,
___I would have said___ (I / say) hello.

2 Sam got to the station just in time to catch the train to the airport. If _____
(he / miss) the train, _____ (he / miss) his flight too.

3 I'm glad that you reminded me about Rachel's birthday. _____
(I / forget) if _____ (you / not / remind) me.

4 I wanted to send you an email, but I didn't have your email address. If _____
(I / have) your address, _____ (I / send) you an email.

5 A: How was your trip? Was it good?
 B: It was OK, but _____ (we / enjoy) it more if the weather
 _____ (be) better.

6 I took a taxi to the hotel, but the traffic was bad. _____ (it / be)
quicker if _____ (I / walk).

7 I'm not tired. If _____ (I / be) tired, I'd go home now.

8 I wasn't tired last night. If _____ (I / be) tired, I would
have gone home earlier.

40.2 **For each situation, write a sentence beginning with If.**

1 I wasn't hungry, so I didn't eat anything.
 ___If I'd been hungry, I would have eaten something.___

2 The accident happened because the road was icy.
 If the road _____ , the accident _____

3 I didn't know that Joe had to get up early, so I didn't wake him up.
 If I _____ that he had to get up early, _____

4 Unfortunately I lost my phone, so I couldn't call you.
 If _____

5 Karen wasn't injured in the crash because she was wearing a seat belt.
 _____

6 You didn't have breakfast – that's why you're hungry now.
 _____

7 I didn't get a taxi because I didn't have enough money.
 _____

40.3 **Imagine that you are in these situations. For each situation, write a sentence with I wish.**

1 You've eaten too much and now you feel sick.
 You say: ___I wish I hadn't eaten so much.___

2 There was a job advertised in the paper. You decided not to apply for it. Now you think that
your decision was wrong.
 You say: I wish I _____

3 When you were younger, you never learned to play a musical instrument. Now you regret this.
 You say: _____

4 You've painted the gate red. Now you think that red was the wrong colour.
 You say: _____

5 You are walking in the country. You'd like to take some pictures, but you didn't bring your
camera.
 You say: _____

6 You have some unexpected guests. They didn't phone you first to say they were coming. You are
very busy and you are not prepared for them.
 You say (to yourself): _____

A You can say 'I **wish you luck / all the best / a happy birthday**' etc. :
- ○ **I wish you all the best** in the future.
- ○ I saw Mark before the exam and **he wished me luck**.

We say 'wish somebody *something*' (**luck / a happy birthday** etc.). But you cannot say 'I wish that something *happens*'. We use **hope** in this situation. For example:
- ○ I'm sorry you're not well. I **hope** you **feel** better soon. (*not* I wish you feel)

Compare **I wish** and **I hope**:
- ○ **I wish** you **a pleasant stay** here.
- ○ **I hope** you **have** a pleasant stay here. (*not* I wish you have)

B We also use **wish** to say that we regret something, that something is not as we would like it. When we use **wish** in this way, we use the *past* (**knew/lived** etc.), but the meaning is *present:*
- ○ I **wish** I **knew** what to do about the problem. (I don't know and I regret this)
- ○ I **wish** you **didn't** have to go so soon. (you have to go)
- ○ Do you **wish** you **lived** near the sea? (you don't live near the sea)
- ○ Jack's going on a trip to Mexico soon. I **wish** I **was** going too. (I'm not going)

To say that we regret something in the past, we use **wish + had** … (**had known / had said**) etc. :
- ○ I **wish** I**'d known** about the party. I would have gone if I'd known. (I didn't know)
- ○ It was a stupid thing to say. I **wish** I **hadn't said** it. (I said it)

For more examples, see Units 39 and 40.

C **I wish I could** (**do** something) = I regret that I cannot do it:
- ○ I'm sorry I have to go. I **wish** I **could stay** longer. (but I can't)
- ○ I've met that man before. I **wish** I **could remember** his name. (but I can't)

I wish I could have (**done** something) = I regret that I could not do it:
- ○ I hear the party was great. I **wish** I **could have gone**. (but I couldn't go)

D You can say '**I wish** (somebody) **would** (do something)'. For example:

I wish it would stop raining.

It's been raining all day. Tanya doesn't like it. She says:
I wish it **would stop** raining.

Tanya would like the rain to stop, but this will probably not happen.

We use **I wish … would** when we would like something to happen or change. Usually, the speaker doesn't expect this to happen.

We often use **I wish … would** to complain about a situation:
- ○ The phone has been ringing for five minutes. **I wish** somebody **would answer** it.
- ○ **I wish** you**'d do** (= you **would** do) something instead of just sitting and doing nothing.

You can use **I wish … wouldn't …** to complain about things that people do repeatedly:
- ○ **I wish** you **wouldn't keep** interrupting me. (= please don't interrupt me)

We use **I wish … would …** to say that we want something to happen. But we do not use **I wish … would …** to say how we would like things *to be*. Compare:
- ○ **I wish** Sarah **would** come. (= I want her to come)
- *but*   **I wish** Sarah **was** (*or* **were**) here now. (*not* I wish Sarah would be)

- ○ **I wish** somebody **would buy** me a car.
- *but*   **I wish** I **had** a car. (*not* I wish I would have)

| Would → Unit 36 | I wish I knew → Unit 39 | I wish I was / I wish I were → Unit 39C |
| I wish I had known → Unit 40 | | |

Exercises

41.1 Put in wish(ed) or hope(d).

1 I ___wish___ you a pleasant stay here.
2 Enjoy your holiday. I .... you have a great time.
3 Goodbye. I .... you all the best.
4 We said goodbye to each other and .... each other luck.
5 We're going to have a picnic tomorrow, so I .... the weather is nice.
6 I .... you luck in your new job. I .... it works out well for you.

41.2 What do you say in these situations? Write sentences with I wish ... would ... .

1 It's raining. You want to go out, but not in the rain.
   You say: ___I wish it would stop raining.___
2 You're waiting for Jane. She's late and you're getting impatient.
   You say to yourself: I wish ....
3 You're looking for a job – so far without success. Nobody will give you a job.
   You say: I wish somebody ....
4 You can hear a baby crying. It's been crying for a long time and you're trying to study.
   You say: ....
5 Brian has been wearing the same clothes for years. You think he needs some new clothes.
   You say to Brian: ....

For the following situations, write sentences with I wish ... wouldn't ... .

6 Your friend drives very fast. You don't like this.
   You say to your friend: I wish you ....
7 Joe leaves the door open all the time. This annoys you.
   You say to Joe: ....
8 A lot of people drop litter in the street. You don't like this.
   You say: I wish people ....

41.3 Are these sentences right or wrong? Correct them where necessary.

1 I wish Sarah would be here now.   ___I wish Sarah were here now.___
2 I wish you would listen to me.   ....
3 I wish I would have more free time.   ....
4 I wish our flat would be a bit bigger.   ....
5 I wish the weather would change.   ....
6 I wish you wouldn't complain all the time. ....
7 I wish everything wouldn't be so expensive. ....

41.4 Put the verb into the correct form.

1 It was a stupid thing to say. I wish ___I hadn't said___ it. (I / not / say)
2 I'm fed up with this rain. I wish ___it would stop___ . (it / stop)
3 It's a difficult question. I wish .... the answer. (I / know)
4 I should have listened to you. I wish .... your advice. (I / take)
5 You're lucky to be going away. I wish .... with you. (I / can / come)
6 I have no energy at the moment. I wish .... so tired. (I / not / be)
7 Aren't they ready yet? I wish .... (they / hurry up)
8 It would be nice to stay here longer. I wish .... to go now.
   (we / not / have)
9 When we were in London last year, we didn't have time to see all the things we wanted to see.
   I wish .... longer. (we / can / stay)
10 It's freezing today. I wish .... so cold. I hate cold weather.
   (it / not / be)
11 Joe still doesn't know what he wants to do. I wish .... (he / decide)
12 I really didn't enjoy the party. I wish .... (we / not / go)

83

Passive 1 (**is done / was done**)

A

Study this example:

This house **was built** in 1961.

Was built is *passive*.

Compare active and passive:

Somebody **built** [this house] in 1961. *(active)*
 subject   object

[This house] **was built** in 1961. *(passive)*
 subject

When we use an active verb, we say *what the subject does:*
- ○ My grandfather was a builder. **He built** this house in 1961.
- ○ It's a big company. **It employs** two hundred people.

When we use a passive verb, we say *what happens to the subject:*
- ○ 'How old is this house?' '**It was built** in 1961.'
- ○ **Two hundred people are employed** by the company.

B

When we use the passive, who or what causes the action is often unknown or unimportant:
- ○ A lot of money **was stolen** in the robbery. (somebody stole it, but we don't know who)
- ○ **Is** this room **cleaned** every day? (does somebody clean it? – it's not important who)

If we want to say who does or what causes the action, we use **by**:
- ○ This house was built **by my grandfather**.
- ○ Two hundred people are employed **by the company**.

C

The passive is **be** (**is/was** etc.) + *past participle* (**done/cleaned/seen** etc.):
 (**be**) **done**   (**be**) **cleaned**   (**be**) **damaged**   (**be**) **built**   (**be**) **seen** etc.

For irregular past participles (**done/seen/known** etc.), see Appendix 1.

Study the active and passive forms of the *present simple* and *past simple*:

Present simple
active   **clean(s) / see(s)** etc.   Somebody **cleans** [this room] every day.

passive   **am/is/are** + **cleaned/seen** etc.   [This room] **is cleaned** every day.

- ○ Many accidents **are caused** by careless driving.
- ○ I'**m not invited** to parties very often.
- ○ How **is** this word **pronounced**?

Past simple
active   **cleaned/saw** etc.   Somebody **cleaned** [this room] yesterday.

passive   **was/were** + **cleaned/seen** etc.   [This room] **was cleaned** yesterday.

- ○ We **were woken** up by a loud noise during the night.
- ○ 'Did you go to the party?' 'No, I **wasn't invited**.'
- ○ How much money **was stolen** in the robbery?

Passive 2–3 ➜ Units 43–44   By ➜ Unit 128

Exercises

42.1 Complete the sentences using one of these verbs in the correct form, present or past:

~~cause~~	damage	hold	invite	make
overtake	show	surround	translate	write

1 Many accidents ___are caused___ by dangerous driving.
2 Cheese _____ from milk.
3 The roof of the building _____ in a storm a few days ago.
4 You _____ to the wedding. Why didn't you go?
5 A cinema is a place where films _____ .
6 In the United States, elections for president _____ every four years.
7 Originally the book _____ in Spanish, and a few years ago it
  _____ into English.
8 Although we were driving fast, we _____ by a lot of other cars.
9 You can't see the house from the road. It _____ by trees.

42.2 Write questions using the passive. Some are present and some are past.

1 Ask about glass. (how / make?) ___How is glass made?___
2 Ask about television. (when / invent?) _____
3 Ask about mountains. (how / form?) _____
4 Ask about antibiotics. (when / discover?) _____
5 Ask about silver. (what / use for?) _____

42.3 Put the verb into the correct form, present simple or past simple, active or passive.

1 It's a big factory. Five hundred people ___are employed___ (employ) there.
2 ___Did somebody clean___ (somebody / clean) this room yesterday?
3 Water _____ (cover) most of the earth's surface.
4 How much of the earth's surface _____ (cover) by water?
5 The park gates _____ (lock) at 6.30 p.m. every evening.
6 The letter _____ (send) a week ago and it (arrive) _____ yesterday.
7 The boat hit a rock and _____ (sink) quickly. Fortunately everybody
  _____ (rescue).
8 Robert's parents _____ (die) when he was very young. He and his sister
  _____ (bring up) by their grandparents.
9 I was born in London, but I _____ (grow up) in Canada.
10 While I was on holiday, my camera _____ (steal) from my hotel room.
11 While I was on holiday, my camera _____ (disappear) from my hotel room.
12 Why _____ (Sue / resign) from her job? Didn't she enjoy it?
13 Why _____ (Ben / fire) from his job? Did he do something wrong?
14 The company is not independent. It _____ (own) by a much larger company.
15 I saw an accident last night. Somebody _____ (call) an ambulance but nobody
  _____ (injure), so the ambulance _____ (not / need).
16 Where _____ (these pictures / take)? In London?
  _____ (you / take) them, or somebody else?
17 Sometimes it's quite noisy living here, but it's not a problem for me –
  I _____ (not / bother) by it.

42.4 Rewrite these sentences. Instead of using **somebody, they, people** etc., write a passive sentence.

1 Somebody cleans the room every day.   ___The room is cleaned every day.___
2 They cancelled all flights because of fog.   All _____
3 People don't use this road much.   _____
4 Somebody accused me of stealing money.   I _____
5 How do people learn languages?   How _____
6 People warned us not to go out alone.   _____

Passive 2 (be done / been done / being done)

Study the following active and passive forms:

A

Infinitive

active   (to) **do/clean/see** etc.

Somebody **will clean** this room later.

passive   (to) **be + done/cleaned/seen** etc.

This room **will be cleaned** later.

- ○ The situation is serious. Something must **be done** before it's too late.
- ○ A mystery is something that can't **be explained**.
- ○ The music was very loud and could **be heard** from a long way away.
- ○ A new supermarket is going **to be built** next year.
- ○ Please go away. I want **to be left** alone.

B

Perfect infinitive

active   (to) **have + done/cleaned/seen** etc.

Somebody **should have cleaned** the room .

passive   (to) **have been + done/cleaned/seen** etc.

The room **should have been cleaned**.

- ○ I should have received the letter by now. It might **have been sent** to the wrong address.
- ○ If you had locked the car, it wouldn't **have been stolen**.
- ○ There were some problems at first, but they seem **to have been solved**.

C

Present perfect

active   **have/has + done** etc.

The room looks nice. Somebody **has cleaned** it .

passive   **have/has been + done** etc.

The room looks nice. It **has been cleaned**.

- ○ Have you heard? The trip **has been cancelled**.
- ○ **Have** you ever **been bitten** by a dog?
- ○ 'Are you going to the party?' 'No, I **haven't been invited**.'

Past perfect

active   **had + done** etc.

The room looked nice. Somebody **had cleaned** it .

passive   **had been + done** etc.

The room looked nice. It **had been cleaned**.

- ○ The vegetables didn't taste good. They **had been cooked** too long.
- ○ The car was three years old, but **hadn't been used** very much.

D

Present continuous

active   **am/is/are + (do)ing**

Somebody **is cleaning** the room at the moment.

passive   **am/is/are + being (done)**

The room **is being cleaned** at the moment.

- ○ There's somebody walking behind us. I think we **are being followed**.
- ○ (in a shop) 'Can I help you?' 'No, thanks. I**'m being served**.'

Past continuous

active   **was/were + (do)ing**

Somebody **was cleaning** the room when I arrived.

passive   **was/were + being (done)**

The room **was being cleaned** when I arrived.

- ○ There was somebody walking behind us. I think we **were being followed**.

Passive 1, 3 ➜ Units 42, 44

Exercises

43.1 What do these words mean? Use **it can** … or **it can't** … . Use a dictionary if necessary.

If something is
1 **washable**, _it can be washed_ .   4 **unusable**, _____ .
2 **unbreakable**, it _____ .   5 **invisible**, _____ .
3 **edible**, _____ .   6 **portable**, _____ .

43.2 Complete these sentences with the following verbs (in the correct form):

| arrest | carry | cause | ~~do~~ | make | repair | ~~send~~ | spend | wake up |

Sometimes you need have (might have, should have etc.).

1 The situation is serious. Something must _be done_ before it's too late.
2 I should have received the letter by now. It might _have been sent_ to the wrong address.
3 A decision will not _____ until the next meeting.
4 Do you think that more money should _____ on education?
5 This road is in very bad condition. It should _____ a long time ago.
6 The injured man couldn't walk and had to _____ .
7 I told the hotel receptionist I wanted to _____ at 6.30 the next morning.
8 If you hadn't pushed the policeman, you wouldn't _____ .
9 It's not certain how the fire started, but it might _____ by an electrical fault.

43.3 Rewrite these sentences. Instead of using **somebody** or **they** etc., write a passive sentence.

1 Somebody has cleaned the room.
  The room has been cleaned.
2 Somebody is using the computer right now.
  The computer _____
3 I didn't realise that somebody was recording our conversation.
  I didn't realise that _____
4 When we got to the stadium, we found that they had cancelled the game.
  When we got to the stadium, we found that _____
5 They are building a new ring road round the city.

6 They have built a new hospital near the airport.

43.4 Make sentences from the words in brackets. Sometimes the verb is active, sometimes passive.

1 There's somebody behind us.   (I think / we / follow)   _I think we're being followed._
2 This room looks different.   (you / paint / the walls?)   _Have you painted the walls?_
3 My car has disappeared.   (it / steal!)   It _____
4 My umbrella has disappeared.   (somebody / take)   Somebody _____
5 Sam gets a higher salary now.   (he / promote)   He _____
6 Ann can't use her office this week.   (it / redecorate)   It _____
7 There was a problem with the photocopier yesterday, but now it's OK.
  (it / work) It _____ again.   (it / repair) It _____
8 When I went into the room, I saw that the table and chairs were not in the same place.
  (the furniture / move)   The _____
9 A neighbour of mine disappeared six months ago.   (he / not / see / since then)
  He _____
10 I wonder how Jane is these days.   (I / not / see / for ages)
  I _____
11 A friend of mine was mugged on his way home a few nights ago.   (you / ever / mug?)

A
I was offered … / **we were given** … etc.

Some verbs can have two objects. For example, **give**:

- ☐ Somebody gave **the police the information**. (= somebody gave the information to the police)

object 1   object 2

So it is possible to make two passive sentences:

- ☐ **The police** were given the information. *or*
  The information was given to the police.

Other verbs which can have two objects are:

    ask   **offer**   **pay**   **show**   **teach**   **tell**

When we use these verbs in the passive, most often we begin with the *person*:

- ☐ **I've been offered** the job, but I don't think I'll accept it. (= they have offered me the job)
- ☐ **You will be given** plenty of time to decide. (= we will give you plenty of time)
- ☐ I didn't see the original document but **I was shown** a copy. (= somebody showed me)
- ☐ Tim has an easy job – **he's paid** a lot of money to do very little. (= they pay him a lot)

B
I don't like being …

The passive of **doing/seeing** etc. is **being done / being seen** etc. Compare:

active   I don't like **people telling me** what to do.
passive   I don't like **being told** what to do.

- ☐ I remember **being taken** to the zoo when I was a child.
  (= I remember somebody taking me to the zoo)
- ☐ Steve hates **being kept** waiting. (= he hates people keeping him waiting)
- ☐ We managed to climb over the wall without **being seen**. (= without anybody seeing us)

C
I was born …

We say '**I was** born …' (*not* I am born):

- ☐ I **was born** in Chicago.
- ☐ Where **were** you **born**? (*not* Where are you born?) } *past*

but

- ☐ How many babies **are born** every day?   *present*

D
Get

You can use **get** instead of **be** in the passive:

- ☐ There was a fight at the party, but nobody **got hurt**. (= nobody **was** hurt)
- ☐ I don't **get invited** to many parties. (= I'**m** not invited)
- ☐ I'm surprised Liz **didn't get offered** the job. (= Liz **wasn't offered** the job)

We use **get** only when things *happen*. For example, you cannot use **get** in these sentences:

- ☐ Jessica **is liked** by everybody. (*not* gets liked – this is not a 'happening')
- ☐ Peter was a mystery man. Very little **was known** about him. (*not* got known)

We use **get** mainly in informal spoken English. You can use **be** in all situations.

We also use **get** in the following expressions (which are not passive in meaning):

    get married, **get divorced**   **get dressed** (= put on your clothes)
    get lost (= not know where you are)   **get changed** (= change your clothes)

Passive 1–2 ➜ Units 42–43

Exercises

44.1 Write these sentences in another way, beginning in the way shown.

1 They didn't give me the information I needed.
I _wasn't given the information I needed._

2 They asked me some difficult questions at the interview.
I ....

3 Amy's colleagues gave her a present when she retired.
Amy ....

4 Nobody told me about the meeting.
I wasn't ....

5 How much will they pay you for your work?
How much will you ....

6 I think they should have offered Tom the job.
I think Tom ....

7 Has anybody shown you what to do?
Have you ....

44.2 Complete the sentences using **being** + the following verbs (in the correct form):

| give | invite | ~~keep~~ | knock down | stick | treat |

1 Steve hates ....._being kept_..... waiting.
2 We went to the party without ....
3 I like giving presents and I also like .... them.
4 It's a busy road and I don't like crossing it. I'm afraid of ....
5 I'm an adult. I don't like .... like a child.
6 You can't do anything about .... in a traffic jam.

44.3 When were they born? Choose five of these people and write a sentence for each.
(Two of them were born in the same year.)

Ludwig van Beethoven	Mahatma Gandhi	Elvis Presley	1452	1869	1935
~~Walt Disney~~	Michael Jackson	William Shakespeare	1564	~~1901~~	1958
Galileo	Martin Luther King	Leonardo da Vinci	1770	1929	

1 .....Walt Disney was born in 1901.....
2 ....
3 ....
4 ....
5 ....
6 ....
7 And you? I ....

44.4 Complete the sentences using **get/got** + the following verbs (in the correct form):

| ask | damage | ~~hurt~~ | pay | steal | sting | stop | use |

1 There was a fight at the party, but nobody ....._got hurt._....
2 Alex .... by a bee while he was sitting in the garden.
3 These tennis courts don't .... very often. Not many people want to play.
4 I used to have a bicycle, but it .... a few months ago.
5 Rachel works hard but doesn't .... very much.
6 Last night I .... by the police as I was driving home. One of the lights
on my car wasn't working.
7 Please pack these things very carefully. I don't want them to ....
8 People often want to know what my job is. I .... that question a lot.

→ Additional exercises 22–24 (pages 314–15)

It is said that ...   He is said to ...
He is supposed to ...

Study this example situation:

George is very old. Nobody knows exactly how old he is, but:

It is said that [he] is 108 years old.

or [He] **is said to be** 108 years old.

Both these sentences mean: 'People say that he is 108 years old.'

You can use these structures with a number of other verbs, especially:

alleged   believed   considered   expected   known   reported   thought   understood

Compare the two structures:

- ○ Cathy loves running.
  It is said that she runs ten miles a day.   *or*   She **is said to run** ten miles a day.
- ○ The police are looking for a missing boy.
  It is believed that the boy is wearing a white sweater and blue jeans.   *or*   The boy **is believed to be wearing** a white sweater and blue jeans.
- ○ The strike started three weeks ago.
  It is expected that the strike will end soon.   *or*   The strike **is expected to end** soon.
- ○ A friend of mine has been arrested.
  It is alleged that he hit a policeman.   *or*   He **is alleged to have hit** a policeman.
- ○ The two houses belong to the same family.
  It is said that there is a secret tunnel between them.   *or*   There **is said to be** a secret tunnel between them.

These structures are often used in news reports. For example, in a report about an accident:
- ○ **It is reported that** two people were injured in the explosion.   *or*   Two people **are reported to have been injured** in the explosion.

(Be) supposed to

Sometimes (**it is**) **supposed to** ... = (it is) said to ... :
- ○ I want to see that film. It**'s supposed to be** good.   (= it is said to be good)
- ○ Fireworks **are supposed to have been invented** in China. Is it true?

But sometimes **supposed to** has a different meaning. We use **supposed to** to say what is intended, arranged or expected. Often this is different from the real situation:
- ○ The plan **is supposed to be** a secret, but everybody seems to know about it.
  (= the plan is intended to be a secret)
- ○ What are you doing at work? You**'re supposed to be** on holiday.
  (= you arranged to be on holiday)
- ○ Our guests **were supposed to come** at 7.30, but they were late.
- ○ Jane **was supposed to phone** me last night, but she didn't.
- ○ I'd better hurry. I**'m supposed to be meeting** Chris in ten minutes.

You're **not supposed to** do something = it is not allowed or advisable:
- ○ You**'re not supposed to park** your car here. It's private parking only.
- ○ Jeff is much better after his illness, but he**'s** still **not supposed to do** any heavy work.

Exercises

45.1 Write these sentences in another way, beginning as shown. Use the <u>underlined</u> word each time.

1 It is <u>expected</u> that the strike will end soon. The strike *is expected to end soon.*
2 It is <u>expected</u> that the weather will be good tomorrow.
   The weather is
3 It is <u>believed</u> that the thieves got in through a window in the roof.
   The thieves
4 It is <u>reported</u> that many people are homeless after the floods.
   Many people
5 It is <u>thought</u> that the prisoner escaped by climbing over a wall.
   The prisoner
6 It is <u>alleged</u> that the man was driving at 110 miles an hour.
   The man
7 It is <u>reported</u> that the building has been badly damaged by the fire.
   The building
8 a It is <u>said</u> that the company is losing a lot of money.
      The company
   b It is <u>believed</u> that the company lost a lot of money last year.
      The company
   c It is <u>expected</u> that the company will make a loss this year.
      The company

45.2 There are a lot of rumours about Alan. Here are some of the things people say about him:

1 Alan speaks ten languages.

2 He knows a lot of famous people.

3 He is very rich.

4 He has twelve children.

5 He was an actor when he was younger.

Alan

Nobody is sure whether these things are true. Write sentences about Alan using **supposed to**.

1 *Alan is supposed to speak ten languages.*
2 He
3
4
5

45.3 Complete the sentences using **supposed to be** + the following:

on a diet	a flower	my friend	a joke	~~a secret~~	working

1 How is it that everybody seems to know about the plan? It *is supposed to be a secret.*
2 You shouldn't criticise me all the time. You
3 I shouldn't be eating this cake really. I
4 I'm sorry for what I said. I was trying to be funny. It
5 What's this drawing? Is it a tree? Or maybe it
6 You shouldn't be reading the paper now. You

45.4 Write sentences with **supposed to** + the following verbs:

block	depart	~~park~~	phone	start

Use the negative (**not supposed to**) where necessary.

1 You *'re not supposed to park* here. It's private parking only.
2 We   work at 8.15, but we rarely do anything before 8.30.
3 Oh, I   Helen last night, but I completely forgot.
4 This door is a fire exit. You   it.
5 My flight   at 11.30, but it was an hour late.

→ Additional exercises 22–24 (pages 314–15)

Have something done

Study this example situation:

LISA

The roof of Lisa's house was damaged in a storm. So she called a builder, and yesterday a man came and repaired it.

Lisa **had** the roof **repaired** yesterday.

This means: Lisa arranged for somebody else to repair the roof. She didn't repair it herself.

We use **have something done** to say that we arrange for somebody else to do something for us. Compare:

- Lisa **repaired** the roof. (= she repaired it herself)
  Lisa **had** the roof **repaired**. (= she arranged for somebody else to repair it)

- 'Did you **make** those curtains yourself?' 'Yes, I enjoy making things.'
  'Did you **have** those curtains **made**?' 'No, I made them myself.'

Be careful with word order. The *past participle* (**repaired/cut** etc.) is after the *object*:

have	*object*	*past participle*
Lisa **had**	the roof	**repaired** yesterday.
Where did you **have**	your hair	**cut**?
Your hair looks nice. Have you **had**	it	**cut**?
Our neighbour has just **had**	a garage	**built**.
We are **having**	the house	**painted** this week.
How often do you **have**	your car	**serviced**?
I think you should **have**	that coat	**cleaned**.
I don't like **having**	my picture	**taken**.

Get something done

You can also say '**get** something done' instead of '**have** something done':

- When are you going to **get the roof repaired**? (= have the roof repaired)
- I think you should **get your hair cut** really short.

Sometimes **have something done** has a different meaning. For example:

- Paul and Karen **had their bags stolen** while they were travelling.

This does not mean that they arranged for somebody to steal their bags. 'They **had their bags stolen**' means only: 'Their bags were stolen'.

With this meaning, we use **have something done** to say that something happens to somebody or their belongings. Often what happens is not nice:

- Gary **had** his nose **broken** in a fight. (= his nose was broken)
- Have you ever **had** your bike **stolen**?

Exercises

46.1 Tick (✓) the correct sentence, (a) or (b), for each picture.

① 	② 	③ 	④ 
SARAH	BILL	JOHN	SUE

1. (a) Sarah is cutting her hair.
   (b) Sarah is having her hair cut.

2. (a) Bill is cutting his hair.
   (b) Bill is having his hair cut.

3. (a) John is cleaning his shoes.
   (b) John is having his shoes cleaned.

4. (a) Sue is taking a picture.
   (b) Sue is having her picture taken.

46.2 Put the words in the correct order.

1 had / a few weeks ago / the house / we / painted
   We had the house painted a few weeks ago.

2 serviced / her car / Sarah / once a year / has
   Sarah ....

3 twelve pounds / have / cleaned / it / my suit / cost / to
   ....

4 my eyes / I / two years ago / had / tested / the last time / was
   ....

5 had / in the kitchen / fitted / some new cupboards / we've
   ....

6 as soon as possible / need / translated / we / to get / this document
   ....

46.3 Write sentences in the way shown.

1 Lisa didn't repair the roof herself.   She ...*had it repaired.*...............................

2 I didn't cut my hair myself.   I ....

3 We didn't clean the carpets ourselves.   We ....

4 John didn't build that wall himself.   ....

5 I didn't deliver the flowers myself.   ....

46.4 Use the words in brackets to complete the sentences. Use the structure **have something done**.

1 ...*We're having the house painted*....... (we / the house / paint) this week.

2 I lost my key. I'll have to .... (another key / make).

3 When was the last time .... (you / your hair / cut)?

4 .... (you / a newspaper / deliver) to
   your house every day, or do you go out and buy one?

5 A: What's happening in your garden?
   B: Oh, ... (we / a garage / build).

6 A: .... (you / the washing machine / fix)?
   B: Not yet. There's someone coming to look at it next week.

7 If you want to wear earrings, why don't you ....
   (you / your ears / pierce)?

Now use 'have something done' with its second meaning (see Section D).

8 Gary was in a fight last night. He ...*had his nose broken*.... (he / his nose / break).

9 Did I tell you about Jane?   ....
   (she / her credit cards / steal).

10 Security was very strict at the airport.   ....
   (we all / our bags / search).

A

Study this example situation:

I'm feeling ill.

PAUL

You want to tell somebody what Paul said.
There are two ways of doing this:

You can repeat Paul's words (direct speech):
Paul said '**I'm feeling ill**.'

Or you can use reported speech:
Paul said **that he was feeling ill**.

Compare:

direct   Paul said ' I   am feeling ill.'

reported   Paul said that **he   was** feeling ill.

In writing we use these quotation marks to show direct speech.

B

When we use reported speech, the main verb of the sentence is usually past (Paul **said** that ... / I **told** her that ... etc.). The rest of the sentence is usually past too:
- ○ Paul **said** that he **was feeling** ill.
- ○ I **told** Lisa that I **didn't have** any money.

You can leave out **that**. So you can say:
- ○ Paul **said that** he was feeling ill. *or* Paul **said** he was feeling ill.

In general, the *present* form in direct speech changes to the *past* form in reported speech:

am/is → **was**	do/does → **did**	will → **would**
are → **were**	have/has → **had**	can → **could**
want/like/know/go etc. → **wanted/liked/knew/went** etc.		

Compare direct speech and reported speech:

You met Anna. Here are some of the things she said in *direct* speech:

My parents **are** fine.
I'**m** going to learn to drive.

I **want** to buy a car.
John **has** a new job.
I **can't** come to the party on Friday.
I **don't** have much free time.
I'**m** going away for a few days.
I'**ll** phone you when I **get** back.

ANNA

Later you tell somebody what Anna said. You use *reported* speech:

- ○ Anna said that her parents **were** fine.
- ○ She said that she **was** going to learn to drive.
- ○ She said that she **wanted** to buy a car.
- ○ She said that John **had** a new job.
- ○ She said that she **couldn't** come to the party on Friday.
- ○ She said she **didn't** have much free time.
- ○ She said that she **was** going away for a few days and **would** phone me when she **got** back.

C

The *past simple* (**did/saw/knew** etc.) can usually stay the same in reported speech, or you can change it to the *past perfect* (**had done / had seen / had known** etc.):

- ○   *direct*   Paul said 'I **woke** up feeling ill, so I **didn't go** to work.'
     reported   Paul said (that) he **woke** up feeling ill, so he **didn't go** to work.   *or*
             Paul said (that) he **had woken** up feeling ill, so he **hadn't gone** to work.

Reported speech 2 → Unit 48   Reported questions → Unit 50B

Exercises

47.1 Yesterday you met a friend of yours, Steve. You hadn't seen him for a long time. Here are some of the things Steve said to you:

1 I'm living in London.

2 My father isn't very well.

3 Rachel and Mark are getting married next month.

4 My sister has had a baby.

5 I don't know what Joe is doing.

6 I saw Helen at a party in June and she seemed fine.

Steve

7 I haven't seen Amy recently.

8 I'm not enjoying my job very much.

9 You can come and stay at my place if you're ever in London.

10 My car was stolen a few days ago.

11 I want to go on holiday, but I can't afford it.

12 I'll tell Chris I saw you.

Later that day you tell another friend what Steve said. Use reported speech.

1 _Steve said that he was living in London._

2 He said that ....

3 He ....

4 ....

5 ....

6 ....

7 ....

8 ....

9 ....

10 ....

11 ....

12 ....

47.2 Somebody says something to you which is not what you expected. Use your own ideas to complete your answers.

1 A: It's quite a long way from the hotel to the station.
   B: Is it? The man on the reception desk said _it was only five minutes' walk_ .

2 A: Sue is coming to the party tonight.
   B: Is she? I saw her a few days ago and she said she ....

3 A: Sarah gets on fine with Paul.
   B: Does she? Last week you said .... each other.

4 A: Joe knows lots of people.
   B: That's not what he told me. He said .... anyone.

5 A: Jane will be here next week.
   B: Oh, really? When I spoke to her, she said .... away.

6 A: I'm going out tonight.
   B: Are you? I thought you said .... home.

7 A: John speaks French quite well.
   B: Does he? He told me .... any other languages.

8 A: I haven't seen Ben recently.
   B: That's strange. He told me .... last weekend.

➜ Additional exercise 25 (page 316)

A

It is not always necessary to change the verb in reported speech. If the situation *is still the same*, you do not need to change the verb to the past. For example:

- ○ *direct*   Paul said 'My new job **is** boring.'
  reported   Paul said that his new job **is** boring.
  (The situation is still the same. His job **is** still boring now.)

- ○ *direct*   Helen said '**I want** to go to Canada next year.'
  reported   Helen told me that **she wants** to go to Canada next year.
  (Helen still wants to go to Canada next year.)

You can also change the verb to the past:

- ○ Paul said that his new job **was** boring.
- ○ Helen told me that she **wanted** to go to Canada next year.

But if the situation has changed or finished, you *must* use a past verb:

- ○ Paul left the room suddenly. He said **he had** to go. (*not* has to go)

B

You need to use a past form when there is a difference between what was said and what is really true.
For example:

You met Sonia a few days ago.
She said: **Joe is in hospital**.

Later that day you meet Joe in the street. You say:
Hi, Joe. I didn't expect to see you. Sonia said you **were** in hospital.
(*not* 'Sonia said you are in hospital', because clearly he is not)

C

Say and **tell**

If you say *who* somebody is talking to, use **tell**:

- ○ Sonia **told me** that you were in hospital. (*not* Sonia said me)
- ○ What did you **tell the police**? (*not* say the police)

Otherwise use **say**:

- ○ Sonia **said** that you were in hospital. (*not* Sonia told that …)
- ○ What did you **say**?

But you can '**say** something **to** somebody':

- ○ Ann **said** goodbye **to** me and left. (*not* Ann said me goodbye)
- ○ What did you **say to** the police?

- · TELL **SOMEBODY**
- · SAY ~~SOMEBODY~~

D

Tell/ask somebody **to** do something

We also use the infinitive (**to do / to be** etc.) in reported speech, especially with **tell** and **ask** (for orders and requests):

- ○ *direct*   '**Drink** plenty of water,' the doctor said to me.
  reported   The doctor **told me to drink** plenty of water.
- ○ *direct*   '**Don't be** late,' I said to Joe.
  reported   I **told Joe not to be** late.
- ○ *direct*   '**Can you help** me, please,' Jackie said to me.
  reported   Jackie **asked me to help** her.

You can also say 'Somebody **said** (**not**) **to** do something':

- ○ Paul **said not to worry** about him. (*but not* Paul said me)

Reported speech 1 → Unit 47   Reported questions → Unit 50B

Exercises

48.1 Here are some things that Sarah said to you:

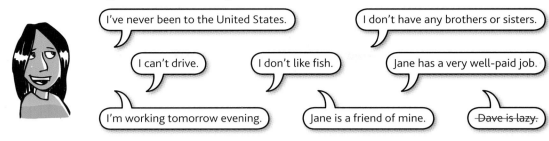

I've never been to the United States.

I don't have any brothers or sisters.

I can't drive.

I don't like fish.

Jane has a very well-paid job.

I'm working tomorrow evening.

Jane is a friend of mine.

~~Dave is lazy.~~

But later Sarah says something different to you. What do you say?

	Sarah	You
1	Dave works very hard.	But you said he was lazy.
2	Let's have fish for dinner.	But
3	I'm going to buy a car.	
4	Jane is always short of money.	
5	My sister lives in Paris.	
6	I think New York is a great place.	
7	Let's go out tomorrow evening.	
8	I've never spoken to Jane.	

48.2 Complete the sentences with **say** or **tell** (in the correct form). Use only one word each time.

1. Ann ....*said*.... goodbye to me and left.
2. .... us about your holiday. Did you have a nice time?
3. Don't just stand there! .... something!
4. I wonder where Sue is.   She .... she would be here at 8 o'clock.
5. Dan .... me that he was bored with his job.
6. The doctor .... that I should rest for at least a week.
7. Don't .... anybody what I .... It's a secret just between us.
8. 'Did she .... you what happened?' 'No, she didn't .... anything to me.'
9. Gary couldn't help me.   He .... me to ask Chris.
10. Gary couldn't help me.   He .... to ask Chris.

48.3 The following sentences are direct speech:

Don't wait for me if I'm late.

Mind your own business.

Don't worry, Sue.

Please slow down!

Can you open your bag, please?

Could you get me a paper?

~~Hurry up!~~

Will you marry me?

Do you think you could give me a hand, Tom?

Now choose one of these to complete each of the sentences below. Use <u>reported</u> speech.

1. Will was taking a long time to get ready, so I ....*told him to hurry up*.................... .
2. Sarah was driving too fast, so I asked ....
3. Sue was nervous about the situation. I told ....
4. I couldn't move the piano alone, so I ....
5. The security guard looked at me suspiciously and ....
6. Tom was going to the shop, so I ....
7. The man started asking me personal questions, so I ....
8. John was in love with Marianne, so he ....
9. I didn't want to delay Helen, so I ....

→ Additional exercise 25 (page 316)

Questions 1

A

In questions we usually put the subject after the first verb:

subject	+ verb		verb	+ subject
Tom	will	→	will	Tom?
you	have	→	have	you?
the house	was	→	was	the house?

- ○ **Will Tom** be here tomorrow?
- ○ **Have you** been working hard?
- ○ When **was the house b**uilt?

Remember that the subject comes after the *first* verb:
- ○ **Is Katherine** working today? (*not* Is working Katherine)

B

In *present simple* questions, we use **do/does**:

you	live	→	**do**	you **live**?
the film	starts	→	**does**	the film **start**?

- ○ **Do** you **live** near here?
- ○ What time **does** the film **start**?

In *past simple* questions, we use **did**:

you	sold	→	**did**	you **sell**?
the train	stopped	→	**did**	the train **stop**?

- ○ **Did** you **sell** your car?
- ○ Why **did** the train **stop**?

But do not use **do/does/did** if **who/what** etc. is the subject of the sentence. Compare:

who *object*

Emma phoned somebody .
└── *object* ──┘

 Who **did** Emma **phone**?

who *subject*

 Somebody phoned Emma.
subject ──┘

 Who **phoned** Emma?

In these examples, **who/what** etc. is the subject:
- ○ **Who wants** something to eat? (*not* Who does want)
- ○ **What happened** to you last night? (*not* What did happen)
- ○ **How many people came** to the meeting? (*not* did come)
- ○ **Which bus goes** to the centre? (*not* does go)

C

Note the position of prepositions in questions beginning **Who/What/Which/Where** … ?:
- ○ **Who** do you want to speak **to**?
- ○ **Which** job has Tina applied **for**?
- ○ **What** was the weather **like** yesterday?
- ○ **Where** are you **from**?

You can use *preposition* + **whom** in formal style:
- ○ **To whom** do you wish to speak?

D

Isn't it … ? / **Didn't you** … ? etc. (negative questions)

We use negative questions especially to show surprise:
- ○ **Didn't you** hear the doorbell? I rang it three times.

or when we expect the listener to agree with us:
- ○ '**Haven't we** met before?' 'Yes, I think we have.'

Note the meaning of **yes** and **no** in answers to negative questions:
- ○ **Don't you** want to go? { **Yes**. (= Yes, I want to go)
   { **No**. (= No, I don't want to go)

Note the word order in negative questions beginning **Why** … ?:
- ○ **Why don't we** eat out tonight? (*not* Why we don't eat)
- ○ **Why wasn't Emma** at work yesterday? (*not* Why Emma wasn't)

Questions 2 ➜ Unit 50   Question tags (**do you?** **isn't it?** etc.) ➜ Unit 52

Exercises

49.1 Ask Joe questions. (Look at his answers before you write the questions.)

1 (where / live?)   *Where do you live?*   In Manchester.
2 (born there?)   ....   No, I was born in London.
3 (married?)   ....   Yes.
4 (how long / married?)   ....   17 years.

5 (children?)   ....   Yes, two boys.

6 (how old / they?)   ....   12 and 15.
7 (what / do?)   ....   I'm a journalist.
8 (what / wife / do?)   ....   She's a doctor.

Joe

49.2 Make questions with **who** or **what**.

1   Somebody hit me.   *Who hit you?*
2   I hit somebody.   *Who did you hit?*
3   Somebody paid the bill.   Who ....
4   Something happened.   What ....
5   Diane said something.
6   This book belongs to somebody.
7   Somebody lives in that house.
8   I fell over something.
9   Something fell off the shelf.
10   This word means something.
11   I borrowed the money from somebody.
12   I'm worried about something.

49.3 Put the words in brackets in the correct order. All the sentences are questions.

1 (when / was / built / this house)   *When was this house built?*
2 (how / cheese / is / made)   ....
3 (when / invented / the computer / was)   ....
4 (why / Sue / working / isn't / today)   ....
5 (what time / coming / your friends / are)   ....
6 (why / was / cancelled / the trip)   ....
7 (where / your mother / was / born)   ....
8 (why / you / to the party / didn't / come)   ....
9 (how / the accident / did / happen)   ....
10 (why / this machine / doesn't / work)   ....

49.4 Write negative questions from the words in brackets. In each situation you are surprised.

1 A: We won't see Lisa this evening.
   B: Why not? (she / not / come / out with us?)   *Isn't she coming out with us?*
2 A: I hope we don't meet Luke tonight.
   B: Why? (you / not / like / him?)   ....
3 A: Don't go and see that film.
   B: Why not? (it / not / good?)   ....
4 A: I'll have to borrow some money.
   B: Why? (you / not / have / any?)   ....

Questions 2 (**Do you know where ... ? / He asked me where ...**)

Do you **know where** ... ? / **I don't know why** ... / **Could you tell me what** ... ? etc.

We say: Where **has Tom** gone?

but Do you know where **Tom has** gone? (*not* Do you know where has Tom gone?)

When the question (**Where has Tom gone?**) is part of a longer sentence (**Do you know** ... ? / **I don't know** ... / **Can you tell me** ... ? etc.), the word order changes. We say:

○ What time **is it**?	*but* **Do you know** what time **it is**?
○ Who **are those people**?	**I don't know** who **those people are**.
○ Where **can I** find Louise?	**Can you tell me** where **I can** find Louise?
○ How much **will it** cost?	**Do you have any idea** how much **it will** cost?

Be careful with **do/does/did** questions. We say:

○ What time **does the film start**?	*but* **Do you know** what time **the film starts**?
	(*not* does the film start)
○ What **do you mean**?	**Please explain** what **you mean**.
○ Why **did she leave** early?	**I wonder** why **she left** early.

Use **if** or **whether** where there is no other question word (**what**, **why** etc.):

○ Did anybody see you?	*but* Do you know **if** anybody saw you?
	or ... **whether** anybody saw you?

He asked me where ... (reported questions)

The same changes in word order happen in reported questions. Compare:

○ *direct*	The police officer said to us 'Where	**are you going** ?'
reported	The police officer asked us where	**we were going** .
○ *direct*	Clare said 'What time	**do the banks close** ?'
reported	Clare wanted to know what time	**the banks closed** .

In reported speech the verb usually changes to the past (**were**, **closed** etc.). See Unit 47.

Study these examples. You had an interview for a job and these were some of the questions the interviewer asked you:

Are you willing to travel?

Why **did you apply** for the job?

What **do you do** in your spare time?

Can you speak any other languages?

How long **have you** been working in your present job?

Do you have a driving licence?

Later you tell a friend what the interviewer asked you. You use *reported* speech:
- ○ She asked if (*or* whether) **I was** willing to travel.
- ○ She wanted to know what **I did** in my spare time.
- ○ She asked how long **I had** been working in my present job.
- ○ She asked why **I had** applied for the job. (*or* ... why I **applied**)
- ○ She wanted to know if (*or* whether) **I could** speak any other languages.
- ○ She asked if (*or* whether) **I had** a driving licence.

Reported speech → Units 47–48

Exercises

50.1 Which is right? Tick (✓) the correct alternative.

1 a Do you know what time the film starts? ✓
  b Do you know what time does the film start?
  c Do you know what time starts the film?

2 a Why Amy does get up so early every day?
  b Why Amy gets up so early every day?
  c Why does Amy get up so early every day?

3 a I want to know what this word means.
  b I want to know what does this word mean.
  c I want to know what means this word.

4 a I can't remember where did I park the car.
  b I can't remember where I parked the car.
  c I can't remember where I did park the car.

5 a Why you didn't phone me yesterday?
  b Why didn't you phone me yesterday?
  c Why you not phoned me yesterday?

6 a Do you know where does Helen work?
  b Do you know where Helen does work?
  c Do you know where Helen works?

7 a How much it costs to park here?
  b How much does it cost to park here?
  c How much it does cost to park here?

8 a Tell me what you want.
  b Tell me what you do want.
  c Tell me what do you want.

50.2 Put the words in the correct order.

1 (don't / Tom / where / know / gone / has) I _don't know where Tom has gone_ .
2 (is / to the airport / far / it) How _don't know where Tom has gone_ ?
3 (wonder / is / how / old / Tom) I _don't know where Tom has gone_ .
4 (Lisa / on holiday / going / is) When _don't know where Tom has gone_ ?
5 (tell / the post office / you / me / is / where)
Could .... ?
6 (in the accident / injured / anyone / don't / whether / know / was)
I ....
7 (what / tomorrow / know / time / will / arrive / you / you)
Do .... ?

50.3 You have been away for a while and have just come back to your home town. You meet Tony, a friend of yours. He asks you a lot of questions:

1 How are you?
2 Where have you been?
3 How long have you been back?
4 What are you doing now?
5 Why did you come back?
6 Where are you living?
7 Are you glad to be back?
8 Do you have any plans to go away again?
9 Can you help me find a job?

Tony

Now you tell another friend what Tony asked you. Use reported speech.

1 _He asked me how I was._
2 He asked me ....
3 He ....
4 ....
5 ....
6 ....
7 ....
8 ....
9 ....

➜ Additional exercise 25 (page 316)

Auxiliary verbs (have/do/can etc.)
I think so / I hope so etc.

A

In each of these sentences there is an auxiliary verb and a main verb:

I	**have**	**lost**	my keys.
She	**can't**	**come**	to the party.
The hotel	**was**	**built**	ten years ago.
Where	**do** you	**live**?	

In these examples **have/can't/was/do** are auxiliary (= helping) verbs.

You can use an auxiliary verb when you don't want to repeat something:
- ○ 'Have you locked the door?'   'Yes, I **have**.' (= I have *locked the door*)
- ○ Gary wasn't working, but Laura **was**. (= Laura was *working*)
- ○ Jessica could lend me the money, but she **won't**. (= she won't *lend me the money*)

Use **do/does/did** for the present and past simple:
- ○ 'Do you like onions?'   'Yes, I **do**.' (= I *like onions*)
- ○ 'Does Simon live in London?'   'He **did**, but he **doesn't** any more.'

You can use auxiliary verbs to deny what somebody says (= say it is not true):
- ○ 'You're sitting in my place.'   'No, I**'m not**.' (= I'm not *sitting in your place*)
- ○ 'You didn't lock the door before you left.'   'Yes, I **did**.' (= I *locked the door*)

B

We use **have you**? / **isn't she**? / **do they**? etc. to show interest in what somebody has said, or to show surprise:
- ○ 'I've just seen Stephen.'   'Oh, **have you**? How is he?'
- ○ 'Lisa isn't very well today.'   'Oh, **isn't she**? What's wrong with her?'
- ○ 'It rained every day during our holiday.'   '**Did it**? What a shame!'
- ○ 'James and Tanya are getting married.'   '**Are they**? Really?'

C

We use auxiliary verbs with **so** and **neither**:
- ○ 'I'm tired.'   '**So am I**.' (= I'm tired too)
- ○ 'I never read newspapers.'   '**Neither do I**.' (= I never read newspapers either)
- ○ Sarah hasn't got a car and **neither has Mark**.

Note the word order after **so** and **neither** (verb before subject):
- ○ I passed the exam and **so did Paul**. (*not* so Paul did)

Instead of **neither**, you can use **nor**. You can also use **not** … **either**:
- ○ 'I don't know.' '**Neither** do I.' *or* '**Nor** do I.' *or* 'I do**n't either**.'

D

I think so / I hope so etc.

After some verbs we use **so** when we don't want to repeat something:
- ○ 'Are those people Korean?'   '**I think so**.' (= I think *they are Korean*)
- ○ 'Will you be at home this evening?'   '**I expect so**. (= I expect *I'll be at home* …)
- ○ 'Do you think Kate has been invited to the party?'   '**I suppose so**.'

In the same way we say: **I hope so**, **I guess so** and **I'm afraid so**.

The usual negative forms are:

I think so / I expect so	→	I **don't think so** / I **don't expect so**
I hope so / I'm afraid so / I guess so	→	I **hope not** / I**'m afraid not** / I **guess not**
I suppose so	→	I **don't suppose so** *or* I **suppose not**

- ○ 'Is that woman American?'   '**I think so. / I don't think so**.'
- ○ 'Do you think it will rain?'   '**I hope so. / I hope not**.' (*not* I don't hope so)

American English ➔ **Appendix 7**

Exercises

51.1 Complete each sentence with an auxiliary verb (**do/was/could** etc.). Sometimes the verb must be negative (**don't/wasn't** etc.).

1 I wasn't tired, but my friends ......were...... .
2 I like hot weather, but Ann ....
3 'Is Andy here?' 'He .... five minutes ago, but I think he's gone home now.'
4 Liz said she might call me later this evening, but I don't think she ....
5 'Are you and Chris coming to the party?' 'I ...., but Chris ....'
6 I don't know whether to apply for the job or not. Do you think I .... ?
7 'Please don't tell anybody what I said.' 'Don't worry. I ....'
8 'You never listen to me.' 'Yes, I ....!'
9 I thought it was going to rain, but it ....
10 'Please help me.' 'I'm sorry. I .... if I ...., but I ....'

51.2 You never agree with Sue. Answer in the way shown.

1 I'm hungry.   Are you? I'm not.
2 I'm not tired.   Aren't you? I am.
3 I like football.   ....
4 I didn't enjoy the film. ....   You
5 I've never been to Australia. ....
6 I thought the exam was easy. ....

Sue

51.3 You are talking to Tina. If you're in the same position as Tina, reply with **So** ... or **Neither** ... , as in the first example. Otherwise, ask questions as in the second example.

1 I'm tired.   So am I.
2 I work hard.   Do you? What do you do?
3 I watched television last night.   ....
4 I won't be at home tomorrow.   ....   You
5 I like reading. I read a lot.   ....
6 I'd like to live somewhere else.   ....
7 I can't go out tonight.   ....

Tina

51.4 In these conversations, you are B. Read the information in brackets and then answer with **I think so**, **I hope not** etc.

1 (You don't like rain.)
   A: Is it going to rain?   B: (hope)   I hope not.
2 (You need more money quickly.)
   A: Do you think you'll get a pay rise soon?   B: (hope) ....
3 (You think Katherine will probably get the job that she applied for.)
   A: Do you think Katherine will get the job?   B: (expect) ....
4 (You're not sure whether Amy is married – probably not.)
   A: Is Amy married?   B: (think) ....
5 (You are the receptionist at a hotel. The hotel is full.)
   A: Have you got a room for tonight?   B: (afraid) ....
6 (You're at a party. You have to leave early.)
   A: Do you have to leave already?   B: (afraid) ....
7 (Ann normally works every day, Monday to Friday. Tomorrow is Wednesday.)
   A: Is Ann working tomorrow?   B: (suppose) ....
8 (You are going to a party. You can't stand John.)
   A: Do you think John will be at the party?   B: (hope) ....
9 (You're not sure what time the concert is – probably 7.30.)
   A: Is the concert at 7.30?   B: (think) ....

Question tags (**do you? isn't it?** etc.)

Study these examples:

You haven't seen Lisa today, **have you**?

No, I haven't.

It was a good film, **wasn't it**?

Yes, it was great.

Have you? and **wasn't it**? are *question tags* (= mini-questions that we often put on the end of a sentence in spoken English). In question tags, we use an auxiliary verb (**have/was/will** etc.). We use **do/does/did** for the present and past simple (see Unit 51):

- ○ 'Karen plays the piano, **doesn't** she?' 'Well, yes, but not very well.'
- ○ 'You didn't lock the door, **did** you?' 'No, I forgot.'

Normally we use a *negative* question tag after a *positive* sentence:

… and a *positive* question tag after a *negative* sentence:

positive sentence +	*negative tag*
Kate **will** be here soon,	**won't she**?
There **was** a lot of traffic,	**wasn't there**?
Joe **should** pass the exam,	**shouldn't he**?

negative sentence +	*positive tag*
Kate **won't** be late,	**will she**?
They **don't** like us,	**do they**?
You **haven't** eaten yet,	**have you**?

Notice the meaning of **yes** and **no** in answer to a negative sentence:

- ○ You're **not** going out today, **are you**? { **Yes.** (= Yes, I am going out)
  No. (= No, I am not going out)

The meaning of a question tag depends on how you say it. If your voice goes *down*, you are not really asking a question; you are only inviting the listener to agree with you:

- ○ 'It's a nice day, **isn't it**?' 'Yes, beautiful.'
- ○ 'Paul doesn't look well today, **does he**?' 'No, he looks very tired.'
- ○ 'Lisa's very funny. She's got a great sense of humour, **hasn't she**?' 'Yes, she has.'

But if the voice goes *up*, it is a real question:

- ○ 'You haven't seen Lisa today, **have you**?' 'No, I haven't.'
  (= Have you by chance seen Lisa today?)

You can use a *negative sentence + positive tag* to ask for things or information, or to ask somebody to do something. The voice goes *up* at the end of the tag in sentences like these:

- ○ 'You haven't got a pen, **have you**?' 'Yes, here you are.'
- ○ 'You couldn't do me a favour, **could you**?' 'It depends what it is.'
- ○ 'You don't know where Karen is, **do you**?' 'Sorry, I have no idea.'

After **Let's** … , the question tag is **shall we**:

- ○ **Let's** go for a walk, **shall we**? (the voice goes *up*)

After **Don't** … , the question tag is **will you**:

- ○ **Don't** be late, **will you**? (the voice goes *down*)

After **I'm** … , the negative question tag is **aren't I** (= am I not):

- ○ 'I'm right, **aren't I**?' 'Yes, you are.'

Auxiliary verbs (**have/do/can** etc.) ➔ Unit 51

Exercises

52.1 Put a question tag on the end of these sentences.

1	Kate won't be late,	_will she_ ?	No, she's never late.
2	You're tired,	_aren't you_ ?	Yes, a little.
3	You travel a lot,	?	Yes, I love travelling.
4	You weren't listening,	?	Yes, I was!
5	Sarah doesn't know Ann,	?	No, they've never met.
6	Jack's on holiday,	?	Yes, he's in Australia.
7	Kate's been to China before,	?	Yes, two or three times.
8	You can speak German,	?	Yes, but not fluently.
9	They won't mind if I take a photo,	?	No, of course they won't.
10	There are a lot of people here,	?	Yes, more than I expected.
11	Let's go out tonight,	?	Yes, that would be great.
12	This isn't very interesting,	?	No, not really.
13	I'm too impatient,	?	Yes, you are sometimes.
14	You wouldn't tell anyone,	?	No, of course not.
15	Ann has lived here a long time,	?	Yes, 20 years.
16	I shouldn't have lost my temper,	?	No, but that's all right.
17	He'd never met her before,	?	No, that was the first time.
18	Don't drop that vase,	?	Don't worry. I won't.

52.2 Read the situation and write a sentence with a question tag. In each situation you are asking your friend to agree with you.

1 You look out of the window. The sky is blue and the sun is shining. What do you say to your friend? (beautiful day) _It's a beautiful day, isn't it?_

2 You're with a friend outside a restaurant. You're looking at the prices, which are very high. What do you say? (expensive) It ....

3 You and a colleague have just finished a training course. You really enjoyed it. What do you say to your colleague? (great) The course ....

4 Your friend's hair is much shorter than when you last met. What do you say to her/him? (have / your hair / cut) You ....

5 You and a friend are listening to a woman singing. You like her voice very much. What do you say to your friend? (a good voice) She ....

6 You are trying on a jacket in a shop. You look in the mirror and you don't like what you see. What do you say to your friend? (not / look / very good)
It ....

7 You and a friend are walking over a small wooden bridge. The bridge is very old and some parts are broken. What do you say? (not / very safe)
This bridge ....

52.3 In these situations you are asking for information, asking people to do things etc.

1 You need a pen. Perhaps Jane has got one. Ask her.
   Jane, you haven't got a pen, have you?

2 You have to move a heavy table. You want Joe to give you a hand with it. Ask him.
   Joe, you ....

3 You're looking for Sarah. Perhaps Kate knows where she is. Ask her.
   Kate, you ....

4 You need a bicycle pump. Perhaps Helen has got one. Ask her.
   Helen, ...

5 Ann has a car and you need a lift to the station. Perhaps she'll take you. Ask her.
   Ann, ...

6 You're looking for your keys. Perhaps Robert has seen them. Ask him.
   Robert, ...

Verb + -ing (enjoy doing / stop doing etc.)

A Look at these examples:
- I **enjoy reading**. (*not* I enjoy to read)
- Would you **mind closing** the door? (*not* mind to close)
- Chris **suggested going** to the cinema. (*not* suggested to go)

> Would you **mind closing** the door?

After **enjoy**, **mind** and **suggest**, we use -ing (*not* to ...).

Some more verbs that are followed by -ing:

stop	postpone	admit	avoid	imagine
finish	consider	deny	risk	fancy

- Suddenly everybody **stopped talking**. There was silence.
- I'll do the shopping when I've **finished cleaning** the flat.
- He tried to **avoid answering** my question.
- I don't **fancy going** out this evening. (= I'm not enthusiastic about it)
- Have you ever **considered going** to live in another country?
- They said they were innocent. They **denied doing** anything wrong.

The negative form is **not -ing**:
- When I'm on holiday, I enjoy **not having** to get up early.

B We also use -ing after:

> **give up** (= stop)
> **put off** (= postpone)
> **go on** or **carry on** (= continue)
> **keep** or **keep on** (= do something continuously or repeatedly)

- I've **given up reading** newspapers. I think it's a waste of time.
- Catherine doesn't want to retire. She wants to **go on working**. (*or* ... to **carry on working**.)
- You **keep interrupting** when I'm talking! *or* You **keep on interrupting** ...

C With some verbs you can use the structure *verb* + somebody + -ing:
- I can't **imagine George riding** a motorbike.
- You can't **stop me doing** what I want.
- Did you really say that? I don't **remember you saying** that.
- 'Sorry to **keep you waiting** so long.' 'That's all right.'

Note the passive form (**being done/seen/kept** etc.):
- I don't **mind being kept** waiting. (= I don't mind **people keeping** me ...)

D When you are talking about finished actions, you can say **having done/stolen/said** etc. :
- They admitted **having stolen** the money.

But it is not necessary to use **having** (done). You can also say:
- They admitted **stealing** the money.
- I now regret **saying** (*or* **having said**) what I said.

E After some of the verbs on this page (especially **admit/deny/suggest**) you can also use **that** ... :
- They **denied that** they had stolen the money. (*or* They **denied stealing** ...)
- Chris **suggested that** we went to the cinema. (*or* Chris **suggested going** ...)

Suggest ➜ Unit 34   Being done (passive) ➜ Unit 44B   Verb + to ... ➜ Unit 54   Verb + to ... and -ing ➜ Units 55C, 56–58   Remember / regret / go on ➜ Unit 56B   Go on / carry on / keep on ➜ Unit 141A

Exercises

53.1 Complete the sentences for each situation using -ing.

1
What shall we do? | We could go to the zoo.
She suggested __going to the zoo__ .

2
Do you want to play tennis? | No, not really.
He didn't fancy ....

3
You were driving too fast. | You're right. Sorry!
She admitted ....

4
Let's go swimming. | Good idea!
She suggested ....

5
You broke the DVD player. | No, I didn't!
He denied ....

6
Can you wait a few minutes? | Sure, no problem.
They didn't mind ....

53.2 Complete each sentence with one of the following verbs (in the correct form):

~~answer~~	apply	be	forget	listen	live
lose	make	pay	read	try	use

1 He tried to avoid __answering__ my question.
2 Could you please stop .... so much noise?
3 I enjoy .... to music.
4 I considered .... for the job, but in the end I decided against it.
5 Have you finished .... the newspaper yet?
6 We need to change our routine. We can't go on .... like this.
7 I don't mind you .... my phone, but please ask me first.
8 My memory is getting worse. I keep .... things.
9 I've put off .... this bill so many times. I really must do it today.
10 What a stupid thing to do! Can you imagine anybody .... so stupid?
11 I've given up .... to lose weight – it's impossible.
12 If you gamble, you risk .... your money.

53.3 Complete the sentences so that they mean the same as the first sentence.

1 I can do what I want and you can't stop me.
   You __can't stop me doing__ what I want.
2 It's not a good idea to travel during the rush hour.
   It's better to avoid .... during the rush hour.
3 Shall we paint the kitchen next weekend instead of this weekend?
   Shall we postpone .... until next weekend?
4 Could you turn the music down, please?
   Would you mind ...., please?
5 Please don't interrupt all the time.
   Would you mind .... all the time?

53.4 Use your own ideas to complete these sentences. Use -ing.

1 She's a very interesting person. I always enjoy __talking to her__ .
2 I'm not feeling very well. I don't fancy ....
3 I'm afraid there aren't any chairs. I hope you don't mind ....
4 It was a beautiful day, so I suggested ....
5 It was very funny. I couldn't stop ....
6 My car isn't very reliable. It keeps ....

107

Verb + **to** … (**decide to** … / **forget to** … etc.)

A

offer	decide	hope	deserve	promise
agree	plan	manage	afford	threaten
refuse	arrange	fail	forget	learn

After these verbs you can use **to** … (*infinitive*):
- ○ It was late, so we **decided to take** a taxi home.
- ○ Simon was in a difficult situation, so I **agreed to help** him.
- ○ How old were you when you **learnt to drive**? (*or* learnt **how** to drive)
- ○ I waved to Karen, but **failed to attract** her attention.

The negative is **not to** … :
- ○ We **decided not to go** out because of the weather.
- ○ I **promised not to be** late.

After some verbs **to** … is not possible. For example, **enjoy/think/suggest**:
- ○ I **enjoy reading**. (*not* enjoy to read)
- ○ Andy **suggested meeting** for coffee. (*not* suggested to meet)
- ○ Are you **thinking of buying** a car? (*not* thinking to buy)

For verb + -**ing**, see Unit 53. For verb + preposition + -**ing**, see Unit 62.

B

After **dare** you can use the infinitive with or without **to**:
- ○ I wouldn't **dare to tell** him. *or* I wouldn't **dare tell** him.

But after **dare not** (*or* **daren't**), you must use the infinitive without **to**:
- ○ I **daren't tell** him what happened. (*not* I daren't to tell him)

C

We also use **to** … after:

seem   **appear**   **tend**   **pretend**   **claim**

For example:
- ○ They **seem to have** plenty of money.
- ○ I like Dan, but I think he **tends to talk** too much.
- ○ Ann **pretended not to see** me when she passed me in the street.

There is also a *continuous* infinitive (**to be** do**ing**) and a *perfect* infinitive (**to have** done):
- ○ I **pretended to be reading** the paper. (= I pretended that I **was reading**)
- ○ You **seem to have lost** weight. (= it seems that you **have lost** weight)
- ○ Joe **seems to be enjoying** his new job. (= it seems that he **is enjoying** it)

D

After some verbs you can use a question word (**what/whether/how** etc.) + **to** … .
We use this structure especially after:

ask   **decide**   **know**   **remember**   **forget**   **explain**   **learn**   **understand**   **wonder**

We **asked**	how	**to get**	to the station.
Have you **decided**	where	**to go**	for your holidays?
I don't **know**	whether	**to apply**	for the job or not.
Do you **understand**	what	**to do**?	

Also
show/tell/ask/advise/teach somebody **what/how/where** to do something:
- ○ Can somebody **show me how to use** this camera?
- ○ Ask Jack. He'll **tell you what to do**.

Verb + -**ing** ➜ Unit 53   Verb + object + **to** … (**want** etc.) ➜ Unit 55
Verb + **to** … and -**ing** ➜ Units 55C, 56–58

Exercises

54.1 Complete the sentences for these situations.

1 Shall we get married? — Yes, let's.
They decided _to get married_ .

2 Please help me. — OK.
She agreed ....

3 Can I carry your bag for you? — No, thanks. I can manage.
He offered ....

4 Let's meet at 8 o'clock. — OK, fine.
They arranged ....

5 What's your name? — I'm not going to tell you.
She refused ....

6 Please don't tell anyone. — I won't. I promise.
She promised ....

54.2 Complete each sentence with a suitable verb.

1 Don't forget _to lock_ the door when you go out.
2 There was a lot of traffic, but we managed .... to the airport in time.
3 We couldn't afford .... in London. It's too expensive.
4 We've got new computer software in our office. I haven't learnt .... it yet.
5 Mark doesn't know what happened. I decided not .... him.
6 We were all afraid to speak. Nobody dared .... anything.

54.3 Put the verb into the correct form, **to** … or **-ing**. (See Unit 53 for verbs + **-ing**.)

1 When I'm tired, I enjoy _watching_ television. It's relaxing. (watch)
2 I've decided .... for another job. I need a change. (look)
3 Let's get a taxi. I don't fancy .... home. (walk)
4 I'm not in a hurry. I don't mind .... (wait)
5 Tina ran in a marathon last week, but she failed .... (finish)
6 I wish that dog would stop .... It's driving me crazy. (bark)
7 Our neighbour threatened .... the police if we didn't stop the noise. (call)
8 We were hungry, so I suggested .... dinner early. (have)
9 Hurry up! I don't want to risk .... the train. (miss)
10 They didn't know I was listening to them. I pretended .... asleep. (be)

54.4 Make a new sentence using the verb in brackets.

1 You've lost weight. (seem) _You seem to have lost weight._
2 Tom is worried about something. (appear) Tom appears ....
3 You know a lot of people. (seem) You ....
4 My English is getting better. (seem) ....
5 That car has broken down. (appear) ....
6 David forgets things. (tend) ....
7 They have solved the problem. (claim) ....

54.5 Complete each sentence using **what/how/where/whether** + these verbs:

> do ~~get~~ go put ride use

1 Do you know _how to get_ to John's house?
2 Would you know .... if there was a fire in the building?
3 You'll never forget .... a bicycle once you've learnt.
4 I've been invited to the party, but I haven't decided .... or not.
5 My room is very untidy. I've got so many things and I don't know .... them.
6 I have some clothes to wash. Can you show me .... the washing machine?

→ Additional exercises 26–28 (pages 317–19)

Verb (+ object) + **to** ... (**I want you to** ... etc.)

A

want	ask	help		would like
expect	beg	mean (= intend)		would prefer

These verbs are followed by **to** ... *(infinitive)*. The structure can be:

> *verb* + **to** ...   *or*   *verb* + *object* + **to** ...

- ○ We **expected to be** late.
- ○ **Would** you **like to go** now?
- ○ He doesn't **want to know**.

- ○ We expected **Dan to be** late.
- ○ Would you like **me to go** now?
- ○ He doesn't want **anybody to know**.

Do not say 'want that':
- ○ Do you **want me to come** with you?   *(not* Do you want that I come*)*

After **help** you can use the infinitive with or without **to**. So you can say:
- ○ Can you help me **to move** this table?   *or*   Can you help me **move** this table?

B

tell	remind	force	encourage	teach	enable
order	warn	invite	persuade	get (= persuade)	

These verbs have the structure *verb* + *object* + **to** ... :
- ○ Can you **remind me to call** Sam tomorrow?
- ○ Who **taught you to drive**?
- ○ I didn't move the piano by myself. I **got somebody to help** me.
- ○ Joe said the switch was dangerous and **warned me not to touch** it.

In the next example, the verb is *passive* (**I was warned** / **we were told** etc.):
- ○ **I was warned not to touch** the switch.

You cannot use **suggest** with the structure *verb* + *object* + **to** ... :
- ○ Jane **suggested that I ask** your advice.   *(not* Jane suggested me to ask*)*

C

After **advise** and **allow**, two structures are possible. Compare:

> *verb* + **-ing** (without an object)   *verb* + *object* + **to** ...

- ○ I wouldn't **advise staying** in that hotel.
- ○ They don't **allow parking** in front of the building.

- ○ I wouldn't **advise anybody to stay** in that hotel.
- ○ They don't **allow people to park** in front of the building.

Study these examples with (**be**) **allowed** *(passive)*:
- ○ Parking **isn't allowed** in front of the building.

- ○ You **aren't allowed to park** in front of the building.

D

Make and **let**

These verbs have the structure *verb* + *object* + *infinitive* (without **to**):
- ○ I **made him promise** that he wouldn't tell anybody what happened.   *(not* to promise*)*
- ○ Hot weather **makes me feel** tired. (= causes me to feel tired)
- ○ Her parents wouldn't **let her go** out alone. (= wouldn't allow her to go out)
- ○ **Let me carry** your bag for you.

We say '**make** somebody **do**' *(not* to do*)*, but in the *passive* we say '**made to** do' (with **to**):
- ○ **We were made to wait** for two hours. (= They **made us wait** ...)

| Suggest ➔ Units 34, 53 | Tell/ask somebody to ... ➔ Unit 48D | Verb + -ing ➔ Unit 53 |
| Verb + to ... ➔ Unit 54 | Verb + to ... and -ing ➔ Units 56–58 | Help ➔ Unit 57C |

Exercises

55.1 Complete the questions. Use **do you want me to** … ? or **would you like me** to … ? with these
verbs (+ any other necessary words):

| come | lend | repeat | show | shut | wait |

1 Do you want to go alone, or _do you want me to come with you_ ?
2 Do you have enough money, or do you want .... ?
3 Shall I leave the window open, or would you .... ?
4 Do you know how to use the machine, or would .... ?
5 Did you hear what I said, or do .... ?
6 Can I go now, or do .... ?

55.2 Complete the sentences for these situations.

1 Meet me at the station. — OK.
She told _him to meet_ _her at the station_ .

2 Why don't you come and stay with us? — That would be nice.
They invited him ....

3 Don't forget to call Joe. — No, I won't forget.
He reminded her ....

4 Be careful. — Don't worry. I will.
She warned ....

5 Can you give me a hand? — Sure.
He asked ....

55.3 Complete each second sentence so that the meaning is similar to the first sentence.

1 My father said I could use his car.   My father allowed _me to use his car._
2 I was surprised that it rained.   I didn't expect ....
3 Don't stop him doing what he wants.   Let ....
4 Tim looks older when he wears glasses.   Tim's glasses make ....
5 I think you should know the truth.   I want ....
6 At first I didn't want to apply for the   Sarah persuaded ....
  job, but Sarah persuaded me.   ....
7 My lawyer said I shouldn't say   My lawyer advised ....
  anything to the police.   ....
8 I was told that I shouldn't believe   I was warned ....
  everything he says.
9 If you've got a car, you are able to get Having a car enables ....
  around more easily.   ....

55.4 Put the verb into the correct form: infinitive (**do/make/eat** etc.), to + infinitive, or **-ing**.

1 They don't allow people ..._to park_.. in front of the building. (park)
2 I've never been to Hong Kong, but I'd like .... there. (go)
3 I'm in a difficult position. What do you advise me .... ? (do)
4 The film was very sad. It made me .... (cry)
5 Lisa's parents always encouraged her .... hard at school. (study)
6 If you want to get a cheap flight, I'd advise .... early. (book)
7 Sarah wouldn't let me .... her car. She doesn't trust me. (borrow)
8 If you enter a country with a tourist visa, you are normally not allowed ....
  there. (work)
9 'I don't think Alex likes me.' 'What makes you .... that?' (think)

→ Additional exercises 26–28 (pages 317–19)

Verb + -ing or to ... 1 (remember/regret etc.)

A Some verbs are followed by **-ing** and some are followed by **to** ... .

Verbs usually followed by **-ing**:	Verbs usually followed by **to** ... :

admit	fancy	postpone
avoid	finish	risk
consider	imagine	stop
deny	keep (on)	suggest
enjoy	mind	

afford	fail	offer
agree	forget	plan
arrange	hope	promise
decide	learn	refuse
deserve	manage	threaten

For examples, see Unit 53.　　　　　　For examples, see Unit 54.

B Some verbs can be followed by **-ing** or **to** ... with a difference of meaning:

remember

I **remember doing** something = I did it and now I remember this.
You **remember doing** something *after* you have done it.
- ○ I know I locked the door. I clearly **remember locking** it.
  (= I locked it, and now I remember this)
- ○ He could **remember driving** along the road just before the accident, but he couldn't remember the accident itself.

I **remembered to do** something = I remembered that I had to do it, so I did it.
You **remember to do** something *before* you do it.
- ○ I **remembered to lock** the door, but I forgot to shut the windows.
  (= I remembered that I had to lock it, and so I locked it)
- ○ I must **remember to pay** the electricity bill. (= I must not forget to pay it)

regret

I **regret doing** something = I did it and now I'm sorry about it:
- ○ I now **regret saying** what I said. I shouldn't have said it.
- ○ Do you **regret not going** to college?

I **regret to say** / **to tell** you / **to inform** you = I'm sorry that I have to say (etc.):
- ○ (*from a formal letter*) We **regret to inform** you that your application has been unsuccessful.

go on

Go on doing something = continue with the same thing:
- ○ The president paused for a moment and then **went on talking**.
- ○ We need to change. We can't **go on living** like this.

Go on to do something = do or say something new:
- ○ After discussing the economy, the president then **went on to talk** about foreign policy.

C The following verbs can be followed by **-ing** or **to** ... with no difference of meaning:
　　begin　　start　　continue　　intend　　bother

So you can say:
- ○ It **started raining**. *or* It **started to rain**.
- ○ Andy **intends buying** a house. *or* Andy **intends to buy** ...
- ○ Don't **bother locking** the door. *or* Don't **bother to lock** ...

But normally we do not use **-ing** after **-ing**:
- ○ It's **starting to rain**. (*not* It's starting raining)

Verb + -ing ➜ Unit 53　　　Verb + to ... ➜ Units 54–55　　　Other verbs + -ing or to ... ➜ Units 57–58

Exercises

56.1 Put the verb into the correct form, **-ing** or **to** ... .

1 They denied ____stealing____ the money. (steal)
2 I don't enjoy _____ very much. (drive)
3 I can't afford _____ out tonight. I don't have enough money. (go)
4 Has it stopped _____ yet? (rain)
5 We were unlucky to lose the game. We deserved _____ . (win)
6 Why do you keep _____ me questions? Can't you leave me alone? (ask)
7 Please stop _____ me questions! (ask)
8 I refuse _____ any more questions. (answer)
9 The driver of one of the cars admitted _____ the accident. (cause)
10 Mark needed our help, and we promised _____ what we could. (do)
11 I don't mind _____ alone, but it's better to be with other people. (be)
12 The wall was quite high, but I managed _____ over it. (climb)
13 'Does Sarah know about the meeting?' 'No, I forgot _____ her.' (tell)
14 I've enjoyed _____ to you. I hope _____ you again soon. (talk, see)

56.2 Tom can remember some things about his childhood, but he can't remember others. Complete the sentences.

1 He was in hospital when he was a small child. He can still remember this.
   ____He can remember being in hospital____ when he was a small child.
2 He went to Paris with his parents when he was eight. He remembers this.
   He remembers _____ with his parents
   when he was eight.
3 He cried on his first day at school. He doesn't remember this.
   He doesn't _____ on his first day at school.
4 Once he fell into the river. He can remember this.
   He _____ .
5 He said he wanted to be a doctor. He can't remember this.
   _____ to be a doctor.
6 Once he was bitten by a dog. He doesn't remember this.
   _____ a dog.

56.3 Complete each sentence with a verb in the correct form, **-ing** or **to** ... . Sometimes either form is possible.

1 a Please remember ____to lock____ the door when you go out.
  b A: You lent me some money a few months ago.
    B: Did I? Are you sure? I don't remember _____ you any money.
  c A: Did you remember _____ your sister?
    B: Oh no, I completely forgot. I'll phone her tomorrow.
  d When you see Steve, remember _____ hello to him from me.
  e Someone must have taken my bag. I clearly remember _____ it by the window
    and now it has gone.
2 a I believe that what I said was right. I don't regret _____ it.
  b I knew they were in trouble, but I regret _____ I did nothing to help them.
  c It started to get cold, and he regretted not _____ his coat.
3 a Ben joined the company nine years ago. He became assistant manager after two years, and a
    few years later he went on _____ manager of the company.
  b I can't go on _____ here any more. I want a different job.
  c When I came into the room, Lisa was reading a newspaper. She looked up and said hello, and
    then went on _____ her newspaper.
4 a If the company continues _____ money, the factory may be closed.
  b Julia has been ill, but now she's beginning _____ better.
  c The baby started _____ in the middle of the night.

➔ Additional exercises 26–28 (pages 317–19)

A Try to ... and try -ing

Try to do = attempt to do, make an effort to do:
- ○ I was very tired. I **tried to keep** my eyes open, but I couldn't.
- ○ Please **try to be** quiet when you come home. Everyone will be asleep.

Try also means 'do something as an experiment or test'. For example:
- ○ These cakes are delicious. You should **try** one.
  (= you should have one to see if you like it)
- ○ We couldn't find anywhere to stay. We **tried** every hotel in the town, but they were all full.
  (= we went to every hotel to see if they had a room)

If **try** (with this meaning) is followed by a verb, we say **try -ing**:
- ○ A: The photocopier doesn't seem to be working.
     B: **Try pressing** the green button.
       (= press the green button – perhaps this will help to solve the problem)

Compare:
- ○ I **tried to move** the table, but it was too heavy.   (so I couldn't move it)
- ○ I didn't like the way the furniture was arranged, so I **tried moving** the table to the other side of the room. But it didn't look right, so I moved it back again.

B Need to ... and need -ing

I need to do something = it is necessary for me to do it:
- ○ I **need to get** more exercise.
- ○ He **needs to work** harder if he wants to make progress.
- ○ I don't **need to come** to the meeting, do I?

Something **needs doing** = it needs to be done:
- ○ My phone **needs charging**.
  (= it needs to be charged)
- ○ Do you think this jacket **needs cleaning**?
  (= ... needs to be cleaned)
- ○ It's a difficult problem. It **needs thinking** about very carefully.   (= it needs to be thought about)

My phone **needs charging**.

C Help and can't help

You can say **help to do** or **help do** (with or without **to**):
- ○ Everybody **helped to clean** up after the party. *or*
     Everybody **helped clean** up ...
- ○ Can you **help** me **to move** this table? *or*
     Can you **help** me **move** ...

I **can't help doing** something = I can't stop myself doing it:
- ○ I don't like him, but he has a lot of problems. I **can't help feeling** sorry for him.
- ○ She tried to be serious, but she **couldn't help laughing**.
  (= she couldn't stop herself laughing)
- ○ I'm sorry I'm so nervous. I **can't help it**.
  (= I can't help **being** nervous)

She **couldn't help laughing**.

Verb + -ing ➜ Unit 53   Verb + to ... ➜ Units 54–55   Other verbs + -ing or to ... ➜ Units 56, 58

Exercises

57.1 Make suggestions. Use **try** + one of the following:

phone his office	restart it	~~change the batteries~~
turn it the other way	take an aspirin	

1 The radio isn't working. Have you __tried changing the batteries?__

2 I can't open the door. The key won't turn. Try _____

3 The computer isn't working properly. Have you tried _____

4 Fred isn't answering his phone. What shall I do? You could _____

5 I've got a terrible headache. I wish it would go. Have you _____

57.2 For each picture, write a sentence with **need(s)** + one of the following verbs:

| ~~clean~~ | cut | empty | paint | tighten |

1 This jacket is dirty. __It needs cleaning.__
2 The room isn't very nice. It _____
3 The grass is very long. _____
4 The screws are loose. _____
5 The bin is full. _____

57.3 Put the verb into the correct form.

1 a I was very tired. I tried __to keep__ (keep) my eyes open, but I couldn't.

   b I rang the doorbell, but there was no answer. Then I tried _____ (knock) on the door, but there was still no answer.

   c We tried _____ (put) the fire out but without success. We had to call the fire brigade.

   d Sue needed to borrow some money. She tried _____ (ask) Gary, but he was short of money too.

   e I tried _____ (reach) the shelf, but I wasn't tall enough.

   f Please leave me alone. I'm trying _____ (concentrate).

2 a I need a change. I need _____ (go) away for a while.

   b My grandmother isn't able to look after herself any more. She needs _____ (look) after.

   c The windows are dirty. They need _____ (clean).

   d Your hair is getting very long. It needs _____ (cut).

   e You don't need _____ (iron) that shirt. It doesn't need _____ (iron).

3 a They were talking very loudly. I couldn't help _____ (overhear) what they said.

   b Can you help me _____ (get) the dinner ready?

   c He looks so funny. Whenever I see him, I can't help _____ (smile).

   d The fine weather helped _____ (make) it a really nice holiday.

A | **Like / love / hate**

When you talk about repeated actions, you can use **-ing** or **to** ... after these verbs.
So you can say:

- Do you **like getting** up early? *or* Do you **like to get** up early?
- Stephanie **hates flying**. *or* Stephanie **hates to fly**.
- I **love meeting** people. *or* I **love to meet** people.
- I don't **like being** kept waiting. *or* ... **like to be** kept waiting.
- I don't **like** friends **calling** me at work. *or* ... friends **to call** me at work.

but

(1) We use **-ing** (*not* **to** ...) when we talk about a situation that already exists (or existed).
     For example:
- Paul lives in Berlin now. He **likes living** there. (He **likes living** in Berlin = He lives there and he likes it)
- Do you **like being** a student? (You are a student – do you like it?)
- The office I worked in was horrible. I **hated working** there. (I worked there and I hated it)

(2) There is sometimes a difference between **I like to do** and **I like doing**:

I like doing something = I do it and I enjoy it:
- I **like cleaning** the kitchen. (= I enjoy it)

I like to do something = I think it is a good thing to do, but I don't necessarily enjoy it:
- It's not my favourite job, but I **like to clean** the kitchen as often as possible.

Note that **enjoy** and **mind** are always followed by **-ing** (*not* **to** ...):
- I **enjoy cleaning** the kitchen. (*not* I enjoy to clean)
- I **don't mind cleaning** the kitchen. (*not* I don't mind to clean)

B | **Would like / would love / would hate / would prefer**

Would like / would love etc. are usually followed by **to** ... :
- I'**d like** (= I **would** like) to go away for a few days.
- **Would** you **like to come** to dinner on Friday?
- I **wouldn't like to go** on holiday alone.
- I'**d love to meet** your family.
- **Would** you **prefer to have** dinner now or later?

Compare **I like** and **I would like** (**I'd** like):
- I **like playing** tennis. / I **like to play** tennis. (= I like it in general)
- I'**d like to play** tennis today. (= I want to play today)

Would mind is always followed by **-ing** (*not* **to** ...):
- **Would** you **mind closing** the door, please?

C | I would like **to have done** something = I regret now that I didn't or couldn't do it:
- It's a shame we didn't see Anna when we were in London. I **would like to have seen** her again.
- We'**d like to have gone** away, but we were too busy at home.

You can use the same structure after **would love / would hate / would prefer**:
- Poor David! I **would hate to have been** in his position.
- I'**d love to have gone** to the party, but it was impossible.

Enjoy/mind ➜ Unit 53   Would like ➜ Units 37E, 55A   Prefer ➜ Unit 59

58.1 Write sentences about yourself. Say whether you like or don't like these activities. Choose one of these verbs for each sentence:

> like / don't like   love   hate   enjoy   don't mind

1 (fly)   *I don't like flying.*   or   *I don't like to fly.*
2 (play cards) ....
3 (be alone) ....
4 (go to museums) ....
5 (cook) ....

58.2 Make sentences from the words in brackets. Use **-ing** or **to** ... . Sometimes either form is possible.

1 Paul lives in Berlin now. It's nice. He likes it.
   (he / like / live / there)   *He likes living there.*
2 Jane is a biology teacher. She likes her job.
   (she / like / teach / biology)   She ....
3 Joe always has his camera with him and takes a lot of pictures.
   (he / like / take / pictures) ....
4 I used to work in a supermarket. I didn't like it much.
   (I / not / like / work / there) ....
5 Rachel is studying medicine. She likes it.
   (she / like / study / medicine) ....
6 Dan is famous, but he doesn't like it.
   (he / not / like / be / famous) ....
7 Jennifer is a very careful person. She doesn't take many risks.
   (she / not / like / take / risks) ....
8 I don't like surprises.
   (I / like / know / things / in advance) ....

58.3 Complete each sentence with a verb in the correct form, **-ing** or **to** ... . In one sentence either form is possible.

1 It's good to visit other places – I enjoy ..... *travelling* ..... .
2 'Would you like .... down?' 'No, thanks. I'll stand.'
3 I'm not quite ready yet. Would you mind .... a little longer?
4 When I was a child, I hated .... to bed early.
5 When I have to catch a train, I'm always worried that I'll miss it. So I like ....
   to the station in plenty of time.
6 I enjoy .... busy. I don't like it when there's nothing to do.
7 I would love .... to your wedding, but I'm afraid it isn't possible.
8 I don't like .... in this part of town. I want to move somewhere else.
9 Do you have a minute? I'd like .... to you about something.
10 If there's bad news and good news, I like .... the bad news first.

58.4 Write sentences using **would** ... **to have (done)**. Use the verbs in brackets.

1 It's a shame I couldn't go to the party. (like)   *I would like to have gone to the party.*
2 It's a shame I didn't see the programme. (like) ....
3 I'm glad I didn't lose my watch. (hate) ....
4 It's too bad I didn't meet your parents. (love) ....
5 I'm glad I wasn't alone. (not / like) ....
6 It's a shame I couldn't travel by train. (prefer) ....

Prefer and would rather

A Prefer to do and prefer doing

You can use '**prefer to** (do)' or '**prefer -ing**' to say what you prefer in general:

○ I don't like cities. I **prefer to live** in the country. *or* I **prefer living** in the country.

Study the differences in structure after **prefer**. We say:

	I prefer	something	**to** something else.
	I prefer	**doing** something	**to doing** something else.
but	I prefer	**to do** something	**rather than (do)** something else.

○ I **prefer** this coat to the coat you were wearing yesterday.
○ I **prefer driving to travelling** by train.
but ○ I **prefer to drive rather than travel** by train.
○ Sarah **prefers to live** in the country **rather than (live)** in a city.

B Would prefer (I'd prefer …)

We use **would prefer** to say what somebody wants in a specific situation (not in general):

○ '**Would** you **prefer** tea or coffee?' 'Coffee, please.'

We say 'would prefer **to do** something' (*not usually* would prefer doing):

○ 'Shall we go by train?' 'I**'d prefer to drive**.' (*not* I'd prefer driving)
○ I**'d prefer to stay** at home tonight **rather than go** to the cinema.

C Would rather (I'd rather …)

Would rather (do) = **would prefer** (to do). We use **would rather** + *infinitive* (without **to**).
Compare:

○ 'Shall we go by train?' { 'I'd **prefer to drive**.'
'I'd **rather drive**.' (*not* to drive)
○ '**Would** you **rather have** tea or coffee?' 'Coffee, please.'

The negative is 'I**'d rather not** (do something)':

○ I'm tired. I**'d rather not go** out this evening, if you don't mind.
○ 'Do you want to go out this evening?' 'I**'d rather not**.'

We say '**would rather do** something **than do** something else':

○ I**'d rather stay** at home tonight **than go** to the cinema.

D I'd rather somebody did something

We say '**I'd rather you did** something' (*not* I'd rather you do). For example:

○ 'Who's going to drive, you or me?' 'I**'d rather** you **drove**.' (= I would prefer this)
○ 'Jack says he'll repair your bike tomorrow, OK?' 'I**'d rather** he **did** it today.'
○ Are you going to tell Anna what happened, or **would** you **rather** I **told** her?

In this structure we use the *past* (**drove**, **did** etc.), but the meaning is present *not* past.
Compare:

○ I'd rather **make** dinner now.
I'd rather **you made** dinner now. (*not* I'd rather you make)

I'd rather you **didn't** (do something) = I'd prefer you not to do it:

○ I**'d rather you didn't tell** anyone what I said.
○ 'Are you going to tell Anna what happened?' 'No. I**'d rather** she **didn't** know.'
○ 'Shall I tell Anna what happened?' 'I**'d rather you didn't**.'

Would prefer ➜ Unit 58B   Prefer (one thing) to (another) ➜ Unit 136D

Exercises

59.1 Which do you prefer? Write sentences using 'I prefer (something) to (something else)'. Put the verb into the correct form where necessary.

1 (drive / travel by train)
   I prefer driving to travelling by train.
2 (basketball / football)
   I prefer ....
3 (go to the cinema / watch DVDs at home)
   I .... to .... at home.
4 (be very busy / have nothing to do)
   I ....

Now rewrite sentences 3 and 4 using the structure 'I prefer to (do something)'.

5 (1)   I prefer to drive rather than travel by train.
6 (3) I prefer to ....
7 (4) ....

59.2 Complete the sentences. Sometimes you need one word, sometimes more.

A	B
1 Shall we walk home?	I'd rather get a taxi.
2 Do you want to eat now?	I'd prefer to wait till later.
3 Would you like to watch TV?	I'd .... to listen to some music.
4 Do you want to go to a restaurant?	I'd rather .... at home.
5 Let's leave now.	.... wait a few minutes.
6 What about a game of tennis?	I'd prefer .... for a swim.
7 I think we should decide now.	I'd .... think about it for a while.
8 Would you like to sit down?	.... to stand.
9 Do you want me to come with you?	I'd rather .... alone.

Now use the same ideas to complete these sentences using **than** and **rather than**.

10 I'd rather get a taxi than walk home.
11 I'd prefer .... for a swim ....
12 I'd rather .... at home ....
13 I'd prefer .... about it for a while ....
14 I'd rather .... some music ....

59.3 Complete the sentences using **would you rather I** ... .

1 Are you going to make dinner or would you rather I made it .... ?
2 Are you going to pay the bill or would you rather .... ?
3 Are you going to do the shopping or .... ?
4 Are you going to phone Tanya or .... ?

59.4 Use your own ideas to complete these sentences.

1 'Shall I tell Anna what happened?' 'No, I'd rather she didn't know.'
2 Do you want me to go now or would you rather I .... here?
3 Do you want to go out this evening or would you rather .... at home?
4 This is a private matter. I'd rather you .... tell anybody else.
5 I don't want to make a decision without Jack and Sue. I'd rather they .... here.
6 A: Do you mind if I put some music on?
   B: I'd rather you .... I'm trying to study.

→ Additional exercises 27–28 (pages 318–19)   **119**

Preposition (in/for/about etc.) + -ing

If a preposition (**in/for/about** etc.) is followed by a verb, the verb ends in **-ing**:

	preposition	verb (-ing)	
Are you interested	**in**	**working**	for us?
I'm not good	**at**	**learning**	languages.
Sue must be fed up	**with**	**studying**.	
What are the advantages	**of**	**having**	a car?
Thanks very much	**for**	**inviting**	me to your party.
How	**about**	**meeting**	for lunch tomorrow?
Why don't you go out	**instead of**	**sitting**	at home all the time?
Amy went to work	**in spite of**	**feeling**	ill.

You can also say 'instead of **somebody** doing something', 'fed up with **people** doing something' etc. :
- ○ I'm fed up with **people** telling me what to do.

Note the use of the following prepositions + **-ing**:

> **before -ing** and **after -ing**:
> - ○ **Before going** out, I phoned Sarah.   (*not* Before to go out)
> - ○ What did you do **after finishing** school?
> You can also say '**Before I went** out …' and '… **after you finished** school'.
>
> **by -ing** (to say *how* something happens):
> - ○ The burglars got into the house **by breaking** a window and **climbing** in.
> - ○ You can improve your English **by reading** more.
> - ○ She made herself ill **by** not **eating** properly.
> - ○ Many accidents are caused **by** people **driving** too fast.
>
> **without -ing**:
> - ○ We ran ten kilometres **without stopping**.
> - ○ It was a stupid thing to say. I said it **without thinking**.
> - ○ She needs to work **without** people **disturbing** her.   (*or* … **without being** disturbed.)
> - ○ I have enough problems of my own **without having** to worry about yours.

To -ing (look forward **to doing** something etc.)

To is often part of the *infinitive* (**to** do / **to** see etc.):
- ○ We decided **to travel** by train.
- ○ Would you like **to meet** for lunch tomorrow?

But **to** is also a *preposition* (like **in/for/about/with** etc.). For example:
- ○ We went from Paris **to Geneva**.
- ○ I prefer tea **to coffee**.
- ○ Are you looking forward **to the weekend**?

If a preposition is followed by a verb, the verb ends in **-ing**:
- ○ I'm fed up **with travelling** by train.
- ○ How **about going** away this weekend?

So, when **to** is a preposition and it is followed by a verb, you must say **to -ing**:
- ○ I prefer driving **to travelling** by train.   (*not* to travel)
- ○ Are you looking forward **to going** on holiday?   (*not* looking forward to go)

Be/get used to -ing ➔ Unit 61   Verb + preposition + -ing ➔ Unit 62
While/when -ing ➔ Unit 68B   In spite of ➔ Unit 113   Prepositions ➔ Units 121–136

Exercises

60.1 Complete the second sentence so that it means the same as the first.

1 Why is it useful to have a car?
What are the advantages of ....*having a car*....?

2 I don't intend to apply for the job.
I have no intention of ....

3 Helen has a good memory for names.
Helen is good at ....

4 You probably won't win the lottery. You have little chance.
You have little chance of ....

5 Did you get into trouble because you were late?
Did you get into trouble for ....?

6 We didn't eat at home. We went to a restaurant instead.
Instead of ....

7 We got into the exhibition. We didn't have to queue.
We got into the exhibition without ....

8 We played very well, but we lost the game.
We lost the game despite ....

60.2 Complete the sentences using **by -ing**. Use the following (with the verb in the correct form):

borrow too much money	~~break a window~~	drive too fast
put some pictures on the walls	stand on a chair	turn a key

1 The burglars got into the house ...*by breaking a window*... .
2 I was able to reach the top shelf ....
3 You start the engine of a car ....
4 Kevin got himself into financial trouble ....
5 You can put people's lives in danger ....
6 We made the room look nicer ....

60.3 Complete the sentences with a suitable word. Use only one word each time.

1 We ran ten kilometres without .....*stopping*..... .
2 He left the hotel without .... his bill.
3 It's a nice morning. How about .... for a walk?
4 We were able to translate the letter into English without .... a dictionary.
5 Before .... to bed, I like to have a hot drink.
6 It was a long trip. I was very tired after .... on a train for 36 hours.
7 I was annoyed because the decision was made without anybody .... me.
8 After .... the same job for ten years, I felt I needed a change.
9 We got lost because we went straight on instead of .... left.
10 I like these pictures you took. You're good at .... pictures.

60.4 For each situation, write a sentence with **I'm (not) looking forward to**.

1 You are going on holiday next week. How do you feel?
....*I'm looking forward to going on holiday.*....

2 Kate is a good friend of yours and she is coming to visit you soon. So you will see her again
soon. How do you feel? I'm ....

3 You are going to the dentist tomorrow. You don't enjoy going to the dentist. How do you feel?
I'm not ....

4 Rachel hates school, but she's leaving next summer. How does she feel?
....

5 You've arranged to play tennis tomorrow. You haven't played for a while and you like tennis a
lot. How do you feel?
....

Be/get used to something (I'm used to ...)

A Study this example situation:

Lisa is American, but she lives in Britain. When she first drove a car in Britain, she found it very difficult because she had to drive on the left, not on the right. Driving on the left was strange and difficult for her because:

She **wasn't used to it**.
She **wasn't used to driving** on the left.

But after a lot of practice, driving on the left became less strange. So:
She **got used to driving** on the left.

Now it's no problem for Lisa:
She **is used to driving** on the left.

B **I'm used to** something = it is not new or strange for me:

- ○ Paul lives alone. He doesn't mind this because he has lived alone for 15 years. It is not strange for him. He **is used to it**. He **is used to living** alone.
- ○ I bought some new shoes. They felt a bit strange at first because I **wasn't used to them**.
- ○ Our new apartment is on a very busy street. I expect we'll **get used to the noise**, but at the moment it's very disturbing.
- ○ Helen has a new job. She has to get up much earlier now than before – at 6.30. She finds this difficult because she **isn't used to getting** up so early.
- ○ Katherine's husband is often away from home. She doesn't mind this. She **is used to him being** away.

C After **be/get used** you cannot use the infinitive (**to do** / **to drive** etc.). We say:
- ○ She is used **to driving** on the left. (*not* She is used to drive)

When we say '**I am used to** something', **to** is a *preposition*, not a part of the infinitive.
So we say:
- ○ We're not used **to the noise**. / We're not used **to it**.
- ○ Paul is used **to living** alone. (*not* Paul is used to live)
- ○ Lisa had to get used **to driving** on the left. (*not* get used to drive)

D Do not confuse **I am used to doing** and **I used to do**:

I **am** used **to** (**doing**) something = it isn't strange or new for me:
- ○ I **am** used **to the weather** in this country.
- ○ I **am** used **to driving** on the left because I've lived in Britain a long time.

I used **to do** something = I did it regularly in the past but no longer do it. You can use this only for the past, not for the present. (See Unit 18.)

The structure is 'I **used** to do' (*not* I **am** used to do):
- ○ I **used to drive** to work every day, but these days I usually go by bike.
- ○ We **used to live** just outside the town, but now we live near the centre.

Used to (do) ➜ Unit 18   To + -ing ➜ Unit 60C

Exercises

61.1 Look again at the situation in Section A on the opposite page ('Lisa is American …').
The following situations are similar. Complete the sentences using **used to**.

1 Jack has to drive two hours to his work every morning. Many years ago, when he first had to do
   this, it was difficult for him. But now it's OK.
      When Jack started working in this job, he wasn't .... driving
      two hours to work every morning, but after some time he .... it.
      Now it's no problem for him. He .... two hours every morning.

2 Julia is a nurse. A year ago she started working nights. At first she found it hard and didn't like it.
      She .... nights and it took her a few months
      to .... it. Now, after a year, it's OK for her.
      She .... nights.

61.2 What do you say in these situations? Use **I'm (not) used to …** .

1 You live alone. You don't mind this. You have always lived alone.
   FRIEND: Do you get lonely sometimes?
   YOU: No, *I'm used to living alone.*
2 You sleep on the floor. You don't mind this. You have always slept on the floor.
   FRIEND: Wouldn't you prefer to sleep in a bed?
   YOU: No, I ....
3 You have to work long hours in your job. This is not a problem for you. You have always worked
   long hours.
   FRIEND: You have to work very long hours in your job, don't you?
   YOU: Yes, but I don't mind that. I ....
4 You usually go to bed early. Last night you went to bed very late (for you) and as a result you are
   very tired this morning.
   FRIEND: You look tired this morning.
   YOU: Yes, ...

61.3 Read the situations and complete the sentences using **get/got used to**.

1 Some friends of yours have just moved into an apartment on a busy street. It is very noisy.
   They'll have to ....*get used to the noise.*..
2 The children at school got a new teacher. She was different from the teacher before her, but this
   wasn't a problem for the children. They soon ....
3 Sue moved from a big house to a much smaller one. She found it strange at first. She had to
   .... in a much smaller house.
4 Some people you know from Britain are going to live in your country. What will they have to get
   used to?
   They'll have to ....

61.4 Complete the sentences using only one word each time.

1 Lisa had to get used to ....*driving*..... on the left.
2 Dan used to .... a lot of coffee. Now he prefers tea.
3 I feel very full after that meal. I'm not used to .... so much.
4 I wouldn't like to share an office. I'm used to .... my own office.
5 I used to .... a car, but I sold it a few months ago.
6 When we were children, we used to .... swimming very often.
7 There used to .... a school here, but it was knocked down a few years ago.
8 I'm the boss here! I'm not used to .... told what to do.
9 We used to .... in a village. We moved to London a few years ago and had to get
   used to .... in a big city.

→ Additional exercises 26–28 (pages 317–19)

Verb + preposition + -ing (succeed in -ing / accuse somebody of -ing etc.)

A

Many verbs have the structure *verb + preposition* (**in/for/about** etc.) *+ object*.
For example:

	verb +	*preposition*	*+ object*
	We **talked**	about	the problem.
	You must **apologise**	for	what you said.

If the *object* is another verb, it ends in -**ing**:

	verb +	*preposition*	*+ object*
	We **talked**	about	**going** to South America.
	You must **apologise**	for	not **telling** the truth.

Some more verbs with this structure:

approve (of)	He doesn't **approve**	of	**swearing**.
decide (against)	We have **decided**	against	**moving** to London.
dream (of)	I wouldn't **dream**	of	**asking** them for money.
feel (like)	Do you **feel**	like	**going** out tonight?
insist (on)	They **insisted**	on	**paying** for the meal.
look forward (to)	I'm **looking forward**	to	**meeting** her.
succeed (in)	Have you **succeeded**	in	**finding** a job yet?
think (of/about)	I'm **thinking**	of/about	**buying** a house.

You can also say 'approve of **somebody** doing something', 'look forward to **somebody** doing something' etc :

- ☐ I don't approve **of people killing** animals for fun.
- ☐ We are all looking forward **to Andy coming** home.

B

The following verbs can have the structure *verb + object + preposition + -ing*:

	verb +	*object*	*+ preposition*	*+ -ing (object)*
accuse (of)	They **accused**	us	of	**telling** lies.
congratulate (on)	We all **congratulated**	Lisa	on	**winning** the first prize.
excuse (for)	**Excuse**	me	for	**phoning** you so late.
prevent (from)	What **prevented**	you	from	**coming** to see us?
stop (from)	The rain didn't **stop**	us	from	**enjoying** our holiday.
suspect (of)	Nobody **suspected**	the general	of	**being** a spy.
thank (for)	I forgot to **thank**	them	for	**helping** me.

You can say '**stop** somebody **doing**' or '**stop** somebody **from doing**':

- ☐ You can't **stop** me **doing** what I want. *or* You can't **stop** me **from doing** what I want.

The following examples are with **not -ing**:

- ☐ They accused us of **not telling** the truth.
- ☐ Excuse me for **not replying** to your email until now.

Some of these verbs are often used in the *passive*. For example:

- ☐ We **were accused of telling** lies.
- ☐ The general **was suspected of being** a spy.

Note that we say 'apologise **to somebody** for …':

- ☐ I apologised **to them** for keeping them waiting. (*not* I apologised them)

Decide to … ➜ Unit 54A   Preposition + -ing ➜ Unit 60   Verb + preposition ➜ Units 132–136

Exercises

62.1 Complete each sentence using only one word.

1 Our neighbours apologised for ....*making*.... so much noise.
2 I feel lazy. I don't feel like .... any work.
3 I wanted to go out alone, but Joe insisted on .... with me.
4 Where are you thinking of .... your holiday this year?
5 We have decided against .... a car because we can't really afford it.
6 It's good Dan and Amy are coming to stay with us. I'm looking forward to ....
   them again.
7 Some parents don't approve of their children .... a lot of TV.
8 It took us a long time, but we finally succeeded in .... the problem.
9 I've always dreamed of .... a small house by the sea.

62.2 Complete each sentence using a preposition + one of the following verbs (in the correct form):

be	cause	do	eat	escape	~~go~~
interrupt	invite	tell	use	walk	wear

1 Do you feel ...*like going*.... out this evening?
2 The driver of the other car accused me .... the accident.
3 There's a fence around the lawn to stop people .... on the grass.
4 Excuse me .... you, but may I ask you something?
5 The man who has been arrested is suspected .... a false passport.
6 I'm fed up with my job. I'm thinking .... something else.
7 The guards weren't able to prevent the prisoner ....
8 I didn't want to hear the story, but Dan insisted .... me.
9 I'm getting hungry. I'm really looking forward .... something.
10 I think you should apologise to Sue .... so rude to her.
11 I'm sorry I can't come to your party, but thank you very much .... me.
12 The police stopped the car because they suspected the driver .... not ....
   a seat belt.

62.3 Complete the sentences on the right.

1 YOU KEVIN *It was nice of you to help me. Thanks very much.*
   Kevin thanked ...*me for helping him*.... .

2 ANN TOM *I'll take you to the station. I insist.*
   Tom insisted .... Ann
   ....

3 YOU DAN *I hear you got married. Congratulations!*
   Dan congratulated me ....
   ....

4 SUE JENNY *It was nice of you to come to see me. Thank you.*
   Jenny thanked ....
   ....

5 YOU KATE *I'm sorry I didn't phone earlier.*
   Kate apologised ....
   ....

6 YOU JANE *You're selfish.*
   Jane accused ....
   ....

→ Additional exercises 27–28 (pages 318–19)

Expressions + -ing

A

When these expressions are followed by a verb, the verb ends in **-ing**:

It's no use / It's no good ...
- ☐ There's nothing you can do about the situation, so **it's no use worrying** about it.
- ☐ **It's no good trying** to persuade me. You won't succeed.

There's no point in ...
- ☐ **There's no point in having** a car if you never use it.
- ☐ **There was no point in waiting** any longer, so we left.

But we usually say '**the** point **of doing** something':
- ☐ **What's the point of having** a car if you never use it?

B

It's (not) worth ...
- ☐ I live only a short walk from here, so **it's not worth taking** a taxi.
- ☐ Our flight was very early in the morning, so **it wasn't worth going** to bed.

You can say that a film is **worth seeing**, a book is **worth reading** etc. :
- ☐ What was the film like? Was it **worth seeing**?
- ☐ Thieves broke into the house, but didn't take anything. There was nothing **worth stealing**.

C

Have trouble -ing, **have difficulty -ing** etc.

Have **trouble / difficulty / a problem   doing** something:
- ☐ I had no **trouble finding** a place to stay. (*not* trouble to find)
- ☐ Did you have any **difficulty getting** a visa?
- ☐ People sometimes have **problems reading** my writing.

D

Spend time / waste time / be busy

spend/waste (time) **doing** something:
- ☐ He **spent** hours **trying** to repair the clock.
- ☐ I **waste** a lot of time **doing** nothing.

(be) **busy doing** something:
- ☐ She said she couldn't see me. She was too **busy doing** other things.

E

Go swimming / go fishing etc.

We use **go -ing** for a number of activities (especially sports).
For example, you can say:

go sailing	go swimming	go fishing	go skiing
go camping	go surfing	go scuba diving	go jogging
go riding	go hiking	go sightseeing	go shopping

- ☐ How often do you **go swimming**?
- ☐ I'd like to **go skiing**.
- ☐ When was the last time you **went shopping**?
- ☐ I've never **been sailing**. (For **gone** and **been**, see Unit 7C.)

Exercises

63.1 Make sentences beginning **There's no point** … .

1 Why have a car if you never use it?
    There's no point in having a car if you never use it.

2 Why work if you don't need money?

3 Don't try to study if you feel tired.

4 Why hurry if you've got plenty of time?

63.2 Complete the sentences on the right.

1 Shall we get a taxi home?
No, it isn't far. It's not worth ___*getting a taxi*___ .

2 If you need help, why don't you ask David?
It's no use _____ . He won't be able to do anything.

3 I don't really want to go out tonight.
Well, stay at home! There's no point _____ if you don't want to.

4 Shall I phone Lisa now?
No, it's no good _____ now. She won't be at home.

5 Are you going to complain about what happened?
No, it's not worth _____ . Nobody will do anything about it.

6 Do you want to keep these old clothes?
No, let's throw them away. They're not worth _____ .

63.3 Complete the sentences.

1 I managed to get a visa, but it was difficult.
I had difficulty ___*getting a visa*___ .

2 I find it hard to remember people's names.
I have a problem _____ .

3 Lucy managed to get a job. It wasn't a problem.
She had no trouble _____ .

4 It won't be difficult to get a ticket for the game.
You won't have any problem _____ .

5 Do you find it difficult to understand him?
Do you have difficulty _____ ?

63.4 Complete the sentences. Use only <u>one</u> word each time.

1 I waste a lot of time ___*doing*___ nothing.
2 Every morning I spend about an hour _____ the newspaper.
3 'What's Karen doing?' 'She's going away tomorrow, so she's busy _____ .'
4 I think you waste too much time _____ TV.
5 There's a beautiful view from that hill. It's worth _____ to the top.
6 Just stay calm. There's no point in _____ angry.

63.5 Complete these sentences with the following (with the verb in the correct form):

go riding	~~go sailing~~	go shopping	go skiing	go swimming

1 Ben lives by the sea and he's got a boat, so he often ___*goes sailing*___ .
2 It was a very hot day, so we _____ in the lake.
3 There's plenty of snow in the mountains, so we'll be able to _____ .
4 Helen has got two horses. She _____ regularly.
5 'Where's Dan?' 'He's _____ . There were a few things he needed to buy.'

→ Additional exercises 27–28 (pages 318–19)

To ... , for ... and so that ...

Study these examples:
- ○ I phoned the restaurant **to reserve** a table.
- ○ What do you need **to make** bread?
- ○ We shouted **to warn** everybody of the danger.
- ○ This letter is **to confirm** the decisions we made at our meeting last week.
- ○ The president has a team of bodyguards **to protect** him.

In these examples **to** ... (**to reserve** ... / **to make** ... etc.) tells us the *purpose* of something: why somebody does something, has something, needs something etc., or why something exists.

We say 'a place **to park**', 'something **to eat**', 'work **to do**' etc. :
- ○ It's difficult to find **a place to park** in the centre. (= a place where you can park)
- ○ Would you like **something to eat**? (= something that you can eat)
- ○ Do you have **much work to do**? (= work that you must do)
- ○ I get lonely if there's **nobody to talk to**.
- ○ I need **something to open** this bottle **with**.

Also **money/time/chance/opportunity/energy/courage** (etc.) **to** do something:
- ○ They gave us **money to buy** food.
- ○ Do you have **much opportunity to practise** your English?
- ○ I need **a few days to think** about your proposal.

Compare **for** ... and **to** ... :

for + *noun*	**to** + *verb*
○ We stopped **for petrol**.	○ We stopped **to get** petrol.
○ I had to run **for the bus**.	○ I had to run **to catch the bus**.

You can say '**for** somebody **to do** something':
- ○ There weren't any chairs **for us to sit on**, so we sat on the floor.

You can use **for** -ing or **to** ... to talk about the *general* purpose of something, or what it is generally used for:
- ○ I use this brush **for washing** the dishes. *or* ... **to wash** the dishes.

But we do not use **for** -ing to say why somebody does something:
- ○ I went into the kitchen **to wash** the dishes. (*not* for washing)

You can use **What** ... **for**? to ask about purpose:
- ○ **What** is this switch **for**?
- ○ **What** did you do that **for**?

So that

We use **so that** (*not* **to** ...) especially

when the purpose is *negative* (**so that** ... **won't/wouldn't**):
- ○ I hurried **so that** I **wouldn't** be late. (= because I didn't want to be late)
- ○ Eat something now **so that** you **won't** (*or* **don't**) **get** hungry later.

with **can** and **could** (**so that** ... **can/could**):
- ○ She's learning English **so that** she **can** study in Canada.
- ○ We moved to London **so that** we **could** see our friends more often.

You can leave out **that**. So you can say:
- ○ I hurried **so that** I wouldn't be late. *or* I hurried **so** I wouldn't be late.

Exercises

64.1 Choose from Box A and Box B to make a new sentence with **to** ... .

A
1 ~~I shouted~~
2 I opened the box
3 I'm saving money
4 I need a knife
5 I'm wearing two sweaters
6 I phoned the police

B
I want to keep warm
I want to go to Canada
I wanted to report the accident
~~I wanted to warn people of the danger~~
I want to chop these onions
I wanted to see what was in it

1   I shouted to warn people of the danger.
2   I opened the box ....
3   I ....
4   ....
5   ....
6   ....

64.2 Complete these sentences using **to** + a suitable verb.

1 The president has a team of bodyguards ....to protect.... him.
2 I didn't have enough time .... the newspaper today.
3 I came home by taxi. I didn't have the energy ....
4 'Would you like something .... ?'   'Yes, please. A cup of coffee.'
5 We need a bag .... these things in.
6 There will be a meeting next week .... the problem.
7 Do you need a visa .... to the United States?
8 I saw Helen at the party, but we didn't have a chance .... to each other.
9 I need some new clothes. I don't have anything nice ....
10 They've just passed their exams. They're having a party ....
11 I can't do all this work alone. I need somebody .... me.

64.3 Put in **to** or **for**.

1 We stopped ....for.... petrol.
2 You need a lot of experience .... this job.
3 You need a lot of experience .... do this job.
4 We'll need more time .... make a decision.
5 I went to the dentist .... a check-up.
6 I had to put on my glasses .... read the paper.
7 Do you have to wear glasses .... reading?
8 I wish we had a garden .... the children .... play in.

64.4 Make one sentence from two, using **so that**.

1 I hurried. I didn't want to be late.   I hurried ....so that I wouldn't be late.....
2 I wore warm clothes. I didn't want to be cold.
   I wore warm clothes ....
3 I gave Dan my phone number. I wanted him to be able to contact me.
   I gave Dan my phone number ....
4 We whispered. We didn't want anybody else to hear our conversation.
   We whispered .... nobody ....
5 Please arrive early. We want to be able to start the meeting on time.
   Please arrive early ....
6 We made a list of things to do. We didn't want to forget anything.
   We made a list of things to do ....
7 I slowed down. I wanted the car behind me to be able to overtake.
   I slowed down ....

Adjective + **to** ...

A   **Difficult to understand** etc.

> Compare sentences (a) and (b):
>
> ○   James doesn't speak very clearly. {
> (a) **It** is difficult to understand him .
> (b) He is **difficult to understand**.
>
> Sentences (a) and (b) have the same meaning. Note that we say:
> ○   He is difficult **to understand**.   (*not* He is difficult to understand him.)

You can use the same structures with:

easy	nice	safe	cheap	exciting	impossible
hard	good	dangerous	expensive	interesting	

○   Do you think it is **safe** (for us) **to drink this water**?
    Do you think this water is **safe** (for us) **to drink**?   (*not* to drink it)
○   The questions in the exam were very difficult. It was **impossible to answer them**.
    The questions in the exam were very difficult. They were **impossible to answer**.
    (*not* to answer them)
○   Nicola has lots of interesting ideas. It's **interesting to talk** to her.
    Nicola is **interesting to talk to**.   (*not* to talk to her.)

You can also use this structure with *adjective + noun*:
○   This is a **difficult question** (for me) **to answer**.   (*not* to answer it)

B   **Nice of (you) to** ...

You can say 'It's **nice of** somebody **to** do something':
○   It was **nice of you to take** me to the airport. Thank you very much.

You can use many other adjectives in this way. For example:

kind	(in)considerate	generous	mean	careless	silly	stupid	unfair

○   It's **silly of Ruth to give up** her job when she needs the money.
○   I think it was **unfair of him to criticise** me.

C   **Sorry to** ... / **surprised to** ... etc.

You can use *adjective* + **to** ... to say how somebody reacts to something:
○   I'm **sorry to hear** that your mother isn't well.

You can use many other adjectives in this way. For example:

glad	pleased	relieved	surprised	amazed	sad	disappointed

○   Was Julia **surprised to see** you?
○   It was a long and tiring journey. We were **glad to get** home.

D   **The first / the next** (etc.) + **to** ...

You can use **to** ... after **the first/second/third** etc., and also after **the last / the next / the only** ... :
○   If I have any more news, you will be **the first** (person) **to know**.
○   **The next** train **to arrive** at platform 4 will be the 10.50 to Liverpool.
○   Everybody was late except me. I was **the only** one **to arrive** on time.

E

You can say that something is **sure/certain/likely/bound to** happen:
○   Carla is a very good student. She's **bound to pass** the exam.   (= she is sure to pass)
○   I'm **likely to get** home late tonight.   (= I will probably get home late)

> **Afraid/interested/sorry** ➜ Unit 66   **It** ... ➜ Unit 84C   **Enough** and **too** + adjective ➜ Unit 103

Exercises

65.1 (Section A) Write these sentences in another way, beginning as shown.

1 It's difficult to understand him.   He _is difficult to understand._
2 It's easy to use this machine.   This machine is ....
3 It was very difficult to open the window.   The window ....
4 It's impossible to translate some words.   Some words ....
5 It's expensive to maintain a car.   A ....
6 It's not safe to stand on that chair.   That ....

65.2 (Section A) Complete the second sentence. Use the adjective in brackets and **to** ... as in the example.

1 I couldn't answer the question.   (difficult)   It was a _difficult question to answer._
2 Everybody makes that mistake.   (easy)   It's an ....
3 I like living in this place.   (nice)   It's a ....
4 We enjoyed watching the game.   (good)   It was a ....

65.3 (Section B) Make a new sentence beginning **It** ... . Use one of these adjectives each time:

careless   inconsiderate   ~~kind~~   nice

1 Sue has offered to help me.   _It's kind of Sue to offer to help me._
2 You make the same mistake again and again.
   It ....
3 Dan and Jenny invited me to stay with them.

   ....
4 The neighbours make so much noise.

   ....

65.4 (Section C) Use the following words to complete these sentences:

~~I / sorry / hear~~   I / glad / hear   pleased / meet   we / surprised / see

1 _I'm sorry to hear_ that your mother isn't well. I hope she gets better soon.
2 I got your message. .... that you're keeping well.
3 .... Paula at the party last night. We didn't expect her to come.
4 'Tom, this is Chris.' 'Hi Chris. .... you.'

65.5 (Section D) Complete the second sentence using the words in brackets + **to** ... .

1 Nobody spoke before me. (the first) I was _the first person to speak._
2 Everybody else arrived before Paul.
   (the last) Paul was the ....
3 Emily passed the exam. All the other students failed.
   (the only) Emily was ....
4 I complained to the restaurant manager about the service. Another customer had already complained.
   (the second) I was ....
5 Neil Armstrong walked on the moon in 1969. Nobody had done this before him.
   (the first) Neil Armstrong was ....

65.6 (Section E) Complete these sentences using the words in brackets and a suitable verb.

1 Carla is a very good student. She _is bound to pass_ the exam. (bound)
2 I'm not surprised you're tired. After such a long journey you .... tired. (bound)
3 Andy has a very bad memory. He .... what you tell him. (sure)
4 I don't think you need to take an umbrella. It .... (not likely)
5 The holidays begin this weekend. There .... a lot of traffic on the roads. (likely)

To ... (afraid **to do**) and preposition + **-ing** (afraid **of -ing**)

A

Afraid to (do) and **afraid of** (do)ing

I am **afraid to do** something = I don't want to do it because it is dangerous or the result could be bad.
We use **afraid to do** for things we do intentionally; we can choose to do them or not:
- ⃝ This part of town is dangerous. People are **afraid to walk** here at night.
  (= they don't want to walk here because it is dangerous – so they don't)
- ⃝ James was **afraid to tell** his parents what had happened.
  (= he didn't want to tell them because he knew they would be angry or worried)

I am **afraid of** something **happening** = it is possible that something bad will happen (for example, an accident).
We do not use **afraid of -ing** for things we do intentionally:
- ⃝ The path was icy, so we walked very carefully. We were **afraid of falling**.
  (= it was possible that we would fall – *not* we were afraid to fall)
- ⃝ I don't like dogs. I'm always **afraid of being** bitten. (*not* afraid to be bitten)

So, you are **afraid to do** something because you are **afraid of something happening** as a result:
- ⃝ I was **afraid to go** near the dog because I **was afraid of being** bitten.

B

Interested in (do)ing and **interested to** (do)

I'm **interested in doing** something = I'm thinking of doing it, I would like to do it:
- ⃝ Let me know if you're **interested in joining** the club. (*not* to join)
- ⃝ I tried to sell my car, but nobody was **interested in buying** it. (*not* to buy)

We use **interested to** ... to say how somebody reacts to what they **hear/see/read/learn/know/find**.
For example, 'I was **interested to hear** it' = I heard it and it was interesting for me:
- ⃝ I was **interested to hear** that Tanya left her job.
- ⃝ Ask Mike for his opinion. I would be **interested to know** what he thinks. (= it would be interesting for me to know it)

This structure is the same as **surprised to** ... / **glad to** ... etc. (see Unit 65C):
- ⃝ I was **surprised to hear** that Tanya left her job.

C

Sorry to (do) and **sorry for/about** (do)ing

We use **sorry to** ... to say we regret something that happens (see Unit 65C):
- ⃝ I was **sorry to hear** that Nicky lost her job. (= I was sorry when I heard that ...)
- ⃝ I've enjoyed my stay here. I'll be **sorry to leave**.

We also say **sorry to** ... to apologise at the time we do something:
- ⃝ I'm **sorry to phone** you so late, but I need to ask you something.

You can use **sorry for** or **sorry about** (doing something) to apologise for something you did before:
- ⃝ I'm **sorry for** (*or* **about**) **shouting** at you yesterday. (*not* sorry to shout)

You can also say:
- ⃝ I'm **sorry I shouted** at you yesterday.

D

We say:

I want to (do) / **I'd like to** (do)	*but*	I'm **thinking of** (do)ing / I **dream of** (do)ing
I failed to (do)	*but*	I **succeeded in** (do)ing
I allowed them to (do)	*but*	I **prevented** them **from** (do)ing
		I **stopped** them **from** (do)ing

For examples, see Units 54–55 and 62.

Verb + preposition + **-ing** ➜ Unit 62   Adjective + preposition ➜ **Units 130–131**
Sorry about/for ➜ Unit 130

Exercises

66.1 Use the words in brackets to write sentences. Use **afraid to ...** or **afraid of -ing**.

1 The streets are unsafe at night.
(a lot of people / afraid / go / out)   _A lot of people are afraid to go out._
2 We walked very carefully along the icy path.
(we / afraid / fall)   _We were afraid of falling._
3 I don't usually carry my passport with me.
(I / afraid / lose / it) ....
4 I thought she would be angry if I told her what had happened.
(I / afraid / tell / her) ....
5 We rushed to the station.
(we / afraid / miss / our train) ....
6 In the middle of the film there was an especially horrifying scene.
(we / afraid / look) ....
7 The vase was very valuable, so I held it carefully.
(I / afraid / drop / it) ....
8 I thought the food on my plate didn't look fresh.
a (I / afraid / eat / it) ....
b (I / afraid / get / sick) ....

66.2 Complete the sentences using **in ...** or **to ...** . Use these verbs:

> ~~buy~~   get   know   look   read   start

1 I'm trying to sell my car, but nobody is interested ....._in buying_..... it.
2 Julia is interested .... her own business.
3 I was interested .... your article in the newspaper last week. It was very well written.
4 Ben wants to stay single. He's not interested .... married.
5 I heard from Mark recently. You'll be interested .... that he's now working in Paris.
6 I don't enjoy sightseeing. I'm not interested .... at old buildings.

66.3 Complete each sentence using **sorry for/about ...** or **sorry to ...** . Use the verb in brackets.

1 I'm ....._sorry to phone_.... you so late, but I need to ask you something. (phone)
2 I was .... that you didn't get the job you applied for. (hear)
3 I'm .... all those bad things about you. I didn't mean them. (say)
4 I'm .... you, but do you have a pen I could borrow? (disturb)
5 I'm .... the book you lent me. I'll buy you another one. (lose)

66.4 Complete each sentence using the verb in brackets.

1 a We wanted ...._to leave_.... the building. (leave)
  b We weren't allowed .... the building. (leave)
  c We were prevented .... the building. (leave)
2 a Peter failed .... the problem. (solve)
  b Chris succeeded .... the problem. (solve)
3 a I'm thinking .... away next week. (go)
  b I'm hoping .... away next week. (go)
  c I'd like .... away next week. (go)
  d I'm looking forward .... away next week. (go)
4 a Helen wanted .... me lunch. (buy)
  b Helen insisted .... me lunch. (buy)
  c Helen promised .... me lunch. (buy)
  d Helen wouldn't dream .... me lunch. (buy)

→ Additional exercise 27 (page 318)   **133**

See somebody do and see somebody doing

A

Study this example situation:

Tom got into his car and drove away. You saw this.
You can say:

- ○ I saw Tom **get** into his car and **drive** away.

In this structure we use **get/drive/do** etc.
(*not* to get / to drive / to do).

| Somebody **did** something | + | I saw this |

I **saw** somebody **do** something

TOM

But after a *passive* ('he **was seen**' etc.), we use **to**:

- ○ He was seen **to** get in the car.

B

Study this example situation:

Yesterday you saw Kate. She was waiting for a bus.
You can say:

- ○ I saw Kate **waiting** for a bus.

In this structure we use -**ing** (**waiting/doing** etc.):

| Somebody **was doing** something | + | I saw this |

I **saw** somebody **doing** something

KATE

C

Study the difference in meaning between the two structures:

I saw him **do** something = he **did** something (*past simple*) and I saw this. I saw the complete action from beginning to end:

- ○ He **fell** off the wall. I saw this. → I saw him **fall** off the wall.
- ○ The accident **happened**. Did you see it? → Did you see the accident **happen**?

I saw him **doing** something = he **was doing** something (*past continuous*) and I saw this. I saw him when he was in the middle of doing it. This does not mean that I saw the complete action:

- ○ He **was walking** along the street.
  I saw this when I drove past in my car. } I saw him **walking** along the street.

Sometimes the difference is not important and you can use either form:

- ○ I've never seen her **dance**. *or* I've never seen her **dancing**.

D

We use these structures with **see** and **hear**, and a number of other verbs:

- ○ I didn't **hear** you **come** in. (you came in – I didn't hear this)
- ○ Lisa suddenly **felt** somebody **touch** her on the shoulder.
- ○ Did you **notice** anyone **go** out?

- ○ I could **hear** it **raining**. (it was raining – I could hear it)
- ○ A man was **seen running** away a short time after the break-in.
- ○ **Listen to** the birds **singing**!
- ○ Can you **smell** something **burning**?
- ○ We looked everywhere for Paul, and finally we **found** him **sitting** under a tree in the garden and **eating** an apple.

Exercises

67.1 Complete the answers to the questions.

1	Did anybody go out?	I don't think so. I didn't see _anybody go out_ .
2	Has Sarah arrived yet?	Yes, I think I heard her ....
3	How do you know I took the money?	I know because I saw you ....
4	Did the doorbell ring?	I don't think so. I didn't hear ....
5	Can Tom play the piano?	I've never heard ....
6	Did I lock the door when I went out?	Yes, I saw ....
7	How did the woman fall?	I don't know. I didn't see ....

67.2 In each of these situations you and a friend saw, heard or smelt something. Look at the pictures and complete the sentences.

1 _We saw Kate waiting for a bus_ .
2 We saw David and Helen ....
3 We saw .... in a restaurant.
4 We heard ....
5 We could ....
6 ....

67.3 Complete these sentences. Use the following verbs (in the correct form):

climb	~~come~~	crawl	cry	explode	ride
run	say	~~sing~~	slam	sleep	tell

1 Listen to the birds _singing_ !
2 I didn't hear you _come_ in.
3 We listened to the old man .... his story from beginning to end.
4 Listen! Can you hear a baby .... ?
5 I looked out of the window and saw Dan .... his bike along the road.
6 I thought I heard somebody .... 'Hi', so I looked round.
7 We watched two men .... across the garden and .... through an open window into the house.
8 Everybody heard the bomb .... It was a tremendous noise.
9 Oh! I can feel something .... up my leg! It must be an insect.
10 I heard somebody .... the door in the middle of the night. It woke me up.
11 When we got home, we found a cat .... on the kitchen table.

-ing clauses (**Feeling tired**, I went to bed early.)

A Study these situations:

Joe was playing football. He hurt his knee.
You can say:
- ○ Joe hurt his knee **playing football**.

You were feeling tired. So you went to bed early.
You can say:
- ○ **Feeling tired**, I went to bed early.

'**Playing football**' and '**feeling tired**' are -**ing** clauses.
If the -**ing** clause is at the beginning of the sentence (as in the second example), we write a comma (,) after it.

B When two things happen at the same time, you can use an -**ing** clause:
- ○ Kate is in the kitchen **making coffee**.
  (= she is in the kitchen *and* she is making coffee)
- ○ A man ran out of the house **shouting**.
  (= he ran out of the house *and* he was shouting)
- ○ Do something! Don't just stand there **doing nothing**!

We also use -**ing** when one action happens during another action. We use -**ing** for the longer action:
- ○ Joe hurt his knee **playing football**. (= while he was playing)
- ○ Did you cut yourself **shaving**? (= while you were shaving)

You can also use -**ing** after **while** or **when**:
- ○ Joe hurt his knee **while playing** football.
- ○ Be careful **when crossing** the road. (= when you are crossing)

C When one action happens before another action, we use **having** (**done**) for the first action:
- ○ **Having found** a hotel, we looked for somewhere to have dinner.
- ○ **Having finished** her work, she went home.

You can also say **after** -**ing**:
- ○ **After finishing** her work, she went home.

If one short action follows another short action, you can use the simple -**ing** form (**doing** instead of **having done**) for the first action:
- ○ **Taking** a key out of his pocket, he opened the door.

These structures are used more in written English than in spoken English.

D You can use an -**ing** clause to explain something, or to say why somebody does something.

The -**ing** clause usually comes at the beginning of the sentence:
- ○ **Feeling** tired, I went to bed early. (= because I felt tired)
- ○ **Being** unemployed, he doesn't have much money. (= because he is unemployed)
- ○ **Not having** a car, she finds it difficult to get around.
  (= because she doesn't have a car)

Use **having** (**done**) for something that happened before something else:
- ○ **Having** already **seen** the film twice, I didn't want to see it again.
  (= because I had already seen it twice)

These structures are used more in written English than in spoken English.

-ing and -ed clauses ➜ Unit 97

Exercises

68.1 Choose from Box A and Box B to make sentences. Use an **-ing** clause.

A
1	~~Kate was in the kitchen.~~
2	Amy was sitting in an armchair.
3	Sue opened the door carefully.
4	Sarah went out.
5	Lisa was in London for two years.
6	Anna walked around the town.

B
| She was trying not to make a noise. |
| She looked at the sights and took pictures. |
| She said she would be back in an hour. |
| She was reading a book. |
| ~~She was making coffee.~~ |
| She worked in a bookshop. |

1   *Kate was in the kitchen making coffee.*
2   Amy was sitting ....
3   Sue ....
4   ....
5   ....
6   ....

68.2 Make one sentence from two using an **-ing** clause.

1   Joe was playing football. He hurt his knee.   *Joe hurt his knee playing football.*
2   I was watching TV. I fell asleep. I ....
3   A friend of mine slipped and fell. He was getting off a bus.
    A friend of mine ....
4   I was walking home in the rain. I got very wet.
    I ....
5   Laura was driving to work yesterday. She had an accident.
    ....
6   Two people were overcome by smoke. They were trying to put out the fire.
    ....

68.3 Make sentences beginning **Having** … . Put the words in the correct order.

1   (went / she / work / her / home / finished)
    Having *finished her work, she went home* .
2   (tickets / the theatre / bought / into / our / went / we)
    Having .... , ...
3   (journey / their / had / they / lunch / continued)
    Having .... , ...
4   (the / coffee / shopping / I / a cup / went / done / for / of)
    Having .... , ...

68.4 Make one sentence from two. Begin with **-ing** or **Not** **-ing** (like the examples in Section D).
Sometimes you need to begin with **Having** (done something).

1   I felt tired. So I went to bed early.
    Feeling tired,   I went to bed early.
2   I thought they might be hungry. So I offered them something to eat.
    .... , I offered them something to eat.
3   Robert is a vegetarian. So he doesn't eat any kind of meat.
    .... , Robert doesn't eat any kind of meat.
4   I didn't know his email address. So I wasn't able to contact him.
    .... , I wasn't able to contact him.
5   Sarah has travelled a lot. So she knows a lot about other countries.
    .... , Sarah knows a lot about other countries.
6   I wasn't able to speak the local language. So I had trouble communicating.
    .... , I had trouble communicating.
7   We had spent nearly all our money. So we couldn't afford to stay at a hotel.
    .... , we couldn't afford to stay at a hotel.

A

A noun can be *countable* or *uncountable*:

Countable
- ☐ I eat **a banana** every day.
- ☐ I like **bananas**.

Banana is a *countable* noun.

A countable noun can be singular (**banana**) or plural (**bananas**).

We can use numbers with countable nouns. So we can say 'one banana', 'two bananas' etc.

Examples of nouns usually countable:
- ☐ Kate was singing **a song**.
- ☐ There's **a** nice **beach** near here.
- ☐ Do you have **a** ten-pound **note**?
- ☐ It wasn't your fault. It was **an accident**.
- ☐ There are no **batteries** in the radio.
- ☐ We don't have enough **cups**.

Uncountable
- ☐ I eat **rice** every day.
- ☐ I like **rice**.

Rice is an *uncountable* noun.

An uncountable noun has only one form (**rice**).

We cannot use numbers with uncountable nouns. We cannot say 'one rice', 'two rices' etc.

Examples of nouns usually uncountable:
- ☐ Kate was listening to (some) **music**.
- ☐ There's **sand** in my shoes.
- ☐ Do you have any **money**?
- ☐ It wasn't your fault. It was bad **luck**.
- ☐ There is no **electricity** in this house.
- ☐ We don't have enough **water**.

B

You can use **a/an** with singular countable nouns:

  a beach   **a student**   **an umbrella**

You cannot use singular countable nouns alone (without **a/the/my** etc.):
- ☐ I want **a banana**. (*not* I want banana)
- ☐ There's been **an accident**. (*not* There's been accident)

You can use *plural* countable nouns alone:
- ☐ I like **bananas**. (= bananas in general)
- ☐ **Accidents** can be prevented.

You cannot normally use **a/an** with uncountable nouns. We do not say 'a sand', 'a music', 'a rice'.
But you can often use **a … of**. For example:
  a bowl / a packet / a grain of rice

You can use uncountable nouns alone (without **the/my/some** etc.):
- ☐ I eat **rice** every day.
- ☐ There's **blood** on your shirt.
- ☐ Can you hear **music**?

C

You can use **some** and **any** with plural countable nouns:
- ☐ We sang **some songs**.
- ☐ Did you buy **any apples**?

We use **many** and **few** with plural countable nouns:
- ☐ We didn't take **many pictures**.
- ☐ I have a **few things** to do.

You can use **some** and **any** with uncountable nouns:
- ☐ We listened to **some music**.
- ☐ Did you buy **any** apple **juice**?

We use **much** and **little** with uncountable nouns:
- ☐ We didn't do **much shopping**.
- ☐ I have a **little work** to do.

Countable and uncountable 2 ➜ Unit 70   **Some** and **any** ➜ Unit 85
Many/much/few/little ➜ Unit 87   **Children / the children** ➜ Unit 75

Exercises

69.1 Some of these sentences need **a/an**. Correct the sentences where necessary.

1   Joe goes everywhere by bike. He hasn't got car.   _He hasn't got a car._
2   Helen was listening to music when I arrived.   _OK_
3   We went to very nice restaurant last weekend.   ....
4   I brush my teeth with toothpaste.   ....
5   I use toothbrush to brush my teeth.   ....
6   Can you tell me if there's bank near here?   ....
7   My brother works for insurance company in Frankfurt.   ....
8   I don't like violence.   ....
9   Can you smell paint?   ....
10 When we were in Rome, we stayed in big hotel.   ....
11 We need petrol. I hope we come to petrol station soon. ....
12 I wonder if you can help me. I have problem.   ....
13 I like your suggestion. It's very interesting idea.   ....
14 John has interview for job tomorrow.   ....
15 I like volleyball. It's good game.   ....
16 Lisa doesn't usually wear jewellery.   ....
17 Jane was wearing beautiful necklace.   ....

69.2 Complete the sentences using the following words. Use **a/an** where necessary.

~~accident~~	biscuit	blood	coat	decision	electricity
interview	key	moment	~~music~~	question	sugar

1   It wasn't your fault. It was _an accident_ .
2   Listen! Can you hear _music_ ?
3   I couldn't get into the house because I didn't have ....
4   It's very warm today. Why are you wearing .... ?
5   Do you take .... in your coffee?
6   Are you hungry? Would you like .... with your coffee?
7   Our lives would be very difficult without ....
8   'I had .... for a job yesterday.'   'Did you? How did it go?'
9   The heart pumps .... through the body.
10 Excuse me, but can I ask you .... ?
11 I'm not ready yet. Can you wait .... , please?
12 We can't delay much longer. We have to make .... soon.

69.3 Complete the sentences using the following words. Sometimes the word needs to be plural (**-s**), and sometimes you need to use **a/an**.

air	day	friend	joke	language	meat
patience	people	~~picture~~	queue	space	umbrella

1   I had my camera, but I didn't take any _pictures_ .
2   There are seven .... in a week.
3   A vegetarian is a person who doesn't eat ....
4   Outside the cinema there was .... of people waiting to see the film.
5   I'm not very good at telling ....
6   Last night I went out with some .... of mine.
7   There were very few .... in town today. The streets were almost empty.
8   I'm going out for a walk. I need some fresh ....
9   Gary always wants things quickly. He doesn't have much ....
10 I think it's going to rain. Do you have .... I could borrow?
11 Do you speak any foreign .... ?
12 Our flat is very small. We don't have much ....

Countable and uncountable 2

Many nouns can be used as countable or uncountable nouns, usually with a difference in meaning.
Compare:

Countable	Uncountable
◯ Did you hear **a noise** just now? (= a specific noise)	◯ I can't work here. There's too much **noise**. (= noise in general)
◯ I bought **a paper** to read. (= a newspaper)	◯ I need **some paper** to write on. (= material for writing on)
◯ There's **a hair** in my soup! (= one single hair)	◯ You've got very long **hair**. (*not* hairs) (= all the hair on your head)
◯ You can stay with us. There's **a spare room**. (= a room in a house)	◯ You can't sit here. There isn't **room**. (= space)
◯ I had some interesting **experiences** while I was travelling. (= things that happened to me)	◯ They offered me the job because I had a lot of **experience**. (*not* experiences)
◯ Enjoy your trip. Have **a** good **time**!	◯ I can't wait. I don't have **time**.

Coffee/tea/juice/beer etc. (drinks) are normally uncountable:
◯ I don't like **coffee** very much.
But you can say **a coffee** (= a cup of coffee), **two coffees** (= two cups) etc. :
◯ **Two coffees** and **an orange juice**, please.

The following nouns are usually uncountable:

accommodation	behaviour	damage	luck	permission	traffic
advice	bread	furniture	luggage	progress	weather
baggage	chaos	information	news	scenery	work

You cannot use **a/an** with these nouns:
◯ I'm going to buy **some bread**. *or* ... **a loaf of bread**. (*not* a bread)
◯ Enjoy your holiday! I hope you have good **weather**. (*not* a good weather)

These nouns are not usually plural (so we do not say 'breads', 'furnitures' etc.):
◯ Where are you going to put all your **furniture**? (*not* furnitures)
◯ Let me know if you need more **information**. (*not* informations)

News is uncountable, not plural:
◯ The **news was** very depressing. (*not* The news were)

Travel (*noun*) means 'travelling in general' (uncountable). We do not say 'a travel' to mean **a trip** or **a journey**:
◯ They spend a lot of money on **travel**.
◯ We had a very good **trip/journey**. (*not* a good travel)

Compare these countable and uncountable nouns:

Countable	Uncountable
◯ I'm looking for **a job**.	◯ I'm looking for **work**. (*not* a work)
◯ What **a** beautiful **view**!	◯ What beautiful **scenery**!
◯ It's **a** nice **day** today.	◯ It's nice **weather** today.
◯ We had a lot of **bags** and **cases**.	◯ We had a lot of **baggage/luggage**.
◯ **These chairs** are mine.	◯ **This furniture** is mine.
◯ That's **a** good **suggestion**.	◯ That's good **advice**.

Countable and uncountable 1 ➜ Unit 69   American English ➜ Appendix 7

Exercises

70.1 **Which of the underlined parts of these sentences is correct?**

1 'Did you hear ~~noise~~ / a noise just now?' 'No, I didn't hear anything.' (a noise *is correct*)
2 a If you want to know the news, you can read paper / a paper.
   b I want to print some documents, but the printer is out of paper / papers.
3 a Light / A light comes from the sun.
   b I thought there was somebody in the house because there was light / a light on inside.
4 a I was in a hurry this morning. I didn't have time / a time for breakfast.
   b 'Did you have a good holiday?' 'Yes, we had wonderful time / a wonderful time.'
5 This is nice room / a nice room. Did you decorate it yourself?
6 Sue was very helpful. She gave us some very useful advice / advices.
7 Did you have nice weather / a nice weather when you were away?
8 We were very unfortunate. We had bad luck / a bad luck.
9 Is it difficult to find a work / job at the moment?
10 Our travel / journey from Paris to Moscow by train was very tiring.
11 When the fire alarm rang, there was total chaos / a total chaos.
12 I had to buy a bread / some bread because I wanted to make some sandwiches.
13 Bad news don't / doesn't make people happy.
14 Your hair is / Your hairs are too long. You should have it / them cut.
15 The damage / The damages caused by the storm will cost a lot to repair.

70.2 **Complete the sentences using the following words. Use the plural (-s) where necessary.**

advice	chair	experience	experience	furniture	hair
information	job	~~luggage~~	permission	progress	work

1 I didn't have much ___luggage___ – just two small bags.
2 They'll tell you all you want to know. They'll give you plenty of _____ .
3 There is room for everybody to sit down. There are plenty of _____ .
4 We have no _____ , not even a bed or a table.
5 'What does Alan look like?' 'He's got a long beard and very short _____ .'
6 Carla's English is better than it was. She's made _____ .
7 Mike is unemployed. He can't get a _____ .
8 Mike is unemployed. He can't get _____ .
9 If you want to leave early, you have to ask for _____ .
10 I didn't know what to do. So I asked Chris for _____ .
11 I don't think Dan should get the job. He doesn't have enough _____ .
12 Nicola has done many interesting things. She could write a book about her _____ .

70.3 **What do you say in these situations? Use a word from Section B (luggage, weather etc.) in each sentence.**

1 Your friends have just arrived at the station. You can't see any cases or bags.
   You ask them: _Do you have any luggage_ ?
2 You go into the tourist office. You want to know about places to see in the town.
   You say: I'd like _____ .
3 You are a student. You want your teacher to advise you about which courses to do.
   You say: Can you give me _____ ?
4 You want to watch the news on TV, but you don't know when it is on.
   You ask your friend: What time _____ ?
5 You are at the top of a mountain. You can see a very long way. It's beautiful.
   You say: It _____ , isn't it?
6 You look out of the window. The weather is horrible – cold, wet and windy.
   You say: What _____ !

A

Countable nouns can be *singular* or *plural*:

a **dog**	a **child**	the **evening**	this **party**	an **umbrella**
dogs	some **children**	the **evenings**	these **parties**	two **umbrellas**

Before singular countable nouns you can use **a/an**:
- ○ Bye! Have a nice **evening**.
- ○ Do you need **an umbrella**?

You cannot use singular countable nouns alone (without **a/the/my** etc.):
- ○ She never wears **a** hat.   (*not* She never wears hat)
- ○ Be careful of **the** dog.   (*not* Be careful of dog)
- ○ What **a** beautiful day!
- ○ I've got **a** headache.

B

We use **a/an** … to say what kind of thing something is, or what kind of person somebody is:
- ○ That's **a nice table**.

In the plural we use the noun alone (*not* some …):
- ○ Those are **nice chairs**.   (*not* some nice chairs)

Compare singular and plural:

○ A dog is **an animal**.	○ Dogs are **animals**.
○ I'm **an optimist**.	○ We're **optimists**.
○ Tom's father is **a doctor**.	○ Most of my friends are **students**.
○ Are you **a good driver**?	○ Are they **good students**?
○ Jane is **a really nice person**.	○ Jane's parents are **really nice people**.
○ What **a lovely dress**!	○ What **awful shoes**!

We say that somebody has **a long nose / a nice face / blue eyes / small hands** etc. :

○ Jack has **a** long **nose**.	○ Jack has **blue eyes**.
(*not* the long nose)	(*not* the blue eyes)

Remember to use **a/an** when you say what somebody's job is:
- ○ Sandra is **a nurse**.   (*not* Sandra is nurse)
- ○ Would you like to be **an English teacher**?

C

You can use **some** with plural countable nouns. We use **some** in two ways.

(1) **Some** = a number of / a few of / a pair of:
- ○ I've seen **some** good **movies** recently.   (*not* I've seen good movies)
- ○ **Some friends** of mine are coming to stay at the weekend.
- ○ I need **some** new **sunglasses**.   (= a new pair of sunglasses)

Do not use **some** when you are talking about things in general (see Unit 75):
- ○ I love **bananas**.   (*not* some bananas)
- ○ My aunt is a writer. She writes **books**.   (*not* some books)

(2) **Some** = some but not all:
- ○ **Some children** learn very quickly.   (but not all children)
- ○ Tomorrow there will be rain in **some places**, but most of the country will be dry.

Countable and uncountable ➜ Units 69–70   A/an and the ➜ Unit 72   Some and any ➜ Unit 85

Exercises

71.1 What are these things? Use a dictionary if necessary.

1 an ant? *It's an insect.*
2 ants and bees? *They're insects.*
3 a cauliflower?
4 chess?
5 a pigeon, an eagle and a crow?

6 a skyscraper?

7 Earth, Mars, Venus and Jupiter?

8 a tulip?
9 the Nile, the Rhine and the Mekong?

10 a violin, a trumpet and a flute?

Who were these people?

11 Beethoven? *He was a composer.*
12 Shakespeare?
13 Albert Einstein?

14 Washington, Lincoln and Kennedy?

15 Marilyn Monroe?

16 Michael Jackson and John Lennon?

17 Van Gogh, Renoir and Picasso?

71.2 Read about what these people do, and say what their jobs are. Choose from:

chef	interpreter	journalist	~~nurse~~
plumber	surgeon	tour guide	waiter

1 Sarah looks after patients in hospital. *She's a nurse.*
2 Gary works in a restaurant. He brings the food to the tables. He
3 Jane writes articles for a newspaper.
4 Kevin works in a hospital. He operates on people.
5 Jonathan cooks in a restaurant.
6 Dave installs and repairs water pipes.
7 Martina takes visitors round her city and tells them about it. She
8 Lisa translates what people are saying from one language into another so that they can understand each other.

71.3 Put in **a/an** or **some** where necessary. If no word is necessary, leave the space empty.

1 I've seen ....*some*.... good films recently.
2 What's wrong with you? Have you got ....*a*.... headache?
3 I know a lot of people. Most of them are ....*–*.... students.
4 When I was .... child, I used to be very shy.
5 Would you like to be .... actor?
6 Questions, questions, questions! You're always asking .... questions!
7 What .... beautiful garden!
8 .... birds, for example the penguin, cannot fly.
9 Do you like staying in .... hotels?
10 I've been walking for three hours. I've got .... sore feet.
11 I don't feel very well this morning. I've got .... sore throat.
12 Maria speaks .... English, but not very much.
13 It's a shame we don't have .... camera. I'd like to take .... picture of that house.
14 Those are .... nice shoes. Where did you get them?
15 I'm going shopping. I want to buy .... new shoes.
16 You need .... visa to visit .... countries, but not all of them.
17 Jane is .... teacher. Her parents were .... teachers too.
18 I don't believe him. He's .... liar. He's always telling .... lies.

A/an and the

Study this example:

I had **a sandwich** and **an apple** for lunch.

The sandwich wasn't very good, but **the apple** was nice.

Joe says 'a sandwich', 'an apple' because this is the first time he talks about them.

Joe now says '**the** sandwich', '**the** apple' because Karen knows which sandwich and which apple he means – **the** sandwich and **the** apple that he had for lunch.

JOE   *KAREN*

Compare **a** and **the** in these examples:

○ **A man** and **a woman** were sitting opposite me. **The man** was American, but I think **the woman** was British.

○ When we were on holiday, we stayed at **a hotel**. Sometimes we ate at **the hotel** and sometimes we went to **a restaurant**.

We use **the** when we are thinking of a specific thing. Compare **a/an** and **the**:

○ Tim sat down on **a chair**. (perhaps one of many chairs in the room)
   Tim sat down on **the chair nearest the door**. (a specific chair)

○ Paula is looking for **a job**. (not a specific job)
   Did Paula get **the job she applied for**? (a specific job)

○ Do you have **a car**? (not a specific car)
   I cleaned **the car** yesterday. (= my car)

We use **the** when it is clear in the situation which thing or person we mean. For example, in a room we talk about **the light / the floor / the ceiling / the door / the carpet** etc. :

○ Can you turn off **the light**, please? (= the light in this room)
○ I took a taxi to **the station**. (= the station in that town)
○ *(in a shop)* I'd like to speak to **the manager**, please. (= the manager of this shop)

In the same way, we say (go to) **the bank / the post office**:

○ I have to go to **the bank** and then I'm going to **the post office**.
   (The speaker is usually thinking of a specific bank or post office.)

We also say (go to) **the doctor / the dentist**:

○ Clare isn't very well. She's gone to **the doctor.** (= her usual doctor)
○ I don't like going to **the dentist**.

Compare **the** and **a**:

○ I have to go to **the bank** today.
   Is there **a bank** near here?
○ I don't like going to **the dentist**.
   My sister is **a dentist**.

We say 'once **a week** / three times **a day** / £1.50 **a kilo**' etc. :

○ 'How often do you go to the cinema?' 'About once **a month**.'
○ 'How much are those potatoes?' '£1.50 **a kilo**.'
○ Helen works eight hours **a day**, six days **a week**.

A/an ➜ Unit 71   The ➜ Units 73–78

Exercises

72.1 Put in **a/an** or **the**.

1 This morning I bought ___*a*___ newspaper and _____ magazine. _____ newspaper is in
   my bag, but I can't remember where I put _____ magazine.
2 I saw _____ accident this morning. _____ car crashed into _____ tree. _____
   driver of _____ car wasn't hurt, but _____ car was badly damaged.
3 There are two cars parked outside: _____ blue one and _____ grey one. _____ blue
   one belongs to my neighbours; I don't know who _____ owner of _____ grey one is.
4 My friends live in _____ old house in _____ small village. There is _____ beautiful
   garden behind _____ house. I would like to have _____ garden like that.

72.2 Put in **a/an** or **the**.

1 a This house is very nice. Has it got _____ garden?
   b It's a beautiful day. Let's sit in _____ garden.
   c I like living in this house, but it's a shame that _____ garden is so small.
2 a Can you recommend _____ good restaurant?
   b We had dinner in _____ very nice restaurant.
   c We had dinner in _____ best restaurant in town.
3 a She has _____ French name, but in fact she's English, not French.
   b What's _____ name of that man we met yesterday?
   c We stayed at a very nice hotel – I can't remember _____ name now.
4 a There isn't _____ airport near where I live. _____ nearest airport is 70 miles away.
   b Our flight was delayed. We had to wait at _____ airport for three hours.
   c Excuse me, please. Can you tell me how to get to _____ airport?
5 a 'Are you going away next week?' 'No, _____ week after next.'
   b I'm going away for _____ week in September.
   c Gary has a part-time job. He works three mornings _____ week.

72.3 Put in **a/an** or **the** where necessary.

1 Would you like apple?   Would you like an apple?
2 How often do you go to dentist?
3 Could you close door, please?
4 I'm sorry. I didn't mean to do that. It was mistake.
5 Excuse me, where is bus station, please?
6 I have problem. Can you help me?
7 I'm just going to post office. I won't be long.
8 There were no chairs, so we sat on floor.
9 Have you finished with book I lent you?
10 My sister has just got job in bank in Zurich.
11 We live in small apartment in city centre.
12 There's supermarket at end of street I live in.

72.4 Answer these questions about yourself. Where possible, use the structure in Section D (**once a week / three times a day** etc.).

1 How often do you go to the cinema?   Three or four times a year.
2 How often do you go to the dentist?
3 How often do you go away on holiday?
4 What's the usual speed limit in towns in your country?
5 How much sleep do you need?
6 How often do you go out in the evening?
7 How much television do you watch (on average)?
8 How much does it cost to rent a small car in your country?

→ Additional exercise 29 (page 319)

A

We use **the** when there is only one of something:
- ○ Have you ever crossed **the equator**?
  (there is only one equator)
- ○ What's **the longest river in Europe**?
- ○ Our apartment is on **the tenth floor**.
- ○ Buenos Aires is **the capital of Argentina**.
- ○ I'm going away at **the end of this month**.

THE EQUATOR →

We use **the** before **same** (**the same**):
- ○ Your sweater is **the same** colour as mine. (*not* is same colour)
- ○ 'Are these keys **the same**?' 'No, they're different.'

B

We say:

the sun	the moon	the earth	the world	the universe
the sky	the sea	the ground	the environment	the internet

- ○ I love to look at the stars in **the sky**. (*not* in sky)
- ○ **The internet** has changed the way we live.
- ○ We need to do more to protect **the environment**. (= the natural world around us)
- ○ **The earth** goes round **the sun**, and **the moon** goes round **the earth**.

We also use '**Earth**' (without **the**) when we think of it as a planet in space (like **Mars**, **Jupiter** etc.).
- ○ Which planet is nearest **Earth**?

We say **space** (without **the**) when we mean 'space in the universe'. Compare
- ○ There are millions of stars **in space**. (*not* in the space)
- ○ I tried to park my car, but **the space** was too small.

We use **a/an** to say what kind of thing something is (see Unit 71B). Compare **the** and **a**:
- ○ **The** sun is **a** star. (= one of many stars)
- ○ **The** hotel we stayed at was **a** very nice hotel.

C

We say: (go to) **the cinema**, **the theatre**.
- ○ I go to **the cinema** a lot, but I haven't been to **the theatre** for ages.

When we say **the cinema / the theatre**, we do not necessarily mean a specific cinema or theatre.

We usually say **the radio**, but **television/TV** (without **the**). Compare:
- ○ I listen to **the radio** a lot.   *but*   I watch **television** a lot.
- ○ We heard it on **the radio**.   *but*   We watched it on **TV**.

The television / **the** TV = the television set:
- ○ Can you turn off **the television**, please?

D

We do not normally use **the** with **breakfast/lunch/dinner**:
- ○ What did you have for **breakfast**?
- ○ We had **lunch** in a very nice restaurant.

But we use **a/an** if we say 'a **big** lunch', 'a **wonderful** dinner', 'an **early** breakfast' etc. :
- ○ We had **a** very **nice lunch**. (*not* We had very nice lunch)

E

We do *not* use **the** before *noun + number*. For example, we say:
- ○ Our train leaves from **Platform 5**. (*not* the Platform 5)
- ○ (*in a shop*) Do you have these shoes in **size 43**? (*not* the size 43)

In the same way, we say: **Room 126** (in a hotel), **page 29** (of a book), **question 3** (in an exam), **Gate 10** (at an airport) etc.

A/an and the → Unit 72   The 2–4 → Units 74–76   Names with and without the → Units 77–78

Exercises

73.1 Put in **the** or **a** where necessary. If no word is necessary, leave the space empty.

1 A: Our apartment is on ___the___ tenth floor.
  B: Is it? I hope there's ___a___ lift.
2 A: Did you have _____ nice holiday?
  B: Yes, it was _____ best holiday I've ever had.
3 A: Where's _____ nearest shop?
  B: There's one at _____ end of this street.
4 A: It's _____ lovely day, isn't it?
  B: Yes, there isn't _____ cloud in _____ sky.
5 A: I've got a problem with my computer. It isn't connecting to _____ internet.
  B: That's interesting. I've got _____ same problem with mine.
6 A: We spent all our money because we stayed at _____ most expensive hotel in town.
  B: Why didn't you stay at _____ cheaper hotel?
7 A: Would you like to travel in _____ space?
  B: Yes, I'd love to go to _____ moon.
8 A: What's Jupiter? Is it _____ star?
  B: No, it's _____ planet. It's _____ largest planet in _____ solar system.

73.2 Put in **the** where necessary. If you don't need **the**, leave the space empty.

1 I haven't been to ___the___ cinema for ages.
2 Sarah spends most of her free time watching _____ TV.
3 Do you ever listen to _____ radio?
4 _____ television was on, but nobody was watching it.
5 Have you had _____ dinner yet?
6 Lisa and I arrived at _____ same time.
7 What's _____ capital city of Canada?
8 What do you want for _____ breakfast?
9 I lay down on _____ ground and looked up at _____ sky.

73.3 Put in **the** or **a** where necessary. (See Unit 72 for **a** and **the** if necessary.)

1 Sun is star. ___The sun is a star.___
2 I'm fed up with doing same thing every day. _____
3 Room 25 is on second floor. _____
4 Moon goes round earth every 27 days. _____
5 It was very hot day. It was hottest day of year. _____
6 We had lunch in nice restaurant by sea. _____
7 What's on at cinema this week? _____
8 I like to eat good breakfast before I go to work. _____
9 We missed our train because we were waiting on wrong platform. _____
10 Next train to London leaves from Platform 3. _____
11 You'll find information you need at top of page 15. _____

73.4 Complete the sentences using the following. Use **the** where necessary.

| breakfast | cinema | ~~dinner~~ | gate | Gate 21 | question 8 | sea |

1 Are you going out this evening?' 'Yes, after ___dinner___.'
2 There was no wind, so _____ was very calm.
3 The test wasn't too difficult, but I couldn't answer _____ .
4 'I'm going to _____ tonight.' 'Are you? What film are you going to see?'
5 I didn't have time for _____ this morning because I was in a hurry.
6 Oh, _____ is open. I must have forgotten to shut it.
7 (airport announcement) Flight AB123 to Rome is now boarding at _____ .

→ Additional exercise 29 (page 319)

The 2 (school / the school etc.)

A

Compare **school** and **the school**:

ELLIE

Ellie is ten years old. Every day she goes **to school**. She's **at school** now. **School** starts at 9 and finishes at 3.

We say a child goes **to school** or is **at school** (as a student). We are not thinking of a specific school. We are thinking of **school** as a general idea – children learning in a classroom.

Today Ellie's mother wants to speak to her daughter's teacher. So she has gone to **the school** to see her. She's at **the school** now.

Ellie's mother is not a student. She is not 'at school', she doesn't 'go to school'. If she wants to see Ellie's teacher, she goes to **the school** (=Ellie's school, a specific building).

B

We use **prison** (or **jail**), **hospital**, **university**, **college** and **church** in a similar way. We do not use **the** when we are thinking of the general idea of these places and what they are used for. Compare:

- Ken's brother is **in prison** for robbery. (He is a prisoner. We are not thinking of a specific prison.)
- Joe had an accident last week. He was taken **to hospital**. He's still **in hospital** now. (as a patient)
- When I leave school, I plan to go **to university** / go **to college**. (as a student)
- Sally's father goes **to church** every Sunday. (to take part in a religious service)

- Ken went to **the prison** to visit his brother. (He went as a visitor, not as a prisoner.)
- Jane has gone to **the hospital** to visit Joe. She's at **the hospital** now. (as a visitor, not as a patient)
- I went to **the university** to meet Professor Thomas. (as a visitor, not as a student)
- Some workmen went to **the church** to repair the roof. (not for a religious service)

With most other places, you need **the**. For example, **the station**, **the cinema**, (see Units 72C and 73C).

C

We say **go to bed / be in bed** etc. (*not* the bed):
- I'm going **to bed** now. Goodnight.
- Do you ever have breakfast **in bed**?
but - I sat down on **the bed**. (a specific piece of furniture)

go to work / be at work / start work / finish work etc. (*not* the work):
- Chris didn't go to **work** yesterday.
- What time do you usually finish **work**?

go home / come home / arrive home / get home / be at home etc. :
- It's late. Let's go **home**.
- Will you be at **home** tomorrow afternoon?

D

We say **go to sea / be at sea** (without **the**) when the meaning is 'go/be on a voyage':
- Keith works on ships. He's **at sea** most of the time.
but - I'd like to live near **the sea**.
- It can be dangerous to swim in **the sea**.

The ➔ Units 72–73, 75–78   Prepositions (**at school / in hospital** etc.) ➔ Units 123–125
Home ➔ Unit 126C   American English ➔ Appendix 7

74.1 Complete each sentence using a preposition (**to/at/in** etc.) + one of these words:

bed   home   ~~hospital~~   hospital   prison   school   university   work

1 Two people were injured in the accident and were taken ...*to hospital*............ .
2 In Britain, children from the age of five have to go ....
3 Mark didn't go out last night. He stayed ....
4 There is a lot of traffic in the morning when everybody is going ....
5 Kate's mother has just had an operation. She is still ....
6 When Sophie leaves school, she wants to study economics ....
7 Ben never gets up before 9 o'clock. It's 8.30 now, so he is still ....
8 If people commit crimes, they may be sent ....

74.2 Complete the sentences with **school** or **the school**.

1 Why aren't your children at ....*school*..... today? Are they ill?
2 When he was younger, Tim hated ....
3 There were some parents waiting outside .... to meet their children.
4 .... usually starts at 8.30 in the morning.
5 A: How do your children get to and from .... ? By bus?
   B: No, they walk. .... isn't very far.
6 What sort of job does Emily want to do when she leaves .... ?

74.3 Some of these sentences need **the**. Correct them where necessary.

1 a 'How old is university?' 'About 200 years.'   ....*the university*....
   b In your country do many people go to university?   ....*OK*....
   c If you want to get a degree, you normally have to study
      at university.   ....
   d This is a small town, but university is the biggest in the country.   ....

2 a My brother has always been healthy. He's never been in hospital.   ....
   b When Ann was ill, I went to hospital to visit her. When I was
      there, I met Lisa, who is a nurse at hospital.   ....
   c A woman was injured in the accident and was taken to hospital.   ....

3 a John's mother is a regular churchgoer. She goes to church every
      Sunday.   ....
   b John himself doesn't go to church.   ....
   c John went to church to take some pictures of the building.   ....

4 a Why is she in prison? What did she do?   ....
   b A few days ago firefighters were called to prison to put out a fire.   ....
   c Do you think too many people are sent to prison?   ....

74.4 Which is correct?

1 How did you <u>get home / ~~get to home~~</u> after the party? (<u>get home</u> *is correct*)
2 I like to read <u>in bed / in the bed</u> before I go to sleep.
3 Shall we meet <u>after work / after the work</u> tomorrow evening?
4 I love swimming <u>in sea / in the sea</u>.
5 It's nice to travel around, but there's no place <u>like home / like the home</u>!
6 Sam likes to <u>go to bed / go to the bed</u> early, and get up early.
7 I didn't sleep well in the hotel. <u>Bed / The bed</u> was uncomfortable.
8 How long did it take to cross the ocean? How long were you <u>at sea / at the sea</u>?
9 What time do you usually start <u>work / the work</u> in the morning?

→ Additional exercise 29 (page 319)

The 3 (children / the children)

A

When we are talking about things or people in general, we do *not* use **the**:
- ○ I'm afraid of **dogs**. (*not* the dogs)
  (**dogs** = dogs in general, not a specific group of dogs)
- ○ **Doctors** are usually paid more than **teachers**.
- ○ Do you know anybody who collects **stamps**?
- ○ **Crime** is a problem in most big cities. (*not* The crime)
- ○ **Life** has changed a lot in the last thirty years. (*not* The life)
- ○ Do you like **classical music / Chinese food / fast cars**?
- ○ My favourite sport is **football/skiing/athletics**.
- ○ My favourite subject at school was **history/physics/English**.

We say '**most** people / **most** books / **most** cars' etc. (*not* the most …):
- ○ **Most shops** accept credit cards. (*not* The most shops)

the

B

We use **the** when we mean specific things or people.
Compare:

In general (without **the**)	*Specific people or things* (with **the**)
○ **Children** learn from playing. (= children in general)	○ We took **the children** to the zoo. (= a specific group, perhaps the speaker's children)
○ I couldn't live without **music**.	○ The film wasn't very good, but I liked **the music**. (= the music in the film)
○ All **cars** have wheels.	○ All **the cars in this car park** belong to people who work here.
○ **Sugar** isn't very good for you.	○ Can you pass **the sugar**, please? (= the sugar on the table)
○ **English people** drink a lot of tea. (= English people in general)	○ **The English people I know** drink a lot of tea. (= only the English people I know, not English people in general)

C

The difference between 'something in general' and 'something specific' is not always very clear.
Compare:

In general (without **the**)	*Specific people or things* (with **the**)
○ I like working with **people**. (= people in general)	
○ I like working with **people who say what they think**. (not all people, but 'people who say what they think' is still a general idea)	○ I like **the people I work with**. (= a specific group of people)
○ Do you like **coffee**? (= coffee in general)	
○ Do you like **strong black coffee**? (not all coffee, but 'strong black coffee' is still a general idea)	○ I didn't like **the coffee we had after dinner**. (= specific coffee)

The 1–2 ➜ Units 73–74   The + adjective (**the young** / **the English** etc.) ➜ Unit 76

Exercises

75.1 Choose four of these things and write whether you like them or not:

bananas	boxing	cats	crowds	fast food	horror movies
~~hot weather~~	maths	opera	snow	supermarkets	zoos

Begin each sentence with one of these:

I like … / I don't like …   **I don't mind …**
I love … / I hate …   **I'm interested in … / I'm not interested in …**

1   *I don't like hot weather very much.*
2   ......
3   ......
4   ......
5   ......

75.2 Complete the sentences using the following. Use **the** where necessary.

~~(the) basketball~~	(the) **grass**	(the) **patience**	(the) **people**
(the) **questions**	(the) **meat**	~~(the) information~~	(the) **hotels**
(the) **history**	(the) **water**	(the) **spiders**	(the) **lies**

1   My favourite sport is ....*basketball*.... .
2   ....*The information*.... we were given wasn't correct.
3   Some people are afraid of ....
4   A vegetarian is somebody who doesn't eat ....
5   The test wasn't very difficult. I answered .... without difficulty.
6   Do you know .... who live next door?
7   .... is the study of the past.
8   It's better to tell the truth. Telling .... usually causes problems.
9   We couldn't find anywhere to stay in the town. .... were full.
10   .... in the pool didn't look very clean, so we didn't go for a swim.
11   Don't sit on .... It's wet after the rain.
12   You need .... to teach young children.

75.3 Choose the correct form, with or without **the**.

1   I'm afraid of <u>dogs / ~~the dogs~~</u>.   (<u>dogs</u> *is correct*)
2   <u>Apples / The apples</u> are good for you.
3   Look at <u>apples / the apples</u> on that tree! They're very big.
4   <u>Women / The women</u> live longer than <u>men / the men</u>.
5   I don't drink <u>tea / the tea</u>. I don't like it.
6   We had a very good meal. <u>Vegetables / The vegetables</u> were especially good.
7   <u>Life / The life</u> is strange sometimes. Some very strange things happen.
8   I enjoy <u>holidays / the holidays</u> by the sea.
9   How much money does the government spend on <u>education / the education</u>?
10   Who are <u>people / the people</u> in this picture?
11   What makes <u>people / the people</u> violent? What causes <u>aggression / the aggression</u>?
12   <u>All books / All the books</u> on the top shelf belong to me.
13   Don't stay in that hotel. It's very noisy and <u>rooms / the rooms</u> are very small.
14   A pacifist is somebody who is against <u>war / the war</u>.
15   <u>First World War / The First World War</u> lasted from 1914 until 1918.
16   I don't like <u>films / the films</u> that don't have happy endings.
17   Someone gave me a book about <u>history / the history</u> of <u>modern art / the modern art</u>.
18   Rob and Louise got married, but <u>marriage / the marriage</u> didn't last very long.
19   <u>Most people / The most people</u> believe that <u>marriage / the marriage</u> and
     <u>family life / the family life</u> are the basis of <u>society / the society</u>.

→ Additional exercise 29 (page 319)

A

Study these sentences:

- ☐ **The giraffe** is the tallest of all animals.
- ☐ **The bicycle** is an excellent means of transport.
- ☐ When was **the telephone** invented?
- ☐ **The dollar** is the currency of the United States.

In these examples, **the** … does not mean one specific thing.
The giraffe = a specific type of animal, not a specific giraffe.
We use **the** in this way to talk about a type of animal, machine etc.

In the same way we use **the** for musical instruments:

- ☐ Can you play **the** guitar?
- ☐ **The** piano is my favourite instrument.

Compare **a** and **the**:

- ☐ I'd like to have **a piano**.　　but　I can't play **the piano**.
- ☐ We saw **a giraffe** at the zoo.　but　**The giraffe** is my favourite animal.

Note that we use **man** (= human beings in general / the human race) without **the**:

- ☐ What do you know about the origins of **man**?　(*not* the man)

B

The + adjective

We use **the** + *adjective* (without a noun) to talk about groups of people. For example:

the young	the rich	the sick	the injured
the old	the poor	the disabled	the dead
the elderly	the homeless	the unemployed	

The young = young people, **the rich** = rich people etc. :

- ☐ Do you think **the rich** should pay higher taxes?
- ☐ We need to do more to help **the homeless**.

The young / **the rich** / **the injured** etc. are *plural* in meaning. For example, you cannot say 'a young' or 'the injured' for one person. You must say '**a young person**', '**the injured woman**' etc.

Note that we say 'the **poor**' (*not* the poors), 'the **young**' (*not* the youngs) etc.

C

The + nationality

You can use **the** + nationality adjectives that end in **-ch** or **-sh** (**the French** / **the English** / **the Spanish** etc.). The meaning is 'the people of that country':

- ☐ **The French** are famous for their food.　(= the people of France)

The French / **the English** etc. are plural in meaning. We do not say 'a French / an English'. You have to say **a Frenchman** / **an Englishwoman** etc.

We also use **the** + nationality words ending in **-ese** (**the Chinese** / **the Sudanese** / **the Japanese** etc.):

- ☐ **The Chinese** invented printing.

But these words can also be singular (**a** Chinese, **a** Japanese etc.).
Note also:　**a Swiss** (singular) and **the Swiss** (= the people of Switzerland)

With other nationalities, the plural noun ends in **-s**. For example:

　　an Italian → **Italians**　　**a Mexican** → **Mexicans**　　**a Turk** → **Turks**

With these words (**Italians** etc.), we do not normally use **the** to talk about the people in general (see Unit 75).

A/an and the ➜ Unit 72　　The 1–3 ➜ Units 73–75　　Names with and without the ➜ Units 77–78

Exercises

76.1 Answer the questions. Choose the right answer from the box. Don't forget **the**. Use a dictionary if necessary.

1	2	3	4
animals	*birds*	*inventions*	*currencies*
tiger elephant	eagle penguin	telephone wheel	dollar peso
rabbit cheetah	swan owl	telescope laser	euro rupee
giraffe kangaroo	parrot pigeon	helicopter typewriter	rouble yen

1 a Which of the animals is tallest? ....the giraffe........

  b Which animal can run fastest?

  c Which of these animals is found in Australia?

2 a Which of these birds has a long neck?

  b Which of these birds cannot fly?

  c Which bird flies at night?

3 a Which of these inventions is oldest?

  b Which one is most recent?

  c Which one was especially important for astronomy?

4 a What is the currency of India?

  b What is the currency of Canada?

  c And the currency of your country?

76.2 Put in **the** or **a**.

1 When was .....the..... telephone invented?

2 Can you play .... musical instrument?

3 Jessica plays .... violin in an orchestra.

4 There was .... piano in the corner of the room.

5 Can you play .... piano?

6 Our society is based on .... family.

7 Martin comes from .... large family.

8 .... computer has changed the way we live.

76.3 Complete these sentences using **the** + the following:

> injured   poor   rich   sick   unemployed   ~~young~~

1 ....The young.... have the future in their hands.

2 Ambulances arrived at the scene of the accident and took .... to hospital.

3 Life is all right if you have a job, but things are not so easy for ....

4 Helen has been a nurse all her life. She has spent her life caring for ....

5 In England there is an old story about a man called Robin Hood. It is said that he robbed .... and gave the money to ....

76.4 What do you call the people of these countries?

	one person (**a/an ...**)	the people in general
1 Canada	a Canadian	Canadians
2 Germany		
3 France		
4 Russia		
5 China		
6 Brazil		
7 England		
8 and your country		

Names with and without **the** 1

A

We do *not* use **the** with names of people ('Helen', 'Helen Taylor' etc.). In the same way, we do *not* use **the** with most names of places. For example:

continents	Africa (*not* the Africa), Europe, South America
countries, states etc.	France (*not* the France), Japan, Brazil, Texas
islands	Sicily, Bermuda, Tasmania
cities, towns etc.	Cairo, New York, Bangkok
mountains	Everest, Etna, Kilimanjaro

But we use **the** in names with **Republic**, **Kingdom**, **States** etc. :
   the Czech **Republic**   **the** United **Kingdom** (**the** UK)
   the Dominican **Republic**   **the** United **States** of America (**the** USA)
Compare:
   ○ Have you been to **Canada** or **the United States**?

B

When we use **Mr/Mrs/Captain/Doctor** etc. + a name, we do not use **the**. So we say:
   Mr Johnson / **Doctor** Johnson / **Captain** Johnson / **President** Johnson etc. (*not* the …)
   Uncle Robert / **Saint** Catherine / **Princess** Maria etc. (*not* the …)
Compare:
   ○ We called **the doctor**.
      We called **Doctor** Johnson. (*not* the Doctor Johnson)

We use **Mount** (= mountain) and **Lake** before a name in the same way (without **the**):
   Mount Everest (*not* the …)   **Mount** Etna   **Lake** Superior   **Lake** Victoria
   ○ They live near **the lake**.
      They live near **Lake Superior**. (*not* the Lake Superior)

C

We use **the** with the names of oceans, seas, rivers and canals:
   the Atlantic (Ocean)   **the** Red Sea   **the** Amazon
   the Indian Ocean   **the** Channel (between   **the** Nile
   the Mediterranean (Sea)   France and Britain)   **the** Suez Canal

We use **the** with the names of deserts:
   the Sahara (Desert)   **the** Gobi Desert

D

We use **the** with *plural* names of people and places:

people	**the** Taylors (= the Taylor family), **the** Johnsons
countries	**the** Netherlands, **the** Philippines, **the** United States
groups of islands	**the** Canaries / **the** Canary Islands, **the** Bahamas
mountain ranges	**the** Rocky Mountains / **the** Rockies, **the** Andes, **the** Alps

   ○ The highest mountain in **the Andes** is (**Mount**) **Aconcagua**.

E

We say:
   the north (of Brazil)   *but*   **northern** Brazil (*without* the)
   the south-east (of Spain) *but*   **south-eastern** Spain
Compare:
   ○ Sweden is in **northern Europe**; Spain is in **the south**.
Also **the** Middle East, **the** Far East

We also use **north/south** etc. (without **the**) in the names of some regions and countries:
   North America   **South Africa**

Note that on maps, **the** is not usually included in the name.

Names with and without **the** 2 → Unit 78

Exercises

77.1 **Put in the where necessary. Leave the space empty if the sentence is already complete.**

1 Who is ......—...... Doctor Johnson? *(the sentence is complete without* the)
2 I was ill, so I went to see .... doctor.
3 The most powerful person in .... United States is .... president.
4 .... President Kennedy was assassinated in 1963.
5 Do you know .... Wilsons? They're a very nice couple.
6 I'm looking for .... Professor Brown. Do you know where she is?

77.2 **Some of these sentences are correct, but some need the (sometimes more than once). Correct the sentences where necessary.**

1 Everest was first climbed in 1953.   *OK*
2 Milan is in north of Italy.   *in the north of Italy*
3 Africa is much larger than Europe.
4 Last year I visited Mexico and United States.
5 South of England is warmer than north.
6 Portugal is in western Europe.
7 France and Britain are separated by Channel.
8 James has travelled a lot in Middle East.
9 Chicago is on Lake Michigan.
10 Next year we're going skiing in Swiss Alps.
11 UK consists of Great Britain and Northern Ireland.
12 Seychelles are a group of islands in Indian Ocean.
13 The highest mountain in Africa is Kilimanjaro.
14 River Volga flows into Caspian Sea.

77.3 **Here are some geography questions. Choose the right answer from one of the boxes and write the if necessary. You do not need all the names in the boxes. Use an atlas if necessary.**

continents	countries	oceans and seas	mountains	rivers and canals	
Africa	Canada	~~Atlantic~~	Alps	Amazon	Rhine
Asia	Denmark	Indian Ocean	Andes	Danube	Thames
Australia	Indonesia	Pacific	Himalayas	Nile	Volga
Europe	Sweden	Black Sea	Rockies	Suez Canal	
North America	Thailand	Mediterranean	Urals	Panama Canal	
South America	United States	Red Sea			

1 What do you have to cross to travel from Europe to America? *the Atlantic*
2 Where is Argentina? ....
3 Which is the longest river in Africa? ....
4 Of which country is Stockholm the capital? ....
5 Of which country is Washington the capital? ....
6 What is the name of the mountain range in the west of North America? ....
7 What is the name of the sea between Africa and Europe? ....
8 Which is the smallest continent in the world? ....
9 What is the name of the ocean between North America and Asia? ....
10 What is the name of the ocean between Africa and Australia? ....
11 Which river flows through London? ....
12 Which river flows through Vienna, Budapest and Belgrade? ....
13 Of which country is Bangkok the capital? ....
14 What joins the Atlantic and Pacific oceans? ....
15 Which is the longest river in South America? ....

Names with and without **the** 2

A

Names without **the**

We do not use **the** with names of most city streets/roads/squares/parks etc. :

| Union **Street** (*not* the …) | Fifth **Avenue** | Hyde **Park** |
| Queens **Road** | **Broadway** | Times **Square** |

Names of important public buildings and institutions (for example, airports, stations, universities) are often two words:

Manchester Airport   **Harvard University**

The first word is the name of a place ('Manchester') or a person ('Harvard'). These names are usually without **the**. In the same way, we say:

| Victoria Station (*not* the …) | **Canterbury Cathedral** | **Edinburgh Castle** |
| **Buckingham Palace** | **Cambridge University** | **Sydney Harbour** |

Compare:

Buckingham Palace (*not* the …)   *but*   **the Royal Palace**
('Royal' is an adjective – it is not a name like 'Buckingham'.)

B

Most other buildings have names with **the**. For example:

hotels	**the** Sheraton Hotel, **the** Holiday Inn
theatres/cinemas	**the** Palace Theatre, **the** Odeon (cinema)
museums/galleries	**the** Guggenheim Museum, **the** National Gallery
other buildings	**the** Empire State (Building), **the** White House, **the** Eiffel Tower

We often leave out the noun:

the Sheraton (Hotel)   **the Palace** (Theatre)   **the Guggenheim** (Museum)

Some names are only **the** + *noun*, for example:

the Acropolis   **the Kremlin**   **the Pentagon**

C

Names with **of** usually have **the**. For example:

| **the** Bank **of** England | **the** Museum **of** Modern Art |
| **the** Great Wall **of** China | **the** Tower **of** London |

Note that we say:

the University **of** Cambridge   *but*   **Cambridge University** (*without* the)

D

Many shops, restaurants, hotels, banks etc. are named after people. These names end in -'s or -s. We do not use **the** with these names:

| **McDonald's** (*not* the …) | **Barclays** (bank) |
| **Joe's Diner** (restaurant) | **Macy's** (department store) |

Churches are often named after saints (St = Saint):

St John's Church (*not* the St Johns Church)   **St Patrick's Cathedral**

E

Most newspapers and many organisations have names with **the**:

| *newspapers* | **the** Washington Post, **the** Financial Times, **the** Sun |
| *organisations* | **the** European Union, **the** BBC, **the** Red Cross |

Names of companies, airlines etc. are usually without **the**:

| **Fiat** (*not* the Fiat) | **Sony** | **Singapore Airlines** |
| **Kodak** | **IBM** | **Yale University Press** |

Names with and without **the** 1 ➡ Unit 77

Exercises

78.1 Use the map to answer the questions. Write the name of the place and the street it is in.
Use **the** if necessary. (Remember that on maps we do not normally use **the**.)

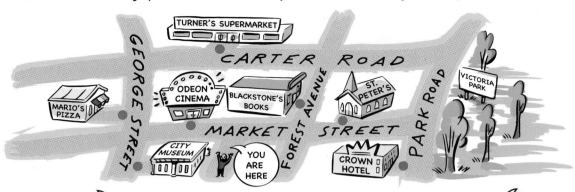

1	Is there a cinema near here?	Yes,	_the Odeon in Market Street_ .
2	Is there a supermarket near here?	Yes,	.... in ....
3	Is there a hotel near here?	Yes,	.... in ....
4	Is there a church near here?	Yes,	.... in ....
5	Is there a museum near here?	Yes,	.... in ....
6	Is there a bookshop near here?	Yes,	.... in ....
7	Is there a restaurant near here?	Yes,	.... in ....
8	Is there a park near here?	Yes,	.... at the end of ....

78.2 Where are the following? Use **the** where necessary.

Acropolis	Broadway	Buckingham Palace	Eiffel Tower
Kremlin	White House	Gatwick Airport	~~Times Square~~

1 _Times Square_ is in New York.   5 .... is in Moscow.
2 .... is in Paris.   6 .... is in New York.
3 .... is in London.   7 .... is in Athens.
4 .... is in Washington.   8 .... is near London.

78.3 Choose the correct form, with or without **the**.

1 Have you ever been to ~~British Museum~~ / the British Museum? (the British Museum *is correct*)
2 The biggest park in New York is Central Park / the Central Park.
3 My favourite park in London is St James's Park / the St James's Park.
4 Imperial Hotel / The Imperial Hotel is in Baker Street / the Baker Street.
5 Dublin Airport / The Dublin Airport is situated about 12 kilometres from the city centre.
6 Jack is a student at Liverpool University / the Liverpool University.
7 If you're looking for a department store, I would recommend Harrison's / the Harrison's.
8 If you're looking for a hotel, I would recommend Park Plaza / the Park Plaza.
9 Statue of Liberty / The Statue of Liberty is at the entrance to New York Harbour / the New York Harbour.
10 You should go to Science Museum / the Science Museum. It's very interesting.
11 Andy works for IBM / the IBM now.   He used to work for British Telecom / the British Telecom.
12 'Which cinema are you going to this evening?' 'Classic / The Classic.'
13 I'd like to go to China and see Great Wall / the Great Wall.
14 'Which newspaper do you want?' 'Times / The Times.'
15 This book is published by Cambridge University Press / the Cambridge University Press.
16 'What's that building?' 'It's College of Art / the College of Art.'

→ Additional exercise 29 (page 319)

A

Sometimes we use a *plural* noun for one thing that has two parts. For example:

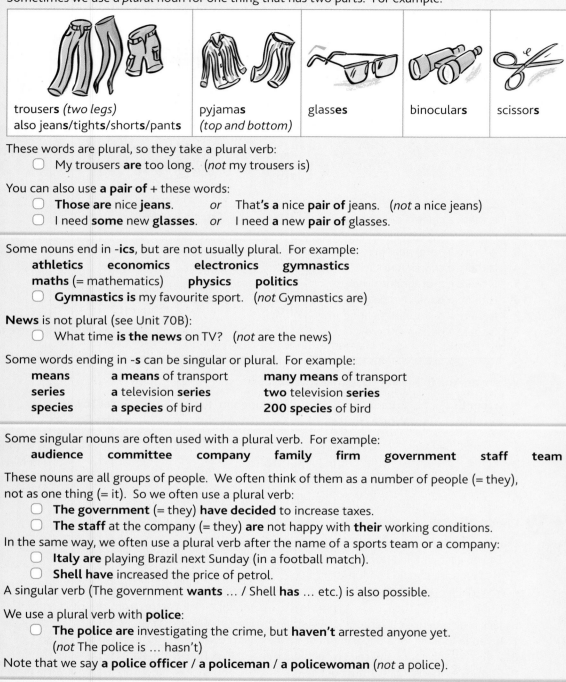

trousers *(two legs)* also jean**s**/tight**s**/short**s**/pant**s**	pyjama**s** *(top and bottom)*	glass**es**	binocular**s**	scissor**s**

These words are plural, so they take a plural verb:
- ○ My trousers **are** too long.   (*not* my trousers is)

You can also use **a pair of** + these words:
- ○ **Those are** nice **jeans**.   *or*   That**'s** a nice **pair of** jeans.   (*not* a nice jeans)
- ○ I need **some** new **glasses**.   *or*   I need **a new pair of** glasses.

B

Some nouns end in **-ics**, but are not usually plural. For example:

athletics   **economics**   **electronics**   **gymnastics**
maths (= mathematics)   **physics**   **politics**
- ○ **Gymnastics is** my favourite sport.   (*not* Gymnastics are)

News is not plural (see Unit 70B):
- ○ What time **is the news** on TV?   (*not* are the news)

Some words ending in **-s** can be singular or plural. For example:

means	**a means** of transport	**many means** of transport
series	**a** television **series**	**two** television **series**
species	**a species** of bird	**200 species** of bird

C

Some singular nouns are often used with a plural verb. For example:

audience   **committee**   **company**   **family**   **firm**   **government**   **staff**   **team**

These nouns are all groups of people. We often think of them as a number of people (= they), not as one thing (= it). So we often use a plural verb:
- ○ **The government** (= they) **have decided** to increase taxes.
- ○ **The staff** at the company (= they) **are** not happy with **their** working conditions.

In the same way, we often use a plural verb after the name of a sports team or a company:
- ○ **Italy are** playing Brazil next Sunday (in a football match).
- ○ **Shell have** increased the price of petrol.

A singular verb (The government **wants** … / Shell **has** … etc.) is also possible.

We use a plural verb with **police**:
- ○ **The police are** investigating the crime, but **haven't** arrested anyone yet.
  (*not* The police is … hasn't)

Note that we say **a police officer / a policeman / a policewoman** (*not* a police).

D

We do not often use the plural of **person** ('persons'). We normally use **people** (a *plural* word):
- ○ He's **a** nice **person**.   *but*   They are nice **people**.   (*not* nice persons)
- ○ **Many people don't** have enough to eat.   (*not* Many people doesn't)

E

We think of a sum of money, a period of time, a distance etc. as *one* thing. So we use a singular verb:
- ○ **Fifty thousand pounds** (= it) **was** stolen in the robbery.   (*not* were stolen)
- ○ **Three years** (= it) **is** a long time to be without a job.   (*not* Three years are)
- ○ **Two miles isn't** very far to walk.

American English ➜ **Appendix 7**

Exercises

79.1 Complete each sentence using a word from Sections A or B. Sometimes you need **a** or **some**.

1 My eyesight isn't very good. I need ___glasses___ .
2 ___A species___ is a group of animals or plants that have the same characteristics.
3 Footballers don't wear trousers when they play. They wear _____ .
4 The bicycle is _____ of transport.
5 The bicycle and the car are _____ of transport.
6 I want to cut this piece of material. I need _____ .
7 A friend of mine is writing _____ of articles for the local newspaper.
8 There are a lot of American TV _____ shown on TV in Britain.
9 While we were out walking, we saw many different _____ of bird.

79.2 In each example the words on the left are connected with an activity (for example, a sport or an academic subject). Write the name of the activity. The beginning of the word is given.

1 calculate   algebra   equation   ___mathematics___
2 government   election   minister   p_____
3 finance   trade   employment   e_____
4 running   jumping   throwing   a_____
5 light   heat   gravity   ph_____
6 exercises   somersault   parallel bars   gy_____
7 processor   silicon chip   gigabyte   el_____

79.3 Choose the correct form of the verb, singular or plural. In two sentences either the singular or plural verb is possible.

1 Gymnastics is / ~~are~~ my favourite sport. (is *is correct*)
2 The trousers you bought for me <u>doesn't / don't</u> fit me.
3 The police <u>want / wants</u> to interview two men about the robbery last week.
4 Physics <u>was / were</u> my best subject at school.
5 Can I borrow your scissors? Mine <u>isn't / aren't</u> sharp enough.
6 It's a nice place to visit. The people <u>is / are</u> very friendly.
7 Fortunately the news <u>wasn't / weren't</u> as bad as we expected.
8 Where <u>does / do</u> your family live?
9 I can't find my binoculars. Do you know where <u>it is / they are</u>?
10 <u>Does / Do</u> the police know how the accident happened?
11 Germany <u>is / are</u> playing Spain tomorrow night, but it's not on TV.
12 Most people <u>enjoy / enjoys</u> music.

79.4 Most of these sentences are wrong. Correct them where necessary.

1 Three years are a long time to be without a job.   ___Three years is a long time___
2 The government have decided to increase taxes.   ___OK (has decided *is also correct*)___
3 Susan was wearing a black jeans.
4 I don't like hot weather. Thirty degrees is too hot for me.
5 I like Martin and Jane. They're very nice persons.
6 Ten pounds aren't enough. I need more money than that.
7 I'm going to buy a new pyjama.
8 The committee haven't made a decision yet.
9 There was a police directing traffic in the street.
10 What is the police going to do?
11 This scissors isn't very sharp.
12 Four days isn't enough for a good holiday.

A

You can use two nouns together *(noun + noun)* to mean *one* thing/person/idea etc. For example:

a **tennis ball**   income **tax**   the **city centre**

The first noun is like an adjective. It tells us what kind of thing/person/idea etc. For example:

a **tennis ball** = a **ball** used to play **tennis**
a **bus driver** = the **driver** of a **bus**
a **road accident** = an **accident** that happens on the **road**
income tax = **tax** that you pay on your **income**
the **city centre** = the **centre** of the **city**
a **Paris hotel** = a **hotel** in **Paris**
my **life story** = the **story** of my **life**

So you can say:

a **television** camera   a **television** programme   a **television** studio   a **television** producer
(these are all different things or people to do with television)
language **problems**   marriage **problems**   health **problems**   work **problems**
(these are all different kinds of problems)

Compare:

garden vegetables (= **vegetables** that are grown in a garden)
a **vegetable garden** (= a **garden** where vegetables are grown)

Sometimes the first word ends in -**ing**. Usually these are things we use for doing something:

a **frying** pan (= a pan for frying)   a **washing** machine   a **swimming** pool

Sometimes there are more than two nouns together:

- I waited at the **hotel reception desk**.
- We watched the **World Swimming Championships** on television.
- If you want to play **table tennis** (= a game), you need a **table tennis table** (= a table).

B

When two nouns are together like this, sometimes we write them as one word and sometimes as two separate words. For example:

a **headache**   **toothpaste**   a **weekend**   a **car park**   a **road sign**

There are no clear rules for this. If you are not sure, write two words.

C

Note the difference between:

a **sugar bowl** (maybe empty) and a **bowl of sugar** (= a bowl with sugar in it)
a **shopping bag** (maybe empty) and a **bag of shopping** (= a bag full of shopping)

D

When we use *noun + noun*, the first noun is like an *adjective*. It is normally singular, but the meaning is often plural. For example: a **book**shop is a shop where you can buy **books**, an **apple** tree is a tree that has **apples**.

In the same way we say:

a **three-hour** journey   (= a journey that takes three **hours**)
a **ten-pound** note   (*not* pounds)
a **four-week** course   (*not* weeks)
a **six-mile** walk   (*not* miles)
two **14-year**-old girls   (*not* years)

Compare:

- It was **a** four-**week** course.

but   The course lasted four **weeks**.

-'s and **of** ... → Unit 81   A **week's** holiday / three **weeks'** holiday etc. → Unit 81E

Exercises

80.1 **What do we call these things and people?**

1 A ticket for a concert is _a concert ticket_ .
2 Problems concerning health are _health problems_ .
3 An interview for a job is _____ .
4 Pictures taken on your holiday are your _____ .
5 Chocolate made with milk is _____ .
6 Somebody whose job is to inspect factories is _____ .
7 A horse that runs in races is _____ .
8 A race for horses is _____ .
9 Shoes for running are _____ .
10 A student studying at university is _____ .
11 The results of your exams are your _____ .
12 The carpet in the living room is _____ .
13 A scandal involving an oil company is _____ .
14 Workers at a car factory are _____ .
15 A scheme for the improvement of a road is _____ .
16 A department store in New York is _____ .
17 A course that lasts five days is _____ .
18 A question that has two parts is _____ .
19 A man who is thirty years old is _____ .

80.2 **Answer the questions using two of the following words each time:**

~~accident~~	belt	birthday	card	credit	driver
editor	forecast	newspaper	number	party	~~road~~
room	seat	shop	truck	weather	window

1 This can be caused by bad driving. _a road accident_
2 You should wear this when you're in a car. a _____
3 You can use this to pay for things instead of cash. a _____
4 If you want to know if it's going to rain, this is what you need. the _____
5 This person is a top journalist. a _____
6 You might stop to look in this when you're walking along a street. a _____
7 If you're staying at a hotel, you need to remember this. your _____
8 This is a way to celebrate getting older. a _____
9 This person transports things by road. a _____

80.3 **Which is correct?**

1 It's quite a long book. There are ~~450 page~~ / 450 pages. (450 pages *is correct*)
2 I didn't have any change. I only had a twenty-pound / twenty pounds note.
3 I looked down and there were two ten-pound / ten pounds notes on the ground.
4 At work in the morning I usually have a 15-minute / 15 minutes break for coffee.
5 There are 60-minute / 60 minutes in an hour.
6 It's only a two-hour / two hours flight from London to Madrid.
7 My office is on the tenth floor of a twelve-storey / twelve storeys building.
8 I work five-day / five days a week. Saturday and Sunday are free.
9 Five-star / Five stars hotels are the most expensive.
10 Sam's daughter is six-year-old / six years old.
11 The oldest building in the city is the 500-year-old / 500 years old castle.
12 Do you use the twelve-hour / twelve hours clock or the 24-hour / 24 hours clock?

A

We use **-'s** (*apostrophe* + **s**) mostly for people or animals:
- ○ **Tom's** computer isn't working. (*not* the computer of Tom)
- ○ How old are **Chris's** children? (*not* the children of Chris)
- ○ What's (= What is) **your sister's** name?
- ○ What's **Tom's sister's** name?
- ○ Be careful. Don't step on **the cat's** tail.

You can use **-'s** without a noun after it:
- ○ This isn't my book. It's **my sister's**. (= my sister's book)

We use **-'s** with a noun (**Tom/friend/teacher** etc.). We do not use **-'s** with a long group of words. So we say:

    your friend's name

but the name **of the woman sitting by the door**

Note that we say **a woman's hat** (= a hat for a woman), **a boy's name** (= a name for a boy), **a bird's egg** (= an egg laid by a bird) etc.

B

With a *singular* noun we use **-'s**:
    my sister's room (= **her** room – one sister)   **Mr Carter's** house (= **his** house)

With a *plural* noun (sister**s**, friend**s** etc.) we put an apostrophe (**'**) at the end of the word:
    my sisters' room (= **their** room – *two or more* sisters)
    the Carters' house (= **their** house – Mr and Mrs Carter)

If a plural noun does not end in **-s** (for example **men/women/children/people**) we use **-'s**:
    the **men's** changing room   a **children's** book (= a book for children)

You can use **-'s** after more than one noun:
    Jack and Karen's wedding   **Mr and Mrs Carter's** house

C

For things, ideas etc., we normally use **of** (... **of the water** / ... **of the book** etc.):
    the temperature **of the water** (*not* the water's temperature)
    the name **of the book**   the owner **of the restaurant**

Sometimes the structure *noun + noun* is possible (see Unit 80):
    the **water temperature**   the **restaurant owner**

We say **the beginning/end/middle of** ... / **the top/bottom of** ... / **the front/back/side of** ... :
    the beginning of the month (*not* the month's beginning)
    the top of the hill   **the back of** the car

D

You can usually use **-'s** or **of** ... for an organisation (= a group of people). So you can say:
    the government's decision *or* the decision **of the government**
    the company's success *or* the success **of the company**

It is also possible to use **-'s** for places. So you can say:
    the city's streets   **the world's** population   **Italy's** prime minister

E

You can also use **-'s** with time words (**yesterday** / **next week** etc.):
- ○ Do you still have **yesterday's** newspaper?
- ○ **Next week's** meeting has been cancelled.

In the same way, you can say **today's** / **tomorrow's** / **this evening's** / **Monday's** etc.

We also use **-'s** (or **-s'** with plural words) with periods of time:
- ○ I've got **a week's** holiday starting on Monday.
- ○ Julia has got **three weeks'** holiday.
- ○ I live near the station – it's only about **ten minutes'** walk.

Noun + noun (**a tennis ball**) ➜ Unit 80   A **three-hour** journey, a **ten-pound** note ➜ Unit 80D

Exercises

81.1 In some of these sentences, it would be more natural to use -'s or -'. Change the underlined parts where necessary.

1 Who is <u>the owner of this restaurant</u>?   OK
2 How old are <u>the children of Chris</u>?   Chris's children
3 Is this <u>the umbrella of your friend</u>?
4 Write your name at <u>the top of the page</u>.
5 I've never met <u>the daughter of Charles</u>.
6 Have you met <u>the son of Helen and Dan</u>?
7 We don't know <u>the cause of the problem</u>.
8 Do we still have <u>the newspaper of last Monday</u>?
9 I don't know <u>the words of this song</u>.
10 What is <u>the cost of a new computer</u>?
11 <u>The friends of your children</u> are here.
12 <u>The garden of our neighbours</u> is very nice.
13 I work on <u>the ground floor of the building</u>.
14 <u>The hair of David</u> is very long.
15 I couldn't go to <u>the party of Katherine</u>.
16 Do you know <u>the number of the man I need to speak to</u>?
17 Have you seen <u>the car of the parents of Mike</u>?
18 What's <u>the meaning of this expression</u>?
19 Do you agree with <u>the economic policy of the government</u>?

81.2 What is another way of saying these things? Use -'s or -s'.

1 a hat for a woman   *a woman's hat*
2 a name for a boy
3 clothes for children
4 a school for girls
5 a nest for a bird
6 a magazine for women

81.3 Read each sentence and write a new sentence beginning with the underlined words.

1 The meeting <u>tomorrow</u> has been cancelled.
   Tomorrow's meeting has been cancelled.
2 The storm <u>last week</u> caused a lot of damage.
   Last
3 The only cinema in <u>the town</u> has closed down.
   The
4 The weather in <u>Britain</u> is very changeable.

5 Tourism is the main industry in <u>the region</u>.

81.4 Use the information given to complete the sentences.

1 If I leave my house at 9 o'clock and drive to the airport, I arrive at about 11.
   So it's about *two hours' drive* from my house to the airport.   (drive)
2 If I leave my house at 8.40 and walk to the centre, I get there at 9 o'clock.
   So it's .... from my house to the centre.   (walk)
3 I'm going on holiday on the 12th. I have to be back at work on the 26th.
   So I've got ....   (holiday)
4 I went to sleep at 3 o'clock this morning and woke up an hour later. After that I couldn't
   sleep. So last night I only had ....   (sleep)

Myself/yourself/themselves etc.

A

Study this example:

Hi, I'm Steve.

STEVE

Steve **introduced himself** to the other guests.

We use **myself/yourself/himself** etc. *(reflexive pronouns)* when the *subject* and *object* are the same:

Steve introduced himself

subject   *object*

The reflexive pronouns are:

singular: **myself**   **yourself** *(one person)*   **himself/herself/itself**
plural: **ourselves**   **yourselves** *(more than one person)*   **themselves**

- ◯ I don't want you to pay for me. **I'll** pay for **myself**. *(not* I'll pay for me)
- ◯ Amy had a great holiday. **She** really enjoyed **herself**.
- ◯ Do **you** talk to **yourself** sometimes? *(said to one person)*
- ◯ If **you** want more to eat, help **yourselves**. *(said to more than one person)*

Compare:
- ◯ It's not our fault. **You** can't blame **us**.
- ◯ It's our own fault. **We** should blame **ourselves**.

B

We do not use **myself** etc. after **feel/relax/concentrate/meet**:
- ◯ I **feel** nervous. I can't **relax**.
- ◯ You must try and **concentrate**. *(not* concentrate yourself)
- ◯ What time shall we **meet**? *(not* meet ourselves, *not* meet us)

We normally use **wash/shave/dress** *without* **myself** etc. :
- ◯ He got up, **washed**, **shaved** and **dressed**. *(not* washed himself etc.)
You can also say **get dressed** (He **got dressed**).

C

Compare **-selves** and **each other**:
- ◯ Kate and Joe stood in front of the mirror and looked at **themselves**. (= *Kate and Joe* looked at *Kate and Joe*)
- ◯ Kate looked at Joe; Joe looked at Kate. They looked at **each other**.

themselves

each other

You can use **one another** instead of **each other**:
- ◯ How long have you and Ben known **each other**? *or* … known **one another**?
- ◯ Sue and Alice don't like **each other**. *or* … don't like **one another**.
- ◯ Do you and Sarah live near **each other**? *or* … near **one another**?

D

We also use **myself/yourself** etc. in another way. For example:
- ◯ 'Who repaired your bike for you?' 'I repaired it **myself**.'

I repaired it myself = I repaired it, not anybody else. Here, **myself** is used to emphasise 'I' (= it makes it stronger). Some more examples:
- ◯ I'm not going to do your work for you. **You** can do it **yourself**. (= you, not me)
- ◯ **Let's** paint the house **ourselves**. It will be much cheaper.
- ◯ **The film itself** wasn't very good, but I loved the music.
- ◯ I don't think Lisa will get the job. **Lisa herself** doesn't think so. *(or* **Lisa** doesn't think so **herself**.)

Get dressed / get married etc. ➔ Unit 44D   By myself / by yourself etc. ➔ Unit 83D

Exercises

82.1 Complete the sentences using **myself/yourself** etc. + these verbs (in the correct form):

blame	burn	enjoy	express	hurt	~~introduce~~	put

1 Steve ___introduced himself___ to the other guests at the party.
2 Ben fell down some steps, but fortunately he didn't _____ .
3 It isn't Sue's fault. She really shouldn't _____ .
4 Please try and understand how I feel. _____ in my position.
5 The children had a great time at the beach. They really _____ .
6 Be careful! That pan is very hot. Don't _____ .
7 Sometimes I can't say exactly what I mean. I wish I could _____ better.

82.2 Put in **myself/yourself/ourselves** etc. or **me/you/us** etc.

1 Amy had a great holiday. She enjoyed ___herself___ .
2 It's not my fault. You can't blame _____ .
3 What I did was really bad. I'm ashamed of _____ .
4 We've got a problem. I hope you can help _____ .
5 'Can I take another biscuit?'   'Of course. Help _____ !'
6 You must meet Sarah. I'll introduce _____ to her.
7 Don't worry about us. We can take care of _____ .
8 Don't worry about the children. I'll take care of _____ .
9 I gave them a key to our house so that they could let _____ in.

82.3 Complete these sentences. Use **myself/yourself** etc. only where necessary. Use these verbs (in the correct form):

concentrate	defend	dry	feel	meet	relax	~~shave~~

1 Martin decided to grow a beard because he was fed up with ___shaving___ .
2 I wasn't very well yesterday, but I _____ much better today.
3 I climbed out of the swimming pool and _____ with a towel.
4 I tried to study, but I couldn't _____ .
5 If somebody attacks you, you need to be able to _____ .
6 I'm going out with Chris this evening. We're _____ at 7.30.
7 You're always rushing around. Why don't you sit down and _____ ?

82.4 Complete the sentences with **ourselves/themselves** or **each other**.

1 How long have you and Ben known ___each other___ ?
2 If people work too hard, they can make _____ ill.
3 I need you and you need me. We need _____ .
4 In Britain friends often give _____ presents at Christmas.
5 Some people are very selfish. They only think of _____ .
6 Tracy and I don't see _____ very often these days.
7 We couldn't get back into the house. We had locked _____ out.
8 They've had an argument. They're not speaking to _____ at the moment.
9 We'd never met before, so we introduced _____ to _____ .

82.5 Complete the answers to the questions using **myself/yourself** etc.

1 Who repaired the bike for you? | Nobody. I ___repaired it myself.___
2 Who cuts Brian's hair for him? | Nobody. He cuts _____
3 Shall I tell Amy about your idea? | No, I'll _____
4 Who told you that Linda was going away? | Linda _____
5 Can you phone John for me? | Why can't you _____ ?

→ Additional exercise 30 (page 320)   **165**

A

A friend of mine / a friend of yours etc.

We say '(a friend) **of mine/yours/his/hers/ours/theirs**'.
A friend of mine = one of my friends:
- ○ I'm going to a wedding on Saturday. **A friend of mine** is getting married. (*not* a friend of me)
- ○ We went on holiday with **some friends of ours**. (*not* some friends of us)
- ○ Mike had an argument with **a neighbour of his**.
- ○ It was **a good idea of yours** to go to the cinema.

In the same way we say '(a friend) **of my sister's** / (a friend) **of Tom's**' etc. :
- ○ That woman over there is **a friend of my sister's**. (= one of my sister's friends)
- ○ It was **a good idea of Tom's** to go to the cinema.

B

My own … / **your own** … etc.

We use **my/your/his/her/its/our/their** before **own**:
> **my own** house   **your own** car   **her own** room
> (*not* an own house, an own car etc.)

My own … / **your own** … etc. = something that is only mine/yours, not shared or borrowed:
- ○ I don't want to share a room with anybody. I want **my own room**.
- ○ Vicky and Gary would like to have **their own house**.
- ○ It's a shame that the apartment hasn't got **its own parking space**.
- ○ It's **my own fault** that I've got no money. I buy too many things I don't need.
- ○ Why do you want to borrow my car? Why don't you use **your own**? (= your own car)

You can also say 'a room **of my own**', 'a house **of your own**', 'problems **of his own**' etc. :
- ○ I'd like to have a room **of my own**.
- ○ He won't be able to help you with your problems. He has too many problems **of his own**.

C

We also use **own** to say that we do something ourselves instead of somebody else doing it for us.
For example:
- ○ Brian usually cuts **his own hair**.
  (= he cuts it himself; he doesn't
  go to a barber)
- ○ I'd like to have a garden so that
  I could grow **my own vegetables**.
  (= grow them myself instead of
  buying them from shops)

BRIAN

D

On my own / by myself

On my own and **by myself** both mean 'alone'. We say:

on	my / your his / her / its our / their	**own**	=	**by**	myself / yourself (*singular*) himself / herself / itself ourselves / yourselves (*plural*) / themselves

- ○ I like living **on my own / by myself**.
- ○ 'Did you go on holiday **on your own / by yourself**?' 'No, with a friend.'
- ○ Jack was sitting **on his own / by himself** in a corner of the café.
- ○ Learner drivers are not allowed to drive **on their own / by themselves**.

Myself/yourself/themselves etc. → Unit 82

Exercises

83.1 Write new sentences with the same meaning. Change the <u>underlined</u> words and use the structure in Section A (**a friend of mine** etc.).

1 I am meeting <u>one of my friends</u> tonight. I'm meeting a friend of mine tonight.
2 We met <u>one of your relatives</u>. We met a ....
3 Jason borrowed <u>one of my books</u>. Jason ....
4 Lisa invited <u>some of her friends</u> to her flat. Lisa .... to her flat.
5 We had dinner with <u>one of our neighbours</u>. ....
6 I went on holiday with <u>two of my friends</u>. ....
7 Is that man <u>one of your friends</u>? ....
8 I met <u>one of Jane's friends</u> at the party. .... at the party.
9 It's always been <u>one of my ambitions</u> to travel round the world. .... to travel round the world.

83.2 Complete the sentences using **my own / our own** etc. + the following:

| ~~bedroom~~   business   opinions   private beach   words |

1 I share a kitchen and bathroom, but I have __my own bedroom__ .
2 Gary doesn't think the same as me. He's got ....
3 Julia is fed up with working for other people. She wants to start ....
4 In the test we had to read a story, and then write it in ....
5 We stayed at a luxury hotel by the sea. The hotel had ....

83.3 Complete the sentences using **my own / your own** etc.

1 Why do you want to borrow my car? Why don't you __use your own car__ ?
2 How can you blame me? It's not my fault. It's ....
3 She's always using my ideas. Why can't she use .... ?
4 Please don't worry about my problems. You've got ....
5 I can't make his decisions for him. He must make ....

83.4 Complete the sentences using **my own / your own** etc. Use the following verbs:

| bake   clean   ~~cut~~   make   write |

1 Brian never goes to a barber.
   He __cuts his own hair__ .
2 Helen doesn't often buy clothes.
   She usually ....
3 We don't often buy bread.
   We usually ....
4 I'm not going to clean your shoes.
   You can ....
5 Paul and Joe are singers.
   They sing songs written by other people, but they also ....

83.5 Complete the sentences using **my own / myself** etc.

1 Did you go on holiday on __your own__ ?
2 I'm glad I live with other people. I wouldn't like to live on ....
3 The box was too heavy for me to lift by ....
4 'Who was Tom with when you saw him?'   'Nobody. He was by ....'
5 Very young children should not go swimming by ....
6 I don't think she knows many people. When I see her, she is always by ....
7 I don't like strawberries with cream. I like them on ....
8 Do you like working with other people or do you prefer working by .... ?
9 We had no help decorating the flat. We did it completely on ....
10 I went out with Sally because she didn't want to go out on ....

A

Study this example:

There's a new restaurant in Hill Street.

Yes, I know. I've heard **it's** very good.

We use **there** ... when we talk about something for the first time, to say that it exists:
- ○ **There's** a new restaurant in Hill Street. (*not* A new restaurant is in Hill Street)
- ○ I'm sorry I'm late. **There was** a lot of traffic. (*not* It was a lot of traffic)
- ○ Things are more expensive now. **There has been** a big rise in the cost of living.

It = a specific thing, place, fact, situation etc. (but see also section C):
- ○ We went to the new restaurant. **It**'s very good. (**It** = the restaurant)
- ○ I wasn't expecting them to come. **It** was a complete surprise. (**It** = that they came)

Compare **there** and **it**:
- ○ I don't like this town. **There**'s nothing to do here. **It**'s a boring place.

There also means 'to/at/in that place':
- ○ When we got to the party, there were already a lot of people **there**. (= at the party)

B

You can say **there will be / there must be / there might be / there used to be** etc.:
- ○ Will you be busy tomorrow? **Will there be** much to do?
- ○ '**Is there** a flight to Rome tonight?' '**There might be**. I'll check the website.'
- ○ If people drove more carefully, **there wouldn't be** so many accidents.

Also **there must have been**, **there should have been** etc. :
- ○ I could hear music coming from the house. **There must have been** somebody at home.

Compare **there** and **it**:
- ○ They live on a busy road. **There must be** a lot of noise from the traffic.
- ○ They live on a busy road. **It must be** very noisy.
- ○ **There used to be** a cinema here, but it closed a few years ago.
- ○ That building is now a supermarket. **It used to be** a cinema.

You can also say **there is sure / bound** (= sure) / **likely** to be ... . Compare **there** and **it**:
- ○ **There's sure to be** a flight to Rome tonight. (*or* **There's bound to be** ...)
- ○ There's a flight to Rome tonight, but **it's sure to be** full. (**it** = the flight)

C

We also use **it** in sentences like this:
- ○ **It**'s dangerous **to walk in the road**.

We do not usually say 'To walk in the road is dangerous'. Normally we begin with **It** ... .
Some more examples:
- ○ **It** didn't take us long **to get here**.
- ○ **It**'s a shame (**that**) **you can't come to the party**.
- ○ Let's go. **It**'s not worth **waiting any longer**.

We also use **it** to talk about distance, time and weather:
- ○ How far is **it** from here to the airport?
- ○ What day is **it** today?
- ○ **It**'s a long time since we saw you last.
- ○ **It** was windy yesterday. (*but* **There** was **a cold wind**.)

It's worth / it's no use / there's no point ➜ Unit 63   Sure to / bound to ... etc. ➜ Unit 65E
There is + -ing/-ed ➜ Unit 97

Exercises

84.1 Put in **there is/was** or **it is/was**. Some sentences are questions (**is there** … ? / **is it** … ? etc.) and some are negative (**isn't/wasn't**).

1 The journey took a long time. _There was_ a lot of traffic.
2 What's this restaurant like? _Is it_ good?
3 .... something wrong with the computer. Can you check it for me?
4 I wanted to visit the museum, but .... enough time.
5 'What's that building? .... a hotel?' 'No, ... a theatre.'
6 How do we get across the river? .... a bridge?
7 A few days ago .... a big storm, which caused a lot of damage.
8 I can't find my phone. .... in my bag – I just looked.
9 It's often cold here, but .... much snow.
10 'How was your trip?' '........................ a disaster. Everything went wrong.'
11 .... anything on television, so I turned it off.
12 '........................ a bookshop near here?' 'Yes, ... one in Hudson Street.'
13 When we got to the cinema, ... a queue outside. .... a very long queue, so we decided not to wait.
14 I couldn't see anything. .... completely dark.
15 .... difficult to get a job right now. .... a lot of unemployment.

84.2 Read the first sentence and then write a sentence beginning **There** … .

1 The roads were busy yesterday. _There was a lot of traffic._
2 This soup is very salty. There .... in the soup.
3 The box was empty. .... in the box.
4 The film is very violent. ....
5 The shopping mall was crowded. ....
6 I like this town – it's lively. ....

84.3 Complete the sentences. Use **there will be**, **there would be** etc. Choose from:

| will | may | ~~would~~ | wouldn't | should | used to | (be) going to |

1 If people drove more carefully, _there would be_ fewer accidents.
2 'Do we have any eggs?' 'I'm not sure. .... some in the fridge.'
3 I think everything will be OK. I don't think .... any problems.
4 Look at the sky. .... a storm.
5 'Is there a school in the village?' 'Not now. .... one, but it closed.'
6 People drive too fast on this road. I think .... a speed limit.
7 If people weren't aggressive, ... any wars.

84.4 Are these sentences right or wrong? Change **it** to **there** where necessary.

1 They live on a busy road. It must be a lot of noise. _There must be a lot of noise._
2 It's a long way from my house to the nearest shop. ....
3 After the lecture it will be an opportunity to ask questions. ....
4 I like where I live, but it would be nicer to live by the sea. ....
5 Why was she so unfriendly? It must have been a reason. ....
6 It's three years since I last went to the theatre. ....
7 A: Where can we park the car?
   B: Don't worry. It's sure to be a car park somewhere. ....
8 It was Ken's birthday yesterday. We had a party. ....
9 The situation is still the same. It has been no change. ....
10 It used to be a church here, but it was knocked down. ....
11 I was told that it would be somebody to meet me at the station, but it wasn't anybody. ....
12 I don't know who'll win, but it's sure to be a good game. ....

A In general we use **some** (*also* **somebody/someone/something**) in positive sentences and **any** (*also* **anybody** etc.) in negative sentences:

some	any
◯ We bought **some** flowers.	◯ We did**n't** buy **any** flowers.
◯ He's busy. He's got **some** work to do.	◯ He's lazy. He **never** does **any** work.
◯ There's **somebody** at the door.	◯ There is**n't anybody** at the door.
◯ I want **something** to eat.	◯ I do**n't** want **anything** to eat.

We use **any** in the following sentences because the meaning is negative:
- ◯ She went out **without any** money. (she **didn't** take **any** money with her)
- ◯ He **refused** to eat **anything**. (he **didn't** eat **anything**)
- ◯ It's a very easy exam. **Hardly anybody** fails. (= almost **nobody** fails)

B We use both **some** and **any** in questions. We use **some/somebody/something** to talk about a person or thing that we know exists, or we think exists:
- ◯ Are you waiting for **somebody**? (I think you are waiting for somebody)

We use **some** in questions when we offer or ask for things:
- ◯ Would you like **something** to eat? (there is something to eat)
- ◯ Can I have **some** sugar, please? (there is probably some sugar I can have)

But in most questions, we use **any**. We do not know if the thing or person exists:
- ◯ 'Do you have **any** luggage?' 'No, I don't.'
- ◯ I can't find my bag. Has **anybody** seen it?

C We often use **any** after **if**:
- ◯ **If anyone** has **any** questions, I'll be pleased to answer them.
- ◯ Let me know **if** you need **anything**.

The following sentences have the idea of **if**:
- ◯ I'm sorry for **any** trouble I've caused. (= if I have caused any trouble)
- ◯ **Anyone** who wants to do the exam should tell me by Friday. (= if there is anyone)

D We also use **any** with the meaning 'it doesn't matter which':
- ◯ You can take **any** bus. They all go to the centre. (= it doesn't matter which bus you take)
- ◯ 'Sing a song.' 'Which song shall I sing?' '**Any** song. I don't mind.' (= it doesn't matter which song)
- ◯ Come and see me **any** time you want.

We use **anybody/anyone/anything/anywhere** in the same way:
- ◯ We forgot to lock the door. **Anybody** could have come in.
- ◯ 'Let's go out somewhere.' 'Where shall we go?' '**Anywhere**. I just want to go out.'

Compare **something** and **anything**:
- ◯ A: I'm hungry. I want **something** to eat.
  - B: What would you like?
  - A: I don't mind. **Anything**. (= it doesn't matter what)

E **Somebody/someone/anybody/anyone** are singular words:
- ◯ **Someone** is here to see you.

But we use **they/them/their** after these words:
- ◯ **Someone** has forgotten **their** umbrella. (= his or her umbrella)
- ◯ If **anybody** wants to leave early, **they** can. (= he or she can)

Not … any ➔ Unit 86   Some of / any of … ➔ Unit 88   Hardly any ➔ Unit 101D

Exercises

85.1 Put in **some** or **any**.

1 We didn't buy ......*any*...... flowers.
2 Tonight I'm going out with .... friends of mine.
3 A: Have you seen .... good movies recently?
  B: No, I haven't been to the cinema for ages.
4 I didn't have .... money, so I had to borrow ....
5 Can I have .... milk in my coffee, please?
6 We wanted to buy .... grapes, but they didn't have .... in the shop.
7 He did everything himself – without .... help.
8 You can use this card to withdraw money at .... cash machine.
9 I'd like .... information about places of interest in the town.
10 With the special tourist train ticket, you can travel on .... train you like.
11 Those apples look nice. Shall we buy .... ?

85.2 Complete the sentences with **some-** or **any-** + **-body/-thing/-where**.

1 I was too surprised to say .....*anything*..... .
2 There's .... at the door. Can you go and see who it is?
3 Does .... mind if I open the window?
4 I wasn't feeling hungry, so I didn't eat ....
5 You must be hungry. Why don't I get you .... to eat?
6 Quick, let's go! There's .... coming and I don't want .... to see us.
7 Sarah was upset about .... and refused to talk to ....
8 This machine is very easy to use. .... can learn to use it very quickly.
9 There was hardly .... on the beach. It was almost deserted.
10 'Do you live .... near Joe?' 'No, he lives in another part of town.'
11 'Where shall we go on holiday?' 'Let's go .... warm and sunny.'
12 They stay at home all the time. They never seem to go ....
13 I'm going to a meeting now. If .... needs me, tell them I'll be back at 11.30.
14 Why are you looking under the bed? Have you lost .... ?
15 This is a no-parking area. .... who parks here will have to pay a fine.
16 Jonathan stood up and left the room without saying ....
17 'Can I ask you .... ?' 'Sure. What do you want to ask?'
18 Sue is very secretive. She never tells .... (*2 words*)

85.3 Complete the sentences. Use **any** (+ noun) or **anybody/anything/anywhere**.

1	Which bus do I have to catch?	....*Any bus*.... . They all go to the centre.
2	Which day shall I come?	I don't mind. ....
3	What do you want to eat?	.... I don't mind. Whatever you have.
4	Where shall I sit?	It's up to you. You can sit .... you like.
5	What sort of job are you looking for?	.... It doesn't matter.
6	What time shall I call you tomorrow?	.... Leave a message if I don't answer and I'll get back to you.
7	Who shall I invite to the party?	I don't mind. .... you like.
8	Which newspaper shall I buy?	.... See what they have in the shop.

A No and none

We use **no** + *noun*. **No** = **not a** or **not any**:
- We had to walk home because there was **no bus**. (= there **wasn't a** bus)
- Sue will have **no trouble** finding a job. (= Sue **won't** have **any** trouble …)
- There were **no shops** open. (= There **weren't any** shops open.)

You can use **no** + *noun* at the beginning of a sentence:
- **No reason** was given for the change of plan.

We use **none** *without* a noun:
- 'How much money do you have?' '**None**.' (= no money)
- All the tickets have been sold. There are **none** left. (= no tickets left)

Or we use **none of** … :
- This money is all yours. **None of it** is mine.

Compare **none** and **any**:
- 'How much luggage do you have?' '**None**.' / 'I **don't** have **any**.'

After **none of** + *plural* (none of **the students**, none of **them** etc.) the verb can be singular or plural.
A plural verb is more usual:
- None of the shops **were** (*or* **was**) open.

B Nothing   nobody/no-one   nowhere

You can use these words at the beginning of a sentence or alone (as answers to questions):
- 'What's going to happen?' '**Nobody** (*or* **No-one**) knows.'
- 'What happened?' '**Nothing**.'
- 'Where are you going?' '**Nowhere**. I'm staying here.'

You can also use these words after a verb, especially after **be** and **have**:
- The house is empty. There**'s nobody** living there.
- We **had nothing** to eat.

Nothing/nobody etc. = **not** + **anything/anybody** etc. :
- I said **nothing**. = I **didn't** say **anything**.
- Jane told **nobody** about her plans. = Jane **didn't** tell **anybody** about her plans.
- They have **nowhere** to live. = They **don't** have **anywhere** to live.

With **nothing/nobody** etc., do *not* use a negative verb (**isn't**, **didn't** etc.):
- I **said** nothing. (*not* I didn't say nothing)

C

After **nobody/no-one** you can use **they/them/their** (see also Unit 85E):
- **Nobody** is perfect, are **they**? (= is he or she perfect)
- **No-one** did what I asked **them** to do. (= him or her)
- **Nobody** in the class did **their** homework. (= his or her homework)

D

Sometimes **any/anything/anybody** etc. means 'it doesn't matter which/what/who' (see Unit 85D).
Compare **no-** and **any-**:
- There was **no** bus, so we walked home.
  You can take **any** bus. They all go to the centre. (= it doesn't matter which)
- 'What do you want to eat?' '**Nothing**. I'm not hungry.'
  I'm so hungry. I could eat **anything**. (= it doesn't matter what)
- The exam was extremely difficult. **Nobody** passed. (= everybody failed)
  The exam was very easy. **Anybody** could have passed. (= it doesn't matter who)

Some and **any** → Unit 85   **None of** … → Unit 88   **Any bigger** / **no better** etc. → Unit 106B

Exercises

86.1 Complete these sentences with **no**, **none** or **any**.

1 It was a public holiday, so there were _...no..._ shops open.
2 I haven't got _...any..._ money. Can you lend me some?
3 We had to walk home because there were _____ taxis.
4 We had to walk home because there weren't _____ taxis.
5 'How many eggs have we got?' '_____ . Do you want me to get some?'
6 We took a few pictures, but _____ of them were very good.
7 'Did you take lots of pictures?' 'No, I didn't take _____ .'
8 What a stupid thing to do! _____ intelligent person would do such a thing.
9 There's nowhere to cross the river. There's _____ bridge.
10 I haven't read _____ of the books you lent me.
11 We cancelled the party because _____ of the people we invited were able to come.
12 'Do you know when Chris will be back?' 'I'm sorry. I have _____ idea.'

86.2 Answer these questions using **none/nobody/nothing/nowhere**.

1	What did you do?	_Nothing._
2	Who were you talking to?	
3	How much sugar do you want?	
4	Where are you going?	
5	How many emails did you get?	
6	How much did you pay?	

Now answer the same questions using complete sentences with **any/anybody/anything/ anywhere**.

7 (1) _I didn't do anything._
8 (2) I _____
9 (3) _____
10 (4) _____
11 (5) _____
12 (6) _____

86.3 Complete these sentences with **no-** or **any-** + **-body/-thing/-where**.

1 I don't want _...anything..._ to drink. I'm not thirsty.
2 The bus was completely empty. There was _____ on it.
3 'Where did you go for your holidays?' '_____ . I stayed at home.'
4 I went to the shops, but I didn't buy _____ .
5 'What did you buy?' '_____ . I couldn't find _____ I wanted.'
6 The town is still the same as it was years ago. _____ has changed.
7 Have you seen my watch? I can't find it _____ .
8 There was complete silence in the room. _____ said _____ .

86.4 Choose the right word.

1 She didn't tell ~~nobody~~ / anybody about her plans. (anybody is correct)
2 The accident looked bad, but fortunately nobody / anybody was badly injured.
3 I looked out of the window, but I couldn't see no-one / anyone.
4 My job is very easy. Nobody / Anybody could do it.
5 'What's in that box?' 'Nothing / Anything. It's empty.'
6 The situation is uncertain. Nothing / Anything could happen.
7 I don't know nothing / anything about economics.
8 I'll try and answer no / any questions you ask me.
9 'Who were you talking to just now?' 'No-one / Anyone. I wasn't talking to no-one / anyone.'

→ Additional exercise 30 (page 320)   **173**

Much, many, little, few, a lot, plenty

A

We use **much** and **little** with *uncountable* nouns:

    much time   **much luck**   **little energy**   **little money**

We use **many** and **few** with *plural* nouns:

    many friends   **many people**   **few cars**   **few countries**

We use **a lot of / lots of / plenty of** with both *uncountable* and *plural* nouns:

    a lot of luck   **lots of time**   **plenty of money**
    a lot of friends   **lots of people**   **plenty of ideas**

Plenty = more than enough:

- There's no need to hurry. We've got **plenty of time**.

B

Much is unusual in positive sentences (especially in spoken English). Compare:

- We **didn't** spend **much** money.

but   We **spent a lot of** money.   (*not* We spent much money)

- **Do** you **see** David **much**?

but   I **see** David **a lot**.   (*not* I see David much)

We use **many** and **a lot of** in all kinds of sentences:

- **Many** people drive too fast.   *or*   **A lot of** people drive too fast.
- Do you know **many** people?   *or*   Do you know **a lot of** people?
- There aren't **many** tourists here.   *or*   There aren't **a lot of** tourists here.

Note that we say **many years / many weeks / many days** (*not* a lot of …):

- We've lived here for **many years**.   (*not* a lot of years)

C

Little = not much, **few** = not many:

- Gary is very busy with his job. He has **little time** for other things.   (= not much time, less time than he would like)
- Vicky doesn't like living in London. She has **few friends** there.   (= not many, not as many as she would like)

You can say **very little** and **very few**:

- Gary has **very little** time for other things.
- Vicky has **very few** friends in London.

D

A little = some, a small amount:

- Let's go and have a coffee. We have **a little** time before the train leaves.
  (a little time = some time, enough time to have a coffee)
- 'Do you speak English?'   '**A little**.' (so we can talk a bit)

A few = some, a small number:

- I enjoy my life here. I have **a few** friends and we meet quite often.
  (a few friends = not many but enough to have a good time)
- 'When was the last time you saw Clare?'   '**A few** days ago.' (= some days ago)

Compare **little** and **a little**, **few** and **a few**:

- He spoke **little** English, so it was difficult to communicate with him.
  He spoke **a little** English, so we were able to communicate with him.
- She's lucky. She has **few** problems. (= not many problems)
  Things are not going so well for her. She has **a few** problems. (= some problems)

You can say **only a little** and **only a few**:

- Hurry! We **only** have **a little** time. (*not* only little time)
- The village was very small. There were **only a few** houses. (*not* only few houses)

Countable and uncountable ➔ Units 69–70

Exercises

87.1 In some of these sentences **much** is incorrect or unnatural. Change **much** to **many** or **a lot (of)** where necessary. Write **'OK'** if the sentence is correct.

1 We didn't spend much money.   OK
2 Sue drinks <u>much tea</u>.   a lot of tea
3 Joe always puts much salt on his food.
4 We'll have to hurry. We don't have much time.
5 It cost much to repair the car.
6 Did it cost much to repair the car?
7 I don't know much people in this town.
8 Mike travels much.
9 There wasn't much traffic this morning.
10 You need much money to travel round the world.

87.2 Complete the sentences using **plenty** or **plenty of** + the following:

> hotels   money   room   ~~time~~   to learn   to see

1 There's no need to hurry. There's ___plenty of time.___
2 He doesn't have any financial problems.   He has
3 Come and sit with us.   There's
4 She knows a lot, but she still has
5 It's an interesting town to visit.   There
6 I'm sure we'll find somewhere to stay.

87.3 Put in **much/many/little/few** (one word only).

1 She isn't very popular. She has ___few___ friends.
2 Ann is very busy these days. She has _____ free time.
3 Did you take _____ pictures when you were on holiday?
4 I'm not very busy today. I don't have _____ to do.
5 This is a very modern city. There are _____ old buildings.
6 The weather has been very dry recently. We've had _____ rain.
7 'Do you know Rome?' 'No, I haven't been there for _____ years.'

87.4 Put in **a (a few, a little)** where necessary. Write **'OK'** if the sentence is already complete.

1 She's lucky. She has <u>few problems</u>.   OK
2 Things are not going so well for her. She has <u>few problems</u>.   a few problems
3 Can you lend me <u>few dollars</u>?
4 There was <u>little traffic</u>, so the journey didn't take very long.
5 I can't give you a decision yet. I need <u>little time</u> to think.
6 It was a surprise that he won the match. <u>Few people</u>
    expected him to win.
7 I don't know much Spanish – <u>only few words</u>.
8 I wonder how Sam is. I haven't seen him for <u>few months</u>.

87.5 Put in **little / a little / few / a few**.

1 Gary is very busy with his job. He has ___little___ time for other things.
2 Listen carefully. I'm going to give you _____ advice.
3 Do you mind if I ask you _____ questions?
4 It's not a very interesting place to visit, so _____ tourists come here.
5 I don't think Amy would be a good teacher. She has _____ patience.
6 'Would you like milk in your coffee?' 'Yes, _____.'
7 This is a very boring place to live. There's _____ to do.
8 'Have you ever been to Paris?' 'Yes, I've been there _____ times.'

All / all of   most / most of   no / none of etc.

A

all	some	any	most	much/many	little/few	no

You can use the words in the box with a noun (**some food / few books** etc.):
- ○ **All cars** have wheels.
- ○ **Some cars** can go faster than others.
- ○ *(on a notice)* **NO CARS**. (= no cars allowed)
- ○ **Many people** drive too fast.
- ○ I don't go out very often. I'm at home **most days**.

You cannot say 'all of cars', 'some of people' etc. (see also Section B):
- ○ **Some people** learn languages more easily than others. (*not* Some of people)

Note that we say **most** (*not* the most):
- ○ **Most tourists** don't visit this part of the town. (*not* The most tourists)

B

all	some	any	most	much/many	little/few	half	none

You can use these words with **of** (**some of** / **most of** etc.).

We use | **some of** **most of** **none of** etc. | + | the ...   my ... this ...   these ... that ...   those ... etc. |

So you can say:
  some **of the people**, some **of those people** (*but not* some of people)
  most **of my time**, most **of the time** (*but not* most of time)

- ○ **Some of the people I work with** are not very friendly.
- ○ **None of this money** is mine.
- ○ Have you read **any of these books**?
- ○ I was sick yesterday. I spent **most of the day** in bed.

You don't need **of** after **all** or **half**. So you can say:
- ○ **All my friends** live in Los Angeles. *or* All **of** my friends …
- ○ **Half this money** is mine. *or* Half **of** this money …

Compare:
- ○ **All flowers** are beautiful. (= all flowers in general)
  All (of) **the flowers in this garden** are beautiful. (= a specific group of flowers)
- ○ **Most problems** have a solution. (= most problems in general)
  We were able to solve **most of the problems we had**. (= a specific group of problems)

C

You can use **all of / some of / none of** etc. + **it/us/you/them**:
- ○ 'How many of these people do you know?' '**None of them. / A few of them**.'
- ○ Do **any of you** want to come to a party tonight?
- ○ 'Do you like this music?' '**Some of it**. Not **all of it**.'

We say: **all of us / all of you / half of it / half of them** etc. You need **of** before **it/us/you/them**:
- ○ **All of us** were late. (*not* all us)
- ○ I haven't finished the book yet. I've only read **half of it**. (*not* half it)

D

You can also use **some/most** etc. alone, *without* a noun:
- ○ Some cars have four doors and **some** have two.
- ○ A few of the shops were open, but **most** (of them) were closed.
- ○ Half this money is mine, and **half** (of it) is yours. (*not* the half)

All ➜ Units 75B, 90, 110D   Some and any ➜ Unit 85   No and none ➜ Unit 86
Much/many/little/few ➜ Unit 87   All of whom / most of which etc. ➜ Unit 96B

Exercises

88.1 Put in **of** where necessary. Leave the space empty if the sentence is already complete.

1 All ____–____ cars have wheels. *(the sentence is already complete)*
2 None ___of___ this money is mine.
3 Some _____ films are very violent.
4 Some _____ the films I've seen recently have been very violent.
5 Joe never goes to museums. He says that all _____ museums are boring.
6 I think some _____ people watch too much TV.
7 'Do you want any _____ these magazines?' 'No, I've finished with them.'
8 Kate has lived in London most _____ her life.
9 Joe has lived in Chicago all _____ his life.
10 Most _____ days I get up before 7 o'clock.

88.2 Choose from the list and complete the sentences. Use **of** (**some of / most of** etc.) where necessary.

accidents	European countries	my dinner	the players
birds	her friends	my spare time	the population
~~cars~~	her opinions	the buildings	~~these books~~

1 I haven't read many ___of these books___ .
2 All ___cars___ have wheels.
3 I spend much _____ gardening.
4 Many _____ are caused by bad driving.
5 It's a historic town. Many _____ are over 400 years old.
6 When she got married, she kept it a secret. She didn't tell any _____ .
7 Not many people live in the north of the country. Most _____ live in the south.
8 Not all _____ can fly. For example, the penguin can't fly.
9 Our team played badly and lost the game. None _____ played well.
10 Emma and I have very different ideas. I don't agree with many _____ .
11 Sarah travels a lot in Europe. She has been to most _____ .
12 I had no appetite. I could only eat half _____ .

88.3 Use your own ideas to complete these sentences.

1 The building was damaged in the explosion. All ___the windows___ were broken.
2 We argue sometimes, but get on well most of _____ .
3 I went to the cinema by myself. None of _____ wanted to come.
4 The test was difficult. I could only answer half _____ .
5 Some of _____ you took at the wedding were very good.
6 'Did you spend all _____ I gave you?' 'No, there's still some left.'

88.4 Complete the sentences. Use:

all of / some of / none of + it/them/us (all of it / some of them etc.)

1 These books are all Jane's.   ___None of them___ belong to me.
2 How many of these books have you read?'   '_____ . Every one.'
3 We all got wet in the rain because _____ had an umbrella.
4 Some of this money is yours and _____ is mine.
5 I asked some people for directions, but _____ was able to help me.
6 She invented the whole story from beginning to end. _____ was true.
7 Not all the tourists in the group were Spanish. _____ were French.
8 I watched most of the film, but not _____ .

Both / both of   neither / neither of
either / either of

A

We use **both/neither/either** for *two* things. You can use these words with a *noun* (**both books**, **neither book** etc.).

For example, you are going out to eat. There are two possible restaurants. You say:
- ☐ **Both restaurants** are very good.   (*not* The both restaurants)
- ☐ **Neither restaurant** is expensive.
- ☐ We can go to **either restaurant**. I don't mind.
  (**either** = one or the other, it doesn't matter which one)

You can also use **both/neither/either** alone, *without* a noun:
- ☐ I couldn't decide which of the two shirts to buy. I liked **both**.   (*or* I liked **both** of them.)
- ☐ 'Is your friend British or American?'   '**Neither**. She's Australian.'
- ☐ 'Do you want tea or coffee?'   '**Either**. I don't mind.'

B

Both of … / **neither of** … / **either of** …

We use **both of / neither of / either of + the/these/my/Tom's** … etc. So we say 'both of **the** restaurants', 'both of **those** restaurants' etc. (*but not* both of restaurants):
- ☐ **Both of these** restaurants are very good.
- ☐ **Neither of the** restaurants we went to was (*or* were) expensive.
- ☐ I haven't been to **either of those** restaurants.   (= I haven't been to one or the other)

You don't need **of** after **both**. So you can say:
- ☐ **Both my parents** are from Egypt.   *or*   Both **of** my parents …

You can use **both of / neither of / either of + us/you/them**:
- ☐ *(talking to two people)* Can **either of you** speak Russian?
- ☐ I asked two people the way to the station, but **neither of them** could help me.

You must say 'both **of**' before **us/you/them**:
- ☐ **Both of us** were very tired.   (*not* Both us were …)

After **neither of** … a *singular* or a *plural* verb is possible:
- ☐ Neither of the children **wants** (*or* **want**) to go to bed.

C

You can say:

both … **and** …	☐ **Both** Chris **and** Paul were late.
	☐ I was **both** tired **and** hungry when I arrived home.
neither … **nor** …	☐ **Neither** Chris **nor** Paul came to the party.
	☐ There was an accident in the street where we live, but we **neither** saw **nor** heard anything.
either … **or** …	☐ I'm not sure where Maria's from. She's **either** Spanish **or** Italian.
	☐ **Either** you apologise, **or** I'll never speak to you again.

D

Compare **either/neither/both** (two things) and **any/none/all** (more than two):

☐ There are **two** good hotels here. You could stay at **either** of them.	☐ There are **many** good hotels here. You could stay at **any** of them.
☐ We tried **two** hotels. { **Neither** of them had any rooms. { **Both** of them were full.	☐ We tried **a lot of** hotels. { **None** of them had any rooms. { **All** of them were full.

Neither do I / I don't either ➜ Unit 51C   Both of whom / neither of which ➜ Unit 96B
Both ➜ Unit 110D

Exercises

89.1 Complete the sentences with **both/neither/either**.

1 'Do you want tea or coffee?'   ' *Either* . I really don't mind.'
2 'What day is it today – the 18th or the 19th?'   '...................... . It's the 20th.'
3 A: Where did you go on your trip – Korea or Japan?
   B: We went to .... A week in Korea and a week in Japan.
4 'Shall we sit in the corner or by the window?'   '...................... . I don't mind.'
5 'Where's Lisa? Is she at work or at home?'   '...................... . She's away on holiday.'

89.2 Complete the sentences with **both/neither/either**. Use **of** where necessary.

1 ...*Both*... my parents are from London.
2 To get to the town centre, you can go along the footpath by the river or you can go along the road. You can go .... way.
3 I tried twice to phone Carl, but .... times he was out.
4 .... Tom's parents is English. His father is Polish and his mother is Italian.
5 I saw an accident this morning. One car drove into the back of another. Fortunately .... driver was injured, but .... cars were badly damaged.
6 I've got two sisters and a brother. My brother is working, but .... my sisters are still at school.

89.3 Complete the sentences with **both/neither/either + of us / of them**.

1 I asked two people the way to the station, but *neither of them* could help me.
2 I was invited to two parties last week, but I couldn't go to ....
3 There were two windows in the room. It was very warm, so I opened ....
4 Sarah and I play tennis together regularly, but we're not very good. .... can play very well.
5 I tried two bookshops for the book I wanted, but .... had it.

89.4 Write sentences with **both ... and ... / neither ... nor ... / either ... or ...** .

1 Chris was late. So was Pat.   *Both Chris and Pat were late.*
2 He didn't say hello, and he didn't smile.   *He neither said hello nor smiled.*
3 Joe is on holiday and so is Sam.
   ....
4 Joe doesn't have a car. Sam doesn't have one either.
   ....
5 Brian doesn't watch TV and he doesn't read newspapers.
   ....
6 It was a boring movie. It was long too.
   The movie ....
7 Is that man's name Richard? Or is it Robert? It's one of the two.
   That man's name ....
8 I haven't got time to go on holiday. And I don't have the money.
   I have ....
9 We can leave today or we can leave tomorrow – whichever you prefer.
   We ....

89.5 Complete the sentences with **neither/either/none/any**.

1 We tried a lot of hotels, but ...*none*... of them had any rooms.
2 I took two books with me on holiday, but I didn't read .... of them.
3 I took five books with me on holiday, but I didn't read .... of them.
4 There are a few shops at the end of the street, but .... of them sells newspapers.
5 You can phone me at .... time during the evening. I'm always at home.
6 I can meet you next Monday or Friday. Would .... of those days suit you?
7 John and I couldn't get into the house because .... of us had a key.

A

All and everybody/everyone

We do not normally use **all** to mean **everybody/everyone**:
- ○ **Everybody** had a great time at the party. (*not* All had a great time)

But we say **all of us / all of you / all of them**:
- ○ **All of us** had a great time at the party. (*not* Everybody of us)

B

All and everything

Sometimes you can use **all** or **everything**:
- ○ I'll do **all I can** to help. *or* I'll do **everything I can** to help.

You can say 'all **I can**' / 'all **you need**' etc., but we do not normally use **all** *alone*:
- ○ He thinks he knows **everything**. (*not* he knows all)
- ○ Our holiday was a disaster. **Everything** went wrong. (*not* All went wrong)

But you can say **all about**:
- ○ He knows **all about** computers.

We also use **all** (*not* everything) to mean 'the only thing(s)':
- ○ **All** I've eaten today is a sandwich. (= the only thing I've eaten today)

C

Every / everybody / everyone / everything are *singular* words, so we use a *singular* verb:
- ○ **Every seat** in the theatre **was** taken.
- ○ **Everybody has** arrived. (*not* have arrived)

But we use **they/them/their** after **everybody/everyone**:
- ○ **Everybody** said **they** enjoyed **themselves**. (= everybody enjoyed himself or herself)

D

Whole and all

Whole = complete, entire. Most often we use **whole** with *singular* nouns:
- ○ Did you read **the whole book**? (= all the book, not just a part of it)
- ○ Emily has lived **her whole life** in the same town.
- ○ I was so hungry, I ate **a whole packet** of biscuits. (= a complete packet)

We use **the/my/her** etc. before **whole**. Compare **whole** and **all**:
- **her whole life** *but* **all her life**

We do not normally use **whole** with *uncountable* nouns. We say:
- ○ I've spent **all the money** you gave me. (*not* the whole money)

E

Every/all/whole with time words

We use **every** to say how often something happens (**every day / every Monday / every ten minutes / every three weeks** etc.):
- ○ When we were on holiday, we went to the beach **every day**. (*not* all days)
- ○ The bus service is excellent. There's a bus **every ten minutes**.
- ○ We don't see each other very often – about **every six months**.

All day / the whole day = the complete day from beginning to end:
- ○ We spent **all day / the whole day** on the beach.
- ○ Dan was very quiet. He didn't say a word **all evening / the whole evening**.

Note that we say **all day** (*not* all the day), **all week** (*not* all the week) etc.

Compare **all the time** and **every time**:
- ○ They never go out. They are at home **all the time**. (= always, continuously)
- ○ **Every time** I see you, you look different. (= each time, on every occasion)

Countable and uncountable ➜ Units 69–70   **All / all of** ➜ Unit 88   **Each** and **every** ➜ Unit 91
Every one ➜ Unit 91D   **All** (word order) ➜ Unit 110D

Exercises

90.1 Complete these sentences with **all**, **everything** or **everybody/everyone**.

1 It was a good party. ___Everybody___ had a great time.
2 ___All___ I've eaten today is a sandwich.
3 _____ has their faults. Nobody is perfect.
4 Nothing has changed. _____ is the same as it was.
5 Kate told me _____ about her new job. It sounds quite interesting.
6 Can _____ write their names on a piece of paper, please?
7 Why are you always thinking about money? Money isn't _____ .
8 I didn't have much money with me. _____ I had was ten pounds.
9 When the fire alarm rang, _____ left the building immediately.
10 Sarah didn't say where she was going. _____ she said was that she was going away.
11 We have completely different opinions. I disagree with _____ she says.
12 We all did well in the exam. _____ in our class passed.
13 We all did well in the exam. _____ of us passed.
14 Why are you so lazy? Why do you expect me to do _____ for you?

90.2 Write sentences with **whole**.

1 I read the book from beginning to end. ___I read the whole book.___
2 Everyone in the team played well.
   The _____
3 Paul opened a box of chocolates. When he finished eating, there were no chocolates left in the box. He ate _____
4 The police came to the house. They were looking for something. They searched everywhere, every room. They _____
5 Everyone in Ed and Jane's family plays tennis. Ed and Jane play, and so do all their children. The _____
6 Ann worked from early in the morning until late in the evening.
   _____
7 Jack and Lisa had a week's holiday by the sea. It rained from the beginning of the week to the end. It _____

Now write sentences 6 and 7 again using **all** instead of **whole**.

8 (6) Ann _____
9 (7) _____

90.3 Complete these sentences using **every** with the following:

| five minutes | ~~ten minutes~~ | four hours | six months | four years |

1 The bus service is very good. There's a bus ___every ten minutes___ .
2 Tom is ill. He has some medicine. He has to take it _____ .
3 The Olympic Games take place _____ .
4 We live near a busy airport. A plane flies over our house _____ .
5 Martin goes to the dentist for a check-up _____ .

90.4 Which is the correct alternative?

1 I've spent ~~the whole money~~ / all the money you gave me. (all the money *is correct*)
2 Sue works every day / all days except Sunday.
3 I'm tired. I've been working hard all the day / all day.
4 It was a terrible fire. Whole building / The whole building was destroyed.
5 I've been trying to contact her, but every time / all the time I phone there's no answer.
6 I don't like the weather here. It rains every time / all the time.
7 When I was on holiday, all my luggage / my whole luggage was stolen.

→ Additional exercise 30 (page 320)

Each and every

A

Each and **every** are similar in meaning. Often it is possible to use **each** or **every**:

- ○ **Each** time (or **Every** time) I see you, you look different.
- ○ There are computers in **each** classroom (or **every** classroom) in the school.

But **each** and **every** are not exactly the same. Study the difference:

We use **each** when we think of things separately, one by one. ○ Study **each sentence** carefully. (= study the sentences one by one) each = X + X + X + X **Each** is more usual for a small number: ○ There were four books on the table. **Each book** was a different colour. ○ (in a card game) At the beginning of the game, **each player** has three cards.	We use **every** when we think of things as a group. The meaning is similar to **all**. ○ **Every sentence** must have a verb. (= all sentences in general) every = (XXXXXXXXXXX XXXXXXXXXXX XXXXXXXXXXX) **Every** is more usual for a large number: ○ Kate loves reading. She has read **every book** in the library. (= all the books) ○ I'd like to visit **every country** in the world. (= all the countries)

Each (but not **every**) can be used for two things:
- ○ In football, **each team** has eleven players. (*not* every team)

We use **every** (not **each**) to say how often something happens:
- ○ 'How often do you use your car?' '**Every day**.' (*not* Each day)
- ○ There's a bus **every ten minutes**. (*not* each ten minutes)

B

Compare the structures we use with **each** and **every**:

You can use **each** with a noun:
  each book   **each student**
You can use **each** alone (without a noun):
○ None of the rooms was the same.
  Each (= each room) was different.
Or you can use **each one**:
○ **Each one** was different.
You can say **each of** (**the** … / **these** … / **them** etc.):
○ Read **each of these** sentences carefully.
○ **Each of the** books is a different colour.
○ **Each of them** is a different colour.
	You can use **every** with a noun:
	  every book **every student**
	You can't use **every** alone, but you can say **every one**:
	○ A: Have you read all these books?
	  B: Yes, **every one**.
	
	You can say **every one of** … (*but not* 'every of'):
	
	○ I've read **every one of those** books.
	(*not* every of those books)
	○ I've read **every one of them**.

C

You can also use **each** in the middle or at the end of a sentence. For example:
- ○ The students were **each** given a book. (= Each student was given a book.)
- ○ These oranges cost 40 pence **each**.

D

Everyone and **every one**

Everyone (one word) is only for people (= everybody).

Every one (two words) is for things or people, and is similar to **each one** (see Section B).
- ○ **Everyone** enjoyed the party. (= **Everybody** …)
- ○ Sarah is invited to lots of parties and she goes to **every one**. (= to **every party**)

Each other ➜ Unit 82C   All and every ➜ Unit 90

Exercises

91.1 Look at the pictures and complete the sentences with **each** or **every**.

1 ....Each.... player has three cards.
2 Kate has read ....every.... book in the library.
3 .... side of a square is the same length.
4 .... seat in the theatre was taken.
5 There are six apartments in the building. .... one has a balcony.
6 There's a train to London .... hour.
7 She was wearing four rings – one on .... finger.
8 Our football team is playing well. We've won .... game this season.

91.2 Put in **each** or **every**.

1 There were four books on the table. ....Each.... book was a different colour.
2 The Olympic Games are held ....every.... four years.
3 .... parent worries about their children.
4 In a game of tennis there are two or four players. .... player has a racket.
5 Nicola plays volleyball .... Thursday evening.
6 I understood most of what they said but not .... word.
7 The book is divided into five parts and .... of these has three sections.
8 I get paid .... four weeks.
9 I called the office two or three times, but .... time it was closed.
10 Car seat belts save lives. .... driver should wear one.
11 A friend of mine has three children. I always give .... of them a present at Christmas.
12 *(from an exam)* Answer all five questions. Write your answer to .... question on a separate sheet of paper.

91.3 Complete the sentences using **each**.

1 The price of one of those oranges is 30 pence. _Those oranges are 30 pence each_ .
2 I had ten pounds and so did Sonia. Sonia and I ....
3 One of those postcards costs 80 pence. Those ....
4 The hotel was expensive. I paid £150 and so did you. We ....

91.4 Put in **everyone** (1 word) or **every one** (2 words).

1 Sarah is invited to a lot of parties and she goes to ....every one.... .
2 As soon as .... had arrived, we began the meeting.
3 I asked her lots of questions and she answered .... correctly.
4 Amy is very popular. .... likes her.
5 I dropped a tray of glasses. Unfortunately .... broke.

A

Look at this example sentence:

> The woman | who lives next door | is a doctor.
> └── relative clause ──┘

A *clause* is a part of a sentence. A *relative clause* tells us which person or thing (or what kind of person or thing) the speaker means:

- The woman **who lives next door** ... ('who lives next door' tells us which woman)
- People **who live in the country** ... ('who live in the country' tells us what kind of people)

We use **who** in a relative clause when we are talking about people (not things):

> the woman – she lives next door – is a doctor
>
> ⟶ The woman **who lives next door** is a doctor.
>
> we know a lot of people – they live in the country
>
> ⟶ We know a lot of people **who live in the country**.

- An architect is someone **who designs buildings**.
- What was the name of the person **who phoned**?
- Anyone **who wants to apply for the job** must do so by Friday.

You can also use **that** (instead of **who**), but you can't use **which** for people:

- The woman **that lives next door** is a doctor. (*not* the woman which)

Sometimes you must use **who** (*not* that) for people – see Unit 95.

B

When we are talking about things, we use **that** or **which** (*not* who) in a relative clause:

> where is the cheese? – it was in the fridge
>
> ⟶ Where is the cheese { **that** / **which** } **was in the fridge?**

- I don't like stories **that have unhappy endings**. (*or* stories **which** have ...)
- Grace works for a company **that makes furniture**. (*or* a company **which** makes furniture)
- The machine **that broke down** is working again now. (*or* The machine **which** broke down)

That is more usual than **which**, but sometimes you must use **which** – see Unit 95.

C

Remember that in relative clauses we use **who/that/which**, not **he/she/they/it**.
Compare:

- 'Who's that woman?' '**She** lives next door to me.'
  I've never spoken to the woman **who** lives next door. (*not* the woman she lives)

- Where is the cheese? **It** was in the fridge.
  Where is the cheese **that** was in the fridge? (*not* the cheese it was)

D

What = 'the thing(s) that'. Compare **what** and **that**:
- **What happened** was my fault. (= the thing that happened)

but

- Everything **that happened** was my fault. (*not* Everything what happened)
- The machine **that broke down** is now working again. (*not* The machine what broke down)

Relative clauses 2–5 ➜ Units 93–96

Exercises

92.1 In this exercise you have to explain what some words mean. Choose the right meaning from the box and then write a sentence with **who**. Use a dictionary if necessary.

he/she { steals from a shop <s>designs buildings</s> doesn't believe in God is not brave	he/she { buys something from a shop pays rent to live in a house or apartment breaks into a house to steal things expects the worst to happen

1 (an architect)   _An architect is someone who designs buildings._
2 (a burglar) A burglar is someone ....
3 (a customer) ....
4 (a shoplifter) ....
5 (a coward) ....
6 (an atheist) ....
7 (a pessimist) ....
8 (a tenant) ....

92.2 Make one sentence from two. Use **who/that/which**.

1 A girl was injured in the accident. She is now in hospital.
    The girl who was injured in the accident is now in hospital.
2 A waitress served us. She was impolite and impatient.
    The ....
3 A building was destroyed in the fire. It has now been rebuilt.
    The ....
4 Some people were arrested. They have now been released.
    The ....
5 A bus goes to the airport. It runs every half hour.
    The ....

92.3 Complete the sentences. Choose from the box and make a relative clause.

invented the telephone **runs away from home** **stole my wallet** **were hanging on the wall**	<s>makes furniture</s> **gives you the meaning of words** **can support life** **cannot be explained**

1 Helen works for a company ......_that makes furniture_.................................... .
2 The book is about a girl ....
3 What happened to the pictures .... ?
4 A mystery is something ....
5 The police have arrested the man ....
6 A dictionary is a book ....
7 Alexander Bell was the man ....
8 It seems that Earth is the only planet ....

92.4 Are these sentences right or wrong? Correct them where necessary.

1 I don't like stories who have unhappy endings.   _stories that have_
2 What was the name of the person who phoned?   _OK_
3 Where's the nearest shop who sells bread?   ....
4 The driver which caused the accident was fined £500.   ....
5 Do you know the person that took these pictures?   ....
6 We live in a world what is changing all the time.   ....
7 Dan said some things about me that were not true.   ....
8 What was the name of the horse it won the race?   ....

Relative clauses 2: clauses with and without **who/that/which**

A

Look at these example sentences from Unit 92:

- ◯ The woman **who** lives next door is a doctor.   (*or* The woman **that** lives …)

    | The woman | lives next door. | **who** (= the woman) is the *subject*

- ◯ Where is the cheese **that** was in the fridge?   (*or* the cheese **which** was …)

    | The cheese | was in the fridge.   **that** (= the cheese) is the *subject*

You must use **who/that/which** when it is the *subject* of the relative clause. So you cannot say 'The woman lives next door is a doctor.' or 'Where is the cheese was in the fridge?'.

B

Sometimes **who/that/which** is the *object* of the verb. For example:

- ◯ The woman **who I wanted to see** was away on holiday.

    | I wanted to see | the woman | **who** (= the woman) is the *object*
    I is the *subject*

- ◯ Have you found the keys **that you lost**?

    | You lost | the keys. | **that** (= the keys) is the *object*
    you is the *subject*.

When **who/that/which** is the object, you can leave it out. So you can say:

- ◯ **The woman I wanted to see** was away.   *or*   The woman **who** I wanted to see …
- ◯ Have you found **the keys you lost**?   *or*   … the keys **that** you lost?
- ◯ **The dress Lisa bought** doesn't fit her very well.   *or*   The dress **that** Lisa bought …
- ◯ Is there **anything I can do**?   *or*   … anything **that** I can do?

Note that we say:

> **the keys you lost**   (*not* the keys you lost them)
> **the dress Lisa bought**   (*not* the dress Lisa bought it)

C

Note the position of prepositions (**in/to/for** etc.) in relative clauses:

> Tom is talking to a woman – do you know her?

> ⟶ Do you know the woman (who/that) Tom is talking to ?

> I slept in a bed last night – it wasn't very comfortable

> ⟶ The bed (that/which) I slept in last night wasn't very comfortable.

- ◯ Are these the books **you were looking for**?   *or*   … the books **that/which** you were …
- ◯ The woman **he fell in love with** left him after a month.   *or*   The woman **who/that** he …
- ◯ The man **I was sitting next to on the plane** talked all the time.   *or*
    The man **who/that** I was sitting next to …

Note that we say:

> **the books you were looking for**   (*not* the books you were looking for them)

D

You cannot use **what** in sentences like these (see also Unit 92D):

- ◯ Everything **(that) they said** was true.   (*not* Everything what they said)
- ◯ I gave her all the money **(that) I had**.   (*not* all the money what I had)

What = the thing(s) that:

- ◯ Did you hear **what they said**?   (= the things that they said)

Relative clauses 1 ➔ **Unit 92**   Relative clauses 3–5 ➔ **Units 94–96**   Whom ➔ **Unit 94B**

Exercises

93.1 **In some of these sentences you need who or that. Correct the sentences where necessary.**

1 The <u>woman lives next door</u> is a doctor.   *The woman who lives next door*
2 Have you found the keys you lost?   *OK*
3 The people we met last night were very nice.
4 The people work in the office are very nice.
5 The people I work with are very nice.
6 What have you done with the money I gave you?
7 What happened to the money was on the table?
8 What's the worst film you've ever seen?
9 What's the best thing it has ever happened to you?

93.2 **What do you say in these situations? Complete each sentence with a relative clause.**

1 Your friend lost some keys. You want to know if he has found them. You say:
Have you found   *the keys you lost* ?
2 A friend is wearing a dress. You like it. You tell her:
I like the dress ....
3 A friend is going to see a film. You want to know the name of the film. You say:
What's the name of the film .... ?
4 You wanted to visit a museum. It was shut when you got there. You tell a friend:
The museum .... was shut when we got there.
5 You invited some people to your party. Some of them couldn't come. You tell someone:
Some of the people .... couldn't come.
6 Your friend had to do some work. You want to know if she has finished. You say:
Have you finished the work .... ?
7 You rented a car. It broke down after a few miles. You tell a friend:
The car .... broke down after a few miles.

93.3 **These sentences all have a relative clause with a preposition. Put the words in the correct order.**

1 Did you find (looking / for / you / the books / were)?
Did you find   *the books you were looking for* ?
2 We couldn't go to (we / invited / to / were / the wedding).
We couldn't go to ....
3 What's the name of (the hotel / about / me / told / you)?
What's the name of .... ?
4 Unfortunately I didn't get (applied / I / the job / for).
Unfortunately I didn't get ....
5 Did you enjoy (you / the concert / to / went)?
Did you enjoy .... ?
6 Gary is a good person to know. He's (on / rely / can / somebody / you).
Gary is a good person to know. He's ....
7 Who was (the man / were / with / you) in the restaurant last night?
Who was .... in the restaurant last night?

93.4 **Put in that or what where necessary. If the sentence is already complete, leave the space empty.**

1 I gave her all the money ......–...... I had. (all the money **that** I had *is also correct*)
2 Did you hear ....*what*.... they said?
3 They give their children everything .... they want.
4 Tell me .... you want and I'll try to get it for you.
5 Why do you blame me for everything .... goes wrong?
6 I won't be able to do much, but I'll do .... I can.
7 I won't be able to do much, but I'll do the best .... I can.
8 I don't agree with .... you've just said.
9 I don't trust him. I don't believe anything .... he says.

Relative clauses 3: **whose/whom/where**

A Whose

We use **whose** in relative clauses instead of **his/her/their**:

> we helped some people – their car had broken down
>
> → We helped some people **whose** **car had broken down**.

We use **whose** mostly for people:

- ○ A widow is a woman **whose husband is dead**.   (**her** husband is dead)
- ○ What's the name of the man **whose car you borrowed**?   (you borrowed **his** car)
- ○ I met someone **whose brother I went to school with**.   (I went to school with **his/her** brother)

Compare **who** and **whose**:

- ○ I met a man **who** knows you.   (**he** knows you)
- ○ I met a man **whose sister** knows you.   (**his sister** knows you)

B Whom

Whom is possible instead of **who** when it is the *object* of the verb in the relative clause (like the sentences in Unit 93B):

- ○ George is a person **whom I admire** very much.   (I admire **him**)

You can also use **whom** with a preposition (**to whom / from whom / with whom** etc.):

- ○ I like the people **with whom I work**.   (I work **with them**)

Whom is a formal word and we do not often use it in this way. We usually prefer **who** or **that**, or nothing (see Unit 93). So we usually say:

- ○ … a person **who/that** I admire a lot   *or*   … a person **I admire** a lot
- ○ … the people **who/that** I work with   *or*   … the people **I work with**

C Where

You can use **where** in a relative clause to talk about a place:

> the restaurant – we had lunch there – it was near the airport
>
> → The restaurant **where** **we had lunch** was near the airport.

- ○ I recently went back to **the town where I grew up**.
  (*or* … the town I grew up in   *or* … the town **that** I grew up in)
- ○ I would like to live in **a place where there is plenty of sunshine**.

D We say:

the day / the year / the time etc. { something happens   *or*
                                          that something happens

- ○ I can't meet you on Friday. That's **the day (that) I'm going away**.
- ○ **The last time (that) I saw Anna**, she looked great.
- ○ I haven't seen Jack and Helen since **the year (that) they got married**.

E We say:

the reason { something happens   *or*
                 that/why something happens

- ○ **The reason I'm phoning** is to ask your advice.
  (*or* The reason that I'm phoning / The reason **why** I'm phoning)

Relative clauses 1–2 → Units 92–93   Relative clauses 4–5 → Units 95–96   Whom → Unit 96

Exercises

94.1 You met these people at a party:

The next day you tell a friend about these people. Complete the sentences using **who** or **whose**.

1 I met somebody ....whose mother writes detective stories........... .
2 I met a man ....
3 I met a woman ....
4 I met somebody ....
5 I met a couple ....
6 I met somebody ....

94.2 Read the situations and complete the sentences using **where**.

1 You grew up in a small town. You went back there recently. You tell someone this.
  I recently went back to ....the small town where I grew up.............. .
2 You're thirsty and you want a drink. You ask a friend where you can get some water.
  Is there a shop near here ....?
3 You work in a factory. The factory is going to close down next month. You tell a friend.
  The .... is going to close down next month.
4 Sue is staying at a hotel. You want to know the name of the hotel. You ask a friend.
  Do you know the name of ....?
5 You play football in a park on Sundays. You show a friend the park. You say:
  This is the .... on Sundays.

94.3 Complete each sentence using **who/whom/whose/where**.

1 What's the name of the man ......whose..... car you borrowed?
2 A cemetery is a place .... people are buried.
3 A pacifist is a person .... believes that all wars are wrong.
4 An orphan is a child .... parents are dead.
5 What was the name of the person to .... you spoke on the phone?
6 The place .... we spent our holidays was really beautiful.
7 This school is only for children .... first language is not English.
8 The woman with .... he fell in love left him after a month.

94.4 Use your own ideas to complete these sentences. They are like the examples in Sections D and E.

1 I can't meet you on Friday. That's the day .....I'm going away.............. .
2 The reason .... was that the salary was too low.
3 I'll never forget the time ....
4 Do you remember the day ....?
5 The reason .... is that they don't need one.
6 .... was the year ....

Relative clauses 4: extra information clauses (1)

A

There are two types of relative clause. In these examples, the relative clauses are <u>underlined</u>. Compare:

Type 1
- ○ The woman <u>who lives next door</u> is a doctor.
- ○ Grace works for a company <u>that makes furniture</u>.
- ○ We stayed at the hotel <u>(that) you recommended</u>.

In these examples, the relative clauses tell you which person or thing (or what kind of person or thing) the speaker means:
'The woman **who lives next door**' tells us *which* woman.
'A company **that makes furniture**' tells us *what kind* of company.
'The hotel (**that**) **you recommended**' tells us *which* hotel.

We do not use commas (,) with these clauses:
- ○ We know a lot of people <u>who live in London</u>.

Type 2
- ○ My brother Ben, <u>who lives in Hong Kong</u>, is an architect.
- ○ Anna told me about her new job, <u>which she's enjoying a lot</u>.
- ○ We stayed at the Park Hotel, <u>which a friend of ours recommended</u>.

In these examples, the relative clauses do not tell you which person or thing the speaker means. We already know which thing or person is meant: 'My brother Ben', 'Anna's new job' and 'the Park Hotel'.
The relative clauses in these sentences give us *extra information* about the person or thing.

We use commas (,) with these clauses:
- ○ My brother Ben, <u>who lives in Hong Kong</u>, is an architect.

B

In both types of relative clause we use **who** for people and **which** for things. But:

Type 1
You can use **that**:
- ○ Do you know anyone **who/that** speaks French and Italian?
- ○ Grace works for a company **which/that** makes furniture.

You can leave out **who/which/that** when it is the object (see Unit 93):
- ○ We stayed at the hotel (that/which) you recommended.
- ○ This morning I met somebody (who/that) I hadn't seen for ages.

We do not often use **whom** in this type of clause (see Unit 94B).

Type 2
You cannot use **that**:
- ○ John, **who** (*not* that) speaks French and Italian, works as a tour guide.
- ○ Anna told me about her new job, **which** (*not* that) she's enjoying a lot.

You cannot leave out **who** or **which**:
- ○ We stayed at the Park Hotel, **which** a friend of ours recommended.
- ○ This morning I met Chris, **who** I hadn't seen for ages.

You can use **whom** for people (when it is the object):
- ○ This morning I met Chris, **whom** I hadn't seen for ages.

C

In both types of relative clause you can use **whose** and **where**:

- ○ We met some people **whose** car had broken down.
- ○ What's the name of the place **where** you went on holiday?

- ○ Lisa, **whose** car had broken down, was in a very bad mood.
- ○ Kate has just been to Sweden, **where** her daughter lives.

Relative clauses (Type 1) → **Units 92–94**   Relative clauses (Type 2) → **Unit 96**

Exercises

95.1 Make one sentence from two. Use the sentence in brackets to make a relative clause (Type 2). You will need to use **who(m)/whose/which/where**.

1 Catherine is very friendly. (She lives next door.)
   Catherine, who lives next door, is very friendly.

2 We stayed at the Park Hotel. (A friend of ours recommended it.)
   We stayed at the Park Hotel, which a friend of ours recommended.

3 We often go to visit our friends in Cambridge. (It is not far from London.)
   We often go to visit our friends in Cambridge ....

4 I went to see the doctor. (She told me I needed to change my diet.)
   I went to see ....

5 Steven is one of my closest friends. (I have known him for a very long time.)
   Steven ....

6 Lisa is away from home a lot. (Her job involves a lot of travelling.)
   Lisa ....

7 The new stadium will be finished next month. (It can hold 90,000 people.)
   ....

8 Alaska is the largest state in the USA. (My brother lives there.)
   ....

9 Our teacher was very kind. (I have forgotten her name.)
   ....

95.2 Read the information and complete each sentence. Use a relative clause of Type 1 or Type 2. Use commas where necessary.

1 There's a woman living next door to me. She's a doctor.
   The woman _who lives next door to me is a doctor._

2 I've got a brother called Ben. He lives in Hong Kong. He's an architect.
   My brother _Ben, who lives in Hong Kong, is an architect._

3 There was a strike at the factory. It began ten days ago. It is now over.
   The strike at the factory ....

4 I was looking for a book this morning. I've found it now.
   I've found ....

5 I've had my car for 15 years. It has never broken down.
   My car ....

6 A job was advertised. A lot of people applied for it. Few of them had the necessary qualifications.
   Few of ....

7 Amy has a son. She showed me a picture of him. He's a police officer.
   Amy showed me ....

95.3 Some of these sentences are wrong. Correct them and put in commas where necessary. If the sentence is correct, write 'OK'.

1 Anna told me about her new job that she's enjoying very much.
   Anna told me about her new job, **which** she's enjoying very much.

2 My office that is on the second floor is very small.
   ....

3 The office I'm using at the moment is very small.
   ....

4 Mark's father that used to be in the army now works for a TV company.
   ....

5 The doctor that examined me couldn't find anything wrong.
   ....

6 The sun that is one of millions of stars in the universe provides us with heat and light.
   ....

Relative clauses 5: extra information clauses (2)

A Prepositions + whom/which

You can use a *preposition* before **whom** (for people) and **which** (for things). So you can say:
to whom / with whom / about which / without which etc.
- ○ Mr Lee, **to whom** I spoke at the meeting, is very interested in our proposal.
- ○ Fortunately we had a good map, **without which** we would have got lost.

In informal English we often keep the preposition after the verb in the relative clause. When we do this, we normally use **who** (*not* whom) for people:
- ○ This is my friend from Canada, **who** I was telling you **about**.
- ○ Yesterday we visited the City Museum, **which** I'd never been **to** before.

B All of / most of etc. + whom/which

Study these examples:

> Helen has three brothers. All of them are married. *(2 sentences)*
>
> → Helen has three brothers, **all of whom** are married. *(1 sentence)*
>
> They asked me a lot of questions. I couldn't answer most of them . *(2 sentences)*
>
> → They asked me a lot of questions, **most of which** I couldn't answer. *(1 sentence)*

In the same way you can say:
none of / neither of / any of / either of
some of / many of / much of / (a) few of   } + **whom** (people)
both of / half of / each of / one of / two of etc. } + **which** (things)

- ○ Martin tried on three jackets, **none of which** fitted him.
- ○ Two men, **neither of whom** I had seen before, came into the office.
- ○ They have three cars, **two of which** they rarely use.
- ○ Sue has a lot of friends, **many of whom** she was at school with.

You can also say **the cause of which / the name of which** etc. :
- ○ The building was destroyed in a fire, **the cause of which** was never established.
- ○ We stayed at a beautiful hotel, **the name of which** I can't remember now.

C Which (*not* what)

Study this example:

> Joe got the job. This surprised everybody. *(2 sentences)*
>
> Joe got the job, **which** surprised everybody. *(1 sentence)*
> ——— relative clause ———

In this example, **which** = 'the fact that he got the job'. You must use **which** (*not* what) in sentences like these:
- ○ Sarah couldn't meet us, **which** was a shame. (*not* what was a shame)
- ○ The weather was good, **which** we hadn't expected. (*not* what we hadn't expected)

For **what**, see Units 92D and 93D.

All of / most of etc. ➡ Unit 88   Both of etc. ➡ Unit 89   Relative clauses 1–4 ➡ Units 92–95

Exercises

96.1 Write the relative clauses in a more formal way using a preposition + **whom/which**.

1 Yesterday we visited the City Museum, which I'd never been to before.
Yesterday we visited the City Museum, _to which I'd never been before_ .

2 My brother showed us his new car, which he's very proud of.
My brother showed us his new car, _____ .

3 This is a picture of our friends Chris and Sam, who we went on holiday with.
This is a picture of our friends Chris and Sam, _____ .

4 The wedding, which only members of the family were invited to, took place on Friday.
The wedding, _____ ,
took place on Friday.

96.2 Use the information in the first sentence to complete the second sentence. Use **all of / most of** etc. or **the … of + whom/which**.

1 All of Helen's brothers are married.
Helen has three brothers, _all of whom are married_ .

2 Most of the information we were given was useless.
We were given a lot of information, _____ .

3 None of the ten people who applied for the job was suitable.
Ten people applied for the job, _____ .

4 Kate hardly ever uses one of her computers.
Kate has got two computers, _____ .

5 Mike won £100,000. He gave half of it to his parents.
Mike won £100,000, _____ .

6 Both of Julia's sisters are lawyers.
Julia has two sisters, _____ .

7 Jane replied to neither of the emails I sent her.
I sent Jane two emails, _____ .

8 I went to a party – I knew only a few of the people there.
There were a lot of people at the party, _____ .

9 The sides of the road we drove along were lined with trees.
We drove along the road, the _____ .

10 The aim of the company's new business plan is to save money.
The company has a new business plan, _____ .

96.3 Join sentences from the boxes to make new sentences. Use **which**.

1 ~~Laura couldn't come to the party.~~
2 Jane doesn't have a phone.
3 Alex has passed his exams.
4 Our flight was delayed.
5 Kate offered to let me stay at her house.
6 The street I live in is very noisy at night.
7 Our car has broken down.

This was very kind of her.
This means we can't go away tomorrow.
This makes it difficult to contact her.
This makes it difficult to sleep sometimes.
~~This was a shame.~~
This is good news.
This meant we had to wait three hours at the airport.

1 Laura couldn't come to the party, _which was a shame._

2 Jane _____

3 _____

4 _____

5 _____

6 _____

7 _____

-ing and -ed clauses (the woman **talking to Tom**, the boy **injured in the accident**)

A

A *clause* is a part of a sentence. Some clauses begin with -**ing** or -**ed**. For example:

TOM

Do you know the woman **talking to Tom** ?
└─── -**ing** *clause* ───┘

the woman talking to Tom

The boy **injured in the accident** was taken to hospital.
└─── -**ed** *clause* ───┘

the boy injured in the accident

B

We use -**ing** clauses to say what somebody (or something) is (or was) doing at a particular time:

- ☐ Do you know the woman **talking to Tom**? (the woman **is talking** to Tom)
- ☐ Police **investigating the crime** are looking for three men. (police **are investigating** the crime)
- ☐ Who were those people **waiting outside**? (they **were waiting**)
- ☐ I was woken up by a bell **ringing**. (a bell **was ringing**)

You can also use an -**ing** clause to say what happens all the time, not just at a particular time. For example:
- ☐ The road **connecting the two villages** is very narrow. (the road **connects** the two villages)
- ☐ I have a large room **overlooking the garden**. (the room **overlooks** the garden)
- ☐ Can you think of the name of a flower **beginning with T**? (the name **begins** with T)

C

-**ed** clauses have a *passive* meaning:
- ☐ The boy **injured in the accident** was taken to hospital.
  (he **was injured** in the accident)
- ☐ George showed me some pictures **painted by his father**.
  (they **had been painted** by his father)

Injured and **painted** are *past participles*. Note that many past participles are irregular and do not end in -**ed** (**stolen/made/written** etc.):
- ☐ The police never found the money **stolen in the robbery**.
- ☐ Most of the goods **made in this factory** are exported.

D

We often use -**ing** and -**ed** clauses after **there is / there was** etc. :
- ☐ **There were** some children **swimming** in the river.
- ☐ **Is there** anybody **waiting**?
- ☐ **There was** a big red car **parked** outside the house.

You can use **left** in this way, with the meaning 'not used, still there':
- ☐ We've eaten nearly all the chocolates. There are only a few **left**.

See/hear somebody **doing** something ➜ Unit 67   -**ing** clauses ➜ Unit 68   **There (is)** ➜ Unit 84
Irregular past participles (**made/stolen** etc.) ➜ Appendix 1

Exercises

97.1 Make one sentence from two. Complete the sentences with an **-ing** clause.

1 A bell was ringing. I was woken up by it.
I was woken up by ___a bell ringing___ .

2 A man was sitting next to me on the plane. I didn't talk much to him.
I didn't talk much to the _____ .

3 A taxi was taking us to the airport. It broke down.
The _____ broke down.

4 There's a path at the end of this street. The path leads to the river.
At the end of the street there's a _____ .

5 A factory has just opened in the town. It employs 500 people.
A _____ has just opened in the town.

6 The company sent me a brochure. It contained the information I needed.
The company sent me _____ .

97.2 Make one sentence from two, beginning as shown. Each time make an **-ed** clause.

1 A boy was injured in the accident. He was taken to hospital.
The boy ___injured in the accident___ was taken to hospital.

2 A gate was damaged in the storm. It has now been repaired.
The gate _____ has now been repaired.

3 A number of suggestions were made at the meeting. Most of them were not very practical.
Most of the _____ were not very practical.

4 Some paintings were stolen from the museum. They haven't been found yet.
The _____ haven't been found yet.

5 A man was arrested by the police. What's his name?
What's the name of _____ ?

97.3 Complete the sentences using the following verbs in the correct form:

| blow | call | ~~invite~~ | live | offer | read | ~~ring~~ | sit | study | work |

1 I was woken up by a bell ___ringing___ .
2 Some of the people ___invited___ to the party can't come.
3 Life must be very unpleasant for people _____ near busy airports.
4 A few days after the interview, I received an email _____ me the job.
5 Somebody _____ Jack phoned while you were out.
6 There was a tree _____ down in the storm last night.
7 The waiting room was empty except for a young man _____ by the window
_____ a magazine.
8 Ian has a brother _____ in a bank in London and a sister _____
economics at university in Manchester.

97.4 Use the words in brackets to make sentences using **There is / There was** etc.

1 That house is empty. (nobody / live / in it) ___There's nobody living in it.___
2 The accident wasn't serious. (nobody / injure) ___There was nobody injured.___
3 I can hear footsteps. (somebody / come)
There _____
4 The train was full. (a lot of people / travel)
_____
5 We were the only guests at the hotel. (nobody else / stay there)
_____
6 The piece of paper was blank. (nothing / write / on it)
_____
7 The college offers English courses in the evening. (a course / begin / next Monday)
_____

A

Many adjectives end in **-ing** and **-ed**, for example: **boring** and **bored**. Study this example situation:

bored

boring

Jane has been doing the same job for a very long time. Every day she does exactly the same thing again and again. She doesn't enjoy her job any more and would like to do something different.

Jane's job is **boring**.

Jane is **bored** (with her job).

Somebody is **bored** if something (or somebody else) is **boring**. Or, if something is **boring**, it makes you **bored**. So:
- ○ Jane is **bored** because her job is **boring**.
- ○ Jane's job is **boring**, so Jane is **bored**.   (*not* Jane is boring)

If a person is **boring**, this means that they make other people **bored**:
- ○ George always talks about the same things. He's really **boring**.

B

Compare adjectives ending in **-ing** and **-ed**:

○ My job is { **boring**. **interesting**. **tiring**. **satisfying**. **depressing**. (etc.)

In these examples, the **-ing** adjective tells you about the job.

- ○ I'm **bored** with my job.
- ○ I'm not **interested** in my job any more.
- ○ I get very **tired** doing my job.
- ○ I'm not **satisfied** with my job.
- ○ My job makes me **depressed**. (etc.)

In these examples, the **-ed** adjective tells you how somebody feels (about the job).

Compare these examples:

interesting
- ○ Julia thinks politics is **interesting**.

- ○ Did you meet anyone **interesting** at the party?

surprising
- ○ It was **surprising** that he passed the exam.

disappointing
- ○ The movie was **disappointing**. We expected it to be much better.

shocking
- ○ The news was **shocking**.

interested
- ○ Julia is **interested** in politics. (*not* interesting in politics)
- ○ Are you **interested** in buying a car? I'm trying to sell mine.

surprised
- ○ Everybody was **surprised** that he passed the exam.

disappointed
- ○ We were **disappointed** with the movie. We expected it to be much better.

shocked
- ○ I was **shocked** when I heard the news.

Exercises

98.1 Complete the sentences for each situation. Use the word in brackets + **-ing** or **-ed**.

1 The movie wasn't as good as we had expected. (**disappoint**…)
   a The movie was __disappointing__ .
   b We were __disappointed__ with the movie.

2 Donna teaches young children. It's a very hard job, but she enjoys it.   (**exhaust**…)
   a She enjoys her job, but it's often _____ .
   b At the end of a day's work, she is often _____ .

3 It's been raining all day. I hate this weather. (**depress**…)
   a This weather is _____ .
   b This weather makes me _____ .
   c It's silly to get _____ because of the weather.

4 Clare is going to Mexico next month. She has never been there before.   (**excit**…)
   a It will be an _____ experience for her.
   b Going to new places is always _____ .
   c She is really _____ about going to Mexico.

98.2 Choose the correct word.

1 I was ~~disappointing~~ / disappointed with the film. I had expected it to be better.
   (disappointed *is correct*)
2 Are you interesting / interested in football?
3 The new project sounds exciting / excited. I'm looking forward to working on it.
4 It's embarrassing / embarrassed when you have to ask people for money.
5 Do you easily get embarrassing / embarrassed?
6 I had never expected to get the job. I was really amazing / amazed when I was offered it.
7 She has really learnt very fast. She has made amazing / amazed progress.
8 I didn't find the situation funny. I was not amusing / amused.
9 It was a really terrifying / terrified experience. Everybody was very shocking / shocked.
10 Why do you always look so boring / bored? Is your life really so boring / bored?
11 He's one of the most boring / bored people I've ever met. He never stops talking and he never
   says anything interesting / interested.

98.3 Complete each sentence using a word from the box.

amusing/amused	annoying/annoyed	boring/bored
confusing/confused	disgusting/disgusted	exciting/excited
exhausting/exhausted	interesting/interested	~~surprising~~/surprised

1 He works very hard. It's not __surprising__ that he's always tired.
2 I've got nothing to do. I'm _____ .
3 The teacher's explanation was _____ . Most of the students didn't
   understand it.
4 The kitchen hadn't been cleaned for ages. It was really _____ .
5 I don't visit art galleries very often. I'm not particularly _____ in art.
6 There's no need to get _____ just because I'm a few minutes late.
7 The lecture was _____ . I fell asleep.
8 I've been working very hard all day and now I'm _____ .
9 I'm starting a new job next week. I'm very _____ about it.
10 Steve is good at telling funny stories. He can be very _____ .
11 Helen is a very _____ person. She knows a lot, she's travelled a lot and
   she's done lots of different things.

Adjectives: a **nice new** house, you look **tired**

A

Sometimes we use two or more adjectives together:
- ○ My brother lives in a **nice new** house.
- ○ In the kitchen there was a **beautiful large round wooden** table.

Adjectives like **new/large/round/wooden** are *fact* adjectives. They give us factual information about age, size, colour etc.

Adjectives like **nice/beautiful** are *opinion* adjectives. They tell us what somebody thinks of something or somebody.
Opinion adjectives usually go before fact adjectives.

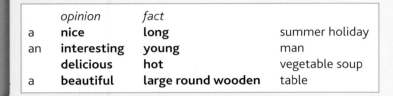

	opinion	*fact*	
a	**nice**	**long**	summer holiday
an	**interesting**	**young**	man
	delicious	**hot**	vegetable soup
a	**beautiful**	**large round wooden**	table

B

Sometimes we use two or more fact adjectives together. Usually (but not always) we put fact adjectives in this order:

1 how big?	→	2 how old?	→	3 what colour?	→	4 where from?	→	5 what is it made of?	→	NOUN

    a **tall young** man (1 → 2)   a **large wooden** table (1 → 5)
    big blue eyes (1 → 3)   an **old Russian** song (2 → 4)
    a **small black plastic** bag (1 → 3 → 5)   an **old white cotton** shirt (2 → 3 → 5)

Adjectives of size and length (**big/small/tall/short/long** etc.) usually go
before adjectives of shape and width (**round/fat/thin/slim/wide** etc.):
    a **large round** table   a **tall thin** girl   a **long narrow** street

When there are two or more colour adjectives, we use **and**:
    a **black and white** dress   a **red, white and green** flag
This does not usually happen with other adjectives before a noun:
    a **long black** dress   (*not* a long and black dress)

C

We use adjectives after **be/get/become/seem**:
- ○ **Be careful**!
- ○ **I'm tired** and **I'm getting hungry**.
- ○ As the film went on, it **became** more and more **boring**.
- ○ Your friend **seems** very **nice**.

We also use adjectives to say how somebody/something looks, feels, sounds, tastes or smells:
- ○ You **look tired**. / I **feel tired**. / She **sounds tired**.
- ○ The dinner **smells good**.
- ○ This tea **tastes** a bit **strange**.

But to say *how* somebody *does something* you must use an *adverb* (see Units 100–101):
- ○ Drive **carefully**! (*not* Drive careful)
- ○ Susan plays the piano very **well**. (*not* plays … very good)

D

We say 'the **first two** days / the **next few** weeks / the **last ten** minutes' etc. :
- ○ I didn't enjoy the **first two** days of the course. (*not* the two first days)
- ○ They'll be away for the **next few** weeks. (*not* the few next weeks)

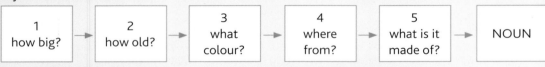

Adverbs ➜ **Units 100–101**   Comparison (**cheaper** etc.) ➜ **Units 105–107**
Superlatives (**cheapest** etc.) ➜ **Unit 108**

99.1 Put the adjectives in brackets in the correct position.

1 a beautiful table (wooden / round)   *a beautiful round wooden table*
2 an unusual ring   (gold)
3 an old house   (beautiful)
4 black gloves   (leather)
5 an American film   (old)
6 a long face   (thin)
7 big clouds   (black)
8 a sunny day   (lovely)
9 an ugly dress   (yellow)
10 a wide avenue   (long)
11 a lovely restaurant   (little)
12 a red car   (old / little)
13 a new sweater   (green / nice)
14 a metal box   (black / small)
15 a big cat   (fat / black)
16 long hair   (black / beautiful)
17 an old painting   (interesting / French)
18 an enormous umbrella   (red / yellow)

99.2 Complete each sentence with a verb (in the correct form) and an adjective from the boxes.

feel	look	~~seem~~
smell	sound	taste

awful	fine	interesting
nice	~~upset~~	wet

1 Helen ___*seemed upset*___ this morning. Do you know what was wrong?
2 I can't eat this. I've just tried it and it ....
3 I wasn't very well yesterday, but I .... today.
4 What beautiful flowers! They .... too.
5 You .... Have you been out in the rain?
6 James was telling me about his new job. It .... – much better than his old job.

99.3 Put in the correct word.

1 This tea tastes a bit ___*strange*___ . (strange / strangely)
2 I always feel .... when the sun is shining. (happy / happily)
3 The children were playing .... in the garden. (happy / happily)
4 The man became .... when the manager of the restaurant asked him to leave.
   (violent / violently)
5 You look .... ! Are you all right? (terrible / terribly)
6 There's no point in doing a job if you don't do it .... (proper / properly)
7 The soup tastes .... (good / well)
8 Hurry up! You're always so .... (slow / slowly)

99.4 Write the following in another way using **the first ... / the next ... / the last ...** .

1 the first day and the second day of the course   *the first two days of the course*
2 next week and the week after   *the next two weeks*
3 yesterday and the day before yesterday
4 the first week and the second week of May
5 tomorrow and a few days after that
6 questions 1, 2 and 3 in the exam
7 next year and the year after
8 the last day of our holiday and the two days
   before that

→ Additional exercise 31 (page 320)

Adjectives and adverbs 1 (**quick/quickly**)

A

Look at these examples:
- ○ Our holiday was too short – the time passed very **quickly**.
- ○ Two people were **seriously** injured in the accident.

Quickly and **seriously** are *adverbs*. Many adverbs are formed from an adjective + **-ly**:

adjective:	quick	serious	careful	quiet	heavy	bad
adverb:	quick**ly**	serious**ly**	careful**ly**	quiet**ly**	heavi**ly**	bad**ly**

For spelling, see Appendix 6.

Not all words ending in **-ly** are adverbs. Some *adjectives* end in **-ly** too, for example:
friendly   lively   elderly   lonely   silly   lovely

B

Adjective or adverb?

Adjectives (**quick/careful** etc.) tell us about a *noun* (somebody or something). We use adjectives before nouns:

- ○ Sam is a **careful driver**. (*not* a carefully driver)
- ○ We didn't go out because of the **heavy rain**.

Adverbs (**quickly/carefully** etc.) tell us about a *verb* (how somebody does something or *how* something happens):

- ○ Sam **drove carefully** along the narrow road. (*not* drove careful)
- ○ We didn't go out because it was **raining heavily**. (*not* raining heavy)

Compare:

- ○ She speaks **perfect English**.
  adjective + noun

- ○ She **speaks English perfectly**.
  verb + noun + adverb

We also use adjectives after some verbs, especially **be**, and also **look/feel/sound** etc.
Compare:

- ○ Please **be quiet**.
- ○ I was disappointed that my exam results **were** so **bad**.
- ○ Why do you always **look** so **serious**?
- ○ I **feel happy**.

- ○ Please **speak quietly**.
- ○ I was unhappy that I **did** so **badly** in the exam. (*not* did so bad)
- ○ Why do you never **take** me **seriously**?
- ○ The children were **playing happily**.

C

We also use adverbs before *adjectives* and *other adverbs*. For example:

reasonably cheap	*(adverb + adjective)*
terribly sorry	*(adverb + adjective)*
incredibly quickly	*(adverb + adverb)*

- ○ It's a **reasonably cheap** restaurant and the food is **extremely good**.
- ○ I'm **terribly sorry**. I didn't mean to push you. (*not* terrible sorry)
- ○ Maria learns languages **incredibly quickly**.
- ○ The exam was **surprisingly easy**.

You can also use an adverb before a *past participle* (**injured/organised/written** etc.):
- ○ Two people were **seriously injured** in the accident. (*not* serious injured)
- ○ The meeting was **badly organised**.

Adjectives after **be/look/feel** etc. → Unit 99C   Adjectives and adverbs 2 → Unit 101

Exercises

100.1 Complete each sentence with an adverb. The first letters of the adverb are given.

1 We didn't go out because it was raining he*avily* .
2 Our team lost the game because we played very ba................................ .
3 I didn't have any problems finding a place to live. I found a flat quite ea................................ .
4 We had to wait for a long time, but we didn't complain. We waited pat................................ .
5 Nobody knew Steve was coming to see us. He arrived unex................................ .
6 Mike keeps fit by playing tennis reg................................ .
7 I don't speak French very well, but I can understand per................................ if people speak
   sl................................ and cl................................ .

100.2 Put in the correct word.

1 Two people were ....*seriously*.... injured in the accident. (serious / seriously)
2 The driver of the car had ....*serious*.... injuries. (serious / seriously)
3 I think you behaved very .... (selfish / selfishly)
4 Tanya is .... upset about losing her job. (terrible / terribly)
5 There was a .... change in the weather. (sudden / suddenly)
6 Everybody at the carnival was .... dressed. (colourful / colourfully)
7 Linda usually wears .... clothes. (colourful / colourfully)
8 Liz fell and hurt herself really .... (bad / badly)
9 Joe says he didn't do well at school because he was .... taught. (bad / badly)
10 Don't go up that ladder. It doesn't look .... (safe / safely)

100.3 Complete each sentence using a word from the box. Sometimes you need the adjective (**careful** etc.) and sometimes the adverb (**carefully** etc.).

| careful(ly) | complete(ly) | continuous(ly) | financial(ly) | fluent(ly) |
| happy/happily | nervous(ly) | perfect(ly) | ~~quick(ly)~~ | special(ly) |

1 Our holiday was too short. The time passed very .....*quickly*..... .
2 Steve doesn't take risks when he's driving. He's always ....
3 Sue works .... She never seems to stop.
4 Rachel and Patrick are very .... married.
5 Maria's English is very .... although she makes quite a lot of mistakes.
6 I cooked this meal .... for you, so I hope you like it.
7 Everything was very quiet. There was .... silence.
8 I tried on the shoes and they fitted me ....
9 Do you usually feel .... before exams?
10 I'd like to buy a car, but it's .... impossible for me at the moment.

100.4 Choose two words (one from each box) to complete each sentence.

absolutely	badly	completely	changed	~~cheap~~	damaged
~~reasonably~~	seriously	slightly	enormous	ill	long
unnecessarily	unusually		planned	quiet	

1 I thought the restaurant would be expensive, but it was ....*reasonably cheap*.... .
2 Will's mother is .... in hospital.
3 What a big house! It's ....
4 It wasn't a serious accident. The car was only ....
5 The children are normally very lively, but they're .... today.
6 When I returned home after 20 years, everything had ....
7 The movie was .... It could have been much shorter.
8 A lot went wrong during our holiday because it was ....

➔ Additional exercise 31 (page 320)

Adjectives and adverbs 2 (well/fast/late, hard/hardly)

A Good/well

Good is an *adjective*. The *adverb* is **well**:

- ○ Your English is **good**.   *but*   You **speak** English **well**.
- ○ Susan is a **good** pianist.   *but*   Susan **plays** the piano **well**.

We use **well** (*not* good) with *past participles* (**dressed/known** etc.):

   well-dressed   **well-known**   **well-educated**   **well-paid**
- ○ Gary's father is a **well-known** writer.

But **well** is also an adjective with the meaning 'in good health':
- ○ 'How are you today?' 'I'm very **well**, thanks.'

B Fast/hard/late

These words are both adjectives and adverbs:

adjective	*adverb*
○ Darren is a very **fast runner**.	Darren can **run** very **fast**.
○ Kate is a **hard worker**.	Kate **works hard**. (*not* works hardly)
○ I was **late**.	I **got up late** this morning.

Lately = recently:
- ○ Have you seen Tom **lately**?

C Hardly

Hardly = very little, almost not. Study these examples:
- ○ Sarah wasn't very friendly at the party. She **hardly** spoke to me.
  (= she spoke to me very little, almost not at all)
- ○ We've only met once or twice. We **hardly** know each other.

Hard and **hardly** are different. Compare:
- ○ He tried **hard** to find a job, but he had no luck. (= he tried a lot, with a lot of effort)
- ○ I'm not surprised he didn't find a job. He **hardly** tried. (= he tried very little)

I **can hardly** do something = it's very difficult for me, almost impossible:
- ○ Your writing is terrible. I **can hardly** read it. (= it is almost impossible to read it)
- ○ My leg was hurting. I **could hardly** walk.

D

You can use **hardly + any/anybody/anyone/anything/anywhere**:
- ○ A: How much money have we got?
  B: **Hardly any**. (= very little, almost none)
- ○ These two cameras are very similar. There's **hardly any** difference between them.
- ○ The exam results were very bad. **Hardly anybody** in our class passed. (= very few students passed)

There's **hardly anything** in the fridge.

Note that you can say:
- ○ She said **hardly anything**.   *or*   She **hardly** said **anything**.
- ○ We've got **hardly any** money.   *or*   We've **hardly** got **any** money.

Hardly ever = almost never:
- ○ I'm nearly always at home in the evenings. I **hardly ever** go out.

Hardly also means 'certainly not'. For example:
- ○ It's **hardly surprising** that you're tired. You haven't slept for three days.
  (= it's certainly not surprising)
- ○ The situation is serious, but it's **hardly a crisis**. (= it's certainly not a crisis)

Adjectives after verbs ('**You look tired**' etc.) ➜ Unit 99C   Adjectives and adverbs 1 ➜ Unit 100

Exercises

101.1 Put in **good** or **well**.

1 I play tennis but I'm not very ___good___ .
2 Your exam results were very _____ .
3 You did _____ in your exams.
4 The weather was _____ while we were away.
5 I didn't sleep _____ last night.
6 Lucy speaks German _____ . She's _____ at languages.
7 Our new business isn't doing very _____ at the moment.
8 I like your hat. It looks _____ on you.
9 I've met her a few times, but I don't know her _____ .

101.2 Complete these sentences using **well** + the following words:

> ~~behaved~~   dressed   informed   kept   known   paid   written

1 The children were very good. They were ___well-behaved___ .
2 I'm surprised you haven't heard of her. She is quite _____ .
3 Our neighbours' garden is neat and tidy. It is very _____ .
4 I enjoyed the book you lent me. It's a great story and it's very _____ .
5 Tanya knows a lot about many things. She is very _____ .
6 Mark's clothes are always smart. He is always _____ .
7 Jane has a lot of responsibility in her job, but she isn't very _____ .

101.3 Are the <u>underlined</u> words right or wrong? Correct them where necessary.

1 I'm tired because I've been working <u>hard</u>.   ___OK___
2 I tried <u>hard</u> to remember her name, but I couldn't.   _____
3 This coat is practically unused. I've <u>hardly</u> worn it.   _____
4 Laura is a good tennis player. She hits the ball <u>hardly</u>. _____
5 Don't walk so <u>fast</u>! I can't keep up with you.   _____
6 I had plenty of time, so I was walking <u>slow</u>.   _____

101.4 Complete the sentences. Use **hardly** + the following verbs (in the correct form):

> change   hear   ~~know~~   recognise   say   sleep   speak

1 Scott and Tracy have only met once before. They ___hardly know___ each other.
2 You're speaking very quietly. I can _____ you.
3 I'm very tired this morning. I _____ last night.
4 We were so shocked when we heard the news, we could _____ .
5 Kate was very quiet this evening. She _____ a word.
6 You look the same now as you looked 15 years ago. You've _____ .
7 I met David a few days ago. I hadn't seen him for a long time and he looks very different now.
   I _____ him.

101.5 Complete these sentences with **hardly** + any/anybody/anything/anywhere/ever.

1 I'll have to go shopping. There's ___hardly anything___ to eat.
2 It was a very warm day and there was _____ wind.
3 'Do you know much about computers?' 'No, _____ .'
4 The hotel was almost empty. There was _____ staying there.
5 I listen to the radio a lot, but I _____ watch television.
6 Our new boss is not very popular. _____ likes her.
7 It was very crowded in the room. There was _____ to sit.
8 We used to be good friends, but we _____ see each other now.
9 It was nice driving this morning. There was _____ traffic.
10 I hate this town. There's _____ to do and _____ to go.

→ Additional exercise 31 (page 320)

So and such

A

Compare **so** and **such**:

We use **so** + *adjective/adverb:*
so stupid	**so quick**
so nice	**so quickly**

- ○ I didn't like the book. The story was **so stupid**.
- ○ I like Liz and Joe. They are **so nice**.

We use **such** + *noun:*
such a story	**such people**

We also use **such** + *adjective + noun:*
such a stupid **story**	**such** nice **people**

- ○ I didn't like the book. It was **such** a stupid **story**. (*not* a so stupid story)
- ○ I like Liz and Joe. They are **such nice people**. (*not* so nice people)

We say **such a** … (*not* a such):
such a big **dog** (*not* a such big dog)

B

So and **such** make the meaning stronger:

- ○ It's a beautiful day, isn't it? It's **so warm**. (= really warm)
- ○ It's difficult to understand him because he talks **so quietly**.

You can use **so** … **that**:
- ○ The book was **so good that** I couldn't put it down.
- ○ I was **so tired that** I fell asleep in the armchair.

We usually leave out **that**:
- ○ I was **so tired** I fell asleep.

- ○ It was a great holiday. We had **such a good time**. (= a really good time)
- ○ You always think good things are going to happen. You're **such an optimist**.

You can use **such** … **that**:
- ○ It was **such a good book that** I couldn't put it down.
- ○ It was **such nice weather that** we spent the whole day on the beach.

We usually leave out **that**:
- ○ It was **such nice weather** we spent …

C

We also use **so** and **such** with the meaning 'like this':

- ○ Somebody told me the house was built 100 years ago. I didn't realise it was **so old**. (= as old as it is)
- ○ I'm tired because I got up at six. I don't usually get up **so early**.
- ○ I expected the weather to be cooler. I'm surprised it is **so warm**.

- ○ I didn't realise it was **such an old house**.
- ○ You know it's not true. How can you say **such a thing**?

Note the expression **no such** … :
- ○ You won't find the word 'blid' in the dictionary. There's **no such word**. (= this word does not exist)

D

Compare:

so long	**such a long time**
○ I haven't seen her for **so long** I've forgotten what she looks like.	○ I haven't seen her for **such a long time**. (*not* so long time)
so far	**such a long way**
○ I didn't know it was **so far**.	○ I didn't know it was **such a long way**.
so much, so many	**such a lot (of)**
○ I'm sorry I'm late – there was **so much** traffic.	○ I'm sorry I'm late – there was **such a lot of** traffic.

Not so … as ➜ Unit 107A   Such as ➜ Unit 117A

Exercises

102.1 Put in **so**, **such** or **such a**.

1 It's difficult to understand him because he speaks ......*so*...... quietly.
2 I like Liz and Joe. They're ......*such*...... nice people.
3 It was a great holiday. We had ......*such a*...... good time.
4 I was surprised that he looked .... well after his recent illness.
5 Everything is .... expensive these days, isn't it?
6 The weather is beautiful, isn't it? I didn't expect it to be .... nice day.
7 I think she works too hard. She looks .... tired all the time.
8 He always looks good. He wears .... nice clothes.
9 It was .... boring movie that I fell asleep while I was watching it.
10 I couldn't believe the news. It was .... shock.
11 I have to go. I didn't realise it was .... late.
12 The food at the hotel was .... awful. I've never eaten .... awful food.
13 They've got .... much money they don't know what to do with it.
14 I didn't realise you lived .... long way from the city centre.
15 The party was really great. It was .... shame you couldn't come.

102.2 Make one sentence from two. Use **so** or **such**.

1 ~~She worked hard.~~	You could hear it from miles away.
2 ~~It was a beautiful day.~~	You would think it was her native language.
3 I was tired.	We spent the whole day indoors.
4 We had a good time on holiday.	~~She made herself ill.~~
5 She speaks English well.	I couldn't keep my eyes open.
6 I've got a lot to do.	I didn't eat anything else for the rest of the day.
7 The music was loud.	~~We decided to go to the beach.~~
8 I had a big breakfast.	I didn't know what to say.
9 It was horrible weather.	I don't know where to begin.
10 I was surprised.	We didn't want to come home.

1 ....*She worked so hard she made herself ill.*....
2 ....*It was such a beautiful day we decided to go to the beach.*....
3 I was ....
4 ....
5 ....
6 ....
7 ....
8 ....
9 ....
10 ....

102.3 Use your own ideas to complete these pairs of sentences.

1 a We enjoyed our holiday. It was so ....*relaxing*.................... .
   b We enjoyed our holiday. We had such ....*a good time*.................... .
2 a I like Catherine. She's so ....
   b I like Catherine. She's such ....
3 a I like New York. It's so ....
   b I like New York. It's such ....
4 a I wouldn't like to be a teacher. It's so ....
   b I wouldn't like to be a teacher. It's such ....
5 a It's great to see you again! I haven't seen you for so ....
   b It's great to see you again! I haven't seen you for such ....

Enough and too

A
Enough goes *after* adjectives and adverbs:
- ○ I can't run very far. I'm not **fit enough**. (*not* enough fit)
- ○ Let's go. We've waited **long enough**.
- ○ I can let you know tomorrow. Is that **soon enough**?

I'm not **fit enough**.

Compare **too** … and **not** … **enough**:
- ○ You never stop working. You work **too hard**.
  (= more than is necessary)
- ○ You're lazy. You **don't** work **hard enough**.
  (= less than is necessary)

B
Enough normally goes *before* nouns:
- ○ I can't run very far. I don't have **enough energy**. (*not* energy enough)
- ○ Do we have **enough petrol**, or should we stop and get some?
- ○ We've got **enough money**. We don't need any more.
- ○ Some of us had to sit on the floor because there weren't **enough chairs**.

We also use **enough** alone (without a noun):
- ○ We don't need to stop for petrol. We've got **enough**.

Compare **too much/many** and **enough**:
- ○ There's **too much furniture** in this room. There's not **enough space**.
- ○ There were **too many people** and not **enough chairs**.

C
We say **enough/too** … **for** somebody/something:
- ○ Does Joe have enough experience **for the job**?
- ○ This bag isn't big enough **for all my clothes**.
- ○ That shirt is too small **for you**. You need a larger size.

But we say **enough/too** … **to** do something. For example:
- ○ Does Joe have enough experience **to do the job**? (*not* for doing)
- ○ We don't have enough money **to go on holiday right now**.
- ○ She's not old enough **to have a driving licence**.
  She's too young **to have a driving licence**.
- ○ Let's get a taxi. It's too far **to walk home from here**.

The following example has both **for** … and **to** … :
- ○ The bridge is just wide enough **for two cars to pass each other**.

D
We say:

	The food was very hot. We couldn't eat **it**.
and	The food was so hot that we couldn't eat **it**.
but	The food was **too** hot **to eat**. (*without* it)

Some more examples like this:
- ○ These boxes are **too heavy to carry**.
  (*not* to carry them)
- ○ The wallet was **too big to put** in my pocket.
  (*not* to put it)
- ○ This chair isn't **strong enough to stand on**.
  (*not* to stand on it)

To … and for … (purpose) ➜ Unit 64   Adjective + to … (difficult to understand etc.) ➜ Unit 65

Exercises

103.1 Complete the sentences using **enough** + the following words:

> big ~~chairs~~ cups ~~fit~~ milk money room time warm well

1 I can't run very far. I'm not .....*fit enough*..... .
2 Some of us had to sit on the floor because there weren't ....*enough chairs*.... .
3 I'd like to buy a car, but I don't have .... at the moment.
4 Do you have .... in your coffee or would you like some more?
5 Are you .... ? Or shall I switch on the heating?
6 It's only a small car. There isn't .... for all of us.
7 Steve didn't feel .... to go to work this morning.
8 I enjoyed my trip to Paris, but there wasn't .... to do everything I wanted.
9 Try this jacket on and see if it's .... for you.
10 There weren't .... for everybody to have coffee at the same time.

103.2 Complete the answers to the questions. Use **too** or **enough** + the word(s) in brackets.

1	Does she have a driving licence?	(old)	No, she's not old enough to have a driving licence.
2	I need to talk to you about something.	(busy)	Well, I'm afraid I'm .... to you now.
3	Let's go to the cinema.	(late)	No, it's .... to the cinema.
4	Why don't we sit outside?	(warm)	It's not .... outside.
5	Would you like to be a politician?	(shy)	No, I'm .... a politician.
6	Would you like to be a teacher?	(patience)	No, I don't have .... a teacher.
7	Did you hear what he was saying?	(far away)	No, we were .... what he was saying.
8	Can he read a newspaper in English?	(English)	No, he doesn't know .... a newspaper.

103.3 Make one sentence from two. Complete the new sentence using **too** or **enough**.

1 We couldn't carry the boxes. They were too heavy.
   .....*The boxes were too heavy to carry.*.....
2 I can't drink this coffee. It's too hot.
   This coffee is ....
3 Nobody could move the piano. It was too heavy.
   The piano ....
4 Don't eat these apples. They're not ripe enough.
   These apples ....
5 I can't explain the situation. It is too complicated.
   The situation ....
6 We couldn't climb over the wall. It was too high.
   The wall ....
7 Three people can't sit on this sofa. It isn't big enough.
   This sofa ....
8 You can't see some things without a microscope. They are too small.
   Some ....

Quite, pretty, rather and fairly

A

You can use **quite/pretty/rather/fairly** + adjectives or adverbs. So you can say:
- ○ It's **quite cold**.   It's **pretty cold**.   It's **rather cold**.   It's **fairly cold**.

Quite/pretty/rather/fairly = less than 'very' but more than 'a little'.

B

Quite and **pretty** are similar in meaning:
- ○ I'm surprised you haven't heard of her. She's **quite famous / pretty famous**.   (= less than 'very famous', but more than 'a little famous')
- ○ Anna lives **quite near** me, so we see each other **pretty often**.

Pretty is an informal word and is used mainly in spoken English.

Quite goes before **a/an**:
- ○ We live in **quite an old house**. (*not* a quite old house)

Compare:
- ○ Sarah has **quite a** good job.
   Sarah has **a pretty** good job.

You can also use **quite** (but not **pretty**) in the following ways:

quite a/an + *noun* (without an adjective):
- ○ I didn't expect to see them. It was **quite a surprise**.   (= quite a big surprise)

quite a lot (**of** …):
- ○ There were **quite a lot of** people at the meeting.

quite + verb, especially **like** and **enjoy**:
- ○ I **quite like** tennis, but it's not my favourite sport.

C

Rather is similar to **quite** and **pretty**. We often use **rather** for negative ideas (things we think are not good):
- ○ The weather isn't so good. It's **rather cloudy**.
- ○ Paul is **rather shy**. He doesn't talk very much.

Quite and **pretty** are also possible in these examples.

When we use **rather** for positive ideas (**good/nice** etc.), it means 'unusually' or 'surprisingly':
- ○ These oranges are **rather good**. Where did you get them?

D

Fairly is weaker than **quite/rather/pretty**. For example, if something is **fairly good**, it is not very good and it could be better:
- ○ My room is **fairly big**, but I'd prefer a bigger one.
- ○ We see each other **fairly often**, but not as often as we used to.

E

Quite also means 'completely'. For example:
- ○ 'Are you sure?'   'Yes, **quite sure**.' (= completely sure)

Quite means 'completely' with a number of adjectives, especially:

sure	right	true	clear	different	incredible	amazing
certain	wrong	safe	obvious	unnecessary	extraordinary	impossible

- ○ She was **quite different** from what I expected. (= completely different)
- ○ Everything they said was **quite true**. (= completely true)

We also use **quite** (= completely) with some verbs. For example:
- ○ I **quite agree** with you. (= I completely agree)

Not quite = not completely:
- ○ They **haven't quite finished** eating yet.
- ○ I **don't quite understand** what you mean.
- ○ 'Are you ready yet?'   '**Not quite**.' (= not completely)

Exercises

104.1 Complete the sentences using **quite** + the following:

~~famous~~	good	hungry	late	noisy	often	old	surprised

1 I'm surprised you haven't heard of her. She's ..... *quite famous* ..... .
2 I'm .... Is there anything to eat?
3 'How were the pictures you took?' '................................. . Better than usual.'
4 I go to the cinema .... – maybe once a month.
5 We live near a very busy road, so it's often ....
6 I didn't expect Laura to contact me. I was .... when she phoned.
7 I went to bed .... last night, so I'm a bit tired this morning.
8 I don't know exactly when these houses were built, but they're ....

104.2 Put the words in the right order to complete the sentences.

1 The weather was better than we had expected.
   It was ..... *quite a nice day* .... (a / nice / quite / day).
2 Tom likes to sing.
   He has .... (voice / quite / good / a).
3 The bus stop wasn't very near the hotel.
   We had to walk .... (quite / way / a / long).
4 It's not so warm today.
   There's .... (a / wind / cold / pretty).
5 The journey took longer than I expected.
   There was .... (lot / traffic / a / of / quite).
6 I'm tired.
   I've had .... (pretty / day / a / busy).

104.3 Use your own ideas to complete these sentences. Use **rather** + adjective.

1 The weather isn't so good. It's ..... *rather cloudy* ..... .
2 I enjoyed the film, but it was ....
3 The hotel we stayed at wasn't very good. I was ....
4 I think it's .... that Chris went away without telling anybody.
5 Lucy doesn't like having to wait. Sometimes she's ....

104.4 What does **quite** mean in these sentences? Tick (✓) the right meaning.

	more than a little, less than very (Section B)	completely (Section E)
1 It's <u>quite cold</u>. You'd better wear your coat.	✓	
2 'Are you sure?' 'Yes, <u>quite sure</u>.'		✓
3 Anna's English is <u>quite good</u>.		
4 I couldn't believe it. It was <u>quite incredible</u>.		
5 My bedroom is <u>quite big</u>.		
6 I'm <u>quite tired</u>. I think I'll go to bed.		
7 I <u>quite agree</u> with you.		

104.5 Complete these sentences using **quite** + the following:

different	impossible	right	safe	sure	~~true~~	unnecessary

1 I didn't believe her at first, but in fact what she said was ..... *quite true* ..... .
2 You won't fall. The ladder is ....
3 I'm afraid I can't do what you ask. It's ....
4 I couldn't agree with you more. You are ....
5 You can't compare the two things. They are ....
6 You needn't have done that. It was ....
7 I think I saw them go out, but I'm not ....

A Study these examples:

> How shall we travel? Shall we drive or go by train?
>
> Let's drive. It's **cheaper**.
> Don't go by train. It's **more expensive**.
>
> **Cheaper** and **more expensive** are *comparative* forms.

After comparatives you can use **than** (see Unit 107):
- ○ It's **cheaper** to drive **than** go by train.
- ○ Going by train is **more expensive than** driving.

B The comparative form is -**er** or **more** … .

We use -**er** for short words (one syllable):

cheap → cheap**er**	fast → fast**er**
large → larg**er**	thin → thin**ner**

We also use -**er** for two-syllable words that end in -**y** (-**y** → **ier**):
- luck**y** → luck**ier**   early → earl**ier**
- eas**y** → eas**ier**   prett**y** → prett**ier**

For spelling, see Appendix 6.

We use **more** … for longer words (two syllables or more):
- more serious   more often
- more expensive   more comfortable

We also use **more** … for adverbs that end in -**ly**:
- more slowly   more seriously
- more easily   more quietly

Compare these examples:

- ○ You're **older** than me.
- ○ The exam was quite easy – **easier** than I expected.
- ○ Can you walk a bit **faster**?
- ○ I'd like to have a **bigger** car.
- ○ Last night I went to bed **earlier** than usual.

- ○ You're **more patient** than me.
- ○ The exam was quite difficult – **more difficult** than I expected.
- ○ Can you walk a bit **more slowly**?
- ○ I'd like to have a **more reliable** car.
- ○ I don't play tennis much these days. I used to play **more often**.

You can use -**er** *or* **more** … with some two-syllable adjectives, especially:
clever   narrow   quiet   shallow   simple
- ○ It's too noisy here. Can we go somewhere **quieter** / **more quiet**?

C A few adjectives and adverbs have irregular comparative forms:

good/well → **better**
- ○ The garden looks **better** since you tidied it up.
- ○ I know him **well** – probably **better** than anybody else knows him.

bad/badly → **worse**
- ○ 'How's your headache? Better?'   'No, it's **worse**.'
- ○ He did very badly in the exam – **worse** than expected.

far → **further** (*or* **farther**)
- ○ It's a long walk from here to the park – **further** than I thought.   (*or* **farther** than)

Further (*but not* farther) can also mean 'more' or 'additional':
- ○ Let me know if you hear any **further** news.   (= any more news)

Comparison 2–3 → Units 106–107   Superlatives (**cheapest** / **most expensive** etc.) → Unit 108

Exercises

105.1 Complete the sentences using a comparative form (**older / more important** etc.).

1 It's too noisy here. Can we go somewhere ....*quieter*.... ?
2 This coffee is very weak. I like it ....
3 The hotel was surprisingly big. I expected it to be ....
4 The hotel was surprisingly cheap. I expected it to be ....
5 The weather is too cold here. I'd like to live somewhere ....
6 My job is a bit boring sometimes. I'd like to do something ....
7 It's a shame you live so far away. I wish you lived ....
8 I was surprised how easy it was to get a job. I thought it would be ....
9 Your work isn't very good. I'm sure you can do ....
10 Don't worry. The situation isn't so bad. It could be ....
11 I was surprised we got here so quickly. I expected the trip to take ....
12 You're talking very loudly. Can you speak .... ?
13 You hardly ever call me. Why don't you call me .... ?
14 You're standing too near the camera. Can you move a bit .... away?
15 You were a little depressed yesterday, but you look .... today.

105.2 Complete the sentences. Use the comparative forms of the words in the box. Use **than** where necessary.

big	crowded	~~early~~	easily	high	important
interested	peaceful	~~reliable~~	serious	simple	thin

1 I was feeling tired last night, so I went to bed ....*earlier than*.... usual.
2 I'd like to have a ....*more reliable*.... car. The one I have keeps breaking down.
3 Unfortunately her illness was .... we thought at first.
4 You look .... Have you lost weight?
5 I want a .... apartment. We don't have enough space here.
6 He doesn't study very hard. He's .... in having a good time.
7 Health and happiness are .... money.
8 The instructions were very complicated. They could have been ....
9 There were a lot of people on the bus. It was .... usual.
10 I like living in the country. It's .... living in a town.
11 You'll find your way around the town .... if you have a good map.
12 In some parts of the country, prices are .... in others.

105.3 Read the situations and complete the sentences. Use a comparative form (**-er** or **more …**).

1 Yesterday the temperature was six degrees. Today it's only three degrees.
  It's ....*colder today than*.... it was yesterday.

2 The journey takes four hours by car and five hours by train.
  It takes .... by car.

3 Dan and I went for a run. I ran ten kilometres. Dan stopped after eight kilometres.
  I ran .... Dan.

4 Chris and Joe both did badly in the test. Chris got 30%, but Joe only got 25%.
  Joe did .... Chris in the test.

5 I expected my friends to arrive at about 4 o'clock. In fact they arrived at 2.30.
  My friends .... I expected.

6 You can go by bus or by train. The buses run every 30 minutes. The trains run every hour.
  The buses .... the trains.

7 We were very busy in the office today. We're not usually so busy.
  We .... usual in the office today.

Comparison 2 (**much better / any better / better and better / the sooner the better**)

A

Before comparatives you can use:

much   **a lot**   **far** (= a lot)   **a bit**   **a little**   **slightly** (= a little)

○ Let's go by car. It's **much cheaper**. (*or* **a lot cheaper**)
○ 'How do you feel now?' '**Much better**, thanks.'
○ Don't go by train. It's **a lot more expensive**. (*or* **much more expensive**)
○ Could you speak **a bit more slowly**? (*or* **a little more slowly**)
○ This bag is **slightly heavier** than the other one.
○ Her illness was **far more serious** than we thought at first. (*or* **much more serious /
a lot more serious**)

B

You can use **any** and **no** + *comparative* (**any longer / no bigger** etc.):
○ I've waited long enough. I'm not waiting **any longer**. (= not even a little longer)
○ We expected their apartment to be very big, but it's **no bigger** than ours. *or*
    … it is**n't any bigger** than ours. (= not even a little bigger)
○ How do you feel now? Do you feel **any better**?
○ This hotel is better than the other one, and it's **no more expensive**.

C

Better and better / more and more etc.

We repeat comparatives (**better and better** etc.) to say that something changes continuously:
○ Your English is improving. It's getting **better and better**.
○ The city has grown fast in recent years. It's got **bigger and bigger**.
○ As I listened to his story, I became **more and more convinced** that he was lying.
○ These days **more and more people** are learning English.

D

The … the …

You can say **the** (sooner/bigger/more etc.) **the better**:
○ 'What time shall we leave?' '**The sooner the better**.' (= as soon as possible)
○ A: What sort of box do you want? A big one?
    B: Yes, **the bigger the better**. (= as big as possible)
○ When you're travelling, **the less luggage** you have **the better**.

We also use **the … the …** to say that one thing depends on another thing:
○ **The warmer** the weather, **the better** I feel. (= if the weather is warmer, I feel better)
○ **The sooner** we leave, **the earlier** we will arrive.
○ **The younger** you are, **the easier** it is to learn.
○ **The more expensive** the hotel, **the better** the service.
○ **The more** electricity you use, **the higher** your bill will be.
○ **The more** I thought about the plan, **the less** I liked it.

E

Older and **elder**

The comparative of **old** is **older**:
○ David looks **older** than he really is.

You can use **elder** (*or* **older**) when you talk about people in a family. You can say
(**my/your** etc.) **elder sister/brother/daughter/son**:
○ **My elder sister** is a TV producer. (*or* My **older** sister …)

We say 'my **elder sister**', but we do not say that 'somebody is elder':
○ My sister is **older** than me. (*not* elder than me)

Any/no ➜ Unit 86   Comparison 1, 3 ➜ Units 105, 107   Eldest ➜ Unit 108C
Even + comparative ➜ Unit 112 C

Exercises

106.1 Use the words in brackets to complete the sentences. Use **much / a bit** etc. + a comparative form. Use **than** where necessary.

1 Her illness was __much more serious than__ we thought at first. (much / serious)
2 This bag is too small. I need something _____ . (much / big)
3 I liked the museum. It was _____ I expected. (much / interesting)
4 It was very hot yesterday. Today it's _____ . (a bit / cool)
5 I'm afraid the problem is _____ it seems. (far / complicated)
6 You're driving too fast. Can you drive _____ ? (a bit / slowly)
7 It's _____ to learn a language in a country where it is spoken. (a lot / easy)
8 I thought she was younger than me, but in fact she's _____ . (slightly / old)

106.2 Complete the sentences using **any/no** + comparative. Use **than** where necessary.

1 I've waited long enough. I'm not waiting __any longer__ .
2 I'm sorry I'm a bit late, but I couldn't get here _____ .
3 This shop isn't expensive. The prices are _____ anywhere else.
4 I need to stop for a rest. I can't walk _____ .
5 The traffic isn't particularly bad today. It's _____ usual.

106.3 Complete the sentences using the structure in Section C (**... and ...**).

1 It's getting __more and more difficult__ to find a job. (difficult)
2 That hole in your sweater is getting _____ . (big)
3 My bags seemed to get _____ as I carried them. (heavy)
4 As I waited for my interview, I became _____ . (nervous)
5 As the day went on, the weather got _____ . (bad)
6 Health care is becoming _____ . (expensive)
7 Since Anna went to Canada, her English has got _____ . (good)
8 As the conversation went on, Paul became _____ . (talkative)

106.4 Complete the sentences using the structure in Section D (**the ... the ...**).

1 I like warm weather.
   The warmer the weather, __the better I feel__ . (feel)
2 I didn't really like him when we first met.
   But the more I got to know him, _____ . (like)
3 If you're in business, you want to make a profit.
   The more goods you sell, _____ . (profit)
4 It's hard to concentrate when you're tired.
   The more tired you are, _____ . (hard)
5 Kate had to wait a very long time.
   The longer she had to wait, _____ . (impatient / become)

106.5 Use the words on the right to complete the sentences.

1 I like to travel light. The __less__ luggage, the better. 2 The problem is getting _____ and more serious. 3 The more time I have, the _____ it takes me to do things. 4 I'm walking as fast as I can. I can't walk _____ faster. 5 The higher your income, _____ more tax you have to pay. 6 I'm surprised Anna is only 25. I thought she was _____ . 7 Jane's _____ sister is a nurse. 8 I was a little late. The journey took _____ longer than I expected. 9 We have a lot to discuss. We need to start the meeting _____ later than 9.30. 10 Don't tell him anything. The _____ he knows, the _____ .	**any** **better** **elder** ~~**less**~~ **less** **longer** **more** **no** **older** **slightly** **the**

A Study this example situation:

SARAH   JOE   DAVID

Sarah, Joe and David are all very rich.
Sarah has $20 million, Joe has $15 million
and David has $10 million. So:

Joe is rich.

He is **richer than** David.

But he **isn't as rich as** Sarah.
(= Sarah is **richer than** he is)

Some more examples of **not as** … (**as**):

- ○ Jack **isn't as old as** he looks. (= he looks **older than** he is)
- ○ The town centre **wasn't as crowded as** usual. (= it is usually **more crowded**)
- ○ Lisa **didn't** do as well in the exam **as** she had hoped. (= she had hoped to do **better**)
- ○ The weather is better today. It's **not as cold**. (= yesterday was **colder than** today)
- ○ I **don't** know **as many** people **as** you do. (= you know **more** people **than** me)
- ○ 'How much did it cost? Fifty pounds?' 'No, **not as much as** that.' (= **less than** fifty pounds)

You can also say **not so** … (**as**):

- ○ It's not warm, but it is**n't so** cold **as** yesterday. (= it isn't **as cold as** …)

Less … **than** is similar to **not as** … **as**:

- ○ I spent **less** money **than** you. (= I **didn't** spend as much money **as** you)
- ○ The city centre was **less** crowded **than** usual. (= it **wasn't as** crowded **as** usual)
- ○ I play tennis **less than** I used to. (= I **don't** play as much **as** I used to)

B We also use **as** … **as** (*but not* so … as) in positive sentences and in questions:

- ○ I'm sorry I'm late. I got here **as fast as** I could.
- ○ There's plenty of food. You can have **as much as** you want.
- ○ Let's walk. It's **just as quick as** taking the bus.
- ○ Can you send me the information **as soon as possible**, please?

Also **twice as** … **as**, **three times as** … **as** etc. :

- ○ Petrol is **twice as expensive as** it was a few years ago.
- ○ Their house is about **three times as big as** ours.

C We say **the same as** (*not* the same like):

- ○ Laura's salary is **the same as** mine.   *or*   Laura gets **the same** salary **as** me.
- ○ David is **the same** age **as** James.
- ○ Sarah hasn't changed. She still looks **the same as** she did ten years ago.

D **Than me / than I am** etc.

You can say:

- ○ You're taller **than me**.   *or*   You're taller **than I am**.
  (*not usually* You're taller than I)
- ○ He's not as clever **as her**.   *or*   He's not as clever **as she is**.
- ○ They have more money **than us**.   *or*   They have more money **than we have**.
- ○ I can't run as fast **as him**.   *or*   I can't run as fast **as he can**.

Comparison 1–2 ➔ Units 105–106   As long as ➔ Unit 115B   As and like ➔ Unit 117

Exercises

107.1 Complete the sentences using **as ... as.**

1 I'm tall, but you are taller. I'm not _as tall as you_ .
2 My salary is high, but yours is higher. My salary isn't ....
3 You know a bit about cars, but I know more.
You don't ....
4 We are busy today, but we were busier yesterday.
We aren't ....
5 I still feel bad, but I felt a lot worse earlier.
I don't ....
6 Our neighbours have lived here for quite a long time, but we've lived here longer.
Our neighbours haven't ....
7 I was a little nervous before the interview, but usually I'm a lot more nervous.
I wasn't ....

107.2 Write a new sentence with the same meaning.

1 Jack is younger than he looks. Jack isn't _as old as he looks_ .
2 I didn't spend as much money as you. You _spent more money than me_ .
3 The station was nearer than I thought. The station wasn't ....
4 The meal didn't cost as much as I expected. The meal cost ....
5 I go out less than I used to. I don't ....
6 Karen's hair isn't as long as it used to be. Karen used to ....
7 I know them better than you do. You don't ....
8 There are fewer people at this meeting than at the last one.
There aren't ....

107.3 Complete the sentences using **as ... as** + the following:

| bad | comfortable | ~~fast~~ | hard | long | often | quietly | soon | well |

1 I'm sorry I'm late. I got here _as fast as_ I could.
2 It was a difficult question. I answered it .... I could.
3 'How long can I stay with you?' 'You can stay .... you like.'
4 I need the information quickly, so let me know .... possible.
5 I like to keep fit, so I go swimming .... I can.
6 I didn't want to wake anybody, so I came in .... I could.

In the following sentences use **just as ... as.**

7 I'm going to sleep on the floor. It's .... the bed.
8 You always say how tiring your job is, but I work .... you.
9 At first I thought he was nice, but really he's .... everybody else.

107.4 Write sentences using **the same as.**

1 David and James are both 22 years old. David _is the same age as_ James.
2 You and I both have dark brown hair. Your hair .... mine.
3 I arrived at 10.25 and so did you. I arrived .... you.
4 My birthday is 5 April. It's Tom's birthday too. My birthday .... Tom's.

107.5 Complete the sentences with **than ...** or **as ...** .

1 I can't reach as high as you. You are taller _than me_ .
2 He doesn't know much. I know more ....
3 I don't work particularly hard. Most people work as hard ....
4 We were very surprised. Nobody was more surprised ....
5 She's not a very good player. I'm a better player ....
6 They've been very lucky. I wish we were as lucky ....

A Study these examples:

> What is **the longest** river in the world?
> What was **the most enjoyable** holiday you've ever had?
>
> **Longest** and **most enjoyable** are *superlative* forms.

The superlative form is **-est** or **most** ... . In general, we use **-est** for short words and **most** ... for longer words. The rules are the same as those for the comparative – see Unit 105.

long → long**est**	**hot** → hott**est**	**easy** → easi**est**	**hard** → hard**est**
but **most** famous	**most** boring	**most** difficult	**most** expensive

A few adjectives are irregular:

good → **best** bad → **worst** far → **furthest/farthest**

For spelling, see Appendix 6.

B We normally use **the** before a superlative (**the** longest / **the** most famous etc.):
- Yesterday was **the hottest** day of the year.
- The movie was really boring. It's **the most boring** movie I've ever seen.
- She is a really nice person – one of **the nicest** people I know.
- Why does he always come to see me at **the worst** possible time?

Compare superlative and comparative:

- This hotel is **the cheapest** in town. *(superlative)*
  It's **cheaper** than all the others in town. *(comparative)*

- He's **the most patient** person I've ever met.
  He's much **more patient** than I am.

C **Oldest** and **eldest**

The superlative of **old** is **oldest**:
- That church is **the oldest** building in the town. *(not the eldest)*

We use **eldest** (*or* **oldest**) when we are talking about people in a family:
- **My eldest son** is 13 years old. (*or* My **oldest** son)
- Are you **the eldest** in your family? (*or* the **oldest**)

D After superlatives we normally use **in** with places:
- What's the longest river **in the world**? *(not of the world)*
- We had a nice room. It was one of the best **in the hotel**. *(not of the hotel)*

We also use **in** for organisations and groups of people (a class / a company etc.):
- Who is the youngest student **in the class**? *(not of the class)*

For a period of time, we normally use **of**:
- Yesterday was the hottest day **of the year**.
- What was the happiest day **of your life**?

E We often use the *present perfect* (I **have done**) after a superlative (see also Unit 8A):
- What's **the most important** decision **you've ever had** to make?
- That was **the best** holiday **I've had** for a long time.

> Comparison (**cheaper** / **more expensive** etc.) → Units 105–107   Elder → Unit 106E

Exercises

108.1 Complete the sentences. Use a superlative (**-est** or **most** ...) + a preposition (**of** or **in**).

1 It's a very good room. It's ___the best room in___ the hotel.
2 It's a very cheap restaurant. It's .... the town.
3 It was a very happy day. It was .... my life.
4 She's a very intelligent student. She's .... the class.
5 It's a very valuable painting. It's .... the gallery.
6 Spring is a very busy time for me. It's .... the year.

In the following sentences use **one of** + a superlative + a preposition.

7 It's a very good room. It's ___one of the best rooms in___ the hotel.
8 He's a very rich man. He's one .... the country.
9 It's a very big castle. It's .... Europe.
10 She's a very good player. She's .... the team.
11 It was a very bad experience. It was .... my life.
12 It's a very famous university. It's .... the world.

108.2 Complete the sentences. Use a superlative (**-est** or **most** ...) or a comparative (**-er** or **more** ...).

1 We stayed at ___the cheapest___ hotel in the town. (cheap)
2 Our hotel was ___cheaper___ than all the others in the town. (cheap)
3 The United States is very large, but Canada is .... (large)
4 What's .... country in the world? (small)
5 I wasn't feeling well yesterday, but I feel a bit .... today. (good)
6 It was an awful day. It was .... day of my life. (bad)
7 What is .... sport in your country? (popular)
8 Everest is .... mountain in the world. It is ....
   than any other mountain. (high)
9 This building is over 250 metres high, but it's not .... in the city.
   (tall)
10 I prefer this chair to the other one. It's .... (comfortable)
11 What's .... way to get to the station? (quick)
12 Which is .... – the bus or the train? (quick)
13 What's .... thing you've ever bought? (expensive)
14 Sue and Kevin have got three daughters. .... is 14 years old. (old)

108.3 What do you say in these situations? Use a superlative + **ever**. Use the words in brackets (in the correct form).

1 You've just been to the cinema. The movie was extremely boring. You tell your friend:
   (boring / movie / see) That's ___the most boring movie I've ever seen___ .

2 Your friend has just told you a joke, which you think is very funny. You say:
   (funny / joke / hear) That's ....

3 You're drinking coffee with a friend. It's really good coffee. You say:
   (good / coffee / taste) This ....

4 You are talking to a friend about Sarah. Sarah is very generous. You tell your friend about her:
   (generous / person / meet) She ....

5 You have just run ten kilometres. You've never run further than this. You say to your friend:
   (far / run) That ....

6 You decided to give up your job. Now you think this was a bad mistake. You say to your friend:
   (bad / mistake / make) It ....

7 Your friend meets a lot of people, some of them famous. You ask your friend:
   (famous / person / meet?) Who .... ?

Word order 1: verb + object; place and time

Verb + object

The *verb* and the *object* normally go together. We do not usually put other words between them:

	verb +	object	
I	**like**	**my job**	very much. (*not* I like very much my job)
Did you	**see**	**your friends**	yesterday?
Helen never	**drinks**	**coffee**.	

Study these examples. The verb and the object go together each time:

- Do you **eat** **meat** every day? (*not* Do you eat every day meat?)

- Everybody **enjoyed** **the party** very much. (*not* enjoyed very much the party)

- Our guide **spoke** **English** fluently. (*not* spoke fluently English)

- I lost all my money and I also **lost** **my passport** . (*not* I lost also my passport)

- At the end of the street you'll **see** **a supermarket** on your left. (*not* see on your left a supermarket)

Place and time

Usually the *verb* and the *place* (where?) go together:
go home   **live in a city**   **walk to work** etc.

If the verb has an *object*, the place comes after the *verb + object*:
take somebody home   **meet a friend in the street**

Time (when? / how often? / how long?) usually goes after *place*:

	place +	time	
Ben walks	**to work**	**every morning**.	(*not* every morning to work)
Sam has been	**in Canada**	**since April**.	
We arrived	**at the airport**	**early**.	

Study these examples. *Time* goes after *place*:

- I'm going **to Paris** **on Monday** . (*not* I'm going on Monday to Paris)

- They have lived **in the same house** **for a long time** .

- Don't be late. Make sure you're **here** **by 8 o'clock** .

- Sarah gave me a lift **home** **after the party** .

- You really shouldn't go **to bed** **so late** .

It is often possible to put *time* at the beginning of the sentence:
- **On Monday** I'm going to Paris.
- **Every morning** Ben walks to work.

Some time words (for example, **always/never/usually**) go with the verb in the middle of the sentence. See Unit 110.

Word order in questions ➔ Units 49–50   Adjective order ➔ Unit 99   Word order 2 ➔ Unit 110

Exercises

109.1 Is the word order right or wrong? Correct the sentences where necessary.

1 Everybody enjoyed the party very much.   *OK*
2 Ben walks every morning to work.   *Ben walks to work every morning.*
3 Joe doesn't like very much football.
4 I drink three or four cups of coffee every morning.
5 I ate quickly my breakfast and went out.
6 Are you going to invite to the party a lot of people?
7 I phoned Tom immediately after hearing the news.
8 Did you go late to bed last night?
9 Did you learn a lot of things at school today?
10 I met on my way home a friend of mine.

109.2 Put the parts of the sentence in the correct order.

1 (the party / very much / everybody enjoyed)   *Everybody enjoyed the party very much.*
2 (we won / easily / the game)
3 (quietly / the door / I closed)
4 (Tanya / quite well / speaks / German)

5 (Sam / all the time / TV / watches)

6 (again / please don't ask / that question)

7 (football / every weekend / does Kevin play?)

8 (some money / I borrowed / from a friend of mine)

109.3 Complete the sentences. Put the parts in the correct order.

1 (for a long time / have lived / in the same house)
They *have lived in the same house for a long time*.
2 (to the supermarket / every Friday / go)
I   .
3 (home / did you come / so late)
Why   ?
4 (her children / takes / every day / to school)
Sarah   .
5 (been / recently / to the cinema)
I haven't   .
6 (at the top of the page / your name / write)
Please   .
7 (her name / after a few minutes / remembered)
I   .
8 (around the town / all morning / walked)
We   .
9 (on Saturday night / didn't see you / at the party)
I   .
10 (some interesting books / found / in the library)
We   .
11 (her umbrella / last night / in a restaurant / left)
Laura   .
12 (opposite the park / a new hotel / are building)
They   .

A Some adverbs (for example, **always**, **also**, **probably**) go with the verb in the middle of a sentence:
- ☐ Helen **always drives** to work.
- ☐ We were feeling very tired and we **were also** hungry.
- ☐ The concert **will probably be cancelled**.

B If the verb is one word (**drives/fell/cooked** etc.), the adverb goes *before* the verb:

	adverb	verb	
Helen	always	**drives**	to work.
I	almost	**fell**	as I was going down the stairs.

- ☐ I cleaned the house and **also cooked** the dinner.   (*not* cooked also)
- ☐ Lucy **hardly ever watches** television and **rarely reads** newspapers.
- ☐ 'Shall I give you my address?' 'No, I **already have** it.'

Note that these adverbs (**always/often/also** etc.) go before **have to** … :
- ☐ Joe never phones me. I **always have** to phone him.   (*not* I have always to phone)

But adverbs go *after* **am/is/are/was/were**:
- ☐ We were feeling very tired and we **were also** hungry.
- ☐ Why are you always late? You**'re never** on time.
- ☐ The traffic **isn't usually** as bad as it was this morning.

C If the verb is two or more words (for example, **can remember / doesn't eat / will be cancelled**), the adverb usually goes *after the first verb* (**can/doesn't/will** etc.):

	verb 1	adverb	verb 2	
I	**can**	**never**	**remember**	her name.
Clare	**doesn't**	**often**	**eat**	meat.
	Are you	**definitely**	**going**	away next week?
The concert	**will**	**probably**	**be**	cancelled.

- ☐ You**'ve always been** very kind to me.
- ☐ Jack can't cook. He **can't even boil** an egg.
- ☐ **Do** you **still work** for the same company?
- ☐ The house **was only built** a year ago and it**'s already falling** down.

Note that **probably** goes before a negative (**isn't/won't** etc.). So we say:
- ☐ I **probably won't see** you.   *or*   I will **probably not** see you.   (*not* I won't probably)

D We also use **all** and **both** in these positions:
- ☐ We **all felt** ill after the meal.   (*not* we felt all ill)
- ☐ My parents **are both** teachers.   (*not* my parents both are teachers)
- ☐ Sarah and Jane **have both applied** for the job.
- ☐ We **are all going** out tonight.

E Sometimes we use **is/will/did** etc. instead of repeating part of a sentence (see Unit 51):
- ☐ Tom says he isn't clever, but I think he **is**.   (= he **is clever**)

When we do this, we put **always/never** etc. *before* the verb:
- ☐ He always says he won't be late, but he **always is**.   (= he **is always** late)
- ☐ I've never done it and I **never will**.   (= I **will never** do it)

Word order 1 → Unit 109

Exercises

110.1 Are the underlined words in the right position or not? Correct the sentences where necessary.

1 Helen drives <u>always</u> to work.   *Helen always drives to work.*
2 I cleaned the house and <u>also</u> cooked the dinner.   *OK*
3 I have <u>usually</u> a shower in the morning.
4 We <u>soon</u> found the solution to the problem.
5 Steve gets <u>hardly ever</u> angry.
6 I did some shopping and I went <u>also</u> to the bank.
7 Jane has <u>always</u> to hurry in the morning.
8 I <u>never</u> have worked in a factory.
9 I <u>never</u> have enough time. I <u>always</u> am busy.

110.2 Rewrite the sentences to include the word in brackets.

1 Clare doesn't eat meat. (often)   *Clare doesn't often eat meat.*
2 Katherine is very generous. (always)
3 I don't have to work on Saturdays. (usually)
4 Do you watch TV in the evenings? (always)
5 Martin is learning Spanish and he is learning Japanese. (also)
  Martin is learning Spanish and he
6 a We were on holiday in Spain. (all)
  b We were staying at the same hotel. (all)
  c We enjoyed ourselves. (all)
7 a The new hotel is very expensive. (probably)
  b It costs a lot to stay there. (probably)
8 a I can help you. (probably)
  b I can't help you. (probably)

110.3 Complete the sentences. Use the words in brackets in the correct order.

1   *I can never remember*   (remember / I / never / can) her name.
2 .... (take / I / usually) sugar in coffee.
3 .... (am / usually / I) hungry when I get home from work.
4 Mark and Amy .... (both / were / born) in Manchester.
5 Lisa is a good pianist. .... (sing / she / also / can) very well.
6 Our cat .... (usually / sleeps) under the bed.
7 They live in the same building as me, but ....
  (never / I / have / spoken) to them.
8 This shop is always very busy. ....
  (have / you / always / to wait) a long time to be served.
9 My eyesight isn't very good.
  (I / read / can / only) with glasses.
10 .... (all / were / we) tired, so ....
  (all / we / fell) asleep.
11 A: Are you tired?
   B: Yes, ... (am / I / always) at this time of day.
12 .... (I / probably / leaving / will / be) early tomorrow.
13 I'm afraid .... (probably / I / be / won't) able to come to
   the party.
14 Helen is away a lot. .... (is / hardly ever / she) at home.
15 .... (we / still / are / living) in the same place. We haven't
   moved.
16 If we hadn't taken the same train, ...
   (never / met / we / would / have) each other.
17 Tanya .... (says / always) that she'll phone me, but
   .... (does / she / never).

A Still

We use **still** to say that a situation or action is continuing. It hasn't changed or stopped:

- ○ It's 10 o'clock and Joe is **still** in bed.
- ○ When I went to bed, Chris was **still** working.
- ○ Do you **still** want to go away or have you changed your mind?

Still usually goes in the middle of the sentence with the verb (see Unit 110).

B Any more / any longer / no longer

We use **not** … **any more** or **not** … **any longer** to say that a situation has changed. **Any more** and **any longer** go at the end of a sentence:

- ○ Lucy **doesn't** work here **any more** (*or* any longer). She left last month.
  (*not* Lucy doesn't still work here.)
- ○ We used to be good friends, but we **aren't any more** (*or* any longer).

You can also use **no longer**. **No longer** goes in the middle of the sentence:

- ○ Lucy **no longer** works here.

Note that we do not normally use **no more** in this way:

- ○ We are **no longer** friends. (*not* We are no more friends.)

Compare **still** and **not** … **any more**:

- ○ Sally **still** works here, but Lucy **doesn't** work here **any more**.

C Yet

Yet = until now. We use **yet** mainly in negative sentences (**He isn't** here **yet**) and questions (**Is he** here **yet**?). **Yet** shows that the speaker is expecting something to happen.
Yet usually goes at the end of a sentence:

- ○ It's 10 o'clock and Joe **isn't** here **yet**.
- ○ **Have** you **met** your new neighbours **yet**?
- ○ 'Where are you going on holiday?' 'We **don't** know **yet**.'

We often use **yet** with the *present perfect* (**Have** you **met** … **yet**?). See Unit 7D.

Compare **yet** and **still**:

- ○ Mike lost his job six months ago and **is still** unemployed.
  Mike lost his job six months ago and **hasn't found** another job **yet**.
- ○ **Is** it **still** raining?
  Has it **stopped** raining **yet**?

Still is also possible in *negative* sentences (before the negative):

- ○ She said she would be here an hour ago and she **still hasn't** come.

This is similar to 'she hasn't come **yet**'. But **still** … **not** shows a stronger feeling of surprise or impatience. Compare:

- ○ I sent him an invitation last week. He **hasn't** replied **yet**. (but I expect he will reply soon)
- ○ I sent him an invitation weeks ago and he **still hasn't** replied. (he should have replied before now)

D Already

We use **already** to say that something happened sooner than expected. **Already** usually goes in the middle of a sentence (see Unit 110):

- ○ 'What time is Sue leaving?' 'She has **already** left.' (= sooner than you expected)
- ○ Shall I tell Joe what happened or does he **already** know?
- ○ I've just had lunch and I'm **already** hungry.

Present perfect + **already/yet** ➔ Unit 7D   Word order ➔ Unit 110

Exercises

111.1 Compare what Paul said a few years ago with what he says now. Some things are the same as before and some things have changed. Write sentences with **still** and **any more**.

Paul a few years ago

I travel a lot.
I work in a shop.
I write poems.
I want to be a teacher.
I'm interested in politics.
I'm single.
I go fishing a lot.

Paul now

I travel a lot.
I work in a hospital.
I gave up writing poems.
I want to be a teacher.
I'm not interested in politics.
I'm single.
I haven't been fishing for years.

1 (travel)   *He still travels a lot.*
2 (shop)   *He doesn't work in a shop any more.*
3 (poems) He
4 (teacher)
5 (politics)
6 (single)
7 (fishing)
8 (beard)

Now write three sentences about Paul using **no longer**.

9   *He no longer works in a shop.*
10
11
12

111.2 For each sentence (with **still**) write a sentence with a similar meaning using **not … yet** + one of the following verbs:

| decide | find | finish | go | ~~stop~~ | take off | wake up |

1 It's still raining.   *It hasn't stopped raining yet.*
2 Gary is still here.   He
3 They're still repairing the road.   They
4 The children are still asleep.
5 Ann is still looking for a place to live.
6 I'm still wondering what to do.
7 The plane is still waiting on the runway.

111.3 Put in **still**, **yet**, **already** or **any more** in the <u>underlined</u> sentence (or part of the sentence). Study the examples carefully.

1 Mike lost his job a year ago and <u>he is unemployed</u>.   *he is still unemployed*
2 Shall I tell Joe what happened or <u>does he know</u>?   *does he already know?*
3 I'm hungry. <u>Is dinner ready?</u>   *Is dinner ready yet?*
4 I was hungry earlier, but <u>I'm not hungry</u>.   *I'm not hungry any more*
5 Can we wait a few minutes? <u>I don't want to go out.</u>
6 Amy used to work at the airport, but <u>she doesn't work there</u>.
7 I used to live in Amsterdam. <u>I have a lot of friends there.</u>
8 'Shall I introduce you to Joe?'   'There's no need. <u>We've met.</u>'
9 <u>Do you live in the same place</u> or have you moved?
10 Would you like to eat with us or <u>have you eaten</u>?
11 'Where's John?'   '<u>He's not here.</u> He'll be here soon.'
12 Tim said he'd be here at 8.30. It's 9 o'clock now and <u>he isn't here</u>.
13 Do you want to join the club or <u>are you a member</u>?
14 It happened a long time ago, but <u>I can remember it very clearly</u>.
15 I've put on weight. <u>These trousers don't fit me.</u>
16 '<u>Have you finished with the paper?</u>' 'No, <u>I'm reading it.</u>'

A

Study this example situation:

Tina loves watching television.

She has a TV in every room of the house, **even** the bathroom.

We use **even** to say that something is unusual or surprising. It is not usual to have a TV in the bathroom.

Some more examples:
- ○ These pictures are really awful. **Even I** take better pictures than these. (and I'm certainly not a good photographer)
- ○ He always wears a coat, **even in hot weather**.
- ○ The print was very small. I couldn't read it, **even with glasses**.
- ○ Nobody would help her, **not even her best friend**.
- *or* **Not even** her best friend would help her.

B

You can use **even** with the verb in the middle of a sentence (see Unit 110):
- ○ Sue has travelled all over the world. She has **even** been to the Antarctic. (It's especially unusual to go to the Antarctic, so she must have travelled a lot.)
- ○ They are very rich. They **even** have their own private jet.

Study these examples with **even** after a negative (**not/can't/don't** etc.):
- ○ I can't cook. I **can't even** boil an egg. (and boiling an egg is very easy)
- ○ They weren't very friendly to us. They **didn't even** say hello.
- ○ Jessica is very fit. She's just run five miles and she's **not even** out of breath.

C

You can use **even** + *comparative* (**cheaper** / **more expensive** etc.):
- ○ I got up very early, but Jack got up **even earlier**.
- ○ I knew I didn't have much money, but I've got **even less** than I thought.
- ○ We were surprised to get an email from her. We were **even more surprised** when she came to see us a few days later.

D

Even though / even when / even if

We use **even though / even when / even if** + *subject* + *verb*:

- ○ **Even though she can't** drive, she bought a car.

       subject + verb

- ○ He never shouts, **even when he's** angry.
- ○ This river is dangerous. It's dangerous to swim in it, **even if you're** a strong swimmer.

You cannot use **even** in this way (+ *subject* + *verb*). We say:
- ○ **Even though she can't** drive, she bought a car. (*not* Even she can't drive)
- ○ I can't reach the shelf **even if I stand** on a chair. (*not* even I stand)

Compare **even if** and **if**:
- ○ We're going to the beach tomorrow. It doesn't matter what the weather is like. We're going **even if** it's raining.
- ○ We want to go to the beach tomorrow, but we won't go **if** it's raining.

If and when ➜ Unit 25D   Though / even though ➜ Unit 113E

Exercises

112.1 Amy, Kate and Lisa are three friends who went on holiday together. Use the information given about them to complete the sentences using **even** or **not even**.

Amy is usually happy is usually on time likes getting up early is very interested in art	*Kate* isn't very keen on art is usually miserable usually hates hotels hasn't got a camera	*Lisa* is almost always late is a keen photographer loves staying in hotels isn't very good at getting up

1 They stayed at a hotel. Everybody liked it, _____even Kate_____ .
2 They arranged to meet. They all arrived on time, _____ .
3 They went to an art gallery. Nobody enjoyed it, _____ .
4 Yesterday they had to get up early. They all managed to do this, _____ .
5 They were together yesterday. They were all in a good mood, _____ .
6 None of them took any pictures, _____ .

112.2 Make sentences with **even**. Use the words in brackets.

1 Sue has been all over the world. (the Antarctic) _She has even been to the Antarctic._
2 We painted the whole room. (the floor) We _____
3 Rachel has met lots of famous people. (the prime minister)
    She _____
4 You could hear the noise from a long way away. (from the next street)
    You _____

In the following sentences you have to use **not** ... **even**.

5 They didn't say anything to us. (hello) _They didn't even say hello._
6 I can't remember anything about her. (her name)
    I _____
7 There isn't anything to do in this town. (a cinema)
    _____
8 He didn't tell anybody where he was going. (his wife)
    _____
9 I don't know anyone in our street. (the people next door)
    _____

112.3 Complete the sentences using **even** + comparative.

1 It was very hot yesterday, but today it's _even hotter_ .
2 The church is 500 years old, but the house next to it is _____ .
3 That's a very good idea, but I've got an _____ one.
4 The first question was very difficult to answer. The second one was _____ .
5 I did very badly in the exam, but most of my friends did _____ .
6 Neither of us was hungry. I ate very little and my friend ate _____ .

112.4 Put in **if**, **even**, **even if** or **even though**.

1 _Even though_ she can't drive, she has bought a car.
2 The bus leaves in five minutes, but we can still catch it _____ we run.
3 The bus leaves in two minutes. We won't catch it now _____ we run.
4 His Spanish isn't very good, _____ after three years in Spain.
5 His Spanish isn't very good, _____ he lived in Spain for three years.
6 _____ with the heating on, it was cold in the house.
7 I couldn't sleep _____ I was very tired.
8 I won't forgive them for what they did, _____ they apologise.
9 _____ I hadn't eaten anything for 24 hours, I wasn't hungry.

→ Additional exercise 32 (page 321)

A

Study this example situation:

Last year Paul and Sarah had a holiday by the sea.
It rained a lot, but they enjoyed it.

You can say:

Although it rained a lot, they enjoyed it.
(= It rained a lot, *but* they …)
or
In spite of
    Despite } **the rain**, they enjoyed it.

B

After **although** we use a *subject + verb*:
- ☐ **Although it rained** a lot, we enjoyed our holiday.
- ☐ I didn't get the job **although I had** the necessary qualifications.

Compare the meaning of **although** and **because**:
- ☐ We went out **although** it was raining heavily.
- ☐ We didn't go out **because** it was raining heavily.

C

After **in spite of** or **despite**, we use a *noun*, a *pronoun* (**this/that/what** etc.) or *-ing*:
- ☐ **In spite of the rain**, we enjoyed our holiday.
- ☐ I didn't get the job **in spite of having** the necessary qualifications.
- ☐ She wasn't well, but **in spite of this** she continued working.
- ☐ **In spite of what** I said yesterday, I still love you.

Despite is the same as **in spite of**. We say **in spite of**, but **despite** (*without* of):
- ☐ She wasn't well, but **despite this** she continued working. (*not* despite of this)

You can say **in spite of the fact (that)** … and **despite the fact (that)** … :
- ☐ I didn't get the job { **in spite of the fact (that)**
                          despite the fact (that) } I had the necessary qualifications.

Compare **in spite of** and **because of**:
- ☐ We went out **in spite of the rain**. (*or* … **despite the rain**.)
- ☐ We didn't go out **because of the rain**.

D

Compare **although** and **in spite of / despite**:
- ☐ **Although the traffic was** bad,
     In spite of the traffic, } we arrived on time. (*not* In spite of the traffic was bad)

- ☐ I couldn't sleep { **although I was** very tired. (*not* despite I was tired)
                      despite being very tired.

E

Though is the same as **although**:
- ☐ I didn't get the job **though** I had the necessary qualifications.

In spoken English we often use **though** at the end of a sentence:
- ☐ The house isn't so nice. I like the garden **though**. (= but I like the garden)
- ☐ I see them every day. I've never spoken to them **though**. (= but I've never spoken to them)

Even though (*but not* 'even' alone) is a stronger form of **although**:
- ☐ **Even though** I was really tired, I couldn't sleep. (*not* Even I was really tired …)

Even ➜ Unit 112

Exercises

113.1 Complete the sentences. Use **although** + a sentence from the box.

I didn't speak the language well	~~he has a very important job~~
I had never seen her before	we don't like them very much
it was quite cold	the heating was on
I'd met her twice before	we've known each other a long time

1 _Although he has a very important job_ , he isn't particularly well-paid.
2 .... , I recognised her from a photograph.
3 She wasn't wearing a coat ....
4 We thought we'd better invite them to the party ....
5 .... , I managed to make myself understood.
6 .... , the room wasn't warm.
7 I didn't recognise her ....
8 We're not very good friends ....

113.2 Complete the sentences with **although / in spite of / because / because of**.

1 _Although_ it rained a lot, we enjoyed our holiday.
2 a .... all our careful plans, a lot of things went wrong.
   b .... we'd planned everything carefully, a lot of things went wrong.
3 a I went home early .... I was feeling unwell.
   b I went to work the next day .... I was still feeling unwell.
4 a She only accepted the job .... the salary, which was very high.
   b She accepted the job .... the salary, which was rather low.
5 a I managed to get to sleep .... there was a lot of noise.
   b I couldn't get to sleep .... the noise.

Use your own ideas to complete the following sentences:

6 a He passed the exam although ....
   b He passed the exam because ....
7 a I didn't eat anything although ....
   b I didn't eat anything in spite of ....

113.3 Make one sentence from two. Use the word(s) in brackets in your sentences.

1 I couldn't sleep. I was very tired. (despite)
   I couldn't sleep despite being very tired.
2 They have very little money. They are happy. (in spite of)
   In spite ....
3 My foot was injured. I managed to walk home. (although)
   ....
4 I enjoyed the film. The story was silly. (in spite of)
   ....
5 We live in the same street. We hardly ever see each other. (despite)
   ....
6 I got very wet in the rain. I was only out for five minutes. (even though)
   ....

113.4 Use the words in brackets to make a sentence with **though** at the end.

1 The house isn't very nice. (like / garden) _I like the garden though._
2 It's warm today. (very windy) ....
3 We didn't like the food. (ate) ....
4 Liz is very nice. (don't like / husband) I ....

→ Additional exercise 32 (page 321)   **227**

A

Study this example situation:

Your car should have a spare wheel because it is possible you will have a puncture.

Your car should have a spare wheel **in case** you have a puncture.

In case you have a puncture = because it is possible you will have a puncture.

Some more examples of **in case**:
- ○ I'll leave my mobile phone switched on **in case Jane calls**. (= because it is possible she will call)
- ○ I'll draw a map for you **in case you have problems finding our house**. (= because it is possible you will have problems)
- ○ I'll remind them about the meeting **in case they've forgotten**. (= because it is possible they have forgotten)

We use **just in case** for a smaller possibility:
- ○ I don't think it will rain, but I'll take an umbrella **just in case**. (= **just in case** it rains)

Do not use **will** after **in case**. Use a present tense for the future (see Unit 25):
- ○ I'll leave my phone switched on **in case** Jane **calls**. (*not* in case Jane will call)

B

In case is not the same as **if**. We use **in case** to say *why* somebody does (or doesn't do) something. You do something *now* **in case** something happens *later*.

Compare:

in case	if
○ We'll buy some more food **in case** Tom comes. (= Maybe Tom will come. We'll buy some more food now, whether he comes or not; then we'll *already* have the food *if* he comes.)	○ We'll buy some more food **if** Tom comes. (= Maybe Tom will come. If he comes, we'll buy some more food; if he doesn't come, we won't buy any more food.)
○ I'll give you my phone number **in case** you need to contact me.	○ You can call me on this number **if** you need to contact me.
○ You should insure your bike **in case** it is stolen.	○ You should inform the police **if** your bike is stolen.

C

You can use **in case** + *past* to say why somebody did something:
- ○ I left my phone switched on **in case Jane called**. (= because it was possible that Jane would call)
- ○ I drew a map for Sarah **in case she had problems finding the house**.
- ○ We rang the doorbell again **in case they hadn't heard it the first time**.

D

In case of is not the same as **in case**. **In case of** ... = if there is ... (especially on notices etc.):
- ○ **In case of fire**, please leave the building as quickly as possible. (= if there is a fire)
- ○ **In case of emergency**, call this number. (= if there is an emergency)

If ➜ Units 25, 38–40

Exercises

114.1 Sophie is going for a long walk in the country. You think she should take:

> ~~some chocolate~~   a map   an anorak   a camera   some water

You think she should take these things because:

> it's possible she'll get lost   ~~she might get hungry~~
> perhaps she'll be thirsty   maybe it will rain
> she might want to take some pictures

What do you say to Sophie? Write sentences with in case.

1 _Take some chocolate in case you get hungry._
2 Take ....
3 ....
4 ....
5 ....

114.2 **What do you say in these situations? Use in case.**

1 It's possible that Jane will need to contact you, so you agree to give her your phone number.
   You say: I'll give you my phone number _in case you need to contact me_ .
2 A friend of yours is going away for a long time. Maybe you won't see her again before she
   goes, so you decide to say goodbye now.
   You say: I'll say goodbye now ....
3 You are shopping in a supermarket with a friend. You think you have everything you need,
   but maybe you forgot something. Your friend has the list. You ask her to check it.
   You say: Can you .... ?
4 You advise a friend about using a computer. You think he should back up (= *copy*) his files
   because maybe there will be a problem with his computer (and he could lose all his data).
   You say: You should back up ....

114.3 **Complete the sentences using in case.**

1 There was a possibility that Jane would call. So I left my phone switched on.
   I left _my phone switched on in case Jane called_ .
2 I thought that I might forget the name of the book. So I wrote it down.
   I wrote down the name of the book ....
3 I thought my parents might be worried about me. So I phoned them.
   I phoned my parents ....
4 I sent an email to Lisa, but she didn't reply. So I sent another email because maybe she didn't
   get the first one.
   I sent her another email ....
5 I met some people when I was on holiday in France. They said they might come to London
   one day. I live in London, so I gave them my phone number.
   I gave them my phone number ....

114.4 **Put in in case or if.**

1 I'll draw a map for you _in case_ you have problems finding our house.
2 You should tell the police _if_ you have any information about the crime.
3 I hope you'll come to Australia sometime. .... you come, you must visit us.
4 This book belongs to Susan. Can you give it to her .... you see her?
5 Write your name and phone number on your bag .... you lose it.
6 Go to the lost property office .... you lose your bag.
7 The burglar alarm will ring .... somebody tries to break into the house.
8 You should lock your bike to something .... somebody tries to steal it.
9 I was advised to get insurance .... I needed medical treatment while I was abroad.

→ Additional exercise 32 (page 321)

A **Unless**

Study this example situation:

> The club is for members only.
>
> You can't go in **unless you are a member**.
>
> This means:
>
> You can't go in *except if* you are a member.
> You can go in *only if* you are a member.
>
> **Unless** = except if.

Some more examples of **unless**:
- ○ I'll see you tomorrow **unless I have to work late**. (= except if I have to work late)
- ○ There are no buses to the beach. **Unless you have a car**, it's difficult to get there.
  (= except if you have a car)
- ○ 'Shall I tell Liz what happened?' '**Not unless** she asks you.' (= only if she asks you)
- ○ Sally hates to complain. She wouldn't complain about something **unless it was really bad**.
  (= except if it was really bad)
- ○ We can take a taxi to the restaurant – **unless you'd prefer to walk**. (= except if you'd prefer
  to walk)

Instead of **unless** it is often possible to say **if** … **not**:
- ○ **Unless we leave now**, we'll be late. *or* **If we don't leave now**, we'll …

B **As long as / provided / providing**

$\left.\begin{array}{l}\textbf{as long as } or \textbf{ so long as}\\ \textbf{provided (that)} or \textbf{ providing (that)}\end{array}\right\}$ All these expressions mean 'if' or 'on condition that'.

For example:
- ○ You can borrow my car $\left\{\begin{array}{l}\textbf{as long as}\\ \textbf{so long as}\end{array}\right\}$ you promise not to drive too fast.
  (= you can borrow my car, but you must promise not to drive too fast – this is a condition)

- ○ Travelling by car is convenient $\left\{\begin{array}{l}\textbf{provided (that)}\\ \textbf{providing (that)}\end{array}\right\}$ you have somewhere to park.
  (= but only if you have somewhere to park)

- ○ $\left.\begin{array}{l}\textbf{Providing (that)}\\ \textbf{Provided (that)}\end{array}\right\}$ the room is clean, I don't mind which hotel we stay at.
  (= the room must be clean – otherwise I don't mind)

C **Unless / as long as** etc. for the future

When you are talking about the future, do *not* use **will** after **unless / as long as / so long as /
provided / providing**. Use a *present* tense (see Unit 25):
- ○ I'm not going out **unless** it **stops** raining. (*not* unless it will stop)
- ○ **Providing** the weather **is** good, we're going to have a picnic tomorrow.
  (*not* providing the weather will be good)

If ➜ Units 25, 38–40

Exercises

115.1 Write a new sentence with the same meaning. Use **unless** in your sentence.

1 You must try a bit harder or you won't pass the exam.
   You won't pass the exam unless you try a bit harder.

2 Listen carefully or you won't know what to do.
   You won't know what to do

3 She must apologise to me or I'll never speak to her again.

4 You have to speak very slowly or he won't be able to understand you.

5 Business must improve soon or the company will have to close.

115.2 Write sentences with **unless**.

1 The club isn't open to everyone. You're allowed in only if you're a member.
   You aren't allowed in the club unless you're a member.

2 I don't want to go to the party alone. I'm going only if you go too.
   I'm not going

3 Don't worry about the dog. It will attack you only if you move suddenly.
   The dog

4 Ben isn't very talkative. He'll speak to you only if you ask him something.
   Ben

5 Today is a public holiday. The doctor will see you only if it's an emergency.
   The doctor

115.3 Which is correct?

1 You can borrow my car <u>unless / as long as</u> you promise not to drive too fast.
   (<u>as long as</u> *is correct*)
2 I'm playing tennis tomorrow <u>unless / providing</u> it rains.
3 I'm playing tennis tomorrow <u>unless / providing</u> it doesn't rain.
4 I don't mind if you come home late <u>unless / as long as</u> you come in quietly.
5 I'm going now <u>unless / provided</u> you want me to stay.
6 I don't watch TV <u>unless / as long as</u> I've got nothing else to do.
7 Children are allowed to use the swimming pool <u>unless / provided</u> they are with an adult.
8 <u>Unless / Provided</u> they are with an adult, children are not allowed to use the swimming pool.
9 We can sit here in the corner <u>unless / as long as</u> you'd rather sit over there by the window.
10 A: Our holiday cost a lot of money.
   B: Did it? Well, that doesn't matter <u>unless / as long as</u> you enjoyed yourselves.

115.4 Use your own ideas to complete these sentences.

1 We'll be late unless _we get a taxi_ .
2 I like hot weather as long as .
3 It takes about 20 minutes to drive to the airport provided .
4 I don't mind walking home as long as .
5 I like to walk to work in the morning unless .
6 We can meet tomorrow unless .
7 I can lend you the money providing .
8 You won't achieve anything unless .

→ Additional exercise 32 (page 321)

As (As I walked along the street ... / As I was hungry ...)

A

As = at the same time as

You can use **as** when two things happen at the same time:
- ○ We all waved goodbye to Liz **as** she drove away.
  (We **waved** and she **drove** away at the same time)
- ○ **As** I walked along the street, I looked in the shop windows.
- ○ Can you turn off the light **as** you go out, please?

Bye!

Or you can say that something happened **as you were doing** something else (in the middle of doing something else):
- ○ Kate slipped **as she was getting off** the bus.
- ○ We met Paul **as we were leaving** the hotel.

For the *past continuous* (**was getting** / **were going** etc.), see Unit 6.

You can also use **just as** (= exactly at that moment):
- ○ **Just as** I sat down, the doorbell rang.
- ○ I had to leave **just as** the conversation was getting interesting.

We also use **as** when two things happen together in a longer period of time:
- ○ **As** the day went on, the weather got worse.
- ○ I began to enjoy the job more **as** I got used to it.

the day went on
the weather got worse

Compare **as** and **when**:

We use **as** only if two things happen at the same time. ○ **As I drove home**, I listened to music. (= at the same time)	Use **when** (*not* as) if one thing happens after another. ○ **When I got home**, I had something to eat. (*not* As I got home)

B

As = because

As also means 'because':
- ○ **As I was hungry**, I decided to find somewhere to eat.   (= because I was hungry)
- ○ **As we have plenty of time** before our flight, let's go and have a coffee.
- ○ We watched TV all evening **as we didn't have anything better to do**.
- ○ **As I don't watch television any more**, I gave my TV to a friend of mine.

You can also use **since** in this way:
- ○ **Since** we have plenty of time, let's go and have a coffee.

Compare **as** (= because) and **when**:

○ I couldn't contact David **as he was on holiday**. (= because he was on holiday)	○ David's passport was stolen **when he was on holiday**. (= during the time he was away)
○ **As they lived near us**, we used to see them quite often. (= because they lived near us)	○ **When they lived near us**, we used to see them quite often. (= at the time they lived near us)

As ... as → Unit 107   Like and as → Unit 117   As if → Unit 118

Exercises

116.1 (Section A) Use **as** to join sentences from the boxes.

1 ~~We all waved goodbye to Liz~~
2 I listened
3 I burnt myself
4 The crowd cheered
5 A dog ran out in front of the car

we were driving along the road
I was taking a hot dish out of the oven
~~she drove away~~
she told me her story
the two teams came onto the field

1   We all waved goodbye to Liz as she drove away.
2
3
4
5

116.2 (Section B) Join sentences from the boxes. Begin each sentence with **as**.

1 ~~I was hungry~~
2 today is a public holiday
3 I didn't want to disturb anybody
4 I don't know what to do
5 none of us had a watch

I need some advice
I was very quiet
~~I decided to find somewhere to eat~~
we didn't know what time it was
many of the shops are shut

1   As I was hungry, I decided to find somewhere to eat.
2
3
4
5

116.3 What does **as** mean in these sentences?

	because	at the same time as
1 **As** they live near us, we see them quite often.	✓	
2 Kate slipped **as** she was getting off the bus.		✓
3 **As** I was tired, I went to bed early.		
4 Unfortunately, **as** I was parking the car, I hit the car behind me.		
5 **As** we climbed the hill, we got more and more tired.		
6 We decided to go out to eat **as** we had no food at home.		
7 **As** we don't use the car very often, we've decided to sell it.		

116.4 In some of these sentences, you need **when** (not as). Correct the sentences where necessary.

1 Julia got married as she was 22.   when she was 22
2 As the day went on, the weather got worse.   OK
3 He dropped the glass as he was taking it out of the cupboard.
4 I lost my phone as I was in London.
5 As I left school, I didn't know what to do.
6 The train slowed down as it approached the station.
7 I used to live near the sea as I was a child.

116.5 Use your own ideas to complete these sentences.

1 I saw you as
2 It started to rain just as
3 As I didn't have enough money for a taxi,
4 Just as I took the picture,

➜ Additional exercise 32 (page 321)   **233**

Like and as

A

Like = 'similar to', 'the same as'. You cannot use **as** in this way:

○ What a beautiful house! It's **like a palace**. (*not* as a palace)
○ 'What does Sandra do?' 'She's a teacher, **like me**.' (*not* as me)
○ Be careful! The floor has been polished. It's **like walking on ice**. (*not* as walking)
○ It's raining again. I hate weather **like this**. (*not* as this)

In these sentences, **like** is a *preposition*. So it is followed by a *noun* (like **a palace**), a *pronoun* (like **me** / like **this**) or **-ing** (like **walking**).

You can also say '... **like** (somebody/something) **doing** something':

○ 'What's that noise?' 'It sounds **like a baby crying**.'

Sometimes **like** = for example:

○ I enjoy water sports, **like surfing, scuba diving and water-skiing**.

You can also use **such as** (= for example):

○ I enjoy water sports, **such as surfing, scuba diving and water-skiing**.

B

As = in the same way as, or in the same condition as. We use **as** before *subject + verb*:

○ I didn't move anything. I left everything **as it was**.
○ You should have done it **as I showed you**.

We also use **like** in this way:

○ I left everything **like it was**.

Compare **as** and **like**:

○ You should have done it **as I showed you**. *or* ... **like I showed you**.
○ You should have done it **like this**. (*not* as this)

Note that we say **as usual** / **as always**:

○ You're late **as usual**.
○ **As always**, Nick was the first to complain.

C

Sometimes **as** (+ *subject + verb*) has other meanings. For example, after **do**:

○ You can do **as you like**. (= do what you like)
○ They did **as they promised**. (= They did what they promised.)

We also say **as you know** / **as I said** / **as she expected** / **as I thought** etc. :

○ **As you know**, it's Emma's birthday next week. (= you know this already)
○ Andy failed his driving test, **as he expected**. (= he expected this before)

Like is not usual in these expressions, except with **say** (**like I said**):

○ **As I said** yesterday, I'm sure we can solve the problem. *or* **Like I said** yesterday ...

D

As can also be a *preposition*, but the meaning is different from **like**.
Compare:

○ **As a taxi driver**, I spend most of my working life in a car. (I am a taxi driver, that is my job)	○ Everyone wants me to drive them to places. I'm **like a taxi driver**. (I'm not a taxi driver, but I'm like one)

As (*preposition*) = in the position of, in the form of etc. :

○ Many years ago I worked **as a photographer**. (*not* like a photographer)
○ Many words, for example 'work' and 'rain', can be used **as verbs or nouns**.
○ London is fine **as a place to visit**, but I wouldn't like to live there.
○ The news of the tragedy came **as a great shock**.

As ... as ➜ Unit 107   As (= at the same time as / because) ➜ Unit 116   As if ➜ Unit 118

Exercises

117.1 In some of these sentences, you need **like** (not **as**). Correct the sentences where necessary.

1 It's raining again. I hate <u>weather as this</u>.　　　　<u>weather like this</u>
2 Andy failed his driving test, as he expected.　　　　<u>OK</u>
3 Do you think Lisa looks as her mother?
4 Tim gets on my nerves. I can't stand people as him.
5 Why didn't you do it as I told you to do it?
6 Brian is a student, as most of his friends.
7 You never listen. Talking to you is as talking to the wall.
8 As I said before, I'm thinking of changing my job.
9 Tom's idea seems a good one. Let's do as he suggests.
10 I'll phone you tomorrow as usual, OK?
11 Suddenly there was a terrible noise. It was as a bomb exploding.
12 She's a very good swimmer. She swims as a fish.

117.2 Complete the sentences using **like** or **as** + the following:

a beginner	blocks of ice	~~a palace~~	a birthday present
a child	a theatre	winter	a tour guide

1 This house is beautiful. It's __like a palace__ .
2 My feet are really cold. They're _____ .
3 I've been playing tennis for years, but I still play _____ .
4 Marion once had a part-time job _____ .
5 I wonder what that building is. It looks _____ .
6 My brother gave me this watch _____ a long time ago.
7 It's very cold for the middle of summer. It's _____ .
8 He's 22 years old, but he sometimes behaves _____ .

117.3 Put in **like** or **as**. Sometimes either word is possible.

1 We heard a noise __like__ a baby crying.
2 Your English is very fluent. I wish I could speak _____ you.
3 Don't take my advice if you don't want to. You can do _____ you like.
4 You waste too much time doing things _____ sitting in cafés all day.
5 I wish I had a car _____ yours.
6 You don't need to change clothes. You can go out _____ you are.
7 My neighbour's house is full of interesting things. It's _____ a museum.
8 We saw Kevin last night. He was very cheerful, _____ always.
9 Sally has been working _____ a waitress for the last two months.
10 In several countries in Asia, _____ Japan, Indonesia and Thailand, traffic drives on the left.
11 You're different from the other people I know. I don't know anyone else _____ you.
12 We don't need all the bedrooms in the house, so we use one of them _____ a study.
13 The news that Sarah and Gary were getting married came _____ a complete surprise to me.
14 _____ her father, Catherine has a very good voice.
15 At the moment I've got a temporary job in a bookshop. It's not great, but it's OK _____ a temporary job.
16 _____ you can imagine, we were very tired after such a long journey.
17 This tea is awful. It tastes _____ water.
18 I think I prefer this room _____ it was, before we decorated it.

Like / as if / as though

A

You can use **like** to say how somebody or something **looks/sounds/feels**:
- ○ That house **looks like** it's going to fall down.
- ○ Helen **sounded like** she had a cold, didn't she?
- ○ I've just got back from holiday, but I feel very tired. I don't **feel like** I've had a holiday.

> That house **looks like** it's going to fall down.

You can also use **as if** or **as though** in all these examples:
- ○ That house **looks as if** it's going to fall down.
- ○ Helen **sounded as if** she had a cold, didn't she?
- ○ I don't **feel as though** I've had a holiday.

Compare:
- ○ You **look tired**.   (**look** + *adjective*)
  You **look like you haven't slept**.   (**look like** + *subject* + *verb*)

As if and **as though** are more formal than **like**.

B

You can say **It looks like** … / **It sounds like** … :
- ○ Sarah is very late, isn't she? **It looks like** she isn't coming.
- ○ We took an umbrella because **it looked like** it was going to rain.
- ○ The noise is very loud next door. **It sounds like** they're having a party.

> **It sounds like** they're having a party next door.

You can also use **as if** or **as though**:
- ○ It **looks as if** she isn't coming. *or*
  It **looks as though** she isn't coming.
- ○ It **looked as if** it was going to rain.
- ○ It **sounds as though** they're having a party.

C

You can use **like** / **as if** / **as though** with other verbs to say how somebody does something:
- ○ He ran **like he was running for his life**.
- ○ After the interruption, the speaker went on talking **as if nothing had happened**.
- ○ When I told them my plan, they looked at me **as though I was mad**.

D

After **as if** (or **as though**), we sometimes use the *past* when we are talking about the *present*.
For example:
- ○ I don't like Tim. He talks as if he **knew** everything.

The meaning is not past in this sentence. We use the past (as if he **knew**) because the idea is not real: Tim does *not* know everything. We use the past in the same way in other sentences with **if** and **wish** (see Unit 39).
Like is not normally used in this way.

Some more examples:
- ○ She's always asking me to do things for her – **as if I didn't** have enough to do already.
  (I *do* have enough to do)
- ○ Gary's only 40. Why do you talk about him **as if he was** an old man? (he isn't an old man)

When you use the past in this way, you can use **were** instead of **was**:
- ○ Why do you talk about him **as if he were** (*or* was) an old man?
- ○ They treat me **as if I were** (*or* was) their own son.   (I'm not their son)

If I was/were ➜ Unit 39C   Look/sound etc. + adjective ➜ Unit 99C   Like and as ➜ Unit 117

Exercises

118.1 What do you say in these situations? Use the words in brackets to make your sentence.

1 You meet Bill. He has a black eye and some plasters on his face. (look / like / be / a fight)
You say to him: *You look like you've been in a fight.*

2 Claire comes into the room. She looks absolutely terrified. (look / like / see / a ghost)
You say to her: What's the matter? You _____

3 Joe is on holiday. He's talking to you on the phone and sounds happy. (sound / as if / have / a good time)
You say to him: You _____

4 You have just run one kilometre. You are absolutely exhausted. (feel / like / run / a marathon)
You say to a friend: I _____

118.2 Make sentences beginning **It looks like** … / **It sounds like** … .

you should see a doctor	there's been an accident	they're having an argument
it's going to rain	~~she isn't coming~~	we'll have to walk

1 Sarah said she would be here an hour ago.
You say: *It looks like she isn't coming.*

2 The sky is full of black clouds.
You say: It _____

3 You hear two people shouting at each other next door.
You say: _____

4 You see an ambulance, some policemen and two damaged cars at the side of the road.
You say: _____

5 You and a friend have just missed the last bus home.
You say: _____

6 Dave isn't feeling well. He tells you all about it.
You say: _____

118.3 Complete the sentences with **as if**. Choose from the box, putting the verbs in the correct form.

she / enjoy / it	I / go / be sick	he / not / eat / for a week
~~he / need / a good rest~~	she / hurt / her leg	he / mean / what he / say
I / not / exist	she / not / want / come	

1 Mark looks very tired. He looks *as if he needs a good rest* .

2 I don't think Paul was joking. He looked _____ .

3 What's the matter with Amanda? She's walking _____ .

4 Peter was extremely hungry and ate his dinner very quickly.
He ate _____ .

5 Tanya had a bored expression on her face during the movie.
She didn't look _____ .

6 I've just eaten too many chocolates. Now I don't feel well.
I feel _____ .

7 I phoned Liz and invited her to the party, but she wasn't very enthusiastic about it.
She sounded _____ .

8 I went into the office, but nobody spoke to me or looked at me.
Everybody ignored me _____ .

118.4 These sentences are like the ones in Section D. Complete each sentence using **as if**.

1 Andy is a terrible driver. He drives *as if he were* the only driver on the road.

2 I'm 20 years old, so please don't talk to me _____ I _____ a child.

3 Steve has never met Nicola, but he talks about her _____ his best friend.

4 It was a long time ago that we first met, but I remember it _____ yesterday.

A

For and during

We use **for** + a period of time to say how long something goes on:

for **two hours**   for **a week**   for **ages**

- ○ We watched TV **for two hours** last night.
- ○ Jess is going away **for a week** in September.
- ○ Where have you been? I've been waiting **for ages**.
- ○ Are you going away **for the weekend**?

We use **during** + *noun* to say when something happens (*not* how long):

during **the movie**   during **our holiday**   during **the night**

- ○ I fell asleep **during the movie**.
- ○ We met some really nice people **during our holiday**.
- ○ The ground is wet. It must have rained **during the night**.

I fell asleep **during the movie**.

With 'time words' (for example: **the morning / the afternoon / the summer**), you can usually say **in** or **during**:

- ○ It must have rained **in the night**. *or* ... **during the night**.
- ○ I'll phone you sometime **during the afternoon**. *or* ... **in the afternoon**.

You cannot use **during** to say how long something goes on:

- ○ It rained **for** three days without stopping. (*not* during three days)

Compare **during** and **for**:

- ○ I fell asleep **during the movie**. I was asleep **for half an hour**.

B

During and while

Compare:

We use **during** + *noun:*
○ I fell asleep **during the movie**.
  ⌞*noun*⌟
	We use **while** + *subject + verb:*
	○ I fell asleep **while I was watching TV**.
	  ⌞*subject + verb*⌟

○ We met a lot of interesting people **during our holiday**.	○ We met a lot of interesting people **while we were on holiday**.
○ Robert suddenly began to feel ill **during the exam**.	○ Robert suddenly began to feel ill **while he was doing the exam**.

Some more examples of **while**:

- ○ We saw Clare **while we were waiting** for the bus.
- ○ **While you were** out, there was a phone call for you.
- ○ Alex read a book **while I watched** TV.

When you are talking about the future, use the *present* (*not* will) after **while**:

- ○ I'm going to Singapore next week. I hope to see some friends of mine **while I'm** there. (*not* while I will be there)
- ○ What are you going to do **while** you're waiting? (*not* while you'll be waiting)

Alex read a book **while I watched** TV.

See also Unit 25.

For and **since** ➔ Unit 12A   **While** + -ing ➔ Unit 68B

Exercises

119.1 Put in **for** or **during**.

1 It rained ___for___ three days without stopping.
2 I fell asleep ___during___ the movie.
3 I went to the theatre last night. I met Sue _____ the interval.
4 Martin hasn't lived in Britain all his life. He lived in Brazil _____ four years.
5 Production at the factory was seriously affected _____ the strike.
6 I felt really ill last week. I could hardly eat anything _____ three days.
7 I waited for you _____ half an hour and decided that you weren't coming.
8 Sarah was very angry with me. She didn't speak to me _____ a week.
9 We usually go out at weekends, but we don't go out _____ the week very often.
10 Jack started a new job a few weeks ago. Before that he was out of work _____ six months.
11 I need a break. I think I'll go away _____ a few days.
12 The president gave a long speech. She spoke _____ two hours.
13 We were hungry when we arrived. We hadn't had anything to eat _____ the journey.
14 We were hungry when we arrived. We hadn't had anything to eat _____ eight hours.

119.2 Put in **during** or **while**.

1 We met a lot of interesting people ___while___ we were on holiday.
2 We met a lot of interesting people ___during___ our holiday.
3 I met Mike _____ I was shopping.
4 _____ I was on holiday, I didn't read any newspapers or watch TV.
5 _____ our stay in Paris, we went to a lot of museums and galleries.
6 My phone rang _____ we were having dinner.
7 There was a lot of noise _____ the night. What was it?
8 I'd been away for many years. _____ that time, many things had changed.
9 What did they say about me _____ I was out of the room?
10 I went out for dinner last night. Unfortunately I began to feel ill _____ the meal and had to go home.
11 Please don't interrupt me _____ I'm speaking.
12 There were many interruptions _____ the president's speech.
13 Can you hold my bag _____ I try on this jacket?
14 We were hungry when we arrived. We hadn't had anything to eat _____ we were travelling.

119.3 Use your own ideas to complete these sentences.

1 I fell asleep while ___I was watching TV.___
2 I fell asleep during ___the movie.___
3 Nobody came to see me while _____
4 Can you wait for me while _____
5 Most of the students looked bored during _____
6 I was asked a lot of questions during _____
7 Don't open the car door while _____
8 The lights suddenly went out while _____
9 It started to rain during _____
10 It started to rain while _____
11 What are you going to do while _____

By and until   By the time …

A

By … = not later than:

- ☐ I sent the documents to them today, so they should receive them **by Monday**. (= on or before Monday, not later than Monday)

- ☐ We'd better hurry. We have to be home **by 5 o'clock**. (= at or before 5 o'clock, not later than 5 o'clock)

- ☐ Where's Sarah? She should be here **by now**. (= now or before now – so she should have already arrived)

Use by 14 August

This milk has to be used **by 14 August**.

B

We use **until** (*or* **till**) to say *how long* a situation continues:

- ☐ 'Shall we go now?'   'No, let's **wait until** it stops raining.' *or* '… **till** it stops raining.'

- ☐ I couldn't get up this morning. { I **stayed in bed until** half past ten.
  { I **didn't** get up **until** half past ten.

Compare **until** and **by**:

Something *continues* **until** a time in the future:	Something *happens* **by** a time in the future:
☐ Joe **will be away until** Monday. (so he'll be back *on* Monday)	☐ Joe **will be back by** Monday. (= he'll be back not later than Monday)
☐ I**'ll be working until** 11.30. (so I'll stop working *at* 11.30)	☐ I**'ll have finished my work by** 11.30. (= I'll finish my work not later than 11.30.)

C

You can say '**by the time** something happens'. Study these examples:
- ☐ It's too late to go to the bank now. **By the time we get there**, it will be closed. (= the bank will close between now and the time we get there)

- ☐ *(from a postcard)* Our holiday ends tomorrow. So **by the time you receive this postcard**, I'll be back home. (= I will arrive home between tomorrow and the time you receive this postcard)

- ☐ Hurry up! **By the time we get to the cinema**, the film will already have started.

You can say '**by the time** something happened' (for the past):
- ☐ Karen's car broke down on the way to the party last night. **By the time she arrived**, most of the other guests had left. (= it took her a long time to get to the party and most of the guests left during this time)

- ☐ I had a lot of work to do yesterday evening. I was very tired **by the time I finished**. (= it took me a long time to do the work, and I became more and more tired during this time)

- ☐ We went to the cinema last night. It took us a long time to find somewhere to park the car. **By the time we got to the cinema**, the film had already started.

Also **by then** *or* **by that time**:
- ☐ Karen finally got to the party at midnight, but **by then**, most of the other guests had left.
  or … but **by that time**, most of the other guests had left.

Will be doing and **will have done** ➔ Unit 24   **By** (other uses) ➔ Units 42B, 60B, 128

Exercises

120.1 Complete the sentences with **by**.

1 We have to be home not later than 5 o'clock.
We have to be home __by 5 o'clock__.

2 I have to be at the airport not later than 8.30.
I have to be at the airport ....

3 Let me know not later than Saturday whether you can come to the party.
.... whether you can come to the party.

4 Please make sure that you're here not later than 2 o'clock.
Please make sure that ....

5 If we leave now, we should arrive not later than lunchtime.
If we leave now, ...

120.2 Put in **by** or **until**.

1 Steve has gone away. He'll be away __until__ Monday.

2 Sorry, but I must go. I have to be home .... 5 o'clock.

3 I've been offered a job. I haven't decided yet whether to accept it or not. I have to decide
.... Friday.

4 I think I'll wait .... Thursday before making a decision.

5 It's too late to go shopping. The shops are open only .... 5.30 today. They'll be
closed .... now.

6 I need to pay the phone bill. It has to be paid .... tomorrow.

7 Don't pay the bill today. Wait .... tomorrow.

8 A: Have you finished redecorating your house?
B: Not yet. We hope to finish .... the end of the week.

9 A: I'm going out now. I'll be back at about 10.30. Will you still be here?
B: I don't think so. I'll probably have gone out .... then.

10 I'm moving into my new flat next week. I'm staying with a friend .... then.

11 I've got a lot of work to do. .... the time I finish, it will be time to go to bed.

12 If you want to take part in the competition, you have to apply .... 3 April.

120.3 Use your own ideas to complete these sentences. Use **by** or **until**.

1 David is away at the moment. He'll be away __until Monday__.

2 David is away at the moment. He'll be back __by Monday__.

3 I'm just going out. I won't be very long. Wait here ....

4 I'm going out to buy a few things. It's 4.30 now. I won't be long. I'll be back ....

5 If you want to apply for the job, your application must be received ....

6 Last night I watched TV ....

120.4 Read the situations and complete the sentences using **By the time** ... .

1 I was invited to a party, but I got there much later than I intended.
__By the time I got to the party__, most of the other guests had left.

2 I intended to catch a train, but it took me longer than expected to get to the station.
...., my train had already left.

3 I wanted to go shopping after finishing my work. But I finished much later than expected.
...., it was too late to go shopping.

4 I saw two men who looked as if they were trying to steal a car. I called the police, but it was
some time before they arrived.
...., the two men had disappeared.

5 We climbed a mountain and it took us a very long time to get to the top. There wasn't
much time to enjoy the view.
...., we had to come down again.

→ Additional exercise 33 (page 321)

At/on/in (time)

A

Compare **at**, **on** and **in**:

- ○ They arrived **at 5 o'clock**.
- ○ They arrived **on Friday**.
- ○ They arrived **in October**. / They arrived **in 1998**.

We use:

at for the time of day	
at five o'clock at 11.45 at midnight at lunchtime at sunset etc.	

on for days and dates	
on Friday / on Fridays on 16 May 2009 on Christmas Day on my birthday	

in for longer periods (for example: months/years/seasons)

in October	in 1998	in the 18th century	in the past
in (the) winter	in the 1990s	in the Middle Ages	in (the) future

B

We use **at** in these expressions:

at night	○ I don't like working **at night**.
at the weekend / at weekends	○ Will you be here **at the weekend**?
at Christmas	○ Do you give each other presents **at Christmas**?
at the moment / at present	○ The manager isn't here **at the moment / at present**.
at the same time	○ Kate and I arrived **at the same time**.

C

We say:

in the morning(s)	*but*	**on Friday morning(s)**
in the afternoon(s)		**on Sunday afternoon(s)**
in the evening(s)		**on Monday evening(s)** etc.

- ○ I'll see you **in the morning**.
- ○ Do you work **in the evenings**?

- ○ I'll see you **on Friday morning**.
- ○ Do you work **on Saturday evenings**?

D

We do not use **at/on/in** before **last/next/this/every**:

- ○ I'll see you **next Friday**.   (*not* on next Friday)
- ○ They got married **last March**.

In spoken English we often leave out **on** before days (**Sunday/Monday** etc.). So you can say:

- ○ I'll see you **on Friday**.   *or* I'll see you **Friday**.
- ○ I don't work **on Monday mornings**.   *or* I don't work **Monday mornings**.

E

In a few minutes / in six months etc.

- ○ The train will be leaving **in a few minutes**.   (= a few minutes from now)
- ○ Andy has gone away. He'll be back **in a week**.   (= a week from now)
- ○ They'll be here **in a moment**.   (= a moment from now)

You can also say: in six months' **time**, in a week's **time** etc.

- ○ They're getting married in **six months' time**.   *or*   … **in six months**.

We also use **in** … to say how long it takes to do something:

- ○ I learnt to drive **in four weeks**.   (= it took me four weeks to learn)

On/in time, at/in the end ➔ Unit 122   In/at/on (position) ➔ Units 123–125
In/at/on (other uses) ➔ Unit 127   American English ➔ Appendix 7

Exercises

121.1 Put in **at**, **on** or **in**.

1 Mozart was born in Salzburg __in__ 1756.
2 I've been invited to a wedding _____ 14 February.
3 Electricity prices are going up _____ October.
4 _____ weekends, we often go for long walks in the country.
5 I haven't seen Kate for a few days. I last saw her _____ Tuesday.
6 Jonathan is 63. He'll be retiring from his job _____ two years' time.
7 I'm busy right now, but I'll be with you _____ a moment.
8 My brother is an engineer, but he doesn't have a job _____ the moment.
9 There are usually a lot of parties _____ New Year's Eve.
10 I don't like driving _____ night.
11 My car is being repaired at the garage. It will be ready _____ two hours.
12 My phone and the doorbell rang _____ the same time.
13 Mary and David always go out for dinner _____ their wedding anniversary.
14 It was a short book and easy to read. I read it _____ a day.
15 _____ Saturday night I went to bed _____ midnight.
16 We travelled overnight and arrived _____ 5 o'clock _____ the morning.
17 The course begins _____ 7 January and ends sometime _____ April.
18 I might not be at home _____ Tuesday morning, but I'll be there _____ the afternoon.

121.2 Complete the sentences. Use **at**, **on** or **in** + the following:

the evening	about 20 minutes	~~1492~~	the same time
the moment	21 July 1969	the 1920s	night
Saturdays	the Middle Ages	11 seconds	

1 Columbus made his first voyage from Europe to America __in 1492__ .
2 If the sky is clear, you can see the stars _____ .
3 After working hard during the day, I like to relax _____ .
4 Neil Armstrong was the first man to walk on the moon _____ .
5 It's difficult to listen if everyone is speaking _____ .
6 Jazz became popular in the United States _____ .
7 I'm just going out to the shop. I'll be back _____ .
8 'Can I speak to Dan?' 'I'm afraid he's busy _____ ,'
9 Many of Europe's great cathedrals were built _____ .
10 Ben is a very fast runner. He can run 100 metres _____ .
11 Liz works from Monday to Friday. Sometimes she also works _____ .

121.3 Which is correct: **a**, **b**, or both of them?

1 a I'll see you on Friday. b I'll see you Friday. __both__
2 a I'll see you on next Friday. b I'll see you next Friday. __b__
3 a Paul got married in April. b Paul got married April. ___
4 a They never go out on Sunday evenings. b They never go out Sunday evenings. ___
5 a We often have a short holiday on Christmas. b We often have a short holiday at Christmas. ___
6 a What are you doing the weekend? b What are you doing at the weekend? ___
7 a Will you be here on Tuesday? b Will you be here Tuesday? ___
8 a We were ill at the same time. b We were ill in the same time. ___
9 a Sue got married at 18 May 2008. b Sue got married on 18 May 2008. ___
10 a He left school last June. b He left school in last June. ___

→ Additional exercise 33 (page 321)

On time and in time   At the end and in the end

A   On time and in time

On time = punctual, not late. If something happens **on time**, it happens at the time that was planned:

- ☐ The 11.45 train left **on time**. (= it left at 11.45)
- ☐ 'I'll meet you at 7.30.' 'OK, but please be **on time**.' (= don't be late, be there at 7.30)
- ☐ The conference was well-organised. Everything began and finished **on time**.

The opposite of **on time** is **late**:

- ☐ Be **on time**. Don't be **late**.

In time (for something / to do something) = soon enough:

- ☐ Will you be home **in time for dinner**? (= soon enough for dinner)
- ☐ I've sent Tracey a birthday present. I hope it arrives **in time** (for her birthday).
  (= on or before her birthday)
- ☐ I'm in a hurry. I want to get home **in time to see** the game on TV.
  (= soon enough to see the game)

The opposite of **in time** is **too late**:

- ☐ I got home **too late** to see the game on TV.

You can say **just in time** (= almost too late):

- ☐ We got to the station **just in time** for our train.
- ☐ A child ran into the road in front of the car – I managed to stop **just in time**.

B   At the end and in the end

At the end (of something) = at the time when something ends. For example:

at the end of the month	**at the end of January**	**at the end of the game**
at the end of the film	**at the end of the course**	**at the end of the concert**

- ☐ I'm going away **at the end of January / at the end of the month**.
- ☐ **At the end of the concert**, everyone applauded.
- ☐ The players shook hands **at the end of the game**.

We do not say 'in the end of …'. So you cannot say 'in the end of January' or 'in the end of the concert'.

The opposite of **at the end** (of …) is **at the beginning** (of …):

- ☐ I'm going away **at the beginning of January**. (*not* in the beginning)

In the end = finally.

We use **in the end** when we say what the final result of a situation was:

- ☐ We had a lot of problems with our car. We sold it **in the end**. (= finally we sold it)
- ☐ He got more and more angry. **In the end** he just walked out of the room.
- ☐ Alan couldn't decide where to go for his holidays. He didn't go anywhere **in the end**.
  (*not* at the end)

The opposite of **in the end** is usually **at first**:

- ☐ **At first** we didn't get on very well, but **in the end** we became good friends.

At/on/in (time) ➔ Unit 121

Exercises

122.1 Complete the sentences with **on time** or **in time**.

1 The bus was late this morning, but it's usually _on time_ .
2 The film was supposed to start at 8.30, but it didn't begin ....
3 I like to get up .... to have a big breakfast before going to work.
4 We want to start the meeting .... , so please don't be late.
5 I've just washed this shirt. I want to wear it this evening, so I hope it will be dry
   ....
6 The train service isn't very good. The trains are rarely ....
7 I nearly missed my flight this morning. I got to the airport just ....
8 I almost forgot that it was Joe's birthday. Fortunately I remembered ....
9 Why are you never .... ? You always keep everybody waiting.

122.2 Read the situations and make sentences using **just in time**.

1 A child ran into the road in front of your car. You saw the child at the last moment.
   (manage / stop) _I managed to stop just in time._
2 You were walking home. Just after you got home, it started to rain very heavily.
   (get / home) I ....
3 Tim was going to sit on the chair you had just painted. You said, 'Don't sit on that chair!',
   so he didn't. (stop / him) I ....
4 You and a friend went to the cinema. You were late, and you thought you would miss the
   beginning of the film. But the film began just as you sat down in the cinema.
   (get / cinema / beginning / film)
   We ....

122.3 Complete the sentences using **at the end** + the following:

the course	~~the game~~	the interview	the month	the race

1 The players shook hands _at the end of the game_ .
2 I usually get paid ....
3 The students had a party ....
4 Two of the runners collapsed ....
5 To my surprise, I was offered the job ....

122.4 Write sentences with **In the end**. Use the verb in brackets.

1 We had a lot of problems with our car. (sell) _In the end we sold it._
2 Anna got more and more fed up with her job.
   (resign) ....
3 I tried to learn German, but I found it too difficult.
   (give up) ....
4 We couldn't decide whether to go to the party or not.
   (not / go) ....

122.5 Put in **at** or **in**.

1 I'm going away _at_ the end of the month.
2 It took me a long time to find a job. .... the end I got a job in a hotel.
3 Are you going away .... the beginning of August or .... the end?
4 I couldn't decide what to buy Laura for her birthday. I didn't buy her anything .... the end.
5 We waited ages for a taxi. We gave up .... the end and walked home.
6 I'll be moving to a new address .... the end of September.
7 We had a few problems at first, but .... the end everything was OK.
8 I'm going away .... the end of this week.
9 A: I didn't know what to do.
   B: Yes, you were in a difficult position. What did you do .... the end?

A In

in a room
in a building
in a box

in a garden
in a town/country
in the city centre

in a pool
in the sea
in a river

- There's no-one **in the room** / **in the building** / **in the garden**.
- What have you got **in your hand** / **in your mouth**?
- When we were **in Italy**, we spent a few days **in Venice**.
- I have a friend who lives **in a small village in the mountains**.
- There were some people swimming **in the pool** / **in the sea** / **in the river**.

B At

at the bus stop   **at** the door   **at** the roundabout   **at** reception

- Who is that man standing **at the bus stop** / **at the door** / **at the window**?
- Turn left **at the traffic lights** / **at the church** / **at the roundabout** / **at the junction**.
- We have to get off the bus **at the next stop**.
- When you leave the hotel, please leave your key **at reception**. (= at the reception desk)

C On

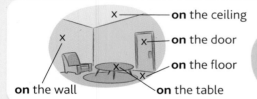

on the ceiling   **on** her nose

on the door

on the floor

on the wall   **on** the table   **on** a page   **on** an island

- I sat **on the floor** / **on the ground** / **on the grass** / **on the beach** / **on a chair**.
- There's a dirty mark **on the wall** / **on the ceiling** / **on your nose** / **on your shirt**.
- Have you seen the notice **on the notice board** / **on the door**?
- You'll find details of TV programmes **on page seven** (of the newspaper).
- The hotel is **on a small island** in the middle of a lake.

D

Compare **in** and **at**:
- There were a lot of people **in the shop**. It was very crowded.
  Go along this road, then turn left **at the shop**.
- I'll meet you **in the hotel lobby**.
  I'll meet you **at the entrance to the hotel**.

Compare **in** and **on**:
- There is some water **in the bottle**.
  There is a label **on the bottle**.

in the bottle

on the bottle

Compare **at** and **on**:
- There is somebody **at the door**. Shall I go and see who it is?
  There is a notice **on the door**. It says 'Do not disturb'.

In/at/on (position) 2–3 ➔ Units 124–125

Exercises

123.1 Answer the questions about the pictures. Use **in**, **at** or **on** with the words below the pictures.

① (bottle)	② (arm)	③ (traffic lights)	④ (door)
⑤ (wall)	⑥ (Paris)	⑦ (gate)	⑧ (beach)

1 Where's the label?   _On the bottle._
2 Where's the fly?   ....
3 Where is the car waiting?   ....
4 a Where's the notice?   ....
   b Where's the key?   ....
5 Where are the shelves?   ....
6 Where's the Eiffel Tower?   ....
7 a Where's the man standing?   ....
   b Where's the bird?   ....
8 Where are the children playing?   ....

123.2 Complete the sentences. Use **in**, **at** or **on** + the following:

the window	your coffee	the mountains	that tree
my guitar	~~the river~~	the island	the next petrol station

1 Look at those people swimming ....._in the river_.... .
2 One of the strings .... is broken.
3 There's something wrong with the car. We'd better stop ....
4 Would you like sugar .... ?
5 The leaves .... are a beautiful colour.
6 Last year we had a wonderful skiing holiday ....
7 There's nobody living .... It's uninhabited.
8 He spends most of the day sitting .... and looking outside.

123.3 Complete the sentences with **in**, **at** or **on**.

1 There was a long queue of people ....._at_.... the bus stop.
2 Nicola was wearing a silver ring .... her little finger.
3 There was an accident .... the crossroads this morning.
4 I wasn't sure whether I had come to the right office. There was no name .... the door.
5 There are some beautiful trees .... the park.
6 You'll find the sports results .... the back page of the newspaper.
7 I wouldn't like an office job. I couldn't spend the whole day sitting .... a computer.
8 My brother lives .... a small village .... the south-west of England.
9 The man the police are looking for has a scar .... his right cheek.
10 The headquarters of the company are .... Milan.
11 I like that picture hanging .... the wall .... the kitchen.
12 If you come here by bus, get off .... the stop after the traffic lights.

→ Additional exercise 34 (page 322)

In/at/on (position) 2

A

We say that somebody/something is:

in a line / **in a row** / **in a queue**	**in bed**
in the sky / **in the world**	**in the country** / **in the countryside**
in an office / **in a department**	**in a picture** / **in a photo** / **in a photograph**
in a book / **in a paper** (= newspaper) / **in a magazine** / **in a letter**	

○ When I go to the cinema, I like to sit **in the front row**.
○ James isn't up yet. He's still **in bed**.
○ It was a lovely day. There wasn't a cloud **in the sky**.
○ I've just started working **in the sales department**.
○ Who is the woman **in that photo**?
○ Have you seen this picture **in today's paper**?

in a row

B

on the left / **on the right**   **on the left-hand side** / **on the right-hand side**
on the ground floor / **on the first floor** / **on the second floor** etc.
on a map / **on a menu** / **on a list**
on a farm

○ In Britain we drive **on the left**. *or* ... **on the left-hand side**.
○ Our apartment is **on the second floor** of the building.
○ Here's a shopping list. Don't buy anything that's not **on the list**.
○ Have you ever worked **on a farm**?

We say that a place is **on a river** / **on a road** / **on the coast**:
○ Budapest is **on the** (River) **Danube**.
○ The town where you live – is it **on the coast** or inland?

Also **on the way**:
○ We stopped to buy some things in a shop **on the way** home.

BUDAPEST

DANUBE

C

at the top (of) / **at the bottom** (of) / **at the end** (of)
○ Write your name **at the top of the page**.
○ Jane's house is **at the other end of the street**.

at the top (of the page)

at the bottom (of the page)

D

in the front / **in the back** of a car
○ I was sitting **in the back** (of the car) when we crashed.

at the back

at the front / **at the back** of a building / theatre / group of people etc.
○ The garden is **at the back of the house**.
○ Let's sit **at the front** (of the cinema).
○ We were **at the back**, so we couldn't see very well.

on the front / **on the back** of a letter / piece of paper etc.
○ I wrote the date **on the back of the photo**.

at the front

E

in the corner of a room
○ The TV is **in the corner** of the room.

at the corner *or* **on the corner** of a street
○ There is a small shop **at/on the corner** of the street.

in the corner   **at/on** the corner

In the world → Unit 108D   In/at/on (position) → Units 123, 125   American English → Appendix 7

Exercises

124.1 Answer the questions about the pictures. Use **in**, **at** or **on** with the words below the pictures.

① SUE SALES	②	③	④	⑤
(sales department)	(second floor)	(corner)	(corner)	(top / stairs)
⑥	⑦ LIZ	⑧ POST OFFICE	⑨ GARY	⑩
(back / car)	(front)	left	(back row)	(farm)

1 Where does Sue work? ..In the sales department...
2 Sue lives in this building. Where's her flat exactly? ....
3 Where is the woman standing? ....
4 Where is the man standing? ....
5 Where's the cat? ....
6 Where's the dog? ....
7 Liz is in this group of people. Where is she? ....
8 Where's the post office? ....
9 Gary is at the cinema. Where is he sitting? ....
10 Where does Kate work? ....

124.2 Complete the sentences. Use **in**, **at** or **on** + the following:

the west coast	the world	the back of the class	~~the sky~~
the front row	the right	the back of this card	the way to work

1 It was a lovely day. There wasn't a cloud ...in the sky... .
2 In most countries people drive ....
3 What is the tallest building ....?
4 I usually buy a newspaper .... in the morning.
5 San Francisco is .... of the United States.
6 We went to the theatre last night. We had seats ....
7 I couldn't hear the teacher. She spoke quietly and I was sitting ....
8 I don't have your address. Could you write it ....?

124.3 Complete the sentences with **in**, **at** or **on**.

1 Write your name ...at... the top of the page.
2 Is your sister .... this photograph? I don't recognise her.
3 I didn't feel very well when I woke up, so I stayed .... bed.
4 We normally use the front entrance to the building, but there's another one .... the back.
5 Is there anything interesting .... the paper today?
6 There was a list of names, but my name wasn't .... the list.
7 .... the end of the street, there is a path leading to the river.
8 I love to look up at the stars .... the sky at night.
9 When I'm a passenger in a car, I prefer to sit .... the front.
10 I live in a very small village. You probably won't find it .... your map.
11 Joe works .... the furniture department of a large store.
12 Paris is .... the River Seine.
13 I don't like cities. I'd much prefer to live .... the country.
14 My office is .... the top floor. It's .... the left as you come out of the lift.

➔ Additional exercise 34 (page 322)

In/at/on (position) 3

A   In hospital / at work etc.

We say that somebody is **in hospital** / **in prison** / **in jail**:
- ○ Anna's mother is **in hospital**.

We say that somebody is **at work** / **at school** / **at university** / **at college**:
- ○ I'll be **at work** until 5.30.
- ○ Julia is studying chemistry **at university**.

We say that somebody **is at home** or **is home** (with or without **at**), but we say **do something at home** (with **at**):
- ○ I'll **be at home** all evening. or I'll **be home** all evening.
- ○ Shall we go to a restaurant or **eat at home**?

B   At a party / at a concert etc.

We say that somebody is **at** an event (**at a party** / **at a conference** etc.):
- ○ Were there many people **at the party** / **at the meeting** / **at the wedding**?
- ○ I saw Steve **at a conference** / **at a concert** on Saturday.

C   In and at for buildings

You can often use **in** or **at** with buildings. For example, you can eat **in a restaurant** or **at a restaurant**; you can buy something **in a supermarket** or **at a supermarket**. We usually say **at** when we say where an event takes place (for example: a concert, a film, a party, a meeting):
- ○ We went to a concert **at the National Concert Hall**.
- ○ The meeting took place **at the company's head office** in Frankfurt.
- ○ There was a robbery **at the supermarket**.

We say **at the station** / **at the airport**:
- ○ There's no need to meet me **at the station**. I can get a taxi.

We say **at** somebody's house:
- ○ I was **at Helen's house** last night. or I was **at Helen's** last night.

Also **at the doctor's** / **at the hairdresser's** etc.

We use **in** when we are thinking about the building itself. Compare:
- ○ We had dinner **at the hotel**.
     All the rooms **in the hotel** have air conditioning. (*not* at the hotel)
- ○ I was **at Helen's** (**house**) last night.
     It's always cold **in Helen's house**. The heating doesn't work well. (*not* at Helen's house)

D   In and at for towns etc.

We normally use **in** with cities, towns and villages:
- ○ The Louvre is a famous art museum **in Paris**. (*not* at Paris)
- ○ Sam's parents live **in a village** in the south of France. (*not* at a village)

We use **at** when we think of the place as a point or station on a journey:
- ○ Does this train stop **at Oxford**? (= at Oxford station)

E   On a bus / in a car etc.

We usually say **on a bus** / **on a train** / **on a plane** / **on a ship** but **in a car** / **in a taxi**:
- ○ **The bus** was very full. There were too many people **on it**.
- ○ Laura arrived **in a taxi**.

We say **on a bike** (= bicycle) / **on a motorbike** / **on a horse**:
- ○ Jane passed me **on her bike**.

At school / in hospital etc. → Unit 74   In/at/on (position) → Units 123–24
To/at/in/into → Unit 126   By car / by bike etc. → Unit 128B

Exercises

125.1 Complete the sentences about the pictures. Use **in**, **at** or **on** with the words below the pictures.

1 AIRPORT CAR HIRE
(the airport)

2 DAVE
(a train)

3 CONFERENCE
KAREN
(a conference)

4 MARTIN
(hospital)

5 JUDY
(the hairdresser's)

6 GARY
(his bike)

7
(New York)

8 THE Savoy Theatre
(the Savoy Theatre)

1 You can hire a car ___at the airport___ .
2 Dave is ....
3 Karen is ....
4 Martin is ....
5 Judy is ....
6 I saw Gary ....
7 We spent a few days ....
8 We went to a show ....

125.2 Complete the sentences. Use **in**, **at** or **on** + the following:

| the plane | hospital | a taxi | ~~the station~~ | the cinema |
| Tokyo | school | prison | the airport | the sports centre |

1 My train arrives at 11.30. Can you meet me ___at the station___ ?
2 We walked to the restaurant, but we went home ....
3 I'd like to see a film. What's on .... this week?
4 Some people are .... for crimes that they did not commit.
5 'What does your sister do? Does she have a job?' 'No, she's still .... ,'
6 I play basketball .... on Friday evenings.
7 A friend of mine was injured in an accident a few days ago. She's still ....
8 Our flight was delayed. We had to wait .... for four hours.
9 I enjoyed the flight, but the food .... wasn't very nice.
10 Vicky has gone to Japan. She's living ....

125.3 Complete these sentences with **in**, **at** or **on**.

1 We went to a concert ___at___ the National Concert Hall.
2 It was a very slow train. It stopped .... every station.
3 My parents live .... a small village about 50 miles from London.
4 I haven't seen Kate for some time. I last saw her .... David's wedding.
5 We stayed .... a very comfortable hotel when we were .... Amsterdam.
6 There were about fifty rooms .... the hotel.
7 I don't know where my umbrella is. Perhaps I left it .... the bus.
8 'Where were you on Monday evening?' 'I was .... a friend's house.'
9 There must be somebody .... the house. The lights are on.
10 The exhibition .... the Museum of Modern Art finishes on Saturday.
11 Shall we travel .... your car or mine?
12 I didn't expect you to be .... home. I thought you'd be .... work.
13 'Did you like the movie?' 'Yes, but it was too hot .... the cinema.'
14 Paul lives .... Birmingham. He's a student .... Birmingham University.

→ Additional exercise 34 (page 322)

A

We say **go/come/travel** (etc.) **to** a place or event. For example:

go to China	**go to** bed	**come to** my house
go back to Italy	**go to** the bank	**be taken to** hospital
return to London	**go to** a concert	**be sent to** prison
welcome somebody **to** a place		**drive to** the airport

TO → ☐

- ○ When are your friends **going back to** Italy? (*not* going back in Italy)
- ○ Three people were injured in the accident and **taken to** hospital.
- ○ **Welcome to** our country! (*not* Welcome in)

In the same way we say 'a **journey to** / a **trip to** / a **visit to** / on **my way to** …' etc. :
- ○ Did you enjoy **your trip to** Paris / **your visit to** the zoo?

Compare **to** (for *movement*) and **in/at** (for *position*):
- ○ They are **going to** France. *but* They **live in** France.
- ○ Can you **come to** the party? *but* I'll **see you at** the party.

We say **been to** a place or an event:
- ○ I've **been to Italy** four times, but I've never **been to Rome**.
- ○ Amanda has never **been to a football match** in her life.

B

Get and **arrive**

We say **get to** a place:
- ○ What time did they **get to London / to work / to the hotel**?

But we say **arrive in** … or **arrive at** … (*not* arrive to).
We say **arrive in** a town, city or country:
- ○ They **arrived in London / in Spain** a week ago.

For other places (buildings etc.) or events, we say **arrive at**:
- ○ When did they **arrive at the hotel / at the airport / at the party**?

C

Home

We say **go home / come home / get home / arrive home / on the way home** etc. (no preposition).
We do not say 'to home':
- ○ I'm tired. Let's **go home** now. (*not* go to home)
- ○ I met Lisa **on my way home**. (*not* my way to home)

D

Into

Go into, **get into** … etc. = enter (a room / a building / a car etc.):
- ○ I opened the door, **went into** the room and sat down.
- ○ A bird **flew into** the kitchen through the window.
- ○ Every month, my salary **is paid** directly **into** my bank account.

INTO → ☐

With some verbs (especially **go/get/put**) we often use **in** (instead of **into**):
- ○ She **got in** the car and drove away. (*or* She **got into** the car …)
- ○ I read the letter and **put it** back **in** the envelope.

The opposite of **into** is **out of**:
- ○ She **got out of** the car and **went into** a shop.

We usually say '**get on/off** a bus / a train / a plane' (*not usually* into/out of):
- ○ She **got on the bus** and I never saw her again.

Been to → Units 7–8   **In/at/on** (position) → Units 123–125   **At home** → Unit 125A
Into and **in** → Unit 138A

Exercises

126.1 Put in **to/at/in/into** where necessary. If no preposition is necessary, leave the space empty.

1 Three people were taken __to__ hospital after the accident.
2 I met Kate on my way __–__ home. *(no preposition)*
3 We left our luggage _____ the station and went to find something to eat.
4 Shall we take a taxi _____ the station or shall we walk?
5 I have to go _____ the bank today. What time does it open?
6 The Amazon flows _____ the Atlantic Ocean.
7 'Do you have your camera with you?' 'No, I left it _____ the car.'
8 Have you ever been _____ China?
9 I had lost my key, but I managed to climb _____ the house through a window.
10 We got stuck in a traffic jam on our way _____ the airport.
11 We had lunch _____ the airport while we were waiting for our plane.
12 Welcome _____ the hotel. We hope you enjoy your stay here.
13 We drove along the main road for about a kilometre and then turned _____ a narrow side street.
14 Did you enjoy your visit _____ the museum?
15 I'm tired. As soon as I get _____ home, I'm going _____ bed.
16 Marcel is French. He has just returned _____ France after two years _____ Brazil.
17 Carl was born _____ Chicago, but his family moved _____ New York when he was three. He still lives _____ New York.

126.2 Have you been to these places? If so, how many times? Choose three of the places and write a sentence using **been to**.

Athens	Australia	Hong Kong	Mexico	Paris
Rome	Singapore	Sweden	Tokyo	the United States

1 *(example answers)*   I've never been to Australia. / I've been to Mexico once.
2 _____
3 _____
4 _____

126.3 Put in **to/at/in** where necessary. If no preposition is necessary, leave the space empty.

1 What time does this train get __to__ London?
2 We arrived _____ Barcelona a few days ago.
3 What time did you get _____ home last night?
4 What time do you usually arrive _____ work in the morning?
5 When we got _____ the cinema, there was a long queue outside.
6 I arrived _____ home feeling very tired.

126.4 Write sentences using **got + into / out of / on / off**.

1 You were walking home. A friend passed you in her car. She saw you, stopped and offered you a lift. She opened the door. What did you do?   I got into the car.
2 You were waiting for the bus. At last your bus came. The doors opened. What did you do then? I _____ the bus.
3 You drove home in your car. You stopped outside your house and parked the car. What did you do then? _____
4 You were travelling by train to Manchester. When the train got to Manchester, what did you do?
   _____
5 You needed a taxi.   After a few minutes a taxi stopped for you. You opened the door. What did you do then? _____
6 You were travelling by air. At the end of your flight, your plane landed at the airport and stopped. The doors were opened, you took your bag and stood up. What did you do then?
   _____

→ Additional exercise 34 (page 322)

A

In

in the rain / in the sun / in the shade / in the dark / in bad weather etc.
- ○ We sat **in the shade**. It was too hot to sit **in the sun**.
- ○ Don't go out **in the rain**. Wait until it stops.

(write) **in ink / in pen / in pencil**
- ○ When you do the exam, you're not allowed to write **in pencil**.

Also (write) **in words / in figures / in capital letters** etc.
- ○ Please write your name **in capital letters**.
- ○ Write the story **in your own words**. (= don't copy somebody else)

in the shade

(be/fall) **in love** (**with** somebody)
- ○ They're very happy together. They're **in love**.

in (my) **opinion**
- ○ **In my opinion**, the movie wasn't very good.

B

On

on TV / on television / on the radio
- ○ I didn't watch the news **on television**, but I heard it **on the radio**.

on the phone
- ○ I've never met her, but I've spoken to her **on the phone** a few times.

(be/go) **on strike**
- ○ There are no trains today. The drivers are **on strike**.

(be/go) **on a diet**
- ○ I've put on a lot of weight. I'll have to go **on a diet**.

(be) **on fire**
- ○ Look! That car is **on fire**.

on the whole (= in general)
- ○ Sometimes I have problems at work, but **on the whole** I enjoy my job.

on purpose (= intentionally)
- ○ I'm sorry. I didn't mean to annoy you. I didn't do it **on purpose**.

C

On holiday / on a trip etc.

We say: (be/go) **on holiday / on business / on a trip / on a tour / on a cruise** etc.
- ○ I'm going **on holiday** next week.
- ○ Emma's away **on business** at the moment.
- ○ One day I'd like to go **on a world tour**.

You can also say 'go to a place **for a** holiday / **for my** holiday(s)':
- ○ Steve has gone to France **for a holiday**.

D

At the age of … etc.

We are now flying **at a speed** of 800 kilometres an hour and **at an altitude** of 9,000 metres.

We say **at the age of 16 / at 120 miles an hour / at 100 degrees** etc. :
- ○ Tracy left school **at 16**. *or* … **at the age** of 16.
- ○ The train was travelling **at 120 miles an hour**.
- ○ Water boils **at 100 degrees Celsius**.

In/at/on (time) ➜ Unit 121   In/at/on (position) ➜ Units 123–125

Exercises

127.1 Complete the sentences using **in** + the following:

capital letters	cold weather	love	my opinion
pencil	~~the rain~~	the shade	

1 Don't go out ___in the rain___ . Wait until it stops.
2 Matt likes to keep warm, so he doesn't go out much ....
3 If you write .... and make a mistake, you can rub it out and correct it.
4 They fell .... almost immediately and were married in a few weeks.
5 Please write your address clearly, preferably ....
6 It's too hot in the sun. I'm going to sit ....
7 Amanda thought the restaurant was OK, but .... it wasn't very good.

127.2 Complete the sentences using **on** + the following:

business	a diet	~~fire~~	holiday	the phone
purpose	strike	TV	a tour	the whole

1 Look! That car is ___on fire___ ! Somebody call the fire brigade.
2 Workers at the factory have gone .... for better pay and conditions.
3 Soon after we arrived, we were taken .... of the city.
4 I feel lazy this evening. Is there anything worth watching .... ?
5 I'm sorry. It was an accident. I didn't do it ....
6 Richard has put on a lot of weight recently. I think he should go ....
7 Jane's job involves a lot of travelling. She often has to go away ....
8 A: I'm going .... next week.
  B: Where are you going? Somewhere nice?
9 A: Is Sarah here?
  B: Yes, but she's .... at the moment. She won't be long.
10 A: How was your exam?
  B: Well, there were some difficult questions, but .... it was OK.

127.3 Complete the sentences with **in**, **on** or **at**.

1 Water boils ___at___ 100 degrees Celsius.
2 When I was 14, I went .... a trip to France organised by my school.
3 There was panic when people realised that the building was .... fire.
4 Julia's grandmother died recently .... the age of 79.
5 Can you turn the light on, please? I don't want to sit .... the dark.
6 We didn't go .... holiday last year. We stayed at home.
7 I hate driving .... fog. You can't see anything.
8 I won't be here next week. I'll be .... holiday.
9 Technology has developed .... great speed.
10 Alan got married .... 17, which is rather young to get married.
11 I heard an interesting programme .... the radio this morning.
12 .... my opinion, violent films should not be shown .... television.
13 I wouldn't like to go .... a cruise. I think I'd get bored.
14 I shouldn't eat too much. I'm supposed to be .... a diet.
15 I wouldn't like his job. He spends most of his time talking .... the phone.
16 The earth travels round the sun .... 107,000 kilometres an hour.
17 'Did you enjoy your holiday?' 'Not every minute, but .... the whole, yes.'
18 A lot of houses were damaged .... the storm last week.

→ Additional exercise 34 (page 322)

A

We use **by** in many expressions to say how we do something. For example, you can:

send something **by post**	contact somebody **by phone** / **by email**
do something **by hand**	pay **by credit card** / **by cheque**

- ○ Can I pay **by credit card**?
- ○ You can contact me **by phone** or **by email**.

But we say **pay cash** or **pay in cash** (*not usually* by cash).

We also say that something happens **by mistake** / **by accident** / **by chance**:
- ○ We hadn't arranged to meet. We met **by chance**.

But we say 'do something **on purpose**' (= you mean to do it):
- ○ I didn't do it **on purpose**. It was an accident.

Note that we say **by chance**, **by credit card** etc. (*not* by the chance / by a credit card). In these expressions we use **by** + *noun* without **the** or **a**.

B

In the same way we use **by** … to say how somebody travels:

by car / **by train** / **by plane** / **by boat** / **by ship** / **by bus** / **by bike** etc.
by road / **by rail** / **by air** / **by sea**
- ○ Jess usually goes to work **by bus**.

But we say **on foot**:
- ○ Did you come here **by car** or **on foot**?

You cannot use **by** if you say <u>my</u> car / <u>the</u> train / <u>a</u> taxi etc. We say:

by car	*but*	**in my** car (*not* by my car)
by train	*but*	**on the** train (*not* by the train)

We use **in** for cars and taxis:
- ○ They didn't come **in their car**. They came **in a taxi**.

We use **on** for bikes and public transport (buses, trains etc.):
- ○ We travelled **on the 6.45 train**.

C

We say that 'something is done **by** somebody/something' (*passive*):
- ○ Have you ever been bitten **by a dog**?
- ○ The programme was watched **by millions of people**.

Compare **by** and **with**:
- ○ The door must have been opened **with a key**.   (*not* by a key) (= somebody used a key to open it)
- ○ The door must have been opened **by somebody** with a key.

We say 'a play **by Shakespeare**' / 'a painting **by Rembrandt**' / 'a novel **by Tolstoy**' etc. :
- ○ Have you read anything **by** Ernest Hemingway?

D

By also means 'next to / beside':
- ○ Come and sit **by me**.   (= next to me)
- ○ 'Where's the light switch?' '**By the door**.'

SWITCH →

E

Note the following use of **by**:
- ○ Clare's salary has just gone up **from** £2,500 a month **to** £2,750. So it has increased **by £250** / **by ten per cent**.
- ○ Carl and Mike had a race over 200 metres. Carl won **by** about **three metres**.

new salary ——— £2,750

increased **by** £250

old salary ——— £2,500

Passive + by → Unit 42B	By + -ing → Unit 60B	By myself → Unit 83D	By (time) → Unit 120

Exercises

128.1 Complete the sentences using **by** + the following:

canal	~~chance~~	credit card	hand	mistake

1 We hadn't arranged to meet. We met ____by chance____ .
2 I didn't intend to take your umbrella. I took it _____ .
3 Don't put the sweater in the washing machine. It has to be washed _____ .
4 I don't need cash. I can pay the bill _____ .
5 The town is not on the coast, but is connected to the sea _____ .

128.2 Put in **by**, **in** or **on**.

1 Jess usually goes to work ____by____ bus.
2 I saw Jane this morning. She was _____ the bus.
3 How did you get here? Did you come _____ train?
4 I decided not to go _____ car. I went _____ my bike instead.
5 I didn't feel like walking home, so I came home _____ a taxi.
6 Sorry we're late. We missed the bus, so we had to come _____ foot.
7 How long does it take to cross the Atlantic _____ ship?

128.3 All these sentences have a mistake. Correct them.

1 Did you come here by Kate's car or yours?   ____in Kate's car____
2 I don't like travelling on bus.   _____
3 These photographs were taken by a very good camera.   _____
4 I know this music is from Beethoven, but I can't remember what it's called.   _____
5 I couldn't pay by cash – I didn't have any money on me.   _____
6 We lost the game because of a mistake of one of our players.   _____

128.4 Write three sentences like the examples. Write about a song, a painting, a film, a book etc.

1 ____War and Peace is a book by Tolstoy.____
2 ____Romeo and Juliet is a play by Shakespeare.____
3 _____
4 _____
5 _____

128.5 Put in **by**, **in**, **on** or **with**.

1 Have you ever been bitten ____by____ a dog?
2 The plane was badly damaged _____ lightning.
3 We managed to put the fire out _____ a fire extinguisher.
4 Who is that man standing _____ the window?
5 These photographs were taken _____ a friend of mine.
6 I don't mind going _____ car, but I don't want to go _____ your car.
7 There was a small table _____ the bed _____ a lamp and a clock _____ it.

128.6 Complete the sentences using **by**.

1 Clare's salary was £2,500 a month. Now it is £2,750.
   Her salary ____has increased by £250.____
2 My daily newspaper used to cost 80 pence. From today it costs 90.
   The price has gone up _____
3 There was an election. Helen won. She got 25 votes and James got 23.
   Helen won _____
4 I went to Kate's house to see her, but she had gone out five minutes before I arrived.
   I missed _____

→ Additional exercise 34 (page 322)

Noun + preposition (**reason for**, **cause of** etc.)

A   *Noun +* **for** …

a demand / a need FOR …
- ☐ The company closed down because there wasn't enough **demand for** its product.
- ☐ There's no excuse for behaviour like that. There's no **need for** it.

a reason FOR …
- ☐ The train was late, but nobody knew the **reason for** the delay.   (*not* reason of)

B   *Noun +* **of** …

an advantage / a disadvantage OF …
- ☐ The **advantage of living alone** is that you can do what you like.

but

there is an advantage **in** (*or* **to**) doing something
- ☐ **There are** many advantages **in** living alone. *or* … many advantages **to** living alone.

a cause OF …
- ☐ The **cause of** the explosion is unknown.

a picture / a photo / a photograph / a map / a plan / a drawing (etc.) **OF** …
- ☐ Rachel showed me some **pictures of** her family.
- ☐ I had a **map of** the town, so I was able to find my way around.

C   *Noun +* **in** …

an increase / a decrease / a rise / a fall IN (prices etc.)
- ☐ There has been an **increase in** the number of road accidents recently.
- ☐ Last year was a bad one for the company. There was a big **fall in** sales.

D   *Noun +* **to** …

damage TO …
- ☐ The accident was my fault, so I had to pay for the **damage to** the other car.

an invitation TO … (a party / a wedding etc.)
- ☐ Did you get an **invitation to** the party?

a solution TO (a problem) / a **key TO** (a door) / an **answer TO** (a question) / a **reply TO** (a letter) / a **reaction TO** …
- ☐ I hope we find a **solution to** the problem.   (*not* a solution of the problem)
- ☐ I was surprised at her **reaction to** my suggestion.

an attitude TO …   *or* an **attitude TOWARDS** …
- ☐ His **attitude to** his job is very negative. *or* His **attitude towards** his job …

E   *Noun +* **with** … / **between** …

a relationship / a connection / contact WITH …
- ☐ Do you have a good **relationship with** your parents?
- ☐ The police want to question a man in **connection with** the robbery.

but

a relationship / a connection / contact / a difference BETWEEN two things or people
- ☐ The police believe that there is no **connection between** the two crimes.
- ☐ There are some **differences between** British and American English.

Exercises

129.1 Complete the second sentence so that it has the same meaning as the first.

1   What caused the explosion? What was the cause ___of the explosion___ ?
2   We're trying to solve the problem.
    We're trying to find a solution _____ .
3   Sue gets on well with her brother.
    Sue has a good relationship _____ .
4   The cost of living has gone up a lot.
    There has been a big increase _____ .
5   I don't know how to answer your question.
    I can't think of an answer _____ .
6   I don't think that a new road is necessary.
    I don't think there is any need _____ .
7   I think that working at home has many advantages.
    I think that there are many advantages _____ .
8   The number of people without jobs fell last month.
    Last month there was a fall _____ .
9   Nobody wants to buy shoes like these any more.
    There is no demand _____ .
10 In what way is your job different from mine?
    What is the difference _____ ?

129.2 Complete the sentences using these nouns + a preposition:

cause	connection	contact	damage	invitation
key	~~map~~	photographs	reason	reply

1   On the wall there were some pictures and a ___map of___ the world.
2   Thank you for the _____ your party next week.
3   Since she left home two years ago, Sophie has had little _____ her family.
4   I can't open this door. Do you have a _____ the other door?
5   The _____ the fire at the hotel last week is still unknown.
6   Did you get a _____ the email you sent to the company?
7   The two companies are completely independent. There is no _____ them.
8   Jane showed me some old _____ the city as it looked 100 years ago.
9   Carol has decided to give up her job. I don't know her _____ doing this.
10 It wasn't a bad accident. The _____ the car wasn't serious.

129.3 Complete the sentences with the correct preposition.

1   There are some differences ___between___ British and American English.
2   Money isn't the solution _____ every problem.
3   There has been an increase _____ the amount of traffic using this road.
4   The advantage _____ having a car is that you don't have to rely on public transport.
5   There are many advantages _____ being able to speak a foreign language.
6   Everything can be explained. There's a reason _____ everything.
7   When Paul left home, his attitude _____ his parents seemed to change.
8   Ben and I used to be good friends, but I don't have much contact _____ him now.
9   There has been a sharp rise _____ property prices in the past few years.
10 What was Sarah's reaction _____ the news?
11 If I give you the camera, can you take a picture _____ me?
12 The company has rejected the workers' demands _____ a rise _____ pay.
13 What was the answer _____ question 3 in the test?
14 The fact that Jane was offered a job has no connection _____ the fact that she is a friend of
    the managing director.

→ Additional exercise 35 (page 322)

Adjective + preposition 1

A

It was **nice of** you to ...

nice / kind / good / generous / polite / stupid / silly etc. **OF** somebody (to do something)
- ☐ Thank you. It was very **kind of you** to help me.
- ☐ It is **stupid of me** to go out without a coat in such cold weather.

but

(be) **nice / kind / good / generous / polite / rude / friendly / cruel** etc. **TO** somebody
- ☐ They have always been very **nice to** me. (*not* with me)
- ☐ Why were you so **unfriendly to** Lucy?

B

Adjective + **about / with**

angry / annoyed / furious / upset {
ABOUT something
WITH somebody **FOR** doing something
}
- ☐ There's no point in getting **angry about** things that don't matter.
- ☐ Are you **annoyed with** me **for** being late?
- ☐ Lisa is **upset about** not being invited to the party.

excited / worried / nervous / happy etc. **ABOUT** a situation
- ☐ Are you **nervous about** the exam?

pleased / satisfied / happy / delighted / disappointed WITH something you receive, or the result of something
- ☐ They were **delighted with** the present I gave them.
- ☐ Were you **happy with** your exam results?

C

Adjective + **at / by / with / of**

surprised / shocked / amazed / astonished / upset AT *or* **BY** something
- ☐ Everybody was **surprised at** (*or* **by**) the news.
- ☐ I hope you weren't **shocked by** (*or* **at**) what I said.

impressed WITH *or* **BY** somebody/something
- ☐ I'm very **impressed with** (*or* **by**) her English. It's very good.

fed up / bored WITH something
- ☐ I don't enjoy my job any more. I'm **fed up with** it. / I'm **bored with** it.

tired / sick OF something
- ☐ Come on, let's go! I'm **tired of** waiting. / I'm **sick of** waiting.

D

Sorry about / for

sorry ABOUT a situation or something that happened
- ☐ I'm **sorry about** the mess. I'll clear it up later.
- ☐ **Sorry about** last night. (= Sorry about something that happened last night)

sorry FOR *or* **ABOUT** something you did
- ☐ Alex is very **sorry for** what he said. (*or* **sorry about** what he said)
- ☐ I'm **sorry for** shouting at you yesterday. (*or* **sorry about** shouting)

You can also say 'I'm sorry I (did something)':
- ☐ I'm **sorry I shouted** at you yesterday.

feel / be sorry FOR somebody who is in a bad situation
- ☐ I **feel sorry for** Matt. He's had a lot of bad luck. (*not* I feel sorry about Matt)

Preposition + -ing ➔ Unit 60   Adjective + to ... ➔ Unit 65   **Sorry to ... / sorry for ...** ➔ Unit 66C
Adjective + preposition 2 ➔ **Unit 131**

Exercises

130.1 Complete the sentences using **nice of** ... , **kind of** ... etc.

1	I went out in the cold without a coat.	(silly) *That was silly of you.*
2	Tom offered to drive me to the airport.	(nice) That was _____ him.
3	I needed money and Sue gave me some.	(generous) That _____ .
4	They didn't invite us to their party.	(not very nice) That wasn't _____ .
5	Can I help you with your luggage?	(very kind) _____ .
6	Kevin never says 'thank you'.	(not very polite) _____ .
7	They've had an argument and now they refuse to speak to each other.	(a bit childish) _____ .

130.2 Complete the sentences using these adjectives + a preposition:

> amazed   angry   bored   careless   excited   impressed   kind   ~~nervous~~

1 Are you ___nervous about___ the exam?
2 Thank you for all you've done. You've been very _____ me.
3 What have I done wrong? Why are you _____ me?
4 You must be very _____ your trip next week. It sounds really great.
5 I wasn't _____ the service in the restaurant. We had to wait ages before our food arrived.
6 Ben isn't very happy at college. He says he's _____ the course he's doing.
7 I'd never seen so many people before. I was _____ the crowds.
8 It was _____ you to leave the door unlocked when you went out.

130.3 Put in the correct preposition.

1 They were delighted ___with___ the present I gave them.
2 It was nice _____ you to come and see me when I was ill.
3 Why are you so rude _____ people? Why can't you be more polite?
4 We always have the same food every day. I'm fed up _____ it.
5 We enjoyed our holiday, but we were a bit disappointed _____ the hotel.
6 I can't understand people who are cruel _____ animals.
7 I was surprised _____ the way he behaved. It was completely out of character.
8 I've been trying to learn Spanish, but I'm not very satisfied _____ my progress.
9 Tanya doesn't look very well. I'm worried _____ her.
10 They told me they were sorry _____ the situation, but there was nothing they could do.
11 I wouldn't like to be in her position. I feel sorry _____ her.
12 Are you still upset _____ what I said to you yesterday?
13 Some people say Kate is unfriendly, but she's always been very nice _____ me.
14 I'm tired _____ doing the same thing every day. I need a change.
15 The man we interviewed for the job was intelligent and we were impressed _____ the way he answered our questions.
16 I'm sorry _____ the smell of paint in this room. I've just finished redecorating it.
17 I was shocked _____ what I saw. I'd never seen anything like it before.
18 Our neighbours were very angry _____ the noise we made.
19 Our neighbours were furious _____ us _____ making so much noise.
20 I'm sorry _____ what I did. I hope you're not angry _____ me.

➜ Additional exercise 35 (page 322)

A Adjective + **of** (1)

afraid / frightened / terrified / scared OF …
- ☐ 'Are you **afraid of** spiders?' 'Yes, I'm **terrified of** them.'

fond / proud / ashamed / jealous / envious OF …
- ☐ Why are you always so **jealous of** other people?

suspicious / critical / tolerant OF …
- ☐ He didn't trust me. He was **suspicious of** my motives.

B Adjective + **of** (2)

aware / conscious OF …
- ☐ 'Did you know he was married?' 'No, I wasn't **aware of** that.'

capable / incapable OF …
- ☐ I'm sure you are **capable of** passing the examination.

full / short OF …
- ☐ Amy is a very active person. She's always **full of** energy.
- ☐ I'm **short of** money. Can you lend me some?

typical OF …
- ☐ He's late again. It's **typical of** him to keep everybody waiting.

certain / sure OF or **ABOUT** …
- ☐ I think she's arriving this evening, but I'm not **sure of** that. *or* … not **sure about** that.

C Adjective + **at / to / from / in / on / with / for**

good / bad / brilliant / better / hopeless etc. **AT** …
- ☐ I'm not very **good at** repairing things. (*not* good in repairing things)

married / engaged TO …
- ☐ Louise is **married to** an American. (*not* married with)
- *but* Louise is married **with three children**. (= she is married and has three children)

similar TO …
- ☐ Your writing is **similar to** mine.

different FROM or **different TO** …
- ☐ The film was **different from** what I'd expected. *or* … **different to** what I'd expected.

interested IN …
- ☐ Are you **interested in** art?

keen ON …
- ☐ We stayed at home because Chris wasn't very **keen on** going out.

dependent ON … (*but* **independent OF** …)
- ☐ I don't want to be **dependent on** anybody.

crowded WITH (people etc.)
- ☐ The streets were **crowded with** tourists. (*but* … **full of** tourists)

famous FOR …
- ☐ The Italian city of Florence is **famous for** its art treasures.

responsible FOR …
- ☐ Who was **responsible for** all that noise last night?

Preposition + -ing → Unit 60   Afraid of/to … → Unit 66A   Adjective + preposition 1 → Unit 130
American English → Appendix 7

Exercises

131.1 Complete the sentences using these adjectives + the correct preposition:

> afraid   capable   different   interested   proud   responsible   similar   ~~sure~~

1 I think she's arriving this evening, but I'm not ..... sure of ..... that.
2 Your camera is .... mine, but it isn't exactly the same.
3 Don't worry. I'll look after you. There's nothing to be ....
4 I never watch the news on TV. I'm not .... the news.
5 The editor is the person who is .... what appears in a newspaper.
6 Sarah is a keen gardener. She's very .... her garden and loves showing it to visitors.
7 I was surprised when I met Lisa for the first time. She was .... what I expected.
8 He could become world champion one day. He's .... it.

131.2 Complete the second sentence so that it means the same as the first.

1 There were lots of tourists in the streets.   The streets were crowded ..... with tourists ..... .
2 There was a lot of furniture in the room.   The room was full ....
3 I don't like sport very much.   I'm not very keen ....
4 We don't have enough time.   We're short ....
5 I'm not a very good tennis player.   I'm not very good ....
6 Catherine's husband is Russian.   Catherine is married ....
7 I don't trust Robert.   I'm suspicious ....
8 My problem is not the same as yours.   My problem is different ....

131.3 Put in the correct preposition.

1 Amy is always full ..... of ..... energy.
2 My home town is not a very interesting place. It's not famous .... anything.
3 Kate is very fond .... her younger brother.
4 I don't like going up ladders. I'm scared .... heights.
5 You look bored. You don't seem interested .... what I'm saying.
6 'Our flight departs at 10.35.' 'Are you sure .... that?'
7 I'm not ashamed .... what I did. In fact I'm quite proud .... it.
8 I wanted to go out for a meal, but nobody else was keen .... the idea.
9 These days everybody is aware .... the dangers of smoking.
10 The station platform was crowded .... people waiting for the train.
11 Sue is much more successful than I am. Sometimes I feel a bit jealous .... her.
12 Do you know anyone who might be interested .... buying an old car?
13 We've got plenty to eat. The fridge is full .... food.
14 She's very honest. I don't think she is capable .... telling a lie.
15 Helen works hard and she's extremely good .... her job.
16 It's typical .... him to change his mind at the last minute.
17 Mark has no money of his own. He's totally dependent .... his parents.
18 We're short .... staff in our office at the moment. We need more people to do the work.

131.4 Write sentences about yourself. Are you good at these things or not? Use the following:

> good   pretty good   not very good   hopeless

1 (repairing things)   I'm not very good at repairing things.
2 (telling jokes) ....
3 (maths) ....
4 (remembering names) ....
5 (sport) ....

→ Additional exercise 35 (page 322)

A   Verb + **to**

talk / speak TO somebody (**with** is also possible but less usual)
- ○ Who was that man you were **talking to**?

listen TO …
- ○ We spent the evening **listening to** music.   (*not* listening music)

apologise TO somebody (**for** …)
- ○ They **apologised to me** for what happened.   (*not* They apologised me)

explain something **TO** somebody
- ○ Can you **explain** this word **to me**?   (*not* explain me this word)

explain / describe (**to** somebody) what/how/why …
- ○ I **explained to them** why I was worried.   (*not* I explained them)
- ○ Let me **describe to you** what I saw.   (*not* Let me describe you)

B   We do not use **to** with these verbs:

phone / call / email / text somebody
- ○ I **called the airline** to cancel my flight.   (*not* called to the airline)
but   **write** (a letter) **to** somebody

answer somebody/something
- ○ He refused to **answer my question**.   (*not* answer to my question)
but   **reply to** an email / a letter etc.

ask somebody
- ○ Can I **ask you** a question?   (*not* ask to you)

thank somebody (**for** something)
- ○ He **thanked me** for helping him.   (*not* He thanked to me)

C   Verb + **at**

look / stare / glance AT … , **have a look / take a look AT** …
- ○ Why are you **looking at** me like that?

laugh AT …
- ○ I look stupid with this haircut. Everybody will **laugh at** me.

aim / point (something) **AT** … , **shoot / fire** (a gun) **AT** …
- ○ Don't **point** that knife **at** me. It's dangerous.
- ○ We saw someone with a gun **shooting at** birds, but he didn't hit any.

D   Some verbs can be followed by **at** or **to**, with a difference in meaning. For example:

shout AT somebody (when you are angry)
- ○ He got very angry and started **shouting at** me.

shout TO somebody (so that they can hear you)
- ○ He **shouted to** me from the other side of the street.

throw something **AT** somebody/something (in order to hit them)
- ○ Somebody **threw** an egg **at** the minister.

throw something **TO** somebody (for somebody to catch)
- ○ Lisa shouted 'Catch!' and **threw** the keys **to** me from the window.

Verb + preposition 2–5 ➜ Units 133–136   Ask for ➜ Unit 133B
Apologise for / thank somebody for ➜ Unit 135B   Other verbs + to ➜ Unit 136D

Exercises

132.1 **Which is correct?**

1　a　<u>Can you explain this word to me?</u> .... ☑
　　b　Can you explain me this word? .... ☐

2　a　I got angry with Mark. Afterwards, I apologised to him. .... ☐
　　b　I got angry with Mark. Afterwards I apologised him. .... ☐

3　a　Amy won't be able to help you. There's no point in asking to her. .... ☐
　　b　Amy won't be able to help you. There's no point in asking her. .... ☐

4　a　I need somebody to explain me what I have to do. .... ☐
　　b　I need somebody to explain to me what I have to do. .... ☐

5　a　They didn't understand the system, so I explained it to them. .... ☐
　　b　They didn't understand the system, so I explained it them. .... ☐

6　a　I like to sit on the beach and listen to the sound of the sea. .... ☐
　　b　I like to sit on the beach and listen the sound of the sea. .... ☐

7　a　I asked them to describe me exactly what happened. .... ☐
　　b　I asked them to describe to me exactly what happened. .... ☐

8　a　We'd better phone the restaurant to reserve a table. .... ☐
　　b　We'd better phone to the restaurant to reserve a table. .... ☐

9　a　It was a difficult question. I couldn't answer to it. .... ☐
　　b　It was a difficult question. I couldn't answer it. .... ☐

10　a　I explained everybody the reasons for my decision. .... ☐
　　b　I explained to everybody the reasons for my decision. .... ☐

11　a　I thanked everybody for all the help they had given me. .... ☐
　　b　I thanked to everybody for all the help they had given me. .... ☐

12　a　My friend texted to me to let me know she was going to be late. .... ☐
　　b　My friend texted me to let me know she was going to be late. .... ☐

132.2 **Complete the sentences. Use these verbs + the correct preposition:**

~~explain~~　　~~laugh~~　　listen　　look　　point　　reply　　speak　　throw　　throw

1　I look stupid with this haircut. Everybody will ___laugh at___ me.
2　I don't understand this. Can you ___explain___ it ___to___ me?
3　Sue and Kevin had an argument and now they're refusing to .... each other.
4　Be careful with those scissors! Don't .... them .... me!
5　I'm not sure where we are. I'll have to .... the map.
6　Please .... me! I've got something important to tell you.
7　Don't .... stones .... the birds! It's cruel.
8　If you don't want that sandwich, ... it .... the birds. They'll eat it.
9　I tried to contact Tina, but she didn't .... my emails.

132.3 **Put in to or at.**

1　They apologised ___to___ me for what happened.
2　I glanced .... my watch to see what time it was.
3　Please don't shout .... me! Try to calm down.
4　I saw Sue as I was cycling along the road. I shouted .... her, but she didn't hear me.
5　Don't listen .... what he says. He doesn't know what he's talking about.
6　What's so funny? What are you laughing .... ?
7　Could I have a look .... your magazine, please?
8　I'm lonely. I need somebody to talk ....
9　She was so angry she threw a book .... the wall.
10　The woman sitting opposite me on the train kept staring .... me.
11　Can I speak .... you a moment? There's something I want to ask you.

→ Additional exercise 36 (page 323)

A   Verb + **about**

talk / read / know ABOUT … , **tell** somebody **ABOUT** …
- ○ We **talked about** a lot of things at the meeting.

have a discussion ABOUT something, *but* **discuss** something (no preposition)
- ○ We had **a discussion about** what we should do.
- ○ We **discussed** a lot of things at the meeting.   (*not* discussed about)

do something **ABOUT** something = *do something to improve a bad situation*
- ○ If you're worried about the problem, you should **do** something **about** it.

B   Verb + **for**

ask (somebody) **FOR** …
- ○ I sent an email to the company **asking** them **for** more information about the job.
- *but*   'I **asked** him **the way** to …', 'She **asked** me **my name**' (no preposition)

apply (**TO** a person, a company etc.) **FOR** a job etc.
- ○ I think you'd be good at this job. Why don't you **apply for** it?

wait FOR …
- ○ Don't **wait for** me. I'll join you later.
- ○ I'm not going out yet. I'm **waiting for** the rain to stop.

search (a person / a place / a bag etc.) **FOR** …
- ○ I've **searched** the house **for** my keys, but I still can't find them.

leave (a place) **FOR** another place
- ○ I haven't seen her since she **left** (home) **for** the office this morning.
  (*not* left to the office)

C   Care about, care for and take care of

care ABOUT somebody/something = *think that somebody/something is important*
- ○ He's very selfish. He doesn't **care about** other people.

We say '**care what/where/how** …' etc. (*without* about):
- ○ You can do what you like. I don't **care what** you do.

care FOR somebody/something
(1) = *like something* (usually negative sentences)
- ○ I don't **care for** very hot weather. (= I don't like …)
(2) = *look after somebody*
- ○ Alan is 85 and lives alone. He needs somebody to **care for** him.

take care OF … = *look after, keep safe, take responsibility for*
- ○ Don't worry about me. I can **take care of** myself.
- ○ I'll **take care of** the travel arrangements. You don't need to do anything.

D   Look for and look after

look FOR … = *search for, try to find*
- ○ I've lost my keys. Can you help me to **look for** them?

look AFTER … = *take care of, keep safe or in good condition*
- ○ Alan is 85 and lives alone. He needs somebody to **look after** him.   (*not* look for)
- ○ You can borrow this book, but you must promise to **look after** it.

Verbs + **about/of** (think/hear etc.) → Unit 134   Other verbs + **for** → Unit 135B

Exercises

133.1 **Put in the correct preposition. If no preposition is necessary, leave the space empty.**

1 I'm not going out yet. I'm waiting __for__ the rain to stop.
2 Don't ask me _____ money. I don't have any.
3 I've applied _____ a job at the factory. I don't know if I'll get it.
4 I've applied _____ three colleges. I hope one of them accepts me.
5 I've searched everywhere _____ Joe, but I haven't been able to find him.
6 I don't want to talk _____ what happened last night. Let's forget it.
7 I don't want to discuss _____ what happened last night. Let's forget it.
8 We had an interesting discussion _____ the problem, but we didn't reach a decision.
9 We discussed _____ the problem, but we didn't reach a decision.
10 I sent her an email. Now I'm waiting _____ her to reply.
11 Ken and Sonia are travelling in Italy. They're in Rome right now, and tomorrow they leave
   _____ Venice.
12 The roof of the house is in very bad condition. I think we ought to do something _____ it.
13 We waited _____ Steve for half an hour, but he never came.
14 Tomorrow morning I have to catch a plane. I'm leaving my house _____ the airport at 7.30.

133.2 **Put in the correct preposition after care. If no preposition is necessary, leave the space empty.**

1 He's very selfish. He doesn't care __about__ other people.
2 Who's going to take care _____ you when you are old?
3 She doesn't care _____ the exam. She doesn't care whether she passes or fails.
4 'Do you like this coat?' 'Not really. I don't care _____ the colour.'
5 Don't worry about the shopping. I'll take care _____ that.
6 He gave up his job to care _____ his elderly father.
7 I want to have a good holiday. I don't care _____ the cost.
8 I want to have a good holiday. I don't care _____ how much it costs.

133.3 **Complete the sentences with look for or look after. Use the correct form of look (looks/
looked/looking).**

1 I __looked for__ my keys, but I couldn't find them anywhere.
2 Kate is _____ a job. I hope she finds one soon.
3 Who _____ you when you were ill?
4 I'm _____ Liz. I need to ask her something. Have you seen her?
5 The car park was full, so we had to _____ somewhere else to park.
6 A babysitter is somebody who _____ other people's children.

133.4 **Complete the sentences with these verbs (in the correct form) + a preposition:**

apply	ask	do	leave	look	~~search~~	talk	wait

1 Police are __searching for__ the man who escaped from prison.
2 Sarah wasn't ready. We had to _____ her.
3 I think Ben likes his job, but he doesn't _____ it much.
4 When I'd finished my meal, I _____ the waiter _____ the bill.
5 Cathy is unemployed. She has _____ several jobs, but she hasn't had any
   luck.
6 If something is wrong, why don't you _____ something _____ it?
7 Helen's car is very old, but it's in excellent condition. She _____ it very well.
8 Diane is from Boston, but now she lives in Paris. She _____ Boston _____ Paris
   when she was 19.

→ Additional exercise 36 (page 323)

Verb + preposition 3 **about** and **of**

A

hear ABOUT … = *be told about something*
- ☐ Did you **hear about** the fire at the hotel yesterday?

hear OF … = *know that somebody/something exists*
- ☐ 'Who is Tom Hart?' 'I have no idea. I've never **heard of** him.' (*not* heard from him)

hear FROM … = *be in contact with somebody*
- ☐ 'Have you **heard from** Jane recently?' 'Yes, she called me a few days ago.'

B

think ABOUT … and **think OF** …

When you **think ABOUT** something, you consider it, you concentrate your mind on it:
- ☐ I've **thought about** what you said and I've decided to take your advice.
- ☐ 'Will you lend me the money?' 'I'll **think about** it.'

When you **think OF** something, the idea comes to your mind:
- ☐ It was my idea. I **thought of** it first. (*not* thought about it)
- ☐ I felt embarrassed. I couldn't **think of** anything to say. (*not* think about anything)

We also use **think of** when we ask or give an opinion:
- ☐ 'What did you **think of** the movie?' 'I didn't **think** much **of** it.' (= I didn't like it much)

The difference is sometimes very small and you can use **of** or **about**:
- ☐ When I'm alone, I often **think of** (*or* **about**) you.

You can say **think of** *or* **think about** doing something (for possible future actions):
- ☐ My sister is **thinking of** (*or* **about**) going to Canada. (= she is considering it)

C

dream ABOUT … (when you are asleep)
- ☐ I **dreamt about** you last night.

dream OF *or* **ABOUT** being something / doing something = *imagine*
- ☐ Do you **dream of** (*or* **about**) being rich and famous?

I **wouldn't dream OF** doing something = *I would never do it*
- ☐ 'Don't tell anyone what I said.' 'No, I **wouldn't dream of** it.' (= I would never do it)

D

complain (**TO** somebody) **ABOUT** … = *say that you are not satisfied*
- ☐ We **complained to** the manager of the restaurant **about** the food.

complain OF a pain, an illness etc. = *say that you have a pain etc.*
- ☐ We called the doctor because George was **complaining of** a pain in his stomach.

E

remind somebody **ABOUT** … = *tell somebody not to forget*
- ☐ I'm glad you **reminded** me **about** the meeting. I'd completely forgotten about it.

remind somebody **OF** … = *cause somebody to remember*
- ☐ This house **reminds** me **of** the one I lived in when I was a child.
- ☐ Look at this photograph of Richard. Who does he **remind** you **of**?

F

warn somebody **ABOUT** a person or thing which is bad, dangerous, unusual etc.
- ☐ I knew he was a strange person. I had been **warned about** him. (*not* warned of him)
- ☐ Vicky **warned me** about the traffic. She said it would be bad.

warn somebody **ABOUT** *or* **OF** a danger, something bad which might happen later
- ☐ Scientists have **warned** us **about** (*or* **of**) the effects of climate change.

Remind/warn somebody **to** … → Unit 55B

Exercises

134.1 Complete the sentences using **hear** or **heard** + a preposition (**about/of/from**).

1 I've never ___heard of___ Tom Hart. Who is he?
2 'Did you _____ the accident last night?' 'Yes, Vicky told me.'
3 Jane used to call me quite often, but I haven't _____ her for a long time now.
4 A: Have you _____ a writer called William Hudson?
   B: No, I don't think so. What sort of writer is he?
5 Thanks for your email. It was good to _____ you.
6 'Do you want to _____ our holiday?' 'Not now. Tell me later.'
7 I live in a small town in the north of England. You've probably never _____ it.

134.2 Complete the sentences using **think about** or **think of**. Sometimes both **about** and **of** are possible. Use the correct form of **think (think/thinking/thought)**.

1 You look serious. What are you ___thinking about___ ?
2 I need time to make decisions. I like to _____ things carefully.
3 That's a good idea. Why didn't I _____ that?
4 A: I've finished reading the book you lent me.
   B: What did you _____ it? Did you think it was good?
5 We're _____ going out to eat this evening. Would you like to come?
6 I don't really want to go out with Tom tonight. I'll have to _____ an excuse.
7 When I was offered the job, I didn't accept immediately. I went away and
   _____ it for a while. In the end I decided to take the job.
8 I don't _____ much _____ this coffee. It's like water.
9 Katherine is homesick. She's always _____ her family back home.
10 A: Do you think I should apply to do the course?
    B: I can't _____ any reason why not.

134.3 Put in the correct preposition.

1 Did you hear ___about___ the fire at the hotel yesterday?
2 'I had a strange dream last night.' 'Did you? What did you dream _____ ?'
3 Our neighbours complained _____ us _____ the noise we made last night.
4 Kevin was complaining _____ pains in his chest, so he went to the doctor.
5 I love this music. It reminds me _____ a warm day in spring.
6 He loves his job. He thinks _____ his work all the time, he dreams _____ it, he talks
   _____ it and I'm fed up with hearing _____ it.
7 'We've got no money. What can we do?' 'Don't worry. I'll think _____ something.'
8 Jackie warned me _____ the water. She said it wasn't safe to drink.
9 We warned our children _____ the dangers of playing in the street.

134.4 Complete the sentences using these verbs (in the correct form) + a preposition:

complain	dream	hear	remind	remind	~~think~~	think	warn

1 It was my idea. I ___thought of___ it first.
2 Ben is never satisfied. He's always _____ something.
3 I can't make a decision yet. I need time to _____ your proposal.
4 Before you go into the house, I must _____ you _____ the dog. He's bitten
   people before, so be careful.
5 She's not a well-known singer. Not many people have _____ her.
6 A: You wouldn't go away without telling me, would you?
   B: Of course not. I wouldn't _____ it.
7 I would have forgotten my appointment if Jane hadn't _____ me _____ it.
8 Do you see that man over there? Does he _____ you _____ anybody you know?

→ Additional exercise 36 (page 323)

Verb + preposition 4   of/for/from/on

A   Verb + **of**

accuse / suspect somebody **OF** …
- ☐ Sue **accused** me **of** being selfish.
- ☐ Some students were **suspected of** cheating in the exam.

approve / disapprove OF …
- ☐ His parents don't **approve of** what he does, but they can't stop him.

die OF *or* **FROM** an illness etc.
- ☐ 'What did he **die of**?' 'A heart attack.'

consist OF …
- ☐ We had an enormous meal. It **consisted of** seven courses.

B   Verb + **for**

pay (somebody) **FOR** …
- ☐ I didn't have enough money to **pay for** the meal.   (*not* pay the meal)

but **pay** a bill / a fine / a fee / tax / rent / a sum of money etc.   (no preposition)
- ☐ I didn't have enough money to **pay the rent**.

thank / forgive somebody **FOR** …
- ☐ I'll never **forgive** them **for** what they did.

apologise (**TO** somebody) **FOR** …
- ☐ When I realised I was wrong, I **apologised** (**to** them) **for** my mistake.

blame somebody/something **FOR** … , somebody is **to blame FOR** …
- ☐ Everybody **blamed** me **for** the accident.
- ☐ Everybody said that I was **to blame for** the accident.

blame (a problem etc.) **ON** …
- ☐ The accident wasn't my fault. Don't **blame** it **on** me.

C   Verb + **from**

suffer FROM an illness etc.
- ☐ There's been an increase in the number of people **suffering from** heart disease.

protect somebody/something **FROM** …
- ☐ Sun block **protects** the skin **from** the sun.

D   Verb + **on**

depend / rely ON …
- ☐ 'What time will you be home?'   'I don't know. It **depends on** the traffic.'
- ☐ You can **rely on** Anna. She always keeps her promises.

You can use **depend** + **when/where/how** etc. with or without **on**:
- ☐ 'Are you going to buy it?'   'It **depends how much** it is.'   (*or* It depends **on** how much)

live ON money/food
- ☐ Michael's salary is very low. It isn't enough to **live on**.

congratulate / compliment somebody **ON** …
- ☐ **I congratulated** her **on** doing so well in her exams.
- ☐ The meal was really good. I **complimented** Mark **on** his cooking skills.

Verb + preposition + -ing ➜ Unit 62   Other verbs + for ➜ Unit 133   Other verbs + on ➜ Unit 136E

Exercises

135.1 Put in the correct preposition. If no preposition is necessary, leave the space empty.

1 Some students were suspected __of__ cheating in the exam.
2 Are you going to apologise _____ what you did?
3 The apartment consists _____ three rooms, a kitchen and bathroom.
4 I was accused _____ lying, but I was telling the truth.
5 We finished our meal, paid _____ the bill, and left the restaurant.
6 The accident was my fault, so I had to pay _____ the repairs.
7 Some people are dying _____ hunger, while others eat too much.
8 I called Helen to thank her _____ the present she sent me.
9 The government is popular. Most people approve _____ what they're doing.
10 Do you blame the government _____ the economic situation?
11 When something goes wrong, you always blame it _____ other people.

135.2 Complete the second sentence so that it means the same as the first.

1 Sue said that I was selfish.
Sue accused me __of being selfish__ .
2 The misunderstanding was my fault, so I apologised.
I apologised _____ .
3 Jane won the tournament, so I congratulated her.
I congratulated _____ .
4 He has enemies, and he has a bodyguard to protect him.
He has a bodyguard to protect _____ .
5 There are eleven players in a football team.
A football team consists _____ .
6 Sandra eats only bread and eggs.
Sandra lives _____ .
7 You can't say that your problems are my fault.
You can't blame _____ .

135.3 Complete the sentences using these verbs (in the correct form) + a preposition:

| accuse | apologise | ~~approve~~ | congratulate | depend | live | pay | suffer |

1 His parents don't __approve of__ what he does, but they can't stop him.
2 When you went to the theatre with Paul, who _____ the tickets?
3 It's not pleasant when you are _____ something you didn't do.
4 We hope to go to the beach tomorrow, but it _____ the weather.
5 Things are cheap there. You can _____ very little money.
6 You were rude to Lisa. I think you should _____ her.
7 Alex _____ back pain. He spends too much time working at his desk.
8 When I saw David, I _____ him _____ passing his driving test.

135.4 Put in the correct preposition. If no preposition is necessary, leave the space empty.

1 I'll never forgive them __for__ what they did.
2 They wore warm clothes to protect themselves _____ the cold.
3 You know you can always rely _____ me if you need any help.
4 Sophie doesn't have enough money to pay _____ her college fees.
5 She's often unwell. She suffers _____ very bad headaches.
6 I don't know whether I'll go out tonight. It depends _____ how I feel.
7 She hasn't got a job. She depends _____ her parents for money.
8 My usual breakfast consists _____ fruit, cereal and coffee.
9 I complimented her _____ her English. She spoke really well.

→ Additional exercise 36 (page 323)

Verb + preposition 5 in/into/with/to/on

A Verb + **in**

believe IN …
- ○ Do you **believe in** God? (= Do you believe that God exists?)
- ○ I **believe in** saying what I think. (= I believe it is right to say what I think)

but **believe** something (= believe it is true), **believe** somebody (= believe they are telling the truth)
- ○ The story can't be true. I don't **believe it**. (*not* believe in it)

specialise IN …
- ○ Helen is a lawyer. She **specialises in** company law.

succeed IN …
- ○ I hope you **succeed in** finding the job you want.

B Verb + **into**

break INTO …
- ○ Our house was **broken into** a few days ago, but nothing was stolen.

crash / drive / bump / run INTO …
- ○ He lost control of the car and **crashed into** a wall.

divide / cut / split something **INTO** two or more parts
- ○ The book is **divided into** three parts.

translate a book etc. **FROM** one language **INTO** another
- ○ She's a famous writer. Her books have been **translated into** many languages.

C Verb + **with**

collide WITH …
- ○ There was an accident this morning. A bus **collided with** a car.

fill something **WITH** … (*but* **full of** … – see Unit 131B)
- ○ Take this saucepan and **fill** it **with** water.

provide / supply somebody **WITH** …
- ○ The school **provides** all its students **with** books.

D Verb + **to**

happen TO …
- ○ What **happened to** that gold watch you used to have? (= where is it now?)

invite somebody **TO** a party / a wedding etc.
- ○ They only **invited** a few people **to** their wedding.

prefer one thing/person **TO** another
- ○ I **prefer** tea **to** coffee.

E Verb + **on**

concentrate ON …
- ○ I tried to **concentrate on** my work, but I kept thinking about other things.

insist ON …
- ○ I wanted to go alone, but some friends of mine **insisted on** coming with me.

spend (money) **ON** …
- ○ How much do you **spend on** food each week?

Verb + preposition + **-ing** ➜ Unit 62   Other verbs + **to** ➜ Unit 132   Other verbs + **on** ➜ Unit 135D

Exercises

136.1 Complete the sentences using these verbs (in the correct form) + a preposition:

> believe   concentrate   divide   drive   fill   happen   ~~insist~~   invite   succeed

1 I wanted to go alone, but my friends *insisted on* coming with me.
2 I haven't seen Mike for ages. I wonder what has .... him.
3 We've been .... the party, but unfortunately we can't go.
4 It's a very large house. It's .... four apartments.
5 I don't .... ghosts. I think people imagine that they see them.
6 Steve gave me an empty bucket and told me to .... it .... water.
7 I was driving along when the car in front stopped suddenly. I couldn't stop in time and
 .... the back of it.
8 Don't try and do two things together. .... one thing at a time.
9 It wasn't easy, but in the end we .... finding a solution to the problem.

136.2 Complete the second sentence so that it means the same as the first.

1 There was a collision between a bus and a car.
 A bus collided *with a car* .
2 I don't mind big cities, but I prefer small towns.
 I prefer ....
3 I got all the information I needed from Jane.
 Jane provided me ....
4 This morning I bought a pair of shoes which cost £70.
 This morning I spent ....
5 There are ten districts in the city.
 The city is divided ....

136.3 Put in the correct preposition. If the sentence is already complete, leave the space empty.

1 The school provides all its students *with* books.
2 A strange thing happened .... me a few days ago.
3 Mark decided to give up sport to concentrate .... his studies.
4 Money should be used well. I don't believe .... wasting it.
5 My present job isn't wonderful, but I prefer it .... what I did before.
6 I hope you succeed .... getting what you want.
7 As I was coming out of the room, I collided .... somebody who was coming in.
8 There was an awful noise as the car crashed .... a tree.
9 Patrick is a photographer. He specialises .... sports photography.
10 Do you spend a lot of money .... clothes?
11 I was amazed when Joe walked into the room. I couldn't believe .... it.
12 Somebody broke .... my car and stole the radio.
13 I was quite cold, but Tom insisted .... having the window open.
14 The teacher decided to split the class .... four groups.
15 I filled the tank, but unfortunately I filled it .... the wrong kind of petrol.
16 Some words are difficult to translate .... one language .... another.

136.4 Use your own ideas to complete these sentences. Use a preposition.

1 I wanted to go out alone, but my friend insisted *on coming with me* .
2 I spend a lot of money ....
3 I saw the accident. The car crashed ....
4 Chris prefers basketball ....
5 The restaurant we went to specialises ....
6 Shakespeare's plays have been translated ....

➜ Additional exercise 36 (page 323)

273

Phrasal verbs 1 General points

We often use verbs with the following words:

in	on	up	away	by	about	over	round *or* around
out	off	down	back	through	along	forward	

So you can say **look out / get on / take off / run away** etc. These are *phrasal verbs*.

We often use **on/off/out** etc. with verbs of movement. For example:

get on	○	The bus was full. We couldn't **get on**.
drive off	○	A woman got into the car and **drove off**.
come back	○	Sarah is leaving tomorrow and **coming back** on Saturday.
turn round	○	When I touched him on the shoulder, he **turned round**.

But often the second word (**on/off/out** etc.) gives a special meaning to the verb. For example:

break down	○	Sorry I'm late. The car **broke down**. (= the engine stopped working)
look out	○	**Look out**! There's a car coming. (= be careful)
take off	○	It was my first flight. I was nervous as the plane **took off**. (= went into the air)
get on	○	How was the exam? How did you **get on**? (= How did you do?)
get by	○	My French isn't very good, but it's enough to **get by**. (= manage)

For more phrasal verbs, see Units 138–145.

Sometimes a phrasal verb is followed by a *preposition*. For example:

phrasal verb	*preposition*		
run away	**from**	○	Why did you **run away from** me?
keep up	**with**	○	You're walking too fast. I can't **keep up with** you.
look up	**at**	○	We **looked up at** the plane as it flew above us.
look forward	**to**	○	Are you **looking forward to** your trip?

Sometimes a phrasal verb has an *object*. Usually there are two possible positions for the object.
So you can say:

I **turned on** the light.   *or*   I **turned** the light **on**.
    object   *object*

If the object is a *pronoun* (**it/them/me/him** etc.), only one position is possible:

I **turned** it **on**. (*not* I turned on it)

Some more examples:

○ Can you ⎰ **fill in** this form?
           ⎱ **fill** this form **in**?

but   They gave me a form and told me to **fill it in**. (*not* fill in it)

○ Don't ⎰ **throw away** this box.
          ⎱ **throw** this box **away**.

but   I want to keep this box, so don't **throw it away**. (*not* throw away it)

○ I'm going to ⎰ **take off** my shoes.
                 ⎱ **take** my shoes **off**.

but   These shoes are uncomfortable. I'm going to **take them off**. (*not* take off them)

○ Don't ⎰ **wake up** the baby.
          ⎱ **wake** the baby **up**.

but   The baby is asleep. Don't **wake her up**. (*not* wake up her)

Phrasal verbs 2–9 ➜ **Units 138–145**   American English ➜ **Appendix 7**

Exercises

137.1 Complete each sentence using a verb from A (in the correct form) + a word from B. You can use a word more than once.

A	fly	get	go		B	away	by	down	on
	look	sit	speak			out	round	up	

1 The bus was full. We couldn't ....._get on_...... .
2 I've been standing for the last two hours. I'm going to .... for a bit.
3 A cat tried to catch the bird, but it .... just in time.
4 We were trapped in the building. We couldn't ....
5 I can't hear you very well. Can you .... a little?
6 'Do you speak German?' 'Not very well, but I can ....'
7 Everything has got so expensive. Prices have .... a lot.
8 I thought there was somebody behind me, but when I ...., there was nobody there.

137.2 Complete the sentences using a word from A and a word from B. You can use a word more than once.

A	away	back	forward	in	up		B	at	through	to	with

1 You're walking too fast. I can't keep ...._up with_..... you.
2 My holidays are nearly over. Next week I'll be .... work.
3 We went .... the top floor of the building to admire the view.
4 The meeting tomorrow is going to be difficult. I'm not looking .... it.
5 There was a bank robbery last week. The robbers got .... £50,000.
6 I love to look .... the stars in the sky at night.
7 I was sitting in the kitchen when a bird flew .... the open window.

137.3 Complete the sentences using these phrasal verbs + **it/them/me**:

~~fill in~~	get out	give back	switch on	take off	wake up

1 They gave me a form and told me to ...._fill it in_.... .
2 I'm going to bed now. Can you .... at 6.30?
3 I've got something in my eye and I can't ....
4 I don't like it when people borrow things and don't ....
5 I want to use the hair dryer. How do I ....?
6 My shoes are dirty. I'd better .... before going into the house.

137.4 Use your own ideas to complete the sentences. Use a noun (**this box** etc.) or a pronoun (**it/them** etc.) + the word in brackets (**away/up** etc.).

1 Don't throw ...._away this box_.... . I want to keep it. (away)
2 I don't want this newspaper. You can throw ...._it away_..... . (away)
3 I borrowed these books from the library. I have to take ....
   tomorrow. (back)
4 We can turn .... Nobody is watching it. (off)
5 A: How did the vase get broken?
   B: I'm afraid I knocked .... while I was cleaning. (over)
6 Shh! My mother is asleep. I don't want to wake .... (up)
7 It's cold today. You should put .... if you're going out. (on)
8 It was only a small fire. I was able to put .... easily. (out)
9 A: Is this hotel more expensive than when we stayed here last year?
   B: Yes, they've put .... (up)
10 It's a bit dark in this room. Shall I turn ....? (on)

➜ Additional exercises 37–41 (pages 323–25)

A
Compare **in** and **out**:

in = into a room, a building, a car etc.
- How did the thieves **get in**?
- Here's a key, so you can **let yourself in**.
- Lisa walked up to the edge of the pool and **dived in**. (= into the water)
- I've got a new apartment. I'm **moving in** on Friday.
- As soon as I got to the airport, I **checked in**.

In the same way you can say **go in**, **come in**, **walk in**, **break in** etc.

Compare **in** and **into**:
- I'm moving **in** next week.
- I'm moving **into my new flat** on Friday.

out = out of a room, building, a car etc.
- He just stood up and **walked out**.
- I had no key, so I was **locked out**.
- She swam up and down the pool, and then **climbed out**.
- Andy opened the window and **looked out**.
- (at a hotel) What time do we have to **check out**?

In the same way you can say **go out**, **get out**, **move out**, **let** somebody **out** etc.

Compare **out** and **out of**:
- He walked **out**.
- He walked **out of the room**.

B
Other verbs + **in**

drop in = visit somebody for a short time without arranging to do this
- I **dropped in** to see Chris on my way home.

join in = take part in an activity that is already going on
- They were playing cards, so I **joined in**.

plug in an electrical machine = connect it to the electricity supply
- The fridge isn't working because you haven't **plugged** it **in**.

PLUG IN

fill in a form, a questionnaire etc. = write the necessary information on a form
- Please **fill in** the application form and send it to us by 28 February.
You can also say **fill out** a form.

take somebody **in** = deceive somebody
- The man said he was a policeman and I believed him. I was completely **taken in**.

C
Other verbs + **out**

eat out = eat at a restaurant, not at home
- There wasn't anything to eat at home, so we decided to **eat out**.

drop out of college, university, a course, a race = stop before you have completely finished a course/race etc.
- Gary went to university but **dropped out** after a year.

get out of something that you arranged to do = avoid doing it
- I promised I'd go to the wedding. I don't want to go, but I can't **get out** of it now.

cut something **out** (of a newspaper etc.)
- There was a beautiful picture in the magazine, so I **cut** it **out** and kept it.

leave something **out** = omit it, not include it
- In the sentence 'She said that she was ill', you can **leave out** the word 'that'.

cross something **out** / **rub** something **out**
- Some of the names on the list had been **crossed out**.   ~~Sarah~~ cross out

Phrasal verbs 1 (General points) ➜ **Unit 137**   More verbs + **out** ➜ **Unit 139**

Exercises

138.1 Complete the sentences using a verb in the correct form.

1 Here's a key so that you can ....*let*.... yourself in.
2 Liz doesn't like cooking, so she .... out a lot.
3 Amy isn't living in this apartment any more. She .... out a few weeks ago.
4 If you're in our part of town, you should .... in and say hello.
5 When I .... in at the airport, I was told my flight would be delayed.
6 There was an article in the paper that I wanted to keep, so I .... it out.
7 I wanted to iron some clothes, but there was nowhere to .... the iron in.
8 I hate .... in questionnaires.
9 Steve was upset because he'd been .... out of the team.
10 Be careful! The water's not very deep here, so don't .... in.
11 If you write in pencil and you make a mistake, you can .... it out.
12 Paul started doing a Spanish course, but he .... out after a few weeks.

138.2 Complete the sentences with **in**, **into**, **out** or **out of**.

1 I've got a new flat. I'm moving ....*in*.... on Friday.
2 We checked .... the hotel as soon as we arrived.
3 As soon as we arrived at the hotel, we checked ....
4 The car stopped and the driver got ....
5 Thieves broke .... the house while we were away.
6 Why did Sarah drop .... college? Did she fail her exams?

138.3 Complete the sentences using a verb + **in** or **out (of)**.

1 Lisa walked to the edge of the pool, ...*dived in*... and swam to the other end.
2 Not all the runners finished the race. Three of them ....
3 I went to see Joe and Sophie in their new house. They .... last week.
4 I've told you everything you need to know. I don't think I've .... anything.
5 Some people in the crowd started singing. Then a few more people .... and soon everybody was singing.
6 We go to restaurants a lot. We like ....
7 Don't be .... by him. If I were you, I wouldn't believe anything he says.
8 I .... to see Laura a few days ago. She was fine.
9 A: Can we meet tomorrow morning at 10?
    B: Probably. I'm supposed to go to another meeting, but I think I can .... it.

138.4 Complete the sentences. Use the word in brackets in the correct form.

1 A: The fridge isn't working.
    B: That's because you haven't ...*plugged it in*... . (plug)

2 A: What do I have to do with these forms?
    B: .... and send them to this address. (fill)

3 A: I've made a mistake on this form.
    B: That's all right. Just .... and correct it. (cross)

4 A: Did you believe the story they told you?
    B: Yes, I'm afraid they completely .... (take)

5 A: Have you been to that new club in Bridge Street?
    B: We wanted to go there a few nights ago, but they wouldn't .... because we weren't members. (let)

→ Additional exercises 37–41 (pages 323–25)

A

out = not burning, not shining

go out	○ Suddenly all the lights in the building **went out**.
put out a fire / a cigarette / a light	○ We managed to **put** the fire **out**.
turn out a light	○ I **turned** the lights **out** before leaving.
blow out a candle	○ We don't need the candle. You can **blow** it **out**.

B   work out

work out = *do physical exercises*
- ○ Rachel **works out** at the gym three times a week.

work out = *develop, progress*
- ○ Good luck for the future. I hope everything **works out** well for you.
- ○ A: Why did James leave the company?
  B: Things didn't **work out**. (= things didn't work out well)

work out (for mathematical calculations)
- ○ The total bill for three people is £84.60. That **works out** at £28.20 each.

work something **out** = *calculate, think about a problem and find the answer*
- ○ 345 × 76? I need to do this on paper. I can't **work** it **out** in my head.

C   Other verbs + **out**

carry out an order, an experiment, a survey, an investigation, a plan etc.
- ○ Soldiers are expected to **carry out** orders.
- ○ An investigation into the accident will be **carried out** as soon as possible.

fall out (**with** somebody) = *stop being friends*
- ○ They used to be very good friends. I'm surprised to hear that they have **fallen out**.
- ○ David **fell out with** his father and left home.

find out that/what/when … etc., **find out about** something = *get information*
- ○ The police never **found out** who committed the murder.
- ○ I just **found out** that it's Helen's birthday today.
- ○ I checked a few websites to **find out about** hotels in the town.

give/hand things **out** = *give to each person*
- ○ At the end of the lecture, the speaker **gave out** information sheets to the audience.

point something **out** (**to** somebody) = *draw attention to something*
- ○ As we drove through the city, our guide **pointed out** all the sights.
- ○ I didn't realise I'd made a mistake until somebody **pointed** it **out to** me.

run out (**of** something)
- ○ We **ran out of** petrol on the motorway. (= we used all our petrol)

sort something **out** = *find a solution to, put in order*
- ○ There are a few problems we need to **sort out**.
- ○ All these papers are mixed up. I'll have to **sort** them **out**.

turn out to be … , **turn out** good/nice etc. , **turn out** that …
- ○ Nobody believed Paul at first, but he **turned out** to be right. (= it became clear in the end that he was right)
- ○ The weather wasn't so good in the morning, but it **turned out** nice later.
- ○ I thought they knew each other, but it **turned out** that they'd never met.

try out a machine, a system, a new idea etc. = *test it to see if it is OK*
- ○ The company is **trying out** a new computer system at the moment.

Phrasal verbs 1 (General points) ➔ **Unit 137**   More verbs + **out** ➔ **Unit 138**

Exercises

139.1 Which words can go together? Choose from the list.

| a candle | a cigarette | ~~a light~~ | a mess | a mistake | a new product | an order |

1 turn out _a light_
2 point out ....
3 blow out ....
4 carry out ....

5 put out ....
6 try out ....
7 sort out ....

139.2 Complete the sentences using a verb + **out**.

1 The company is ..._trying out_... a new computer system at the moment.
2 Steve is very fit. He does a lot of sport and .... regularly.
3 The road will be closed for two days next week while building work is ....
4 We didn't manage to discuss everything at the meeting. We .... of time.
5 You have to .... the problem yourself. I can't do it for you.
6 I don't know what happened exactly. I need to ....
7 The new drug will be .... on a small group of patients.
8 I thought the two books were the same until a friend of mine .... the difference.
9 They got married a few years ago, but it didn't .... and they separated.
10 There was a power cut and all the lights ....
11 We thought she was American at first, but she .... to be Swedish.
12 Sometimes it .... cheaper to eat in a restaurant than to cook at home.
13 I haven't applied for the job yet. I want to .... more about the company first.
14 It took the fire brigade two hours to .... the fire.

139.3 For each picture, complete the sentence using a verb + **out**.

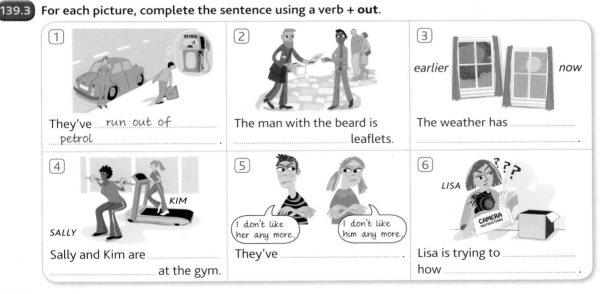

1 They've _run out of petrol_ .
2 The man with the beard is .... leaflets.
3 earlier   now
   The weather has ....
4 SALLY KIM
   Sally and Kim are .... at the gym.
5 I don't like her any more. I don't like him any more.
   They've ....
6 LISA
   Lisa is trying to .... how ....

139.4 Complete the sentences. Each time use a verb + **out**.

1 A: Was the fire serious?
   B: No, we were able to _put it out_ .
2 A: This recipe looks interesting.
   B: Yes, let's ....
3 A: How much money do I owe you exactly?
   B: Just a moment. I'll have to ....
4 A: What happened about your problem with your bank?
   B: It's OK now. I went to see them and we ....

→ Additional exercises 37–41 (pages 323–25)

A   On and off for lights, machines etc.

> We say: the light **is on** / **put** the light **on** / **leave** the light **on** etc.
> **turn** the light **on/off**   *or*   **switch** the light **on/off**

- ○ Shall **I leave** the lights **on** or **turn** them **off**?
- ○ '**Is** the heating **on**?' 'No, I **switched** it **off**.'
- ○ We need some boiling water, so I'll **put** the kettle **on**.

Also **put on** some music / a CD etc.
- ○ I haven't listened to this CD yet. Shall I **put** it **on**?   (= shall I play it)

B   On and off for events etc.

> **go on** = *happen*
- ○ What's all that noise? What's **going on**?   (= what's happening)

> **call** something **off** = *cancel it*
- ○ The open air concert had to be **called off** because of the weather.

> **put** something **off**, **put off** doing something = *delay it*
- ○ The wedding has been **put off** until January.
- ○ We can't **put off** making a decision. We have to decide now.

C   On and off for clothes etc.

> **put on** clothes, glasses, make-up, a seat belt etc.
- ○ My hands were cold, so I **put** my gloves **on**.

Also **put on** weight = *get heavier*
- ○ I've **put on** two kilograms in the last month.

> **try on** clothes (to see if they fit)
- ○ I **tried on** a jacket in the shop, but it didn't fit me very well.

> **take off** clothes, glasses etc.
- ○ It was warm, so I **took off** my jacket.

D   Off = away from a person or place

> **be off** (to a place)
- ○ Tomorrow I'**m off** to Paris / I'**m off** on holiday.
  (= I'm going to Paris / I'm going on holiday)

> **walk off** / **run off** / **drive off** / **ride off** / **go off** (similar to **walk away** / **run away** etc.)
- ○ Diane got on her bike and **rode off**.
- ○ Mark left home at the age of 18 and **went off** to Canada.

> **set off** = *start a journey*
- ○ We **set off** very early to avoid the traffic.   (= We left early)

> **take off** = *leave the ground (for planes)*
- ○ After a long delay the plane finally **took off**.

> **see** somebody **off** = *go with them to the airport/station to say goodbye*
- ○ Helen was going away. We went to the station with her to **see her off**.

Phrasal verbs 1 (General points) → **Unit 137**   More verbs + **on/off** → **Unit 141**

Exercises

140.1 Complete the sentences using **put on** + the following:

| a CD | the heating | the kettle | ~~the light~~ | the oven |

1 It was getting dark, so I ___put the light on___ .
2 It was getting cold, so I _____ .
3 I wanted to bake a cake, so I _____ .
4 I wanted to make some tea, so I _____ .
5 I wanted to listen to some music, so I _____ .

140.2 Complete the sentences. Each time use a verb + **on** or **off**.

1 It was warm, so I ___took off___ my jacket.
2 What are all these people doing? What's _____ ?
3 The weather was too bad for the plane to _____ , so the flight was delayed.
4 I didn't want to be disturbed, so I _____ my phone.
5 Rachel got into her car and _____ at high speed.
6 Tim has _____ weight since I last saw him. He used to be quite thin.
7 A: What time are you leaving tomorrow?
    B: I'm not sure yet, but I'd like to _____ as early as possible.
8 Don't _____ until tomorrow what you can do today.
9 There was going to be a strike by bus drivers, but now they have been offered more money and
    the strike has been _____ .
10 Are you cold? Shall I get you a sweater to _____ ?
11 When I go away, I prefer to be alone at the station or airport. I don't like it when people come to
    _____ me _____ .

140.3 Look at the pictures and complete the sentences.

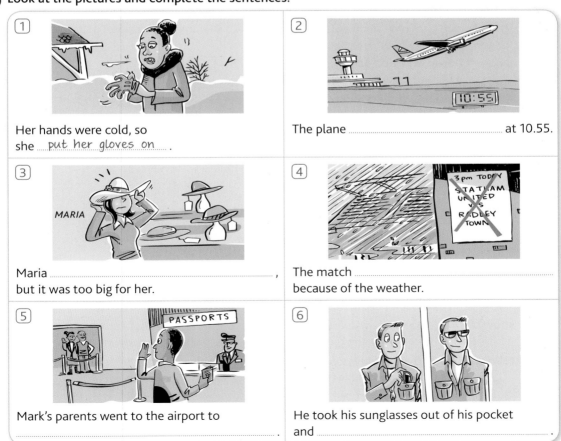

[1] Her hands were cold, so
     she ___put her gloves on___ .

[2] The plane _____ at 10.55.

[3] Maria _____ ,
     but it was too big for her.

[4] The match _____
     because of the weather.

[5] Mark's parents went to the airport to
     _____ .

[6] He took his sunglasses out of his pocket
     and _____ .

→ Additional exercises 37–41 (pages 323–25)

A   Verb + on = continue doing something

drive on / walk on / play on = *continue driving/walking/playing etc.*
- ☐ Shall we stop at this petrol station or shall we **drive on** to the next one?

go on = *continue*
- ☐ The party **went on** until 4 o'clock in the morning.

go on / carry on doing something = *continue doing something*
- ☐ We can't **go on** spending money like this. We'll have nothing left soon.
- ☐ I don't want to **carry on** working here. I'm going to look for another job.

Also **go on with / carry on with** something
- ☐ Don't let me disturb you. Please **carry on with** what you're doing.

keep on doing something = *do it continuously or repeatedly*
- ☐ He **keeps on** criticising me. I'm fed up with it!

B   Get on

get on = *progress*
- ☐ How are you **getting on** in your new job?   (= How is it going?)

get on (**with** somebody) = *have a good relationship*
- ☐ Joanne and Karen don't **get on**. They're always arguing.
- ☐ Richard **gets on** well **with** his neighbours. They're all very friendly.

get on with something = *continue doing something you have to do, usually after an interruption*
- ☐ I must **get on with** my work. I have a lot to do.

C   Verb + off

doze off / drop off / nod off = *fall asleep*
- ☐ The lecture wasn't very interesting. In fact I **dozed off** in the middle of it.

finish something **off** = *do the last part of something*
- ☐ A: Have you finished painting the kitchen?
- B: Nearly. I'll **finish** it **off** tomorrow.

go off = *explode*
- ☐ A bomb **went off** in the city centre, but fortunately nobody was hurt.
Also an alarm can **go off** = *ring*
- ☐ Did you hear the alarm **go off**?

put somebody **off** (doing something) = *cause somebody not to want something or to do something*
- ☐ We wanted to go to the exhibition, but we were **put off** by the long queue.
- ☐ What **put** you **off** applying for the job? Was the salary too low?

rip somebody **off** = *cheat somebody (informal)*
- ☐ Did you really pay £2,000 for that painting? I think you were **ripped off**.
(= you paid too much)

show off = *try to impress people with your ability, your knowledge etc.*
- ☐ Look at that boy on the bike riding with no hands. He's just **showing off**.

tell somebody **off** = *speak angrily to somebody because they did something wrong*
- ☐ Clare's mother **told** her **off** for wearing dirty shoes in the house.

Go on / carry on / keep on ➔ Unit 53B   Phrasal verbs 1 (General points) ➔ Unit 137
More verbs + on/off ➔ Unit 140   American English ➔ Appendix 7

Exercises

141.1 Change the <u>underlined</u> words. Keep the same meaning, but use a verb + **on** or **off**.

1 Did you hear the bomb <u>explode</u>?
   Did you hear the bomb ___go off___ ?

2 The meeting <u>continued</u> longer than I expected.
   The meeting _____ longer than I expected.

3 We didn't stop to rest. We <u>continued walking</u>.
   We didn't stop to rest. We _____ .

4 I <u>fell asleep</u> while I was watching TV.
   I _____ while I was watching TV.

5 Gary doesn't want to retire. He wants to <u>continue</u> working.
   Gary doesn't want to retire. He wants to _____ working.

6 The fire alarm <u>rang</u> in the middle of the night.
   The fire alarm _____ in the middle of the night.

7 Martin <u>phones me continuously</u>. It's very annoying.
   Martin _____ . It's very annoying.

141.2 Complete each sentence using a verb + **on** or **off**.

1 We can't ___go on___ spending money like this. We'll have nothing left soon.
2 I was standing by the car when suddenly the alarm _____ .
3 I'm not ready to go home yet. I have a few things to _____ .
4 'Shall I stop the car here?' 'No, _____ .'
5 Bill paid too much for the car he bought. I think he was _____ .
6 'Is Emma enjoying her course at university?' 'Yes, she's _____ very well.'
7 I was very tired at work today. I nearly _____ at my desk a couple of times.
8 Ben was _____ by his boss for being late for work repeatedly.
9 I really like working with my colleagues. We all _____ really well together.
10 There was a very loud noise. It sounded like a bomb _____ .
11 I _____ making the same mistake. It's very frustrating.
12 I've just had a coffee break, and now I must _____ with my work.
13 Peter is always trying to impress people. He's always _____ .
14 We decided not to go to the concert. We were _____ by the cost of tickets.

141.3 Complete the sentences. Use the following verbs (in the correct form) + **on** or **off**. Sometimes you will need other words as well:

carry	finish	~~get~~	get	get	go	rip	tell

1 A: How ___are you getting on___ in your new job?
   B: Fine, thanks. It's going very well.

2 A: Have you written the letter you had to write?
   B: I've started it. I'll _____ in the morning.

3 A: We took a taxi to the airport. It cost £40.
   B: £40! Normally it costs about £20. You _____ .

4 A: Why were you late for work this morning?
   B: I overslept. My alarm clock didn't _____ .

5 A: How _____ in your interview? Do you think you'll get the job?
   B: I hope so. The interview was OK.

6 A: Did you stop playing tennis when it started to rain?
   B: No, we _____ . The rain wasn't very heavy.

7 A: Some children at the next table in the restaurant were behaving very badly.
   B: Why didn't their parents _____ ?

8 A: Why does Paul want to leave his job?
   B: He _____ his boss.

→ Additional exercises 37–41 (pages 323–25)

A   Compare **up** and **down**:

put something **up** (on a wall etc.)
- ☐ I **put** a picture **up** on the wall.

pick something **up**
- ☐ There was a letter on the floor. I **picked** it **up** and looked at it.

stand up
- ☐ Alan **stood up** and walked out.

turn something **up**
- ☐ I can't hear the TV. Can you **turn** it **up** a bit?

take something **down** (from a wall etc.)
- ☐ I didn't like the picture, so I **took** it **down**.

put something **down**
- ☐ I stopped writing and **put down** my pen.

sit down / bend down / lie down
- ☐ I **bent down** to tie my shoelace.

turn something **down**
- ☐ The oven is too hot. **Turn** it **down** to 150 degrees.

B   **Knock down**, **cut down** etc.

knock down a building, **blow** something **down**, **cut** something **down** etc.
- ☐ Some old houses were **knocked down** to make way for the new shopping centre.
- ☐ Why did you **cut down** the tree in your garden?

be **knocked down** (by a car etc.)
- ☐ A man was **knocked down** by a car and taken to hospital.

burn down = *be destroyed by fire*
- ☐ They were able to put out the fire before the house **burnt down**.

C   **Down** = getting less

slow down = *go more slowly*
- ☐ You're driving too fast. **Slow down**.

calm (somebody) **down** = *become calmer, make somebody calmer*
- ☐ **Calm down**. There's no point in getting angry.

cut down (**on** something) = *eat, drink or do something less often*
- ☐ I'm trying to **cut down on** coffee. I drink too much of it.

D   Other verbs + **down**

break down = *stop working (for machines, cars, relationships etc.)*
- ☐ The car **broke down** and I had to phone for help.
- ☐ Their marriage **broke down** after only a few months.

close down / shut down = *stop doing business*
- ☐ There used to be a shop at the end of the street; it **closed down** a few years ago.

let somebody **down** = *disappoint them because you didn't do what they hoped*
- ☐ You can always rely on Paul. He'll never **let** you **down**.

turn somebody/something **down** = *refuse an application, an offer etc.*
- ☐ I applied for several jobs, but I was **turned down** for all of them.
- ☐ Rachel was offered the job, but she decided to **turn** it **down**.

write something **down** = *write something on paper because you may need the information later*
- ☐ I can't remember Tim's address. I **wrote** it **down**, but I can't find it.

Phrasal verbs 1 (General points) → **Unit 137**   More verbs + **up** → **Units 143–144**

Exercises

142.1 For each picture, complete the sentences using a verb + **up** or **down**. In most sentences you will need other words as well.

1 before now
2 before now
3
4 VOLUME
5 BUS STOP
6
7
8 LISA

1 There used to be a tree next to the house, but we ___cut it down___ .
2 There used to be some shelves on the wall, but I ....
3 The ceiling was so low, he couldn't .... straight.
4 She couldn't hear the radio very well, so she ....
5 While they were waiting for the bus, they .... on the ground.
6 A few trees .... in the storm last week.
7 We've got some new curtains, but we haven't .... yet.
8 Lisa dropped her keys, so she .... and ....

142.2 Complete the sentences. Use the following verbs (in the correct form) + **down**:

> calm   let   ~~take~~   turn   turn   write

1 I don't like this picture on the wall. I'm going to ___take it down___ .
2 The music is too loud. Can you .... ?
3 David was very angry. I tried to ....
4 Sarah gave me her phone number. I .... on a piece of paper.
5 I promised I would help Anna. I don't want to ....
6 I was offered the job, but I decided I didn't want it. So I ....

142.3 Complete each sentence using a verb (in the correct form) + **down**.

1 I stopped writing and ___put down___ my pen.
2 I was really angry. It took me a long time to ....
3 The train .... as it approached the station.
4 Sarah applied to study medicine at university, but she ....
5 Our car is very reliable. It has never ....
6 I need to spend less money. I'm going to .... on things I don't really need.
7 I didn't play very well. I felt that I had .... the other players in the team.
8 The shop .... because it was losing money.
9 This is a very ugly building. Many people would like it to ....
10 I can't understand why you .... the chance of working abroad for a year. It would have been a great experience for you.
11 A: Did you see the accident? What happened exactly?
   B: A man .... by a car as he was crossing the road.
12 Peter got married when he was 20, but unfortunately the marriage .... a few years later.

→ Additional exercises 37–41 (pages 323–25)

A

go up / come up / walk up (to …**)** = *approach*
- ○ A man **came up to** me in the street and asked me for money.

catch up (with somebody**), catch** somebody **up** = *move faster than somebody in front of you* so *that you reach them*
- ○ I'm not ready to go yet. You go on and I'll **catch up with** you / I'll **catch** you **up**.

keep up (with somebody**)** = *continue at the same speed or level*
- ○ You're walking too fast. I can't **keep up (with** you**)**.
- ○ You're doing well. **Keep** it **up**!

B

set up an organisation, a company, a business, a system, a website etc. = *start it*
- ○ The government has **set up** a committee to investigate the problem.

take up a hobby, a sport, an activity etc. = *start doing it*
- ○ Laura **took up** photography a few years ago. She takes really good pictures.

fix up a meeting etc. = *arrange it*
- ○ We've **fixed up** a meeting for next Monday.

C

grow up = *become an adult*
- ○ Ann was born in Hong Kong but **grew up** in Australia.

bring up a child = *raise, look after a child*
- ○ Her parents died when she was a child and she was **brought up** by her grandparents.

D

clean up / clear up / tidy up something = *make it clean, tidy etc.*
- ○ Look at this mess! Who's going to **tidy up**? (*or* **tidy** it **up**)

wash up = *wash the plates, dishes etc. after a meal*
- ○ I hate **washing up**. (*or* I hate **doing the washing-up**.)

E

end up somewhere, **end up** doing something etc.
- ○ There was a fight in the street and three men **ended up** in hospital. (= that's what happened to these men in the end)
- ○ I couldn't find a hotel and **ended up** sleeping on a bench at the station. (= that's what happened to me in the end)

give up = *stop trying*, **give** something **up** = *stop doing it*
- ○ Don't **give up**. Keep trying!
- ○ Sue got bored with her job and decided to **give** it **up**. (= stop doing it)

make up something, be **made up of** something
- ○ Children under 16 **make up** half the population of the city. (= half the population are children under 16)
- ○ Air is **made up** mainly **of** nitrogen and oxygen. (= Air consists of …)

take up space or time = *use space or time*
- ○ Most of the space in the room was **taken up** by a large table.

turn up / show up = *arrive, appear*
- ○ We arranged to meet David last night, but he didn't **turn up**.

use something **up** = *use all of it so that nothing is left*
- ○ I'm going to make some soup. We have a lot of vegetables and I want to **use them up**.

Phrasal verbs 1 (General points) ➜ **Unit 137**   More verbs + **up** ➜ **Units 142, 144**

Exercises

143.1 Look at the pictures and complete the sentences. Use <u>three</u> words each time, including a verb from Section A.

1 A man ___came up to___ me in the street and asked me the way to the station.

2 Sue _____ the front door of the house and rang the doorbell.

3 Tom was a long way behind the other runners, but he managed to _____ them.

4 Tanya was running too fast for Paul. He couldn't _____ her.

143.2 Complete the sentences. Use the following verbs (in the correct form) + **up**:

~~end~~	end	give	give	grow	make	take	take	turn	use	wash

1 I couldn't find a hotel and ___ended up___ sleeping on a bench at the station.
2 I'm feeling very tired now. I've _____ all my energy.
3 After dinner I _____ and put the dishes away.
4 People often ask children what they want to be when they _____ .
5 We invited Tom to the party, but he didn't _____ .
6 Two years ago James _____ his studies to be a professional footballer.
7 A: Do you do any sports?
   B: Not at the moment, but I'm thinking of _____ tennis.
8 You don't have enough determination. You _____ too easily.
9 Karen travelled a lot for a few years and _____ in Canada, where she still lives.
10 I do a lot of gardening. It _____ most of my free time.
11 There are two universities in the city, and students _____ 20 per cent of the population.

143.3 Complete the sentences. Use the following verbs + **up** (with any other necessary words):

bring	~~catch~~	fix	~~give~~	go	keep	keep	make	set	tidy

1 Sue got bored with her job and decided to ___give it up___ .
2 I'm not ready yet. You go on and I'll ___catch up with___ you.
3 The room is in a mess. I'd better _____ .
4 We expect to go away on holiday sometime in July, but we haven't _____ yet.
5 Stephen is having problems at school. He can't _____ the rest of the class.
6 Although I _____ in the country, I have always preferred cities.
7 Our team started the game well, but we couldn't _____ and in the end we lost.
8 I saw Mike at the party, so I _____ him and said hello.
9 When I was on holiday, I joined a tour group. The group _____ two Americans, three Germans, five Italians and myself.
10 Helen has her own internet website. A friend of hers helped her to _____ .

→ Additional exercises 37–41 (pages 323–25)

A

bring up a topic etc. = *introduce it in a conversation*
- ◯ I don't want to hear any more about this matter. Please don't **bring** it **up** again.

come up = *be introduced in a conversation*
- ◯ Some interesting points **came up** in our discussion yesterday.

come up with an idea, a suggestion etc. = *produce an idea*
- ◯ Sarah is very creative. She's always **coming up with** new ideas.

make something **up** = *invent something that is not true*
- ◯ What Kevin told you about himself wasn't true. He **made** it all **up**.

B

cheer up = *be happier*, **cheer** somebody **up** = *make somebody feel happier*
- ◯ You look so sad! **Cheer up**!
- ◯ Helen is depressed at the moment. What can we do to **cheer her up**?

save up for something / to do something = *save money to buy something*
- ◯ Dan is **saving up** for a trip round the world.

clear up = *become bright (for weather)*
- ◯ It was raining when I got up, but it **cleared up** later.

C

blow up = *explode*, **blow** something **up** = *destroy it with a bomb etc.*
- ◯ The engine caught fire and **blew up**.
- ◯ The bridge was **blown up** during the war.

tear something **up** = *tear it into pieces*
- ◯ I didn't read the letter. I just **tore** it **up** and threw it away.

beat somebody **up** = *hit someone repeatedly so that they are badly hurt*
- ◯ A friend of mine was attacked and **beaten up** a few days ago. He was badly hurt and had to go to hospital.

D

break up / **split up** (with somebody) = *separate*
- ◯ I'm surprised to hear that Sue and Paul have **split up**. They seemed very happy together.

do up a coat, a shoelace, buttons etc. = *fasten, tie etc.*
- ◯ It's quite cold. **Do up** your coat before you go out.

do up a building, a room etc. = *repair and improve it*
- ◯ The kitchen looks great now that it has been **done up**.

look something **up** in a dictionary, encyclopaedia etc.
- ◯ If you don't know the meaning of a word, you can **look** it **up** in a dictionary.

put up with something = *tolerate it*
- ◯ We live on a busy road, so we have to **put up with** a lot of noise from the traffic.

hold up a person, a plan etc. = *delay*
- ◯ Don't wait for me. I don't want to **hold** you **up**.
- ◯ Plans to build a new factory have been **held up** because of the company's financial problems.

mix up people/things, **get** people/things **mixed up** = *you think one is the other*
- ◯ The two brothers look very similar. Many people **mix** them **up**. (*or* … **get** them **mixed up**)

Phrasal verbs 1 (General points) → **Unit 137**   More verbs + **up** → **Units 142–143**
American English → **Appendix 7**

Exercises

144.1 Which goes with which?

1 I'm going to tear up	a a new camera	1	_f_
2 Jane came up with	b a lot of bad weather	2	
3 Paul is always making up	c your jacket	3	
4 I think you should do up	d an interesting suggestion	4	
5 I don't think you should bring up	e excuses	5	
6 I'm saving up for	f ~~the letter~~	6	
7 We had to put up with	g that subject	7	

144.2 Look at the pictures and complete the sentences. You will need two or three words each time.

1 *this morning* / *now*

The weather was horrible this morning, but it's ___cleared up___ now.

2 Sorry I'm late.

AMY

Amy was late because she was _____ in the traffic.

3

They bought an old house and _____. It's really nice now.

4 Come out for a meal with us!

JOE

Joe was really depressed. We took him out for a meal to _____.

144.3 Complete the sentences using a verb (in the correct form) + **up**. Sometimes you will need other words as well.

1 Some interesting matters ___came up___ in our discussion yesterday.
2 The ship _____ and sank. The cause of the explosion was never discovered.
3 Two men have been arrested after a man was _____ outside a restaurant last night. The injured man was taken to hospital.
4 'Is Robert still going out with Tina?' 'No, they've _____.'
5 My hands were so cold, I found it hard to _____ my shoelaces.
6 I wish it would stop raining! I hope it _____ soon.
7 I wanted to phone Chris, but I dialled Laura's number by mistake. I got their phone numbers _____.

144.4 Complete the sentences using a verb + **up**. You will need other words as well.

1 Don't wait for me. I don't want to ___hold you up___.
2 I don't know what this word means. I'll have to _____.
3 There's nothing we can do about the problem. We'll just have to _____ it.
4 'Was that story true?' 'No, I _____.'
5 I think we should follow Tom's suggestion. Nobody has _____ a better plan.
6 I hate this photo. I'm going to _____.
7 I'm trying to spend less money at the moment. I'm _____ a trip to Australia.

→ Additional exercises 37–41 (pages 323–25)

A Compare away and back:

away = away from home ☐ We're **going away** on holiday today. **away** = away from a place, a person etc. ☐ The woman got into her car, started the engine and **drove away**. ☐ I tried to take a picture of the bird, but it **flew away**. ☐ I dropped the ticket and it **blew away** in the wind. ☐ The police searched the house and **took away** a computer. In the same way you can say: 　**walk away**, **run away**, **look away** etc.	**back** = back home ☐ We'll **be back** in three weeks. **back** = back to a place, a person etc. ☐ A: I'm going out now. 　B: What time will you **be back**? ☐ After eating at a restaurant, we **walked back** to our hotel. ☐ I've still got Jane's keys. I forgot to **give** them **back** to her. ☐ When you've finished with that book, can you **put** it **back** on the shelf? In the same way you can say: 　**go back**, **come back**, **get back**, 　**take** something **back** etc.

B Other verbs + away

get away = *escape, leave with difficulty*
☐ We tried to catch the thief, but she managed to **get away**.

get away with something = *do something wrong without being caught*
☐ I parked in a no-parking zone, but I **got away with** it. I didn't have to pay a fine.

keep away (from …) = *don't go near*
☐ **Keep away from** the edge of the pool. You might fall in.

give something **away** = *give it to somebody else because you don't want it any more*
☐ 'Did you sell your old computer?' 'No, I **gave** it **away**.'

put something **away** = *put it in the place where it is kept, usually out of sight*
☐ When the children had finished playing with their toys, they **put** them **away**.

throw something **away** = *put it in the rubbish*
☐ I kept the letter, but I **threw away** the envelope.

C Other verbs + back

wave back / smile back / shout back / write back / hit somebody **back**
☐ I waved to her and she **waved back**.

call/phone/ring (somebody) **back** = *return a phone call*
☐ I can't talk to you now. I'll **call** you **back** in ten minutes.

get back to somebody = *reply to them by phone etc.*
☐ I sent him an email, but he never **got back to** me.

look back (on something) = *think about what happened in the past*
☐ My first job was in a travel agency. I didn't like it very much at the time but, **looking back on** it, I learnt a lot and it was a very useful experience.

pay back money, **pay** somebody **back**
☐ If you borrow money, you have to **pay** it **back**.
☐ Thanks for lending me the money. I'll **pay** you **back** next week.

Phrasal verbs 1 (General points) → Unit 137

Exercises

145.1 Look at the pictures and complete the sentences.

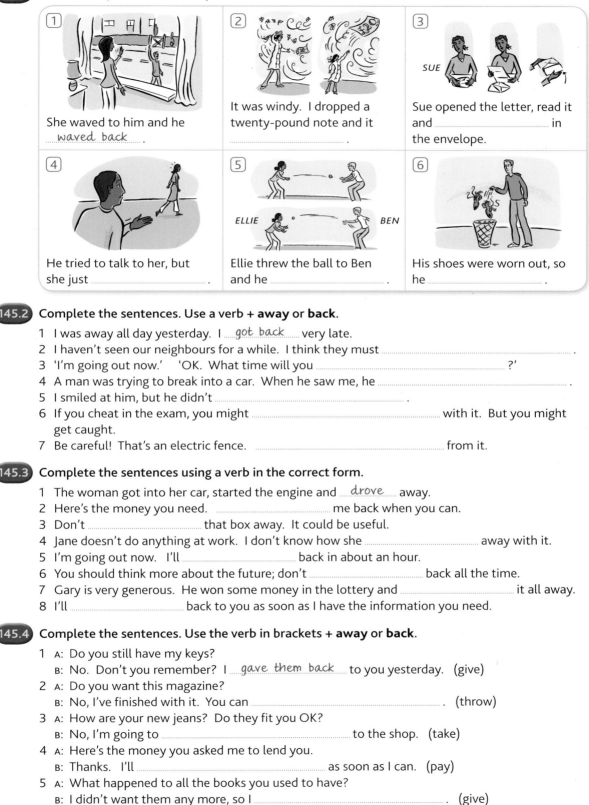

1. She waved to him and he _waved back_ .

2. It was windy. I dropped a twenty-pound note and it ....

3. SUE — Sue opened the letter, read it and .... in the envelope.

4. He tried to talk to her, but she just ....

5. ELLIE — BEN — Ellie threw the ball to Ben and he ....

6. His shoes were worn out, so he ....

145.2 Complete the sentences. Use a verb + **away** or **back**.

1. I was away all day yesterday. I _got back_ very late.
2. I haven't seen our neighbours for a while. I think they must ....
3. 'I'm going out now.' 'OK. What time will you .... ?'
4. A man was trying to break into a car. When he saw me, he ....
5. I smiled at him, but he didn't ....
6. If you cheat in the exam, you might .... with it. But you might get caught.
7. Be careful! That's an electric fence. .... from it.

145.3 Complete the sentences using a verb in the correct form.

1. The woman got into her car, started the engine and _drove_ away.
2. Here's the money you need. .... me back when you can.
3. Don't .... that box away. It could be useful.
4. Jane doesn't do anything at work. I don't know how she .... away with it.
5. I'm going out now. I'll .... back in about an hour.
6. You should think more about the future; don't .... back all the time.
7. Gary is very generous. He won some money in the lottery and .... it all away.
8. I'll .... back to you as soon as I have the information you need.

145.4 Complete the sentences. Use the verb in brackets + **away** or **back**.

1. A: Do you still have my keys?
   B: No. Don't you remember? I _gave them back_ to you yesterday. (give)
2. A: Do you want this magazine?
   B: No, I've finished with it. You can .... (throw)
3. A: How are your new jeans? Do they fit you OK?
   B: No, I'm going to .... to the shop. (take)
4. A: Here's the money you asked me to lend you.
   B: Thanks. I'll .... as soon as I can. (pay)
5. A: What happened to all the books you used to have?
   B: I didn't want them any more, so I .... (give)
6. A: Did you phone Sarah?
   B: She wasn't there. I left a message asking her to .... (call)

→ Additional exercises 37–41 (pages 323–25)

Appendix 1
Regular and irregular verbs

1.1 *Regular verbs*

If a verb is regular, the past simple and past participle end in **-ed**. For example:

infinitive	clean	finish	use	paint	stop	carry
past simple ⎫ *past participle* ⎰	cleaned	finished	used	painted	stopped	carry

For spelling rules, see Appendix 6.

For the *past simple* (I **cleaned** / they **finished** / she **carried** etc.), see Unit 5.

We use the *past participle* to make the perfect tenses and all the passive forms.
Perfect tenses (**have/has/had** cleaned):
- ○ I **have cleaned** the windows.   (*present perfect* – see Units 7–8)
- ○ They were still working. They **had**n't **finished**.   (*past perfect* – see Unit 15)

Passive (**is** clean**ed** / **was** clean**ed** etc.):
- ○ He **was carried** out of the room.   (*past simple passive*) ⎫
- ○ This gate **has** just **been painted**.   (*present perfect passive*) ⎰ see Units 42–44

1.2 *Irregular verbs*

When the past simple and past participle do *not* end in **-ed** (for example, **I saw** / **I have seen**), the verb is *irregular*.

With some irregular verbs, all three forms (*infinitive*, *past simple* and *past participle*) are the same. For example, **hit**:
- ○ Don't **hit** me.   (*infinitive*)
- ○ Somebody **hit** me as I came into the room.   (*past simple*)
- ○ I've never **hit** anybody in my life.   (*past participle – present perfect*)
- ○ George was **hit** on the head by a stone.   (*past participle – passive*)

With other irregular verbs, the past simple is the same as the past participle (but different from the infinitive). For example, **tell → told**:
- ○ Can you **tell** me what to do?   (*infinitive*)
- ○ She **told** me to come back the next day.   (*past simple*)
- ○ Have you **told** anybody about your new job?   (*past participle – present perfect*)
- ○ I was **told** to come back the next day.   (*past participle – passive*)

With other irregular verbs, all three forms are different. For example, **wake → woke/woken**:
- ○ I'll **wake** you up.   (*infinitive*)
- ○ I **woke** up in the middle of the night.   (*past simple*)
- ○ The baby has **woken** up.   (*past participle – present perfect*)
- ○ I was **woken** up by a loud noise.   (*past participle – passive*)

1.3 The following verbs can be regular or irregular:

burn	→ burn**ed** *or* burn**t**		**smell**	→ smell**ed** *or* smel**t**	
dream	→ dream**ed** *or* dream**t** [dremt]*		**spell**	→ spell**ed** *or* spel**t**	
lean	→ lean**ed** *or* lean**t** [lent]*		**spill**	→ spill**ed** *or* spil**t**	
learn	→ learn**ed** *or* learn**t**		**spoil**	→ spoil**ed** *or* spoil**t**	* *pronunciation*

So you can say:
- ○ I **leant** out of the window.   *or*   I **leaned** out of the window.
- ○ The dinner has been **spoiled**.   *or*   The dinner has been **spoilt**.

In British English the irregular form (**burnt/learnt** etc.) is more usual. For American English, see Appendix 7.

1.4 List of irregular verbs

infinitive	past simple	past participle
be	was/were	been
beat	beat	beaten
become	became	become
begin	began	begun
bend	bent	bent
bet	bet	bet
bite	bit	bitten
blow	blew	blown
break	broke	broken
bring	brought	brought
broadcast	broadcast	broadcast
build	built	built
burst	burst	burst
buy	bought	bought
catch	caught	caught
choose	chose	chosen
come	came	come
cost	cost	cost
creep	crept	crept
cut	cut	cut
deal	dealt	dealt
dig	dug	dug
do	did	done
draw	drew	drawn
drink	drank	drunk
drive	drove	driven
eat	ate	eaten
fall	fell	fallen
feed	fed	fed
feel	felt	felt
fight	fought	fought
find	found	found
flee	fled	fled
fly	flew	flown
forbid	forbade	forbidden
forget	forgot	forgotten
forgive	forgave	forgiven
freeze	froze	frozen
get	got	got/gotten
give	gave	given
go	went	gone
grow	grew	grown
hang	hung	hung
have	had	had
hear	heard	heard
hide	hid	hidden
hit	hit	hit
hold	held	held
hurt	hurt	hurt
keep	kept	kept
kneel	knelt	knelt
know	knew	known
lay	laid	laid
lead	led	led
leave	left	left
lend	lent	lent
let	let	let
lie	lay	lain

infinitive	past simple	past participle
light	lit	lit
lose	lost	lost
make	made	made
mean	meant	meant
meet	met	met
pay	paid	paid
put	put	put
read	read [red]*	read [red]*
ride	rode	ridden
ring	rang	rung
rise	rose	risen
run	ran	run
say	said	said
see	saw	seen
seek	sought	sought
sell	sold	sold
send	sent	sent
set	set	set
sew	sewed	sewn/sewed
shake	shook	shaken
shine	shone	shone
shoot	shot	shot
show	showed	shown/showed
shrink	shrank	shrunk
shut	shut	shut
sing	sang	sung
sink	sank	sunk
sit	sat	sat
sleep	slept	slept
slide	slid	slid
speak	spoke	spoken
spend	spent	spent
spit	spat	spat
split	split	split
spread	spread	spread
spring	sprang	sprung
stand	stood	stood
steal	stole	stolen
stick	stuck	stuck
sting	stung	stung
stink	stank	stunk
strike	struck	struck
swear	swore	sworn
sweep	swept	swept
swim	swam	swum
swing	swung	swung
take	took	taken
teach	taught	taught
tear	tore	torn
tell	told	told
think	thought	thought
throw	threw	thrown
understand	understood	understood
wake	woke	woken
wear	wore	worn
weep	wept	wept
win	won	won
write	wrote	written

* pronunciation

Appendix 2
Present and past tenses

	simple	*continuous*
present	**I do** *present simple* (→ Units 2–4) ○ Ann often **plays** tennis. ○ I **work** in a bank, but I **don't enjoy** it much. ○ **Do** you **like** parties? ○ It **doesn't rain** so much in summer.	**I am doing** *present continuous* (→ Units 1, 3–4) ○ 'Where's Ann?' 'She**'s playing** tennis.' ○ Please don't disturb me now. I**'m working**. ○ Hello. **Are** you **enjoying** the party? ○ It **isn't raining** at the moment.
present perfect	**I have done** *present perfect simple* (→ Units 7–8, 10–14) ○ Ann **has played** tennis many times. ○ I**'ve lost** my key. **Have** you **seen** it anywhere? ○ How long **have** you and Sam **known** each other? ○ A: Is it still raining? B: No, it **has stopped**. ○ The house is dirty. I **haven't cleaned** it for weeks.	**I have been doing** *present perfect continuous* (→ Units 9–11) ○ Ann is tired. She **has been playing** tennis. ○ You're out of breath. **Have** you **been running**? ○ How long **have** you **been learning** English? ○ It's still raining. It **has been raining** all day. ○ I **haven't been feeling** well recently. Perhaps I should go to the doctor.
past	**I did** *past simple* (→ Units 5–6, 13–14) ○ Ann **played** tennis yesterday afternoon. ○ I **lost** my key a few days ago. ○ There was a film on TV last night, but we **didn't watch** it. ○ What **did** you **do** when you finished work yesterday?	**I was doing** *past continuous* (→ Unit 6) ○ I saw Ann at the sports centre yesterday. She **was playing** tennis. ○ I dropped my key when I **was trying** to open the door. ○ The television was on, but we **weren't watching** it. ○ What **were** you **doing** at this time yesterday?
past perfect	**I had done** *past perfect* (→ Unit 15) ○ It wasn't her first game of tennis. She **had played** many times before. ○ They couldn't get into the house because they **had lost** the key. ○ The house was dirty because I **hadn't cleaned** it for weeks.	**I had been doing** *past perfect continuous* (→ Unit 16) ○ Ann was tired yesterday evening because she **had been playing** tennis in the afternoon. ○ James decided to go to the doctor because he **hadn't been feeling** well.

For the passive, see Units 42–44.

Appendix 3
The future

3.1 List of future forms:

☐ I**'m leaving** tomorrow.	*present continuous*	(→ Unit 19A)
☐ My train **leaves** at 9.30.	*present simple*	(→ Unit 19B)
☐ I**'m going to leave** tomorrow.	**(be) going to**	(→ Units 20, 23)
☐ I**'ll leave** tomorrow.	**will**	(→ Units 21–23)
☐ I**'ll be leaving** tomorrow.	*future continuous*	(→ Unit 24)
☐ I**'ll have left** by this time tomorrow.	*future perfect*	(→ Unit 24)
☐ I hope to see you before I **leave** tomorrow.	*present simple*	(→ Unit 25)

3.2 Future actions

We use the present continuous (**I'm doing**) for arrangements:
- ☐ I**'m leaving** tomorrow. I've got my plane ticket. (already planned and arranged)
- ☐ 'When **are** they **getting** married?' 'On 24 July.'

We use the present simple (I **leave** / it **leaves** etc.) for timetables, programmes etc. :
- ☐ My train **leaves** at 11.30. (according to the timetable)
- ☐ What time **does** the film **begin**?

We use (**be**) **going to** ... to say what somebody has already decided to do:
- ☐ I've decided not to stay here any longer. I**'m going to leave** tomorrow. (*or* I**'m leaving** tomorrow.)
- ☐ 'Your shoes are dirty.' 'Yes, I know. I**'m going to clean** them.'

We use **will** (**'ll**) when we decide or agree to do something at the time of speaking:
- ☐ A: I don't want you to stay here any longer.
  B: OK. I**'ll leave** tomorrow. (B decides this at the time of speaking)
- ☐ That bag looks heavy. I**'ll help** you with it.
- ☐ I **won't tell** anybody what happened. I promise. (**won't** = **will not**)

3.3 Future happenings and situations

Most often we use **will** to talk about future happenings ('something **will happen**') or situations ('something **will be**'):
- ☐ I don't think John is happy at work. I think he**'ll leave** soon.
- ☐ This time next year I**'ll be** in Japan. Where **will** you **be**?

We use (**be**) **going to** when the situation *now* shows what **is going to happen** *in the future:*
- ☐ Look at those black clouds. It**'s going to rain**. (you can see the clouds *now*)

3.4 Future continuous and future perfect

Will be (do)**ing** = will be in the middle of (doing something):
- ☐ This time next week I'll be on holiday. I**'ll be lying** on a beach or **swimming** in the sea.

We also use **will be -ing** for future actions (see Unit 24C):
- ☐ What time **will** you **be leaving** tomorrow?

We use **will have** (**done**) to say that something will already be complete before a time in the future:
- ☐ I won't be here this time tomorrow. I**'ll have** already **left**.

3.5
We use the *present* (*not* will) after **when/if/while/before** etc. (see Unit 25):
- ☐ I hope to see you **before** I **leave** tomorrow. (*not* before I will leave)
- ☐ **When** you **are** in London again, come and see us. (*not* When you will be)
- ☐ **If** we **don't hurry**, we'll be late.

Appendix 4
Modal verbs (**can/could/will/would** etc.)

This appendix is a summary of modal verbs. For more information, see Units 21–41.

4.1 Compare **can/could** etc. for actions:

can	○ I **can go** out tonight. (= there is nothing to stop me)
	○ I **can't go** out tonight.
could	○ I **could go** out tonight, but I'm not very keen.
	○ I **couldn't go** out last night. (= I wasn't able)
can *or* **may**	○ **Can** / **May** } I **go** out tonight? (= do you allow me?)
will/won't	○ I think I**'ll go** out tonight.
	○ I promise I **won't go** out.
would	○ I **would go** out tonight, but I have too much to do.
	○ I promised I **wouldn't go** out.
shall	○ **Shall I go** out tonight? (do you think it is a good idea?)
should *or* **ought to**	○ I { **should** / **ought to** } **go** out tonight. (= it would be a good thing to do)
must	○ I **must go** out tonight. (= it is necessary)
	○ I **mustn't go** out tonight. (= it is necessary that I do *not* go out)
needn't	○ I **needn't go** out tonight. (= it is not necessary)

Compare **could have** … / **would have** … etc. :

could	○ I **could have gone** out last night, but I decided to stay at home.
would	○ I **would have gone** out last night, but I had too much to do.
should *or* **ought to**	○ I { **should** / **ought to** } **have gone** out last night. I'm sorry I didn't.
needn't	○ I **needn't have gone** out last night. (= I went out, but it was not necessary)

4.2 We use **will/would/may** etc. to say whether something is possible, impossible, probable, certain etc. Compare:

will	○ 'What time **will** she **be** here?' 'She**'ll be** here soon.'
would	○ She **would be** here now, but she's been delayed.
should *or* **ought to**	○ She { **should** / **ought to** } **be** here soon. (= I expect she will be here soon)
may *or* **might** *or* **could**	○ She { **may** / **might** / **could** } **be** here now. I'm not sure. (= it's possible that she is here)
must	○ She **must be** here. I saw her come in.
can't	○ She **can't** possibly **be** here. I know for certain that she's away on holiday.

Compare **would have** … / **should have** … etc. :

will	○ She **will have arrived** by now. (= before now)
would	○ She **would have arrived** earlier, but she was delayed.
should *or* **ought to**	○ I wonder where she is. She { **should** / **ought to** } **have arrived** by now.
may *or* **might** *or* **could**	○ She { **may** / **might** / **could** } **have arrived**. I'm not sure. (= it's possible that she has arrived)
must	○ She **must have arrived** by now. (= I'm sure – there is no other possibility)
can't	○ She **can't** possibly **have arrived** yet. It's much too early. (= it's impossible)

Appendix 5
Short forms (**I'm** / **you've** / **didn't** etc.)

5.1 In spoken English we usually say **I'm** / **you've** / **didn't** etc. (*short forms* or *contractions*) rather than **I am** / **you have** / **did not** etc. We also use these short forms in informal writing (for example, a letter or message to a friend).

When we write short forms, we use an *apostrophe* (') for the missing letter(s):

I'm = I <u>a</u>m   you've = you <u>have</u>   didn't = did n<u>o</u>t

5.2 List of short forms:

'm = am 's = is *or* has 're = are 've = have 'll = will 'd = would *or* had	I'm I've I'll I'd	 he's he'll he'd	 she's she'll she'd	 it's	 you're you've you'll you'd	 we're we've we'll we'd	 they're they've they'll they'd

's can be **is** or **has**:
- ○ She**'s** ill. (= She **is** ill.)
- ○ She**'s** gone away. (= She **has** gone)

but **let's** = let **us**:
- ○ Let**'s** go now. (= Let **us** go)

'd can be **would** or **had**:
- ○ I**'d** see a doctor if I were you. (= I **would** see)
- ○ I**'d** never seen her before. (= I **had** never seen)

We use some of these short forms (especially **'s**) after question words (**who/what** etc.) and after **that/there/here**:

who**'s**   what**'s**   where**'s**   how**'s**   that**'s**   there**'s**   here**'s**   who**'ll**   there**'ll**   who**'d**
- ○ **Who's** that woman over there? (= who **is**)
- ○ **What's** happened? (= what **has**)
- ○ Do you think **there'll** be many people at the party? (= there **will**)

We also use short forms (especially **'s**) after a noun:
- ○ **Katherine's** going out tonight. (= Katherine **is**)
- ○ **My best friend's** just got married. (= My best friend **has**)

You cannot use **'m** / **'s** / **'re** / **'ve** / **'ll** / **'d** at the end of a sentence (because the verb is stressed in this position):
- ○ 'Are you tired?' 'Yes, I **am**.' (*not* Yes, I'm.)
- ○ Do you know where she **is**? (*not* Do you know where she's?)

5.3 Negative short forms

isn't	(= is not)	don't	(= do not)	haven't	(= have not)
aren't	(= are not)	doesn't	(= does not)	hasn't	(= has not)
wasn't	(= was not)	didn't	(= did not)	hadn't	(= had not)
weren't	(= were not)				
can't	(= cannot)	couldn't	(= could not)	mustn't	(= must not)
won't	(= will not)	wouldn't	(= would not)	needn't	(= need not)
shan't	(= shall not)	shouldn't	(= should not)	daren't	(= dare not)

Negative short forms for **is** and **are** can be:

he **isn't** / she **isn't** / it **isn't**   *or* he**'s not** / she**'s not** / it**'s not**
you **aren't** / we **aren't** / they **aren't** *or* you**'re not** / we**'re not** / they**'re not**

Appendix 6
Spelling

6.1 Nouns, verbs and adjectives can have the following endings:

noun + -**s**/-**es** (plural)	boo**ks**	idea**s**	match**es**
verb + -**s**/-**es** (after **he**/**she**/**it**)	wor**ks**	enjoy**s**	wash**es**
verb + -**ing**	work**ing**	enjoy**ing**	wash**ing**
verb + -**ed**	work**ed**	enjoy**ed**	wash**ed**
adjective + -**er** (comparative)	cheap**er**	quick**er**	bright**er**
adjective + -**est** (superlative)	cheap**est**	quick**est**	bright**est**
adjective + -**ly** (adverb)	cheap**ly**	quick**ly**	bright**ly**

When we use these endings, there are sometimes changes in spelling. These changes are listed below.

6.2 Nouns and verbs + -**s**/-**es**

The ending is -**es** when the word ends in -**s**/-**ss**/-**sh**/-**ch**/-**x**:

     bu**s**/bus**es**   mi**ss**/miss**es**   wa**sh**/wash**es**
     mat**ch**/match**es**   sear**ch**/search**es**   bo**x**/box**es**

Note also:

     potato/potato**es**   tomato/tomato**es**
     do/do**es**   go/go**es**

6.3 Words ending in -**y** (bab**y**, carr**y**, eas**y** etc.)

> If a word ends in a *consonant** + **y** (-**by**/-**ry**/-**sy**/-**vy** etc.)
>
> **y** changes to **ie** before the ending -**s**:
>   bab**y**/bab**ies**   stor**y**/stor**ies**   countr**y**/countr**ies**   secretar**y**/secretar**ies**
>   hurr**y**/hurr**ies**   stud**y**/stud**ies**   appl**y**/appl**ies**   tr**y**/tr**ies**
>
> **y** changes to **i** before the ending -**ed**:
>   hurr**y**/hurr**ied**   stud**y**/stud**ied**   appl**y**/appl**ied**   tr**y**/tr**ied**
>
> **y** changes to **i** before the endings -**er** and -**est**:
>   eas**y**/eas**ier**/eas**iest**   heav**y**/heav**ier**/heav**iest**   luck**y**/luck**ier**/luck**iest**
>
> **y** changes to **i** before the ending -**ly**:
>   eas**y**/eas**ily**   heav**y**/heav**ily**   temporar**y**/temporar**ily**

y does *not* change before -**ing**:

     hurry**ing**   study**ing**   apply**ing**   try**ing**

y does *not* change if the word ends in a *vowel** + **y** (-**ay**/-**ey**/-**oy**/-**uy**):

     pl**ay**/pl**ays**/pl**ayed**   monk**ey**/monk**eys**   enj**oy**/enj**oys**/enj**oyed**   b**uy**/b**uys**

An exception is: d**ay**/d**aily**

Note also: p**ay**/p**aid**   l**ay**/l**aid**   s**ay**/s**aid**

6.4 Verbs ending in -**ie** (d**ie**, l**ie**, t**ie**)

If a verb ends in -**ie**, **ie** changes to **y** before the ending -**ing**:

     d**ie**/d**ying**   l**ie**/l**ying**   t**ie**/t**ying**

---

* a e i o u are *vowel* letters.
The other letters (b c d f g etc.) are *consonant* letters.

6.5 Words ending in -**e** (hop**e**, dan**ce**, wid**e** etc.)

Verbs

If a verb ends in -**e**, we leave out **e** before the ending -**ing**:

hop**e**/hop**ing**   smil**e**/smil**ing**   danc**e**/danc**ing**   confus**e**/confus**ing**

Exceptions are **be/being**

and verbs ending in -**ee**:   **see/seeing**   agr**ee**/agr**eeing**

If a verb ends in -**e**, we add -**d** for the past (of regular verbs):

hop**e**/hop**ed**   smil**e**/smil**ed**   danc**e**/danc**ed**   confus**e**/confus**ed**

Adjectives and adverbs

If an adjective ends in -**e**, we add -**r** and -**st** for the comparative and superlative:

wid**e**/wid**er**/wid**est**   lat**e**/lat**er**/lat**est**   larg**e**/larg**er**/larg**est**

If an adjective ends in -**e**, we *keep* **e** before -**ly** in the adverb:

polit**e**/polit**ely**   extrem**e**/extrem**ely**   absolut**e**/absolut**ely**

If an adjective ends in -**le** (sim**ple**, terri**ble** etc.), the adverb ending is -**ply**, -**bly** etc. :

sim**ple**/sim**ply**   terri**ble**/terri**bly**   reasona**ble**/reasona**bly**

6.6 Doubling consonants (**stop/stopping/stopped, wet/wetter/wettest** etc.)

Sometimes a word ends in *vowel + consonant*. For example:

st**op**   pl**an**   r**ub**   b**ig**   w**et**   th**in**   pref**er**   regr**et**

Before the endings -**ing**/-**ed**/-**er**/-**est,** we double the consonant at the end. So **p → pp, n → nn** etc.
For example:

sto**p**	p → **pp**	sto**pp**ing	sto**pp**ed
pla**n**	n → **nn**	pla**nn**ing	pla**nn**ed
ru**b**	b → **bb**	ru**bb**ing	ru**bb**ed
bi**g**	g → **gg**	bi**gg**er	bi**gg**est
we**t**	t → **tt**	we**tt**er	we**tt**est
thi**n**	n → **nn**	thi**nn**er	thi**nn**est

If the word has more than one syllable (**prefer**, **begin** etc.), we double the consonant at the end
only if the final syllable is stressed:

preFER / preferring / preferred   perMIT / permitting / permitted
reGRET / regretting / regretted   beGIN / beginning

If the final syllable is not stressed, we do *not* double the final consonant:

VISit / visiting / visited   deVELop / developing / developed
HAPpen / happening / happened   reMEMber / remembering / remembered

In British English, verbs ending in -**l** have -**ll**- before -**ing** and -**ed** whether the final syllable is stressed
or not:

travel / travelling / travelled   cancel / cancelling / cancelled

For American spelling, see Appendix 7.

Note that

we do *not* double the final consonant if the word ends in *two* consonants (-**rt**, -**lp**, -**ng** etc.):

sta**rt** / starting / started   he**lp** / helping / helped   lo**ng** / longer / longest

we do *not* double the final consonant if there are *two* vowel letters before it (-**oil**, -**eed** etc.):

b**oil** / boiling / boiled   n**eed** / needing / needed   expl**ain** / explaining / explained
ch**eap** / cheaper / cheapest   l**oud** / louder / loudest   qu**iet** / quieter / quietest

we do *not* double **y** or **w** at the end of words. (At the end of words **y** and **w** are not consonants.)

sta**y** / staying / stayed   gro**w** / growing   ne**w** / newer / newest

Appendix 7
American English

There are a few grammatical differences between British English and American English:

Unit	BRITISH	AMERICAN
7A–B, 7D and 13A	The *present perfect* or *past simple* can be used for new or recent happenings. The *present perfect* is more common: ○ I**'ve lost** my key. **Have** you **seen** it? (*or* I **lost** my key. **Did** you **see** it?) ○ Sally isn't here. She**'s gone** out. The *present perfect* or *past simple* can be used with **just, already** and **yet**. The *present perfect* is more common: ○ I'm not hungry. I**'ve just had** lunch. (*or* I **just had** lunch.) ○ A: What time is Mark leaving? B: He**'s already left**. ○ **Have** you **finished** your work **yet**?	The *present perfect* or *past simple* can be used for new or recent happenings. The *past simple* is more common: ○ I **lost** my key. **Did** you **see** it? (*or* I**'ve** lost my key. **Have** you **seen** it?) ○ Sally isn't here. She **went** out. The *present perfect* or *past simple* can be used with **just, already** and **yet**. The *past simple* is more common: ○ I'm not hungry. I **just had** lunch. (*or* I**'ve just had** lunch.) ○ A: What time is Mark leaving? B: He **already left**. ○ **Did** you **finish** your work **yet**?
17C	British speakers usually say: **have** a bath **have** a shower **have** a break **have** a holiday	American speakers say: **take** a bath **take** a shower **take** a break **take** a vacation
21D and 22D	**Will** or **shall** can be used with **I/we**: ○ I **will/shall** be late this evening. **Shall I** … ? and **shall we** … ? are used to ask for advice etc. : ○ Which way **shall we** go?	**Shall** is unusual: ○ I **will** be late this evening. **Should I** … ? and **should we** … ? are more usual to ask for advice etc. : ○ Which way **should we** go?
28	British speakers use **can't** to say they believe something is not probable: ○ Sarah hasn't contacted me. She **can't** have got my message.	American speakers use **must not** in this situation: ○ Sarah hasn't contacted me. She **must not** have gotten my message.
32	You can use **needn't** or **don't need to**: ○ We **needn't** hurry. *or* We **don't need to** hurry.	**Needn't** is unusual. The usual form is **don't need to**: ○ We **don't need to** hurry.
34A–B	After **insist**, **demand** etc. you can use **should**: ○ I insisted that he **should apologise**. ○ Many people are demanding that something **should be** done about the problem.	The *subjunctive* is normally used. **Should** is unusual after **insist**, **demand** etc. : ○ I insisted that he **apologize**.* ○ Many people are demanding that something **be done** about the problem.
51B	British speakers generally use **Have you? / Isn't she?** etc. : ○ A: Lisa isn't very well today. B: **Isn't she?** What's wrong with her?	American speakers generally use **You have? / She isn't?** etc. : ○ A: Lisa isn't very well today. B: **She isn't?** What's wrong with her?
70B	**Accommodation** is usually uncountable: ○ There isn't enough **accommodation**.	**Accommodation** can be countable: ○ There aren't enough **accommodations**.

* Many verbs ending in -**ise** in British English (apolog**ise**/organ**ise**/special**ise** etc.) are spelt with -**ize** (apolog**ize**/organ**ize**/special**ize** etc.) in American English.

Unit	BRITISH	AMERICAN
74B	to/in **hospital** (without **the**): ☐ Three people were injured and taken to **hospital**.	to/in **the hospital**: ☐ Three people were injured and taken to **the hospital**.
79C	Nouns like **government/team/family** etc. can have a singular or plural verb: ☐ The team **is/are** playing well.	These nouns normally take a singular verb in American English: ☐ The team **is** playing well.
121B	**at the weekend / at weekends**: ☐ Will you be here **at the weekend**?	**on the weekend / on weekends**: ☐ Will you be here **on the weekend**?
124D	**at** the front / **at** the back (of a group etc.): ☐ Let's sit **at** the front (of the cinema).	**in** the front / **in** the back (of a group etc.): ☐ Let's sit **in** the front (of the movie theater).
131C	**different from** or **different to**: ☐ It was **different from/to** what I'd expected.	**different from** or **different than**: ☐ It was **different from/than** what I'd expected.
137A	British speakers use both **round** and **around**: ☐ He turned **round**. *or* He turned **around**.	American speakers use **around** (not usually 'round'): ☐ He turned **around**.
137C	British speakers use both **fill in** and **fill out**: ☐ Can you **fill in** this form? *or* Can you **fill out** this form?	American speakers use **fill out**: ☐ Can you **fill out** this form?
141B	**get on** = *progress*: ☐ How are you **getting on** in your new job? **get on** (with somebody): ☐ Richard **gets on** well with his new neighbours.	American speakers do not use **get on** in this way. American speakers use **get along** (with somebody): ☐ Richard **gets along** well with his new neighbors.
144D	**do up** a house etc. : ☐ That old house looks great now that it has been **done up**.	**fix up** a house etc. : ☐ That old house looks great now that it has been **fixed up**.

Appendix	BRITISH	AMERICAN
1.3	The verbs in this section (**burn, spell** etc.) can be regular or irregular (**burned** *or* **burnt**, **spelled** *or* **spelt** etc.). The past participle of **get** is **got**: ☐ Your English has **got** much better. (= has become much better) **Have got** is also an alternative to **have**: ☐ I**'ve got** two brothers. (= I have two brothers.)	The verbs in this section are normally regular (**burned, spelled** etc.). The past participle of **get** is **gotten**: ☐ Your English has **gotten** much better. **Have got** = have (as in British English): ☐ I**'ve got** two brothers.
6.6	British spelling: travel → travelling / travelled cancel → cancelling / cancelled	American spelling: travel → traveling / traveled cancel → canceling / canceled

Additional exercises

These exercises are divided into the following sections:

Present and past

Units 1–6, Appendix 2

1 Put the verb into the correct form: present simple (**I do**), present continuous (**I am doing**), past simple (**I did**) or past continuous (**I was doing**).

1 We can go out now.   _It isn't raining_ (it / not / rain) any more.
2 Katherine _was waiting_ (wait) for me when _I arrived_ (I / arrive).
3 .... (I / get) hungry. Let's go and have something to eat.
4 What .... (you / do) in your spare time? Do you have any hobbies?
5 The weather was horrible when .... (we / arrive). It was cold and .... (it / rain) hard.
6 Louise usually .... (phone) me on Fridays, but .... (she / not / phone) last Friday.
7 A: When I last saw you, ... (you / think) of moving to a new flat.
   B: That's right, but in the end .... (I / decide) to stay where I was.
8 Why .... (you / look) at me like that? What's the matter?
9 It's usually dry here at this time of the year. .... (it / not / rain) much.
10 Sorry I'm late. My phone .... (ring) three times while .... (I / get) ready to go out.
11 Lisa was busy when .... (we / go) to see her yesterday. She had an exam today and .... (she / prepare) for it. .... (we / not / want) to disturb her, so .... (we / not / stay) very long.
12 When I first .... (tell) Tom what happened, ... (he / not / believe) me. .... (he / think) that .... (I / joke).

Present and past

2 Which is correct?

1 Everything is going well. We ~~didn't have~~ / haven't had any problems so far.
  (haven't had *is correct*)
2 Lisa didn't go / hasn't gone to work yesterday. She wasn't feeling well.
3 Look! That man over there wears / is wearing the same sweater as you.
4 I went / have been to New Zealand last year.
5 I didn't hear / haven't heard from Jess recently. I hope she's OK.
6 I wonder why James is / is being so nice to me today. He isn't usually like that.
7 Jane had a book open in front of her, but she didn't read / wasn't reading it.
8 I wasn't very busy. I didn't have / wasn't having much to do.
9 It begins / It's beginning to get dark. Shall I turn on the light?
10 After finishing school, Tim got / has got a job in a factory.
11 When Sue heard the news, she wasn't / hasn't been very pleased.
12 This is a nice restaurant, isn't it? Is this the first time you are / you've been here?
13 I need a new job. I'm doing / I've been doing the same job for too long.
14 'Anna has gone out.' 'Oh, has she? What time did she go / has she gone?'
15 'You look tired.' 'Yes, I've played / I've been playing basketball.'
16 Where are you coming / do you come from? Are you American?
17 I'd like to see Tina again. It's a long time since I saw her / that I didn't see her.
18 Robert and Maria have been married since 20 years / for 20 years.

3 Complete each question using a suitable verb.

1 A: I'm looking for Paul. _Have you seen_ him?
  B: Yes, he was here a moment ago.

2 A: Why _did you go_ to bed so early last night?
  B: I was feeling very tired.

3 A: Where .... ?
  B: Just to the shop at the end of the street. I'll be back in a few minutes.

4 A: .... TV every evening?
  B: No, only if there's something special on.

5 A: Your house is very beautiful. How long .... here?
  B: Nearly ten years.

6 A: How was your holiday? .... a nice time?
  B: Yes, thanks. It was great.

7 A: .... Sarah recently?
  B: Yes, we had lunch together a few days ago.

8 A: Can you describe the woman you saw? What .... ?
  B: A red sweater and black jeans.

9 A: I'm sorry to keep you waiting. .... long?
  B: No, only about ten minutes.

10 A: How long .... you to get to work in the morning?
  B: Usually about 45 minutes. It depends on the traffic.

11 A: .... a horse before?
  B: No, this is the first time. I'm a little nervous.

12 A: .... to the United States?
  B: No, never, but I went to Canada a few years ago.

Additional exercises

4   **Use your own ideas to complete B's sentences.**

1   A: What's the new restaurant like? Is it good?
    B: I've no idea.   _I've never been_ .... there.

2   A: How well do you know Ben?
    B: Very well.   We .... since we were children.

3   A: Did you enjoy your holiday?
    B: Yes, it was really good. It's the best holiday ....

4   A: Is David still here?
    B: No, I'm afraid he isn't. .... about ten minutes ago.

5   A: I like your suit. I haven't seen it before.
    B: It's new. It's the first time ....

6   A: How did you cut your knee?
    B: I slipped and fell when .... tennis.

7   A: Do you ever go swimming?
    B: Not these days. I haven't .... a long time.

8   A: How often do you go to the cinema?
    B: Very rarely. It's nearly a year .... to the cinema.

9   A: I've bought some new shoes. Do you like them?
    B: Yes, they're very nice. Where .... them?

Present and past   **Units 1–17, 110, Appendix 2**

5   **Put the verb into the correct form: past simple (I did), past continuous (I was doing), past perfect (I had done) or past perfect continuous (I had been doing).**

Yesterday afternoon Sarah ...._went_...... (go) to the station to meet Paul. When she
.... (get) there, Paul .... (already / wait)
for her. His train .... (arrive) early.

When I got home, Ben .... (lie) on the sofa. The TV was on, but
he .... (not / watch) it. He .... (fall) asleep
and .... (snore) loudly. I .... (turn) the TV
off and just then he .... (wake) up.

Last night I .... (just / go) to bed and .... (read)
a book when suddenly I .... (hear) a noise. I ....
(get) up to see what it was, but I .... (not / see) anything, so I
.... (go) back to bed.

Lisa had to go to New York last week, but she almost .... (miss) the
plane. She .... (stand) in the queue at the check-in desk when she
suddenly .... (realise) that she .... (leave) her
passport at home. Fortunately she lives near the airport, so she .... (have)
time to take a taxi home to get it. She .... (get) back to the airport
just in time for her flight.

I .... (meet) Peter and Lucy yesterday as I ....
(walk) through the park. They .... (be) to the sports centre where they
.... (play) tennis. They .... (go) to a café and
.... (invite) me to join them, but I .... (arrange)
to meet another friend and .... (not / have) time.

6 Make sentences from the words in brackets. Put the verb into the correct form: present perfect
(**I have done**), present perfect continuous (**I have been doing**), past perfect (**I had done**) or past
perfect continuous (**I had been doing**).

1 Amanda is sitting on the ground. She's out of breath.
(she / run) _She has been running._

2 Where's my bag? I left it under this chair.
(somebody / take / it) ....

3 We were all surprised when Jess and Nick got married last year.
(they / only / know / each other / a few weeks)
....

4 It's still raining. I wish it would stop.
(it / rain / all day) ....

5 Suddenly I woke up. I was confused and didn't know where I was.
(I / dream) ....

6 I wasn't hungry at lunchtime, so I didn't have anything to eat.
   (I / have / a big breakfast) ....
7 Every year Robert and Tina spend a few days at the same hotel by the sea.
   (they / go / there for years) ....
8 I've got a headache.
   (I / have / it / since I got up) ....
9 Next month Gary is going to run in a marathon.
   (he / train / very hard for it) ....

7 **Put the verb into the correct form.**

Sarah and Joe are old friends. They meet by chance at a train station.

SARAH: Hello, Joe. (1) .... (I / not / see)
you for ages. How are you?

JOE: I'm fine. How about you?
(2) .... (you / look) good.

SARAH: Thanks. You too.
So, (3) .... (you / go) somewhere or
(4) .... (you / meet) somebody?

JOE: (5) .... (I / go) to London for a business meeting.

SARAH: Oh. (6) .... (you / often / go) away on business?

JOE: Quite often, yes. And you? Where (7) .... (you / go)?

SARAH: Nowhere. (8) .... (I / meet) a friend.
Unfortunately her train (9) .... (be) delayed –
(10) .... (I / wait) here for nearly an hour.

JOE: How are your children?

SARAH: They're all fine, thanks. The youngest (11) .... (just / start)
school.

JOE: How (12) .... (she / get) on?
(13) .... (she / like) it?

SARAH: Yes, (14) .... (she / think) it's great.

JOE: (15) .... (you / work) at the moment? The last time I
(16) .... (speak) to you, (17) ....
(you / work) in a travel agency.

SARAH: That's right. Unfortunately the company (18) .... (go) out
of business a couple of months after (19) .... (I / start) work
there, so (20) .... (I / lose) my job.

JOE: And (21) .... (you / not / have) a job since then?

SARAH: Not a permanent job. (22) .... (I / have) a few temporary
jobs. By the way, (23) .... (you / see) Matt recently?

JOE: Matt? He's in Canada.

SARAH: Really? How long (24) .... (he / be) in Canada?

JOE: About a year now. (25) .... (I / see) him a few days before
(26) .... (he / go). (27) .... (he / be)
unemployed for months, so (28) .... (he / decide) to try his
luck somewhere else. (29) .... (he / really / look forward)
to going.

SARAH: So, what (30) .... (he / do) there?

JOE: I have no idea. (31) .... (I / not / hear) from him since
(32) .... (he / leave). Anyway, I have to go and catch my train.
It was really nice to see you again.

SARAH: You too. Bye. Have a good trip.

JOE: Thanks. Bye.

8 Put the verb into the most suitable form.

1 Who _____ (invent) the bicycle?

2 'Do you still have a headache?' 'No, _____ (it / go). I'm OK now.'

3 I was the last to leave the office last night. Everybody else _____ (go) home when I _____ (leave).

4 What _____ (you / do) last weekend? _____ (you / go) away?

5 I like your car. How long _____ (you / have) it?

6 It's a shame the trip was cancelled. I _____ (look) forward to it.

7 Jane is an experienced teacher and loves her job. _____ (she / teach) for 15 years.

8 _____ (I / buy) a new jacket last week, but _____ (I / not / wear) it yet.

9 A few days ago _____ (I / see) a man at a party whose face _____ (be) very familiar. At first I couldn't think where _____ (I / see) him before. Then suddenly _____ (I / remember) who _____ (it / be).

10 _____ (you / hear) of Agatha Christie? _____ (she / be) a writer who _____ (die) in 1976. _____ (she / write) more than 70 detective novels. _____ (you / read) any of them?

11 A: What _____ (this word / mean)?
    B: I've no idea. _____ (I / never / see) it before. Look it up in the dictionary.

12 A: _____ (you / get) to the theatre in time for the play last night?
    B: No, we were late. By the time we got there, _____ (it / already / start).

13 I went to Sarah's room and _____ (knock) on the door, but there _____ (be) no answer.   Either _____ (she / go) out or _____ (she / not / want) to see anyone.

14 Patrick asked me how to use the photocopier. _____ (he / never / use) it before, so _____ (he / not / know) what to do.

15 Lisa _____ (go) for a swim after work yesterday. _____ (she / need) some exercise because _____ (she / sit) in an office all day in front of a computer.

Past continuous and used to   Units 6, 18

9 Complete the sentences using the past continuous (**was/were -ing**) or **used to** … . Use the verb in brackets.

1 I haven't been to the cinema for ages now. We ___used to go___ a lot. (go)

2 Ann didn't see me wave to her. She ___was looking___ in the other direction. (look)

3 I _____ a lot, but I don't use my car very much these days. (drive)

4 I asked the taxi driver to slow down. She _____ too fast. (drive)

5 Rosemary and Jonathan met for the first time when they _____ in the same bank. (work)

6 When I was a child, I _____ a lot of bad dreams. (have)

7 I wonder what Joe is doing these days.   He _____ in Spain when I last heard from him. (live)

8 'Where were you yesterday afternoon?' 'I _____ volleyball.' (play)

9 'Do you do any sports?' 'Not these days, but I _____ volleyball.' (play)

10 George looked very nice at the party. He _____ a very smart suit. (wear)

The future

10 **What do you say to your friend in these situations? Use the words given in brackets. Use the present continuous (I am doing), going to or will (I'll).**

1 You have made all your holiday arrangements. Your destination is Jamaica.
   FRIEND: Have you decided where to go for your holiday yet?
   YOU: *I'm going to Jamaica.*   (I / go)

2 You have made an appointment with the dentist for Friday morning.
   FRIEND: Shall we meet on Friday morning?
   YOU: I can't on Friday. .... (I / go)

3 You and some friends are planning a holiday in Spain. You have decided to hire a car, but you haven't arranged this yet.
   FRIEND: How do you plan to travel round Spain? By train?
   YOU: No, ... (we / hire)

4 Your friend has two young children. She wants to go out tomorrow evening. You offer to look after the children.
   FRIEND: I want to go out tomorrow evening, but I don't have a babysitter.
   YOU: That's no problem. .... (I / look after)

5 You have already arranged to have lunch with Sue tomorrow.
   FRIEND: Are you free at lunchtime tomorrow?
   YOU: No, ... (have lunch)

6 You are in a restaurant. You and your friend are looking at the menu. Maybe your friend has decided what to have. You ask her/him.
   YOU: What ....? (you / have)
   FRIEND: I don't know. I can't make up my mind.

7 You and a friend are reading. It's getting a bit dark and your friend is having trouble reading. You decide to turn on the light.
   FRIEND: It's getting a bit dark, isn't it? It's difficult to read.
   YOU: Yes. .... (I / turn on)

8 You and a friend are reading. It's getting a bit dark and you decide to turn on the light. You stand up and walk towards the light switch.
   FRIEND: What are you doing?
   YOU: .... (I / turn on)

11 **Put the verb into the most suitable form. Use a present tense (simple or continuous), will (I'll) or shall.**

Conversation 1 *(in the morning)*

JENNY: (1) *Are you doing* (you / do) anything tomorrow evening, Helen?
HELEN: No, why?
JENNY: Well, would you like to go to the cinema? *Strangers on a Plane* is on. I want to see it, but I don't want to go alone.
HELEN: OK, (2) .... (I / come) with you. What time
          (3) .... (we / meet)?
JENNY: Well, the film (4) .... (start) at 8.45, so
          (5) .... (I / meet) you at about 8.30 outside the cinema, OK?
HELEN: Fine. (6) .... (I / see) Tina later this evening.
          (7) .... (I / ask) her if she wants to come too?
JENNY: Yes, do that. (8) .... (I / see) you tomorrow then. Bye.

Conversation 2 *(later the same day)*

HELEN: Jenny and I (9) .... (go) to the cinema tomorrow night to see
Strangers on a Plane. Why don't you come too?
TINA: I'd love to come. What time (10) .... (the film / start)?
HELEN: 8.45.
TINA: (11) .... (you / meet) outside the cinema?
HELEN: Yes, at 8.30. Is that OK for you?
TINA: Yes, (12) .... (I / be) there at 8.30.

12 **Put the verb into the most suitable form. Sometimes there is more than one possibility.**

1 *A has decided to learn a language.*
   A: I've decided to try and learn a foreign language.
   B: Have you? Which language (1) *are you going to learn* (you / learn)?
   A: Spanish.
   B: (2) .... (you / do) a course?
   A: Yes, (3) .... (it / start) next week.
   B: That's great. I'm sure (4) .... (you / enjoy) it.
   A: I hope so. But I think (5) .... (it / be) difficult.

2 *A wants to know about B's holiday plans.*
   A: I hear (1) .... (you / go) on holiday soon.
   B: That's right. (2) .... (we / go) to Finland.
   A: I hope (3) .... (you / have) a nice time.
   B: Thanks. (4) .... (I / send) you a postcard and
      (5) .... (I / get) in touch with you when
      (6) .... (I / get) back.

3 *A invites B to a party.*
   A: (1) .... (I / have) a party next Saturday. Can you come?
   B: On Saturday? I'm not sure. Some friends of mine (2) .... (come)
      to stay with me next week, but I think (3) .... (they / leave)
      by Saturday. But if (4) .... (they / be) still here,
      (5) .... (I / not / be) able to come to the party.
   A: OK. Well, tell me as soon as (6) .... (you / know).
   B: Right. (7) .... (I / call) you during the week.

4 *A and B are two secret agents arranging a meeting. They are talking on the phone.*
   A: Well, what time (1) .... (we / meet)?
   B: Come to the café by the station at 4 o'clock.
      (2) .... (I / wait) for you
      when (3) .... (you / arrive).
      (4) .... (I / sit) by the window
      and (5) .... (I / wear) a bright green sweater.
   A: OK. (6) .... (Agent 307 / come) too?
   B: No, she can't be there.
   A: Oh. (7) .... (I / bring) the documents?
   B: Yes. (8) .... (I / explain) everything when
      (9) .... (I / see) you. And don't be late.
   A: OK. (10) .... (I / try) to be on time.

Additional exercises

13 Put the verb into the correct form. Choose from the following:

present continuous (**I am doing**)	**will ('ll) / won't**
present simple (**I do**)	**will be doing**
going to (**I'm going to do**)	**shall**

1 I feel a bit hungry. I think .... (I / have) something to eat.
2 Why are you putting on your coat? .... (you / go) somewhere?
3 What time .... (I / phone) you tonight? About 7.30?
4 Look! That plane is flying towards the airport. .... (it / land).
5 We must do something soon, before .... (it / be) too late.
6 I'm sorry you've decided to leave the company. .... (I / miss) you
   when .... (you / go).
7 .... (I / give) you my phone number? If ....
   (I / give) you my number, ... (you / call) me?
8 Are you still watching that programme? What time .... (it / end)?
9 .... (I / go) to a wedding next weekend. A friend of mine
   .... (get) married.
10 I'm not ready yet. .... (I / tell) you when ....
   (I / be) ready. I promise .... (I / not / be) very long.
11 A: Where are you going?
   B: To the hairdresser's. .... (I / have) my hair cut.
12 She was very rude to me. I refuse to speak to her again until ....
   (she / apologise).
13 I wonder where .... (we / live) ten years from now?
14 What do you plan to do when .... (you / finish) your course at
   college?

---

14 Use your own ideas to complete B's sentences.

1 A: How did the accident happen?
   B: I ....*was going*.... too fast and couldn't stop in time.
2 A: Is that a new camera?
   B: No, I .... it a long time.
3 A: Is that a new computer?
   B: Yes, I .... it a few weeks ago.
4 A: I can't talk to you right now. You can see I'm very busy.
   B: OK. I .... back in about half an hour.
5 A: This is a nice restaurant. Do you come here often?
   B: No, it's the first time I .... here.
6 A: Do you do any sport?
   B: No, I .... football, but I gave it up.
7 A: I'm sorry I'm late.
   B: That's OK. I .... long.
8 A: When you went to the US last year, was it your first visit?
   B: No, I .... there twice before.
9 A: Do you have any plans for the weekend?
   B: Yes, I .... to a party on Saturday night.
10 A: Do you know what Steve's doing these days?
    B: No, I .... him for ages.
11 A: Will you still be here by the time I get back?
    B: No, I .... by then.

15 Robert is travelling in North America. He sends an email to a friend in Winnipeg (Canada). Put the verb into the most suitable form.

CANADA
Winnipeg — USA — Minneapolis
Kansas City

Delete Junk Reply Reply All Forward Print To Do

Subject:
    To:

Hi

(1) __I've just arrived__ (I / just / arrive) in Minneapolis. (2) ....
(I / travel) for more than a month now, and (3) .... (I / begin) to
think about coming home. Everything (4) .... (I / see) so far
(5) .... (be) really interesting, and (6) .... (I / meet)
some really kind people.

(7) .... (I / leave) Kansas City a week ago. (8) ....
(I / stay) there with Emily, the aunt of a friend from college. She was really helpful and
hospitable and although (9) .... (I / plan) to stay only a couple of
days, (10) .... (I / end up) staying more than a week.

(11) .... (I / enjoy) the journey from Kansas City to here.
(12) .... (I / take) the Greyhound bus and (13) .... (meet)
some really interesting people – everybody was really friendly.

So now I'm here, and (14) .... (I / stay) here for a few days before
(15) .... (I / continue) up to Canada. I'm not sure exactly when
(16) .... (I / get) to Winnipeg – it depends what happens while
(17) .... (I / be) here. But (18) .... (I / let) you
know as soon as (19) .... (I / know) myself.

(20) .... (I / stay) with a family here – they're friends of some
people I know at home. Tomorrow (21) .... (we / visit) some people
they know who (22) .... (build) a house in the mountains. It isn't
finished yet, but (23) .... (it / be) interesting to see what it's like.

Anyway, that's all for now. (24) .... (I / be) in touch again soon.

Robert

Modal verbs (can/must/would etc.)   Units 26–36, Appendix 4

16 Which alternatives are correct? Sometimes only one alternative is correct, and sometimes two of the alternatives are possible.

1 'What time will you be home tonight?' 'I'm not sure. I .... late.'
   Ⓐ may be   Ⓑ might be   **C** can be   (*both* A *and* B *are correct*)

2 I can't find the theatre tickets. They .... out of my pocket.
   A must have fallen   **B** should have fallen   **C** had to fall

3 Somebody ran in front of the car as I was driving. Fortunately I .... just in time.
   A could stop   **B** could have stopped   **C** managed to stop

4 We've got plenty of time. We .... yet.
   A mustn't leave   **B** needn't leave   **C** don't need to leave

5 I .... out but I didn't feel like it, so I stayed at home.
   A could go   **B** could have gone   **C** must have gone

6 I'm sorry I .... come to your party last week.
   A couldn't come   **B** couldn't have come   **C** wasn't able to come

7 'What do you think of my theory?' 'I'm not sure. You .... right.'
   A could be   **B** must be   **C** might be

8 I couldn't wait for you any longer. I .... , and so I went.
   A must go   **B** must have gone   **C** had to go

9 'Do you know where Sarah is?' 'No. I suppose she .... shopping.'
   A should have gone   **B** may have gone   **C** could have gone

10 At first they didn't believe me when I told them what had happened, but in the end
   I .... them that I was telling the truth.
   A was able to convince   **B** managed to convince   **C** could convince

11 I promised I'd call Gary this evening. I ....
   A mustn't forget   **B** needn't forget   **C** don't have to forget

12 Why did you leave without me? You .... for me.
   A must have waited   **B** had to wait   **C** should have waited

13 Lisa called me and suggested .... lunch together.
   A we have   **B** we should have   **C** to have

14 You look nice in that jacket, but you hardly ever wear it. .... it more often.
   A You'd better wear   **B** You should wear   **C** You ought to wear

15 Shall I buy a car? What's your advice? What .... ?
   A will you do   **B** would you do   **C** shall you do

17 **Complete the sentences using the words in brackets.**

1 Don't phone them now.
   They _might be having_ lunch. (might / have)

2 I've eaten too much. Now I feel sick.
   I .... so much. (shouldn't / eat)

3 I wonder why Tom didn't phone me.
   He .... (must / forget)

4 Why did you go home so early?
   You .... home so early. (needn't / go)

5 You've signed the contract.
   It .... now. (can't / change)

6 'What's Linda doing?' 'I'm not sure.'
   She .... TV. (may / watch)

7 Laura was standing outside the cinema.
   She .... for somebody. (must / wait)

8 He was in prison at the time that the crime was committed.
   He .... it. (couldn't / do)

9 Why weren't you here earlier?
   You .... here earlier. (ought / be)

10 Why didn't you ask me to help you?
   I .... you. (would / help)

11 I'm surprised you weren't told that the road was dangerous.
   You .... about it. (should / warn)

12 Gary was in a strange mood yesterday.
   He .... very well. (might not / feel)

18 Complete B's sentences using **can/could/might/must/should/would** + the verb in brackets. In some sentences you need to use **have: must have ... / should have ...** etc. In some sentences you need the negative (**can't/couldn't** etc.).

1 A: I'm hungry.
  B: But you've just had lunch. You __can't be__ hungry already. (be)

2 A: I haven't seen our neighbours for ages.
  B: No. They __must have gone__ away. (go)

3 A: What's the weather like? Is it raining?
  B: Not at the moment, but it _____ later. (rain)

4 A: Where's Julia?
  B: I'm not sure. She _____ out. (go)

5 A: I didn't see you at Michael's party last week.
  B: No, I had to work that night, so I _____ . (go)

6 A: I think I saw you at Michael's party last week.
  B: No, you _____ me. I didn't go to Michael's party. (see)

7 A: What time will we get to Sue's house?
  B: Well, it takes about one and a half hours, so if we leave at 3 o'clock, we _____ there by 4.30. (get)

8 A: When was the last time you saw Bill?
  B: Years ago. I _____ him if I saw him now. (recognise)

9 A: Did you hear the explosion?
  B: What explosion?
  A: There was a loud explosion about an hour ago. You _____ it. (hear)

10 A: We weren't sure which way to go. In the end we turned right.
  B: You went the wrong way. You _____ left. (turn)

---

if (conditional)

Units 25, 38–40

19 Put the verb into the correct form.

1 If __you found__ a wallet in the street, what would you do with it? (you / find)

2 I must hurry. My friend will be annoyed if __I'm not__ on time. (I / not / be)

3 I didn't realise that Gary was in hospital. If __I'd known__ he was in hospital, I would have gone to visit him. (I / know)

4 If the phone _____ , can you answer it? (ring)

5 I can't decide what to do. What would you do if _____ in my position? (you / be)

6 A: What shall we do tomorrow?
  B: Well, if _____ a nice day, we can go to the beach. (it / be)

7 A: Let's go to the beach.
  B: No, it's too cold. If _____ warmer, I wouldn't mind going. (it / be)

8 A: Did you go to the beach yesterday?
  B: No, it was too cold. If _____ warmer, we might have gone. (it / be)

9 If _____ enough money to go anywhere in the world, where would you go? (you / have)

10 I'm glad we had a map. I'm sure we would have got lost if _____ one. (we / not / have)

11 The accident was your fault. If _____ more carefully, it wouldn't have happened. (you / drive)

12 A: Why do you read newspapers?
  B: Well, if _____ newspapers, I wouldn't know what was happening in the world. (I / not / read)

Additional exercises

20 Complete the sentences.

1 Lisa is tired all the time. She shouldn't go to bed so late.
  If Lisa ___didn't go___ to bed so late, she ___wouldn't be___ tired all the time.
2 It's getting late. I don't think Sarah will come to see us now.
  I'd be surprised if Sarah _____ to see us now.
3 I'm sorry I disturbed you. I didn't know you were busy.
  If _____ you were busy, I _____ you.
4 I don't want them to be upset, so I've decided not to tell them what happened.
  _____ upset if I _____ them what happened.
5 The dog attacked you, but only because you frightened it.
  If you _____ the dog, it _____ you.
6 Unfortunately I didn't have an umbrella and so I got very wet in the rain.
  I _____ so wet if _____ an umbrella.
7 Martin failed his driving test. He was very nervous and that's why he failed.
  If he _____ so nervous, he _____ the test.

21 Use your own ideas to complete the sentences.

1 I'd go out tonight if _____ .
2 I'd have gone out last night if _____ .
3 If you hadn't reminded me, _____ .
4 If I had my camera, _____ .
5 If you give me the camera, _____ .
6 Who would you phone if _____ ?
7 We wouldn't have been late if _____ .
8 If I'd been able to get a ticket, _____ .
9 If I'd done better at the interview, _____ .
10 You wouldn't be hungry now if _____ .
11 Cities would be nicer places if _____ .
12 If there was no TV, _____ .

Passive Units 42–45

22 Put the verb into the most suitable passive form.

1 There's somebody behind us. I think ___we're being followed___ (we / follow).
2 A mystery is something that ___can't be explained___ (can't / explain).
3 We didn't play football yesterday. The game _____ (cancel).
4 The TV _____ (repair). It's working again now.
5 In the middle of the village there is a church which _____ (restore) at the moment. The work is almost finished.
6 The tower is the oldest part of the church. _____ (it / believe) to be over 600 years old.
7 If I didn't do my job properly, _____ (I / would / sack).
8 A: I left a newspaper on the desk last night and it isn't there now.
   B: _____ (it / might / throw) away.
9 I learnt to swim when I was very young. _____ (I / teach) by my mother.
10 After _____ (arrest), I was taken to the police station.
11 '_____ (you / ever / arrest)?' 'No, never.'
12 Two people _____ (report) to _____ (injure) in an explosion at a factory in Birmingham early this morning.

23 Put the verb into the correct form, active or passive.

1 This house is quite old. It __was built__ (build) over 100 years ago.
2 My grandfather was a builder. He __built__ (build) this house many years ago.
3 'Is your car still for sale?' 'No, I _____ (sell) it.'
4 A: Is the house at the end of the street still for sale?
  B: No, it _____ (sell).
5 Sometimes mistakes _____ (make). It's inevitable.
6 I wouldn't leave your car unlocked. It _____ (might / steal).
7 My bag has disappeared. It _____ (must / steal).
8 I can't find my hat. Somebody _____ (must / take) it by mistake.
9 It's a serious problem. I don't know how it _____ (can / solve).
10 We didn't leave early enough. We _____ (should / leave) earlier.
11 Nearly every time I travel by plane, my flight _____ (delay).
12 A new bridge _____ (build) across the river. Work started last year
   and the bridge _____ (expect) to open next year.

24 Read these newspaper reports and put the verbs into the most suitable form.

① **Castle Fire**

Winton Castle (1) __was damaged__ (damage)
in a fire last night. The fire, which
(2) _____ (discover) at about
9 o'clock, spread very quickly. Nobody
(3) _____ (injure), but two
people had to (4) _____
(rescue) from an upstairs room. A number of
paintings (5) _____
_____ (believe / destroy).
It (6) _____
(not / know) how the fire started.

③ **ROAD DELAYS**

Repair work started yesterday on the
Paxham–Longworth road. The road
(1) _____ (resurface)
and there will be long delays. Drivers
(2) _____ (ask) to use
an alternative route if possible. The work
(3) _____ (expect) to
last two weeks. Next Sunday the road
(4) _____ (close), and
traffic (5) _____ (divert).

② **SHOP ROBBERY**

In Paxham yesterday a shop assistant
(1) _____ (force) to hand
over £500 after (2) _____
(threaten) by a man with a knife. The man
escaped in a car which (3) _____
_____ (steal) earlier in the day.
The car (4) _____
(later / find) in a car park where it (5) _____
_____ (abandon) by the
thief. A man (6) _____
(arrest) in connection with the robbery and
(7) _____
(still / question) by the police.

④ **Accident**

A woman (1) _____ (take)
to hospital after her car collided with a
lorry near Norstock yesterday.   She
(2) _____ (allow)
home later after treatment. The road
(3) _____ (block)
for an hour after the accident, and traffic
had to (4) _____ (divert).
A police inspector said afterwards: 'The
woman was lucky. She could (5) _____
_____ (kill).'

Reported speech Units 47–48, 50

25 Complete the sentences using reported speech.

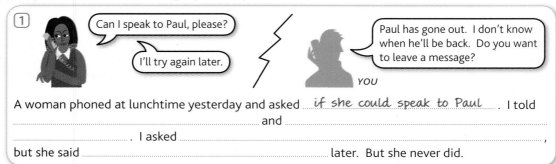

① A woman phoned at lunchtime yesterday and asked *if she could speak to Paul* . I told
.... and ....
.... I asked .... ,
but she said .... later. But she never did.

② I went to London recently, but my visit didn't begin well. I had reserved a hotel room, but
when I got to the hotel they told ....
.... When I asked .... ,
they said .... , but ....
There was nothing I could do. I just had to look for somewhere else to stay.

③ After getting off the plane, we had to queue for an hour to get through immigration. Finally
it was our turn. The immigration official asked us ....
.... , and we told ....
Then he wanted to know .... and
....
He seemed satisfied with our answers, checked our passports and wished us a pleasant stay.

④ A: What time is Sue arriving this afternoon?
B: About three. She said .... us ....
....

A: Aren't you going to meet her?
B: No, she said .... She said
....

⑤

A few days ago a man phoned from a marketing company and started asking me questions.
He wanted to know .... and asked ....
.... I don't like people phoning and asking questions like that,
so I told .... and I put the phone down.

⑥

Louise and Sarah are in a restaurant waiting for Paul.

SARAH: I wonder where Paul is. He said ....
LOUISE: Maybe he's got lost.
SARAH: I don't think so. He said ....
        And I told ....

⑦

Five minutes later

JOE: Is there anything to eat?
JANE: You just said ....
JOE: Well, I am now. I'd love a banana.
JANE: A banana? But you said ....
      You told ....

-ing and to ...   **Units 53–66**

26 **Put the verb into the correct form.**

1 How old were you when you learnt __to drive__ ? (drive)
2 I don't mind __walking__ home, but I'd rather __get__ a taxi. (walk, get)
3 I can't make a decision. I keep .... my mind. (change)
4 He had made his decision and refused .... his mind. (change)
5 Why did you change your decision? What made you .... your mind?
   (change)
6 It was a really good holiday. I really enjoyed .... by the sea again. (be)
7 Did I really tell you I was unhappy? I don't remember .... that. (say)
8 'Remember .... Tom tomorrow.' 'OK. I won't forget.' (call)

Additional exercises

9 The water here is not very good. I'd avoid _____ it if I were you. (drink)

10 I pretended _____ interested in the conversation, but really it was very boring. (be)

11 I got up and looked out of the window _____ what the weather was like. (see)

12 I have a friend who claims _____ able to speak five languages. (be)

13 I like _____ carefully about things before _____ a decision. (think, make)

14 I had a flat in the centre of town but I didn't like _____ there, so I decided _____ . (live, move)

15 Steve used _____ a footballer. He had to stop _____ because of an injury. (be, play)

16 After _____ by the police, the man admitted _____ the car, but denied _____ at 100 miles an hour. (stop, steal, drive)

17 A: How do you make this machine _____ ? (work)

   B: I'm not sure. Try _____ that button and see what happens. (press)

27 Make sentences from the words in brackets.

1 I can't find the tickets. (I / seem / lose / them)
   I seem to have lost them.

2 I don't have far to go. (it / not / worth / take / a taxi)
   It's not worth taking a taxi.

3 I'm feeling a bit tired. (I / not / fancy / go / out)

4 Tim isn't very reliable. (he / tend / forget / things)

5 I've got a lot of luggage. (you / mind / help / me?)

6 There's nobody at home. (everybody / seem / go out)

7 We don't like our apartment. (we / think / move)

8 The vase was very valuable. (I / afraid / touch / it)

9 Ben never carries a lot of money with him. (he / afraid / robbed)

10 I wouldn't go to see the film. (it / not / worth / see)

11 I'm very tired after that long walk. (I / not / used / walk / so far)

12 Sue is on holiday. I received a postcard from her yesterday. (she / seem / enjoy / herself)

13 Dan had lots of photographs he'd taken while on holiday. (he / insist / show / them to me)

14 I don't want to do the shopping. (I'd rather / somebody else / do / it)

28 Complete the second sentence so that the meaning is similar to the first.

1 I was surprised I passed the exam.
   I didn't expect _to pass the exam_ .

2 Did you manage to solve the problem?
   Did you succeed _in solving the problem_ ?

3 I don't read newspapers any more.
   I've given up ....

4 I'd prefer not to go out tonight.
   I'd rather ....

5 He finds it difficult to sleep at night.
   He has trouble ....

6 Shall I phone you this evening?
   Do you want .... ?

7 Nobody saw me come in.
   I came in without ....

8 They said I was a cheat.
   I was accused ....

9 It will be good to see them again.
   I'm looking forward ....

10 What do you think I should do?
   What do you advise me .... ?

11 It's a pity I couldn't go out with you last night.
   I'd like ....

12 I wish I'd taken your advice.
   I regret ....

---

a/an and the   **Units 69–76**

29 Put in **a/an** or **the** where necessary. Leave the space empty if the sentence is already complete.

1 I don't usually like staying at ...–... hotels, but last summer we spent two weeks at ...a... very nice hotel by ...the... sea.

2 If you go to live in .... foreign country, you should try and learn .... language.

3 Helen is .... economist. She lives in .... United States and works for .... investment company.

4 I love .... sport, especially .... tennis . I play two or three times .... week if I can, but I'm not .... very good player.

5 I won't be home for .... dinner this evening. I'm meeting some friends after .... work and we're going to .... cinema.

6 When .... unemployment is high, it's difficult for .... people to find .... work. It's .... big problem.

7 There was .... accident as I was going .... home last night. Two people were taken to .... hospital. I think .... most accidents are caused by .... people driving too fast.

8 A: What's .... name of .... hotel where you're staying?
   B: .... Ambassador. It's in .... Queen Street in .... city centre. It's near .... station.

9 I have two brothers. .... older one is training to be .... pilot with .... British Airways. .... younger one is still at .... school. When he leaves .... school, he wants to go to .... university to study .... law.

319

Pronouns and determiners

30 Which alternatives are correct? Sometimes only one alternative is correct, and sometimes two alternatives are possible.

1 I don't remember .... about the accident.
   (A) anything   **B** something   **C** nothing   (A *is correct*)

2 Chris and I have known .... for quite a long time.
   A us   **B** each other   **C** ourselves

3 'How often do the buses run?' '............................... twenty minutes.'
   A All   **B** Each   **C** Every

4 I shouted for help, but .... came.
   A nobody   **B** no-one   **C** anybody

5 Last night we went out with some friends of ....
   A us   **B** our   **C** ours

6 It didn't take us a long time to get here. .... traffic.
   A It wasn't much   **B** There wasn't much   **C** It wasn't a lot

7 Can I have .... milk in my coffee, please?
   A a little   **B** any   **C** some

8 Sometimes I find it difficult to ....
   A concentrate   **B** concentrate me   **C** concentrate myself

9 There's .... on at the cinema that I want to see, so there's no point in going.
   A something   **B** anything   **C** nothing

10 I drink .... water every day.
   A much   **B** a lot of   **C** lots of

11 .... in the centre are open on Sunday.
   A Most of shops   **B** Most of the shops   **C** The most of the shops

12 There were about twenty people in the photo. I didn't recognise .... of them.
   A any   **B** none   **C** either

13 I've been waiting .... for Sarah to phone.
   A all morning   **B** the whole morning   **C** all the morning

14 I can't afford to buy anything in this shop. .... so expensive.
   A All is   **B** Everything is   **C** All are

Adjectives and adverbs

31 There are mistakes in some of these sentences. Correct the sentences where necessary. Write 'OK' if the sentence is already correct.

1 The building was total destroyed in the fire.   *totally destroyed*

2 I didn't like the book. It was such a stupid story.   *OK*

3 The city is very polluted. It's the more polluted place I've ever been to.

4 I was disappointing that I didn't get the job. I was well-qualified and the interview went well.

5 It's warm today, but there's quite a strong wind.

6 Joe works hardly, but he doesn't get paid very much.

7 The company's offices are in a modern large building.

8 Dan is a very fast runner. I wish I could run as fast as him.

9 I missed the three last days of the course because I was ill. ....

10 You don't look happy. What's the matter? ....

11 The weather has been unusual cold for the time of the year. ....

12 The water in the pool was too dirty to swim in it. ....

13 I got impatient because we had to wait so long time. ....

14 Is this box big enough or do you need a bigger one? ....

15 This morning I got up more early than usual. ....

Conjunctions   Units 25, 38, 112–118

32 Which is correct?

1 I'll try to be on time, but don't worry if / ~~when~~ I'm late. (if *is correct*)

2 Don't throw that bag away. <u>If / When</u> you don't want it, I'll have it.

3 Please report to reception <u>if / when</u> you arrive at the hotel.

4 We've arranged to go to the beach tomorrow, but we won't go <u>if / when</u> it's raining.

5 Tanya is in her final year at school. She still doesn't know what she's going to do <u>if / when</u> she leaves.

6 What would you do <u>if / when</u> you lost your keys?

7 I hope I'll be able to come to the party, but I'll let you know <u>if / unless</u> I can't.

8 I don't want to be disturbed, so don't phone me <u>if / unless</u> it's something important.

9 Please sign the contract <u>if / unless</u> you're happy with the conditions.

10 I like travelling by ship <u>as long as / unless</u> the sea is not rough.

11 You might not remember the name of the hotel, so write it down <u>if / in case</u> you forget it.

12 It's not cold now, but take your coat with you <u>if / in case</u> it gets cold later.

13 Take your coat with you and then you can put it on <u>if / in case</u> it gets cold later.

14 They always have the TV on, <u>even if / if</u> nobody is watching it.

15 <u>Even / Although</u> I left home early, I got to work late.

16 <u>Despite / Although</u> we've known each other a long time, we're not particularly close friends.

17 'When did you leave school?' '<u>As / When</u> I was 17.'

18 I think Ann will be very pleased <u>as / when</u> she hears the news.

Prepositions (time)   Units 12, 119–122

33 Put in one of the following: **at   on   in   during   for   since   by   until**

1 Jack has gone away. He'll be back ....*in*.... a week.

2 We're having a party .... Saturday. Can you come?

3 I've got an interview next week. It's .... 9.30 .... Tuesday morning.

4 Sue isn't usually here .... weekends. She goes away.

5 The train service is very good. The trains are nearly always .... time.

6 It was a confusing situation. Many things were happening .... the same time.

7 I couldn't decide whether or not to buy the sweater. .... the end I decided not to.

8 The road is busy all the time, even .... night.

9 I met a lot of nice people .... my stay in New York.

10 I saw Helen .... Friday, but I haven't seen her .... then.

11 Robert has been doing the same job .... five years.

12 Lisa's birthday is .... the end of March. I'm not sure exactly which day it is.

13 We have some friends staying with us .... the moment. They're staying .... Friday.

14 If you're interested in applying for the job, your application must be received .... Friday.

15 I'm just going out. I won't be long – I'll be back .... ten minutes.

Prepositions (position and other uses)   **Units 123–128**

34 **Put in the missing preposition.**

1 I'd love to be able to visit every country _____ the world.

2 Jessica White is my favourite author. Have you read anything _____ her?

3 'Is there a bank near here?' 'Yes, there's one _____ the end of this road.'

4 Tim is away at the moment. He's _____ holiday.

5 We live _____ the country, a long way from the nearest town.

6 I've got a stain _____ my jacket. I'll have to have it cleaned.

7 We went _____ a party _____ Lisa's house on Saturday.

8 Boston is _____ the east coast of the United States.

9 Look at the leaves _____ that tree. They're a beautiful colour.

10 'Have you ever been _____ Tokyo?' 'No, I've never been _____ Japan.'

11 Mozart died _____ Vienna in 1791 _____ the age of 35.

12 'Are you _____ this photo?' 'Yes, that's me, _____ the left.'

13 We went _____ the theatre last night. We had seats _____ the front row.

14 'Where's the light switch?' 'It's _____ the wall _____ the door.'

15 It was late when we arrived _____ the hotel.

16 I couldn't decide what to eat. There was nothing _____ the menu that I liked.

17 We live _____ a tower block. Our apartment is _____ the fifteenth floor.

18 A: What did you think of the film?

    B: Some parts were a bit stupid, but _____ the whole I enjoyed it.

19 'When you paid the restaurant bill, did you pay cash?' 'No, I paid _____ credit card.'

20 'How did you get here? Did you come _____ the bus?' 'No, _____ car.'

21 A: I wonder what's _____ TV this evening. Do you have a newspaper?

    B: Yes, the TV programmes are _____ the back page.

22 Helen works for a telecommunications company. She works _____ the customer services department.

23 Anna spent two years working _____ Chicago before returning _____ Italy.

24 'Did you enjoy your trip _____ the beach?' 'Yes, it was great.'

25 Next summer we're going _____ a trip to Canada.

Noun/adjective + prepositions   **Units 129–131**

35 **Put in the missing preposition.**

1 The plan has been changed, but nobody seems to know the reason _____ this.

2 Don't ask me to decide. I'm not very good _____ making decisions.

3 Some people say that Sue is unfriendly, but she's always very nice _____ me.

4 What do you think is the best solution _____ the problem?

5 There has been a big increase _____ the price of oil recently.

6 He lives a rather lonely life. He doesn't have much contact _____ other people.

7 Paul is a keen photographer. He likes taking pictures _____ people.

8 Michael got married _____ a woman he met when he was studying at college.

9 He's very brave. He's not afraid _____ anything.

10 I'm surprised _____ the amount of traffic today. I didn't think it would be so busy.

11 Thank you for lending me the guidebook. It was full _____ useful information.

12 I'm afraid I've had to change my plans, so I can't meet you tomorrow. I'm sorry _____ that.

Verb + preposition

36 Complete each sentence with a preposition where necessary. If no preposition is necessary, leave the space empty.

1 She works quite hard. You can't accuse her .... being lazy.
2 Who's going to look .... your children while you're at work?
3 The problem is becoming serious. We have to discuss .... it.
4 The problem is becoming serious. We have to do something .... it.
5 I prefer this chair .... the other one. It's more comfortable.
6 I need to phone .... the office to tell them I won't be at work today.
7 The river divides the city .... two parts.
8 'What do you think .... your new boss?' 'She's all right, I suppose.'
9 Can somebody please explain .... me what I have to do?
10 I said hello to her, but she didn't answer .... me.
11 'Do you like staying at hotels?' 'It depends .... the hotel.'
12 'Have you ever been to Borla?' 'No, I've never heard .... it. Where is it?'
13 You remind me .... somebody I knew a long time ago. You look just like her.
14 This is wonderful news! I can't believe .... it.
15 George is not an idealist – he believes .... being practical.
16 What's funny? What are you laughing .... ?
17 What did you do with all the money you had? What did you spend it .... ?
18 If Alex asks .... you .... money, don't give him any.
19 I apologised .... Sarah .... keeping her waiting so long.
20 Lisa was very helpful. I thanked .... her .... everything she'd done.

Phrasal verbs

37 A says something and B replies. Which goes with which?

A

1 ~~I've made a mistake on this form.~~
2 I'm too warm with my coat on.
3 This jacket looks nice.
4 My phone number is 576920.
5 This room is in a mess.
6 What's 45 euros in dollars?
7 How did you find the mistake?
8 I'm not sure whether to accept their offer or not.
9 I need a place to stay when I'm in London.
10 It's a subject he doesn't like to talk about.
11 I don't know what this word means.

B

a Don't worry. I'll clear it up.
b No problem. I can fix it up.
c Kate pointed it out.
d ~~That's OK. Cross it out and correct it.~~
e Yes, why don't you try it on?
f OK, I won't bring it up.
g Just a minute. I'll write it down.
h Why don't you take it off then?
i You can look it up.
j I think you should turn it down.
k Give me a moment. I'll work it out.

1 _d_
2 ....
3 ....
4 ....
5 ....
6 ....
7 ....
8 ....
9 ....
10 ....
11 ....

Additional exercises

38 Only one alternative is correct. Which is it?

1 Nobody believed Paul at first but he ___B___ to be right. (B *is correct*)
   A came out   **B** turned out   C worked out   D carried out

2 Here's some good news. It will _____ .
   A turn you up   **B** put you up   **C** blow you up   **D** cheer you up

3 I was annoyed with the way the children were behaving, so I _____ .
   A told them up   **B** told them off   **C** told them out   **D** told them over

4 The club committee is _____ of the president, the secretary and seven other members.
   A set up   **B** made up   **C** set out   **D** made out

5 You were going to apply for the job, and then you decided not to. So what _____ ?
   A put you off   **B** put you out   **C** turned you off   **D** turned you away

6 I had no idea that he was lying to me. I was completely _____ .
   A taken in   **B** taken down   **C** taken off   **D** taken over

7 Helen started a course at college, but she _____ after six months.
   A went out   **B** fell out   **C** turned out   **D** dropped out

8 You can't predict everything. Often things don't _____ as you expect.
   A make out   **B** break out   **C** work out   **D** get out

9 Why are all these people here? What's _____ ?
   A going off   **B** getting off   **C** going on   **D** getting on

10 It's a very busy airport. There are planes _____ or landing every few minutes.
   A going up   **B** taking off   **C** getting up   **D** driving off

11 The traffic was moving slowly because a bus had _____ and was blocking the road.
   A broken down   **B** fallen down   **C** fallen over   **D** broken up

12 How are you _____ in your new job? Are you enjoying it?
   A keeping on   **B** going on   **C** carrying on   **D** getting on

39 Complete the sentences. Use two words each time.

1 Keep ___away from___ the edge of the pool. You might fall in.
2 I didn't notice that the two pictures were different until Tanya pointed it _____ me.
3 I asked Dan if he had any suggestions about what we should do, but he didn't come _____ anything.
4 I'm glad Sarah is coming to the party. I'm really looking _____ seeing her again.
5 Things are changing all the time. It's difficult to keep _____ all these changes.
6 I don't want to run _____ food for the party. Are you sure we have enough?
7 Don't let me interrupt you. Carry _____ your work.
8 Steve was very happy in his job until he fell _____ his boss. After that, it was impossible for them to work together, and Steve decided to leave.
9 I've had enough of being treated like this. I'm not going to put _____ it any more.
10 I didn't enjoy the trip very much at the time, but when I look _____ it now, I realise it was a good experience and I'm glad I went on it.
11 The wedding was supposed to be a secret, so how did you find _____ it? Did Jess tell you?
12 There is a very nice atmosphere in the office where I work. Everybody gets _____ everybody else.

40 Complete each sentence using a phrasal verb that means the same as the words in brackets.

1 The football match had to be ....*called off*.... because of the weather. (cancelled)
2 The story Kate told wasn't true. She ....*made it up*.... . (invented it)
3 A bomb .... near the station, but no-one was injured. (exploded)
4 Paul finally .... nearly an hour late. (arrived)
5 Here's an application form. Can you .... and sign it, please? (complete it)
6 A number of buildings are going to be .... to make way for the new road.
   (demolished)
7 I'm having a few problems with my computer which need to be .... as soon
   as possible. (put right)
8 Be positive! You must never .... ! (stop trying)
9 I was very tired and .... in front of the television. (fell asleep)
10 After eight years together, they've decided to .... (separate)
11 The noise is terrible. I can't .... any longer. (tolerate it)
12 We don't have a lot of money, but we have enough to .... (manage)
13 I'm sorry I'm late. The meeting .... longer than I expected. (continued)
14 We need to make a decision today at the latest. We can't .... any longer.
   (delay it)

41 Complete the sentences. Use one word each time.

1 You're driving too fast. Please ....*slow*.... down.
2 It was only a small fire and I managed to .... it out with a bucket of water.
3 The house is empty at the moment, but I think the new tenants are .... in
   next week.
4 I've .... on weight. My clothes don't fit any more.
5 Their house is really nice now. They've .... it up really well.
6 I was talking to the woman sitting next to me on the plane, and it .... out
   that she works for the same company as my brother.
7 'Do you know what happened?' 'Not yet, but I'm going to .... out.'
8 There's no need to get angry. .... down!
9 If you're going on a long walk, plan your route carefully before you .... off.
10 Sarah has just phoned to say that she'll be late. She's been .... up.
11 You've written my name wrong. It's Martin, not Marin – you .... out the T.
12 Three days at £45 a day – that .... out at £135.
13 We had a really interesting discussion, but Jane didn't .... in. She just
   listened.
14 Jonathan is pretty fit. He .... out in the gym every day.
15 Come and see us more often. You can .... in any time you like.
16 We are still discussing the contract. There are still a couple of things to ....
   out.
17 My alarm clock .... off in the middle of the night and ....
   me up.

Study guide

This guide is to help you decide which units you need to study. The sentences in the guide are grouped together (*Present and past*, *Articles and nouns* etc.) in the same way as the units in the *Contents* (pages iii–vi).

Each sentence can be completed using one or more of the alternatives (A, B, C etc.). There are between two and five alternatives each time. IN SOME SENTENCES MORE THAN ONE ALTERNATIVE IS POSSIBLE.

If you don't know or if you are not sure which alternatives are correct, then you probably need to study the unit(s) in the list on the right. You will also find the correct sentence in this unit. (If two or three units are listed, you will find the correct sentence in the first one.)

There is a key to this study guide on page 372.

IF YOU ARE NOT SURE WHICH IS RIGHT	STUDY UNIT

Present and past

1.1	At first I didn't like my job, but .... to enjoy it now. **A** I'm beginning **B** I begin	1, 3
1.2	I don't understand this sentence. What .... ? **A** does mean this word **B** does this word mean **C** means this word	2, 49
1.3	Robert .... away two or three times a year. **A** is going usually **B** is usually going **C** usually goes **D** goes usually	2, 3, 110
1.4	How .... now? Better than before? **A** you are feeling **B** do you feel **C** are you feeling	4
1.5	It was a boring weekend. .... anything. **A** I didn't **B** I don't do **C** I didn't do	5
1.6	Matt .... while we were having dinner. **A** phoned **B** was phoning **C** has phoned	6, 14

Present perfect and past

2.1	James is on holiday. He .... to Italy. **A** is gone **B** has gone **C** has been	7
2.2	Everything is going well. We .... any problems so far. **A** didn't have **B** don't have **C** haven't had	8
2.3	Sarah has lost her passport again. It's the second time this .... **A** has happened **B** happens **C** happened **D** is happening	8
2.4	You're out of breath. .... ? **A** Are you running **B** Have you run **C** Have you been running	9
2.5	Where's the book I gave you? What .... with it? **A** have you done **B** have you been doing **C** are you doing	10
2.6	'............................. each other for a long time?' 'Yes, since we were at school.' **A** Do you know **B** Have you known **C** Have you been knowing	11, 10
2.7	Sally has been working here .... **A** for six months **B** since six months **C** six months ago	12

IF YOU ARE NOT SURE WHICH IS RIGHT

STUDY UNIT

2.8 It's two years .... Joe.   12
   A that I don't see   **B** that I haven't seen   **C** since I didn't see
   D since I last saw

2.9 It .... raining for a while, but now it's raining again.   13
   A stopped   **B** has stopped   **C** was stopped

2.10 My mother .... in Italy.   13
   A grew up   **B** has grown up   **C** had grown up

2.11 .... a lot of sweets when you were a child?   14
   A Have you eaten   **B** Had you eaten   **C** Did you eat

2.12 Jack .... in New York for ten years. Now he lives in Los Angeles.   14, 11
   A lived   **B** has lived   **C** has been living

2.13 The man sitting next to me on the plane was very nervous. He   15
   before.
   A hasn't flown   **B** didn't fly   **C** hadn't flown   **D** wasn't flying

2.14 Katherine was sitting in an armchair resting. She was tired because
   .... very hard.   16
   A she was working   **B** she's been working   **C** she'd been working

2.15 .... a car when you were living in Paris?   17, 14
   A Had you   **B** Were you having   **C** Have you had   **D** Did you have

2.16 I .... tennis a lot, but I don't play very much now.   18
   A was playing   **B** was used to play   **C** used to play

Future

3.1 I'm tired. .... to bed now. Goodnight.   19
   A I go   **B** I'm going

3.2 .... tomorrow, so we can go out somewhere.   19, 21
   A I'm not working   **B** I don't work   **C** I won't work

3.3 That bag looks heavy. .... you with it.   21
   A I'm helping   **B** I help   **C** I'll help

3.4 I think the weather .... be nice later.   23, 22
   A will   **B** shall   **C** is going to

3.5 'Anna is in hospital.'   'Yes, I know. .... her this evening.'   23, 20
   A I visit   **B** I'm going to visit   **C** I'll visit

3.6 We're late. The film .... by the time we get to the cinema.   24
   A will already start   **B** will be already started   **C** will already have started

3.7 Don't worry .... late tonight.   25
   A if I'm   **B** when I'm   **C** when I'll be   **D** if I'll be

IF YOU ARE NOT SURE WHICH IS RIGHT

Modals

4.1	The fire spread through the building very quickly, but fortunately everybody .... **A** was able to escape **B** managed to escape **C** could escape	26
4.2	I'm so tired I .... for a week. **A** can sleep **B** could sleep **B** could have slept	27
4.3	The story .... be true, but I don't think it is. **A** might **B** can **C** could **D** may	27, 29
4.4	Why did you stay at a hotel when you were in Paris? You .... with Sarah. **A** can stay **B** could stay **C** could have stayed	27
4.5	'I've lost one of my gloves.' 'You .... it somewhere.' **A** must drop **B** must have dropped **C** must be dropping **D** must have been dropping	28
4.6	'Why wasn't Amy at the meeting yesterday?' 'She .... about it.' **A** might not know **B** may not know **C** might not have known **D** may not have known	29
4.7	What was the problem? Why .... leave early? **A** had you to **B** did you have to **C** must you **D** you had to	31
4.8	We've got plenty of time. We .... hurry. **A** don't need to **B** mustn't **C** needn't	32
4.9	You missed a great party last night. You .... Why didn't you? **A** must have come **B** should have come **C** ought to have come **D** had to come	33
4.10	Jane won the lottery. I .... a car with the money she'd won. **A** suggested that she buy **B** suggested that she should buy **C** suggested her to buy **D** suggested that she bought	34
4.11	You're always at home. You .... out more often. **A** should go **B** had better go **C** had better to go	35
4.12	It's late. It's time .... home. **A** we go **B** we must go **C** we should go **D** we went **E** to go	35
4.13	.... a little longer, but I really have to go now. **A** I'd stay **B** I'll stay **C** I can stay **D** I'd have stayed	36

If and wish

5.1	I'm not going to bed yet. I'm not tired. If I .... to bed now, I wouldn't sleep. **A** go **B** went **C** had gone **D** would go	38
5.2	If I were rich, ... a lot. **A** I'll travel **B** I can travel **C** I would travel **D** I travelled	39
5.3	I wish I .... have to work tomorrow, but unfortunately I do. **A** don't **B** didn't **C** wouldn't **D** won't	39, 41

IF YOU ARE NOT SURE WHICH IS RIGHT

5.4   The view was wonderful. If _____ a camera with me, I would have taken some pictures.
       A I had   **B** I would have   **C** I would have had   **D** I'd had

40

5.5   The weather is horrible. I wish it _____ raining.
       A would stop   **B** stopped   **C** stops   **D** will stop

41

Passive

6.1   We _____ by a loud noise during the night.
       A woke up   **B** are woken up   **C** were woken up   **D** were waking up

42

6.2   A new supermarket is going to _____ next year.
       A build   **B** be built   **C** be building   **D** building

43

6.3   There's somebody walking behind us. I think _____ .
       A we are following   **B** we are being following   **C** we are followed
       D we are being followed

43

6.4   'Where _____ ?' 'In Chicago.'
       A were you born   **B** are you born   **C** have you been born
       D did you born

44

6.5   There was a fight at the party, but nobody _____ .
       A was hurt   **B** got hurt   **C** hurt

44

6.6   Jane _____ to phone me last night, but she didn't.
       A supposed   **B** is supposed   **C** was supposed

45

6.7   Where _____ ? Which hairdresser did you go to?
       A did you cut your hair   **B** have you cut your hair
       C did you have cut your hair   **D** did you have your hair cut

46

Reported speech

7.1   Paul left the room suddenly. He said he _____ to go.
       A had   **B** has   **C** have

48, 47

7.2   Hi, Joe. I didn't expect to see you. Sonia said you _____ in hospital.
       A are   **B** were   **C** was   **D** should be

48, 47

7.3   Ann _____ and left.
       A said goodbye to me   **B** said me goodbye   **C** told me goodbye

48

Questions and auxiliary verbs

8.1   'What time _____ ?' 'At 8.30.'
       A starts the film   **B** does start the film   **C** does the film start

49

8.2   'Do you know where _____ ?' 'No, he didn't say.'
       A Tom has gone   **B** has Tom gone   **C** has gone Tom

50

8.3   The police officer stopped us and asked us where _____ .
       A were we going   **B** are we going   **C** we are going   **D** we were going

50

IF YOU ARE NOT SURE WHICH IS RIGHT

8.4 'Do you think it will rain?' '_____.'

A I hope not.   B I don't hope.   C I don't hope so.

51

8.5 'You don't know where Karen is, _____?' 'Sorry, I have no idea.'

A don't you   B do you   C is she   D are you

52

-ing and to ...

9.1 You can't stop me _____ what I want.

A doing   B do   C to do   D that I do

53

9.2 I must go now. I promised _____ late.

A not being   B not to be   C to not be   D I wouldn't be

54, 36

9.3 Do you want _____ with you or do you want to go alone?

A me coming   B me to come   C that I come   D that I will come

55

9.4 I know I locked the door. I clearly remember _____ it.

A locking   B to lock   C to have locked

56

9.5 She tried to be serious, but she couldn't help _____.

A laughing   B to laugh   C that she laughed   D laugh

57

9.6 Paul lives in Berlin now. He likes _____ there.

A living   B to live

58

9.7 It's not my favourite job, but I like _____ the kitchen as often as possible.

A cleaning   B clean   C to clean   D that I clean

58

9.8 I'm tired. I'd rather _____ out this evening, if you don't mind.

A not going   B not to go   C don't go   D not go

59

9.9 I'd rather _____ anyone what I said.

A you don't tell   B not you tell   C you didn't tell   D you wouldn't tell

59

9.10 Are you looking forward _____ on holiday?

A going   B to go   C to going   D that you go

60, 62

9.11 When Lisa came to Britain, she had to get used _____ on the left.

A driving   B to driving   C to drive

61

9.12 I'm thinking _____ a house. Do you think that's a good idea?

A to buy   B of to buy   C of buying   D about buying

62, 66

9.13 I had no _____ a place to stay. In fact it was surprisingly easy.

A difficulty to find   B difficulty finding   C trouble to find
D trouble finding

63

9.14 I phoned the restaurant _____ a table.

A for reserve   B to reserve   C for reserving   D for to reserve

64

9.15 James doesn't speak very clearly. _____

A It is difficult to understand him.   B He is difficult to understand.
C He is difficult to understand him.

65

IF YOU ARE NOT SURE WHICH IS RIGHT

STUDY UNIT

9.16	The path was icy, so we walked very carefully. We were afraid .... **A** of falling **B** from falling **C** to fall **D** to falling	66
9.17	I didn't hear you .... in. You must have been very quiet. **A** come **B** to come **C** came	67
9.18	.... a hotel, we looked for somewhere to have dinner. **A** Finding **B** After finding **C** Having found **D** We found	68

Articles and nouns

10.1	It wasn't your fault. It was .... **A** accident **B** an accident **C** some accident	69
10.2	Where are you going to put all your .... ? **A** furniture **B** furnitures	70
10.3	'Where are you going?' 'I'm going to buy ....' **A** a bread **B** some bread **C** a loaf of bread	70
10.4	Sandra is .... She works at a large hospital. **A** nurse **B** a nurse **C** the nurse	71, 72
10.5	Helen works six days .... week. **A** in **B** for **C** a **D** the	72
10.6	There are millions of stars in .... **A** space **B** a space **C** the space	73
10.7	Every day .... begins at 9 and finishes at 3. **A** school **B** a school **C** the school	74
10.8	.... a problem in most big cities. **A** Crime is **B** The crime is **C** The crimes are	75
10.9	When .... invented? **A** was telephone **B** were telephones **C** were the telephones **D** was the telephone	76
10.10	Have you been to .... ? **A** Canada or United States **B** the Canada or the United States **C** Canada or the United States **D** the Canada or United States	77
10.11	On our first day in Moscow, we visited .... **A** Kremlin **B** a Kremlin **C** the Kremlin	78
10.12	What time .... on TV? **A** is the news **B** are the news **C** is news **D** is the new	79, 70
10.13	It took us quite a long time to get here. It was .... journey. **A** three hour **B** a three-hours **C** a three-hour	80
10.14	This isn't my book. It's .... **A** my sister **B** my sister's **C** from my sister **D** of my sister **E** of my sister's	81

IF YOU ARE NOT SURE WHICH IS RIGHT	STUDY UNIT

Pronouns and determiners

11.1   What time shall we .... tomorrow?   **82**
     A meet   **B** meet us   **C** meet ourselves

11.2   I'm going to a wedding on Saturday. .... is getting married.   **83**
     A A friend of me   **B** A friend of mine   **C** One my friends

11.3   They live on a busy road. .... a lot of noise from the traffic.   **84**
     A It must be   **B** It must have   **C** There must have   **D** There must be

11.4   He's lazy. He never does .... work.   **85**
     A some   **B** any   **C** no

11.5   'What would you like to eat?' 'I don't mind. **85**
     – whatever you have.'
     A Something   **B** Anything   **C** Nothing

11.6   We couldn't buy anything because .... of the shops were open.   **86**
     A all   **B** no-one   **C** none   **D** nothing

11.7   We went shopping and spent .... money.   **87**
     A a lot of   **B** much   **C** lots of   **D** many

11.8   .... don't visit this part of the town.   **88**
     A The most tourists   **B** Most of tourists   **C** Most tourists

11.9   I asked two people the way to the station, but .... of them could   **89**
     help me.
     A none   **B** either   **C** both   **D** neither

11.10   .... had a great time at the party.   **90**
     A Everybody   **B** All   **C** All of us   **D** Everybody of us

11.11   The bus service is excellent. There's a bus .... ten minutes.   **90, 91**
     A each   **B** every   **C** all

Relative clauses

12.1   I don't like stories .... have unhappy endings.   **92**
     A that   **B** they   **C** which   **D** who

12.2   I didn't believe them at first, but in fact everything .... was true.   **93**
     A they said   **B** that they said   **C** what they said

12.3   What's the name of the man .... ?   **94**
     A you borrowed his car   **B** which car you borrowed
     C whose car you borrowed   **D** his car you borrowed

12.4   Anna told me about her new job, ... a lot.   **95**
     A that she's enjoying   **B** which she's enjoying   **C** she's enjoying
     D she's enjoying it

12.5   Sarah couldn't meet us, ... was a shame.   **96**
     A that   **B** it   **C** what   **D** which

12.6   George showed me some pictures .... by his father.   **97, 92**
     A painting   **B** painted   **C** that were painted   **D** they were painted

IF YOU ARE NOT SURE WHICH IS RIGHT

Adjectives and adverbs

13.1 Jane doesn't enjoy her job any more. She's _____ because every day she does exactly the same thing.
A boring **B** bored
98

13.2 Lisa was carrying a _____ bag.
A black small plastic **B** small and black plastic **C** small black plastic
D plastic small black
99

13.3 Maria's English is excellent. She speaks _____ .
A perfectly English **B** English perfectly **C** perfect English
D English perfect
100

13.4 He _____ to find a job, but he had no luck.
A tried hard **B** tried hardly **C** hardly tried
101

13.5 I haven't seen her for _____ , I've forgotten what she looks like.
A so long **B** so long time **C** a such long time **D** such a long time
102

13.6 We don't have _____ on holiday right now.
A money enough to go **B** enough money to go
C money enough for going **D** enough money for go
103

13.7 Sarah is doing OK at the moment. She has _____ .
A a quite good job **B** quite a good job **C** a pretty good job
104

13.8 The exam was quite easy – _____ I expected.
A more easy that **B** more easy than **C** easier than **D** easier as
105

13.9 The more electricity you use, _____ .
A your bill will be higher **B** will be higher your bill
C the higher your bill will be **D** higher your bill will be
106

13.10 Patrick is a fast runner. I can't run as fast as _____ .
A he **B** him **C** he can
107

13.11 The movie was really boring. It's _____ I've ever seen.
A most boring movie **B** the more boring movie **C** the movie more boring
D the most boring movie
108

13.12 Ben likes walking. _____
A Every morning he walks to work. **B** He walks to work every morning.
C He walks every morning to work. **D** He every morning walks to work.
109

13.13 Joe never phones me. _____
A Always I have to phone him. **B** I always have to phone him.
C I have always to phone him. **D** I have to phone always him.
110

13.14 Lucy _____ . She left last month.
A still doesn't work here **B** doesn't still work here
C no more works here **D** doesn't work here any more
111

13.15 _____ she can't drive, she bought a car.
A Even **B** Even when **C** Even if **D** Even though
112, 113

IF YOU ARE NOT SURE WHICH IS RIGHT

Conjunctions and prepositions

14.1   I couldn't sleep .... very tired.
       A although I was   **B** despite I was   **C** despite of being   **D** in spite of being

> 113

14.2   You should insure your bike .... stolen.
       A in case it will be   **B** if it will be   **C** in case it is   **D** if it is

> 114

14.3   The club is for members only.   You .... you're a member.
       A can't go in if   **B** can go in only if   **C** can't go in unless
       D can go in unless

> 115

14.4   We watched TV all evening .... we didn't have anything better to do.
       A when   **B** as   **C** while   **D** since

> 116

14.5   'What's that noise?'   'It sounds .... a baby crying.'
       A as   **B** like   **C** as if   **D** as though

> 117, 118

14.6   They are very kind to me.   They treat me .... their own son.
       A as I am   **B** as if I would be   **C** as if I am   **D** as if I were

> 118

14.7   I'll be in Singapore next week.   I hope to see some friends of mine
       .... there.
       A while I'll be   **B** while I'm   **C** during my visit   **D** during I'm

> 119

14.8   Joe is away at the moment.   I don't know exactly when he's coming back, but I'm
       sure he'll be back .... Monday.
       A by   **B** until

> 120

Prepositions

15.1   Bye!   I'll see you ....
       A at Friday morning   **B** on Friday morning   **C** in Friday morning
       D Friday morning

> 121

15.2   I'm going away .... the end of January.
       A at   **B** on   **C** in

> 122

15.3   When we were in Italy, we spent a few days .... Venice.
       A at   **B** to   **C** in

> 123, 125

15.4   Our apartment is .... the second floor of the building.
       A at   **B** on   **C** in   **D** to

> 124

15.5   I saw Steve .... a conference on Saturday.
       A at   **B** on   **C** in   **D** to

> 125

15.6   When did they .... the hotel?
       A arrive to   **B** arrive at   **C** arrive in   **D** get to   **E** get in

> 126

15.7   I'm going .... holiday next week.   I'll be away for two weeks.
       A at   **B** on   **C** in   **D** for

> 127

15.8   We travelled .... 6.45 train, which arrived at 8.30.
       A in the   **B** on the   **C** by the   **D** by

> 128

15.9   'Have you read anything .... Ernest Hemingway?'   'No, what sort
       of books did he write?'
       A of   **B** from   **C** by

> 128

IF YOU ARE NOT SURE WHICH IS RIGHT	STUDY UNIT

15.10 The accident was my fault, so I had to pay for the damage .... the other car.   **129**
    A of   **B** for   **C** to   **D** on   **E** at

15.11 I like them very much. They have always been very nice .... me.   **130**
    A of   **B** for   **C** to   **D** with

15.12 I'm not very good .... repairing things.   **131**
    A at   **B** for   **C** in   **D** about

15.13 I don't understand this sentence. Can you .... ?   **132**
    A explain to me this word   **B** explain me this word
    C explain this word to me

15.14 If you're worried about the problem, you should do something .... it.   **133**
    A for   **B** about   **C** against   **D** with

15.15 'Who is Tom Hart?' 'I have no idea. I've never heard .... him.'   **134**
    A about   **B** from   **C** after   **D** of

15.16 'What time will you be home?' 'I don't know. It depends .... the traffic.'   **135**
    A of   **B** for   **C** from   **D** on

15.17 I prefer tea .... coffee.   **136, 59**
    A to   **B** than   **C** against   **D** from

Phrasal verbs

16.1 These shoes are uncomfortable. I'm going to **137**
    A take off   **B** take them off   **C** take off them

16.2 They were playing cards, so I **138**
    A joined in   **B** came in   **C** got in   **D** broke in

16.3 Nobody believed Paul at first, but he .... to be right.   **139**
    A worked out   **B** came out   **C** found out   **D** turned out

16.4 We can't .... making a decision. We have to decide now.   **140**
    A put away   **B** put over   **C** put off   **D** put out

16.5 'Have you finished painting the kitchen?' 'Nearly. I'll .... tomorrow.'   **141**
    A finish it out   **B** finish it over   **C** finish it off

16.6 You can always rely on Paul. He'll never **142**
    A put you up   **B** let you down   **C** take you over   **D** see you off

16.7 Children under 16 .... half the population of the city.   **143**
    A make up   **B** put up   **C** take up   **D** bring up

16.8 I'm surprised to hear that Sue and Paul have .... They seemed very happy together.   **144**
    A broken up   **B** ended up   **C** finished up   **D** split up

16.9 I parked in a no-parking zone, but I .... it.   **145**
    A came up with   **B** got away with   **C** made off with   **D** got on with

Key to Exercises

In some of the exercises you have to use your own ideas to write sentences. Example answers are given in the Key. If possible, check your answers with somebody who speaks English well.

UNIT 1

1.1
2 e
3 g
4 a
5 d
6 h
7 b
8 c

1.2
1 What's / What is   he studying
   Is he enjoying
2 's / is   your new job going
   it's getting / it is getting
   he isn't enjoying / he's not enjoying
   he's beginning / he is beginning

1.3
3 I'm not listening / I am not listening
4 She's having / She is having
5 I'm not eating / I am not eating
6 He's learning / He is learning
7 They aren't speaking / They're not speaking / They are not speaking
8 I'm getting / I am getting
9 isn't working / 's not working / is not working
10 I'm looking / I am looking

1.4
2 is changing
3 's getting / is getting
4 is rising
5 is starting

UNIT 2

2.1
2 drink
3 opens
4 causes
5 live
6 take
7 connects

2.2
2 do the banks close
3 don't use
4 does Ricardo come
5 do you do
6 takes … does it take
7 does this word mean
8 doesn't do

2.3
3 rises
4 make
5 don't eat
6 doesn't believe
7 translates
8 don't tell
9 flows

2.4
2 Does your sister play tennis?
3 Which newspaper do you read?
4 What does your brother do?
5 How often do you go to the cinema?
6 Where do your grandparents live?

2.5
2 I promise
3 I insist
4 I apologise
5 I recommend

UNIT 3

3.1
3 is trying
4 are they talking
5 OK
6 It's getting / It is getting
7 OK
8 I'm coming / I am coming
9 are you getting
10 He always gets
11 OK

3.2
3 Everybody's waiting / Everybody is waiting
4 Are you listening
5 Do you listen
6 flows
7 's flowing / is flowing
8 We usually grow … we aren't growing / we're not growing / we are not growing
9 it's improving / it is improving
10 She's staying / She is staying … She always stays
11 I'm starting / I am starting
12 I'm learning / I am learning … 's teaching / is teaching
13 I finish … I'm working / I am working
14 live … do your parents live
15 's looking / is looking … She's staying / She is staying
16 does your brother do … he isn't working / he's not working / he is not working
17 I usually enjoy … I'm not enjoying / I am not enjoying

3.3
2 It's always breaking down.
3 I'm always making the same mistake. / … that mistake.
4 You're always forgetting your glasses.

UNIT 4

4.1
2 I'm using / I am using
3 I need
4 does he want
5 is he looking
6 believes
7 I don't remember / I do not remember or I can't remember
8 I'm thinking / I am thinking
9 I think … You don't use
10 consists

4.2
2 What are you doing?
   I'm thinking.
3 Who does this umbrella belong to?
4 The dinner smells good.
5 Is anybody sitting there?
6 These gloves don't fit me.

4.3
2 Do you believe
3 OK (I feel *is also correct*)
4 It tastes
5 I think

4.4
2 's being / is being
3 's / is
4 are you being
5 Is he

UNIT 5

5.1
2 She had
3 She walked to work
4 It took her (about) half an hour
5 She started work
6 She didn't have (any) lunch. / … eat (any) lunch.
7 She finished work
8 She was tired when she got home.
9 She cooked
10 She didn't go
11 She went to bed
12 She slept

5.2

2 taught
3 sold
4 fell … hurt
5 threw … caught
6 spent … bought … cost

5.3

2 did you travel / did you go
3 did it take (you)
4 did you stay
5 Was the weather
6 Did you go to / Did you see /
Did you visit

5.4

3 didn't disturb   7 didn't cost
4 left   8 didn't have
5 didn't sleep   9 were
6 flew

UNIT 6

6.1

Example answers:

3 I was working.
4 I was in bed asleep.
5 I was getting ready to go out.
6 I was watching TV at home.

6.2

Example answers:

2 was having a shower
3 were driving home
4 was reading the paper
5 was watching it

6.3

1 didn't see … was looking
2 met … were going … was going …
had … were waiting / waited
3 was cycling … stepped …
was going … managed …
didn't hit

6.4

2 were you doing
3 Did you go
4 were you driving … happened
5 took … wasn't looking
6 didn't know
7 saw … was trying
8 was walking … heard … was
following … started
9 wanted
10 dropped … was doing … didn't break

UNIT 7

7.1

2 Lisa has broken her leg.
3 The bus fare has gone up.
4 Her English has improved.
5 Dan has grown a beard.
6 The letter has arrived.
7 The temperature has fallen.

7.2

2 been
3 gone
4 gone
5 been

7.3

2 Yes, I've just seen her. /
Yes, I have just seen her. *or*
Yes, I just saw her.
3 He's already left. / He has
already left. *or* He already left.
4 I haven't read it yet. *or*
I didn't read it yet.
5 No, she's already seen the film. /
No, she has already seen … *or*
No, she already saw …
6 Yes, they've just arrived. /
Yes, they have just arrived. *or*
Yes, they just arrived.
7 We haven't told him yet. *or*
We didn't tell him yet.

7.4

2 he's just gone out / he has just
gone out *or* he just went out
3 I haven't finished yet *or*
I didn't finish yet
4 I've already done it / I have
already done it *or* I already did it
5 Have you found a place to live yet?
or Did you find a place … ?
6 I haven't decided yet *or*
I didn't decide yet
7 she's just come back / she has just
come back *or* she just came back

UNIT 8

8.1

2 Have you ever been to California?
3 Have you ever run (in) a marathon?
4 Have you ever spoken to a famous
person?
5 What's the most beautiful place
you've ever visited? / … you have
ever visited?

8.2

3 haven't eaten
4 I haven't played (it)
5 I've had / I have had
6 I haven't read
7 I've never been / I haven't been
8 it's happened / it has happened *or*
that's happened / that has happened
9 I've never tried / I haven't tried *or*
I've never eaten / I haven't eaten
10 's been / has been
11 I've never seen / I haven't seen

8.3

Example answers:

2 I haven't travelled by bus this week.
3 I haven't been to the cinema
recently.
4 I haven't read a book for ages.
5 I haven't lost anything today.

8.4

2 Have you played tennis before?
No, this is the first time I've played
tennis.
3 Have you ridden a horse before? /
Have you been on a horse before?
No, this is the first time I've ridden a
horse. / … I've been on a horse.
4 Have you been to Japan before?
No, this is the first time I've been to
Japan.

UNIT 9

9.1

2 She's been watching television. /
She has been watching television.
3 They've been playing tennis. /
They have been playing tennis.
4 He's been running. / He has been
running.

9.2

2 Have you been waiting long?
3 What have you been doing?
4 How long have you been working
there?
5 How long have you been selling
mobile phones?

9.3

2 've been waiting / have been waiting
3 've been learning Spanish /
have been learning Spanish
4 She's been working there /
She has been working there
5 They've been going there /
They have been going there

9.4

2 I've been looking / I have been
looking
3 are you looking
4 She's been teaching / She has been
teaching
5 I've been thinking / I have been
thinking
6 he's working / he is working
7 She's been working / She has been
working

Key to Exercises

UNIT 10

10.1

2 She's been travelling / She has been travelling
She's visited / She has visited

3 He's won / He has won …
He's / He has been playing tennis

4 They've / They have been making (films …)
They've / They have made (five films …)

10.2

2 Have you been waiting long?
3 Have you caught any fish?
4 How many people have you invited?
5 How long have you been teaching?
6 How many books have you written?
How long have you been writing books?
7 How long have you been saving?
How much money have you saved?

10.3

2 Somebody's broken / Somebody has broken
3 Have you been working
4 Have you ever worked
5 has she gone
6 He's appeared / He has appeared
7 I haven't been waiting
8 it's stopped / it has stopped
9 I've lost / I have lost … Have you seen
10 I've been reading / I have been reading … I haven't finished
11 I've read / I have read
12 I've had / I have had

UNIT 11

11.1

3 have been married
4 OK
5 It's been raining / It has been raining
6 have you been living or have you lived
7 has been working
8 OK
9 I haven't drunk
10 have you had

11.2

2 How long have you been teaching English? or
How long have you taught …
3 How long have you known Katherine?
4 How long has your brother been in Australia?
5 How long have you had that jacket?

6 How long has Joe been working at the airport? or
How long has Joe worked …
7 How long have you been having guitar lessons?
8 Have you always lived in Chicago?

11.3

3 's been / has been
4 've been waiting / have been waiting
5 've known / have known
6 haven't played
7 's been watching / has been watching
8 haven't watched
9 've had / have had
10 hasn't been
11 've been feeling / have been feeling or 've felt / have felt
12 's lived / has lived or 's been living / has been living
13 haven't been
14 've always wanted / have always wanted

UNIT 12

12.1

2 since
3 for
4 for
5 since
6 for
7 since
8 since
9 for

12.2

2 How long has Kate been learning Japanese?
When did Kate start learning Japanese?
3 How long have you known Simon?
When did you first meet Simon? / When did you and Simon first meet?
4 How long have Rebecca and David been married?
When did Rebecca and David get married? / When did Rebecca and David marry?

12.3

3 He has been ill since Sunday.
4 He has been ill for a few days.
5 She got married a year ago.
6 I've had a headache since I woke up.
7 She went to Italy three weeks ago.
8 I've been working in a hotel for six months. or I've worked in a hotel for six months.

12.4

2 No, I haven't seen Laura/her for about a month.
3 No, I haven't been to the cinema for a long time.
4 No, I haven't eaten in a restaurant for ages. / No, I haven't been to a restaurant for ages.
6 No, it's about a month since I (last) saw Laura/her. / No, it's been about a month since …
7 No, it's a long time since I (last) went to the cinema. / No, it's been a long time since …
8 No, it's ages since I (last) ate in a restaurant. / No, it's been ages since … or
… since I went to a restaurant.

UNIT 13

13.1

2 has gone
3 forgot
4 went
5 had
6 has broken

13.2

3 did William Shakespeare write
4 OK
5 OK
6 Who invented
7 were you born
8 OK
9 Albert Einstein was … who developed

13.3

3 I've forgotten / I have forgotten
4 arrested
5 it's improved / it has improved
6 I've finished / I have finished (I'm finished is also correct)
7 I applied
8 It was
9 There's been / There has been
10 He broke or He's broken / He has broken … did that happen … he fell

UNIT 14

14.1

3 OK
4 I bought
5 Where were you
6 Lucy left school
7 OK
8 OK
9 OK
10 When was this book published?

14.2

2 The weather has been cold recently.
3 It was cold last week.
4 I didn't read a newspaper yesterday.
5 I haven't read a newspaper today.
6 Emily has earned a lot of money this year.
7 She didn't earn so much last year.
8 Have you had a holiday recently?

14.3

3 Have you seen … I saw
4 I didn't sleep
5 There were
6 worked … he gave
7 She's lived / She has lived
8 Did you go … it was … was
9 died … I never met
10 I've never met / I have never met
11 I haven't seen
12 have you lived *or* have you been living … did you live … did you live

14.4

Example answers:

2 I haven't bought anything today.
3 I didn't watch TV yesterday.
4 I went out with some friends yesterday evening.
5 I haven't been to the cinema recently.
6 I've read a lot of books recently.

UNIT 15

15.1

2 It had changed a lot.
3 She'd arranged to do something else. / She had arranged …
4 The film had already started.
5 I hadn't seen him for five years.
6 She'd just had breakfast. / She had just had …

15.2

2 I'd never heard it before. / I had never heard …
3 He'd never played (tennis) before. / He had never played …
4 We'd never been there before. / We had never been …

15.3

1 we called
2 there was …
    She'd gone / She had gone
3 He'd just come back from / He had just come back from …
    He looked
4 got a phone call
    He was
    He'd sent her / He had sent her …
    she'd never replied to them /
    she had never replied to them

15.4

2 went
3 had gone
4 broke
5 saw … had broken … stopped

UNIT 16

16.1

2 They'd been playing football. / They had been playing …
3 I'd been looking forward to it. / I had been looking forward …
4 She'd been dreaming. / She had been dreaming.
5 He'd been watching a film. / He had been watching …

16.2

2 I'd been waiting for 20 minutes when I realised that I was in the wrong restaurant. *or* … that I had come to the wrong restaurant.
3 At the time the factory closed down, Sarah had been working there for five years.
4 The orchestra had been playing for about ten minutes when a man in the audience started shouting.
5 *Example answer:*
    I'd been walking along the road for about ten minutes when a car suddenly stopped just behind me.

16.3

3 he was walking
4 She'd been running / She had been running
5 They were eating
6 They'd been eating / They had been eating
7 He was looking
8 was waiting … she'd been waiting / she had been waiting
9 I'd had / I had had
10 We'd been travelling / We had been travelling

UNIT 17

17.1

3 I don't have a ladder. / I haven't got a ladder.
4 We didn't have enough time.
5 He didn't have a map.
6 She doesn't have any money. / She hasn't got any money.
7 I don't have enough energy. / I haven't got enough energy.
8 They didn't have a camera.

17.2

2 B
3 A *or* C
4 A *or* C
5 A
6 C

17.3

3 he didn't have
4 I have *or* I've got
5 *OK*
6 I didn't have
7 *OK* (*or* He hasn't got)
8 Did you have
9 *OK*

17.4

2 has a break
3 had a party
4 have a look
5 's having / is having   a nice time
6 had a chat
7 Did you have trouble
8 had a baby
9 was having a shower
10 Did you have a good flight?

UNIT 18

18.1

2 used to have/ride
3 used to live
4 used to eat/like/love
5 used to be
6 used to take
7 used to be
8 did you use to go

18.2

2–10

- She used to have lots of friends, but she doesn't know many people these days.
- She used to be very lazy, but she works very hard these days.
- She didn't use to like cheese, but she eats lots of cheese now.
- She used to be a hotel receptionist, but she works in a bookshop now.
- She used to play the piano, but she hasn't played the piano for years. / … played it for years.
- She never used to read / She didn't use to read newspapers, but she reads a newspaper every day now.
- She didn't use to drink tea, but she likes it now.
- She used to have a dog, but it died two years ago.
- She used to go to a lot of parties, but she hasn't been to a party for ages.

18.3

Example answers:

3 I used to be a vegetarian, but now I eat meat sometimes.
4 I used to watch TV a lot, but I don't watch it much now.
5 I used to hate getting up early, but now it's no problem.
7 I didn't use to drink coffee, but I drink it every day now.
8 I didn't use to like hot weather, but now I love it.

UNIT 19

19.1

2 How long are you going for?
3 When are you leaving?
4 Are you going alone?
5 Are you travelling by car?
6 Where are you staying?

19.2

2 I'm working late. / I'm working till 9 o'clock.
3 I'm going to the theatre.
4 I'm meeting Julia.

19.3

Example answers:

2 I'm working tomorrow morning.
3 I'm not doing anything tomorrow evening.
4 I'm playing football next Sunday.
5 I'm going to a party this evening.

19.4

3 We're having / We are having
4 finishes
5 I'm not going / I am not going … I'm staying / I am staying
6 Are you doing
7 We're going / We are going … It starts
8 I'm leaving / I am leaving
9 we're meeting / we are meeting
10 does this train get
11 I'm going / I am going … Are you coming
12 does it end
13 I'm not using / I am not using
14 's coming / is coming … She's travelling / She is travelling … arrives

UNIT 20

20.1

2 What are you going to wear?
3 Where are you going to put it?
4 Who are you going to invite?

20.2

2 I'm going to take it back to the shop.
3 I'm not going to accept it.
4 I'm going to phone her tonight.
5 I'm going to complain.

20.3

2 He's going to be late.
3 The boat is going to sink.
4 They're going to run out of petrol.

20.4

2 was going to buy
3 were going to play
4 was going to phone
5 was going to give up
6 were you going to say

UNIT 21

21.1

2 I'll turn / I'll switch / I'll put
3 I'll send
4 I'll do
5 I'll show
6 I'll have
7 I'll stay / I'll wait
8 I'll pay / I'll give
9 I'll try

21.2

2 I'll go to bed.
3 I think I'll walk.
4 I'll eat anything.
5 I don't think I'll go swimming.

21.3

3 I'll meet
4 I'll lend
5 I'm having
6 I won't forget
7 does your train leave
8 won't tell
9 Are you doing
10 Will you come

21.4

2 Shall I buy it?
3 What shall I give/buy/get Helen (for her birthday)?
4 Where shall we go (on holiday)?
5 Shall we go by car or (shall we) walk? / … or (shall we go) on foot?
6 What time shall I come?

UNIT 22

22.1

2 I'm going
3 will get
4 is coming
5 we're going
6 It won't hurt

22.2

2 won't
3 'll / will
4 won't
5 'll / will
6 won't

22.3

2 It will look
3 you'll like / you will like
4 You'll get / You will get
5 people will live
6 we'll meet / we will meet
7 she'll come / she will come
8 it will be

22.4

2 Do you think it will rain?
3 When do you think it will end?
4 How much do you think it will cost?
5 Do you think they'll get married? / … they will get married?
6 What time do you think you'll be back? / … you will be back?
7 What do you think will happen?

22.5

Example answers:

2 I'll be in bed.
3 I'll be at work.
4 I'll probably be at home.
5 I don't know where I'll be this time next year.

UNIT 23

23.1

2 I'll lend
3 I'll get
4 I'm going to wash
5 are you going to paint
6 I'm going to buy
7 I'll show
8 I'll have
9 I'll call
10 He's going to have … he's going to do

23.2

2 I'm going to take … I'll join
3 you'll find ('you're going to find' *is possible*)
4 I'm not going to apply *or* I'm not applying
5 We're going to be late.
6 it's going to fall down
7 I'll take … I'll pick … Kate is going to take *or* Kate is taking

UNIT 24

24.1
2 b *is true*
3 a *and* c *are true*
4 b *and* d *are true*
5 c *and* d *are true*
6 c *is true*

24.2
2 We'll have finished
3 we'll be playing
4 I'll be working
5 the meeting will have ended
6 he'll have spent
7 you'll still be doing
8 she'll have travelled
9 I'll be staying
10 Will you be seeing

UNIT 25

25.1
2 she goes
3 you know
4 Will you be … I get
5 there are … I'll call / I will call
6 it's / it is
7 you see … you won't recognise /
   you will not recognise
8 I'll be / I will be … he gets
9 you need … I'm / I am
10 I'll wait / I will wait …
   you're / you are

25.2
2 I'll give you my address when
   I find somewhere to live. *or*
   … when I've found somewhere to
   live.
3 I'll come straight back home after I
   do the shopping. *or*
   … after I've done the shopping.
4 Let's go home before it gets dark.
5 I won't speak to her until she
   apologises. *or*
   … until she has apologised.

25.3
2 you go / you leave
3 you decide *or* you've decided /
   you have decided
4 you're in Hong Kong / you go to
   Hong Kong
5 build the new road *or* 've built the
   new road / have built the new road

25.4
2 if
3 When
4 If
5 If
6 when
7 if
8 if

UNIT 26

26.1
3 can
4 be able to
5 been able to
6 can *or* will be able to
7 be able to

26.2
Example answers:
2 I used to be able to run fast.
3 I'd like to be able to play the piano.
4 I've never been able to get up early.

26.3
2 could run
3 can wait
4 couldn't eat
5 can't hear
6 couldn't sleep

26.4
2 was able to finish it
3 were able to find it
4 was able to get away

26.5
4 couldn't
5 managed to
6 could
7 managed to
8 could
9 managed to
10 couldn't

UNIT 27

27.1
2 We could have fish.
3 You could phone (her) now.
4 You could give her a book.
5 We could hang it in the kitchen.

27.2
3 I could kill him!
4 *OK* (could have *is also possible*)
5 I could stay here all day
6 it could be in the car
   (may/might *are also possible*)
7 *OK*
8 *OK* (could borrow *is also possible*)
9 You could fall.
   (may/might *are also possible*)

27.3
2 could have come/gone
3 could apply
4 could have been
5 could have got/taken
6 could come

27.4
3 couldn't wear
4 couldn't have found
5 couldn't get
6 couldn't have been
7 couldn't have come/gone

UNIT 28

28.1
2 must   6 can't
3 can't   7 must
4 must   8 must
5 must   9 can't

28.2
3 go
4 have taken / have stolen /
   have moved
5 be
6 have been
7 be looking
8 have been
9 have heard
10 be following

28.3
3 It must have been very expensive.
4 They must have gone away.
5 I must have left it in the restaurant
   last night.
6 It can't have been easy for her.
7 He must have been waiting for
   somebody.
8 She can't have understood what
   I said. *or* She couldn't have
   understood what I said.
9 I must have forgotten to lock it.
10 My neighbours must have been
   having a party.
11 The driver can't have seen the red
   light. *or*
   The driver couldn't have seen …

UNIT 29

29.1
2 She might be busy.
3 She might be working.
4 She might want to be alone.
5 She might have been ill yesterday.
6 She might have gone home early.
7 She might have had to go home
   early.
8 She might have been working
   yesterday.
9 She might not want to see me.
10 She might not be working today.
11 She might not have been feeling
   well yesterday.
You can use **may** *instead of* **might** *in all
these sentences.*

29.2

2 be
3 have been
4 be waiting
5 have arrived / have come / be here

29.3

2 a She might be watching TV.
   b She might have gone out.
3 a It might be in the car.
   b You might have left it in the restaurant.
4 a He might have gone to bed early.
   b He might not have heard the doorbell.
   c He might have been in the shower.

You can use **may** *instead of* **might** *in all these sentences.*

29.4

3 might not have received it / might not have got it
4 couldn't have been an accident
5 couldn't have tried
6 might not have been American

UNIT 30

30.1

2 I might buy a Honda.
3 He might come on Saturday.
4 I might hang it in the dining room.
5 She might go to university.

You can use **may** *instead of* **might** *in all these sentences.*

30.2

2 might wake
3 might bite
4 might need
5 might slip
6 might break

You can use **may** *instead of* **might** *in all these sentences.*

30.3

2 might be able to meet
3 might have to work
4 might have to leave
5 might have to sell
6 might be able to fix

You can use **may** *instead of* **might** *in all these sentences.*

30.4

2 I might not go out this evening.
3 We might not be able to get tickets for the game.
4 Sam might not be able to go out with us tonight.

You can use **may** *instead of* **might** *in all these sentences.*

30.5

2 I might as well go
3 We might as well paint the bathroom.
4 We might as well watch it. / ... watch the film.

You can use **may** *instead of* **might** *in all these sentences.*

UNIT 31

31.1

3 We had to close
4 She has to leave *or* She'll have to leave / She will have to leave
5 do you have to be
6 I have to go *or* I'll have to go / I will have to go
7 Does he have to travel
8 do you have to go *or* will you have to go
9 did you have to wait
10 had to do

31.2

3 have to make
4 don't have to do
5 had to ask
6 don't have to pay *or* won't have to pay / will not have to pay
7 didn't have to go
8 has to make
9 will have to drive *or* is going to have to drive

31.3

3 *OK* (have to *is also correct*)
4 He **has to** work.
5 I **had to** work late yesterday evening.
6 *OK* (have to *is also correct*)
7 She **has had to** wear glasses since she was very young.
   For the present perfect (**has had**) *with* **for** *and* **since**, *see Units* **11–12**.

31.4

3 don't have to
4 mustn't
5 don't have to
6 mustn't
7 doesn't have to
8 mustn't
9 mustn't
10 don't have to

UNIT 32

32.1

2 don't need to
3 must
4 mustn't
5 don't need to
6 needn't
7 must ... mustn't
8 needn't ... must

32.2

2 needn't come
3 needn't walk
4 needn't ask
5 needn't explain

32.3

2 You needn't have walked home. You could have taken a taxi.
3 You needn't have stayed at a hotel. You could have stayed with us.
4 She needn't have phoned me in the middle of the night. She could have waited until the morning.
5 You needn't have shouted at me. You could have been more patient.
6 You needn't have left without saying anything. You could have said goodbye to me.

32.4

3 You needn't worry / You don't need to worry / You don't have to worry
4 You needn't wait / You don't need to wait / You don't have to wait
5 *OK* (You needn't keep *is also correct*)
6 I didn't need to go / I didn't have to go
7 *OK*

UNIT 33

33.1

2 You should look for another job.
3 He shouldn't go to bed so late.
4 You should take a photo.
5 She shouldn't use her car so much.
6 He should put some pictures on the walls.

33.2

2 I don't think you should go out. / I think you should stay at home.
3 I think you should apply for it. / ... for the job.
4 I don't think the government should increase taxes.

33.3

3 should come
4 should do
5 should have done
6 should have won
7 should win
8 should be
9 should have turned

33.4

3 We should have reserved a table.
4 The shop should be open (now). /
   The shop should have
   opened by now. *or*
   It should …
5 She shouldn't be doing 50. /
   She shouldn't be driving so fast. /
   She should be driving more slowly.
6 I should have written down her
   address. / I should have written her
   address down. *or*
   I should have written it down.
7 The driver in front shouldn't have
   stopped without warning. / …
   shouldn't have stopped so suddenly.
8 I should have been looking where I
   was going. / I shouldn't have been
   looking behind me.

UNIT 34

34.1

2 I should stay / I stay / I stayed
   a little longer
3 they should visit / they visit / they
   visited the museum after lunch
4 we should pay / we pay / we paid
   the rent by Friday
5 I should go / I go / I went away for
   a few days

34.2

1 b *OK*
   c *OK*
   d *wrong*
2 a *OK*
   b *wrong*
   c *OK*

34.3

2 should say
3 should worry
4 should leave
5 should ask
6 should listen

34.4

2 If it should rain
3 If there should be any problems
4 If anyone should ask
5 Should there be any problems
6 Should anyone ask (where I'm going)

34.5

2 I should keep
3 I should phone
4 I should get

UNIT 35

35.1

2 You'd better put a plaster on it.
3 We'd better reserve a table.
4 You'd better not go to work (this
   morning).
5 I'd better pay my phone bill (soon). /
   I'd better pay it (soon).
6 I'd better not disturb him.

35.2

3 'd better
4 should
5 should
6 'd better
7 should
8 should

35.3

1 b 'd/had
   c close/shut
   d hadn't
2 a did
   b was done
   c thought

35.4

2 It's time I had a holiday.
3 It's time the train left.
4 It's time I/we had a party.
5 It's time some changes were made. /
   It's time the company made some
   changes.
6 It's time he tried something else.

UNIT 36

36.1

Example answers:

2 I wouldn't like to be a teacher.
3 I'd love to learn to fly a plane.
4 It would be nice to have a big garden.
5 I'd like to go to Mexico.

36.2

2 'd enjoy / would enjoy
3 'd have enjoyed / would have
   enjoyed
4 would you do
5 'd have stopped / would have
   stopped
6 would have been
7 'd be / would be
8 'd have passed / would have passed
9 would have

36.3

2 e
3 b
4 f
5 a
6 d

36.4

2 He promised he'd call. /
   … he would call.
3 You promised you wouldn't tell her.
4 They promised they'd wait (for us). /
   … they would wait.

36.5

2 wouldn't tell
3 wouldn't speak
4 wouldn't let

36.6

2 would shake
3 would always help
4 would share
5 would always forget

UNIT 37

37.1

2 Can/Could I leave a message (for
   her)? *or*
   Can/Could you give her a message?
3 Can/Could you tell me how to get to
   the station? *or*
   … the way to the station? *or*
   … where the station is?
4 Can/Could I try on these trousers?
   or
   Can/Could I try these (trousers) on?
5 Can I give/offer you a lift?

37.2

3 Do you think you could check these
   forms (for me)? / … check them
   (for me)?
4 Do you mind if I leave work early?
5 Do you think you could turn the
   music down? / … turn it down?
6 Is it OK if I close the window?
7 Do you think I could have a look at
   your paper? / … at your newspaper?

37.3

2 Can/Could/Would you show me?
   or Do you think you could show
   me? *or* … do it for me?
3 Would you like to sit down?
   or Would you like a seat?
   or Can I offer you a seat?
4 Can/Could/Would you slow down?
   or Do you think you could … ?
5 Can/Could/May I/we have the
   bill, please? *or* Do you think I/we
   could have … ?
6 Would you like to borrow it?

UNIT 38

38.1

2	b	5	b
3	a	6	a
4	b	7	b

Key to Exercises

38.2

2 bought
3 asked
4 would lose
5 'd be / would be
6 were … stopped
7 gave … 'd have / would have

38.3

2 If he did his driving test now, he'd fail (it) / … he would fail (it).
3 If we stayed at a hotel, it would cost too much.
4 If she left her job, she wouldn't get another one.
5 If we invited Ben (to the party), we'd have to invite his friends too. / … we would have to …
6 If I told him what happened, he wouldn't believe me.

38.4

Example answers:
2 I'd be very angry if somebody broke into my house.
3 If you bought a car, it would cost you a lot to maintain it.
4 I'd be surprised if the economic situation improved.
5 Would you mind if I didn't go out with you tonight?

UNIT 39

39.1

3 I'd help / I would help
4 we lived
5 we'd live / we would live
6 It would taste
7 were/was
8 I wouldn't wait … I'd go / I would go
9 you didn't go
10 there weren't … there wouldn't be

39.2

2 I'd buy it / I would buy it if it weren't/wasn't so expensive.
3 We'd go out / We would go out more often if we could afford it.
4 If I didn't have to work late, I could meet you tomorrow. *or* … I'd meet / I would meet … *or* … I'd be able to meet …
5 We could have lunch outside if it weren't raining / wasn't raining.
6 If I wanted his advice, I'd ask for it / I would ask for it.

39.3

2 I wish I had a computer.
3 I wish Helen were/was here.
4 I wish it weren't/wasn't (so) cold.
5 I wish I didn't live in a big city.
6 I wish I could go to the party.
7 I wish I didn't have to get up early tomorrow.
8 I wish I knew something about cars.
9 I wish I were feeling / was feeling better.

39.4

Example answers:
1 I wish I was at home.
2 I wish I had a big garden.
3 I wish I could tell jokes.
4 I wish I was taller.

UNIT 40

40.1

2 If he'd missed / he had missed (the train), he'd have missed / he would have missed (his flight too).
3 I'd have forgotten / I would have forgotten (if) you hadn't reminded
4 I'd had / I had had (your address), I'd have sent / I would have sent (you an email)
5 we'd have enjoyed / we would have enjoyed (it more if the weather) had been (better)
6 It would have been (quicker if) I'd walked / I had walked
7 I were / I was
8 I'd been / I had been

40.2

2 If the road hadn't been icy, the accident wouldn't have happened.
3 If I'd known / If I had known that Joe had to get up early, I'd have woken / I would have woken him up.
4 If I hadn't lost my phone (*or* If I'd had my phone), I'd have called you / I would have called you / I would have been able to call you / I could have called you
5 If Karen hadn't been wearing a seat belt, she'd have been injured / she would have been injured (in the crash). *or* … she might/could have been injured
6 If you'd had / If you had had breakfast, you wouldn't be hungry now.
7 If I'd had / If I had had enough money, I'd have got / I would have got a taxi.

40.3

2 I wish I'd applied / I wish I had applied for it. *or* … for the job.
3 I wish I'd learned / I wish I had learned to play a musical instrument (when I was younger). *or* I wish I could play … / I wish I was able to play
4 I wish I hadn't painted it red. *or* … the gate red.
5 I wish I'd brought / I wish I had brought my camera. *or* I wish I had my camera (with me)
6 I wish they'd phoned / I wish they had phoned me first (to say they were coming). *or* I wish I'd known / I wish I had known they were coming.

UNIT 41

41.1

2 hope
3 wish
4 wished
5 hope
6 wish … hope

41.2

2 I wish Jane/she would come. *or* … would hurry up.
3 I wish somebody would give me a job.
4 I wish the/that baby would stop crying.
5 I wish you would buy some new clothes. *or* I wish you would get some new clothes.
6 I wish you wouldn't drive so fast.
7 I wish you wouldn't leave the door open (all the time).
8 I wish people wouldn't drop litter in the street.

41.3

2 *OK*
3 I wish I had more free time.
4 I wish our flat was/were a bit bigger.
5 *OK*
6 *OK*
7 I wish everything wasn't/weren't so expensive.

41.4

3 I knew
4 I'd taken / I had taken
5 I could come
6 I wasn't / I weren't
7 they'd hurry up / they would hurry up
8 we didn't have
9 we could have stayed
10 it wasn't / it weren't
11 he'd decide / he would decide
12 we hadn't gone

UNIT 42

42.1

2 is made
3 was damaged
4 were invited
5 are shown
6 are held
7 was written … was translated
8 were overtaken
9 is surrounded

42.2

2 When was television invented?
3 How are mountains formed?
4 When were antibiotics discovered?
5 What is silver used for?

42.3

3 covers
4 is covered
5 are locked
6 was sent … arrived
7 sank … was rescued
8 died … were brought up
9 grew up
10 was stolen
11 disappeared
12 did Sue resign
13 was Ben fired
14 is owned
15 called … was injured …
     wasn't needed
16 were these pictures taken …
     Did you take
17 'm not bothered / am not bothered

42.4

2 All flights were cancelled because of
    fog.
3 This road isn't used much.
4 I was accused of stealing money.
5 How are languages learned/learnt?
6 We were warned not to go out
    alone.

UNIT 43

43.1

2 it can't be broken
3 it can be eaten
4 it can't be used
5 it can't be seen
6 it can be carried

43.2

3 be made
4 be spent
5 have been repaired
6 be carried
7 be woken up
8 have been arrested
9 have been caused

43.3

2 The computer is being used at the
    moment.
3 I didn't realise that our conversation
    was being recorded.
4 … we found that the game had been
    cancelled.
5 A new ring road is being built round
    the city.
6 A new hospital has been built near
    the airport.

43.4

3 It's been stolen! / It has been stolen!
4 Somebody has taken it. *or*
     … taken my umbrella.
5 He's been promoted. / He has been
    promoted.
6 It's being redecorated. / It is being
    redecorated.
7 It's working again. / It is working
    again.
     It's been repaired. / It has been
    repaired.
8 The furniture had been moved.
9 He hasn't been seen since then.
10 I haven't seen her for ages.
11 Have you ever been mugged?

UNIT 44

44.1

2 I was asked some difficult questions
    at the interview.
3 Amy was given a present by her
    colleagues when she retired.
4 I wasn't told about the meeting.
5 How much will you be paid for your
    work?
6 I think Tom should have been
    offered the job.
7 Have you been shown what to do?

44.2

2 being invited
3 being given
4 being knocked down
5 being treated
6 being stuck

44.3

2–6

• Ludwig van Beethoven was born in
  1770.
• Galileo was born in 1564.
• Mahatma Gandhi was born in 1869.
• Michael Jackson was born in 1958.
  Martin Luther King was born in 1929.
• Elvis Presley was born in 1935.
• William Shakespeare was born in
  1564.
• Leonardo da Vinci was born in 1452.

7 I was born in …

44.4

2 got stung
3 get used
4 got stolen
5 get paid
6 got stopped
7 get damaged
8 get asked

UNIT 45

45.1

2 The weather is expected to be good
    tomorrow.
3 The thieves are believed to have got
    in through a window in the roof.
4 Many people are reported to be
    homeless after the floods.
5 The prisoner is thought to have
    escaped by climbing over a wall.
6 The man is alleged to have been
    driving at 110 miles an hour.
7 The building is reported to have
    been badly damaged by the fire.
8 a The company is said to be losing a
       lot of money.
    b The company is believed to have
       lost a lot of money last year.
    c The company is expected to make
       a loss this year.

45.2

2 He is supposed to know a lot of
    famous people.
3 He is supposed to be very rich.
4 He is supposed to have twelve
    children.
5 He is supposed to have been an
    actor when he was younger.

45.3

2 You're / You are supposed to be my
    friend.
3 I'm / I am supposed to be on a diet.
4 It was supposed to be a joke.
5 Or maybe it's / it is supposed to
    be a flower.
6 You're / You are supposed to be
    working.

45.4

2 're / are supposed to start
3 was supposed to phone
4 aren't / 're not / are not supposed
    to block
5 was supposed to depart

UNIT 46

46.1

1 b
2 a
3 a
4 b

46.2

2 Sarah has her car serviced once a year.
3 It cost twelve pounds to have my suit cleaned.
4 The last time I had my eyes tested was two years ago.
5 We've had some new cupboards fitted in the kitchen.
6 We need to get this document translated as soon as possible.

46.3

2 I had it cut.
3 We had them cleaned.
4 He had it built.
5 I had them delivered.

46.4

2 have another key made
3 you had your hair cut
4 Do you have a newspaper delivered
5 we're having / we are having a garage built
6 Have you had the washing machine fixed / Did you have the washing machine fixed
7 have your ears pierced
9 She had her credit cards stolen.
10 We all had our bags searched.

UNIT 47

47.1

2 He said (that) his father wasn't very well.
3 He said (that) Rachel and Mark were getting married next month.
4 He said (that) his sister had had a baby.
5 He said (that) he didn't know what Joe was doing.
6 He said (that) he'd seen / he had seen Helen at a party in June and she'd seemed / she had seemed fine. *or* He said (that) he saw Helen ... and she seemed ...
7 He said (that) he hadn't seen Amy recently.
8 He said (that) he wasn't enjoying his job very much.
9 He said (that) I could come and stay at his place if I was ever in London.
10 He said (that) his car had been stolen a few days ago.
    or ... his car was stolen a few days ago.
11 He said (that) he wanted to go on holiday, but (he) couldn't afford it.
12 He said (that) he'd tell / he would tell Chris he'd seen / he had seen me. *or* ... he saw me.

47.2

Example answers:
2 she wasn't coming / she was going somewhere else / she couldn't come
3 they didn't like each other / they didn't get on with each other / they couldn't stand each other
4 he didn't know anyone
5 she would be away / she was going away
6 you were staying at home
7 he couldn't speak / he didn't speak any other languages
8 he'd seen you / he saw you   last weekend

UNIT 48

48.1

2 But you said you didn't like fish.
3 But you said you couldn't drive.
4 But you said she had a very well-paid job.
5 But you said you didn't have any brothers or sisters.
6 But you said you'd / you had never been to the United States.
7 But you said you were working tomorrow evening.
8 But you said she was a friend of yours.

48.2

2	Tell	7	tell ... said
3	Say	8	tell ... say
4	said	9	told
5	told	10	said
6	said		

48.3

2 her to slow down
3 her not to worry
4 asked Tom to give me a hand
   or ... to help me
5 asked me to open my bag
6 asked him to get (me) a paper
7 told him to mind his own business
8 asked her to marry him
9 told her not to wait (for me) if I was late

UNIT 49

49.1

2 Were you born there?
3 Are you married?
4 How long have you been married?
5 Have you got (any) children?
   or Do you have (any) children?
6 How old are they?
7 What do you do?
8 What does your wife do?

49.2

3 Who paid it? / Who paid the bill?
4 What happened?
5 What did she/Diane say?
6 Who does it / this book belong to?
7 Who lives in that house? / Who lives there?
8 What did you fall over?
9 What fell off the shelf?
10 What does it / this word mean?
11 Who did you borrow it from? / ... borrow the money from?
12 What are you worried about?

49.3

2 How is cheese made?
3 When was the computer invented?
4 Why isn't Sue working today?
5 What time are your friends coming?
6 Why was the trip cancelled?
7 Where was your mother born?
8 Why didn't you come to the party?
9 How did the accident happen?
10 Why doesn't this machine work?

49.4

2 Don't you like him?
3 Isn't it good?
4 Haven't you got any? *or* Don't you have any?

UNIT 50

50.1

2	c	6	c
3	a	7	b
4	b	8	a
5	b		

50.2

2 How far is it to the airport?
3 I wonder how old Tom is.
4 When is Lisa going on holiday?
5 Could you tell me where the post office is?
6 I don't know whether anyone was injured in the accident.
7 Do you know what time you will arrive tomorrow?

50.3

2 He asked me where I'd been. / ... where I had been.
3 He asked me how long I'd been back. / ... how long I had been back.
4 He asked me what I was doing now.
5 He asked me why I'd come back. / ... why I had come back. *or* ... why I came back.
6 He asked me where I was living.
7 He asked me if/whether I was glad to be back.
8 He asked me if/whether I had any plans to go away again.
9 He asked me if/whether I could help him find a job.

UNIT 51

51.1
2 doesn't
3 was
4 will
5 am … isn't *or* 'm not … is *or*
   can … can't *or* can't … can *or*
   am … can't *or* can't … is
6 should
7 won't
8 do
9 didn't
10 would … could … can't

51.2
3 Do you? I don't.
4 Didn't you? I did.
5 Haven't you? I have.
6 Did you? I didn't.

51.3
Example answers:
3 So did I. *or*
   Did you? What did you watch?
4 Neither will I. *or*
   Won't you? Where will you be?
5 So do I. *or*
   Do you? What sort of books do you like?
6 So would I. *or*
   Would you? Where would you like to live?
7 Neither can I. *or*
   Can't you? Why not?

51.4
2 I hope so.
3 I expect so.
4 I don't think so.
5 I'm afraid not.
6 I'm afraid so.
7 I suppose so.
8 I hope not.
9 I think so.

UNIT 52

52.1
3 don't you
4 were you
5 does she
6 isn't he
7 hasn't she
8 can't you
9 will they
10 aren't there
11 shall we
12 is it
13 aren't I
14 would you
15 hasn't she
16 should I
17 had he
18 will you

52.2
2 It's (very) expensive, isn't it?
3 The course was great, wasn't it?
4 You've had your hair cut, haven't you? *or*
   You had your hair cut, didn't you?
5 She has a good voice, hasn't she? *or*
   She's got / She has got a good voice, hasn't she? *or* She has a good voice, doesn't she?
6 It doesn't look very good, does it?
7 This bridge isn't very safe, is it? *or*
   … doesn't look very safe, does it?

52.3
2 Joe, you couldn't give me a hand (with this table), could you?
3 Kate, you don't know where Sarah is, do you? *or* … you haven't seen Sarah, have you?
4 Helen, you haven't got a bicycle pump, have you? *or* … you don't have a bicycle pump, do you?
5 Ann, you couldn't take me to the station, could you? *or*
   … you couldn't give me a lift to the station, could you?
6 Robert, you haven't seen my keys, have you?

UNIT 53

53.1
2 playing tennis
3 driving too fast
4 going swimming
5 breaking the DVD player
6 waiting a few minutes

53.2
2 making
3 listening
4 applying
5 reading
6 living
7 using
8 forgetting
9 paying
10 being
11 trying
12 losing

53.3
2 travelling
3 painting the kitchen
4 turning the music down
5 not interrupting

53.4
Example answers:
2 going out
3 sitting on the floor
4 having a picnic
5 laughing
6 breaking down

UNIT 54

54.1
2 to help him
3 to carry her bag (for her)
4 to meet at 8 o'clock
5 to tell him her name / to give him her name
6 not to tell anyone

54.2
2 to get
3 to live
4 (how) to use
5 to tell
6 say *or* to say

54.3
2 to look
3 walking
4 waiting
5 to finish
6 barking
7 to call
8 having
9 missing
10 to be

54.4
2 Tom appears to be worried about something.
3 You seem to know a lot of people.
4 My English seems to be getting better.
5 That car appears to have broken down.
6 David tends to forget things.
7 They claim to have solved the problem.

54.5
2 what to do
3 how to ride
4 whether to go
5 where to put
6 how to use

UNIT 55

55.1
2 or do you want me to lend you some
3 or would you like me to shut it
4 or would you like me to show you
5 or do you want me to repeat it
6 or do you want me to wait

55.2
2 to stay with them
3 her to call Joe.
4 him to be careful
5 her to give him a hand

55.3

2 I didn't expect it to rain.
3 Let him do what he wants.
4 Tim's glasses make him look older.
5 I want you to know the truth.
6 Sarah persuaded me to apply for the job.
7 My lawyer advised me not to say anything to the police.
8 I was warned not to believe everything he says.
9 Having a car enables you to get around more easily.

55.4

2 to go
3 to do
4 cry
5 to study
6 booking *or* you to book
7 borrow
8 to work
9 think

UNIT 56

56.1

2 driving
3 to go
4 raining
5 to win
6 asking
7 asking
8 to answer
9 causing
10 to do
11 being
12 to climb
13 to tell
14 talking… to see

56.2

2 He remembers going to Paris with his parents when he was eight.
3 He doesn't remember crying on his first day at school.
4 He can remember falling into the river.
5 He can't remember saying he wanted to be a doctor. *or* He can't remember wanting to be a doctor.
6 He doesn't remember being bitten by a dog.

56.3

1 b lending
   c to phone / to call
   d to say
   e leaving/putting
2 a saying
   b to say
   c wearing / having / taking / putting on
3 a to become
   b working
   c reading / looking at
4 a losing *or* to lose
   b to get / to feel
   c crying *or* to cry

UNIT 57

57.1

2 Try turning it the other way.
3 Have you tried restarting it?
4 You could try phoning his office.
5 Have you tried taking an aspirin?

57.2

2 It needs painting.
3 It needs cutting.
4 They need tightening.
5 It needs emptying.

57.3

1 b knocking
   c to put
   d asking
   e to reach
   f to concentrate
2 a to go
   b looking
   c cleaning
   d cutting
   e You don't need to iron …
      It doesn't need ironing
3 a overhearing
   b get *or* to get
   c smiling
   d make *or* to make

UNIT 58

58.1

Example answers:
2 I don't mind playing cards.
3 I don't like being alone. *or* … to be alone.
4 I enjoy going to museums.
5 I love cooking. *or* I love to cook.

58.2

2 She likes teaching biology.
3 He likes taking pictures.
   or He likes to take pictures.
4 I didn't like working there.
5 She likes studying medicine.
6 He doesn't like being famous.
7 She doesn't like taking risks.
   or She doesn't like to take risks.
8 I like to know things in advance.

58.3

2 to sit
3 waiting
4 going *or* to go
5 to get
6 being
7 to come / to go
8 living
9 to talk
10 to have / to know / to get / to hear / to be told

58.4

2 I would like / I'd like to have seen the programme.
3 I would hate / I'd hate to have lost my watch.
4 I would love / I'd love to have met your parents.
5 I wouldn't like to have been alone.
6 I would prefer / I'd prefer to have travelled by train.

UNIT 59

59.1

Example answers:
2 I prefer basketball to football.
3 I prefer going to the cinema to watching DVDs at home.
4 I prefer being very busy to having nothing to do.
6 I prefer to go to the cinema rather than watch DVDs at home.
7 I prefer to be very busy rather than have nothing to do.

59.2

3 prefer
4 eat/stay
5 I'd rather (wait) / I'd prefer to (wait)
6 to go
7 I'd rather (think) / I'd prefer to (think)
8 I'd prefer to stand.
9 go
11 I'd prefer to go for a swim rather than play tennis.
12 I'd rather eat at home than go to a restaurant.
13 I'd prefer to think about it for a while rather than decide now.
14 I'd rather listen to some music than watch TV.

59.3

2 (would you rather) I paid (it)
3 would you rather I did it
4 would you rather I phoned her

59.4

2 stayed/remained/waited
3 stay
4 didn't
5 were
6 didn't

UNIT 60

60.1
2 applying for the job
3 remembering names
4 winning the lottery
5 being late
6 eating at home, we went to a restaurant
7 having to queue *or* queuing
8 playing very well

60.2
2 by standing on a chair
3 by turning a key
4 by borrowing too much money
5 by driving too fast
6 by putting some pictures on the walls

60.3
2 paying/settling
3 going
4 using
5 going
6 being/travelling/sitting
7 asking/telling/consulting
8 doing/having
9 turning/going
10 taking

60.4
2 I'm looking forward to seeing her. / … seeing Kate.
3 I'm not looking forward to going to the dentist (tomorrow).
4 She's looking forward to leaving school (next summer).
5 I'm looking forward to playing tennis (tomorrow).

UNIT 61

61.1
1 When Jack started working in this job, he wasn't **used to driving** two hours to work every morning, but after some time he **got used to** it. Now it's no problem for him. He**'s used to driving** two hours every morning. / He **is used to driving** …
2 She **wasn't used to working** nights and it took her a few months to **get used to** it. Now, after a year, it's OK for her. She**'s used to working** nights. / She **is used to working** …

61.2
2 No, I'm used to sleeping on the floor.
3 I'm used to working long hours.
4 Yes, I'm not used to going to bed so late.

61.3
2 They soon got used to her. / … to the/their new teacher.
3 She had to get used to living in a much smaller house.
4 (*example answers*) They'll have to get used to the weather. / … to the food. / … to speaking a foreign language.

61.4
2 drink
3 eating
4 having
5 have
6 go
7 be
8 being
9 live … living

UNIT 62

62.1
2 doing
3 coming/going
4 spending/having
5 buying/having
6 seeing
7 watching
8 solving
9 buying/having

62.2
2 of causing
3 from walking (*or* stop people walking)
4 for interrupting
5 of using
6 of doing
7 from escaping (*or* prevent the prisoner escaping)
8 on telling
9 to eating
10 for being
11 for inviting
12 of (not) wearing

62.3
2 on taking Ann to the station
3 on getting married
4 Sue for coming to see her
5 (to me) for not phoning earlier
6 me of being selfish

UNIT 63

63.1
2 There's no point in working if you don't need money.
3 There's no point in trying to study if you feel tired.
4 There's no point in hurrying if you've got plenty of time.

63.2
2 asking David
3 in going out
4 phoning her/Lisa
5 complaining (about what happened)
6 keeping

63.3
2 remembering people's names
3 getting a job
4 getting a ticket for the game
5 understanding him

63.4
2 reading
3 packing / getting ready
4 watching
5 going/climbing/walking
6 getting/being

63.5
2 went swimming
3 go skiing
4 goes riding
5 gone shopping

UNIT 64

64.1
2 I opened the box to see what was in it.
3 I'm saving money to go to Canada.
4 I need a knife to chop these onions.
5 I'm wearing two sweaters to keep warm.
6 I phoned the police to report the accident.

64.2
2 to read
3 to walk / to go on foot
4 to drink
5 to put / to carry
6 to discuss / to consider / to talk about
7 to go / to travel
8 to talk / to speak
9 to wear / to put on
10 to celebrate
11 to help / to assist

64.3
2 for
3 to
4 to
5 for
6 to
7 for
8 for … to

64.4

2   so that I wouldn't be cold.
3   so that he could contact me. /
    … would be able to contact me.
4   so that nobody else would hear our
    conversation. / so that nobody else
    could hear … / … would be able to
    hear …
5   so that we can start the meeting
    on time. / so that we'll be able to
    start …
6   so that we wouldn't forget anything.
7   so that the car behind me could
    overtake. / … would be able to
    overtake.

UNIT 65

65.1

2   This machine is easy to use.
3   The window was very difficult to
    open.
4   Some words are impossible to
    translate.
5   A car is expensive to maintain.
6   That chair isn't safe to stand on.

65.2

2   It's an easy mistake to make.
3   It's a nice place to live.   or
    … a nice place to live in.
4   It was a good game to watch.

65.3

2   It's careless of you to make the same
    mistake again and again.
3   It was nice of them to invite me (to
    stay with them). / It was nice of Dan
    and Jenny to …
4   It's inconsiderate of them to make
    so much noise. / It's inconsiderate of
    the neighbours to …

65.4

2   I'm / I am   glad to hear   or
    I was glad to hear
3   We were surprised to see
4   Pleased to meet

65.5

2   Paul was the last (person) to arrive.
3   Emily was the only student to pass
    (the exam). / … the only one to pass
    (the exam).
4   I was the second   customer/person
    to complain (about the service).
5   Neil Armstrong was the first
    person/man   to walk on the moon.

65.6

2   're/are   bound to be
3   's/is   sure to forget
4   's/is   not likely to rain   or
    isn't likely to rain
5   's/is   likely to be

UNIT 66

66.1

3   I'm afraid of losing it.
4   I was afraid to tell her.
5   We were afraid of missing our train.
6   We were afraid to look.
7   I was afraid of dropping it.
8   a   I was afraid to eat it.
    b   I was afraid of getting sick.

66.2

2   in starting
3   to read
4   in getting
5   to know
6   in looking

66.3

2   sorry to hear
3   sorry for saying /
    sorry about saying / sorry I said
4   sorry to disturb
5   sorry for losing / sorry about losing /
    sorry I lost

66.4

1   b   to leave
    c   from leaving
2   a   to solve
    b   in solving
3   a   of/about going
    b   to go
    c   to go
    d   to going
4   a   to buy
    b   on buying
    c   to buy
    d   of buying

UNIT 67

67.1

2   arrive
3   take it / do it
4   it ring
5   him play   or   him playing
6   you lock it / you do it
7   her fall

67.2

2   We saw David and Helen playing
    tennis.
3   We saw Clare eating in a restaurant. /
    … having a meal in a restaurant.
4   We heard Bill playing his guitar.
5   We could smell the dinner burning.
6   We saw Linda   jogging/running.

67.3

3   tell
4   crying
5   riding
6   say
7   run … climb
8   explode
9   crawling
10   slam
11   sleeping

UNIT 68

68.1

2   Amy was sitting in an armchair
    reading a book.
3   Sue opened the door carefully trying
    not to make a noise.
4   Sarah went out saying she would be
    back in an hour.
5   Lisa was in London for two years
    working in a bookshop.
6   Anna walked around the town
    looking at the sights and taking
    pictures.

68.2

2   I fell asleep watching TV.
3   A friend of mine slipped and fell
    getting off a bus.
4   I got very wet walking home in the
    rain.
5   Laura had an accident driving to
    work yesterday.
6   Two people were overcome by
    smoke trying to put out the fire.

68.3

2   Having bought our tickets, we went
    into the theatre.
3   Having had lunch, they continued
    their journey.
4   Having done the shopping, I went for
    a cup of coffee.

68.4

2   Thinking they might be hungry, …
3   Being a vegetarian, …
4   Not knowing his email address, …
5   Having travelled a lot, …
6   Not being able to speak the local
    language, …
7   Having spent nearly all our money, …

UNIT 69

69.1

3   We went to **a** very nice restaurant …
4   OK
5   I use **a** toothbrush …
6   … if there's **a** bank near here?
7   … for **an** insurance company
8   OK
9   OK
10   … we stayed in **a** big hotel.
11   … I hope we come to **a** petrol
    station soon.
12   … I have **a** problem.
13   … It's **a** very interesting idea.
14   John has **an** interview for **a** job
    tomorrow.
15   … It's **a** good game.
16   OK
17   Jane was wearing **a** beautiful
    necklace.

69.2

3   a key
4   a coat
5   sugar
6   a biscuit
7   electricity
8   an interview
9   blood
10 a question
11 a moment
12 a decision

69.3

2   days
3   meat
4   a queue
5   jokes
6   friends
7   people
8   air
9   patience
10 an umbrella
11 languages
12 space

UNIT 70

70.1

2   a a paper
    b paper
3   a Light
    b a light
4   a time
    b a wonderful time
5   a nice room
6   advice
7   nice weather
8   bad luck
9   job
10 journey
11 total chaos
12 some bread
13 doesn't
14 Your hair is … it
15 The damage

70.2

2   information
3   chairs
4   furniture
5   hair
6   progress
7   job
8   work
9   permission
10 advice
11 experience
12 experiences

70.3

2   I'd like some information about places to see in the town.
3   Can you give me (some) advice about which courses to do? / … courses I can do?
4   What time is the news (on)?
5   It's a beautiful view, isn't it?
6   What horrible/awful weather!

UNIT 71

71.1

3   It's a vegetable.
4   It's a game. / It's a board game.
5   They're birds.
6   It's a (tall/high) building.
7   They're planets.
8   It's a flower.
9   They're rivers.
10 They're musical instruments.
12 He was a writer / a poet / a playwright / a dramatist.
13 He was a scientist / a physicist.
14 They were US presidents / American presidents / presidents of the USA.
15 She was an actor / an actress / a film actress / a film star / a movie star.
16 They were singers / musicians.
17 They were painters / artists.

71.2

2   He's a waiter.
3   She's a journalist.
4   He's a surgeon.
5   He's a chef.
6   He's a plumber.
7   She's a tour guide.
8   She's an interpreter.

71.3

4   a
5   an
6   – (You're always asking questions!)
7   a
8   Some
9   – (Do you like staying in hotels?)
10 – (I've got sore feet.)
11 a
12 some
13 a … a
14 – (Those are nice shoes.)
15 some
16 You need **a** visa to visit **some** countries
17 Jane is **a** teacher. Her parents were teachers too.
18 He's **a** liar. He's always telling lies.

UNIT 72

72.1

1   … and **a** magazine. **The** newspaper is in my bag, but I can't remember where I put **the** magazine.
2   I saw **an** accident this morning. **A** car crashed into **a** tree. **The** driver of **the** car wasn't hurt, but **the** car was badly damaged.
3   … **a** blue one and **a** grey one. **The** blue one belongs to my neighbours; I don't know who **the** owner of **the** grey one is.
4   My friends live in **an** old house in **a** small village. There is **a** beautiful garden behind **the** house. I would like to have **a** garden like that.

72.2

1   a a
    b the
    c the
2   a a
    b a
    c the
3   a a
    b the
    c the
4   a an … The
    b the
    c the
5   a the
    b a
    c a

72.3

2   **the** dentist
3   **the** door
4   **a** mistake
5   **the** bus station
6   **a** problem
7   **the** post office
8   **the** floor
9   **the** book
10 **a** job in **a** bank
11 **a** small apartment in **the** city centre
12 **a** supermarket at **the** end of **the** street

72.4

Example answers:

2   About once a year.
3   Once or twice a year.
4   50 kilometres an hour.
5   About seven hours a night.
6   Two or three times a week.
7   About two hours a day.
8   About £20 a day.

UNIT 73

73.1

2 **a** nice holiday ... **the** best holiday
3 **the** nearest shop ... **the** end of this street
4 **a** lovely day ... **a** cloud in **the** sky
5 to **the** internet ... **the** same problem
6 **the** most expensive hotel ... **a** cheaper hotel
7 to travel **in space** ... go to **the** moon
8 **a** star ... **a** planet ... **the** largest planet in **the** solar system

73.2

2 watching TV
3 **the** radio
4 **The** television
5 had dinner
6 **the** same time
7 **the** capital
8 for breakfast
9 **the** ground ... **the** sky

73.3

2 **the** same thing
3 **Room 25** is on **the** second floor.
4 **The** moon goes round **the** earth every 27 days. *or*
   ... goes round **Earth** ...
5 **a** very hot day ... **the** hottest day of **the** year
6 We **had lunch** in **a** nice restaurant by **the** sea.
7 at **the** cinema
8 eat **a** good breakfast
9 on **the** wrong platform
10 **The** next train ... **from Platform 3**
11 You'll find **the** information you need at **the** top **of page 15**.

73.4

2 the sea
3 question 8
4 the cinema
5 breakfast
6 the gate
7 Gate 21

UNIT 74

74.1

2 to school
3 at home
4 to work
5 in hospital
6 at university
7 in bed
8 to prison

74.2

2 school
3 the school
4 School
5 ... get to and from school
   ... The school isn't very far.
6 school

74.3

1 c *OK*
   d the university
2 a *OK*
   b the hospital ... the hospital
   c *OK*
3 a *OK*
   b *OK*
   c the church
4 a *OK*
   b the prison
   c *OK*

74.4

2 in bed
3 after work
4 in the sea
5 like home
6 go to bed
7 The bed
8 at sea
9 work

UNIT 75

75.1

Example answers:
2–5
• I like cats.
• I don't like zoos.
• I don't mind snow.
• I'm not interested in boxing.

75.2

3 spiders
4 meat
5 the questions
6 the people
7 History
8 lies
9 The hotels
10 The water
11 the grass
12 patience

75.3

2 Apples
3 the apples
4 Women ... men
5 tea
6 The vegetables
7 Life
8 holidays (= 'holidays by the sea' in general)
9 education
10 the people
11 people ... aggression
12 All the books
13 the rooms
14 war
15 The First World War
16 films
17 the history of modern art
18 the marriage
19 Most people ... marriage ... family life ... society

UNIT 76

76.1

1 b the cheetah
   c the kangaroo (and the rabbit)
2 a the swan
   b the penguin
   c the owl
3 a the wheel
   b the laser
   c the telescope
4 a the rupee
   b the (Canadian) dollar
   c the ...

76.2

2 a
3 the
4 a
5 the
6 the
7 a
8 The

76.3

2 the injured
3 the unemployed
4 the sick
5 the rich ... the poor

76.4

2 a German   Germans
3 a Frenchman/Frenchwoman the French
4 a Russian   Russians
5 a Chinese   the Chinese
6 a Brazilian   Brazilians
7 an Englishman/Englishwoman the English
8 ...

UNIT 77

77.1

2 the
3 the ... the
4 – (President Kennedy was assassinated in 1963.)
5 the
6 – (I'm looking for Professor Brown.)

77.2

3 *OK*
4 **the** United States
5 **The** south of England ... **the** north
6 *OK*
7 **the** Channel
8 **the** Middle East
9 *OK*
10 **the** Swiss Alps
11 **The** UK
12 **The** Seychelles ... **the** Indian Ocean
13 *OK*
14 **The** river Volga ... **the** Caspian Sea

77.3

2 (in) South America
3 **the** Nile
4 Sweden
5 **the** United States
6 **the** Rockies
7 **the** Mediterranean
8 Australia
9 **the** Pacific
10 **the** Indian Ocean
11 **the** Thames
12 **the** Danube
13 Thailand
14 **the** Panama Canal
15 **the** Amazon

UNIT 78

78.1

2 Turner's in Carter Road
3 **the** Crown (Hotel) in Park Road
4 St Peter's in Market Street
5 **the** City Museum in George Street
6 Blackstone's (Books) in Forest Avenue
7 Mario's (Pizza) in George Street
8 Victoria Park at the end of Market Street

78.2

2 **The** Eiffel Tower
3 Buckingham Palace
4 **The** White House
5 **The** Kremlin
6 Broadway
7 **The** Acropolis
8 Gatwick Airport

78.3

2 Central Park
3 St James's Park
4 The Imperial Hotel … Baker Street
5 Dublin Airport
6 Liverpool University
7 Harrison's
8 the Park Plaza
9 The Statue of Liberty … New York Harbour
10 the Science Museum
11 IBM … British Telecom
12 The Classic
13 the Great Wall
14 The Times
15 Cambridge University Press
16 the College of Art

UNIT 79

79.1

3 shorts
4 a means
5 means
6 some scissors *or* a pair of scissors
7 a series
8 series
9 species

79.2

2 politics
3 economics
4 athletics
5 physics
6 gymnastics
7 electronics

79.3

2 don't
3 want
4 was
5 aren't
6 are
7 wasn't
8 does *or* do
9 they are
10 Do
11 is *or* are
12 enjoy

79.4

3 … wearing black jeans.
4 *OK*
5 … very nice **people**.
6 Ten pounds **isn't** …
7 … buy **some** new **pyjamas**. *or* … buy **a** new **pair of pyjamas**.
8 *OK* (The committee hasn't *is also correct*)
9 There was **a police officer / a policeman / a policewoman** …
10 What **are** the police …
11 **These** scissors **aren't** …
12 *OK*

UNIT 80

80.1

3 a job interview
4 (your) holiday pictures
5 milk chocolate
6 a factory inspector
7 a race horse
8 a horse race
9 running shoes
10 a university student
11 (your) exam results
12 the living room carpet
13 an oil company scandal
14 car factory workers
15 a road improvement scheme
16 a New York department store
17 a five-day course
18 a two-part question
19 a thirty-year-old man

80.2

2 seat belt
3 credit card
4 weather forecast
5 newspaper editor
6 shop window
7 room number
8 birthday party
9 truck driver

80.3

2 twenty-pound
3 ten-pound
4 15-minute
5 60 minutes
6 two-hour
7 twelve-storey
8 five days
9 Five-star
10 six years old
11 500-year-old
12 twelve-hour … 24-hour

UNIT 81

81.1

3 your friend's umbrella
4 *OK*
5 Charles's daughter
6 Helen and Dan's son
7 *OK*
8 last Monday's newspaper
9 *OK*
10 *OK*
11 Your children's friends
12 Our neighbours' garden
13 *OK*
14 David's hair
15 Katherine's party
16 *OK*
17 Mike's parents' car
18 *OK*
19 *OK* (the government's economic policy is *also correct*)

81.2

2 a boy's name
3 children's clothes
4 a girls' school
5 a bird's nest
6 a women's magazine

81.3

2 Last week's storm caused a lot of damage.
3 The town's only cinema has closed down.
4 Britain's weather is very changeable.
5 The region's main industry is tourism.

81.4

2 twenty minutes' walk
3 two weeks' holiday / fourteen days' holiday / a fortnight's holiday
4 an/one hour's sleep

Key to Exercises

UNIT 82

82.1
2 hurt himself
3 blame herself
4 Put yourself
5 enjoyed themselves
6 burn yourself
7 express myself

82.2
2 me
3 myself
4 us
5 yourself
6 you
7 ourselves
8 them
9 themselves

82.3
2 feel
3 dried myself
4 concentrate
5 defend yourself
6 meeting
7 relax

82.4
2 themselves
3 each other
4 each other
5 themselves
6 each other
7 ourselves
8 each other
9 introduced **ourselves** to **each other**

82.5
2 He cuts it himself.
3 No, I'll tell her myself.
4 Linda told me herself. / Linda herself told me. / Linda did herself.
5 Why can't you phone him yourself? / ... do it yourself?

UNIT 83

83.1
2 We met a relative of yours.
3 Jason borrowed a book of mine.
4 Lisa invited some friends of hers to her flat.
5 We had dinner with a neighbour of ours.
6 I went on holiday with two friends of mine.
7 Is that man a friend of yours?
8 I met a friend of Jane's at the party.
9 It's always been an ambition of mine (to travel round the world).

83.2
2 his own opinions
3 her own business
4 our own words
5 its own private beach

83.3
2 your own fault
3 her own ideas
4 your own problems
5 his own decisions

83.4
2 makes her own (clothes)
3 bake/make our own (bread)
4 clean your own (shoes)
5 write their own (songs)

83.5
2 my own
3 myself
4 himself
5 themselves
6 herself
7 their own
8 yourself
9 our own
10 her own

UNIT 84

84.1
3 There's / There is
4 there wasn't
5 Is it ... it's / it is
6 Is there
7 there was
8 It isn't / It's not
9 there isn't
10 It was
11 There wasn't
12 Is there ... there's / there is
13 there was ... It was
14 It was
15 It's / It is ... There's / There is

84.2
2 There's / There is a lot of salt in the soup. *or* ... too much salt ...
3 There was nothing in the box. *or* There wasn't anything in the box.
4 There's / There is a lot of violence in the film.
5 There were a lot of people in the shopping mall.
6 There is a lot to do in this town. / There is a lot happening in this town.

84.3
2 There may be
3 there will be / there'll be *or* there are going to be
4 There's going to be / There is going to be
5 There used to be
6 there should be
7 there wouldn't be

84.4
2 *OK*
3 **there** will be an opportunity
4 *OK*
5 **There** must have been a reason.
6 *OK*
7 **There's** sure to be a car park somewhere.
8 *OK*
9 **There** has been no change.
10 **There** used to be a church here
11 **there** would be somebody ... but **there** wasn't anybody.
12 *OK*

UNIT 85

85.1
2 some
3 any
4 any ... some
5 some
6 some ... any
7 any
8 any
9 some
10 any
11 some

85.2
2 somebody/someone
3 anybody/anyone
4 anything
5 something
6 somebody/someone ... anybody/anyone
7 something ... anybody/anyone
8 Anybody/Anyone
9 anybody/anyone
10 anywhere
11 somewhere
12 anywhere
13 anybody/anyone
14 something
15 Anybody/Anyone
16 anything
17 something
18 anybody/anyone ... anything

85.3

2 Any day
3 Anything
4 anywhere
5 Any job *or* Anything
6 Any time
7 Anybody/Anyone
8 Any newspaper *or* Any one

UNIT 86

86.1

3 no   8 No
4 any   9 no
5 None   10 any
6 none   11 none
7 any   12 no

86.2

2 Nobody/No-one.
3 None.
4 Nowhere.
5 None.
6 Nothing.
8 I wasn't talking to anybody/anyone.
9 I don't want any sugar.
10 I'm not going anywhere.
11 I didn't get any emails.
12 I didn't pay anything.

86.3

2 nobody/no-one
3 Nowhere
4 anything
5 **Nothing**. I couldn't find **anything** …
6 Nothing
7 anywhere
8 **Nobody/No-one** said **anything**.

86.4

2 nobody   6 Anything
3 anyone   7 anything
4 Anybody   8 any
5 Nothing   9 No-one … anyone

UNIT 87

87.1

3 a lot of salt
4 *OK*
5 It cost a lot
6 *OK*
7 many people   *or*   a lot of people
8 Mike travels a lot.
9 *OK*
10 a lot of money

87.2

2 He has (got) plenty of money.
3 There's plenty of room.
4 … she still has plenty to learn.
5 There is plenty to see.
6 There are plenty of hotels.

87.3

2 little   5 few
3 many   6 little
4 much   7 many

87.4

3 a few dollars
4 *OK*
5 a little time
6 *OK*
7 only a few words
8 a few months

87.5

2 a little   6 a little
3 a few   7 little
4 few   8 a few
5 little

UNIT 88

88.1

3 –
4 of
5 –
6 –
7 of
8 of
9 – (of *is also correct*)
10 –

88.2

3 of my spare time
4 accidents
5 of the buildings
6 of her friends
7 of the population
8 birds
9 of the players
10 of her opinions
11 European countries
12 (of) my dinner

88.3

Example answers:

2 the time
3 my friends
4 (of) the questions
5 the pictures / the photos / the photographs
6 (of) the money

88.4

2 All of them
3 none of us
4 some of it
5 none of them
6 None of it
7 Some of them
8 all of it

UNIT 89

89.1

2 Neither   4 Either
3 both   5 Neither

89.2

2 either
3 both
4 Neither of
5 **neither** driver … **both / both the / both of the** cars
6 both / both of

89.3

2 either of them
3 both of them
4 Neither of us
5 neither of them

89.4

3 Both Joe and Sam are on holiday.
4 Neither Joe nor Sam has (got) a car.
5 Brian neither watches TV nor reads newspapers.
6 The movie was both boring and long.
7 That man's name is either Richard or Robert.
8 I have neither the time nor the money to go on holiday.
9 We can leave either today or tomorrow.

89.5

2 either   5 any
3 any   6 either
4 none   7 neither

UNIT 90

90.1

3 Everybody/Everyone
4 Everything
5 all
6 everybody/everyone
7 everything
8 All
9 everybody/everyone
10 All
11 everything/all
12 Everybody/Everyone
13 All
14 everything

90.2

2 The whole team played well.
3 He ate the whole box (of chocolates).
4 They searched the whole house.
5 The whole family play/plays tennis.
6 Ann/She worked the whole day.
7 It rained the whole week.
8 Ann worked all day.
9 It rained all week.

90.3

2 every four hours
3 every four years
4 every five minutes
5 every six months

Key to Exercises

90.4

2 every day
3 all day
4 The whole building
5 every time
6 all the time
7 all my luggage

UNIT 91

91.1

3 Each   6 every
4 Every   7 each
5 Each   8 every

91.2

3 Every   8 every
4 Each   9 each
5 every   10 Every
6 every   11 each
7 each   12 each

91.3

2 Sonia and I had ten pounds each. / Sonia and I each had ten pounds.
3 Those postcards cost 80 pence each. / Those postcards are 80 pence each.
4 We paid £150 each. / We each paid £150.

91.4

2 everyone
3 every one
4 Everyone
5 every one

UNIT 92

92.1

2 A burglar is someone who breaks into a house to steal things.
3 A customer is someone who buys something from a shop.
4 A shoplifter is someone who steals from a shop.
5 A coward is someone who is not brave.
6 An atheist is someone who doesn't believe in God.
7 A pessimist is someone who expects the worst to happen.
8 A tenant is someone who pays rent to live in a house or apartment.

92.2

2 The waitress who/that served us was impolite and impatient.
3 The building that/which was destroyed in the fire has now been rebuilt.
4 The people who/that were arrested have now been released.
5 The bus that/which goes to the airport runs every half hour.

92.3

2 who/that runs away from home
3 that/which were hanging on the wall
4 that/which cannot be explained
5 who/that stole my wallet
6 that/which gives you the meaning of words
7 who/that invented the telephone
8 that/which can support life

92.4

3 the nearest shop **that/which** sells
4 the driver **who/that** caused
5 OK (the person **who** took *is also correct*)
6 a world **that/which** is changing
7 OK (some things about me **which** were *is also correct*)
8 the horse **that/which** won

UNIT 93

93.1

3 OK (the people **who/that** we met *is also correct*)
4 The people **who/that** work in the office
5 OK (the people **who/that** I work with *is also correct*)
6 OK (the money **that/which** I gave you *is also correct*)
7 the money **that/which** was on the table
8 OK (the worst film **that/which** you've ever seen *is also correct*)
9 the best thing **that/which** has ever happened to you

93.2

2 you're wearing   *or* that/which you're wearing
3 you're going to see   *or* that/which you're going to see
4 I/we wanted to visit   *or* that/which I/we wanted to visit
5 I/we invited to the party   *or* who/whom/that we invited …
6 you had to do   *or* that/which you had to do
7 I/we rented   *or* that/which I/we rented

93.3

2 the wedding we were invited to
3 the hotel you told me about
4 the job I applied for
5 the concert you went to
6 somebody you can rely on
7 the man you were with

93.4

3 – (that *is also correct*)
4 what
5 that
6 what
7 – (that *is also correct*)
8 what
9 – (that *is also correct*)

UNIT 94

94.1

2 whose wife is an English teacher
3 who owns a restaurant
4 whose ambition is to climb Everest
5 who have just got married
6 whose parents used to work in a circus

94.2

2 where I can get some water
3 (The) factory where I work
4 the hotel where Sue is staying
5 (the) park where I/we play football

94.3

2 where   6 where
3 who   7 whose
4 whose   8 whom
5 whom

94.4

Example answers:
2 The reason I left my job was that the salary was too low.
3 I'll never forget the time I got stuck in a lift.
4 Do you remember the day we first met?
5 The reason they don't have a car is that they don't need one.
6 2003 was the year Amanda got married.

UNIT 95

95.1

3 We often go to visit our friends in Cambridge, which is not far from London.
4 I went to see the doctor, who told me I needed to change my diet.
5 Steven, who/whom I've known for a very long time, is one of my closest friends.
6 Lisa, whose job involves a lot of travelling, is away from home a lot.
7 The new stadium, which can hold 90,000 people, will be finished next month.
8 Alaska, where my brother lives, is the largest state in the USA.
9 Our teacher, whose name I have forgotten, was very kind.

95.2

3 The strike at the factory, which began ten days ago, is now over.

4 I've found the book I was looking for this morning. *or* ... the book that/which I was looking for.

5 My car, which I've had for 15 years, has never broken down.

6 Few of the people who/that applied for the job had the necessary qualifications.

7 Amy showed me a picture of her son, who is a police officer.

95.3

2 My office, **which** is on the second floor, is very small.

3 *OK* (The office **that/which** I'm using ... *is also correct*)

4 Mark's father, **who** used to be in the army, now works for a TV company.

5 *OK* (The doctor **who** examined me ... *is also correct*)

6 The sun, **which** is one of millions of stars in the universe, provides us with heat and light.

UNIT 96

96.1

2 of which he's very proud

3 with whom we went on holiday

4 to which only members of the family were invited

96.2

2 most of which was useless

3 none of whom was suitable

4 one of which she hardly ever uses

5 half of which he gave to his parents

6 both of whom are lawyers

7 neither of which she replied to

8 only a few of whom I knew

9 (the) sides of which were lined with trees

10 the aim of which is to save money

96.3

2 Jane doesn't have a phone, which makes it difficult to contact her.

3 Alex has passed his exams, which is good news.

4 Our flight was delayed, which meant we had to wait three hours at the airport.

5 Kate offered to let me stay at her house, which was very kind of her.

6 The street I live in is very noisy at night, which makes it difficult to sleep sometimes.

7 Our car has broken down, which means we can't go away tomorrow.

UNIT 97

97.1

2 the man sitting next to me on the plane

3 The taxi taking us to the airport

4 a path leading to the river

5 A factory employing 500 people

6 a brochure containing the information I needed

97.2

2 The gate damaged in the storm

3 Most of the suggestions made at the meeting

4 The paintings stolen from the museum

5 the man arrested by the police

97.3

3 living

4 offering

5 called

6 blown

7 sitting ... reading

8 working ... studying

97.4

3 There's somebody coming.

4 There were a lot of people travelling.

5 There was nobody else staying there.

6 There was nothing written on it.

7 There's a course beginning next Monday.

UNIT 98

98.1

2 a exhausting
   b exhausted

3 a depressing
   b depressed
   c depressed

4 a exciting
   b exciting
   c excited

98.2

2 interested

3 exciting

4 embarrassing

5 embarrassed

6 amazed

7 amazing

8 amused

9 terrifying ... shocked

10 bored ... boring

11 boring ... interesting

98.3

2	bored	7	boring
3	confusing	8	exhausted
4	disgusting	9	excited
5	interested	10	amusing
6	annoyed	11	interesting

UNIT 99

99.1

2 an unusual gold ring

3 a beautiful old house

4 black leather gloves

5 an old American film

6 a long thin face

7 big black clouds

8 a lovely sunny day

9 an ugly yellow dress

10 a long wide avenue

11 a lovely little restaurant

12 a little old red car

13 a nice new green sweater

14 a small black metal box

15 a big fat black cat

16 beautiful long black hair

17 an interesting old French painting

18 an enormous red and yellow umbrella

99.2

2 tastes/tasted awful

3 feel fine

4 smell nice

5 look wet

6 sounds/sounded interesting

99.3

2	happy	6	properly
3	happily	7	good
4	violent	8	slow
5	terrible		

99.4

3 the last two days

4 the first two weeks of May

5 the next few days

6 the first three questions (in the exam)

7 the next two years

8 the last three days of our holiday

UNIT 100

100.1

2 badly

3 easily

4 patiently

5 unexpectedly

6 regularly

7 perfectly ... slowly ... clearly

100.2

3 selfishly

4 terribly

5 sudden

6 colourfully

7 colourful

8 badly

9 badly

10 safe

Key to Exercises

100.3

2 careful
3 continuously
4 happily
5 fluent
6 specially
7 complete
8 perfectly
9 nervous
10 financially *or* completely

100.4

2 seriously ill
3 absolutely enormous
4 slightly damaged
5 unusually quiet
6 completely changed
7 unnecessarily long
8 badly planned

UNIT 101

101.1

2 good
3 well
4 good
5 well
6 well … good
7 well
8 good
9 well

101.2

2 well-known
3 well-kept
4 well-written
5 well-informed
6 well-dressed
7 well-paid

101.3

2 *OK*   5 *OK*
3 *OK*   6 slowly
4 hard

101.4

2 hardly hear
3 hardly slept
4 hardly speak
5 hardly said
6 hardly changed
7 hardly recognised

101.5

2 hardly any
3 hardly anything
4 hardly anybody/anyone
5 hardly ever
6 Hardly anybody/anyone
7 hardly anywhere
8 hardly *or* hardly ever
9 hardly any
10 hardly anything … hardly anywhere

UNIT 102

102.1

4 so
5 so
6 such a
7 so
8 such
9 such a
10 such a
11 so
12 so … such
13 so
14 such a
15 such a

102.2

3 I was so tired (that) I couldn't keep my eyes open.
4 We had such a good time on holiday (that) we didn't want to come home.
5 She speaks English so well (that) you would think it was her native language. *or* She speaks such good English (that) …
6 I've got such a lot to do (that) I don't know where to begin. *or* I've got so much to do (that) …
7 The music was so loud (that) you could hear it from miles away.
8 I had such a big breakfast (that) I didn't eat anything else for the rest of the day.
9 It was such horrible weather (that) we spent the whole day indoors.
10 I was so surprised (that) I didn't know what to say.

102.3

Example answers:
2 a She's so friendly.
  b She's such a nice person.
3 a It's so lively.
  b It's such an exciting place.
4 a It's so exhausting.
  b It's such a difficult job.
5 a I haven't seen you for so long.
  b I haven't seen you for such a long time.

UNIT 103

103.1

3 enough money
4 enough milk
5 warm enough
6 enough room
7 well enough
8 enough time
9 big enough
10 enough cups

103.2

2 too busy to talk
3 too late to go
4 warm enough to sit
5 too shy to be
6 enough patience to be
7 too far away to hear
8 enough English to read

103.3

2 This coffee is too hot to drink.
3 The piano was too heavy to move.
4 These apples aren't / are not ripe enough to eat.
5 The situation is too complicated to explain.
6 The wall was too high to climb over.
7 This sofa isn't / is not big enough for three people (to sit on).
8 Some things are too small to see without a microscope.

UNIT 104

104.1

2 quite hungry
3 Quite good
4 quite often
5 quite noisy
6 quite surprised
7 quite late
8 quite old

104.2

2 quite a good voice
3 quite a long way
4 a pretty cold wind
5 quite a lot of traffic
6 a pretty busy day

104.3

Example answers:
2 rather long
3 rather disappointed
4 rather strange
5 rather impatient

104.4

3 more than a little …
4 completely
5 more than a little …
6 more than a little …
7 completely

104.5

2 quite safe
3 quite impossible
4 quite right
5 quite different
6 quite unnecessary
7 quite sure

UNIT 105

105.1
2 stronger
3 smaller
4 more expensive
5 warmer/hotter
6 more interesting / more exciting
7 nearer/closer
8 more difficult / more complicated
9 better
10 worse
11 longer
12 more quietly
13 more often
14 further/farther
15 happier / more cheerful

105.2
3 more serious than
4 thinner
5 bigger
6 more interested
7 more important than
8 simpler / more simple
9 more crowded than
10 more peaceful than
11 more easily
12 higher than

105.3
2 It takes longer by train than by car.
3 I ran further/farther than Dan.
4 Joe did worse than Chris in the test.
5 My friends arrived earlier than I expected.
6 The buses run more often than the trains. or The buses run more frequently than … or The buses are more frequent than …
7 We were busier than usual in the office today.

UNIT 106

106.1
2 much bigger
3 much more interesting than
4 a bit cooler
5 far more complicated than
6 a bit more slowly
7 a lot easier
8 slightly older

106.2
2 any sooner / any earlier
3 no higher than / no more expensive than / no worse than
4 any further/farther
5 no worse than

106.3
2 bigger and bigger
3 heavier and heavier
4 more and more nervous
5 worse and worse
6 more and more expensive
7 better and better
8 more and more talkative

106.4
2 the more I liked him or the more I got to like him
3 the more profit you (will) make or the higher your profit (will be) or the bigger your profit (will be)
4 the harder it is to concentrate
5 the more impatient she became

106.5
2 more
3 longer
4 any
5 the
6 older
7 elder or older
8 slightly
9 no
10 less … better

UNIT 107

107.1
2 My salary isn't as high as yours.
3 You don't know as much about cars as me. or … as I do.
4 We aren't as busy today as we were yesterday. or … as yesterday.
5 I don't feel as bad as I did earlier. or … as I felt earlier.
6 Our neighbours haven't lived here as long as us. or … as we have.
7 I wasn't as nervous (before the interview) as I usually am.
or … as usual.

107.2
3 The station wasn't as far as I thought.
4 The meal cost less than I expected.
5 I don't go out as much as I used to.
or … as often as I used to.
6 Karen used to have longer hair.
7 You don't know them as well as me.
or … as I do.
8 There aren't as many people at this meeting as at the last one.

107.3
2 as well as
3 as long as
4 as soon as
5 as often as
6 as quietly as
7 just as comfortable as
8 just as hard as
9 just as bad as

107.4
2 Your hair is the same colour as mine.
3 I arrived (at) the same time as you.
4 My birthday is (on) the same day as Tom's. or
My birthday is the same as Tom's.

107.5
2 than him / than he does
3 as me / as I do
4 than us / than we were
5 than her / than she is
6 as them / as they have been

UNIT 108

108.1
2 It's the cheapest restaurant in the town.
3 It was the happiest day of my life.
4 She's the most intelligent student in the class.
5 It's the most valuable painting in the gallery.
6 It's the busiest time of the year.
8 He's one of the richest men in the country.
9 It's one of the biggest castles in Europe.
10 She's one of the best players in the team.   (on the team *is also possible*)
11 It was one of the worst experiences of my life.
12 It's one of the most famous universities in the world.

108.2
3 larger
4 the smallest
5 better
6 the worst
7 the most popular
8 … the highest mountain in the world … It is higher than …
9 the tallest
10 more comfortable
11 the quickest
12 quicker
13 the most expensive
14 The oldest *or* The eldest

108.3
2 That's the funniest joke I've ever heard.
3 This is the best coffee I've ever tasted.
4 She's the most generous person I've ever met.
5 That's the furthest/farthest I've ever run.
6 It's the worst mistake I've ever made. or It was the worst …
7 Who's the most famous person you've ever met?

UNIT 109

109.1

3 Joe doesn't like football very much.
4 OK
5 I ate my breakfast quickly and …
6 … a lot of people to the party?
7 OK
8 Did you go to bed late last night?
9 OK
10 I met a friend of mine on my way home.

109.2

2 We won the game easily.
3 I closed the door quietly.
4 Tanya speaks German quite well.
5 Sam watches TV all the time.
6 Please don't ask that question again.
7 Does Kevin play football every weekend?
8 I borrowed some money from a friend of mine.

109.3

2 I go to the supermarket every Friday.
3 Why did you come home so late?
4 Sarah takes her children to school every day.
5 I haven't been to the cinema recently.
6 Please write your name at the top of the page.
7 I remembered her name after a few minutes.
8 We walked around the town all morning.
9 I didn't see you at the party on Saturday night.
10 We found some interesting books in the library.
11 Laura left her umbrella in a restaurant last night.
12 They are building a new hotel opposite the park.

UNIT 110

110.1

3 I usually have …
4 OK
5 Steve hardly ever gets angry.
6 … and I also went to the bank.
7 Jane always has to hurry …
8 I've never worked / I have never worked …
9 OK (I never have enough time.) I'm always busy. / I am always busy.

110.2

2 Katherine is always very generous.
3 I don't usually have to work on Saturdays.
4 Do you always watch TV in the evenings?
5 … he is also learning Japanese.
6 a We were all on holiday in Spain.
   b We were all staying at the same hotel.
   c We all enjoyed ourselves.
7 a The new hotel is probably very expensive.
   b It probably costs a lot to stay there.
8 a I can probably help you.
   b I probably can't help you.

110.3

2 I usually take
3 I am usually / I'm usually
4 were both born
5 She can also sing
6 usually sleeps
7 I have never spoken / I've never spoken
8 You always have to wait
9 I can only read *or* I can read only
10 We were all … we all fell
11 I always am
12 I will probably be leaving / I'll probably be leaving
13 I probably won't be
14 She is hardly ever / She's hardly ever
15 We are still living / We're still living
16 we would never have met / we'd never have met
17 always says … she never does

UNIT 111

111.1

3 He doesn't write poems any more.
4 He still wants to be a teacher.
5 He isn't / He's not interested in politics any more.
6 He's still single.
7 He doesn't go fishing any more.
8 He doesn't have a beard any more. *or* He hasn't got …

10–12

• He no longer writes poems.
• He is / He's no longer interested in politics.
• He no longer goes fishing.
• He no longer has a beard. *or* He's no longer got a beard.

111.2

2 He hasn't gone yet.
3 They haven't finished (repairing the road) yet.
4 They haven't woken up yet.
5 She hasn't found a place to live yet.
6 I haven't decided (what to do) yet.
7 It hasn't taken off yet.

111.3

5 I don't want to go out yet.
6 she doesn't work there any more
7 I still have a lot of friends there. *or* I've still got …
8 We've already met.
9 Do you still live in the same place
10 have you already eaten
11 He's not here yet.
12 he still isn't here (he isn't here yet *is also possible*)
13 are you already a member
14 I can still remember it very clearly
15 These trousers don't fit me any more.
16 'Have you finished with the paper yet?' 'No, I'm still reading it.'

UNIT 112

112.1

2 even Lisa
3 not even Amy
4 even Lisa
5 even Kate
6 not even Lisa

112.2

2 We even painted the floor.
3 She's even met the prime minister.
4 You could even hear it / You could even hear the noise from the next street. *or* You could hear it / You could hear the noise even from the next street.
6 I can't even remember her name.
7 There isn't even a cinema.
8 He didn't even tell his wife (where he was going).
9 I don't even know the people next door.

112.3

2 even older
3 even better
4 even more difficult
5 even worse
6 even less

112.4

2 if	6 Even
3 even if	7 even though
4 even	8 even if
5 even though	9 Even though

UNIT 113

113.1
2 Although I had never seen her before
3 although it was quite cold
4 although we don't like them very much
5 Although I didn't speak the language well
6 Although the heating was on
7 although I'd met her twice before
8 although we've known each other a long time

113.2
2 a In spite of (or Despite)
  b Although
3 a because
  b although
4 a because of
  b in spite of (or despite)
5 a although
  b because of
Example answers:
6 a he hadn't studied very hard
  b he had studied very hard
7 a I was hungry
  b being hungry / my hunger / the fact (that) I was hungry

113.3
2 In spite of having very little money, they are happy. *or* In spite of the fact (that) they have very little money …
3 Although my foot was injured, I managed to walk home. *or* I managed to walk home although my …
4 I enjoyed the film in spite of the silly story. / … in spite of the story being silly. / … in spite of the fact (that) the story was silly. *or* In spite of … , I enjoyed the film.
5 Despite living in the same street, we hardly ever see each other. *or* Despite the fact (that) we live in … *or* We hardly ever see each other despite …
6 Even though I was only out for five minutes, I got very wet in the rain. *or* I got very wet in the rain even though I was …

113.4
2 It's very windy though.
3 We ate it though.
4 I don't like her husband though.

UNIT 114

114.1
2–5
• Take a map in case you get lost.
• Take an anorak in case it rains.
• Take a camera in case you want to take some pictures.
• Take some water in case you're thirsty. / … in case you are thirsty. *or* … you get thirsty.

114.2
2 I'll say goodbye now in case I don't see you again (before you go).
3 Can you check the list in case we forgot something? *or* … forgot anything?
4 You should back up your files in case there's a problem with your computer. / … there is a problem with your computer.

114.3
2 in case I forgot it.
3 in case they were worried (about me).
4 in case she didn't get the first one. / in case she hadn't got … / in case she hadn't gotten …
5 in case they came to London (one day).

114.4
3 If
4 if
5 in case
6 if
7 if
8 in case
9 in case

UNIT 115

115.1
2 You won't know what to do unless you listen carefully.
3 I'll never speak to her again unless she apologises to me. *or* Unless she apologises to me, I'll …
4 He won't be able to understand you unless you speak very slowly. *or* Unless you speak very slowly, he …
5 The company will have to close unless business improves soon. *or* Unless business improves soon, the company …

115.2
2 I'm not going (to the party) unless you go too. / … unless you're going too.
3 The dog won't attack you unless you move suddenly.
4 Ben won't speak to you unless you ask him something.
5 The doctor won't see you unless it's an emergency.

115.3
2 unless
3 providing
4 as long as
5 unless
6 unless
7 provided
8 Unless
9 unless
10 as long as

115.4
Example answers:
2 it's not too hot
3 there isn't too much traffic
4 it isn't raining
5 I'm in a hurry
6 you have something else to do
7 you pay it back next week
8 you take risks

UNIT 116

116.1
2 I listened as she told me her story.
3 I burnt myself as I was taking a hot dish out of the oven.
4 The crowd cheered as the two teams came onto the field.
5 A dog ran out in front of the car as we were driving along the road.

116.2
2 As today is a public holiday, many of the shops are shut.
3 As I didn't want to disturb anybody, I was very quiet.
4 As I don't know what to do, I need some advice.
5 As none of us had a watch, we didn't know what time it was.

116.3
3 because
4 at the same time as
5 at the same time as
6 because
7 because

116.4
3 OK
4 when I was in London
5 When I left school
6 OK
7 when I was a child

116.5
Example answers:
1 I saw you as you were getting into your car.
2 It started to rain just as we started playing tennis.
3 As I didn't have enough money for a taxi, I had to walk home.
4 Just as I took the picture, somebody walked in front of the camera.

Key to Exercises

UNIT 117

117.1
3 like her mother
4 people like him
5 *OK*
6 like most of his friends *or*
   as most of his friends are
7 like talking to the wall
8 *OK*
9 *OK*
10 *OK*
11 like a bomb exploding
12 like a fish

117.2
2 like blocks of ice
3 like a beginner
4 as a tour guide
5 like a theatre
6 as a birthday present
7 like winter
8 like a child

117.3
2 like
3 as
4 like
5 like
6 as *or* like
7 like
8 as
9 as
10 like *or* such as
11 like
12 as
13 as
14 Like
15 as
16 As
17 like
18 as *or* like

UNIT 118

118.1
2 You look like you've seen a ghost. /
   ... like you saw a ghost.
3 You sound as if you're having a good
   time.
4 I feel like I've (just) run a marathon. /
   ... like I (just) ran a marathon.

118.2
2 It looks like it's going to rain.
3 It sounds like they're having an
   argument.
4 It looks like there's been an accident.
5 It looks like we'll have to walk.
6 It sounds like you should see a
   doctor.

118.3
2 as if he meant what he said
3 as if she's hurt her leg / as if she hurt
   her leg
4 as if he hadn't eaten for a week
5 as if she was enjoying it
6 as if I'm going to be sick
7 as if she didn't want to come
8 as if I didn't exist

118.4
2 as if I was/were
3 as if she was/were
4 as if it was/were

UNIT 119

119.1
3 during
4 for
5 during
6 for
7 for
8 for
9 during
10 for
11 for
12 for
13 during
14 for

119.2
3 while
4 While
5 During
6 while
7 during
8 During
9 while
10 during
11 while
12 during
13 while
14 while

119.3
Example answers:
3 Nobody came to see me while I was
   in hospital.
4 Can you wait for me while I make a
   quick phone call?
5 Most of the students looked bored
   during the lesson.
6 I was asked a lot of questions during
   the interview.
7 Don't open the car door while the
   car is moving.
8 The lights suddenly went out while
   we were watching TV.
9 It started to rain during the game.
10 It started to rain while we were
   walking home.
11 What are you going to do while
   you're on holiday?

UNIT 120

120.1
2 I have to be at the airport by 8.30.
3 Let me know by Saturday whether
   you can come to the party.
4 Please make sure that you're here by
   2 o'clock.
5 If we leave now, we should arrive by
   lunchtime.

120.2
2 by
3 by
4 until
5 until (5.30) ... by (now)
6 by
7 until
8 by
9 by
10 until
11 By
12 by

120.3
Example answers:
3 until I come back
4 by 5 o'clock
5 by next Friday
6 until midnight

120.4
2 By the time I got to the station /
   By the time I'd got to the station
3 By the time I finished (my work) /
   By the time I'd finished (my work)
4 By the time the police arrived /
   By the time the police had arrived
5 By the time we got to the top (of the
   mountain) / By the time we'd got to
   the top (of the mountain)

UNIT 121

121.1
2 on
3 in
4 At *or* On
5 on *or* I last saw her Tuesday. *(no
   preposition)*
6 in
7 in
8 at
9 on *or* There are usually a lot
   of parties New Year's Eve. *(no
   preposition)*
10 at
11 in
12 at
13 on
14 in
15 **On** Saturday night *or*
   Saturday night *(no preposition)*
   ... **at** midnight
16 **at** 5 o'clock **in** the morning
17 **on** 7 January ... **in** April
18 at home **on** Tuesday morning
   or at home Tuesday morning *(no
   preposition)* ... **in** the afternoon

121.2
2 at night
3 in the evening
4 on 21 July 1969
5 at the same time
6 in the 1920s
7 in about 20 minutes
8 at the moment
9 in the Middle Ages
10 in 11 seconds
11 **on** Saturdays *or* ... works
   Saturdays *(no preposition)*

121.3

3 a
4 *both*
5 b
6 b
7 *both*
8 a
9 b
10 a

UNIT 122

122.1

2 on time
3 in time
4 on time
5 in time
6 on time
7 in time
8 in time
9 on time

122.2

2 I got home just in time.
3 I stopped him just in time.
4 We got to the cinema just in time for the beginning of the film. / ... just in time to see the beginning of the film.

122.3

2 at the end of the month
3 at the end of the course
4 at the end of the race
5 at the end of the interview

122.4

2 In the end she resigned (from her job).
3 In the end I gave up (trying to learn German).
4 In the end we decided not to go (to the party). *or*
   In the end we didn't go (to the party).

122.5

2 In	6 at
3 at ... at	7 in
4 in	8 at
5 in	9 in

UNIT 123

123.1

2 On his arm. *or*
   On the man's arm.
3 At the traffic lights.
4 a On the door.
   b In the door.
5 On the wall.
6 In Paris.
7 a At the gate.
   b On the gate.
8 On the beach.

123.2

2 on my guitar
3 at the next petrol station
4 in your coffee
5 on that tree
6 in the mountains
7 on the island
8 at the window

123.3

2 on
3 at
4 on
5 in
6 on
7 at
8 **in** a small village **in** the south-west
9 on
10 in
11 **on** the wall **in** the kitchen
12 at

UNIT 124

124.1

2 On the second floor.
3 At/On the corner.
4 In the corner.
5 At the top of the stairs.
6 In the back of the car.
7 At the front.
8 On the left.
9 In the back row.
10 On a farm.

124.2

2 on the right
3 in the world
4 on the way to work
5 on the west coast
6 in the front row
7 at the back of the class
6 on the back of this card

124.3

2 in		9 in
3 in		10 on
4 at		11 in
5 in		12 on
6 on		13 in
7 At		14 on ... on
8 in		

UNIT 125

125.1

2 on a train
3 at a conference
4 in hospital / in the hospital
5 at the hairdresser's
6 on his bike
7 in New York
8 at the Savoy Theatre

125.2

2 in a taxi
3 at the cinema
4 in prison
5 at school
6 at the sports centre
7 in hospital
8 at the airport
9 on the plane
10 in Tokyo

125.3

2 at
3 in
4 at
5 **at/in** a very comfortable hotel ...
   in Amsterdam
6 in
7 on
8 at
9 in
10 at
11 in
12 **at** home *or* **be** home (*no preposition*) ... **at** work
13 in
14 **in** Birmingham ... **at** Birmingham University

UNIT 126

126.1

3 at
4 to
5 to
6 into
7 in
8 to
9 into
10 to
11 at
12 to
13 into
14 to
15 get home (*no preposition*) ... going **to** bed
16 returned **to** France ... two years **in** Brazil
17 born **in** Chicago ... moved **to** New York ... lives **in** New York

126.2

Example answers:

2–4
• I've been to Sweden once.
• I've never been to the United States.
• I've been to Paris a few times.

126.3

2 in
3 – (no preposition)
4 at
5 to
6 – (no preposition)

Key to Exercises

126.4

2 I got on
3 I got out of the car. / ... my car.
4 I got off the train.
5 I got into the taxi. *or* I got in the taxi.
6 I got off the plane.

UNIT 127

127.1

2 in cold weather
3 in pencil
4 in love
5 in capital letters
6 in the shade
7 in my opinion

127.2

2 on strike
3 on a tour
4 on TV
5 on purpose
6 on a diet
7 on business
8 on holiday
9 on the phone
10 on the whole

127.3

2 on
3 on
4 at
5 in
6 on
7 in
8 on
9 at
10 at
11 on
12 **In** my opinion ... **on** television
13 on
14 on
15 on
16 at
17 on
18 in

UNIT 128

128.1

2 by mistake
3 by hand
4 by credit card
5 by canal

128.2

2 on
3 by
4 **by** car ... **on** my bike
5 in
6 on
7 by

128.3

2 travelling **by** bus *or*
   travelling **on** the bus *or*
   travelling **on buses**
3 taken **with** a very good camera
4 this music is **by** Beethoven
5 **pay cash** *or* pay **in** cash
6 a mistake **by** one of our players

128.4

Example answers:
3–5
• *Ulysses* is a novel by James Joyce.
• *Yesterday* is a song by Paul McCartney.
• *Guernica* is a painting by Pablo Picasso.

128.5

2 by
3 with
4 by
5 by
6 **by** car ... **in** your car
7 **by** the bed **with** a lamp and a clock **on** it

128.6

2 The price has gone up by ten pence.
3 Helen won by two votes.
4 I missed her/Kate by five minutes.

UNIT 129

129.1

2 to the problem
3 with her brother
4 in the cost of living
5 to your question
6 for a new road
7 in *or* to working at home
8 in the number of people without jobs
9 for shoes like these any more
10 between your job and mine

129.2

2 invitation to
3 contact with
4 key to (key for *is also possible*)
5 cause of
6 reply to
7 connection between
8 photographs of
9 reason for
10 damage to

129.3

2 to
3 in
4 of
5 in *or* to
6 for
7 to *or* towards
8 with
9 in
10 to
11 of
12 **for** a rise **in** pay
13 to
14 with

UNIT 130

130.1

2 That was nice of him.
3 That was generous of her.
4 That wasn't very nice of them.
5 That's very kind of you.
6 That isn't very polite of him.
7 That's a bit childish of them.

130.2

2 kind to
3 angry with
4 excited about
5 impressed by / impressed with
6 bored with (bored by *is also possible*)
7 amazed at / amazed by
8 careless of

130.3

2 of
3 to
4 with
5 with (by *or* in *are also possible*)
6 to
7 at/by
8 with
9 about
10 about
11 for
12 about/by/at
13 to
14 of
15 by/with
16 about
17 at/by
18 about
19 **with** us **for** making
20 sorry **for/about** ... angry **with**

UNIT 131

131.1
2 similar to
3 afraid of
4 interested in
5 responsible for
6 proud of
7 different from / different to
(different than *is also possible*)
8 capable of

131.2
2 of furniture
3 on sport
4 of time
5 at tennis
6 to a Russian / to a Russian man /
to a Russian guy
7 of him / of Robert
8 from yours / to yours   *or* from your
problem / to your problem

131.3
2 for
3 of
4 of
5 in
6 of *or* about
7 of ... of
8 on
9 of
10 with
11 of
12 in
13 of
14 of
15 at
16 of
17 on
18 of

131.4
Example answers:
2 I'm hopeless at telling jokes.
3 I'm not very good at maths.
4 I'm pretty good at remembering
names.
5 I'm good at sport.

UNIT 132

132.1
2 a
3 b
4 b
5 a
6 a
7 b
8 a
9 b
10 b
11 a
12 b

132.2
3 speak to
4 point (them) at
5 look at
6 listen to
7 throw (stones) at
8 throw (it) to
9 reply to

132.3
2 at
3 at
4 to
5 to
6 at
7 at
8 to
9 at
10 at
11 to

UNIT 133

133.1
2 for
3 for
4 to
5 for
6 about
7 – *(no preposition)*
8 about
9 – *(no preposition)*
10 for
11 for
12 about
13 for
14 for

133.2
2 of
3 about
4 for
5 of
6 for
7 about
8 – *(no preposition)*

133.3
2 looking for
3 looked after
4 looking for
5 look for
6 looks after

133.4
2 wait for
3 talk about
4 asked (the waiter) for
5 applied for
6 do (something) about
7 looks after *or* has looked after
8 left (Boston) for

UNIT 134

134.1
2 hear about
3 heard from
4 heard of
5 hear from
6 hear about
7 heard of

134.2
2 think about
3 think of
4 think of
5 thinking of/about
6 think of
7 thought about
8 think (much) of
9 thinking about/of
10 think of

134.3
2 about
3 **to** us **about**
4 of
5 of
6 about ... about ... about ...
about
7 of
8 about
9 about/of

134.4
2 complaining about
3 think about
4 warn (you) about
5 heard of
6 dream of
7 reminded (me) about
8 remind (you) of

UNIT 135

135.1
2 for
3 of
4 of
5 – *(no preposition)*
6 for
7 of
8 for
9 of
10 for
11 on

135.2
2 for the misunderstanding
3 her/Jane on winning the tournament
4 him from his enemies
5 of eleven players
6 on bread and eggs
7 me for your problems / your
problems on me

Key to Exercises

135.3
2 paid for
3 accused of
4 depends on
5 live on
6 apologise to
7 suffers from
8 congratulated (him) on

135.4
2 from
3 on
4 – (no preposition)
5 from
6 depends how (no preposition) or depends **on** how
7 on
8 of
9 on

UNIT 136

136.1
2 happened to
3 invited to
4 divided into
5 believe in
6 fill (it) with
7 drove into
8 Concentrate on
9 succeeded in

136.2
2 I prefer small towns to big cities
3 Jane provided me with all the information I needed
4 This morning I spent £70 on a pair of shoes
5 The city is divided into ten districts

136.3
2 to
3 on
4 in
5 to
6 in
7 with
8 into
9 in
10 on
11 – (no preposition)
12 into
13 on
14 into
15 with
16 **from** (one language) **into** another

136.4
Example answers:
2 on petrol
3 into a wall
4 to volleyball
5 in seafood
6 into many languages

UNIT 137

137.1
2 sit down
3 flew away
4 get out
5 speak up
6 get by
7 gone up
8 looked round

137.2
2 back at
3 up to
4 forward to
5 away with
6 up at
7 in through

137.3
2 wake me up
3 get it out
4 give them back
5 switch it on
6 take them off

137.4
3 I have to take **them back**
4 We can turn **the television off**
   or We can turn **off the television**
5 I knocked **it over**
6 I don't want to wake **her up**
7 (example answer) You should put **your coat on** or
   You should put **on your coat**
8 I was able to put **it out**
9 (example answer) they've put **the price(s) up** or
   they've put **up the price(s)**
10 Shall I turn **the light(s) on**? or
   Shall I turn **on the light(s)**?

UNIT 138

138.1
2 eats
3 moved
4 drop
5 checked
6 cut
7 plug
8 filling / to fill
9 left
10 dive
11 rub/cross
12 dropped

138.2
2 into
3 in
4 out
5 into
6 out of

138.3
2 dropped out
3 moved in
4 left out
5 joined in
6 eating out or to eat out
7 taken in
8 dropped in
9 get out of

138.4
2 Fill them in or Fill them out
3 cross it out
4 took me in
5 let us in

UNIT 139

139.1
2 a mistake
3 a candle
4 an order
5 a cigarette / a candle
6 a new product
7 a mess

139.2
2 works out
3 carried out
4 ran out
5 sort out / work out
6 find out
7 tried out
8 pointed out
9 work out
10 went out
11 turned out
12 works out / turns out
13 find out
14 put out

139.3
2 giving out / handing out
3 turned out nice/fine/sunny
4 working out
5 fallen out
6 work out how to use the camera / her new camera

139.4
2 try it out
3 work it out
4 sorted it out / worked it out

UNIT 140

140.1
2 put the heating on
3 put the oven on
4 put the kettle on
5 put a CD on

140.2

2 going on
3 take off
4 switched off / turned off
5 drove off / went off
6 put on
7 set off / be off
8 put off
9 called off
10 put on
11 see (me) off

140.3

2 took off
3 tried on a/the hat or
   tried a/the hat on
4 was called off
5 see him off
6 put them on

UNIT 141

141.1

2 went on / carried on
3 walked on / carried on or
   carried on walking
4 dozed off / dropped off / nodded off
5 go on / carry on / keep on
6 went off
7 keeps on phoning me

141.2

2 went off
3 finish off
4 drive on / carry on
5 ripped off
6 getting on
7 dozed off / dropped off / nodded off
8 told off
9 get on
10 going off
11 keep on
12 get on
13 showing off
14 put off

141.3

2 finish it off
3 were ripped off
4 go off
5 did you get on
6 carried on (playing) / went on
   (playing)
7 tell them off
8 doesn't get on (well) with

UNIT 142

142.1

2 took them down
3 stand up
4 turned it up
5 put their bags down
6 were blown down / fell down
7 put them up
8 bent down (and) picked them up

142.2

2 turn it down
3 calm him down
4 wrote it down
5 let her down
6 turned it down

142.3

2 calm down
3 slowed down
4 was turned down
5 broken down
6 cut down
7 let down
8 (has) closed down
9 be knocked down (or be pulled
   down or be torn down)
10 turned down
11 was knocked down
12 broke down

UNIT 143

143.1

2 went up to / walked up to
3 catch up with
4 keep up with

143.2

2 used up
3 washed up
4 grow up
5 turn up / show up
6 gave up
7 taking up
8 give up
9 ended up
10 takes up
11 make up

143.3

3 tidy it up / tidy up
4 fixed it up
5 keep up with
6 was brought up
7 keep it up
8 went up to
9 was made up of
10 set it up / fix it up

UNIT 144

144.1

2 d
3 e
4 c
5 g
6 a
7 b

144.2

2 held up
3 did it up
4 cheer him up

144.3

2 blew up
3 beaten up
4 broken up / split up
5 do up
6 clears up / will clear up
7 mixed up

144.4

2 look it up
3 put up with
4 made it up
5 come up with
6 tear it up
7 saving up for

UNIT 145

145.1

2 blew away
3 put it back
4 walked away
5 threw it back (to her)
6 threw them away

145.2

2 be away / have gone away
3 be back
4 ran away
5 smile back
6 get away
7 Keep away / Keep back

145.3

2 Pay
3 throw
4 gets
5 be
6 look
7 gave
8 get

145.4

2 throw it away
3 take them back
4 pay you back / pay it back
5 gave them away
6 call back / call me back

1
3 I'm getting / I am getting
4 do you do
5 we arrived … it was raining
6 phones … she didn't phone
7 you were thinking … I decided
8 are you looking
9 It doesn't rain
10 rang … I was getting
11 we went … she was preparing …
We didn't want … we didn't stay
12 told … he didn't believe …
He thought … I was joking

2
2 didn't go
3 is wearing
4 went
5 haven't heard
6 is being
7 wasn't reading
8 didn't have
9 It's beginning
10 got
11 wasn't
12 you've been
13 I've been doing
14 did she go
15 I've been playing
16 do you come
17 since I saw her
18 for 20 years

3
3 are you going
4 Do you watch
5 have you lived / have you been
living / have you been
6 Did you have
7 Have you seen
8 was she wearing
9 Have you been waiting / Have you
been here
10 does it take
11 Have you ridden / Have you ridden
on / Have you been on
12 Have you (ever) been

4
2 've known each other / have known
each other *or* 've been friends /
have been friends
3 I've ever had / I've ever been on /
I've had for ages (*etc.*)
4 He went / He went home / He went
out / He left
5 I've worn it
6 I was playing
7 been swimming for
8 since I've been / since I (last) went
9 did you buy / did you get

5
1 got … was already waiting … had
arrived
2 was lying … wasn't watching …
'd fallen / had fallen … was snoring
… turned … woke
3 'd just gone / had just gone … was
reading … heard … got … didn't see
… went
4 missed … was standing … realised
… 'd left / had left … had … got
5 met … was walking … 'd been / had
been … 'd been playing / had been
playing … were going … invited …
'd arranged / had arranged … didn't
have

6
2 Somebody has taken it.
3 They'd only known / They had only
known each other (for) a few
weeks.
4 It's been raining / It has been raining
all day. *or* It's rained / It has rained
all day.
5 I'd been dreaming. / I had been
dreaming.
6 I'd had / I had had a big breakfast.
7 They've been going / They have
been going there for years.
8 I've had it / I have had it since I got
up.
9 He's been training / He has been
training very hard for it.

7
1 I haven't seen
2 You look / You're looking
3 are you going
4 are you meeting
5 I'm going
6 Do you often go
7 are you going
8 I'm meeting
9 has been
10 I've been waiting
11 has just started / just started
12 is she getting
13 Does she like
14 she thinks
15 Are you working
16 spoke
17 you were working
18 went
19 I started / I'd started
20 I lost
21 you haven't had
22 I've had
23 have you seen
24 has he been
25 I saw

26 he went
27 He'd been
28 he decided / he'd decided
29 He was really looking forward
30 is he doing
31 I haven't heard
32 he left

8
1 invented
2 it's gone / it has gone
3 had gone … left
4 did you do … Did you go
5 have you had
6 was looking *or* 'd been looking /
had been looking
7 She's been teaching / She has been
teaching
8 I bought … I haven't worn *or*
I didn't wear
9 I saw … was … I'd seen / I had seen
… I remembered … it was
10 Have you heard … She was …
died … She wrote … Have you read
11 does this word mean … I've never
seen
12 Did you get … it had already started
13 knocked … was … she'd gone / she
had gone … she didn't want
14 He'd never used / He had never used
… he didn't know
15 went … She needed *or* She'd
needed / She had needed … she'd
been sitting / she had been sitting

9
3 used to drive
4 was driving
5 were working
6 used to have
7 was living
8 was playing
9 used to play
10 was wearing

10
2 I'm going to the dentist.
3 No, we're going to hire a car.
4 I'll look after the children.
5 I'm having lunch with Sue.
6 What are you going to have? / What
are you having?
7 I'll turn on the light.
8 I'm going to turn on the light.

11

2 I'll come
3 shall we meet
4 starts
5 I'll meet
6 I'm seeing
7 Shall I ask
8 I'll see
9 are going
10 does the film start
11 Are you meeting
12 I'll be

12

1 (2) Are you going to do / Are you doing
  (3) it starts
  (4) you'll enjoy / you're going to enjoy
  (5) it will be / it's going to be
2 (1) you're going
  (2) We're going
  (3) you have
  (4) I'll send
  (5) I'll get
  (6) I get
3 (1) I'm having / I'm going to have
  (2) are coming
  (3) they'll have left
  (4) they're
  (5) I won't be / I will not be
  (6) you know
  (7) I'll call
4 (1) shall we meet
  (2) I'll be waiting
  (3) you arrive
  (4) I'll be sitting
  (5) I'll be wearing
  (6) Is Agent 307 coming / Is Agent 307 going to come / Will Agent 307 be coming
  (7) Shall I bring
  (8) I'll explain / I'm going to explain
  (9) I see
  (10) I'll try

13

1 I'll have
2 Are you going
3 shall I phone
4 It's going to land
5 it's / it is
6 I'll miss / I'm going to miss … you go / you've gone
7 Shall I give … I give … will you call
8 does it end
9 I'm going … is getting
10 I'll tell … I'm … I won't be
11 I'm going to have / I'm having
12 she apologises
13 we'll be living / we'll live
14 you finish / you've finished

14

2 I've had / I have had
3 I bought *or* I got
4 I'll come / I will come *or* I'll be / I will be
5 I've been / I have been *or* I've eaten / I have eaten
6 I used to play
7 I haven't been waiting *or* I haven't been here
8 I'd been / I had been *or* I was
9 I'm going / I am going
10 I haven't seen *or* I haven't heard from
11 I'll have gone / I will have gone *or* I'll have left / I will have left

15

2 I've been travelling
3 I'm beginning
4 I've seen
5 has been
6 I've met
7 I left
8 I stayed *or* I was staying
9 I'd planned *or* I was planning
10 I ended up
11 I enjoyed
12 I took
13 met
14 I'm staying *or* I'm going to stay *or* I'll be staying *or* I'll stay
15 I continue
16 I'll get
17 I'm
18 I'll let
19 I know
20 I'm staying
21 we're going to visit *or* we're visiting
22 are building *or* have been building
23 it will be
24 I'll be

16

2 A		9 B *or* C	
3 C		10 A *or* B	
4 B *or* C		11 A	
5 B		12 C	
6 A *or* C		13 A *or* B	
7 A *or* C		14 B *or* C	
8 C		15 B	

17

2 shouldn't have eaten
3 must have forgotten
4 needn't have gone
5 can't be changed
6 may be watching
7 must have been waiting
8 couldn't have done
9 ought to have been
10 would have helped

11 should have been warned
12 might not have been feeling / might not have felt

18

3 could rain / might rain
4 might have gone / could have gone
5 couldn't go
6 couldn't have seen / can't have seen
7 should get
8 wouldn't recognise / might not recognise
9 must have heard
10 should have turned

19

4 rings
5 you were
6 it's / it is
7 it was / it were
8 it had been
9 you had
10 we hadn't had
11 you'd driven / you had driven *or* you'd been driving / you had been driving
12 I didn't read

20

2 came
3 I'd known / I had known … wouldn't have disturbed …
4 They'd be / They would be … told
5 hadn't frightened … wouldn't have attacked
6 wouldn't have got / wouldn't have gotten … I'd had / I had had
7 hadn't been / hadn't got / hadn't gotten … wouldn't have failed *or* would have passed / 'd have passed

21

Example answers:
1 I wasn't feeling so tired
2 I hadn't had so much to do
3 I would have forgotten Jane's birthday
4 I'd take a picture of you
5 I'll take a picture of you
6 you were in trouble
7 you hadn't taken so long to get ready
8 I would have gone to the concert
9 I might have got the job
10 you'd eaten lunch
11 there was less traffic
12 people would go out more

Key to Additional exercises

22
3 was cancelled
4 has been repaired
5 is being restored
6 It's believed / It is believed
7 I'd be sacked / I would be sacked
8 It might have been thrown
9 I was taught
10 being arrested / having been arrested *or* I was arrested
11 Have you ever been arrested
12 are reported … have been injured

23
3 've sold / have sold *or* sold
4 's been sold / has been sold *or* was sold
5 are made
6 might be stolen
7 must have been stolen
8 must have taken
9 can be solved
10 should have left
11 is delayed
12 is being built … is expected

24
Castle Fire
2 was discovered
3 was injured
4 be rescued
5 are believed to have been destroyed
6 is not known
Shop robbery
1 was forced
2 being threatened
3 had been stolen
4 was later found
5 had been abandoned
6 has been arrested / was arrested
7 is still being questioned
Road delays
1 is being resurfaced
2 are asked / are being asked / have been asked
3 is expected
4 will be closed / is going to be closed
5 will be diverted / is going to be diverted
Accident
1 was taken
2 was allowed
3 was blocked
4 be diverted
5 have been killed

25
1 I told **her** (**that**) **Paul had gone out** and **I didn't know when he'd be back**.
   I asked (**her**) **if/whether she wanted to leave a message**, but she said (**that**) **she'd try again** later.

2 I had reserved a hotel room, but when I got to the hotel they told **me** (**that**) **they had no record of a reservation in my name**.
   When I asked (**them**) **if/whether they had any rooms free anyway**, they said (**that**) **they were sorry**, but **the hotel was full**.
3 The immigration official asked us **why we were visiting the country**, and we told **him** (**that**) **we were on holiday**.
   Then he wanted to know **how long we intended to stay** and **where we would be staying during our visit**.
4 She said (**that**) **she'd phone** (**us**) **from the airport when she arrived**. *or* She said (**that**) **she'll phone** (**us**) **from the airport when she arrives**.
   No, she said **not to come to the airport**.
   She said (**that**) **she'd take the bus**. *or* She said (**that**) **she'll take the bus**.
5 He wanted to know **what my job was** and asked (**me**) **how much I earned**. *or*
   He wanted to know **what my job is** and asked (**me**) **how much I earn**.
   … so I told **him to mind his own business** and I put the phone down.
6 He said (**that**) **he'd be at the restaurant at 7.30**.
   He said (**that**) **he knew where the restaurant was**. And I told **him to phone me if there was any problem**.
7 You just said (**that**) **you weren't hungry**.
   But you said (**that**) **you didn't like bananas**. You told **me not to buy any**.

26
3 changing
4 to change
5 change
6 being
7 saying
8 to call
9 drinking
10 to be
11 to see
12 to be
13 to think … making
14 living … to move
15 to be … playing
16 being stopped … stealing … driving
17 work … pressing

27
3 I don't fancy going out.
4 He tends to forget things.
5 Would you mind helping me? / Do you mind helping me?
6 Everybody seems to have gone out.
7 We're / We are thinking of moving.
8 I was afraid to touch it.
9 He's / He is afraid of being robbed.
10 It's / It is not worth seeing.
11 I'm not used to walking so far.
12 She seems to be enjoying herself.
13 He insisted on showing them to me.
14 I'd rather somebody else did it.

28
3 I've given up reading newspapers.
4 I'd rather not go out tonight / … stay at home tonight.
5 He has trouble sleeping at night.
6 Do you want me to phone you this evening?
7 I came in without anybody/anyone seeing me / … without being seen.
8 I was accused of being a cheat / … of cheating.
9 I'm looking forward to seeing them again.
10 What do you advise me to do?
11 I'd like to have gone out with you last night.
12 I regret not taking your advice / … that I didn't take your advice.

29
2 a foreign country … the language
3 an economist … in the United States … for an investment company
4 I love sport, especially tennis … two or three times a week … not a very good player
5 for dinner … after work … to the cinema
6 When unemployment is … for people to find work … a big problem
7 an accident … going home … taken to hospital / taken to the hospital … I think most accidents … by people driving
8 the name of the hotel … The Ambassador … in Queen Street in the city centre … near the station
9 The older one … a pilot with British Airways … The younger one … at school … he leaves school … go to university … study law

30

2 B
3 C
4 A *or* B
5 C
6 B
7 A *or* C
8 A
9 C
10 B *or* C
11 B
12 A
13 A *or* B
14 B

31

3 It's the most polluted place …
4 I was disappointed that …
5 *OK*
6 Joe works hard, but …
7 … in a large modern building.
8 *OK* (as fast as he can *is also correct*)
9 I missed the last three days …
10 *OK*
11 The weather has been unusually cold …
12 The water in the pool was too dirty to swim in.
13 … to wait such a long time. *or* … to wait so long.
14 *OK*
15 … I got up earlier than usual.

32

2 If
3 when
4 if
5 when
6 if
7 if
8 unless
9 if
10 as long as
11 in case
12 in case
13 if
14 even if
15 Although
16 Although
17 When
18 when

33

2 on
3 **at** 9.30 **on** Tuesday morning
4 at / on
5 on
6 at
7 In
8 at
9 during
10 **on** Friday … **since** then
11 for
12 at
13 **at** the moment … **until** Friday
14 by
15 in

34

1 in
2 by
3 at
4 on
5 in
6 on
7 **to** a party **at** Lisa's house
8 on
9 on
10 to … to
11 **in** Vienna … **at** the age of 35
12 **in** this photo … **on** the left
13 **to** the theatre … **in** the front row
14 **on** the wall … **by** the door / **next to** the door / **beside** the door
15 at
16 on
17 **in** a tower block … **on** the fifteenth floor
18 on
19 by
20 **on** the bus … **by** car
21 on … on
22 in
23 **in** Chicago … **to** Italy
24 to
25 on

35

1 for
2 at
3 to
4 to
5 in
6 with
7 of
8 to
9 of
10 at/by
11 of
12 about

36

1 of
2 after
3 – (no preposition)
4 about
5 to
6 – (no preposition)
7 into
8 of (about *is also possible*)
9 to
10 – (no preposition)
11 on
12 of
13 of
14 – (no preposition)
15 in
16 at (about *is also possible*)
17 on
18 If Alex asks you **for** money
19 I apologised **to** Sarah **for** keeping …
20 I thanked her **for** everything

37

2 h
3 e
4 g
5 a
6 k
7 c
8 j
9 b
10 f
11 i

38

2 D
3 B
4 B
5 A
6 A
7 D
8 C
9 C
10 B
11 A
12 D

39

2 out to
3 up with
4 forward to
5 up with
6 out of
7 on with
8 out with
9 up with
10 back on
11 out about
12 on with

40

3 went off
4 turned up / showed up
5 fill it in / fill it out
6 knocked down / pulled down / torn down
7 sorted out
8 give up
9 dozed off / dropped off / nodded off
10 split up / break up
11 put up with it
12 get by / live on
13 went on
14 put it off

41

2 put
3 moving
4 put
5 done
6 turned / turns
7 find
8 Calm
9 set
10 held
11 left / 've left / have left *or* missed / 've missed / have missed
12 works
13 join
14 works
15 drop / call
16 sort / work
17 **went** off … **woke** me up

Key to Study Guide

Present and past
1.1	A
1.2	B
1.3	C
1.4	B, C
1.5	C
1.6	A

Present perfect and past
2.1	B
2.2	C
2.3	A
2.4	C
2.5	A
2.6	B
2.7	A
2.8	D
2.9	A
2.10	A
2.11	C
2.12	A
2.13	C
2.14	C
2.15	D
2.16	C

Future
3.1	B
3.2	A
3.3	C
3.4	A, C
3.5	B
3.6	C
3.7	A

Modals
4.1	A, B
4.2	B
4.3	A, C, D
4.4	C
4.5	B
4.6	C, D
4.7	B
4.8	A, C
4.9	B, C
4.10	A, B, D
4.11	A
4.12	D, E
4.13	A

If and wish
5.1	B
5.2	C
5.3	B
5.4	D
5.5	A

Passive
6.1	C
6.2	B
6.3	D
6.4	A
6.5	A, B
6.6	C
6.7	D

Reported speech
7.1	A
7.2	B
7.3	A

Questions and auxiliary verbs
8.1	C
8.2	A
8.3	D
8.4	A
8.5	B

-ing and to ...
9.1	A
9.2	B, D
9.3	B
9.4	A
9.5	A
9.6	A
9.7	C
9.8	D
9.9	C
9.10	C
9.11	B
9.12	C, D
9.13	B, D
9.14	B
9.15	A, B
9.16	A
9.17	A
9.18	B, C

Articles and nouns
10.1	B
10.2	A
10.3	B, C
10.4	B
10.5	C
10.6	A
10.7	A
10.8	A
10.9	D
10.10	C
10.11	C
10.12	A
10.13	C
10.14	B

Pronouns and determiners
11.1	A
11.2	B
11.3	D
11.4	B
11.5	B
11.6	C
11.7	A, C
11.8	C
11.9	D
11.10	A, C
11.11	B

Relative clauses
12.1	A, C
12.2	A, B
12.3	C
12.4	B
12.5	D
12.6	B, C

Adjectives and adverbs
13.1	B
13.2	C
13.3	B, C
13.4	A
13.5	A, D
13.6	B
13.7	B, C
13.8	C
13.9	C
13.10	B, C
13.11	D
13.12	A, B
13.13	B
13.14	D
13.15	D

Conjunctions and prepositions
14.1	A, D
14.2	C
14.3	B, C
14.4	B, D
14.5	B
14.6	C, D
14.7	B, C
14.8	A

Prepositions
15.1	B, D
15.2	A
15.3	C
15.4	B
15.5	A
15.6	B, D
15.7	B
15.8	B
15.9	C
15.10	C
15.11	C
15.12	A
15.13	C
15.14	B
15.15	D
15.16	D
15.17	A

Phrasal verbs
16.1	B
16.2	A
16.3	D
16.4	C
16.5	C
16.6	B
16.7	A
16.8	A, D
16.9	B

Index

The numbers in the index are unit numbers, not page numbers.

Index